Number Six:

The W. L. Moody, Jr., Natural History Series

Texas Mammals East of the Balcones Fault Zone

Texas Mammals East of the Balcones Fault Zone

BY

David J. Schmidly

PHOTOGRAPHS BY

John L. Tveten

TEXAS A&M UNIVERSITY PRESS

College Station

Library of Congress Cataloging in Publication Data

Schmidly, David J., 1943–
    Texas mammals east of the Balcones Fault zone.

    (The W. L. Moody, Jr., natural history series; no. 6)
    Bibliography: p.
    Includes index.
    1. Mammals—Texas.   I. Title.   II. Title: Balcones
Fault zone.   III. Series.
    QL719.T4S36   1983   599.09764   83-45098
    ISBN 0-89096-158-1
    ISBN 0-89096-171-9 (pbk.)

Manufactured in the United States of America
FIRST EDITION

To my family—
Janet, Kathy, and Brian—
in recognition of their
love and devotion

Contents

FIGURES

TABLES

Preface

TEXAS is a crossroads where four major physiographic subdivisions of
North America come together: the Rocky Mountains region, the Great
Western High Plains, the Great Western Lower Plains, and the Gulf
Coastal Forested Plains. Within the state is such a variation of soils, cli-
mate, and topography that the resultant vegetation and animal life are un-
usually rich.

This diverse environment supports a resident fauna of 139 species of
native terrestrial mammals, a number exceeded in the United States only
by California (165) and New Mexico (143). In addition, Texas is bounded
by the waters of the Gulf of Mexico, and 23 marine mammals enter the
coastal waters of the state. Thus, a total of 162 species of native mammals
occur in Texas or its adjacent waters.

Texas may be conveniently arranged into four regions based on the
geographical distribution of mammals. These are the Trans-Pecos, Plains
country, eastern Texas, and Rio Grande Plain (Map 1). This book repre-

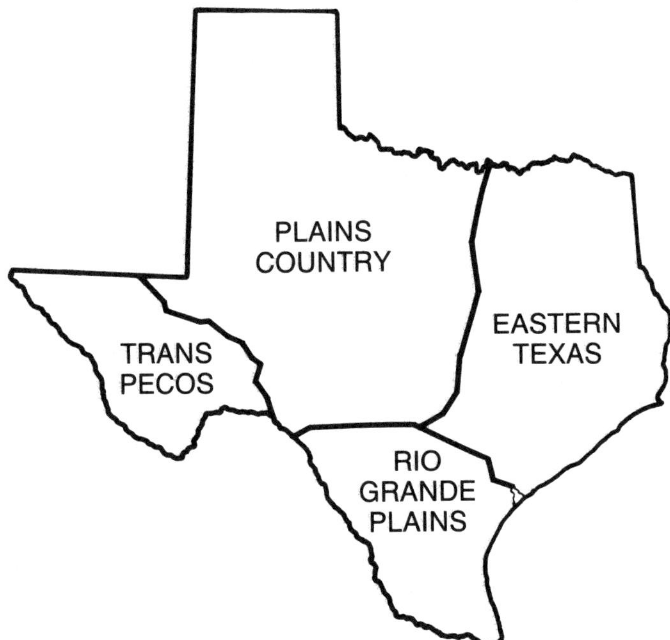

MAP 1. Four regions of Texas based on mammalian distributions.

sents the second in a series designed to document the mammalian fauna of each of these regions. An account of the mammals of the Trans-Pecos region has already been published (Schmidly, 1977).

The subjects of this book are the mammals that inhabit the eastern part of Texas, east of the Balcones Fault Zone. This region includes all of the timbered areas of the state as well as two different kinds of prairies. It is an extremely populous area, containing almost 50 percent of the total human population of Texas. The term "mammal" refers to the class of vertebrate animals possessing hair, with the females having milk-secreting glands. One group of mammals, the cetaceans (whales and dolphins), have a layer of blubber instead of hair. These marine forms are common in the Gulf of Mexico, but only one species, the bottlenosed dolphin (*Tursiops truncatus*), regularly occurs along the Texas coast, and it is the only one discussed in this text. The remainder of the mammals occupy terrestrial environments for much, if not all, of their lives.

The bulk of the text is devoted to accounts of all wild mammals in eastern Texas. These include both the native species that occur in the area naturally as well as five non-native species (the roof rat, the Norway rat, the house mouse, the nutria, and the red fox) that have been introduced by man and that have become established as a part of the free-living fauna. Abbreviated accounts are also included for the domestic species because they have become extensively established throughout the region and because three of them (the wild hog, the cat, and the dog) have taken up a life in the wild state in many places and have significant impacts on other mammals living in the area. Extinct species as well as those of marginal or problematic occurrence are discussed in ancillary fashion in a separate chapter.

The book is organized so that for each species of wild mammal living in eastern Texas today the following categories of information are presented:

Name. For each species the currently accepted scientific and common names are provided following the listing of J. K. Jones, Jr., et al. (1979). The formation or etymology of each name is also provided. The scientific name of a species consists of two words. The first part of the name refers to the genus to which the species belongs; the second part, called the specific epithet, distinguishes a particular species from any others belonging to the same genus. Most scientific names are derived from Latin or Greek, but some are Latinized forms of modern words or names. Frequently the scientific name refers to some physical characteristic or habit of the animal, or to a person or place associated with its collection. The derivation of most names was taken from Brown's *Composition of Scientific Words* (Washington, D.C.: Smithsonian Institution Press, 1979) or Borror's *Dictionary of Word Roots and Combining Forms* (Palo Alto: Mayfield Publ. Co., 1971). In a few cases it was necessary to refer to works dealing specifically with mammals (such as Lowery, 1974, or C. W. Schwartz and Schwartz, 1981) to explain the meaning of particularly complex names.

Identification. For each species one or more photographs as well as brief descriptions of the most important identifying features are provided. Identifications are based on the diagnostic characters of the species such as size, prominent external features, color, and dentition. The types, arrangement, and number of teeth for any species are expressed as a dental formula that aids in identifying species. The dental formula is expressed as the number of teeth on one side of the upper and lower jaw, with the numerator representing upper teeth and the denominator representing lower teeth. The letters *I*, *C*, *Pm*, and *M*, listed from front to rear, represent incisors, canines, premolars, and molars. The total number of teeth is derived by doubling the numbers given in the dental formula.

Four external measurements that are useful in identifying mammals are provided for most species. These are total length, measured from the tip of the nose to the tip of the fleshy part of the tail; tail length, measured from the base of the tail to the tip of the fleshy part; hind foot length, measured from the tip of the longest claw to the heel; and ear length, measured from the notch in the bottom of the ear to the tip of the ear. All measurements are given in the metric system. A conversion table for the metric system and the U.S. customary system is given in Appendix III.

In recent years, a new aid in identifying mammals, the use of chromosome number and morphology (called karyology), has developed. The chromosomes of well-spread cells in metaphase can be counted to determine the diploid number (2N) for an individual, and they can be arranged in pairs according to their size and position of the centromere. The chromosomes are placed in metacentric, submetacentric, or acrocentric groups depending on whether the centromere is median, submedian, or terminal. The chromosomes of an animal arranged in this fashion are referred to as its karyotype (see Fig. 1 for an example). The fundamental number (FN) can then be calculated by totaling the number of chromosome arms: each acrocentric autosome is counted as one; submetacentric and metacentric autosomes are counted as two arms per chromosome. Karyotypes may differ in diploid number, fundamental number, or both. Techniques for preparing mammalian chromosomes are given in Lee (1969) and Robbins and Baker (1978).

The past decade has witnessed an unparalleled trend toward the use of chromosomal characters in mammalian taxonomy. For many taxa, these characters reliably differentiate specimens at the species and population levels and have helped clarify taxonomic problems in instances where cranial and pelage characters have been unrewarding. Excellent examples of the use of chromosomes for clarifying the taxonomic status of mammals in eastern Texas include the pocket gophers of the genus *Geomys* and the subspecies of the deer mouse, *Peromyscus maniculatus*.

Subspecies. Populations of a species from different geographic areas are often distinct morphologically. In some cases, they are so distinct that they might easily be regarded as different species were it not for the fact that where their ranges meet they interbreed freely, as evidenced by morphological intermediacy, and there is no reproductive isolation between them. Such distinct aggregations of individuals within the range of a species are recognized taxonomically as subspecies by adding a third word to the species scientific name. Characteristics used to define subspecies, or races, as they are sometimes called, are largely morphological and depend heavily upon skull measurements.

The delineation of subspecies in eastern Texas reflects my own views based on examining specimens from the region and comparing them with those from surrounding areas. In the cases of those mammals for which subspecies are recognized, I have given the primary citations for the original description and the type locality for each of the subspecies. The subspecies ranges are also shown on an accompanying distribution map. Hall (1981) is the primary reference for subspecies distributions in the areas surrounding eastern Texas.

Distribution and habitat. Here I give the present-day distribution and relative abundance of the species in eastern Texas as well as any local or sectional variations in status. The habitat of the species is described with reference to the major types of vegetation, soil, water, or other factors that are critical to that species survival.

A distribution map is provided for each species with its geographic range in Texas and the surrounding states shaded. Within eastern Texas, dots are placed in the center of a county where a known record exists for the given species in that county. Absence of a dot in any county does not necessarily mean that the species does not occur there, but simply that no record for the species exists for that county. The records as indicated by the dots are based on specimens that I have examined in numerous museums, and the exact localities of all of these records are listed in Appendix I. Closed squares represent significant literature records for which scientific specimens either do not exist or were not examined by me. Closed triangles represent records reported by fur trappers to the Texas Parks and Wildlife Department, but in most instances there are no preserved specimens to verify these records.

Life history. I have tried to give some of the outstanding features of each animal's life history. It was not possible to give a complete catalog of all events in the life of a species, so I concentrated on selected aspects of population structure (including age composition, mortality, and longevity), reproduction, growth and development, activity (including daily and seasonal movements as well as home range and territory), food habits, and behavior (including intra- and interspecific interactions, group aggregations, social hierarchies, and communication). The life histories include observations recorded by other researchers and reported in the literature as well as my personal experiences based on more than ten years of field work in the area. In several instances no detailed studies have been made based on the populations of a species inhabiting eastern Texas, and I have had to rely on investigations made in other regions. In these cases, I attempted to rely on studies conducted in areas adjacent to eastern Texas where environmental conditions were similar. For some poorly known species, the lack of available information prevented any detailed description of the life history.

Remarks. This section includes information of interest about species with economic importance (such as fur-bearing mammals) and those for which the taxonomy is confusing and requires elaboration.

References. Included here is reference to most of the published literature for a particular species that pertains specifically to eastern Texas as well as a few selected references to enable the interested reader to consult more detailed accounts of specific aspects of life history. Complete citations are given in the bibliography at the end of the book.

Acknowledgments

I am grateful to the following people who provided information on mammals, loaned specimens for study, or allowed me to examine collections under their care: John Baccus, Robert J. Baker, Bryce C. Brown, Arthur G. Cleveland, John L. Darling, Dean Fisher, John Hafner, Robert S. Hoffmann, Donald F. Hoffmeister, Robert F. Martin, Howard McCarley, Philip Myers, James L. Patton, Royal Suttkus, William J. Voss, Don Wilson, William E. Wilson, James Yantis, and Earl G. Zimmerman. I also would like to thank William Brownlee and Floyd Potter of the Texas Parks and Wildlife Department for allowing me to use the questionnaires from the fur trapper survey and for providing tables and data pertaining to fur-bearing and game mammals.

My studies of mammals in Big Thicket National Preserve from 1975 to 1980 provide the basis for much of the information presented in this book. My work there was funded by the National Park Service and the U.S. Fish and Wildlife Service, and I am grateful to Milford Fletcher and Clyde Jones, respectively, of those two agencies for their support. My work in the preserve was greatly facilitated by the following National Park Service personnel: Tom Lubbert, Carl Flemming, Jack Bixby, and Harold Timmons. I would also like to acknowledge the field assistance of the following students (listed in decreasing order of total time devoted to the project): W. Glenn Norton, Brian Barnette, Duke Rogers, Gail Dresner, Will Cohen, Mark Engstrom, James Owen, Steve Smith, William Modi, Robert Dowler, Priscilla Tucker, Jim Dean, Scott Gunn, Bill Barber, and Tim Houseal.

Most of the photographs of mammals were taken by John Tveten using animals captured by me or by my graduate students. Mr. Tveten's ability as a wildlife photographer is, in my opinion, extraordinary, and I appreciate the many hours he has taken in preparing these photographs. The following individuals and organizations assisted him in obtaining specimens or by allowing him to use their facilities: Tony Gallucci; Bill and Joyce Morris; William McClure; Marvin Penning; Rory Reynolds; Mike Smolen; Armand Bayou Nature Center, Houston, Texas; Living Desert State Park, Carlsbad, New Mexico; Texas Zoo, Victoria; Gladys Porter Zoo, Brownsville, Texas; and the Houston Zoo. For a few rare species, we could not obtain living animals to photograph, and we borrowed photographs from the following individuals: J. Knox Jones, Jr.; Roger W. Barbour; Woodrow Goodpasture; Susan Shane; Curtis Carley; W. D. Zehr; and Greg K. Yarrow. David Sweeney and Daryl Styblo graciously assisted with the reproduction of the photographs. Last, but certainly not least, I thank Earl Zimmerman, Robert Dowler, and Sarah George for providing photomicrographs of karyotypes.

Several persons aided in the stages of manuscript preparation. Gail Dresner and Judy White assisted with the library work, listed the specimens examined, and made the rough versions of the distribution maps. Connie Norton entered the manuscript on the word-processor, and her ability to organize and pay attention to detail was invaluable throughout the entire project. Helen Finney deserves special mention for working many long and tedious hours to prepare final copies of the distribution maps. Dr. Dwayne Suter, Associate Dean of the College of Agriculture at Texas A&M University, kindly made a TRS-80 Model II™ Radio Shack microcomputer, loaned to him by Charles Phillips, Robert Friedler, and Ron Stegall of Radio Shack, available for use as a word processor.

The Texas Agricultural Experiment Station, under the direction of Neville Clark, graciously provided financial support for some of the field work and for all of the trips to museums and collections. Wallace G. Klussmann, head of the Department of Wildlife and Fisheries Sciences at Texas A&M University, constantly encouraged my work and arranged for me to have time to write the manuscript.

Texas Mammals East of the Balcones Fault Zone

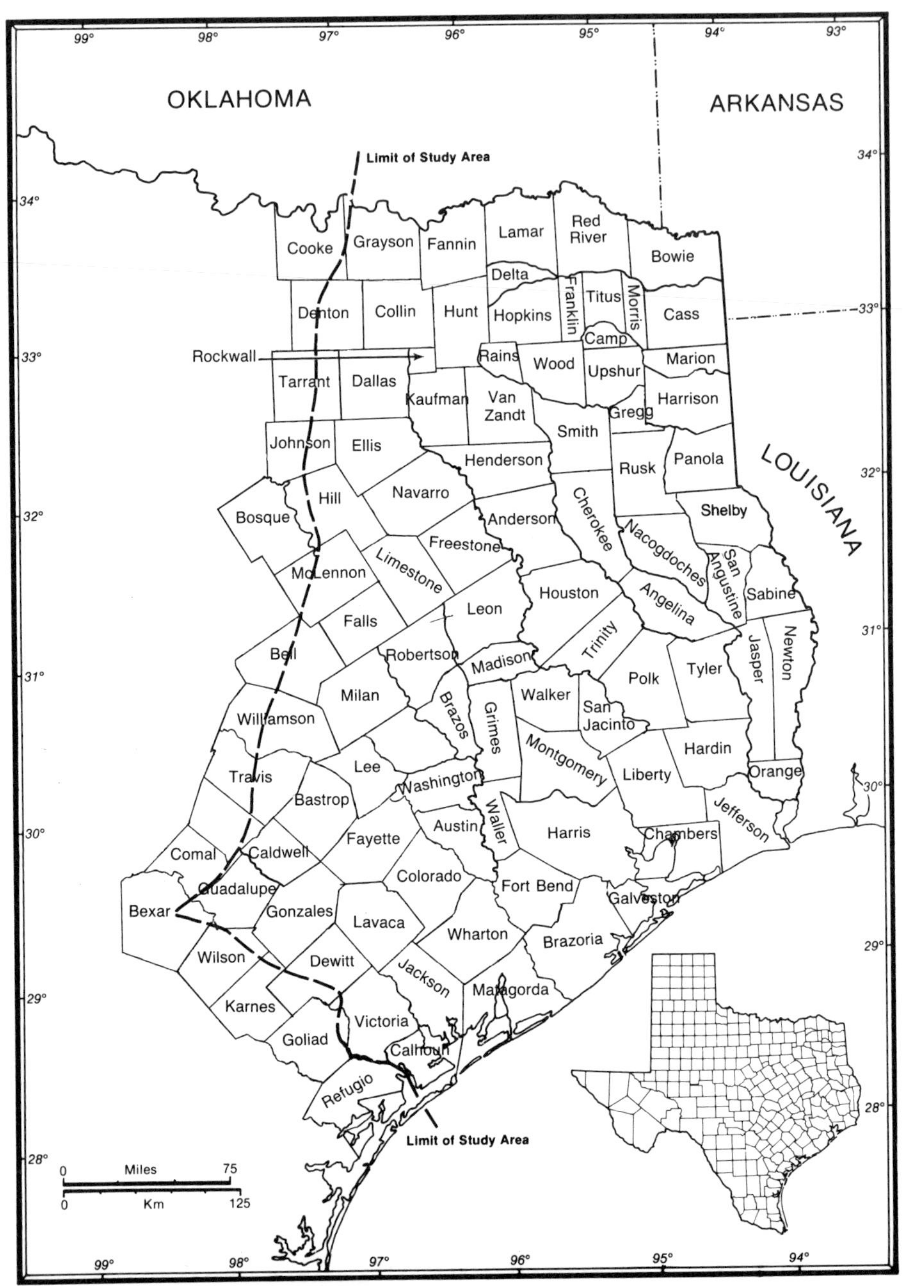

Map 2. Counties of eastern Texas.

1

Description of the Region

THE region of study encompasses all or part of ninety-four counties in eastern Texas and occupies about 17.14 million ha (Map 2). It is delimited by both political and natural boundaries. The political boundaries are on the north, where the Red River divides Texas and Oklahoma, and on the east along the Texas-Louisiana border, much of which corresponds with the course of the Sabine River. The natural boundaries of the region are on the west and south.

To the west, the Balcones Fault Zone forms a striking topographic feature that represents a prominent fracture in the earth's crust forming the boundary between the lowland Gulf coastal plains of eastern Texas and the highly eroded upland plateaus and plains of central and western Texas. The entire stretch of Interstate Highway 35 follows this fault zone, crossing and re-crossing the numerous individual faults of which it is composed. The geological change is evident in most areas from the highway level because the harder rocks to the west of the fault form hills rising noticeably above the more deeply eroded, softer and younger rocks to the east. Displacement in the fault zone has produced an abrupt increase in elevation, known as the Balcones Escarpment. Starting from Waco and extending southward through Austin to San Antonio, this escarpment represents an arc of cliffs, hills, and plateaus that reach a height of about 305 m. There are conspicuous changes in the climate, vegetation, and animal life across this arc. Northward from Waco to the Red River, the escarpment gradually decreases in height until it is recognizable only through the presence of small fault lines. Biotic changes across this portion of the escarpment are not as great as they are to the south of Waco.

The southern boundary of the study region is set about midway between the Guadalupe and San Antonio rivers along a line that separates pedocal soils from pedalfers. This line, which differentiates the Tamaulipan and Texan biotic provinces (as described by Blair, 1950), exists as a belt only a few miles wide that is fairly well defined by differences in basic soil characteristics. Southwest of this line, the pedocals of the humid Tamaulipan province contain soils where some horizon of the developed soil profile contains a greater amount of carbonate of lime than is present in the geological material beneath. A moisture deficit exists, and carbonates are not leached but accumulate at some subsurface level as caliche. Grasslands developed upon soils of this nature are called plains, and the entire South Texas region is often referred to as the Rio Grande Plain. To the northeast of the pedocal-pedalfer boundary, pedalfer soils exhibit mature profiles in which no larger amount of carbonates of lime occurs than is present in the parent material beneath. These acid soils develop in regions of high rainfall and in regions where parent materials are low in basic elements. Pedalfer soils have an excess of moisture, are leached to some extent, and support a vegetational mixture of alternating wooded savannas, tall-grass prairies, and associated ecotones.

Eastern Texas is bisected by ten major rivers that flow generally from northwest to southeast (Map 3). These are, arranged from north to south, the Red, Sulphur, Sabine, Neches, Trinity, San Jacinto, Brazos, Colorado, Lavaca, and Guadalupe rivers. The Sabine River has the largest water discharge, followed in order by the Red, Trinity, Neches, and Brazos. There are major differences in basin characteristics that separate drainages northeast of the Brazos River from those systems southwest of the Brazos. Rivers in the former region, compared to the latter, have comparatively narrow main channels, flat slopes, and low-angled elevation gradients from headwaters to mouth; follow meandering courses; and have wide, timbered floodplains. Usually abundant rainfall produces floods that frequently overflow floodplains for lengthy periods, rise and fall slowly, and generally have low velocities. After flood recessions, there are numerous water-filled oxbow lakes, levee sloughs, and natural depressions within the floodplains. Another major difference in basin characteristics is that the drainages northeast of and including the Brazos River system contain 127 large reservoirs, whereas those drainages southwest of the Brazos contain only 47 small reservoirs.

The floodplain habitats associated with these major river systems constitute dispersal highways by which many forest-dwelling animals extend eastward and westward beyond the forest limits into areas such as the blackland prairies and coastal prairies where vegetational types present barriers to them.

There are four major vegetational areas within eastern Texas. These are (1) the pineywoods, (2) the coastal prairies and marshes, (3) the post oak woodlands, and (4) the blackland prairies. The distribution of these vegetational areas is shown in Map 4, and each area is described below with respect to its climate, dominant plant communities, topography, and soil type. A list of the scientific and vernacular names of all plants referred to in the text is provided in Appendix II.

Pineywoods

The pineywoods area contains approximately 6.1 million ha of gently rolling to hilly forested land. Rainfall is high and fairly uniform, with annual averages of 90 cm to more than 127 cm. Humidity and temperatures are usually high, and the area is comparatively free from persistent winds. Soils are mostly light-colored to dark gray sands or sandy loams.

There are two distinct types of forest in the pineywoods, the pine forest in the southeastern portion and the more extensive pine-oak forest in the central and northern part. The pine forest is characterized by the occurrence of longleaf pine, loblolly pine, and shortleaf pine, listed in the

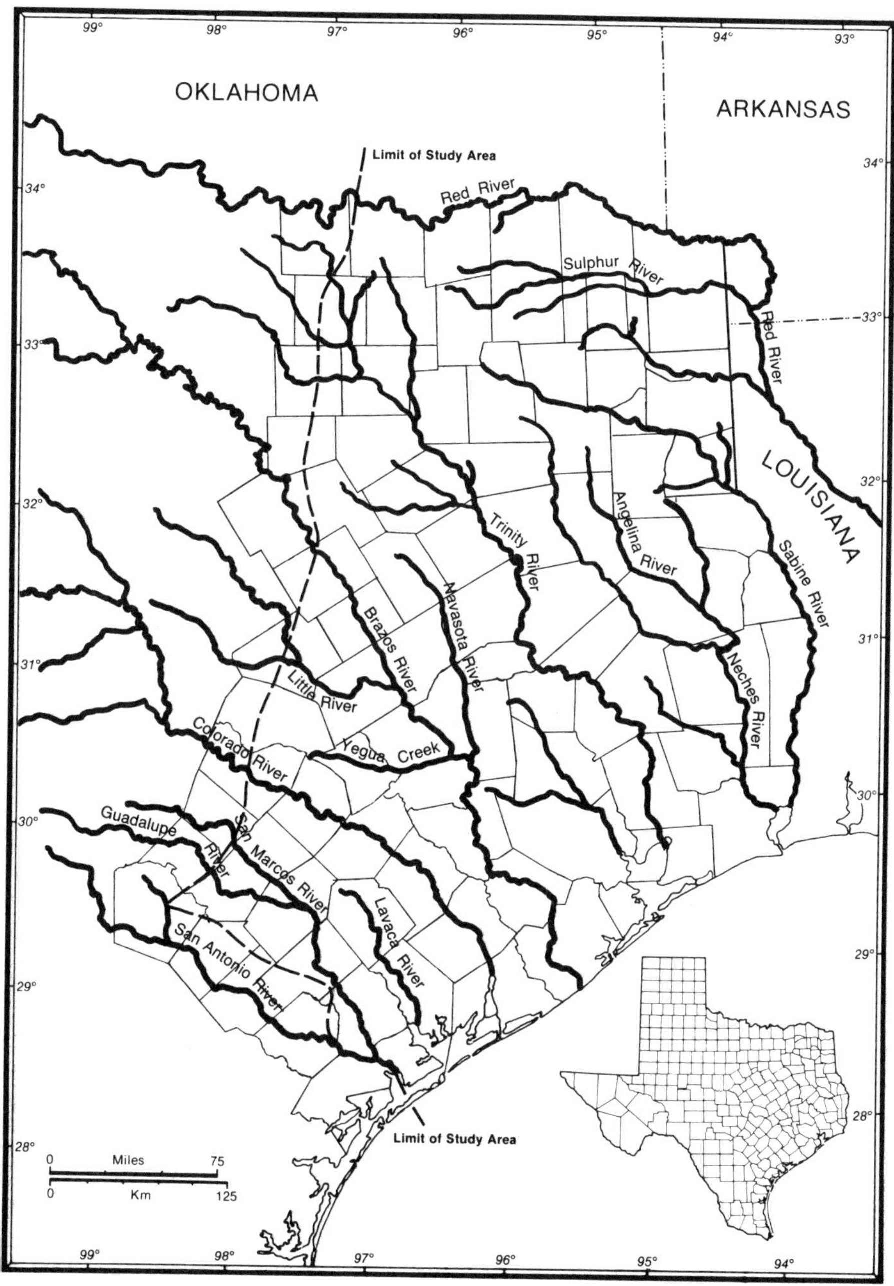

MAP 3. Major river systems of eastern Texas.

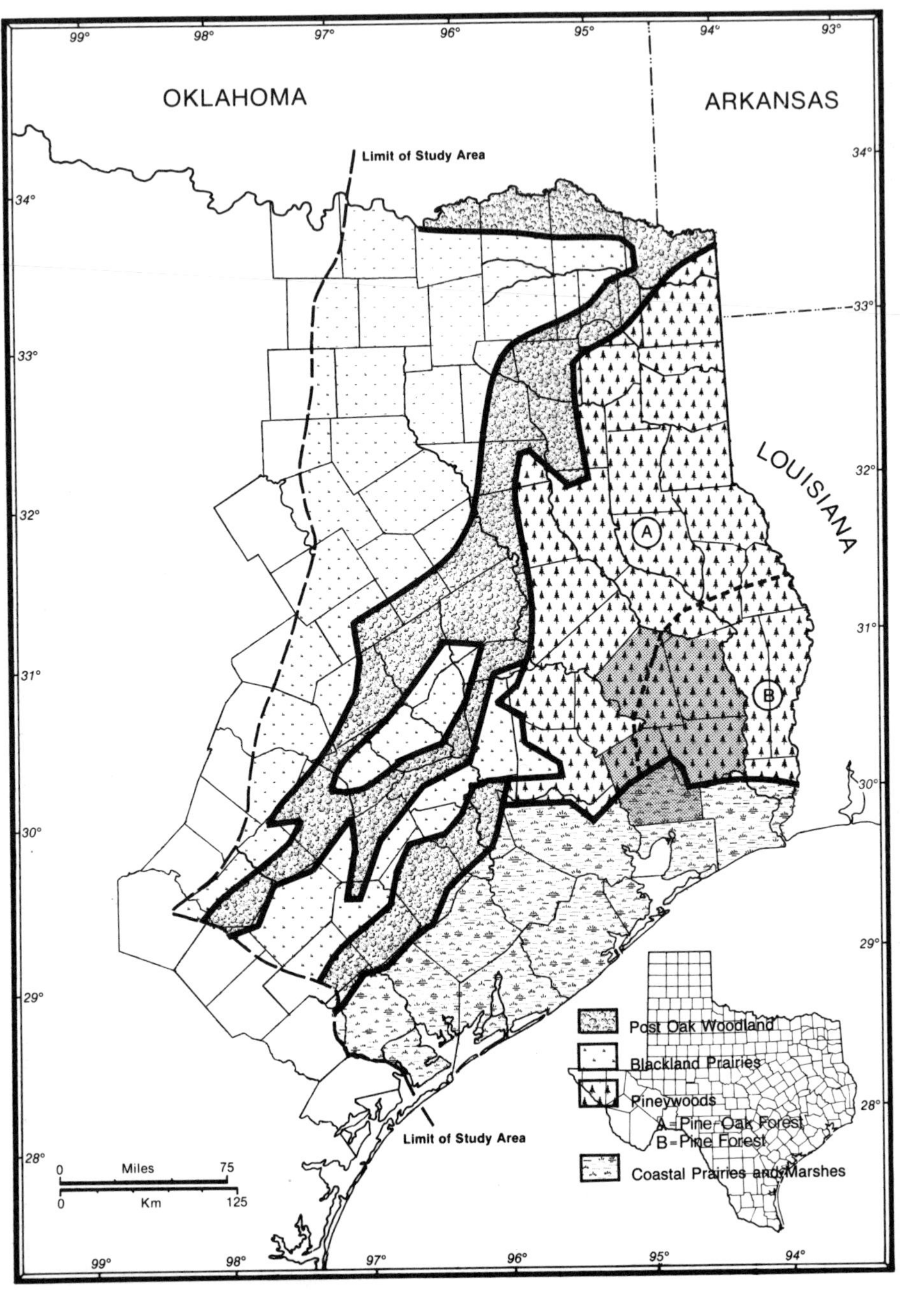

MAP 4. Vegetational areas of eastern Texas. The shaded area represents the four-county area which encompasses most of Big Thicket National Preserve.

order of their decreasing abundance. These three species are considered the climax vegetation in this region. Most of the virgin longleaf pine has been cut, and introduced slash pine has been widely planted over the area. Scattered throughout the stands of the three species of pine are various other woody species that rarely predominate except in disturbed areas. Generally, post oak, blackjack, and wax myrtle are the common subdominants. The elevation of the pine forest region varies from about 8 m above sea level in the south to about 76 m in the north.

The pine-oak forest represents an ecotone between the pine forest and the oak-hickory forest of the post oak woodlands. The topography of this forest region is gently rolling to hilly, and the elevation above sea level varies from about 76 m in the south to about 145 m in the north. The pine-oak forest is characterized by the occurrence of loblolly pine, shortleaf pine, post oak, blackjack, and hickory. Slash pine has also been widely introduced in this forest type. Post oak and blackjack constitute the climax vegetation of the pine-oak forest, but at present loblolly and shortleaf pine are generally dominant.

The pine forest and the pine-oak forest can be divided into two distinct habitats, designated as the upland forest habitat and the lowland forest habitat, according to the natural distribution of the dominant woody species. These two habitats are present in varying admixture throughout the pineywoods area.

The lowland forest habitat is the most mesic habitat in eastern Texas. It occurs wherever there is sufficient moisture to support the dense growth of woody and herbaceous vegetation, and is limited to the floodplains of the numerous streams that drain the timbered region. The dominant vegetation of the lowland forest generally consists of the following trees, listed in the order of their decreasing abundance: water oak, willow oak, sweet gum, black gum, and birch. In some areas, particularly in the pine forest region, cypress and magnolia are among the dominants. Large numbers of fallen and uprooted trees in various stages of decay are usually present in the lowland forest habitat. There are numerous swamps, sloughs, and oxbow lakes in these lowlands, and the water table is usually only a few meters below the surface. All of these factors contribute to the maintenance of the mesic growth of hardwoods.

The lowland forest habitat is most extensive in the southeastern portion of the pine forest in a poorly drained, comparatively low area known as the Big Thicket, because of the dense growth of woody vegetation. The Big Thicket forest is an admixture of evergreens, both conifers and hardwoods. About 50 percent of the forest is composed of evergreens. More specifically, this is a forest of loblolly pine, white oak, beech, and magnolia. Its understory is rich in both evergreen and deciduous shrubs, a variety of climbing vines, and both annual and perennial herbs. Floristically, the Big Thicket may be differentiated into a northern "upper thicket" forest, with American beech as one codominant species, and a southern "lower thicket" forest, in which beech is replaced as the codominant species by the swamp chestnut oak and laurel oak. The upper thicket is best

Pine forest.

Upland pine-oak forest.

Lowland pine-oak forest.

Mesic, lowland swamp.

developed in Polk, Tyler, and Jasper counties, whereas the lower thicket predominates in Montgomery, Liberty, and Hardin counties. In 1974 the U.S. Congress established Big Thicket National Preserve to ensure the protection of the fragile and delicate fauna and flora of this region. The preserve is situated within a four-county region of southeastern Texas (Map 4).

The upland forest is the most xeric natural vegetational type in the timbered region of eastern Texas. It generally occurs on the slopes and summits of the hills. Here, there is always an insufficient amount of available moisture to support typical plant species of the floodplains. The soil of the uplands is generally low in mineral plant nutrients and organic matter. These factors plus the more xeric conditions do not allow as dense a growth of vegetation as in the lowlands. The dominant vegetation of the upland forest habitat varies with the two vegetational regions of the pineywoods. In the pine forest the dominant vegetation is the same as the climax vegetation, and the subdominant vegetation is usually made up of post oak, blackjack, and wax myrtle. In the pine-oak forest the dominant vegetation is usually shortleaf pine, loblolly pine, and post oak. Blackjack, hickory, and sassafras make up the subdominant vegetation in the pine-oak forest. The upland forest habitat is more extensive in the pine-oak forest than in the pine forest.

The forests in the pineywoods area are changing rapidly as a result of lumbering and farming operations, and pine is rapidly becoming more prevalent than hardwoods. One problem of the area is that the predominantly sandy, somewhat sterile soil does not have the strength to develop hardwoods as large as those in heavier soils. In fact, much of the cutting is now for plywood or pulp instead of log timber. Furthermore, many of the hardwoods are along streams, and the creation of reservoirs by dams has flooded these areas.

Coastal Prairies and Marshes

The Gulf Coast portion of eastern Texas is a region of prairies, marshes, and estuaries extending from the San Antonio River on the west along the coast to the Louisiana line and inland some 80 to 96 km from the coast. The topography is level, with elevations varying from near sea level to about 15 m above sea level near its contact with the pine, pine-oak, and oak-hickory forests. It is the smallest natural region in eastern Texas, encompassing 2.98 million ha.

The climate of the region is generally characterized by cool springs, pleasant summers, and mild winters. The region has infrequent hurricanes, usually in summer and early autumn. Most of the killing frosts occur between December 15 and January 20. Rainfall averages from 76 to 152 cm, with the average for the region about 86 cm. The soils over much of the coastal prairies are brown acid clays over clay and soft limestone, known as marl.

Coastal prairie.

The two almost universally dominant grasses of the coastal prairie are bushy bluestem and coastal sacahuiste. Secondary components include other varieties of little bluestem, broomsedge, slender bluestem, purple threeawn, Roemer's threeawn, buffalograss, gulfdune paspalum, brownseed paspalum, rattail smutgrass, and many sedges. Much of the southern part of this region to as far north as the Brazos River has changed drastically since white settlement. At first, intensive grazing so reduced the grass cover that mesquite, live oak, prickly pear, and several acacias had overrun much of it before there was any serious attempt to put the land into cultivation. Recently, brush control programs have been initiated, and in some areas scarcely a trace of either the virgin prairie or the secondary brushlands now remains.

Most of the major rivers of eastern Texas empty into the Gulf of Mexico through this vegetation region. In the upper parts of the coastal prairie these streams have a wooded floodplain characteristic of either the pine forest, pine-oak forest, or oak-hickory forest, but nearer the Gulf this woody vegetation disappears, and the streams meander through prairies and marshes, forming many oxbow lakes.

There are about 105,000 ha of marshland on the southeastern Texas coast between Galveston Bay and Louisiana. Almost all of the marsh lies behind beach ridges of sufficient size to prevent direct influx of seawater except when hurricane winds blow directly inshore. The general topography is level. There are about twenty lakes, with an average size approaching 202 ha. An intercoastal canal, two rivers, and many bayous drain the marshes. The mean annual rainfall is about 132 cm, and the mean annual temperature is 20.5° C, with an average of only six days a year when the temperature is below freezing.

Coastal marsh.

Smooth cordgrass and coastal saltgrass border the tidal inlets and lagoons of the saline marshes. The brackish marshes are marked by marshhay cordgrass, coastal saltgrass, needlegrass rush, Olney bulrush, and saltmarsh bulrush. A cane zone occurs in slightly less brackish sites and apparently on more mineralized soils. It is characterized by common reed and big cordgrass, frequently interspersed with plants typical of the brackish and the fresh marshes. The fresh marsh includes cattail, California bulrush, squarestem spike sedge, arrowhead, and various associated species. In slightly brackish sites with abundant water, there are almost pure stands of Jamaica sawgrass.

Post Oak Woodlands

The post oak woodlands comprise approximately 3.44 million ha. These woodlands, which occupy a narrow strip that is nowhere more than 96 km wide, are located in the central part of eastern Texas and extend in a southwesterly direction, forming a peninsula surrounded by prairies. In the north, the region is situated between the pine forest and blackland prairies. The topography is level to gently rolling and slopes gently from the northwest to the southeast. Elevations are from 92 to 244 m above sea level. Soils on the uplands are light-colored, acid sandy loams or sands. Bottomland soils are light brown to dark gray and acid, ranging in texture from sandy loams to clays. The climate is mild, with 240 to 270 frost-free days. Annual rainfall is 89 to 114 cm.

Vegetatively, the post oak region can best be described as an ecotone between the eastern deciduous forest and the tall-grass prairie. The area

Post oak savanna.

supports a stunted, open forest dotted with small tall-grass prairies. The dominant plants of the uplands are post oak and blackjack oak. To a lesser extent, but also common, are winged elm and black hickory. Red oak is found dominating certain situations in the eastern part of the region, as is bluejack oak, but their range does not extend far beyond that of the pines. Along the southern and western edge of the region, live oak is commonly dominant, at times excluding the post oak. The eastern red cedar is also scattered through wooded areas, particularly on limestone sites.

The trees of the uplands rarely exceed 14 m in height. The wooded areas of the climax are a rather open stand of trees. The crowns in most cases touch to form a thin canopy, but it is not uncommon to find areas in which the crowns do not touch, resulting in irregular gaps and well-lighted ground areas.

Many plants occur in the shrub layer of the post oak belt, but the most important ones are yaupon, deciduous holly, French mulberry, several kinds of hawthorn, and huckleberry. In some sites along the main belt of the association, the whole space beneath the trees and the openings are closed with tight thickets of yaupon in the woods and deciduous holly in the openings. To the west, especially along the western borders of the region, the shrub layer is considerably reduced and altered. Common in these areas are openings where tight soils are found, dominated by mesquite and "brush country" species in the south and mesquite farther north. The eastern border of the post oak belt is invaded by many eastern shrubs that become gradually reduced in numbers toward the west.

As is true in the pineywoods, there is a distinct lowland forest habitat in the post oak region that is also limited to the floodplains of the major streams. This habitat type includes several species for which the upland sites are too dry, such as American elm, pecan, cottonwood, sycamore, black walnut, sweet gum, red bay, white oak, overcup oak, water oak, and black willow. The lowland forest habitat is not nearly as extensive in the post oak region as it is the pine forest or pine-oak forest of the pineywoods region.

In the past it is probable that the grass layer in the entire post oak region was dominated by bluestems and their tall-grass associates wherever light could reach the ground. However, under heavy human use, which has severely affected the whole region, most openings maintain a vegetation of low grasses such as threeawns, panicums, lovegrass, and others.

The land in the post oak region is used primarily for farming and ranching. Much of the region is still in native or improved pastures, although small farms are common. Improved pastures are commonly seeded to Bermudagrass, Dallisgrass, Vaseygrass, carpetgrass, and clovers. About 50 percent of the total area has been cleared, and about one-half of the cleared areas are planted with crops. Clearing of the wooded areas creates extensive edges that are further emphasized by the practice of clearing fairly small, irregular areas.

Blackland Prairies

The blackland prairie forms a narrow band bordered on the east by the timberlands (post oak woodlands and pineywoods), and on the west by the eastern Cross Timbers and extending southward into the Rio Grande Plain. The main prairie is approximately 70 km across in the north and narrows southward to about 12 km. It covers an area of over 4.26 million ha. Several outlier prairies, the largest of which are the Fayette and San Antonio prairies, are also included with the main prairie, so that the entire region encompasses about 4.65 million ha.

Average annual precipitation varies from 115 cm in the north to 75 cm in the south. The growing season increases from north to south and varies from 260 to 290 days. Average annual temperatures vary from 18° C in the northernmost portion to 21° C along the Colorado River. The blackland prairie has a coastward or southeastward orientation. Relief is gently undulating and is marked by numerous mammillary hills with gently rounded slopes. Blackland soils are fairly uniform dark-colored clays interspersed with some gray acid sandy loams.

The blackland prairie has elements of both the true and coastal prairies of the tall-grass prairie and some unique elements of its own. However, because of precipitation and soil moisture retention characteristics, the prairie takes on a lowland grassland appearance even on well-drained upland. At least seven major grassland communities are recognized, and these are distributed across three major soil associations (Collins et al., 1975). The most extensive community type is dominated by Indiangrass and little bluestem. Other important dominants include big bluestem, switchgrass, sideoats grama, hairy grama, tall dropseed, silver bluestem,

Blackland prairie.

and Texas wintergrass. Under heavy grazing, Texas wintergrass, buffalograss, Texas grama, rattail smutgrass, and many annuals increase or invade. Mesquite has also invaded hardland sites of the southern portion of the prairie. The region originally had numerous wooded belts along the streams, but most of these have been cleared to the stream banks.

Current figures reveal that 68 percent of the blackland prairie is cultivated, with an additional 22 percent in tame pasture. As a result of cultivation, overgrazing, and other imprudent land-use practices, there are few if any remnants of climax vegetation in the region. The majority of the remaining prairielands are in Lamar County of northeastern Texas. Another center of remnant prairies is located around Temple and Waco in Bell and McLennan counties. Virtually nothing remains in the southwestern region of the blacklands between the Colorado and San Antonio rivers in the vicinity of Austin and San Antonio.

References. Anonymous, 1952a, 1952b, 1976–77; Blair, 1950; Bray, 1904, 1906; Chambers, 1934; Chambless and Nixon, 1975; Collins et al., 1975; Evans, 1952; F. W. Gould, 1975; E. H. Johnson, 1931; Launchbaugh, 1955; McLeod, 1971; Nixon et al., 1973; Pessin, 1933; Riskind and Collins, 1975; Sullivan and Nixon, 1971; Tharp, 1926; Warner, 1926.

2
Synopsis of Mammals

Status of the Mammalian Fauna

Ninety kinds of mammals presently live in eastern Texas or just outside its boundaries or have inhabited the area within the past 125 years. These animals are listed in a checklist below that includes the scientific name, common name, and status of each species. The checklist is arranged into three sections, one for native mammals, a second for introduced species, and a third for domestic species. Status is defined with the following categories:

Common. A common species is one that is abundant wherever it lives in the region. Most common species are widely distributed over the area.

Uncommon. An uncommon species may or may not be widely distributed, but it does not occur in large numbers and is not well represented in museum collections. Uncommon species are not rare or endangered.

Migrant. A migrant species is one that is not a permanent resident of the region and occurs there only periodically.

Rare. A rare species is one that is present in such small numbers throughout the region that it is seldom seen or collected. Although not presently threatened with extinction, a rare species may become endangered if conditions in its environment worsen.

Endangered. An endangered species is one that is rare and whose prospects of survival and reproduction are in immediate jeopardy.

Peripheral. A peripheral species is one whose range barely infringes (usually by only a few kilometers) on the boundaries of the region.

Possible. A possible species is one that has not yet been recorded from the region but which is known from closely adjacent areas and likely occurs in eastern Texas.

Extinct. An extinct species is one that was once present but no longer occurs in the region.

Accidental. An accidental species is known on the basis of a single record that probably resulted from an unintentional introduction by man.

Native Mammals

MARSUPIALS (ORDER MARSUPICARNIVORA)
  New World Opossums (Family Didelphidae)
    Virginia Opossum, *Didelphis virginiana*   Common

SHREWS AND MOLES (ORDER SORICOMORPHA)
  Shrews (Family Soricidae)

Least Shrew, *Cryptotis parva*	Common
Southeastern Short-tailed Shrew, *Blarina carolinensis*	Uncommon
Southwestern Short-tailed Shrew, *Blarina hylophaga*	Possible
Desert Shrew, *Notiosorex crawfordi*	Possible

  Moles (Family Talpidae)

Eastern Mole, *Scalopus aquaticus*	Common

BATS (ORDER CHIROPTERA)
  Insectivorous Bats (Family Vespertilionidae)

Southeastern Myotis, *Myotis austroriparius*	Uncommon
Cave Myotis, *Myotis velifer*	Peripheral
Silver-haired Bat, *Lasionycteris noctivagans*	Migrant
Eastern Pipistrelle, *Pipistrellus subflavus*	Uncommon
Big Brown Bat, *Eptesicus fuscus*	Uncommon
Red Bat, *Lasiurus borealis*	Common
Seminole Bat, *Lasiurus seminolus*	Common
Hoary Bat, *Lasiurus cinereus*	Migrant
Northern Yellow Bat, *Lasiurus intermedius*	Uncommon
Evening Bat, *Nycticeius humeralis*	Common
Rafinesque's Big-eared Bat, *Plecotus rafinesquii*	Uncommon

  Free-tailed Bats (Family Molossidae)

Brazilian Free-tailed Bat, *Tadarida brasiliensis*	Common

EDENTATES (ORDER EDENTATA)
  Armadillos (Family Dasypodidae)

Nine-banded Armadillo, *Dasypus novemcinctus*	Common

LAGOMORPHS (ORDER LAGOMORPHA)
  Hares and Rabbits (Family Leporidae)

Eastern Cottontail, *Sylvilagus floridanus*	Common
Swamp Rabbit, *Sylvilagus aquaticus*	Uncommon
Black-tailed Jack Rabbit, *Lepus californicus*	Uncommon

RODENTS (ORDER RODENTIA)
  Squirrels (Family Sciuridae)

Thirteen-lined Ground Squirrel, *Spermophilus tridecemlineatus*	Uncommon
Mexican Ground Squirrel, *Spermophilus mexicanus*	Peripheral
Rock Squirrel, *Spermophilus variegatus*	Peripheral
Gray Squirrel, *Sciurus carolinensis*	Common
Fox Squirrel, *Sciurus niger*	Common
Southern Flying Squirrel, *Glaucomys volans*	Common

  Pocket Gophers (Family Geomyidae)

Louisiana Pocket Gopher, *Geomys breviceps*	Common
Attwater's Pocket Gopher, *Geomys attwateri*	Common
Plains Pocket Gopher, *Geomys bursarius*	Common

Pocket Mice and Kangaroo Rats (Family
    Heteromyidae)
    Hispid Pocket Mouse, *Perognathus hispidus*   Uncommon
    Silky Pocket Mouse, *Perognathus flavus*   Uncommon
    Padre Island Kangaroo Rat, *Dipodomys
        compactus*   Peripheral
Beavers (Family Castoridae)
    Beaver, *Castor canadensis*   Common
New World Rats and Mice (Family Cricetidae)
    Marsh Rice Rat, *Oryzomys palustris*   Common
    Plains Harvest Mouse, *Reithrodontomys
        montanus*   Uncommon
    Eastern Harvest Mouse, *Reithrodontomys
        humulis*   Uncommon
    Fulvous Harvest Mouse, *Reithrodontomys
        fulvescens*   Common
    Deer Mouse, *Peromyscus maniculatus*   Uncommon
    Cotton Mouse, *Peromyscus gossypinus*   Common
    White-footed Mouse, *Peromyscus leucopus*   Uncommon
    Encinal Mouse, *Peromyscus pectoralis*   Peripheral
    Golden Mouse, *Ochrotomys nuttalli*   Common
    Northern Pygmy Mouse, *Baiomys taylori*   Common
    Hispid Cotton Rat, *Sigmodon hispidus*   Common
    Eastern Woodrat, *Neotoma floridana*   Common
    Southern Plains Woodrat, *Neotoma micropus*   Uncommon
    Prairie Vole, *Microtus ochrogaster*   Extinct
    Woodland Vole, *Microtus pinetorum*   Uncommon
    Muskrat, *Ondatra zibethicus*   Uncommon
WHALES AND DOLPHINS (ORDER CETACEA)
    Dolphins and Small Whales (Family Delphinidae)
    Bottlenosed Dolphin, *Tursiops truncatus*   Common
CARNIVORES (ORDER CARNIVORA)
    Dogs and Relatives (Family Canidae)
    Coyote, *Canis latrans*   Common
    Red Wolf, *Canis rufus*   Endangered
    Gray Wolf, *Canis lupus*   Extinct
    Gray Fox, *Urocyon cinereoargenteus*   Common
    Bears (Family Ursidae)
    Black Bear, *Ursus americanus*   Extinct
    Raccoons and Relatives (Family Procyonidae)
    Ringtail, *Bassariscus astutus*   Uncommon
    Raccoon, *Procyon lotor*   Common
    Weasels and Relatives (Family Mustelidae)
    Long-tailed Weasel, *Mustela frenata*   Uncommon
    Mink, *Mustela vison*   Common
    Badger, *Taxidea taxus*   Uncommon
    Eastern Spotted Skunk, *Spilogale putorius*   Uncommon

Striped Skunk, *Mephitis mephitis*	Common
Hog-nosed Skunk, *Conepatus mesoleucus*	Uncommon
River Otter, *Lutra canadensis*	Uncommon
Cats (Family Felidae)	
Jaguar, *Felis onca*	Extinct
Mountain Lion, *Felis concolor*	Rare
Ocelot, *Felis pardalis*	Extinct
Bobcat, *Felis rufus*	Common
Even-toed Ungulates (Order Artiodactyla)	
Peccary and Relatives (Family Tayassuidae)	
Collared Peccary, *Dicotyles tajacu*	Extinct
Deer and Relatives (Family Cervidae)	
White-tailed Deer, *Odocoileus virginianus*	Common
Pronghorn (Family Antilocapridae)	
Pronghorn, *Antilocapra americana*	Extinct
Cattle and Relatives (Family Bovidae)	
Bison, *Bison bison*	Extinct

Introduced Mammals

Rodents (Order Rodentia)	
Squirrels (Family Sciuridae)	
Woodchuck, *Marmota monax*	Accidental
Black-tailed Prairie Dog, *Cynomys ludovicianus*	Uncommon
Old World Rats and Mice (Family Muridae)	
Roof Rat, *Rattus rattus*	Common
Norway Rat, *Rattus norvegicus*	Common
House Mouse, *Mus musculus*	Common
Capromyids (Family Capromyidae)	
Nutria, *Myocastor coypus*	Common
Carnivores (Order Carnivora)	
Dogs and Relatives (Family Canidae)	
Red Fox, *Vulpes vulpes*	Uncommon

Domestic Mammals

Carnivores (Order Carnivora)	
Dogs and Relatives (Family Canidae)	
Domestic Dog, *Canis familiaris*	Common
Cats (Family Felidae)	
Domestic Cat, *Felis catus*	Common
Even-toed Ungulates (Order Artiodactyla)	
Pigs (Family Suidae)	
Wild Hog, *Sus scrofa*	Uncommon
Cattle and Relatives (Family Bovidae)	
Domestic Cow, *Bos taurus*	Common
Sheep, *Ovis aires*	Uncommon
Goat, *Capra hircus*	Uncommon

Odd-toed Ungulates (Order Perissodactyla)
  Horses and Relatives (Family Equidae)
    Horse, *Equus caballus*   Common
    Ass, *Equus hemionus*   Uncommon
    Mule, *Equus caballus* × *Equus hemionus*   Uncommon

Geographic and Ecological Affinities of the Mammalian Fauna

The native mammal fauna of eastern Texas is composed of an interesting mixture of species derived from at least four different sources (as defined by Hoffmann and Jones, 1970): steppe or grassland species from the central prairies, deciduous forest species from the eastern and southeastern United States, invaders from the southwest, and invaders from the south. There are few distinctive elements within the fauna. There is but one endemic species (*Geomys attwateri*) and, together with its close sibling (*Geomys breviceps*), these are the only two mammals that probably evolved within the borders of eastern Texas.

The largest segment of the mammal fauna is made up of species that apparently invaded eastern Texas from deciduous forests to the east and southeast, particularly through the lowland forested habitats of the coastal plain. Included in this group of species, most of which live in forested habitats, are the following mammals:

*Blarina carolinensis**	*Sylvilagus aquaticus**
Cryptotis parva	*Sciurus carolinensis**
Scalopus aquaticus	*Sciurus niger*
*Myotis austroriparius**	*Glaucomys volans*
Pipistrellus subflavus	*Oryzomys palustris*
Lasiurus borealis	*Reithrodontomys humulis*
*Lasiurus seminolus**	*Peromyscus leucopus*
Lasiurus intermedius	*Peromyscus gossypinus**
Nycticeius humeralis	*Ochrotomys nuttalli**
*Plecotus rafinesquii**	*Neotoma floridana*
Tadarida brasiliensis	*Microtus pinetorum*
(subspecies *cynocephala*)*	*Canis rufus*
Sylvilagus floridanus	*Urocyon cinereoargenteus*

About one-third of these mammals (indicated by an asterisk) reach the western limits of their distribution in Texas somewhere within the bounds of eastern Texas. Some of these occur westward in the region only approximately to the margins of continuous hardwood forest, whereas others have pushed westward onto the prairies as dendritic segments along the major eastward-flowing river systems.

Eleven species that occur in eastern Texas are associated with the steppe or interior grassland habitats of central North America. Most species of this faunal element probably entered eastern Texas from the west or north, and those that occur in the area today are most common in the blackland prairie region. Included in this steppe assemblage of species are the following:

Spermophilus tridecemlineatus	*Neotoma micropus*
Geomys bursarius	*Microtus ochrogaster*
Perognathus hispidus	*Taxidea taxus*
Reithrodontomys montanus	*Spilogale putorius*
Peromyscus maniculatus	*Antilocapra americana*
(subspecies *pallescens*)	*Bison bison*

A third component of the mammal fauna of eastern Texas consists of southern species characteristic of lowland tropical and subtropical habitats of northeastern Mexico and the Rio Grande Plains of South Texas. Some of these species, such as the armadillo (*Dasypus novemcinctus*) and the northern pygmy mouse (*Baiomys taylori*), are relatively recent invaders of eastern Texas, having arrived only within the past one hundred years. Included in this groups of invaders from the south are the following:

Didelphis virginiana	*Reithrodontomys fulvescens*
Tadarida brasiliensis	*Sigmodon hispidus*
(subspecies *mexicana*)	*Baiomys taylori*
Dasypus novemcinctus	*Felis onca*
Spermophilus mexicanus	*Felis pardalis*
Dipodomys compactus	*Dicotyles tajacu*

Finally, there are a few species that invaded eastern Texas from the west or southwest. All of these species are common in the grassland or desert habitats of Trans-Pecos Texas, and all of them reach their distributional limits in Texas within the study area. At least one of the species, the black-tailed jack rabbit (*Lepus californicus*), may have greatly expanded its range in recent times as a result of the clearing of land associated with agricultural practices. Mammals included in this southwestern assemblage are:

Myotis velifer	*Peromyscus pectoralis*
Lepus californicus	*Bassariscus astutus*
Spermophilus variegatus	*Conepatus mesoleucus*
Perognathus flavus	

Several widespread North American elements occur in the mammalian fauna of eastern Texas. These species have broad geographic ranges and are of little value in determining the relationships of a fauna. The following mammals are included in this category:

Eptesicus fuscus	*Procyon lotor*
Lasionycteris noctivagans	*Mustela frenata*
Lasiurus cinereus	*Mustela vison*
Castor canadensis	*Mephitis mephitis*
Ondatra zibethicus	*Lutra canadensis*
Canis latrans	*Felis rufus*
Canis lupus	*Felis concolor*
Ursus americanus	*Odocoileus virginianus*

With the exception of the fully aquatic bottlenosed dolphin and the semiaquatic beaver, muskrat, and river otter, the complex mosaic of mammals living today in eastern Texas may be arranged into two main assemblages. One of these is made up almost entirely of forest-dwelling species with eastern-southeastern affinities. At present, these mammals occur primarily in the timbered habitats of the pineywoods and post oak woodland regions, although some of them also extend along the wooded streams into the blackland and coastal prairie areas. The other assemblage occupies open lands, including the climax grassland habitats of the blackland and coastal prairies, the grassland savannas of the post oak woodlands, as well as the numerous pastures, old fields, plowed fields, and other cleared areas (such as highway and railroad rights-of-way) scattered throughout eastern Texas. By carefully reading the distribution and habitat section of each species account, it is possible to place most mammals into one of these two assemblages, although there are several species that fit into both categories.

I do not mean to give the impression that there is a distinct geographic division between forest and open-land assemblages because such is not the case. In fact, there is considerable interdigitation of forest and open-land vegetational types throughout eastern Texas. Hence, most mammals are not confined to a specific geographic region because the habitats occupied by a particular species may occur within more than one region. As a result of land-clearing operations in timbered regions, many open-land species have extended their distributions in recent times.

I view eastern Texas as an area of faunal transition between the climax grassland habitats of the Great Plains, as are developed on the High Plains and associated desert scrub subclimaxes in the Trans-Pecos and Rio Grande Plain, and the deciduous forest biome of the eastern United States and its pine-oak and pine subclimaxes. Across this vegetational gradient there is a gradual depletion of grassland and desert faunal elements and a concomitant increase in forest-dwelling mammals.

Economically Important Mammals (Furbearers and Game Species)

Wild mammals played an extremely important role in the history of eastern Texas. Before whites arrived, Indians were dependent to a large extent on mammals for food, clothing, and shelter. Trappers, exploring the wilderness for fur resources (mainly the beaver and otter), were among the first white men to penetrate the region (Lay, 1943). The settlers who followed them used game to tide them over in the period before crops and herds could be developed. Some of the larger plantations employed skilled hunters who provided all of the meat consumed by the slaves or tenants as well as the white families.

The white-tailed deer, in particular, played an important role in the early colonization and development of the region. Railroad construction crews were supplied by professional deer hunters, one of whom claims to have killed 3,000 deer (Anonymous, 1945). Until 1900 market hunting was common throughout eastern Texas, and even as late as 1925 it was not uncomon in the pineywoods region. Deer hides were an important item of trade before 1900, and many professional hunters killed deer for the hides only. Strecker (1927) describes the trade in deer skins in early Texas. One trading post near Waco shipped 75,000 deer hides to New York during the period from 1844 to 1853. In addition to deer skins, the post also shipped large numbers of buffalo, bear, and smaller pelts.

The economic importance of game and fur-bearing mammals is not generally recognized. There are many aesthetic, recreational, and scientific values that cannot be translated into dollars and cents. There are a few items, however, on which statistics present a purely commercial value of the wild mammals.

The economically most important mammals in eastern Texas are the furbearers, of which there are fifteen species. Texas law requires that a "trapper" (one who takes a fur-bearing animal or the pelt of such an animal) must possess a trapping license. License fees are $10.75 for residents and $200.75 for nonresidents. The trapping season for most species opens on December 1 and closes on January 31, lasting only two months (The season for muskrats opens on November 15 and closes on March 15; nutria may be trapped at any time during the year).

During the 1970s the estimated annual income from the harvest of fur-bearing mammals in Texas increased from about $1.2 million in 1972–73 to about $26.2 million in 1978–79, according to estimates from the Texas Parks and Wildlife Department. During this period the average price paid for furs of most species increased substantially (Table 1). For some species, the value of their fur tripled over this nine-year period. The bobcat possesses the most valuable pelt, followed by the otter and red fox. Other valuable furbearers are the gray fox, coyote, and raccoon.

Fur prices are not static throughout a given season. They fluctuate according to supply and demand. Some variation also exists between prices paid by individual dealers. Some buyers prefer to "grade" or sort out furs and set prices according to size, pelage color, or texture. Other buyers pay a "flat" or gross price for all undamaged furs. This price would be substantially lower than the highest price paid for graded furs, but the number of pelts bringing top price and those bringing a lower price provide an average equivalent to those paid on a flat-price basis. The average prices listed in Table 1 were developed by Texas Parks and Wildlife Department biologists based on interviews with representative fur dealers, trappers, and trapper associations.

The increase in prices paid for raw furs during the decade of the seventies produced a 665 percent increase in licenses sold to trappers. In eastern Texas, the greatest number of licensed trappers are in the pineywoods, followed in order by the post oak woodlands, blackland prairies, and coastal prairies and marshes. The mushrooming of license purchases caused concern over the possible adverse effects of increased harvest pressure on the fur-bearing species. In response to this concern, the Texas Parks and Wildlife Department initiated a survey of licensed trappers in the state to assess the man-days spent trapping, harvest techniques, numbers of each species harvested, and the geographic distri-

TABLE 1. Average Prices Paid for Texas Furs.

Species	1936–42	1972–73	1973–74	1974–75	1975–76	1976–77	1977–78	1978–79	1979–80	1980–81
Bobcat	$ 0.85	$22.00	$20.00	$25.00	$50.00	$65.00	$55.00	$85.00	$65.00	$65.00
Red Fox*	—	12.00	20.00	20.00	25.00	38.50	40.00	45.00	45.00	17.00
Gray Fox*	0.90	6.50	12.00	16.50	18.50	22.50	28.50	35.00	35.00	26.00
Coyote	1.99	6.00	13.00	8.50	15.00	13.50	20.00	22.50	15.75	19.50
Raccoon*	1.59	4.50	6.50	5.50	8.75	12.50	16.00	25.50	20.00	11.00
Ringtail*	1.77	3.75	4.50	3.75	4.50	4.50	7.50	7.50	5.75	7.25
Badger*	1.30	2.00	5.00	5.00	5.00	5.00	5.00	5.00	6.26	5.25
Spotted Skunk*	0.30	1.10	1.25	1.25	1.25	1.50	12.00	2.50	2.50	4.25
Striped Skunk*	0.59	.65	1.50	1.50	1.00	1.25	1.50	2.00	3.00	2.00
Opossum*	0.30	.65	1.25	1.75	1.50	1.50	1.75	2.50	2.50	1.50
Mink*										
Male		8.00	10.00	7.00	12.00	12.00	12.00	14.00	14.00	12.00
	5.60									
Female		4.00	5.00	3.50	6.00	6.00	6.00	7.50	7.50	6.00
Nutria*	—	1.25	3.00	2.50	5.50	7.25	6.50	7.25	8.75	8.75
Muskrat*	0.54	1.75	2.50	2.50	5.00	6.25	5.50	6.25	7.25	7.25
Beaver*	8.11	4.00	4.00	4.00	9.00	9.00	7.00	9.00	7.50	5.25
Otter*	—	—	—	—	35.00	40.00	28.00	40.00	40.00	28.00

Source: Texas Parks and Wildlife Department data.
*Indicates those species officially listed as fur-bearing animals in the Texas Parks and Wildlife Code (1981–82).

bution of harvest rates. The survey was distributed to a random sample of 10 percent of the licensed trappers in each county for a five-year period beginning with the 1976–77 trapping season and ending with the 1980–81 season. Cohen (1982) evaluated these questionnaires and calculated harvest levels for each furbearer in the major ecological regions of Texas over the five-year survey period.

Tabulations for the four vegetative areas of eastern Texas are presented in Table 2. Over 2.5 million furbearers were harvested, producing an income in excess of $30 million. Harvest levels and value of the catch were highest in the pineywoods and lowest in the coastal prairies and marshes; the post oak woodland and blackland prairies had intermediate but similar estimates.

Raccoons far outnumbered all other species in the harvest, representing 47 percent of the pelts and 69 percent of the value. The five top-ranking species (raccoon, opossum, nutria, coyote, and striped skunk) constituted about 92 percent of the total pelt harvest and 85 percent of the total value. Raccoons and opossums alone accounted for almost 80 percent of the total harvest and about 75 percent of the total value. These species are taken in such high numbers because both are relatively common in eastern Texas, and both are highly susceptible to the generalized trapping methods utilized by most trappers. Many trappers direct their effort toward raccoons rather than toward those species with more valuable pelts because the return per effort is much greater. The opossum is the only species that even comes close to being taken in similar numbers, but its pelt brings a relatively lower price than other fur-bearing species. Because of this, it is likely that many individuals are discarded by trappers, and the actual number of opossums harvested is probably even higher than the survey indicates.

Species such as the gray fox, nutria, coyote, striped skunk, bobcat, and mink are taken in far fewer numbers than the raccoon and opossum. With the exception of the striped skunk, these species are most likely sought by trappers because of the high value of their pelts. The coyote, gray fox, bobcat, and mink may not have been taken more often because of the difficulty in trapping these species. Another factor that may account for the reduced numbers of these carnivores relates to their density patterns. According to Wood (1952), even when these larger carnivores exist in relatively high densities in a given area, they are still rare compared to smaller carnivores because they are at the upper level of the food web and, hence, tend to be more wide-ranging and more sparsely dispersed. Nutria are relatively easy to trap (Lowery, 1974), which could explain why they are taken in such high numbers by trappers.

Many more striped skunks are probably trapped each year than indicated by the survey. This is because the value of their pelt is low, and the unpleasantness of preparing the pelts is not worth the small monetary gain.

Species harvested in relatively small numbers include the beaver, otter, muskrat, spotted skunk, red fox, and ringtail. The semiaquatic spe-

TABLE 2. Estimated Harvest and Economic Value of Wild Furs in the Major Vegetational Areas of Eastern Texas, 1976–77 to 1980–81.

Species	Pineywoods			Coastal Prairies and Marshes			Post Oak Woodland			Blackland Prairies			TOTALS		
	Harvest	Value($)	Rank	Harvest	Value($)	Rank	Harvest	Value($)	Rank	Harvest	Value($)	Rank	Harvest	Value($)	Rank
Raccoon	393,226	6,750,479	1	241,667	4,329,464	1	300,946	5,236,224	1	276,911	4,675,513	1	1,212,750	20,991,680	1
Ringtail	3,325	23,091	13	11,422	66,854	8	3,452	22,001	10	28,752	184,658	6	46,951	296,604	8
Opossum	275,201	567,122	4	156,682	336,210	4	203,126	411,585	3	200,193	396,688	3	835,202	1,711,605	4
Red Fox	4,941	185,898	7	1,330	51,897	9	1,004	36,187	8	1,168	45,957	9	8,443	319,939	7
Gray Fox	25,474	770,721	3	5,555	173,035	6	6,875	204,379	5	8,584	242,123	5	46,488	1,390,258	5
Bobcat	11,828	789,350	2	4,966	344,989	3	5,411	353,628	4	4,765	316,365	4	26,970	1,804,332	3
Coyote	25,996	494,754	5	14,416	267,098	5	28,515	542,685	2	33,994	632,160	2	102,921	1,936,697	2
Badger	137	839	15	342	2,037	15	22	109	15	127	699	13	628	3,684	15
Spotted Skunk	800	2,898	14	1,379	6,606	13	1,646	6,778	12	4,320	15,979	12	8,145	32,261	14
Striped Skunk	22,733	48,208	9	14,265	31,457	10	21,433	38,991	7	41,083	90,654	7	99,514	209,310	9
Nutria	27,113	208,973	6	87,357	712,649	2	7,195	53,883	6	7,146	54,056	8	128,811	1,029,561	6
Muskrat	4,522	29,967	11	11,313	73,800	7	109	793	14	17	107	14	15,961	104,667	12
Mink	9,613	94,729	12	2,613	25,125	12	1,372	12,665	11	3,097	29,132	11	16,695	161,651	10
Otter	756	24,729	12	778	29,588	13	22	885	13	0	0	15	1,556	55,202	13
Beaver	4,828	40,109	10	426	3,231	9	3,731	29,551	9	5,094	34,502	10	14,079	107,393	11
TOTALS	810,495	10,030,640		337,011	6,454,040		584,859	6,950,344		615,211	6,716,593		2,565,114	30,154,844	

cies (the beaver, otter, and muskrat) are trapped in fewer numbers because all three have restricted distributions and low densities in eastern Texas and because all require specialized techniques to be harvested effectively. Since the majority of trappers use generalized techniques directed toward the raccoon or specialized techniques directed toward species with more valuable pelts, it is not surprising that these species are trapped in such low numbers.

The ringtail is taken in fairly large numbers in other vegetative regions in the state (the Edwards Plateau, and the Cross Timbers and Plains). The low numbers of ringtails taken in eastern Texas reflect its limited distribution in this area.

The red fox was probably taken in low numbers because of its low densities in eastern Texas. The price of its pelt (Table 1) would be a strong incentive to trap this species if it were present in sufficient densities to make the effort worthwhile.

Trappers use a variety of methods to collect furbearers, including steel traps, live traps, guns, dogs, and picking up animals dead on the road (DOR). Many trappers used a combination of these methods, but most use steel traps followed by guns, dogs, live traps, and DORs. Over the five-year period covered by the survey, 85 percent of the trappers in eastern Texas listed steel traps as their most-used method of taking animals, whereas fewer than 10 percent of the trappers used the other methods. By multiplying the estimated number of steel traps by the average number of days each active trapper spent trapping, the number of trap-nights can be estimated. For eastern Texas, the trapper effort relying on steel traps averaged about 2.8 million trap-nights per year.

In order to calculate the average trapper's income from selling furbearing mammals, Schmidly et al. (1980) evaluated the questionnaires returned by 373 trappers in a four-county area (Tyler, Hardin, Liberty, and Polk) encompassing Big Thicket National Preserve after the 1979–80 trapping season. The estimated value of the 14,301 furbearers harvested by trappers during this season was $191,435. The estimated individual income of trappers varied from a low of $5 to a high of $4,848. The average income for all trappers in the study area was $513.23 per trapper; the majority of trappers realized an estimated income of between $100 and $500 for their efforts, as the following table illustrates:

Income (dollars)	Number of Trappers	Percentage of Trappers
0–100	49	13.1
100–500	189	50.7
500–1,000	82	22.0
1,000–2,000	41	11.0
+2,000	12	3.2

These figures represent estimates of gross income realized from selling pelts based on the average price paid per pelt in the state during the

1979–80 trapping season. No estimates are available concerning the expenses incurred by trappers (cost of traps, scent or bait, transportation, or ammunition) in obtaining their pelts; hence, it is impossible to calculate net realized profits for each individual trapper.

By way of comparison, Lay (1939) reported that the average trapper's income during the 1936–37 trapping season was only $57.58 (range, $5.55 to $225.00). Despite the almost tenfold increase in income over the past forty-five years, it is obvious that fortunes are not built on the fur resource. Yet trapping fur animals can be profitable, and it provides both recreation as well as meat. To many of the rural people of eastern Texas, fur is a more important resource than either oil or lumber.

Hunting is another activity of substantial economic importance. The most popular mammals with hunters in eastern Texas are squirrels and white-tailed deer. Several hundred people hunt in the region each year, and this practice contributes significantly to the region's economy. The income generated from the sale of hunting licenses alone amounts to several million dollars annually. However, when the average cost of hunting is considered, it becomes obvious that hunting is more for recreation than for putting meat on the table.

Very little is known about the magnitude of squirrel hunting, either in terms of numbers of individuals or their economic value. More exact information is available for white-tailed deer (Table 3). Deer hunting is more popular and productive in the post oak woodland and pineywoods regions than in the coastal prairies and marshes or the blackland prairies. At one time the pineywoods provided the best deer hunting in Texas (Lay, 1954), but illegal hunting reduced the population to the point that the hunting season was closed. However, as a result of a restocking and protection program implemented by the Texas Parks and Wildlife Department in the 1950s, the deer population has increased to such an extent that hunting is allowed and the region has again become popular with hunters.

TABLE 3. White-tailed Deer Hunter and Harvest Data for the Vegetational Areas of Eastern Texas, 1973–74 through 1979–80.

Ecological Area	Hunting Season	Hunters	Hunter Days	Antlered Kills	Antlerless Kills	Total Kills	Kills per 1,000 Acres	Hunters per 1,000 Acres
Pineywoods	1973–74	83,365	586,883	17,240	466	17,706	1.60	7.53
	1974–75	88,509	651,578	19,075	1,006	20,081	1.81	7.99
	1975–76	103,484	771,950	24,915	554	25,469	2.30	9.34
	1976–77	81,643	611,082	15,938	386	16,324	1.47	7.37
	1977–78	89,610	639,851	20,110	1,261	21,371	1.95	8.16
	1978–79	91,886	671,677	21,480	1,931	23,411	2.13	8.37
	1979–80	101,810	739,802	26,691	2,845	29,536	2.69	9.28
Coastal Prairies and Marshes	1973–74	19,497	144,843	8,123	2,042	10,165	6.13	11.76
	1974–75	19,798	135,527	7,478	1,536	9,014	5.44	11.94
	1975–76	17,812	107,964	8,483	1,070	9,553	5.76	10.75
	1976–77	19,231	101,428	7,468	773	8,241	4.97	11.60
	1977–78	19,739	114,445	6,754	947	7,701	4.64	11.91
	1978–79	22,186	128,082	8,269	938	9,207	5.56	13.39
	1979–80	20,480	113,591	6,568	1,808	8,375	5.05	12.36
Post Oak Savanna	1973–74	103,776	670,660	28,322	4,518	32,840	4.20	13.26
	1974–75	101,773	568,916	28,406	3,551	31,957	4.08	13.00
	1975–76	106,826	638,017	26,859	1,894	28,753	3.67	13.65
	1976–77	96,300	558,047	21,966	2,698	24,664	3.15	12.30
	1977–78	105,410	620,957	23,321	2,751	26,072	3.31	13.38
	1978–79	99,089	569,724	20,859	1,733	22,593	2.87	12.58
	1979–80	100,050	584,293	24,130	2,842	26,972	3.42	12.70
Blackland Prairies	1973–74	2,774	9,433	353	44	397	0.77	5.39
	1974–75	3,618	12,536	584	117	701	1.36	7.03
	1975–76	3,949	19,428	856	122	978	1.90	7.67
	1976–77	2,269	10,900	475	68	543	1.06	4.41
	1977–78	2,510	9,322	154	0	154	0.25	4.15
	1978–79	2,754	13,712	322	0	322	0.53	4.56
	1979–80	2,729	11,880	388	0	388	0.64	4.52

3

Key to the Orders of Mammals

1 Bony plates covering back; almost no hair anywhere on back
. . . . Order Edentata, armadillos (p. 97)
   Back without bony plates; at least part of back (usually entire
   back) covered with hair 2

2 Body torpedo-shaped; hind legs absent; front limbs developed
   into flippers; hairless . . . .
. . . . Order Cetacea, whales and dolphins (p. 226)
   Not as above 3

3 Forelimbs modified for flight . . . .
. . . . Order Chiroptera, bats (p. 54)
   Forelimbs not modified for flight 4

4 Feet with one or more large, hard hoofs 5
   Feet with clawed toes 6

5 Each foot with only one hoof . . . .
. . . . Order Perissodactyla, horse (p. 325)
   Each foot with two or four hoofs . . . .
. . . . Order Artiodactyla, deer, pigs, cattle, etc. (p. 291)

6 Canines present; no pronounced diastema (space between
   teeth) 7
   Canines absent; diastema between incisors and cheek teeth
   pronounced 9

7 Incisors 5/4; hallux (big toe) opposable . . . .
. . . . Order Marsupicarnivora, opossum (p. 34)
   Incisors 3/3 or fewer; hallux not opposable 8

8 Canines not markedly longer than adjacent teeth; size small,
   total length less than 200 mm . . . .
. . . . Order Soricomorpha, shrews and moles (p. 38)
   Canines markedly longer than adjacent teeth; size medium to
   large . . . . Order Carnivora, carnivores (p. 323)

9 Incisors 2/1 . . Order Lagomorpha, rabbits and hares (p. 104)
   Incisors 1/1 . . . . Order Rodentia, rodents (p. 115)

4
Accounts of Wild Mammals

Order Marsupicarnivora

Marsupials were long regarded as a single, extremely diverse order (Marsupialia) that included insectivorous, carnivorous, omnivorous, nectivorous, browsing, and grazing animals. However, recent taxonomic authorities (Ride, 1964) have divided the single order into four separate orders that more properly reflect the antiquity of the different lines of descent. Under this arrangement, the New World opossums, which belong to the family Didelphidae, are placed in the order Marsupicarnivora.

Family Didelphidae (New World Opossums)

Diagnostic features of this family include a primitive brain, epipubic bones on the pelvis, a decided inturning of the angular process of the jaw, young born in an undeveloped state, and the presence of an abdominal pouch or marsupium in which newborns complete embryonic development. The family dates back to Cretaceous time, making it one of the oldest of living mammalian families. Opossums are often referred to as "living fossils" because they have survived relatively unchanged for at least fifty million years. The family includes twelve recent genera and about sixty-five species, with its main area of occurrence in Central America and northern South America. The Virginia opossum (*Didelphis virginiana*) is the only species that ranges north of Mexico.

Virginia Opossum
Didelphis virginiana (Kerr)

Name. The generic name *Didelphis* is derived from the Latin words *di*, meaning "double," and *delphys*, meaning "womb." The word *virginiana* is Latin for "Virginia," which is the type locality.

Identification. Opossums are easily distinguished from other mammals in eastern Texas by their long, scaly, prehensile tail; external, fur-lined abdominal pouch, or marsupium, in the female; five toes on each foot with an opposable and clawless hallux; and long and dense underfur, which is white basally and black terminally and strongly interspersed with exceptionally long, white guard hairs. Their snout is long, slender, and typically white; the ears, feet, and basal part of the tail are black. Two color phases, grayish and blackish, occur in most populations. Average measurements are total length, 809 mm; tail, 347 mm; hind foot, 66 mm; ear, 49 mm. The dental formula is I 5/4, C 1/1, Pm 3/3, M 4/4 × 2 = 50.

Subspecies. Two subspecies of the opossum supposedly occur in

Virginia opossum, *Didelphis virginiana*.

eastern Texas: *D. v. pigra* from the coastal prairie region and *D. v. virginiana* from the remaining area. Supposedly *pigra* may be distinguished from *virginiana* on the basis of its longer tail (usually exceeding 70 percent of head and body) and generally darker color overall; cranial measurements are similar in the two subspecies. I have found that these external features are not sufficient to distinguish opossums from the coastal prairie from those collected in other areas; hence, I have referred all specimens in eastern Texas to *D. v. virginiana*. It was named by Kerr (*The Animal Kingdom* [1792], p. 193) and the type locality is in "Virginia."

Distribution and habitat. Opossums occur throughout the eastern United States. Texas is on the edge of their range, and they occur in all but the extreme western, arid regions of the state. They are widespread throughout eastern Texas and probably occur in every county, although specimens have not been taken in a few counties (Map 5).

Opossums occupy a wide variety of habitats, including wooded areas, old fields, prairies, rice fields, and marshes. They seem to prefer wetter areas, near streams and swamps, but they are also common on the ridges and in the dry heads of small stream courses as well as along creeks and river bottoms.

Next to the raccoon (*Procyon lotor*), opossums are probably the most common medium-sized mammal in eastern Texas. Density estimates of one opossum per 1.6 ha have been made in Walker County (Lay, 1942), but a figure of about one opossum per 4 ha is probably a more reasonable estimate for most of the region.

Life history. Opossums live in dens constructed in ground burrows made by other animals, such as the armadillo (*Dasypus novemcinctus*). Other denning sites include hay stacks, junk heaps, chicken houses, storage sheds, garages, and unused barns. Their dens are seldom exposed to

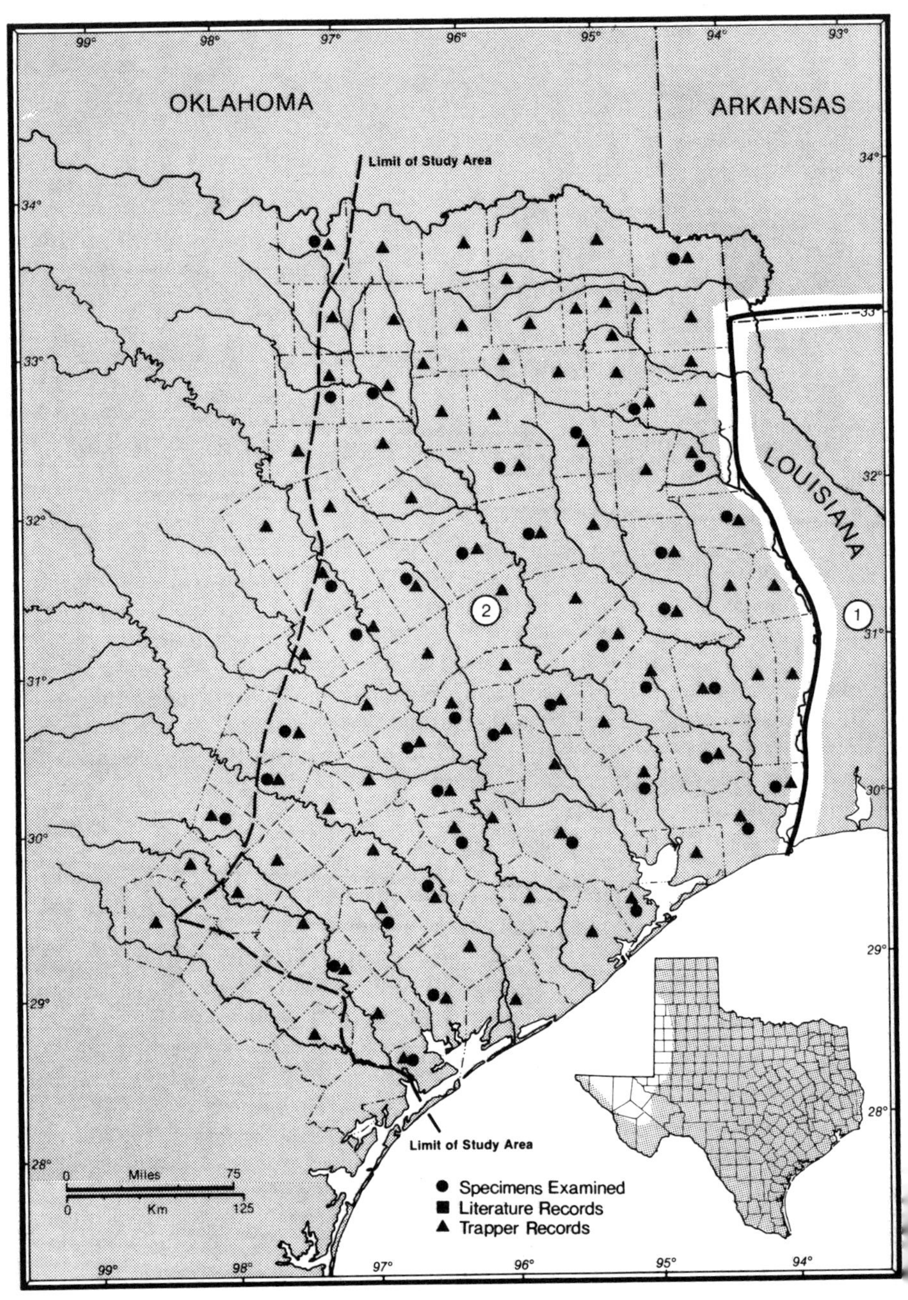

Map 5. Distribution of the Virginia opossum, *Didelphis virginiana*. 1. *D. v. pigra*. 2. *D. v. virginiana*.

direct sunlight, and a single opossum will generally use a variety of denning sites. The average time of occupancy of a den by an individual is about two days, and the average distance traveled between successive den sites is about 300 m. Occasionally two or more opossums may use the same den, and there are records of as many as five individuals of the same sex living in a single den. Opossums construct their nests out of litter.

The opossum is both terrestrial and arboreal, spending almost as much of its existence in trees as on the ground. It can climb fairly well, using its prehensile tail to aid its arboreal activities. Movement on the ground is slow, heavy, plodding, and awkward. The opossum walks with the entire foot—heel, sole, and toes—resting on the ground.

Opossums are almost exclusively nocturnal with a nomadic pattern of activity. Activity begins soon after dark and continues until dawn, with a peak between 11:00 P.M. and 2:00 A.M. Activity declines markedly in late autumn and winter, particularly under conditions of low ambient temperature. Movement is practically negligible below a temperature of $-7°$ C, but opossums do not hibernate.

The average home range size of an individual is about 4.6 ha (range, 0.12 to 23.5 ha). Home ranges are typically elongate instead of circular and often follow water courses, with considerable overlap among different individuals.

Their diet includes the following items: insects, 45 percent; fruit, 11.8 percent; green leaves, 11 percent; leaf and log litter, 10.6 percent; mammal flesh and hair (probably carrion), 7 percent; acorns, 4.7 percent; bird feathers, 4.3 percent; crayfish, 2 percent; snails, 0.8 percent; and seeds, 0.5 percent. Opossums are highly opportunistic feeders, which undoubtedly contributes to their success.

Their mating season is long and extends from January or February to June or July. The female is in heat for about thirty days. Females breed the first season following birth, regardless of whether weaning occurred in spring or summer. The period of receptivity, when mating occurs, is not longer than thirty-six hours and terminates with copulation. Opossums copulate in a manner similar to dogs. The male straddles the female, clasping her hind legs with his hind feet and her nape with his jaws. The pair topple to one side, and insertion of the penis occurs within two minutes. The male maintains his grasp of the female for the duration of coupling, which may last for as long as twenty minutes. At its termination, the female resumes her aggressive attitude and resists all further advances of the male.

Both uteri are inseminated during copulation, and ovulation may be delayed for as long as four days. The gestation period is from eleven to thirteen days. The mean litter size is 6.8 young per litter, with two litters—one from late January to late March and another from mid-May to early July—normally produced each year. Because gestation is shorter than the estrus cycle, nonfertilization or loss of young at parturition does not interrupt the following estrus. It has been suggested that if fewer than three young reach the pouch, the female may remove them and mate again at the next estrus to ensure maximum fecundity.

The young are altricial at birth and weigh about 0.13 g. They immediately migrate to a nipple, which enlarges in their mouth, and to which they remain attached 50 to 65 days. This period from conception to release of the nipple is roughly comparable to the gestation period of placental mammals. Opossums continue to suckle until they are weaned, which takes place about 95 to 105 days following parturition. Their eyes open about 65 days after birth, and after 67 days they move outside of the pouch. They eat solid food after 75 days and actually forage for themselves after 90 days.

Mortality is high during the first year of life. Their trapping-life span is only 83 days, which, in combination with the rapid disappearance of young after weaning, suggests a relatively rapid population turnover. Known predators include foxes, coyotes, horned owls, and barred owls; avian predators serve as an important source of mortality for young of the year. Opossums are commonly seen killed on highways, and this is undoubtedly another major source of mortality.

Opossums appear to be relatively free of ectoparasites, but they sustain a rather high incidence of endoparasites, particularly stomach nematodes and trematodes. They serve as a reservoir host for several important communicable diseases such as tularemia, relapsing fever, and leptospirosis.

Opossums emit a repertoire of sounds, including hisses, growls, screeches, and clicks, in a variety of situations such as mating, aggressive encounters between adults, and females in the presence of young. Social behavior is poorly developed in these mammals and, with the exception of mating, most encounters between adults are agonistic. Death feigning or catatonia is well developed. While feigning death, opossums are immobile, have their mouths open, and lie with a ventral flexion of the body and tail.

Remarks. Next to the raccoon (*Procyon lotor*), the opossum is the second most commonly harvested fur-bearing mammal in eastern Texas (Table 2). However, the value of its pelt is low (averaging $1.95 over a five-year period from 1975–76 to 1980–81), and the species ranks only fourth in terms of economic importance. Many trappers do not consider opossums worth "skinning out." Opossum fur is used primarily for trim on less expensive coats and hats.

References. W. B. Davis, 1958b, 1974; Gardner, 1973; Lay, 1942; Lowery, 1974; McCarley, 1959d; McManus, 1974; C. W. Schwartz and Schwartz, 1981; Sealander, 1979.

Order Soricomorpha

Mammals in this taxon were formerly placed in the order Insectivora along with such Old World groups as the elephant shrews, tree shrews, otter shrews, tenrecs, and hedgehogs. However, modern systematists (Eisenberg, 1981) now separate the true shrews, moles, and solenodons from the others in the order Soricormorpha. This order includes 315 species that are distributed throughout the world except for Australia and most of South America.

Two families of soricomorphs, the Talpidae (moles) and Soricidae (shrews), occur in North America. Both families, represented by three species (two shrews and one mole), occur in eastern Texas. Two other shrews, *Notiosorex crawfordi* in the southwest and *Blarina hylophaga* in the northeast and southeast, probably occur in the region and are included in the accounts given in Chapter 5.

1   Forelimbs highly modified for digging; no pinna; zygomatic arch thin but complete. Family Talpidae ....
.... Eastern mole, *Scalopus aquaticus.*
Forelimbs not modified for digging; zygomatic arch incomplete; pinna present but greatly reduced. Family Soricidae ...   2
2   Tail more than twice as long as hind foot; ears rather conspicuous; three unicuspid teeth in side of upper jaw ....
.... Desert shrew, *Notiosorex crawfordi.*
Tail short, less than twice as long as hind foot; ears nearly hidden in the fur; four or five unicuspid teeth in each side of upper jaw   3
3   Color uniformly lead gray above and below; five unicuspid teeth in each side of lower jaw   4
Color grayish brown above, distinctly paler below; four unicuspid teeth in each side of lower jaw ....
.... Least shrew, *Cryptotis parva.*
4   Karyotype with a diploid number of 52 and a fundamental number of 60, 61, or 62 ....
...... Southwestern short-tailed shrew, *Blarina hylophaga.*
Karyotype with a diploid number of 37 to 46 and a fundamental number of 44 ....
..... Southeastern short-tailed shrew, *Blarina carolinensis.*

Family Soricidae (Shrews)

Members of this family are among the smallest and least conspicuous of mammals, and they have the widest distribution of any soricomorph family. All shrews are characterized by long and pointed snouts, small eyes, and pinnae that are small but usually visible. The feet are five-toed and the foot posture is plantigrade. The narrow and elongate skull has no zygomatic arch or tympanic bulla.

Least Shrew
Cryptotis parva (Say)

Name. The generic name *Cryptotis* comes from Latin and translates as "hidden ear." The specific name *parva* is Latin for "small."

Identification. The least shrew is the smallest mammal in eastern

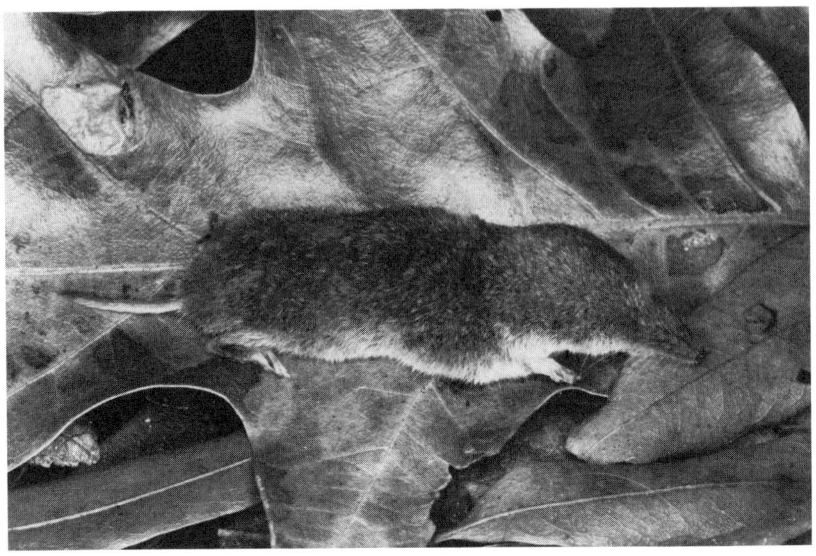

Least shrew, *Cryptotis parva.*

Texas, measuring only about 75 mm in total length. This species is distinguished from the short-tailed shrews (genus *Blarina*) by its smaller size, browner coloration, and by the fact that it is decidedly paler below instead of nearly uniform gray both above and below. Also, the fur is fine, short, and not as velvety as that of the short-tailed shrews. From the desert shrew (*Notiosorex crawfordi*), it differs in that the pinnae do not extend above the fur. *Cryptotis* also has two more teeth in the skull than *Notiosorex*. Average external measurements are total length, 74 mm; tail, 17 mm; hind foot, 10 mm. The dental formula is I 3/1, C 1/1, Pm 2/1, M 3/3 × 2 = 30.

Subspecies. Only one subspecies of *Cryptotis parva*, the nominate race *parva*, occurs in eastern Texas. It was named by Say (*Long's Expedition to the Rocky Mountains*, 1:163, 1823) with type locality on the west bank of the Missouri River near Blair, Engineer Cantonment, Washington County, Nebraska.

Distribution and habitat. This species occurs throughout eastern Texas, and it has been recorded in several counties (Map 6). It occurs in a variety of ecological situations including grassy or weedy fields and vacant lots, railway and highway rights-of-way, fence rows, hedgerows, briar thickets, and other tangles of vegetation adjacent to wooded areas. The critical component of its habitat appears to be the presence of dense herbaceous groundcover, especially of grasses (particularly bluestem, bermudagrass, and Johnson grass). The type of soil seems to be of minor importance in determining its distribution. The least shrew is seldom encountered in marshy or timbered regions, although it is not completely excluded from these ecological situations. Individuals have been trapped in timbered areas near College Station, Brazos County (W. B. Davis and Joeris, 1945), and Nacogdoches, Nacogdoches County (Broadbrooks,

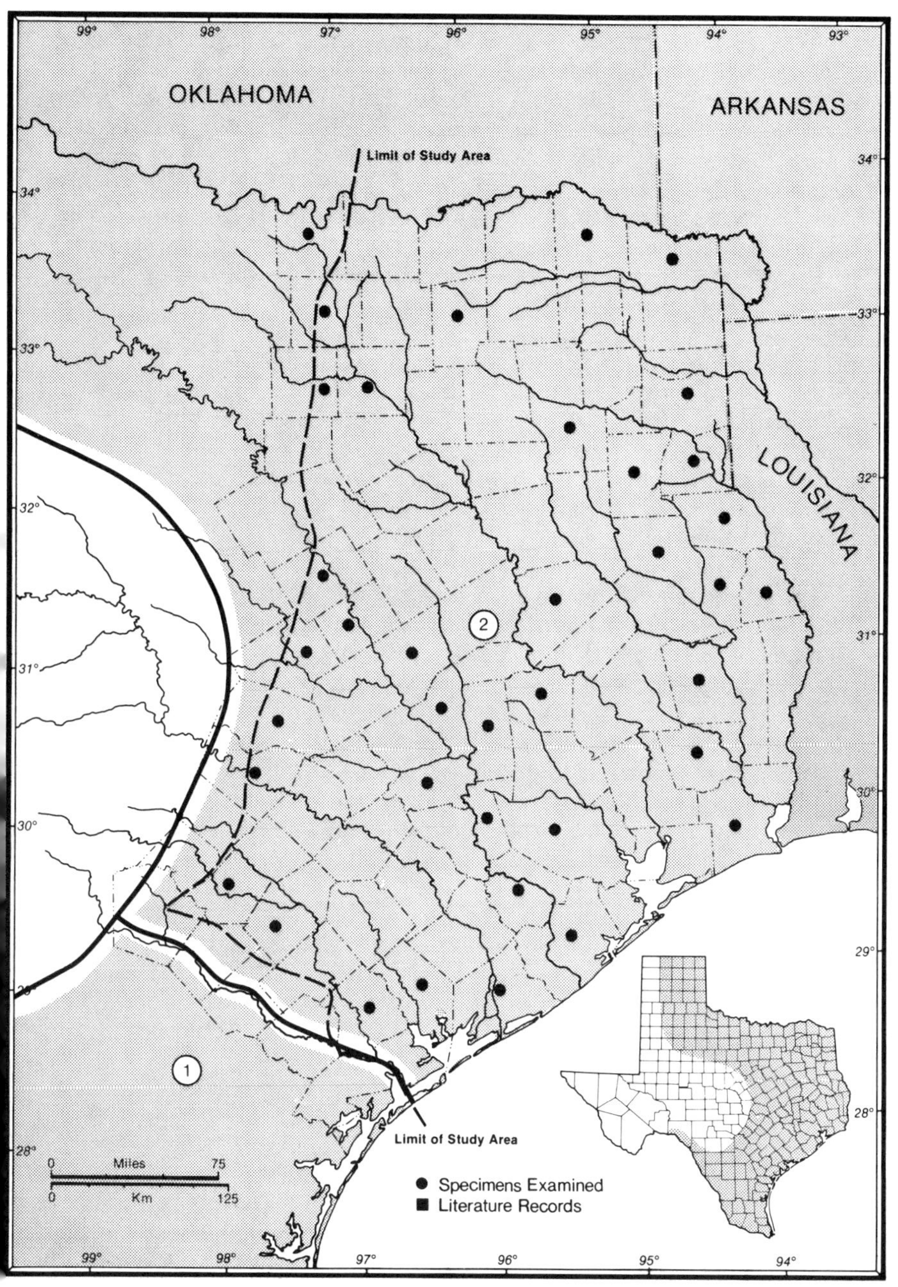

MAP 6. Distribution of the least shrew, *Cryptotis parva*. 1. *C. p. berlandieri*. 2. *C. p. parva*.

1952), and in a marshy area near Simms, Bowie County (Baker, 1942).

Life history. The least shrew commonly uses the surface runways of cotton rats (*Sigmodon hispidus*), with whom it shares its grassy habitats, but may make its own, which are difficult to identify because of similarity to those of certain insects. It also constructs below-ground tunnels about 25 mm in diameter and from 250 mm to 1.5 m in length. These tunnels generally extend about 200 mm below the ground and terminate in a nest. Nests are rather compact, globular-shaped structures normally located in relatively sparsely vegetated situations, such as a bermudagrass pasture or open fields, and often under some object such as a log, board, or piece of sheet metal.

Virtually nothing is known of the population dynamics of *C. parva*, probably because the species is so difficult to trap in numbers using conventional collecting techniques. Population densities of 1.7 shrews per ha have been recorded, but a figure of about 5 per ha is probably more reasonable. Irruptive population increases apparently occur in some places. For example, heavy concentrations of these shrews have been reported in Colorado and Jefferson counties on the basis of large numbers of skulls in barn owl pellets (W. B. Davis, 1938, 1940a).

These shrews do not range very far in their daily activities. The home range is approximately 0.23 ha for females and 0.16 ha for males. Based on observations of captive mammals, least shrews may be active at all hours of the day, with a peak in activity at night. Most of the daylight hours are spent in the nest, sleeping or resting.

Least shrews feed on a variety of items including insect larvae, earthworms, spiders, internal organs of crickets and grasshoppers, centipedes, mollusks, and a small amount of vegetation. Captive animals are fond of sow bugs, grasshoppers, and crickets, but hard-shelled beetles are avoided if other foods are present. If a choice of foods is offered, crickets are preferred over grasshoppers and the latter over sow bugs. Captive shrews will also eat the skinned carcasses of mice and birds. These shrews are cannibalistic to a certain extent. Shrews that die in captivity are often attacked by those that remain. When two shrews are caught together in a live trap, one is often partly eaten by the other, and there are records of females eating their young if they are disturbed or antagonized. When offered an excess amount of food, captive shrews will cache or store the extra food.

The reproductive biology of *Cryptotis* is poorly known. In Brazos County, a female containing four fetuses, each 10 mm in crown-rump length, was captured on October 20 and another containing three embryos on October 24 (W. B. Davis and Joeris, 1945). A shrew with embryos was also taken on October 24 in Bowie County (Baker, 1942). Infant shrews devoid of hair and with eyes and ears unopened have been captured on September 26 (W. B. Davis and Joeris, 1945), February 10 (Broadbrooks, 1952), and February 25 (Hunt, 1951). A slightly digested infant shrew, estimated to be two weeks of age, was discovered in the stomach of a blotched king snake (*Lampropeltis calligaster*) on March 18.

These observations suggest that the breeding period for these shrews extends from January to October, and that more than one litter may be produced annually. The number of young per litter varies from 3 to 7, with a mean of 4.5. The gestation period is between twenty-one and twenty-three days, and most births seem to occur in late afternoon. Newborn young, weighing 0.32 g, are naked at birth; hair becomes visible six days after parturition, and their eyes open after fourteen days. Adult size is reached in about one month.

Known predators of the least shrew include owls, house cats, hawks, spotted skunks, foxes, various snakes, and dogs. Nothing is known of how long these small shrews live in the wild. The only indication of longevity is a record of one individual living twenty-one months in captivity before dying of "old age." It is doubtful that small shrews would live this long in the wild.

This species appears to be somewhat colonial or at least social, inasmuch as they exhibit the unlikely characteristic for shrews of being able to exist together in the same nest. W. B. Davis and Joeris (1945) found a nest in December in Brazos County occupied by twelve individuals, and also reported that captive individuals ate and slept together. McCarley (1959c) found a nest of leaves and grass in January under a log on a hillside in an open field with sparse vegetation in Nacogdoches County. When the nest was gently probed, shrews began to run out, and no fewer than thirty-one individuals were counted. This type of communal behavior is adaptive during the colder months of the year because it permits the little shrews to concentrate and share their body heat and thereby counteract the effect of cool temperature.

Digestion is rapid in these shrews. Pieces of chitin and hair are known to traverse the entire digestive tract in periods of 1.5 to 2 hours. These shrews also have a high metabolic rate, and they normally consume an average amount of food per day that is slightly more than their own body weight.

Least shrews emit a variety of sounds, including low-intensity "clicks," "puts," and "twitters," but the "clicks" are the prominent calls (E. Gould, 1969). These calls are used when shrews are alone and exploring unfamiliar surroundings, and some of them may possibly be used in echolocation.

References. Broadbrooks, 1952; W. B. Davis, 1938, 1940a; W. B. Davis and Joeris, 1945; Hunt, 1951; McCarley, 1959d; Whitaker, 1974.

Southeastern Short-tailed Shrew
Blarina carolinensis (Bachman)

Name. The basis for the generic name *Blarina* is not known. The word *carolinensis* is Latin for "Carolina," in reference to the type locality of this species in South Carolina.

Identification. This small shrew differs, in external appearance, from other shrews in eastern Texas by the lack of contrast in the coloration

Southeastern short-tailed shrew, *Blarina carolinensis.*

of the underparts and upper parts, which are a uniform dark slate gray, and by its larger total length and hind foot. With respect to the skull, *Blarina* is readily distinguished from *Cryptotis* and *Notiosorex* by its larger size, especially that of the braincase, by its bulkier rostrum, and by the more extensive reddish brown tipping to the crowns of its teeth. The number of small unicuspid teeth in *Blarina* is five as opposed to three in *Notiosorex* and four in *Cryptotis.* Average measurements are total length, 88 mm; tail, 17 mm; hind foot, 11 mm. The dental formula is I 3/1, C 1/1, Pm 3/1, M 3/3 × 2 = 32.

B. carolinensis is remarkably similar to *B. hylophaga*, a species known from Louisiana, less than 10 km from the Texas border, and from South Texas at the Aransas National Wildlife Refuge, less than 40 km from the southern boundary of the study area (George et al., 1981). There are no qualitative morphological characters that will distinguish the two species, and their dental formulae are identical. The only morphological difference of note is the slightly larger size of *hylophaga* (see Table 4). The most significant difference between them is in the karyotype (Fig. 1). That of *hylophaga* has a diploid number of 52 and a fundamental number of 60, 61, or 62; *carolinensis* has a diploid number of 37–46 and a fundamental number of 44 (Genoways et al., 1977; George et al., 1982). These differences are such that it is highly unlikely that populations of the two species could interbreed and produce viable offspring where their geographic ranges come into contact.

Subspecies. Two subspecies occur in eastern Texas: *Blarina carolinensis minima* Lowery (*Occas. Pap. Mus. Zool. Louisiana State Univ.,* 13:218, November 22, 1943—type from Comite River, 13 mi. NE Baton Rouge, East Baton Rouge Parish, Louisiana) in the southeast and *B. c.*

TABLE 4. Cranial Measurements (in mm) of specimens of *B. carolinensis* and *B. hylophaga*.

Occipito-premaxillary Length	P^4–M^3 Length	Cranial Breadth	Breadth Zygomatic Plate	Maxillary Breadth	Interorbital Breadth	Mandibular Length	Mandibular Height
Blarina hylophaga from Caddo Parish, Louisiana (16)							
19.62 (19.1–20.5)	5.48 (5.2–5.8)	10.70 (10.2–11.3)	2.11 (2.0–2.3)	7.08 (6.7–7.3)	5.31 (5.0–5.5)	11.16 (10.5–11.6)	5.78 (5.5–6.1)
Blarina hylophaga from Aransas Co., Texas (2)							
19.95 (19.9–20.0)	5.55 (5.5–5.6)	11.00 (10.7–11.3)	2.15 (2.0–2.3)	6.95 (6.8–7.1)	5.35 (5.1–5.6)	11.50 (11.5–11.5)	5.85 (5.6–6.1)
Blarina carolinensis from Red River Co., Texas (2)							
18.52 (18.2–18.8)	4.68 (4.4–4.9)	10.05 (9.9–10.2)	2.25 (2.2–2.3)	6.45 (6.3–6.6)	5.05 (5.0–5.1)	9.60 (9.3–9.9)	5.45 (5.3–5.6)
Blarina carolinensis from Henderson, Gregg, and Harrison counties, Texas (3)							
19.42 (19.2–19.8)	5.37 (5.2–5.6)	10.32 (10.0–10.5)	1.77 (1.6–1.9)	6.77 (6.6–7.1)	5.17 (5.1–5.3)	11.07 (10.8–11.7)	6.03 (5.7–6.2)
Blarina carolinensis from Nacogdoches Co., Texas (5)							
19.25 (18.8–19.8)	5.37 (5.2–5.5)	10.70 (10.2–11.3)	2.02 (1.9–2.2)	6.75 (6.2–7.1)	5.27 (5.1–5.5)	10.88 (10.7–11.1)	5.55 (5.3–5.7)
Blarina carolinensis from Hardin, Tyler, Newton, and Walker counties, Texas (49)							
18.57 (17.9–19.4)	5.18 (4.9–5.5)	10.22 (9.6–10.6)	1.98 (1.6–2.2)	6.53 (6.2–7.0)	5.06 (4.8–5.3)	10.46 (9.9–11.1)	5.26 (4.9–5.7)

Note: See Choate (1972) for an explanation of measurements.

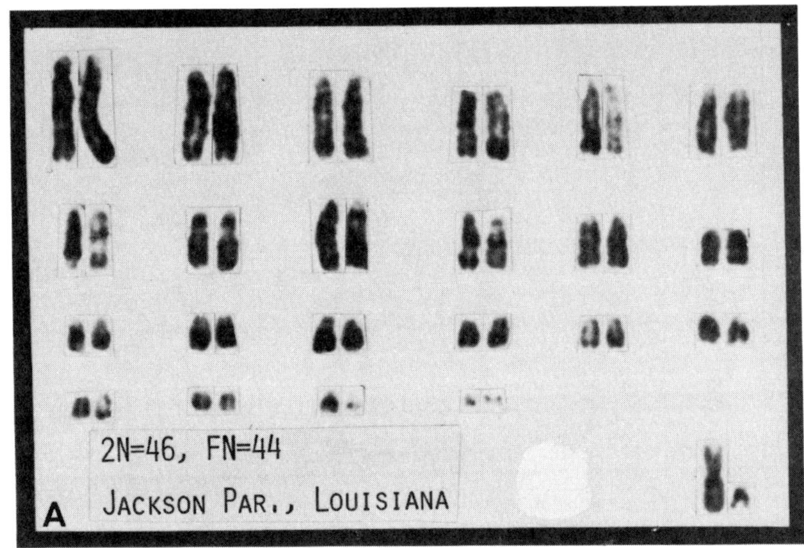

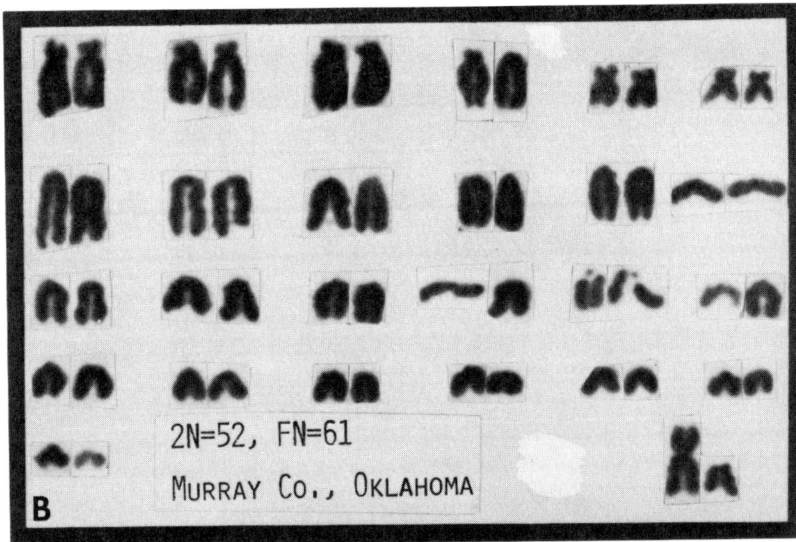

FIGURE 1. Karyotype of (A) *Blarina carolinensis* and (B) *Blarina hylophaga*. From George et al. (1982).

carolinensis (Bachman, *J. Acad. Nat. Sci. Philadelphia*, 7(2):366, 1827—type from eastern South Carolina) in the north (Map 7).

Distribution and habitat. Short-tailed shrews are restricted to the eastern one-third of Texas, where they occur in the pine-oak forest and pine forest regions of the pineywoods (Map 7). They occur in a variety of habitats, including grassy situations, densely wooded floodplains, and pine-oak uplands (McCarley and Bradshaw, 1953). I trapped them occasionally in Big Thicket National Preserve in mixed hardwood-pine forests in traps placed adjacent to or under old logs and in the leafy cover and humus of the forest floor in lower-slope hardwood-pine, upper-slope pine-oak, and flatland hardwood-pine habitats which, during the winter months, are often damp or wet.

Life history. Although they often utilize the runways and tunnels of other small mammals, these shrews will dig their own tunnel systems. Their burrows are located either just beneath the surface of the ground under a rotten log or stump, or at a deeper level about 40 to 56 cm below the surface. Surface tunnels are constructed by merely raising or separating the leaf mold or sod from the soil. Somewhere in the tunnel system they build nests out of partly shredded leaves and dried grass. Small nests used for resting are located in the shrew's shallow runway system; larger nests used for breeding are found in the deeper burrow system.

Little is known of the population dynamics of these shrews, but a considerable amount of information has been published concerning this species elsewhere in eastern North America. Out of 30,394 trap-nights in the Big Thicket, I captured 57 *Blarina* for a trap success percentage of 0.19. This low figure suggests these shrews are not very common, but it must be remembered that they are more difficult to trap than other small mammals. In other geographic areas, their population numbers fluctuate drastically from year to year. In peak periods, there may be as many as 62 or more of these shrews per ha, but a figure of 2.5 to 10 animals per ha is probably more realistic (C. W. Schwartz and Schwartz, 1981).

These shrews are active throughout the year and do not hibernate, but they are much easier to trap in colder months. All shrews are high-strung with a nervous temperament. They spend little time resting and may search for food at any time during the day or night. Their almost constant activity requires a tremendous amount of food and oxygen; this is reflected in their high basal metabolism, which is almost twice that of man. Their home range is usually between 0.2 and 0.4 ha.

These shrews eat a variety of animal and plant materials. Insects (including ants and ground beetles) make up nearly one-half of their diet, followed in abundance by vegetable matter, annelids, crustacea, mollusks, vertebrates, centipedes, inorganic matter, arachnids, and millipedes. There is evidence that *Blarina* may store snails for winter use (W. B. Davis, 1974). Prey are located by the shrew's keen sense of touch, which compensates for their poor eyesight, and are paralyzed by a powerful poison contained in the saliva. This poison is produced by the submaxillary gland and is introduced by wounds made by the teeth. It has been

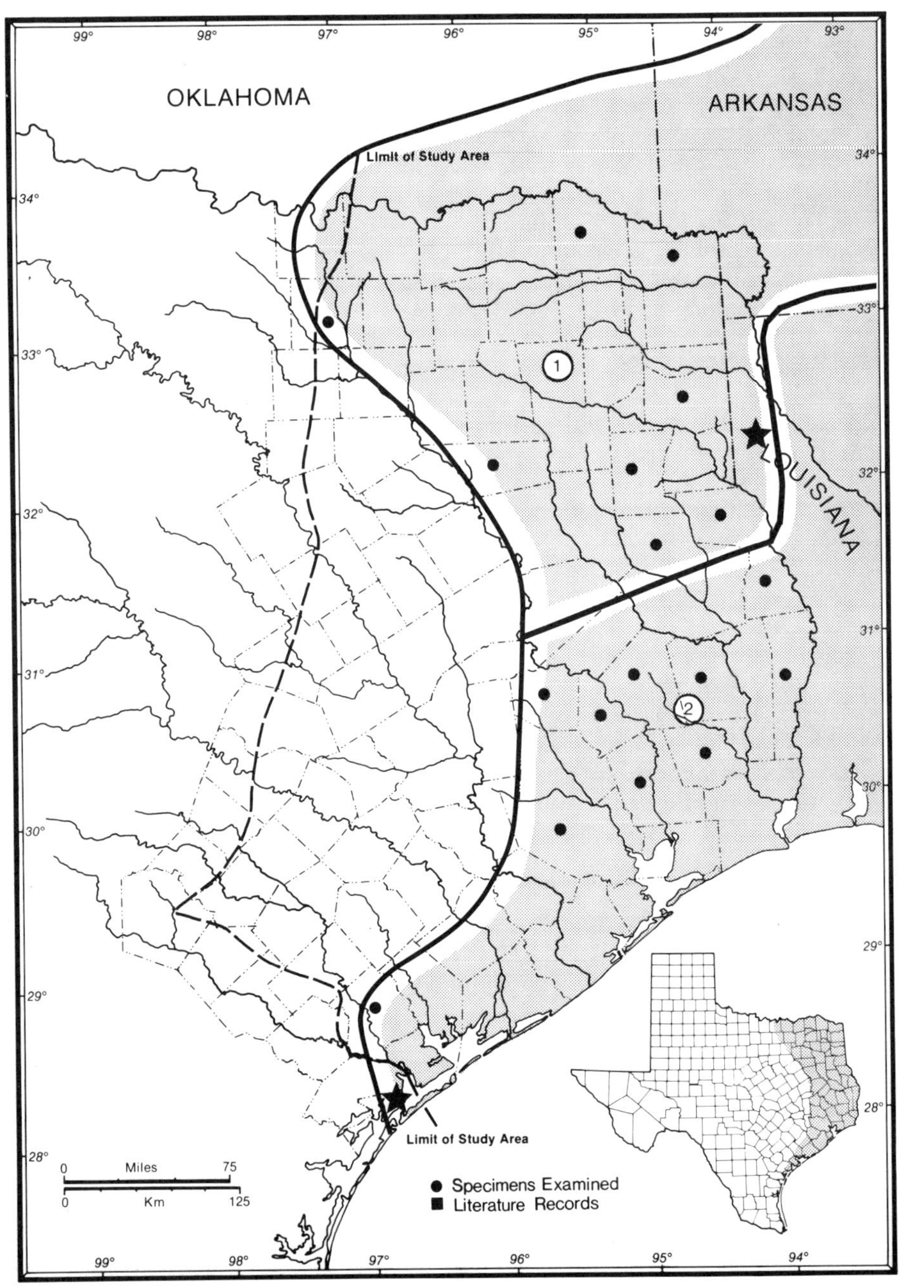

MAP 7. Distribution of the southeastern short-tailed shrew, *Blarina carolinensis*. 1. *B. c. carolinensis*. 2. *B. c. minima*. The stars indicate localities where the closely related species, *Blarina hylophaga*, has been taken.

estimated that there is enough poison in the gland of one adult shrew to kill 200 mice, but the poison is not dangerous to humans. These shrews have an exceedingly pugnacious, energetic nature with an insatiable lust for food. It has been estimated they may consume about one-half of their weight in food per day.

The breeding season of short-tailed shrews extends from February through September. Most adult females have one to two litters annually and bear from three to ten young (average, six to seven) per litter. The gestation period is about twenty-one or twenty-two days. Newborns are pink, blind, and helpless, weighing slightly more than 1 g. They are relatively slow in developing. After one week, they double in size, and hair is present; incisors appear at eighteen days, and shortly afterward (about the twenty-second day) the eyes open. They reach adult size in about one month, at which time they leave the nest. Population turnover is rapid; most shrews live no longer than one winter, and very few individuals reach two years of age.

Predators of short-tailed shrews include snakes, hawks, owls, weasels, skunks, foxes, coyotes, and bobcats. Domestic cats often capture these tiny creatures, but they seldom eat them because of their disagreeable, musky odor, which is produced by a pair of small scent glands located along the flanks of the shrew. The secretions of these glands may play a role in species recognition and as part of the shrew's sex life.

Recent evidence indicates that short-tailed shrews emit a series of ultrasonic clicks that may serve as part of an echolocation system (E. Gould et al., 1964). This technique may be used by the shrews to ascertain in darkness the position of objects and other space relationships.

Remarks. Historically, Texas specimens have been assigned to the species *Blarina brevicauda* (W. B. Davis, 1974; Hall, 1981; McCarley, 1959d). However, recent evidence suggests that *B. brevicauda* is a composite of at least three species in the south central United States (George et al., 1981; Genoways and Choate, 1972; Ellis et al., 1978; Schmidly and Brown, 1979). These include a large northern form, *B. brevicauda*, and two smaller southern species, *B. carolinensis* and *B. hylophaga*. Under this arrangement, Texas specimens are referable to the two smaller southern species, *B. carolinensis*, with two subspecies (*B. c. carolinensis* from northern and east central Texas and *B. c. minima* from southeastern Texas), and *B. hylophaga* with one subspecies (*B. h. plumbea* from Aransas National Wildlife Refuge, Aransas County).

References. W. B. Davis, 1974; McCarley, 1959d; C. W. Schwartz and Schwartz, 1981.

Family Talpidae (Moles)

The family Talpidae comprises one of the most highly specialized groups of insectivores. Living moles are currently classified in fifteen genera and approximately twenty-two species. The one genus occurring in eastern Texas is represented by the single species, *Scalopus aquaticus*.

All moles of the genus *Scalopus* are highly specialized for fossorial life, and it is estimated that 99 percent of their life is spent underground.

Eastern Mole
Scalopus aquaticus (Linnaeus)

Name. The name *Scalopus* is based on the Greek word for mole, *skalopos*, which in turn is derived from words meaning "to dig" and "foot." The Latin name *aquaticus*, which means "water-dwelling," is actually a misnomer that was first applied to this species by Linnaeus in 1758, perhaps because of the "webbed" feet (Lowery, 1974).

Identification. Moles have a body that is robust and depressed. The head is coupled closely to the body with the result that no distinct neck is evident. The tail is short, round, scantily haired, and averages less than one-fourth of the animal's total length. The nose is elongated into a distinctly pointed snout, which is naked anteriorly. The eyes are small with no external opening and are of little use, with the possible exception of light detection. External ears are lacking, and the ear openings are tiny holes buried in the fur. The feet are large, fleshy, and scantily haired. The front feet are broadened, shovel-like, and modified for digging; both the fore toes and hind toes are webbed to the base of the claws. The fur is dense, soft, silky, and velvet-like; color is usually brownish with a silvery sheen. Average external measurements are total length, 147 mm; tail, 26 mm; hind foot, 20 mm. The dental formula is I 3/2, C 1/0, Pm 3/3, M 3/3 × 2 = 36.

Subspecies. Three subspecies of moles occur in eastern Texas: *S. a. aereus* (Bangs, *Proc. Biol. Soc. Washington*, 10:138, December 28, 1896—type locality Stilwell, Adair County, Oklahoma) from extreme eastern Texas in Angelina, Bowie, Hardin, Harrison, Jasper, Rusk, Newton, and Shelby counties; *S. a. cryptus* Davis (*Am. Midland Nat.*, 27:383, March 1942—type locality from College Station, Brazos County, Texas) from the western boundary of the region southeastward to Montgomery County and from the Brazos River eastward to Tyler County; and *S. a. alleni* Baker (*Univ. Kansas Publ. Mus. Nat. Hist.*, 5:22, February 28, 1951—type locality Rockport, Aransas County, Texas) from the southern portion of the region below the Brazos River (Map 8). Yates and Schmidly (1977) recently reviewed geographic variation and the recognition and distribution of subspecies for this species in Texas.

Distribution and habitat. Moles occur throughout eastern Texas except where soil types are not suitable. They also range from extreme southern Texas northward into the Texas Panhandle, and a relict population is known from Presidio County (Map 8).

Since runways of the eastern mole are constructed by digging, the type, condition, and moisture content of the soil are among the most important factors influencing their distribution. They generally prefer loose, well-drained soils, such as those found in sandy floodplains and stream banks, and the light loamy soils of grasslands, pastures, and woodlands.

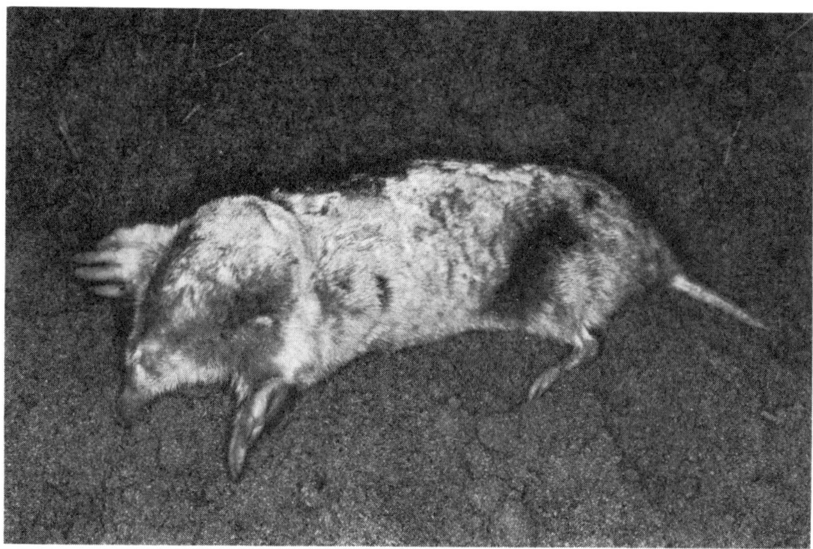

Eastern mole, *Scalopus aquaticus*.

They are scarce or absent in heavy clay and stony or gravelly soils. Moles may persist in suburban housing tracts, especially in gardens and lawns, if the streets do not have curbs. Rivers do not constitute barriers to their dispersal because they are adept swimmers. However, heavy clay soils associated with certain river systems may affect them.

Life history. The tunnel systems of the eastern mole are of two different types: surface runways or ridges, which are used for food collecting, and more permanent deep passages, which are used as living quarters and serve as thoroughfares to feeding grounds.

Due to a need for larger quantities of food, eastern moles range over larger areas than do fossorial rodents and in many cases have home ranges that exceed those of cursorial rodents (Yates and Schmidly, 1977). The average home range of males ranges from 3,616 to 18,041 m^2; that of females from 1,512 to 3,430 m^2 (Barbour and Davis, 1974). This area averages almost twenty-three times larger than that of pocket gophers (genus *Geomys*), which also are fossorial mammals. Population densities of four moles per ha are probably accurate estimates for most places in eastern Texas.

Moles may be active any hour of the day or night and in summer or winter. Activity peaks are from 4:00 to 7:00 A.M. and from 6:00 to 9:00 P.M. They seem to be most active after a warm rain when they take time to extend surface runways. Moles move through loose soil with a breast-stroke motion of the forepaws and with no rotation of the body from side to side. They dig at a rate of from 3.7 to 4.6 m per hour, including stops for rest and food. Moles have a scent gland on the belly. Scent is left on the floor of the tunnel as the mole passes by and may serve as a means of communication between sexes during the breeding season. These glands may also function to render moles undesirable to predators.

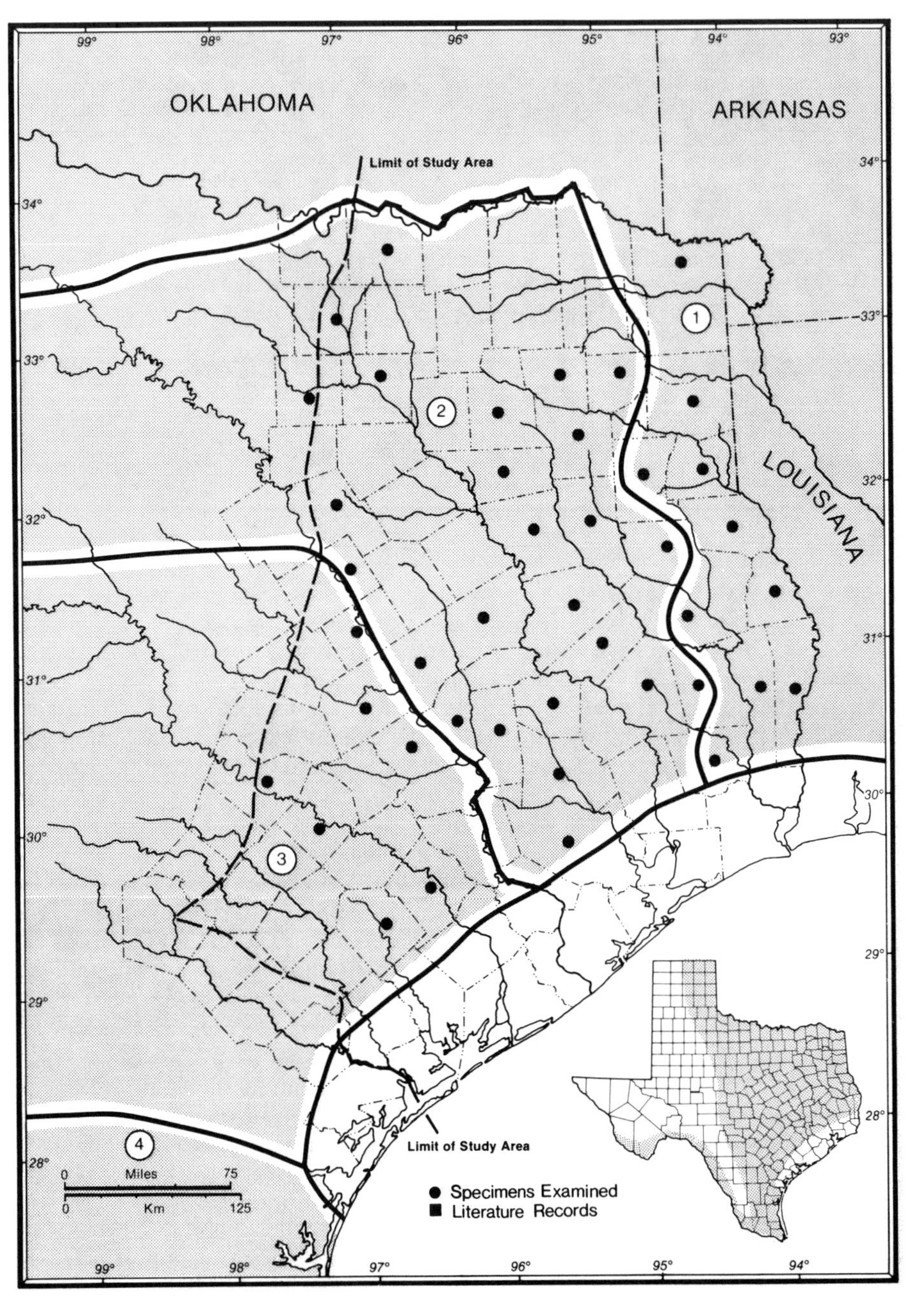

MAP 8. Distribution of the eastern mole, *Scalopus aquaticus*. 1. *S. a. aereus*. 2. *S. a. cryptus*. 3. *S. a. alleni*. 4. *S. a. inflatus*.

Moles have a longer life and a lower reproductive rate than most small mammals. Several adult moles have been recovered two years following tagging, and one individual was recaptured three years after its initial capture (Barbour and Davis, 1974).

The eastern mole has a voracious appetite. Its diet consists primarily of earthworms and insects, although vegetable matter is eaten occasionally; in captivity, it eats almost anything from ground beef to mice and small birds. Factors such as soil acidity, which limits the availability of food items, may, therefore, present barriers to dispersal. Moles locate their food through tactile, olfactory, and vibratory means of discrimination. Eyesight is very poor, and they tend to grab their prey wherever they happen to make contact after determining the direction of prey by vibration and smell. They kill active prey by crushing it against the sides of the burrow with the front feet or by piling loose dirt on the victim and then biting it. Moles kill earthworms by biting them rapidly in several places, often nearly cutting the worm in two. Captive moles are known to consume about 29 g of food per day, which represents between 50 and 55 percent of their total weight.

One of the few times when the eastern mole is known to disperse over the surface of the ground is during the breeding season. Only one litter, of two to five young (average, four), is born each year. The exact gestation period is not known, but it is thought to range from forty-two to forty-five days. The breeding season in eastern Texas probably begins in late fall and extends into winter. Moles taken in November and December were in breeding condition, and a female collected near Jasper, Jasper County, in late February contained three well-developed embryos. Young moles are born in a bulky nest (about 20 cm in length and 10 cm in diameter) made of course grass interspersed with leaves and lined with fine grass. They are rather large (about 50 mm in length) and hairless at birth, and they grow rather slowly. Velvety fur appears at ten to eleven days of age, and they are about half grown in five weeks. Young animals leave the nest and are able to care for themselves at about one month of age, and they reach adult size after about three months. Sexual maturity is reached at about one year of age.

Floods probably represent the greatest natural enemy of the eastern mole. Adults are good swimmers and may survive floods, but young probably perish in large numbers. Few birds of prey catch moles consistently because they spend so little time on the surface, but skulls are occasionally found in owl pellets. Foxes, badgers, coyotes, and perhaps skunks dig moles from their burrow systems; domestic cats and dogs also kill moles, but rarely eat them. W. B. Davis (1951a) reported a mole found in the stomach of a cottonmouth snake (*Agkistrodon piscivorus*).

Moles may be of considerable economic importance where they are abundant. They do damage, by their burrowing activities, to lawns, gardens, and golf greens. However, they eat great quantities of insects and carry humus to lower levels in the soil, which they also help to aereate.

References. Barbour and Davis, 1974; W. B. Davis, 1942; Yates and Schmidly, 1977, 1978.

Order Chiroptera

Bats are an extremely successful group of mammals, second only to rodents in numbers of species, with approximately 850. They are distributed worldwide but attain their greatest diversity and numbers in tropical areas. Remarkable for their structural modifications for flight and echolocatory abilities, bats are perhaps the most unique of all mammals. Their forelimbs are modified for flight, with digits elongated and joined together by a flight membrane extending to the side of the body and hind limb. Their mouselike tail is normally enclosed within the supporting interfemoral membrane, which extends from the tip of the tail to the ankles of the hind feet. A cartilaginous rod (calcar) arises from the inner side of the ankle joint and supports this tail membrane. The knee is directed outward and backward owing to rotation of the leg for supporting the wing membrane; this feature is also an adaptation for the bat's alighting upside down and hanging by its toes. A thin, erect, fleshy projection (called a tragus) rises from the inner base of the ear.

Bats live in a variety of places, including caves, rock crevices, buildings, abandoned houses, the thick foliage of living trees, and cavities of dead trees. Since there are few caves in eastern Texas, most of the species that habitually roost in underground passages are absent from this area. Most bats from temperate areas in the United States either hibernate or migrate to southern latitudes during the winter. However, bats are normally seen on all warm, winter nights in eastern Texas, and it appears that at least some species are resident and active in this region throughout the year.

Bats spend the daytime hanging quietly in a secluded retreat. While at rest, they generally hang downward by their hind feet. Upon leaving the roost as evening approaches, most bats fly to a pond or other body of water to drink. A feeding period follows during which time bats are on the wing catching insects. They use their sonar or echolocation system to identify or track prey as well as to avoid obstacles. They emit a series of brief pulses of high-frequency (ultrasonic) sound which strike an object and are reflected back by it in the form of an echo. By means of their acute sense of hearing, bats are able to convert the echos into information that enables them to ascertain the direction, distance, velocity, and some aspects of the size and shape of the object. Bats are not blind, but their eyes are small and probably of little value in locating prey.

After filling their stomachs with insects, bats retire to a roost where they rest most of the night. This night roost may or may not be located in the same place as the day roost. A second feeding period may occur just before daylight, but by daybreak, or shortly thereafter, bats are back in their daytime roost.

Most bats in eastern Texas mate in fall and winter. The female of most species retains the sperm in the uterus until spring, when ovulation and fertilization occur (hence, they exhibit delayed fertilization). The annual litter is usually produced in May or June. Most bats produce a single young, but several species have twins, and a few often give birth to litters of three or four. Many species congregate in nursery colonies, usually located in buildings or other dark retreats, ranging in size from a dozen or so to several thousand bats, where the young are born. No nest is built. The mother hangs her head upward as the young is born, and the baby is received in a pocket formed by the interfemoral membrane. At birth bats are large and well developed. As soon as they are born, they crawl to the mother's breast and attach to a nipple.

Texas has a varied bat fauna that includes five families and thirty-one species. Compared to the rest of the state, the bat fauna of eastern Texas is somewhat depauperate, with only twelve species and two families, Vespertilionidae and Molossidae. One of the species (*Myotis velifer*) is peripheral and is discussed in Chapter 5.

1 About one-third of the tail projecting beyond the interfemoral membrane (Family Molossidae) . . . .
. . . . Brazilian free-tailed bat, *Tadarida brasiliensis.*
Tail enclosed in interfemoral membrane, with no more than a few millimeters, at most, projecting free (Family Vespertilionidae) 2

2 Ears enormous, over 28 mm from notch to tip; a conspicuous lump present on each side of snout . . . .
. . . . Rafinesque's big-eared bat, *Plecotus rafinesquii*
Ears less than 26 mm from notch to tip; no conspicuous lump on each side of snout 3

3 At least the anterior half of the dorsal surface of the interfemoral membrane well furred 4
Dorsal surface of interfemoral membrane naked, scantily haired, or at most lightly furred on the anterior third 8

4 Color of fur black, with many of the hairs distinctly silver-tipped . . . . Silver-haired bat, *Lasionycteris noctivagans*
Color various, but never uniformly black 5

5 Posterior half of dorsal surface of interfemoral membrane essentially bare; color yellow with no white patches on shoulder or on wrists . . . . Northern yellow bat, *Lasiurus intermedius*
Posterior half of dorsal surface of interfemoral membrane nearly as well furred as the anterior half; color not yellow, white patches on shoulders and wrists 6

6 Forearm more than 45 mm; color wood brown heavily frosted with white . . . . Hoary bat, *Lasiurus cinereus*
Forearm less than 45 mm; upper parts reddish or mahogany 7

7 Color reddish frosted with white (males more reddish than females) . . . . Red bat, *Lasiurus borealis*
Color mahogany frosted with white . . . .
. . . . Seminole bat, *Lasiurus seminolus*

8   Tragus (projection within ear) long, pointed, and straight 9
      Tragus short, blunt, and curved 11
9   Hairs on back dark at base and tip, but lighter in the middle,
      leading edge of wing paler than rest of membrane; space be-
      hind canine with only one small tooth ....
      .... Eastern pipistrelle, *Pipistrellus subflavus*
      Hairs on back dark at base and lighter at tip, or uniformly col-
      ored; no light band in the middle; wing membrane concolor;
      space behind canine with two small teeth 10
10   Forearm 41 to 46 mm; color of upper parts dull to light brown
      .... Cave bat, *Myotis velifer*
      Forearm less than 40 mm; color of upper parts russet to gray
      .... Southeastern myotis, *Myotis austroriparius*
11   Forearm more than 40 mm; two upper incisors on each side of
      upper jaw .... Big brown bat, *Eptesicus fuscus*
      Forearm less than 40 mm; only one upper incisor on each side
      of upper jaw .... Evening bat, *Nycticeius humeralis*

Family Vespertilionidae (Insectivorous Bats)

Eleven of the twelve species of bats occurring in eastern Texas belong to this family. Vespertilionids are rather plain-looking bats that lack
the distinctive facial features characteristic of many families. The ears are
of moderate or large size, and the tragus is present but differs markedly in
shape between species. Most vespertilionids are insectivorous, and they
are unexcelled in their ability to capture flying insects.

Southeastern Myotis
Myotis austroriparius (Rhoads)

Name. The generic name *Myotis* comes from two Greek words, *mys*
for "mouse" and *otis* for "ear." The specific epithet *austroriparius* comes
from two Latin words, *austro* meaning "southern" and *riparius* meaning
"frequenting banks and streams."

Identification. This small bat is most easily confused with the evening bat (*Nycticeius humeralis*), which it closely resembles in color, but
from which it may readily be distinguished by its long, pointed, and
straight—instead of short, blunt, and curved—tragus and by its four, instead of two, upper incisors. Coloration in this species is highly variable,
and two distinct color phases are known. The color of the majority of specimens is best described as dull gray brown, but occasionally the dorsal
pelage is bright orange brown. These color differences are so striking that
it almost appears as if two distinct species of *Myotis* occur in eastern
Texas. LaVal (1970) has reported similar intrapopulational color variation
at other places in the southeastern United States. Average external measurements are total length, 88 mm; tail, 35 mm; hind foot, 10 mm; ear, 15

Southeastern myotis, *Myotis austroriparius* (photograph by Roger W. Barbour).

mm. The dental formula is I 2/3, C 1/1, Pm 3/3, M 3/3 × 2 = 38.

Subspecies. *Myotis austroriparius* is monotypic and distinct subspecies are not recognized.

Distribution and habitat. The southeastern myotis, which ranges from the Ohio River valley into the southeastern states, reaches its western limits in eastern Texas, where specimens have been recorded from Bowie, Panola, Tyler, Newton, Liberty, and Hardin counties (Map 9).

Although this species is abundant in Louisiana (Lowery, 1974), previous collecting records suggest it is uncommon in eastern Texas. The first Texas specimen was reported from Bowie County in 1966 (Packard, 1966), and the second specimen was recorded from Panola County in 1970 (Michael et al., 1970). While collecting in Big Thicket National Preserve and Newton County, I obtained seventeen specimens of this bat in mist nets strung over ponds and along stream courses in the following habitat types: stream floodplain forest, lower-slope hardwood-pine, flatland hardwoods, and upper-slope pine-oak.

Life history. Very little is known about the life history of this bat in eastern Texas. Over most of its range in the southeastern United States, *M. austroriparius* is a cave bat with habits similar to most other cave-dwelling *Myotis*. It hibernates during the severe winter months of the year, during which time it is torpid and apparently does not leave the caves to feed. However, in the western part of its range in Louisiana and

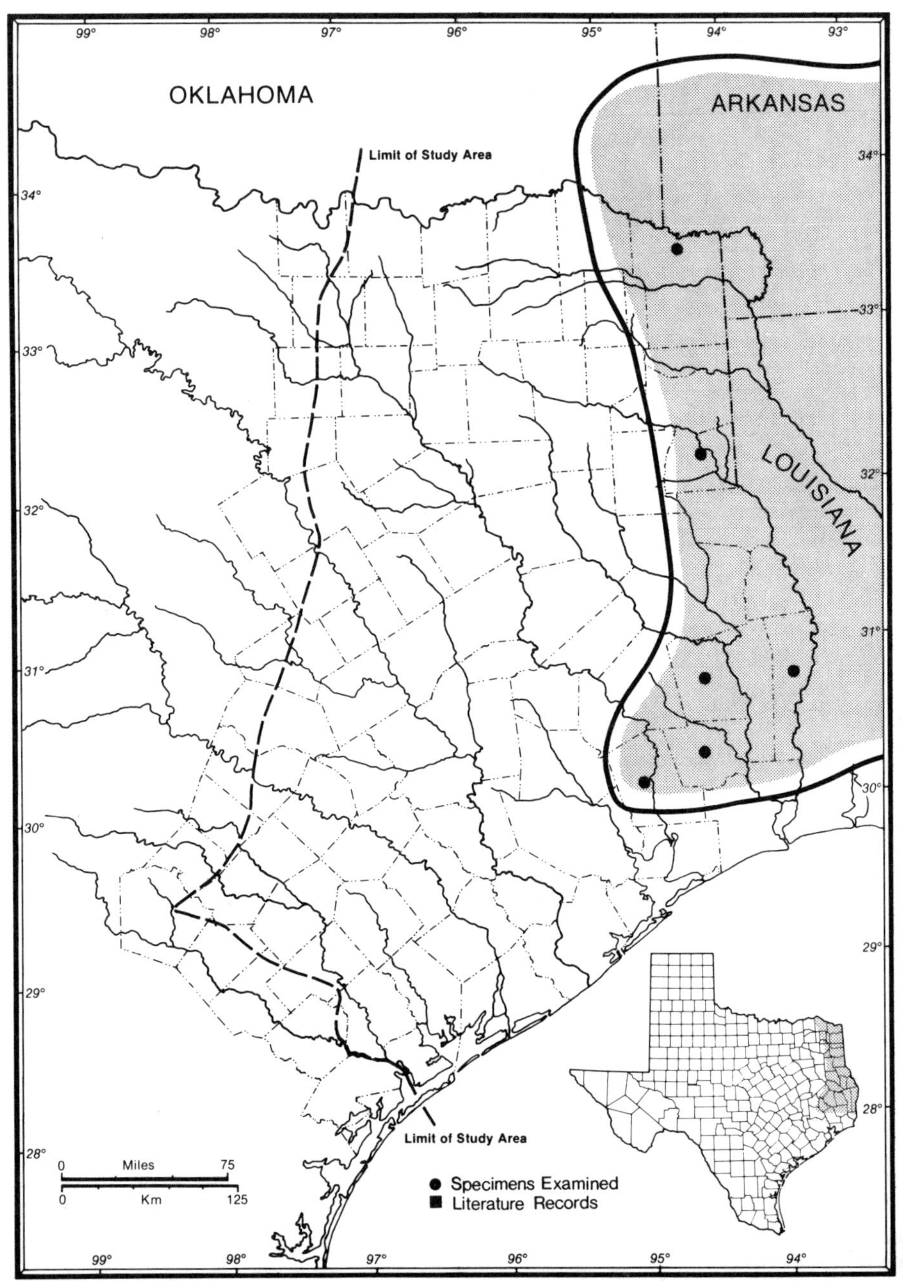

MAP 9. Distribution of the southeastern myotis, *Myotis austroriparius*.

eastern Texas, this species is active throughout the year, feeds regularly, and apparently does not live in caves, which are rare in this region. Specimens have been recorded from eastern Texas in every month except January, September, and November. Exact roosting sites are not known, but this bat probably utilizes such places as hollow trees, attics in abandoned houses, and culverts.

Outdoor roosting populations of this bat in northern Florida mate in both the fall and spring. Parturition extends from the end of April until late May. Females normally give birth to two young, and this is apparently the only member of the genus that ever produces more than one young at a time. No dates or other information are available concerning the birth of bats of this species in eastern Texas, but the situation is probably similar to that in peninsular Florida.

Young bats weigh slightly more than 1 g at birth, and they are capable of flying five to six weeks following birth. Because of this rapid growth, sexual maturity is reached in both sexes before one year of age.

These bats forage over ponds and streams, where they usually fly within 1 m of the surface and capture insects. Known predators include rat snakes, corn snakes, and owls. Large cockroaches have been reported to prey on newborn young.

References. Rice, 1957; Sherman, 1930.

Silver-haired Bat
Lasionycteris noctivagans (Le Conte)

Name. The generic name of this bat is derived from two Greek words, *lasios*, meaning "hair," and *nykteris*, which means "bat." These words refer to the dense fur of the upper parts, including the basal portion of the tail membrane. The specific name is derived from two Latin words, *nox* (for "night") and *vagans* (for "wandering"). The common name denotes the silvery tips of the fur.

Identification. The silver-haired bat is a medium-sized bat (forearm, 39 to 42 mm) that may be easily recognized by its striking black fur tipped with silver and by the dense fur on the dorsal surface of the interfemoral membrane. The skull is broad and flat, with no sagittal crest, such that it is almost straight in dorsal profile. Average external measurements are total length, 98 mm; tail, 38 mm; hind foot, 8 mm; ear, 14 mm. The dental formula is I 2/3, C 1/1, Pm 2/3, M 3/3 × 2 = 36.

Subspecies. Lasionycteris noctivagans is remarkably uniform throughout its range—so much so that no subspecies of it have been distinguished. The species was named by Le Conte (in McMurtrie, *The Animal Kingdom, . . . by the Baron Cuvier . . .* , 1:431, 1831) from individuals taken in the eastern part of the United States.

Distribution and habitat. This bat is widespread through most of the United States and southern Canada. Specimens have been recorded from the pineywoods, coastal plains, Edwards Plateau, Rolling Plains, High Plains, and the Trans-Pecos region of Texas (Map 10). It is rare in

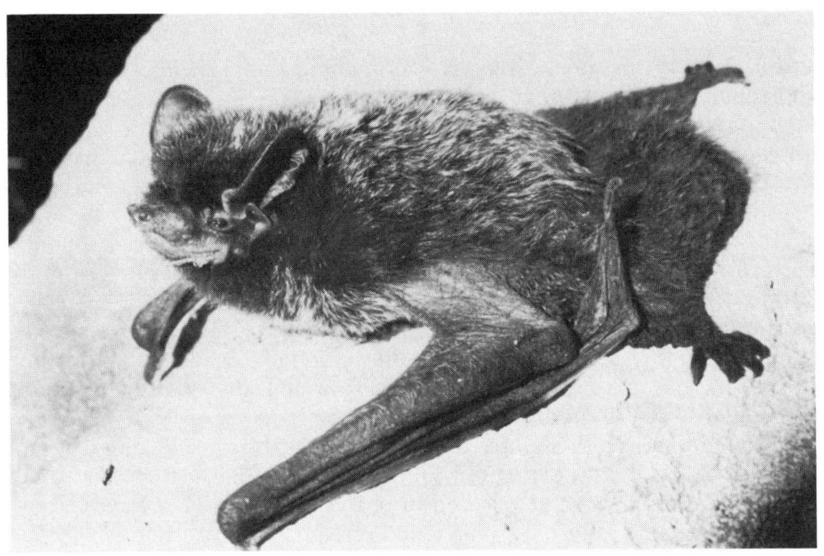

Silver-haired bat, *Lasionycteris noctivagans* (photograph from J. Knox Jones, Jr.).

eastern Texas, as only five specimens have been recorded from three counties (Galveston, Polk, and Tyler).

This tree-inhabiting species reaches its greatest abundance in wooded areas around ponds and streams, where it roosts in hollow trees, behind the loose bark of trees, in clumps of leaves, and occasionally in outbuildings or enclosed attics. It is especially fond of the latter structures during migratory periods.

Life history. L. *noctivagans* is migratory, spending the summer at northern latitudes and migrating to the south during the winter. Specimens have been obtained in eastern Texas during September, November, and January, suggesting that this bat is only a fall and winter resident of the region. It is known to migrate at sea, which probably accounts for the record from Galveston Island.

Adult silver-haired bats are usually solitary roosters, although occasionally they are found in pairs and in groups of three or four. They generally become active three to four hours after sunset, at which time they forage for insects at heights of up to 6 m along water courses or in hardwood groves. They have a distinctive, fluttering flight characterized by a slow wing beat.

Silver-haired bats have a reproductive pattern typical of that of many vespertilionid bats. Mating occurs in late August or September. Sperm are stored through the hibernation period in the uterus of the female, and actual fertilization occurs upon emergence from hibernation in the spring. The young, which normally number two, are born in late June or early July. They are black and wrinkled at birth, but are able to fly at three weeks of age.

References. Barbour and Davis, 1969; W. B. Davis, 1974; Schmidly et al., 1977.

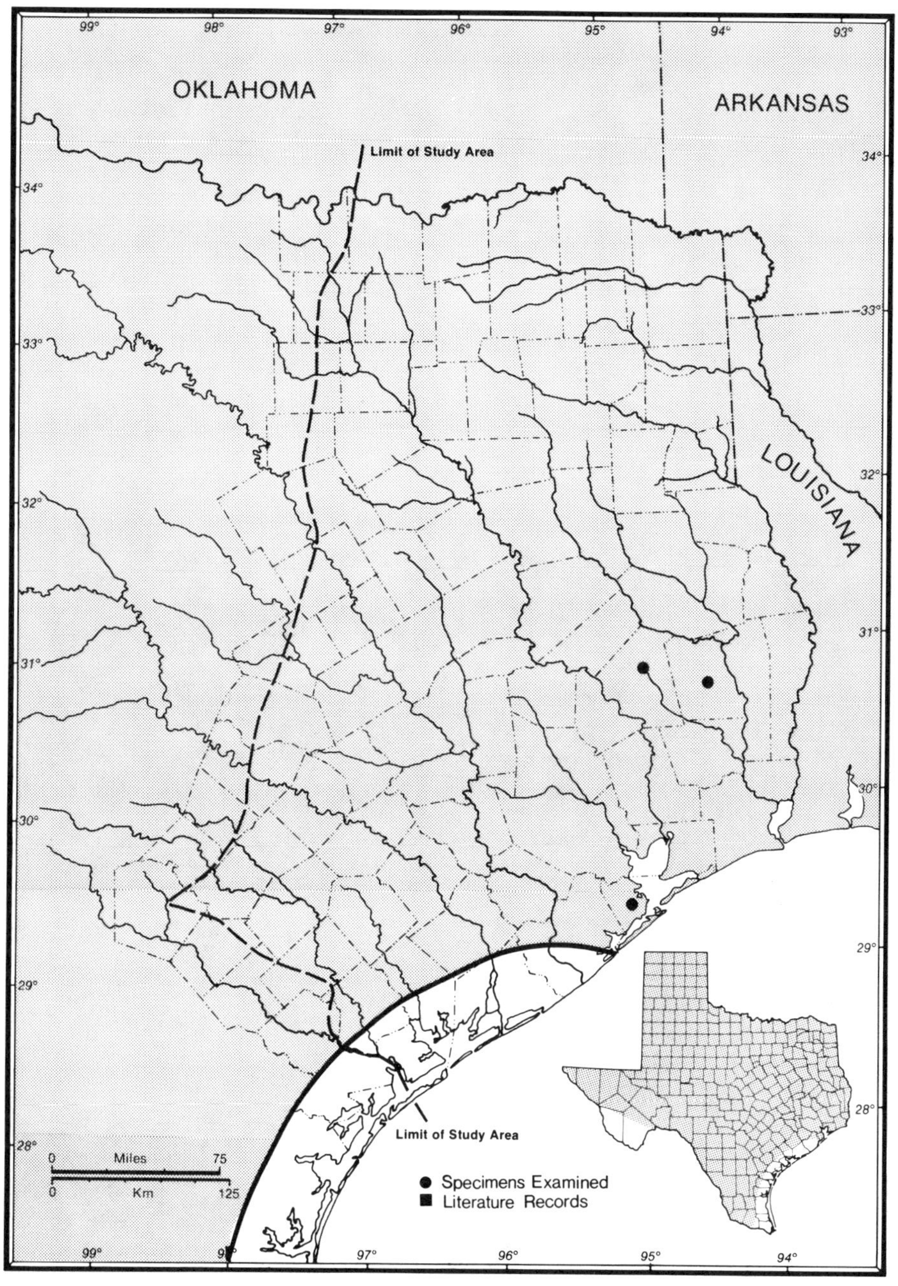

MAP 10. Distribution of the silver-haired bat, *Lasionycteris noctivagans*.

Eastern Pipistrelle
Pipistrellus subflavus (F. Cuvier)

Name. *Pipistrellus* is latinized from the Italian word *pipistrella,* which means "bat." *Subflavus* is derived from the Latin word *sub,* which means "below," and *flavus,* which means "yellowish," in reference to the yellowish belly of this bat.

Identification. The eastern pipistrelle is a small (forearm, 32 to 35 mm), short-winged, pale yellowish brown bat with the anterior third of the interfemoral membrane furred and no keel on the calcar. This species may be easily recognized by its tricolored fur (the base of the hair is dark, the middle band lighter, and the tips dark) and by the fact that the leading edge of the wing membrane is noticeably paler than the rest of the membrane. The tragus is long, narrow, and straight, and closely resembles that of *Myotis austroriparius.* Average external measurements are total length, 90 mm; tail, 42 mm; hind foot, 9 mm; ear, 13 mm. The dental formula is I 2/3, C 1/1, Pm 2/2, M 3/3 × 2 = 34.

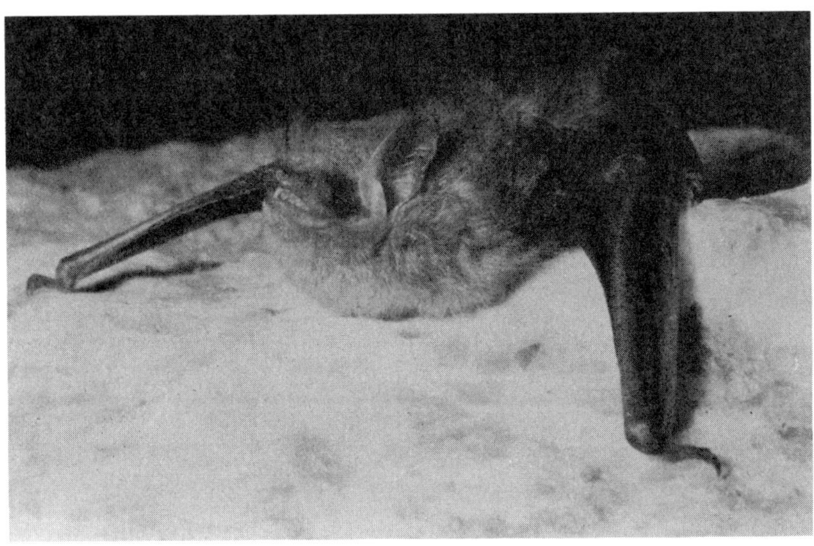

Eastern pipistrelle, *Pipistrellus subflavus* (photograph from J. Knox Jones, Jr.).

Subspecies. Only one subspecies, *Pipistrellus subflavus subflavus,* occurs in eastern Texas, and it was named by F. Cuvier (*Nour. Ann. Mus. Nat. Hist.,* Paris, 1:17, 1832) on the basis of specimens from the eastern United States, probably from Georgia.

Distribution and habitat. This species occurs over most of eastern North America. It reaches the southwestern limits of its range in Texas, where it occurs in all but the Trans-Pecos and High Plains portion of the state. This species has been recorded from seventeen counties scattered

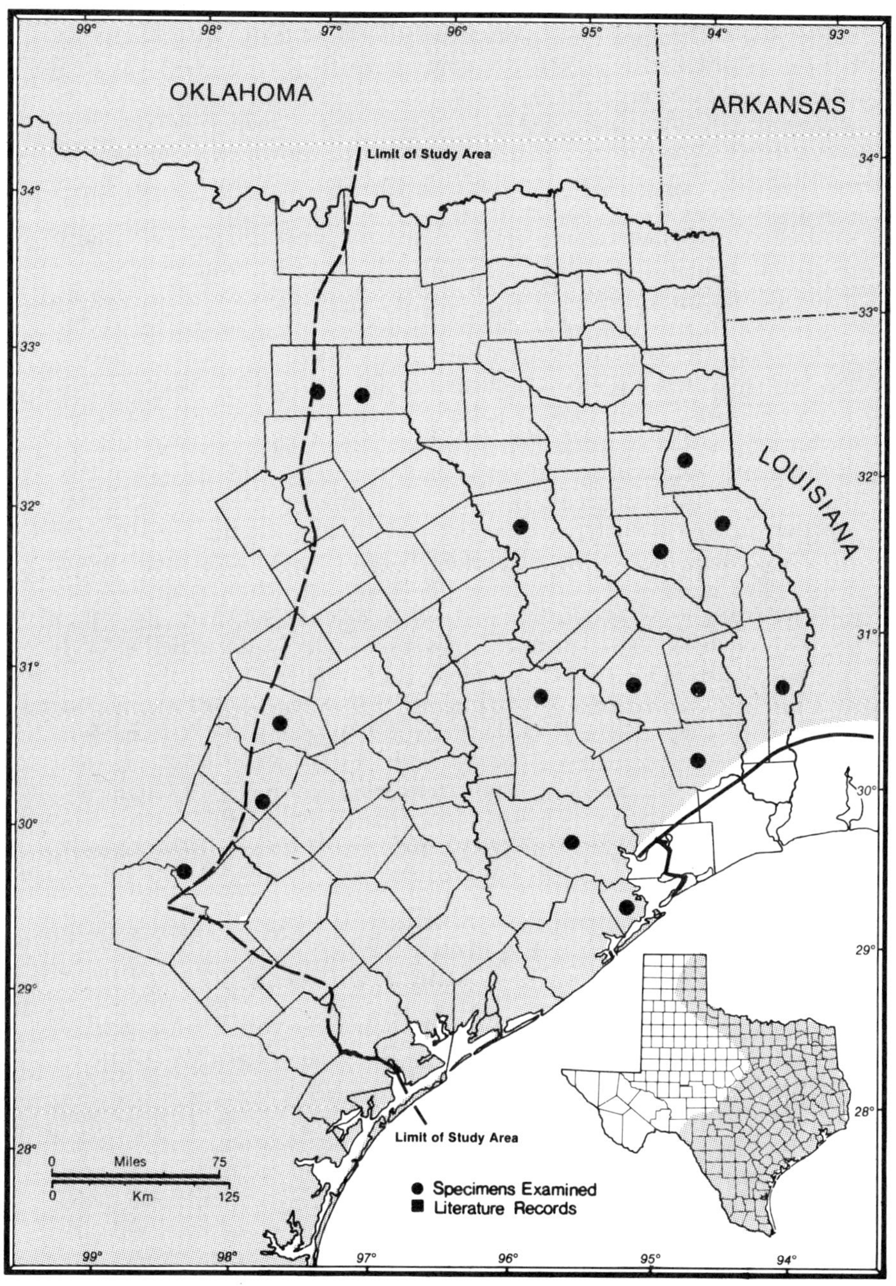

MAP 11. Distribution of the eastern pipistrelle, *Pipistrellus subflavus subflavus*.

throughout eastern Texas (Map 11). It has been collected in every month of the year and is apparently a permanent resident of the area. It appears to be a forest-edge species that seldom forages in deep woods or in open fields unless there are large trees nearby. It is definitely a cave inhabitant wherever possible, and several individuals have been collected from caves in Nacogdoches and Shelby counties. However, caves are absent over most of eastern Texas, so this bat roosts more commonly in hollow stumps, trees, culverts, and attics of old buildings in this area. In other regions of the Deep South, it commonly inhabits clusters of Spanish moss, and it may also utilize this plant, which occurs in many places in eastern Texas, as a roosting site.

Although *P. subflavus* is widely distributed over eastern Texas, it is seldom taken in large numbers. In over three years of collecting bats in the Big Thicket, I was able to collect only five specimens of this species.

Life history. Males and females of this species mate in the fall. Following copulation, sperm is stored and remains viable in the vaginal tract of the female until spring, at which time ovulation and fertilization take place. Litter size is normally two, rarely one; the young are born in May and June. Three of the females I collected in June in the Big Thicket were lactating, which means they had probably just given birth to their young. During the first few days after birth, the young are carried around by the females. They grow rapidly and are able to take care of themselves after about three weeks. This species is remarkably long-lived; banded individuals are known to have lived up to ten years in the wild.

Little is known of the feeding habits of *P. subflavus.* Insects, including small flies, beetles, and moths, constitute its main diet. This bat normally forages over a small area in the shade of trees at the forest edge and often hunts for its prey along water courses or over ponds. Its flight pattern is erratic and fluttering, resembling that of a butterfly.

References. Barbour and Davis, 1969; W. B. Davis, 1974; Lowery, 1974.

Big Brown Bat
Eptesicus fuscus (Palisot de Beauvois)

Name. The generic name is a corruption of the Greek word *ptetikos,* meaning "able to fly" (Lowery, 1974). The name *fuscus* is Latin for "brown," in reference to the coloration of this species.

Identification. This bat is moderately large (forearm, 47 to 51 mm) with a broad nose, a broad rounded tragus, broad wings, and a keeled calcar. The ears, wings, and interfemoral membrane are thick, heavy, and blackish. Its large size and rich, chocolate-brown coloration serve to distinguish it from any other bat in eastern Texas. Average external measurements are total length, 117 mm; tail, 42 mm; hind foot, 10 mm; ear, 16 mm. The dental formula is: I 2/3, C 1/1, Pm 1/2, M 3/3 × 2 = 32.

Subspecies. Specimens from eastern Texas are referable to the subspecies *Eptesicus fuscus fuscus,* named by Beauvois (*Catal. Raisonné Mus. Peale,* p. 18, 1796) with the type locality at Philadelphia, Pennsylvania.

Big brown bat, *Eptesicus fuscus* (photograph from J. Knox Jones, Jr.).

Distribution and habitat. This wide-ranging species occurs from Alaska and Canada south through the United States and Mexico to northern South America. It is not especially widespread in eastern Texas, having been taken in only nine counties in the northern portion of the region (Map 12). With the exception of a single specimen from Waco in McLennan County, all of the records are within the pine-oak forest and long-leaf pine vegetational regions, and no records are available south of the Brazos River.

This is a forest-dwelling species that roosts under the loose bark of dead trees and tree cavities. It also occurs in man-made structures such as outbuildings and attics, behind shutters and awnings, and in chimneys.

Life history. The big brown bat is apparently a year-round resident of eastern Texas, having been collected in all months except November and December. It probably hibernates or enters brief periods of torpor during the winter months. No hibernacula have been discovered in eastern Texas, but buildings are the favorite place for this activity in other places. This bat is rather sedentary and does not make extensive movements from its summer or winter roosts.

Big brown bats emerge from their roost at dusk and forage for insects among the crowns of trees. Their diet is composed primarily of larger insects, such as June beetles, stone flies, May flies, large moths, houseflies, and parasitic wasps. Apparently, an individual uses the same feeding ground each night. When a bat dies, its feeding territory is taken over by another within several days. After feeding, the bats fly to a night roost, often located in places such as a breezeway, porch, or open garage, to rest. Following a second activity period, they depart for their dark, daytime roost.

These bats are seemingly not tolerant of high temperatures in their

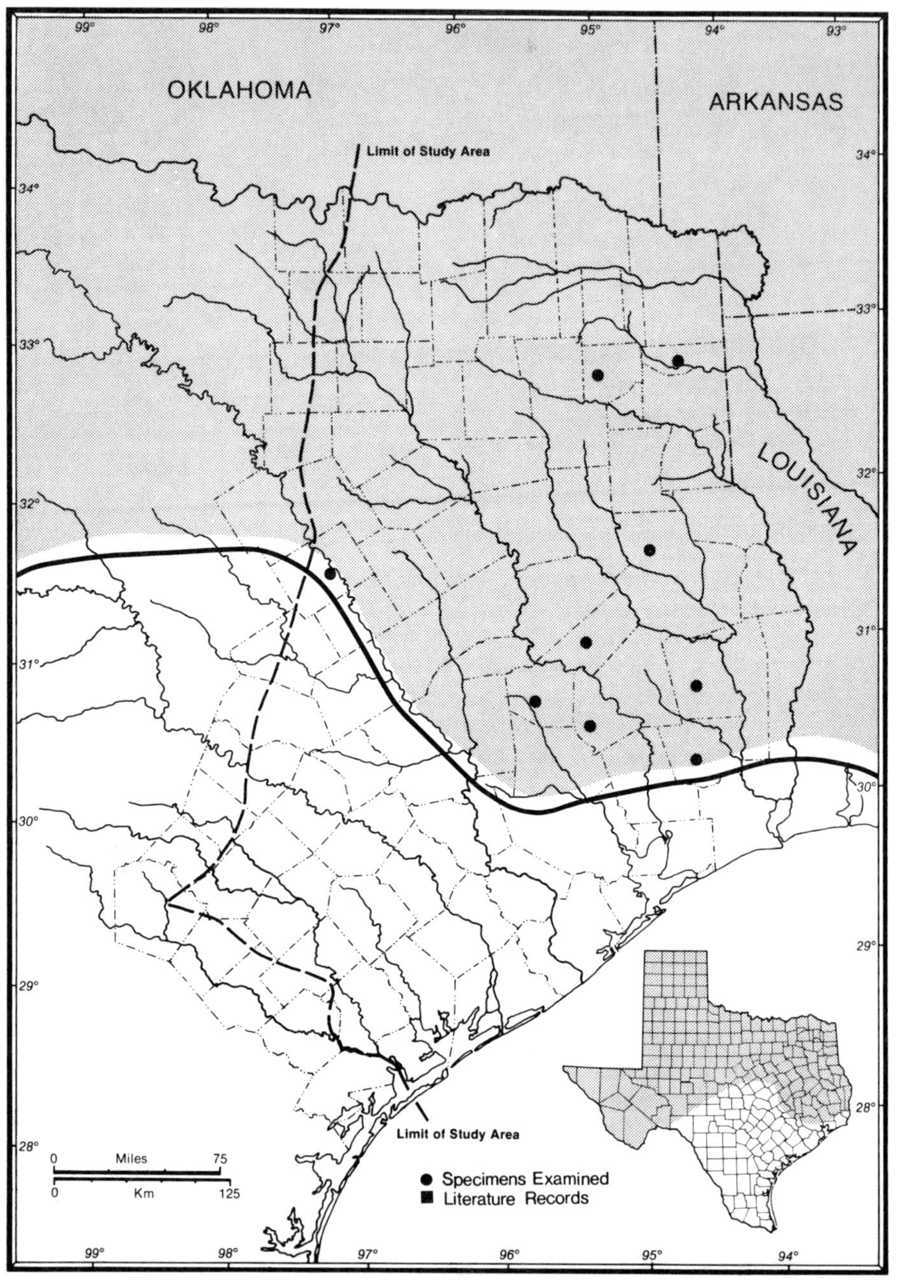

MAP 12. Distribution of the big brown bat, *Eptesicus fuscus fuscus*.

daytime roost. It has been noted among bats roosting in the attic of a house that when the temperature in the roost rises above 33° to 35° C the bats will retreat to a cooler part of the house, such as spaces in the walls, a partition between rooms, crevices at the base of a chimney, or crevices where the roof meets the attic. In these situations, when heat forces the bats to move, they frequently encounter human beings.

These bats mate in the fall, but the young are not born until the following May or June. Maternity colonies, consisting of pregnant females, begin to form in May. These colonies may number up to 300 individuals, but a figure of from 40 to 100 bats is more common. During the period of parturition and lactation, males are largely absent from nursery colonies, although an influx of males into such colonies occurs after the young are mature and begin to fly. The number of young produced per litter is normally only two. At birth the young weigh only about 3 g. They grow rapidly and are weaned at three weeks and able to fly after four weeks; by two months of age they are nearly as large as the adults. These bats are long-lived, and individuals are known to live in captivity for up to twelve years; banded bats in the wild are known to have lived far beyond six years. Predators of big brown bats include barn owls, horned owls, and black snakes.

References. Barbour and Davis, 1969, 1974; W. B. Davis, 1974; Lowery, 1974; Schmidly et al., 1977; Selander, 1979.

Red Bat
Lasiurus borealis (Müller)

Name. *Lasiurus* is derived from two Greek words, *lasios*, meaning "hairy," "woolly," or "shaggy," and *oura*, meaning "tail." The specific name *borealis* is Latin for "northern."

Identification. This medium-sized (forearm, about 42 mm), distinctively reddish bat has short, broad, rounded ears and a densely furred interfemoral membrane. The tragus is triangular in shape, with a slight forward bend at the top. There is a marked sexual dimorphism in coloration in this species; the upper parts of the male are brick red, whereas in the female the reddish upper parts are tipped with white, producing a frosted appearance. Average external measurements are total length, 98 mm; tail, 43 mm; hind foot, 7 mm; ear, 11 mm. The dental formula is I 1/3, C 1/1, Pm 2/2, M 3/3 × 2 = 32.

Subspecies. The subspecies in eastern Texas is *Lasiurus borealis borealis*, named by Müller (*Natursyst. Suppl.*, p. 20, 1776) from New York.

Distribution and habitat. The red bat, which occurs all over the eastern United States, is one of the most common bats in eastern Texas. It has been recorded in thirty-three counties and in all major vegetation regions, although it seems to be more common east than west of the Brazos River (Map 13). This bat prefers wooded regions, where it may occur in a variety of vegetational associations, including pine forest, mixed pine-

Red bat, *Lasiurus borealis.*

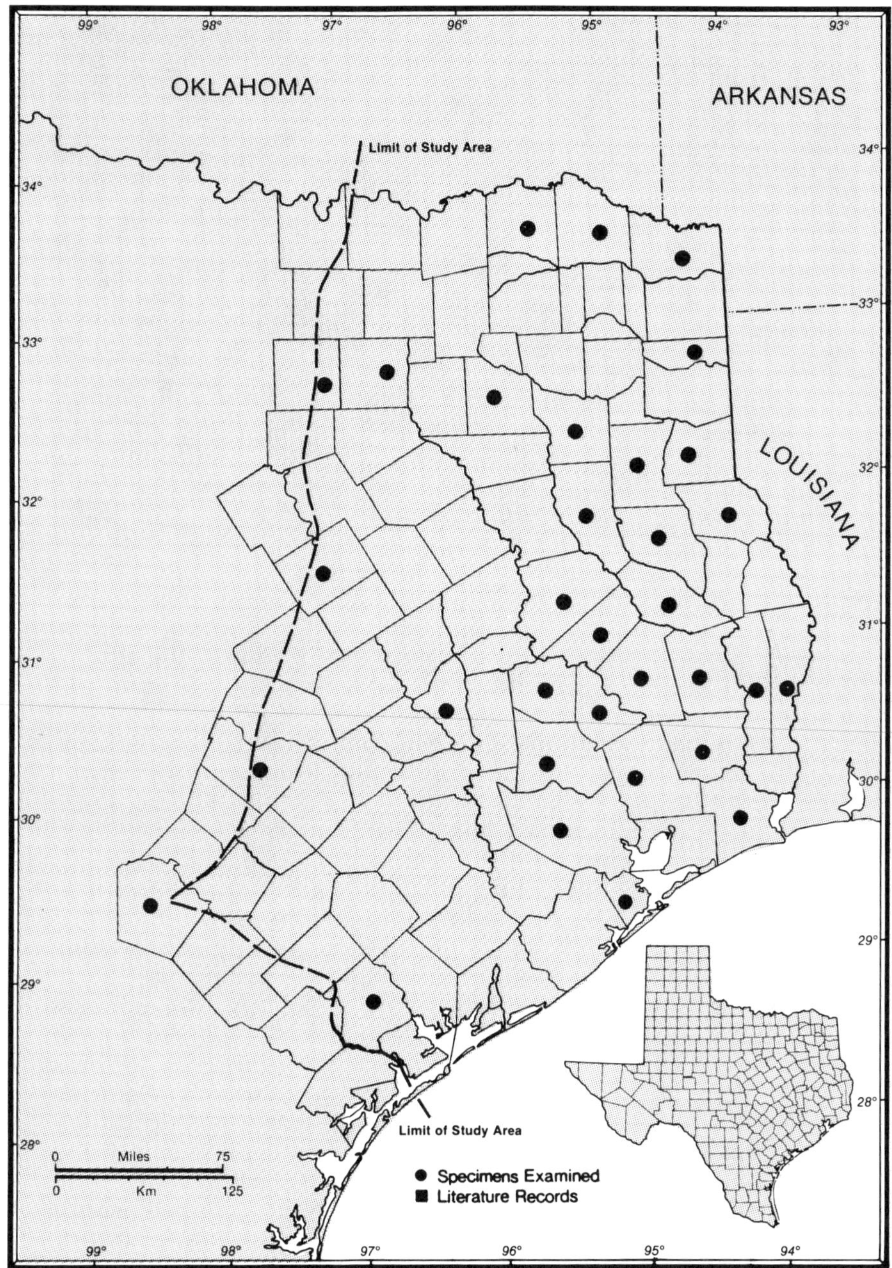

MAP 13. Distribution of the red bat, *Lasiurus borealis borealis*.

Face of the red bat, *Lasiurus borealis*.

hardwood forest, riparian and floodplain forest, oak forest, and agricultural land. I have obtained red bats in mist nets strung over ponds and along waterways in all of these situations.

Life history. Red bats spend the daylight hours of the summer hanging in the foliage of trees. Favorite roosting sites are fence rows and forest edges, with a definite preference for those sites with a south and southwestern exposure. In Iowa they show a definite preference for roosting in American elms (Constantine, 1966), but I do not know whether this is true in eastern Texas. Roosts are generally selected so that they provide dense shade and cover above and at the sides, and are open below so that the bat can drop when taking flight. Red bats are solitary, and the same roosting site may be used by different individuals on different days.

At dusk in the summer red bats typically leave their roost and begin flying near or above treetop level. They are easily distinguished by the musical "chirp" of their ultrasonic flight sounds, as opposed to the nonmusical "beep" of other bats. Later, they fly lower, sometimes within a few meters of the ground, and they may remain active until midnight or later. These bats commonly forage around bright electric lights in towns and occasionally may alight and capture an insect on a light pole. They are also known to forage regularly over the same territory, which may be within a few hundred meters of their day roost. During winter, red bats may be seen flying during the afternoon prior to dusk.

These bats feed on a variety of foods, including crickets, flies, bugs, beetles, cicadas, and other insects. The presence of crickets in their diet suggests they may take some food on the ground. They detect flying insects by echolocation and capture them in flight using the wingtip or occasionally the interfemoral membrane.

Red bats are thought to be highly migratory, moving northward in spring and southward in fall. The details of these movements, however, remain sketchy. They have been collected at all seasons of the year in eastern Texas and appear to be permanent residents of this area. Possibly they undergo seasonal or localized migrations associated with a segregation of sexes, but this is not known. It is also not known whether numbers increase in eastern Texas during the winter as a result of an influx of northern bats.

At northern latitudes red bats breed in August and September; sperm is stored in the uterus and oviducts through the winter, and fertilization and parturition occur in the spring. This same reproductive chronology may also occur in eastern Texas, although copulation may occur in the spring since these bats are present and active in the region throughout the year. The young, which number three or four, are born in May and June. The young are hairless at birth, with their eyes closed, and weigh only 0.5 g. They are capable of flying at three to four weeks and are weaned after five to six weeks.

References. Barbour and Davis, 1969; Constantine, 1966; W. B. Davis, 1974; LaVal and LaVal, 1979; Lowery, 1974; Schmidly et al., 1977.

Seminole Bat
Lasiurus seminolus (Rhoads)

Name. The formation of the generic name *Lasiurus* is the same as given in the preceding account. The specific epithet *seminolus* refers to the Seminole Indians, who inhabited the region from which the bat was first known.

Identification. This bat is very similar to the red bat, from which it differs only in color and by one minor cranial character. The color, instead of being red or reddish, is a deep mahogany, with a light frosting above produced by the white tips of the hairs of the dorsum. The skulls of these species differ in the presence of a more pronounced ridge above the lacrimals in *borealis* as compared to *seminolus*. Otherwise the skull and dentition of the Seminole bat are identical to that of the red bat. Average external measurements are total length, 99 mm; tail, 43 mm; hind foot, 7 mm; ear, 11 mm.

Subspecies. This species is monotypic, and distinct subspecies are not recognized. The species was named by Rhoads (*Proc. Acad. Nat. Sci. Philadelphia*, 47:32, March 19, 1895) with type locality at Tarpon Springs, Pinellas County, Florida.

Distribution and habitat. This bat, which is characteristic of the southeastern United States, reaches the western limits of its distribution in eastern Texas, where it is abundant throughout the pine-oak and long-leaf pine forest regions (Map 14). It is less common in the oak-hickory region and has not been recorded west of the Brazos River. It has been taken from February through November, suggesting it is probably a year-long resident of the area.

Seminole bat, *Lasiurus seminolus*.

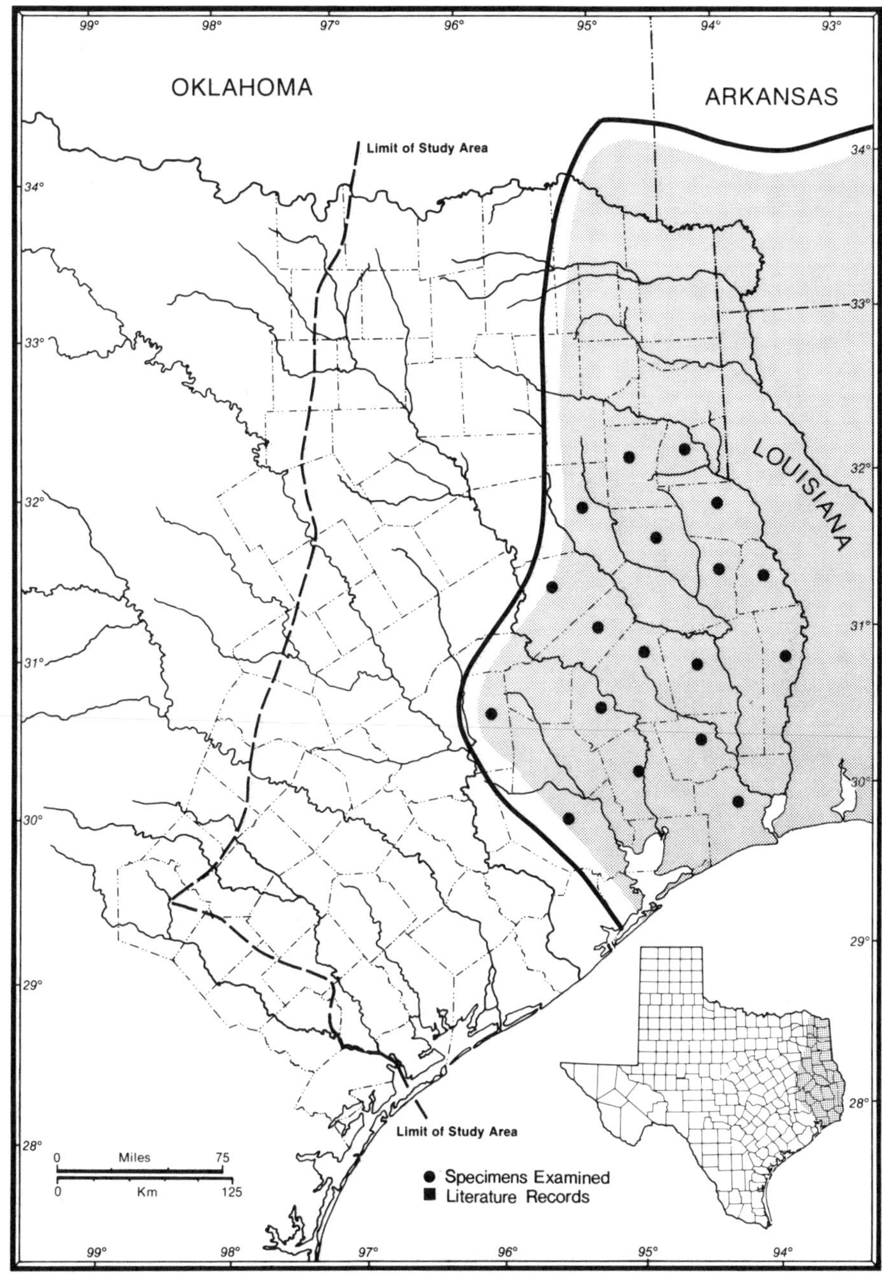

MAP 14. Distribution of the Seminole bat, *Lasiurus seminolus*.

Face of the Seminole bat, *Lasiurus seminolus*.

Life history. The favored roost of this bat during most of the year is the interior of the clumps of Spanish moss that commonly hang on trees in the Deep South. The bats are always solitary, and different individuals sometimes occupy the same clump on different days. Seminole bats may also roost beneath loose bark or in clumps of foliage other than Spanish moss.

This bat emerges early in the evening from its daytime roost and usually feeds at treetop level, about 7 to 15 m above ground. They are active at all seasons, including warm evenings in midwinter. They arise and fly immediately when the air temperature reaches about 21° C, but they rarely fly when the temperature is below 18° C. During periods of extremely cold weather, they become torpid. Just like the red bat, this species is known to feed around streetlights. They eat various species of bugs (Homoptera), flies (Diptera), and beetles (Coleoptera), which they capture on the wing around and in the tree canopy.

The young are probably born in late May or June. There are no records of pregnant females from eastern Texas, but females that I collected in the Big Thicket in late June were lactating. Pregnant females have also been captured in Louisiana on June 2 and 3. Embryo counts for pregnant females in Florida ranged from 1 to 4, with an average of 3.3. The young grow rapidly after birth and are capable of flight after three to four weeks.

References. Barbour and Davis, 1969; Constantine, 1958; W. B. Davis, 1974; Jennings, 1958; Lowery, 1974; Schmidly et al., 1977.

Hoary Bat
Lasiurus cinereus (Palisot de Beauvois)

Name. The derivation of the name *Lasiurus* is the same as that given in the account of *L. borealis*. The name *cinereus* is Latin for "ash-colored" and refers to the white-tipped hairs on the pelage of this bat.

Identification. This is the largest (forearm, 51 to 55 mm) and the most beautiful bat inhabiting eastern Texas. It is easily distinguished by its dark coloration with a frosting of white on the tips of the fur, giving it a hoary appearance. The face, throat, and hairs on the underside of the wing are yellowish; the fur on the back and on the tail membrane, beneath the white tips, is mahogany brown. Its ears are short, round, and rimmed with black. The dental formula is identical to that of the red bat and the Seminole bat. Average external measurements are total length, 134 mm; tail, 51 mm; hind foot, 12 mm; ear, 17 mm.

Subspecies. The subspecies in eastern Texas is *Lasiurus cinereus cinereus*, named by Beauvois (*Catal. Raisonné Mus. Peale*, p. 18, 1796) on the basis of material from Pennsylvania, probably near Philadephia.

Distribution and habitat. The hoary bat occurs throughout the continental United States including Texas. It is not very common in eastern Texas, having been recorded in only seven counties, including four counties (Jasper, Tyler, San Jacinto, and Hardin) in the Big Thicket, two (Tar-

Hoary bat, *Lasiurus cinereus*.

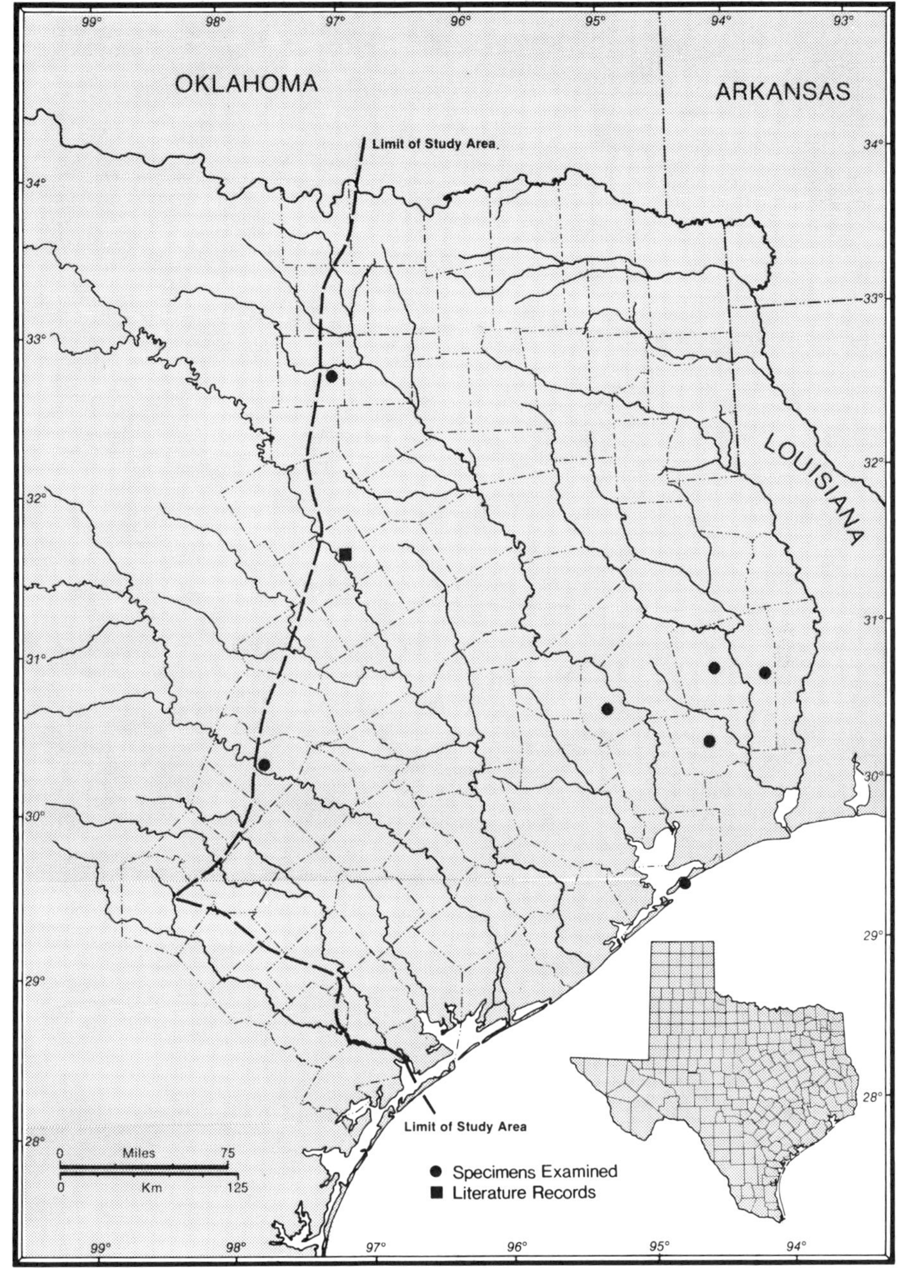

MAP 15. Distribution of the hoary bat, *Lasiurus cinereus cinereus*. The literature record is from W. B. Davis (1974).

Face of the hoary bat, *Lasiurus cinereus*.

rant and Travis) in the blackland prairie, and one (Galveston) on the coastal prairie (Map 15). W. B. Davis (1974) reported a specimen from McLennan County, but I have been unable to locate the specimen or verify the record.

Records of this bat in eastern Texas are scattered throughout the year. However, this species is well known for its migratory habits, and additional data are needed to determine whether it is a permanent resident of the region. Specimens have been obtained in the Big Thicket during January, April, and June; those from the blackland prairie were obtained in residential areas of Austin and Arlington (found hanging alive in a garage) during September and October, respectively. The specimen from Galveston County was obtained in April.

Life history. Hoary bats typically roost in the foliage of trees, generally choosing a leafy site that is covered above, open beneath, and located about 3 to 5 m above the ground. They leave the roost late in the evening and reach their peak activity period several hours after sunset.

Little is known of the food habits of hoary bats. They supposedly feed on insects but may also eat other bats as well as snakes.

There is definite evidence that this species breeds in eastern Texas. On April 19, 1978, I collected a pregnant female (with three embryos each 10 mm in crown–rump length) in the Neches Bottom/Jack Gore Baygall Unit of Big Thicket National Preserve. This record is significant because litter size for this bat is supposedly only two. Newborn young weigh only a few grams at birth. They grow rapidly and are capable of free flight after about one month.

This bat is a swift, direct flier, with the tail and interfemoral membrane curved beneath the body during flight. It regularly utters an audible chattering sound while flying. The hoary bat is also capable of launching itself directly from the water's surface.

References. Barbour and Davis, 1969; Constantine, 1966; Lowery, 1974.

Northern Yellow Bat
Lasiurus intermedius (H. Allen)

Name. The name *intermedius* is derived from the Latin word *inter*, meaning "between" or "among," and *medius*, meaning "in the middle." It refers to the intermediate size of the species compared to other tree bats.

Identification. This rather large bat (forearm, 47 to 54 mm) may be distinguished from other bats by its coloration, which is usually yellowish above and below, although variants are sometimes grayish or even slightly brownish. Its overall yellow color clearly separates it from any other species in eastern Texas except possibly some specimens of *Pipistrellus subflavus*, from which it differs in being decidedly larger. Compared to other lasiurines, this species has decidedly more pointed ears and lacks a completely furred dorsal surface of the interfemoral membrane. Average external measurements are total length, 132 mm; tail, 50 mm; hind foot, 10 mm; ear, 17 mm. The dental formula is I 1/3, C 1/1, Pm 1/2, M 3/3 × 2 = 30.

Subspecies. Lasiurus intermedius floridanus is the only subspecies that occurs in eastern Texas. It was named by Miller (*Proc. Acad. Nat. Sci. Philadephia*, 54:392, September 12, 1902) with type locality at Lake Kissimmee, Osceola County, Florida.

Distribution and habitat. The northern yellow bat occurs in the southeastern United States from southeastern Virginia along the coast to Texas and thence southward along the lowlands of eastern and southern Mexico to the Yucatan Peninsula. It is uncommon in eastern Texas, having been recorded in only six counties (Travis, Colorado, Fort Bend, Harris, Brazos, and Madison) in the southern half of the region (Map 16).

The distribution of the yellow bat is closely associated with Spanish moss, in which it roosts and bears its young. Most specimens have been taken in forested regions where oaks, festooned with Spanish moss, predominate.

Life history. L. intermedius typically forages 5 to 7 m above the ground along the forest edge or over open areas with scattered stumps and clumps of trees. In particular, grassy areas, such as airports, pastures, golf courses, and lake edges, are favored. These bats emerge at dusk to begin feeding on insects that are taken on the wing while the bats forage above treetops.

Little is known of the reproductive biology of this species in eastern Texas. As with many other vespertilionid bats, mating probably occurs in the fall, but the ova are not shed and fertilization does not occur until the following spring. A female yellow bat collected on April 24 at College Station, Brazos County, contained four embryos that measured 5 mm in

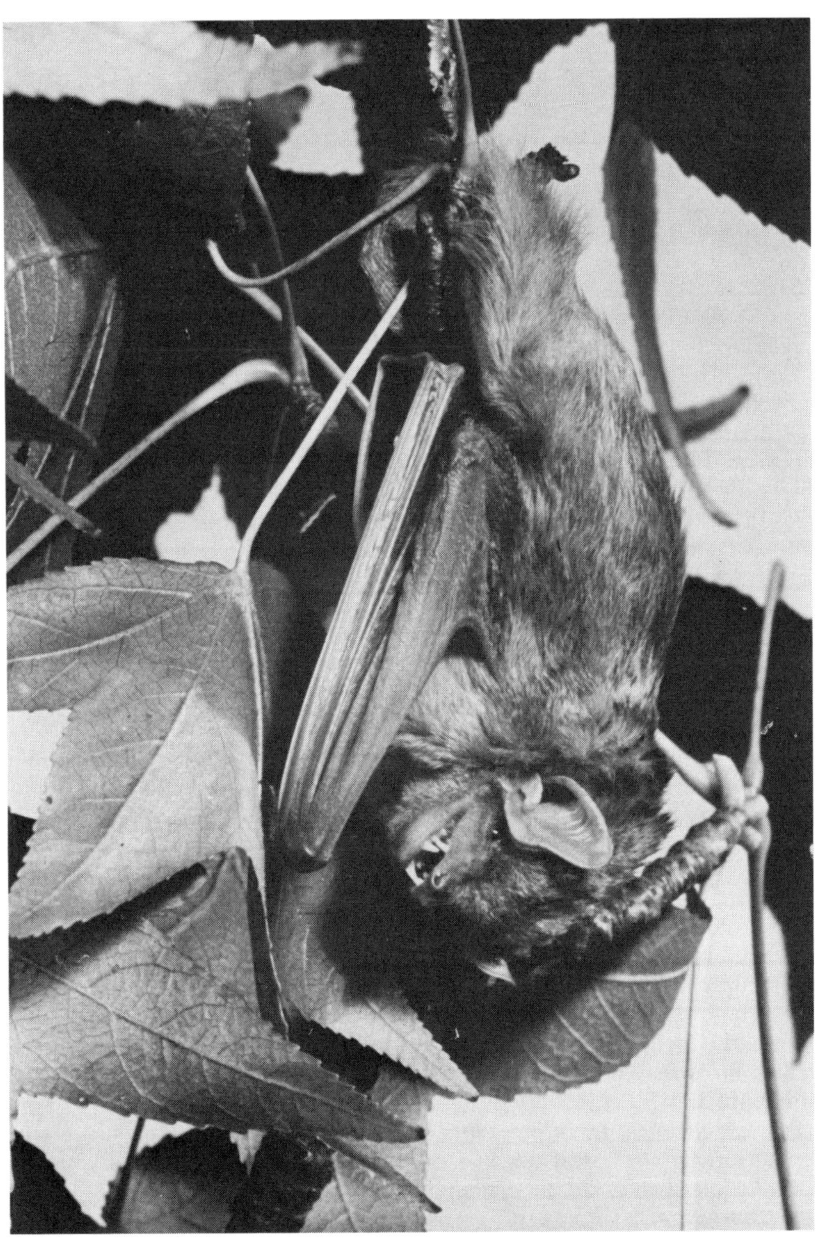

Northern yellow bat, *Lasiurus intermedius* (photograph by Roger W. Barbour).

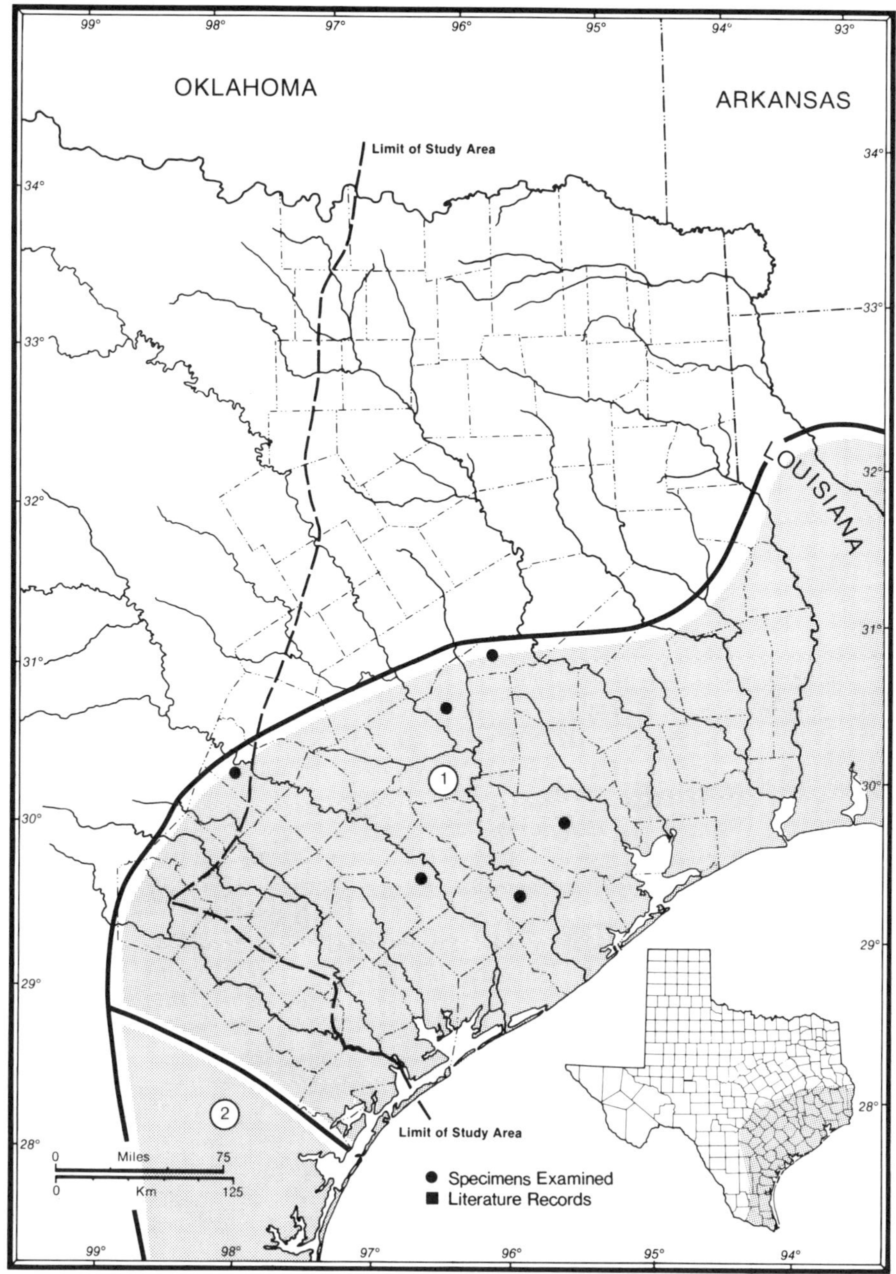

Map 16. Distribution of the northern yellow bat, *Lasiurus intermedius*. 1. *L. i. floridanus*. 2. *L. i. intermedius*.

crown–rump length. This date is consistent with the parturition dates derived from studies in Florida and Louisiana. Litter sizes for bats collected in Florida ranged from 2 to 3, with an average of 2.8.

Virtually nothing is known about the winter habits of this species. Apparently, it does not remain in eastern Texas during the colder months, since there are no collecting records from November to March. The earliest collecting record is from April in Brazos County; the last record is from October in Harris County. Both males and females have been collected during the time this species is resident in the area.

References. Barbour and Davis, 1969; Hall and Jones, 1961; Lowery, 1974; Jennings, 1958; Schmidly et al., 1977.

Evening Bat
Nycticeius humeralis (Rafinesque)

Name. The first part of the scientific name, *Nycticeius*, is of Greek and Latin origin and means "belonging to the night." The second part, *humeralis*, is of Latin origin and means "pertaining to the humerous."

Identification. This is a small to medium-sized bat (forearm, 34 to 38 mm) with a plain nose, pronounced facial glands, and short, narrow wings; coloration is dark brown above and yellowish brown below. The ears, membranes of wings, and tail, for their size, are remarkably thick and leathery. Average external measurements are total length, 88 mm; tail, 34 mm; hind foot, 8 mm; ear, 13 mm. The dental formula is I 1/3, C 1/1, Pm 1/2, M 3/3 × 2 = 30.

The evening bat may be confused only with *Myotis austroriparius*, from which it is distinguished by its short, blunt tragus and by the presence of only one incisor on each side of the upper jaw. *M. austroriparius* has a long, pointed tragus and two incisors on each side of the upper jaw.

Subspecies. Nycticeius humeralis humeralis is the only subspecies that occurs in eastern Texas and was named by Rafinesque (*Amer. Monthly Magazine,* 3:445, October, 1818) with type locality somewhere in the state of Kentucky.

Distribution and habitat. This bat occurs in the southeastern United States west to Texas, where it is known principally east and south of the Balcones Escarpment. It is probably the most common bat in the wooded habitats of eastern Texas, but it has not been recorded from the blackland prairies (Map 17). Both males and females have been collected in all months of the year, although records indicate that it is more abundant in summer and fall than in winter. The species seems to occur more commonly along streams in bottomlands and around man-made ponds.

Life history. The evening bat prefers buildings or trees for roost sites. In the College Station–Bryan area of Brazos County, I have located roosts in hollow trees, attics of houses and apartments in residential areas, warehouses, and barns. One such roosting site, reported to me by an apartment owner in late June, contained several hundred adult females and young bats. The temperature in the attic was extremely warm (about

Evening bat, *Nycticeius humeralis.*

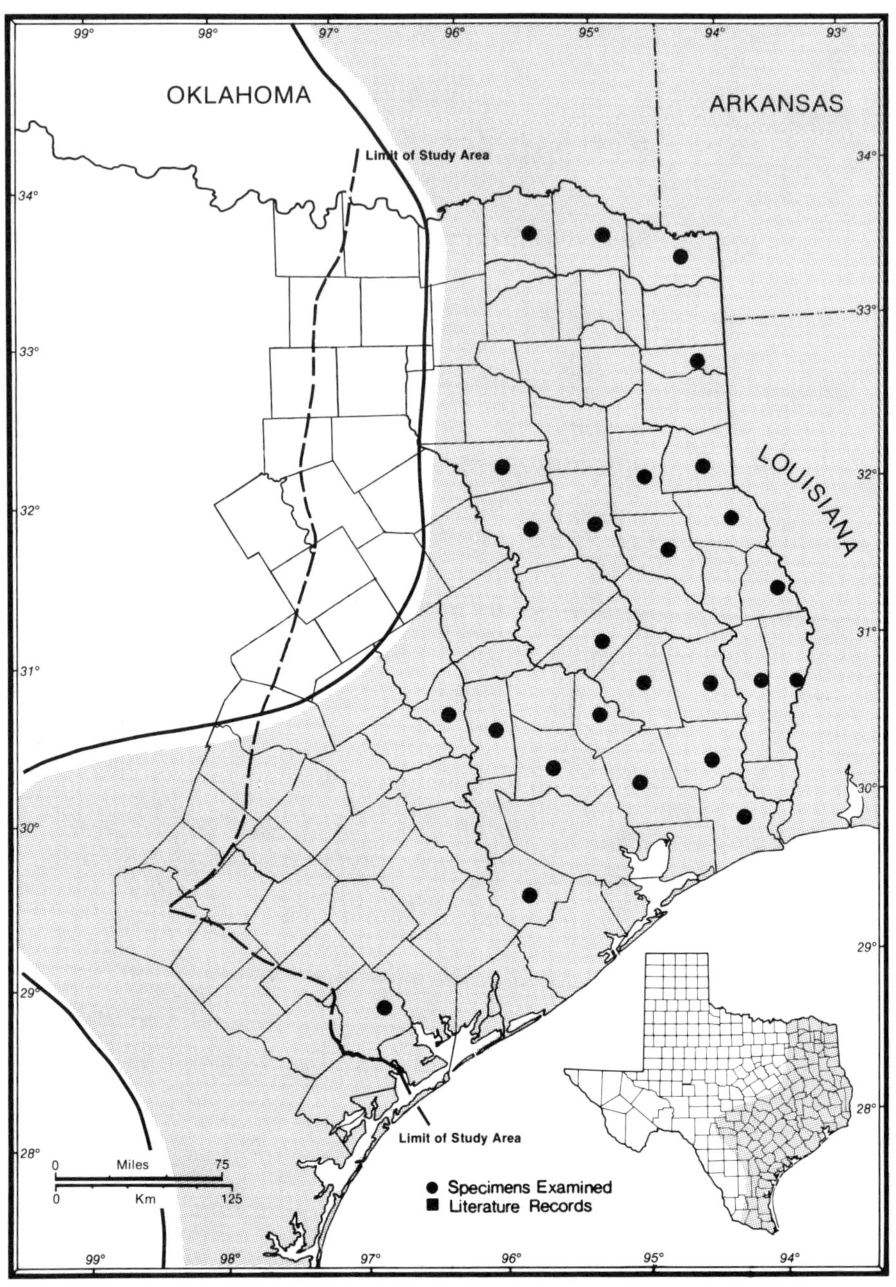

MAP 17. Distribution of the evening bat, *Nycticeius humeralis humeralis*.

Face of the evening bat, *Nycticeius humeralis*.

45° C), and the bats were spaced evenly over the ceiling as well as in the wall spaces. The bats entered and left the attic of the apartment along an open crack between the roof and the wall. The bats remained at this location until late August, at which time they dispersed and left the roost. Although I am not certain where these bats went, another colony of adult male and female bats was subsequently located in a hollow tree in the wooded area adjacent to the apartments.

The evening bat generally begins foraging around sunset, first flying above the trees and gradually descending lower. Typically, it exhibits a bimodal activity pattern with a peak in activity lasting until about one hour after leaving the roost, with little activity through the night, and a second peak period occurring just before dawn. Heavy rain and ambient temperatures approaching 10° C are known to retard activity.

The reproductive cycle of the evening bat is not well documented. Copulation takes place in the fall, but it is not known where this occurs. The young, which normally number two, are born in late May in nursery colonies of various sizes. During this time, the sexes are generally segregated, and the solitary males do not occur in the nursery colony.

The young are born pink and naked with only a few scattered hairs. Their eyes open after twelve to thirty hours. The female carries the young on foraging flights one week to ten days after birth, and the young are capable of free flight at about twenty days of age.

The evening bat is a slow, steady flier that feeds on flying insects. Suspected predators include domestic and feral cats, raccoons, and black snakes. Apparently, the first time of flight from the roost is a highly selective period for this species. Juveniles flying from large, open roosts have low mortality during this first flight, whereas those flying from small, enclosed roosts have high mortality rates.

This bat is suspected of migrating or hibernating at northern latitudes, but there is no evidence for this in eastern Texas. Specimens have been obtained during the colder months of the year, indicating that this species is a winter resident of the area.

References. Lowery, 1974; Schmidly et al., 1977; Sealander, 1979; Watkins, 1972.

Rafinesque's Big-eared Bat
Plecotus rafinesquii (Lesson)

Name. The generic name, *Plecotus*, is derived from the Greek word *pleko* and the Latin word *otus*, which refer to the "twisted ear." The species name refers to the French explorer and naturalist, C. S. Rafinesque, who traveled and studied wildlife in the United States in the early 1800s.

Identification. This medium-sized bat (forearm, 39 to 44 mm) is easily distinguished from other eastern Texas species by its immense ears, which are more than an inch in length (27 to 37 mm) and by prominent lumps on its nose. The color is dark brown above and grayish white below. The bases of the ventral hairs are black or blackish, and the tips are

Rafinesque's big-eared bat, *Plecotus rafinesquii* (photograph by Roger W. Barbour).

white or whitish, with considerable contrast between the two colors. Average external measurements are total length, 96 mm; tail, 45 mm; hind foot, 10 mm; ear, 32 mm. The dental formula is I 2/3, C 1/1, Pm 2/3, M 3/3 × 2 = 36.

Subspecies. The subspecies in eastern Texas is *Plecotus rafinesquii macrotis*, named by Le Conte (in McMurtrie, *The animal kingdom . . . by the Baron Cuvier . . .* , 1:431, 1831) with type locality in Georgia (probably the Le Conte plantation, near Riceboro, in Liberty County).

Distribution and habitat. This bat, which occurs throughout the southeastern United States, reaches the western limits of its range in eastern Texas (Map 18), where specimens have been recorded from seven counties (Marion, Harrison, Nacogdoches, Sabine, Newton, Polk, and Hardin) in the pine-oak and long-leaf pine vegetational regions.

Favored roosting sites include partially lighted, unoccupied buildings and other man-made structures such as wells and cisterns. This bat has been captured in the following situations and on the following dates: Newton County, four individuals found in cisterns during November and December and one mist-netted among eastern red junipers and loblolly pines in June; Polk County, seven individuals captured in a barn in November; Nacogdoches County, thirteen individuals captured in a well in October and November; Sabine County, three individuals collected in an abandoned dwelling in July and September; and Marion County, one male collected in an abandoned dwelling in October. Thus, it appears that this species is found in small numbers at scattered localities and that there are no winter records (January through March) from the region. The lat-

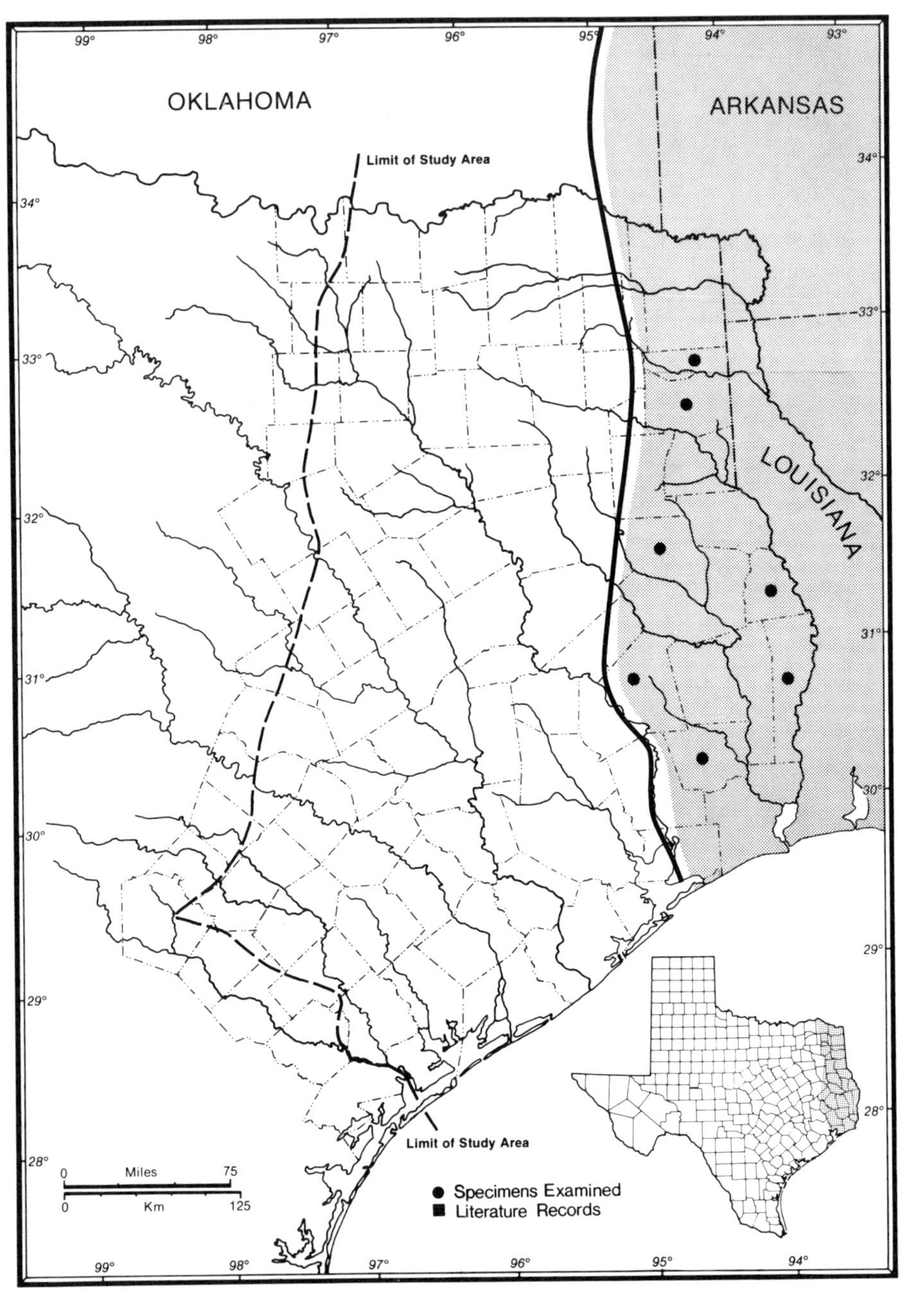

MAP 18. Distribution of Rafinesque's big-eared bat, *Plecotus rafinesquii macrotis*.

ter situation could imply that either the species is absent from the area during this time or that it is in hibernation. *P. rafinesquii* is known to hibernate in other parts of its range.

Life history. Of thirty-two bats of known sex collected in eastern Texas, twenty-one were males and eleven were females. It is interesting that the sex ratio seemed to vary between colonies. For example, fifteen out of seventeen bats taken in a well in Nacogdoches County in October and November were males, whereas six out of seven bats captured in a barn in Polk County in November were females. These bats are known to move frequently within a roosting area, which may account for these differences.

This bat emerges from its roost after dark and returns to the resting site prior to dawn. Apparently, it does not forage in twilight. The flight of adults varies from swift to nearly hovering, and is quite agile. Nothing is known about food habits, but it probably feeds on small, flying insects, as do all other bats in eastern Texas.

The reproductive biology of this species is poorly known. Copulation apparently takes place in autumn and winter, but information is lacking with regard to fertilization, implantation, and the precise gestation period. Females give birth to a single young in late May and early June. Young bats are born naked, and their eyes open after about one week. They are closely associated with adult females for about three weeks after birth, at which time they have permanent dentition and are capable of flight. Adult size is reached in approximately four weeks, and they are weaned at two months.

Because of its roosting habits, *P. rafinesquii* is highly susceptible to predation and other disturbances by man. Potential predators of this bat include snakes, raccoons, opossums, and cats. These bats are long-lived, as evidenced by the fact that some marked animals remained in a colony in Louisiana for eight years.

Several aspects of the behavior of this bat are interesting. At rest the bat hangs by its feet with its head downward and with its long ears coiled in a spiral over the neck. When disturbed at its roost, it begins to move and wave the ears while turning its head to look about. It is also known occasionally to utter a low hoarse bark that sounds much like that of a small dog.

References. C. Jones, 1977; C. Jones and Suttkus, 1975; Michael and Birch, 1967; Schmidly et al., 1977; Schultz et al., 1975.

Family Molossidae (Free-tailed Bats)

The free-tailed bats, as members of this family are called, are important components of tropical and subtropical chiropteran faunas throughout much of the world. In the New World, one species occasionally ranges as far north as Canada, but the main range begins in the southern and southwestern United States and extends southward to South America. The general appearance of molossids is distinctive. The tail extends well beyond the posterior border of the interfemoral membrane, and the fur is usually short and velvety. The ears are broad, project to the side, and are like short wings. Only one species of this family occurs in eastern Texas.

Brazilian Free-tailed Bat
Tadarida brasiliensis (Saussure)

Name. Rafinesque coined the generic name *Tadarida* without giving a clue as to its etymology. The specific name *brasiliensis* is a combination of the name of the country Brazil and the Latin word *ensis*, meaning "belonging to."

Identification. This bat may be easily distinguished from other species in eastern Texas by the fact that a portion of the tail extends free beyond the interfemoral membrane (by about 19 mm). Coloration is brownish black above and grayish brown below. Other highly diagnostic features include the leathery ear, the long hairs on the toes, and the black muzzle with its vertically arranged wrinkles on the upper lip. Average external measurements are total length, 93 mm; tail, 34 mm; hind foot, 10 mm; ear, 17 mm. The dental formula is I 1/2–3, C 1/1, Pm 2/2, M 3/3 × 2 = 30–32.

Subspecies. Two subspecies occur in eastern Texas (Map 19). *Tadarida brasiliensis mexicana* (Saussure, *Revue et Mag. Zool.*, Paris, ser. 2, 12:283, July—type from Cofre de Perote, 13,000 ft, Veracruz, Mexico) is a migratory, cave-dwelling (sometimes house-dwelling) bat of the southwestern United States. It reaches the eastern limits of its range in eastern Texas (approximately in a line beginning with and extending down the Navasota River to the confluence of the Navasota and Brazos rivers and thence continuing southeastward to the Gulf Coast). *T. b. cynocephala* (Le Conte, in McMurtrie, *The animal kingdom . . . by the Baron Cuvier . . .*, 1:432, 1831—type from Georgia, probably near Le Conte plantation, Liberty County) is a sedentary, tree- or house-dwelling bat of the southeastern United States. It reaches the western limits of its range in eastern Texas (in a line extending from Anderson County south to Harris County).

The taxonomic status of *T. b. mexicana* and *T. b. cynocephala* has been debated for years. Carter (1962) and W. B. Davis (1974) consider them as distinct species, but certain recent authors (Lowery, 1974; Schmidly et al., 1977) have preferred to consider them as subspecies of *T. brasiliensis*, as was proposed by A. Schwartz (1955). The primary distinctions between *cynocephala* and *mexicana* are ethological, although some morphological difference is evident between the two (the former, compared to the latter, averages larger in external and cranial measurements).

Distribution and habitat. This bat has an extensive geographic distribution, ranging across the entire southern part of the United States (including all of Texas), south through Mexico, the West Indies, and Central America as well as over most of South America. It probably occurs throughout all of eastern Texas, although it has not been recorded north

Brazilian free-tailed bat, *Tadarida brasiliensis*.

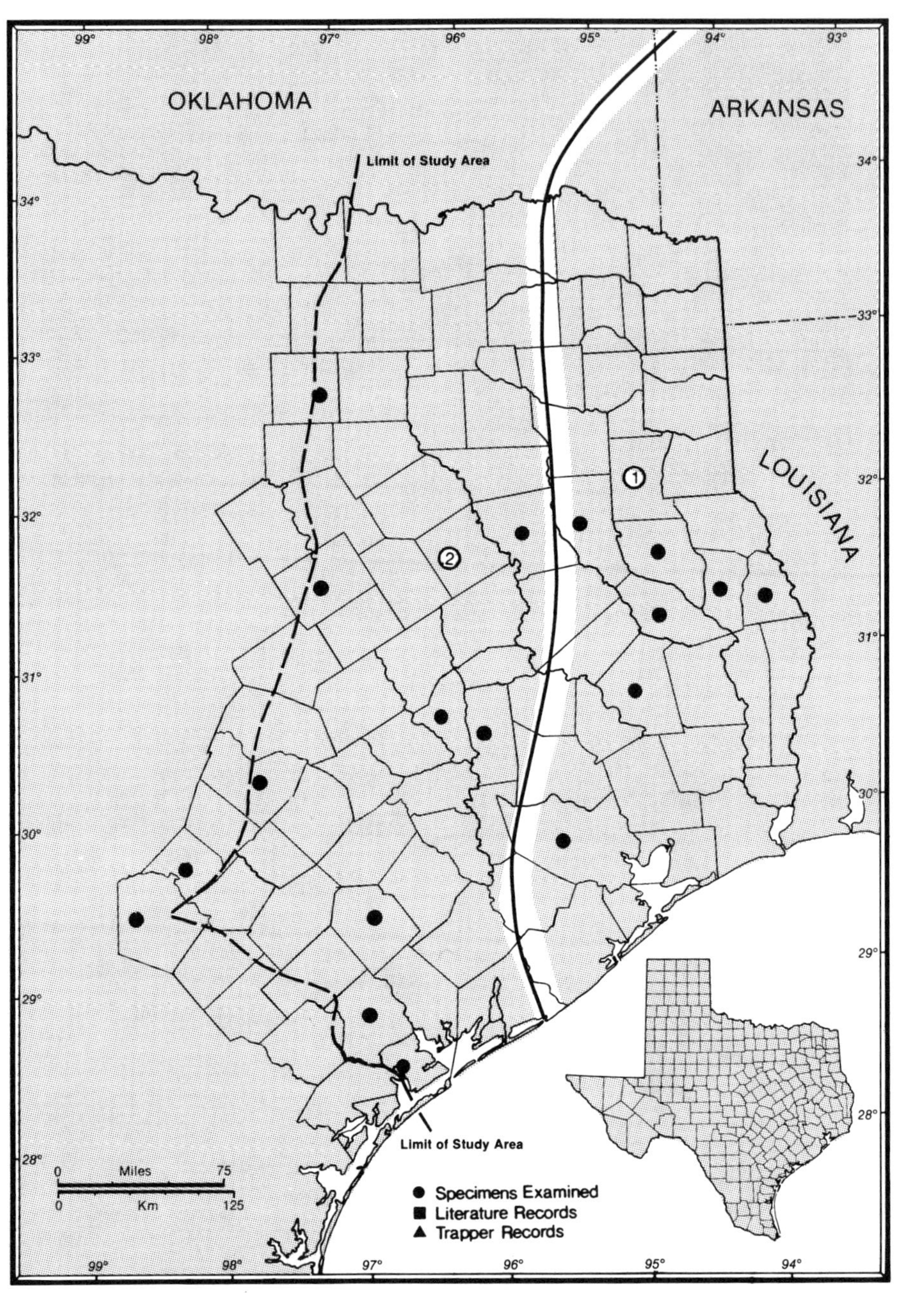

MAP 19. Distribution of the Brazilian free-tailed bat, *Tadarida brasiliensis*. 1. *T. b. cynocephala*. 2. *T. b. mexicana*.

Face of the Brazilian free-tailed bat, *Tadarida brasiliensis.*

of a line extending from Arlington, Tarrant County, eastward to the Sabine River (Map 19).

These bats live entirely in buildings in eastern Texas. W. B. Davis (1974) has estimated that every town in the bat's range is likely to have at least fifteen roosts per 5,000 human population. These bats will use just about any type of building without regard to style, size, age, state of repair, or use by man. The critical feature is whether the building has any accessible small cracks or crevices into which the bats can retreat during the day. Their presence in a building can usually be determined by their musky odor and the presence of guano on the floor. Owners or managers of buildings often have serious problems with these bats. The owner of an old office building in Longview was forced to close the building temporarily because of the resulting odor from the buildup of guano in the attic of the building. Similarly, the owner of a restaurant in Austin had problems with bats in his building, as did one of the large modern hospitals in that town. It is virtually impossible to drive the bats away by killing those present or by using chemical treatments in the roost. The simplest, most effective method is to close the entrance to the roost at a time when most of the bats are on the wing and away from the colony.

Life history. Free-tailed bats generally leave the roost and begin foraging shortly before or after sunset, and they generally do not return until just before dawn. Feeding behavior is characterized by straight, rapid flight, and changes in direction are usually horizontal. Bats may feed at levels of 4.5 m to well over 30 m above the ground. *T. brasiliensis* feeds primarily on moths.

This bat has received considerable attention in Texas because it is a known carrier of rabies. However, not all of its attributes are harmful to

Flight of the Brazilian free-tailed bats out of a cave on the Edwards Plateau. Millions of bats live in these caves, which serve as nursery colonies.

man. Bats are economically important because they consume tens of thousands of tons of insects each year. R. B. Davis et al. (1962) estimated that each free-tailed bat captures a nightly average of 1 g of insects and that the species may destroy about 6,000 tons of insects per year.

Studies have revealed significant differences in the life history strategies of the two subspecies of this species in Texas, particularly with regard to seasonal movements and hibernation. The following discussion treats these aspects of the life history of each subspecies separately.

T. b. cynocephala

Carter (1962) spent several years studying this subspecies, and most of the following information is taken from his findings. This bat lives in colonies that usually contain between 5,000 and 10,000 individuals. It roosts, apparently without exception, in buildings such as churches and old two-story buildings, where two essential, annual activities (hibernation and parturition) take place.

Colonies typically remain in the same roost for a long period of time unless that roost is destroyed. Males and females generally form separate groups within the same roost during spring and summer, but during the period of hibernation prior to copulation the sexes become thoroughly mixed. Some males may leave the main colony during the summer, but most remain at the primary roost, and those leaving tend to locate in suitable auxiliary roosts near the main colony.

Copulation in *T. b. cynocephala* occurs during an intrahibernating period of activity in the winter (presumably brought about by a period of warm weather), and the time and duration of parturition depends on the time and extent of the warm period during which copulation takes place and the severity of the winter after copulation has occurred. One or two weeks of warm weather probably suffices for the completion of copulation since the parturition period may be essentially completed in three weeks and most young are born within a period of about ten days. A series of short warm periods separated by cold periods would conceivably spread copulation over a period of several weeks and result in a similar period for parturition. The length of the gestation period probably depends in part on the severity of the winter after copulation.

During June and July young bats are found in small groups surrounded by adult females. A general uniformity of age seems to be characteristic of any given group of juveniles. The young grow rapidly and are weaned from parental care at an age of about six weeks.

T. b. mexicana

Bats of this subspecies, commonly called guano bats, appear every year in Texas in the multimillions to inhabit a few select caves located on the Balcones Escarpment and the adjacent Edwards Plateau. During the winter these bats migrate to southern latitudes in Mexico, Central America, and possibly South America. In early spring, around March, bats begin arriving in the caves of the Edwards Plateau. The major event in the life of these cave bats summering in Texas is the birth and development of their young.

Guano bats also commmonly occupy buildings, although only a small fraction of the numbers of bats found in caves is ever found roosting in buildings. Most roosts in buildings house fewer than one hundred bats at a time, but a few buildings traditionally house many hundreds each year.

Spenrath and LaVal (1974) spent eighteen months during 1970 and 1971 studying a colony of *Tadarida* that lived in the Animal Husbandry Pavilion on the Texas A&M University campus in College Station. This colony, which is situated near the eastern edge of the distributional limits of *T. b. mexicana*, is located approximately 137 km northeast of the eastern limits of the Edward's Plateau (the region where *mexicana* is known to be abundant) and less than 80 km west of the western edge of the pine-hardwood forest region where *T. b. cynocephala* occurs. I and several of my students have monitored the College Station colony since 1971. Study of this colony is important because of its geographic location (situated between the ranges of *mexicana* and *cynocephala*) and because the bats living there are morphologically and behaviorally intermediate between the two subspecies.

The population size of the Texas A&M University colony peaks in the spring and again in the fall; lows occur in winter and summer. Other roosts (especially caves) on the nearby Edwards Plateau experience lows in winter and highs in summer.

Spenrath and LaVal (1974) gave no precise estimate of the total number of bats present at any one time in the roost. Using the Schnabel mark-recapture formula, I estimated the population size for the spring of 1972 to be 387, with a 95 percent confidence interval ranging from 335 to 439. The population estimate for the fall of 1971 was computed to be 346, with a 95 percent confidence interval ranging from 297 to 395.

It is believed that bats traveling northward in spring to their summer roosts stop over at the College Station roost for short periods. Similarly, they may stop at this roost again in the fall en route to their Latin American breeding grounds, hence causing the spring and fall peaks. However, this assumption has yet to be substantiated, as no bats banded anywhere other than College Station have ever been recaptured at this roost.

There has been some controversy as to whether individuals from this colony migrate or hibernate, the behavioral patterns common to *T. b. mexicana* and *T. b. cynocephala*, respectively. Evidence for overwintering, but not necessarily hibernation, is shown by the fact that bats have been netted during each month of the year. In the study by Spenrath and LaVal (1974), the number of bats netted in winter was nearly half that of the peak populations in spring and fall, and these same trends followed in the subsequent years I studied this colony.

Three individuals banded in College Station have been recaptured elsewhere in Texas. A female banded on June 10, 1970 was taken 58 km south of College Station on June 18, 1970; another female, which was banded on October 22, 1970, was recaptured 533 km southwest of College Station in San Benito, Texas, on November 23, 1970. The third bat was found on October 7, 1972, west of Dilley, Texas, which is about 375 km southwest of the point of banding. The distances at which two of the above bats were taken from the point of banding are of sufficient magnitude to show conclusively that some members of this colony do exhibit migratory behavior.

It is well established in the literature that the sexes of the guano bat roost separately, especially while the young are born and raised from May through August. The Spenrath and LaVal banding efforts involved thirty-three nights of netting, during which time 1,063 bats were banded, including 668 (62.8 percent) males and 395 (37.2 percent) females. The obvious conclusion from these data is that the colony is consistently and predominantly male. Only three times in Spenrath and LaVal's study were females present as a majority (December 1969, October 1970, December 1970), and on only three other occasions was the entire sample as much as 40 percent female (April 1970, September 1970, October 1970). In no average monthly sample netted since 1971 have females ever comprised as much as 40 percent of the sample.

Some females caught in February, March, and April of 1970 and 1971 were dissected, but none contained embryos. These nonreproductive females may have overwintered or been early transients and, therefore, not had the opportunity to breed. Consequently, there was no need for them to move to nursery colonies, and they simply remained in the predominantly male roost. However, some pregnant females apparently do bear their young in the Animal Husbandry Pavilion roost, since two of my students found a very young bat on the floor of the pavilion during the first half of the summer of 1972.

In summary, there appears to be little difference between the College Station colony and other guano bat colonies with respect to seasonal and daily activity patterns. The only major exception is the discrepancy in seasonal fluctuations of population size, which is probably due to College Station's location between northern summer roosts and southern winter roosts and the migration between them. Eastern Texas constitutes a region of morphological intergradation (Schmidly et al., 1977) between *T. b. mexicana* and *T. b. cynocephala*. The simultaneous occurrence of both migration and overwintering offers ethological evidence for intergradation between the two subspecies.

References. Carter, 1962; W. B. Davis, 1974; Schmidly et al., 1977; Spenrath and LaVal, 1974.

Order Edentata

This order of three living families, which includes armadillos, anteaters, and sloths, occurs primarily in South and Central America and Mexico. The nine-banded armadillo (*Dasypus novemcinctus*) is the only species of the order that ranges into the United States, and it is one of the commonest mammals in eastern Texas. Armadillos are unique among all mammals in possessing a bony carapace. The name edentate, which means "toothless," is not literally true of the armadillo. Although it has neither incisor nor canine teeth, the armadillo does possess a series of simple, peglike cheek teeth set well back on the jaws. These teeth lack enamel and are open at the root, a condition incident to continuous growth throughout life.

Family Dasypodidae (Armadillos)

Nine-banded Armadillo
Dasypus novemcinctus Linnaeus

Name. The generic name is from the Greek word *dasypodis*, meaning "hare" or "rabbit," which is taken from the Aztec translation for tortoise-rabbit (*Azotochtli*). Linnaeus apparently found the Aztec name as reported by the conquistador Hernandez unacceptable for latinization and translated the meaning of "rabbit-turtle" into the Greek *Dasypus*. The specific name is a combination of two Latin words, *novem*, meaning "nine," and *cinctus*, meaning "banded" or "girdled."

Identification. The armadillo is about the same size of an opossum and may be easily distinguished from other mammals in eastern Texas by its turtlelike shell or carapace, which is composed of ossified dermal plates (scutes) covered by a leathery skin. This carapace, which accounts for approximately 16 percent of the animal's body weight, is divided into three main regions: a shell that protects the shoulders, another that covers the pelvic region, and a series of eight to eleven (usually nine) telescoping bands connecting the other two parts. There is slight overlap among the bands, each of which is connected to one another by a fold of soft, hairless skin. The head, which tapers to a soft, pinkish, piglike snout, is covered with heavy scales closely attached to the skull. The tail is long (comprising 70 percent or more of head and body length), tapering, and covered by a series of twelve to fifteen bony rings. The ears are large (comprising 40 to 50 percent of head length), grayish to black, and covered with tough, pebbly skin. The legs are short, stout, and adapted for digging. The front feet have four toes and the hind feet five, and all are provided with large, strong claws. Average external measurements are total length, 752 mm; tail, 310 mm; hind foot, 76 mm; ear, 37 mm. There are no incisor or canine teeth. Dentition is 8/8, and all teeth are laterally flattened, peglike, single-rooted, and lack enamel.

Subspecies. In eastern Texas there is only the one subspecies, *Dasypus novemcinctus mexicanus* Peters (*Monatsber. K. preuss. Akad. Wissensch.*, Berlin, p. 180, 1864), with type locality at Matamoros, Tamaulipas, Mexico.

Distribution and habitat. This widely distributed species ranges from Kansas and Missouri southward through Mexico and into South

Nine-banded armadillo, *Dasypus novemcinctus*.

America. The species now occurs throughout Texas except for the Trans-Pecos and Panhandle areas. Armadillos undoubtedly occur in most counties in eastern Texas, although specimens have been collected in only a few of these (Map 20). They are most common in the pineywoods followed in decreasing order by the post oak woodlands, coastal prairies, and blackland prairies.

Although armadillos inhabit many diverse ecological communities, they seem to prefer wooded, riparian areas. They occur in habitats ranging from swampy to relatively dry, but within a given area they are usually found close to water because the food supply is usually more abundant in moist areas and they prefer to burrow in an inclined surface such as the side of a stream bank. During flood periods they migrate away from streams; conversely, in periods of drought, they move toward the remaining water. Soil texture seems to influence the number of armadillos in a given area. Those soils that are more diggable, other factors being equal, will support a greater population density.

Life history. Armadillos live in burrows generally located at the base of a tree or bush. There is no relationship with any particular plant species, although clumps of dewberries and wax myrtle seem to be particularly popular. Armadillos occur in greatest numbers in areas of dense growth probably because such areas support a better food supply. This vegetation may also serve as a protective measure because an armadillo can move with impunity in dense and thorny brush, whereas a would-be predator would experience difficulty.

The location, type, and extent of armadillo burrows depend upon the character of the soil. Generally, the easier the soil is to dig, the more bur-

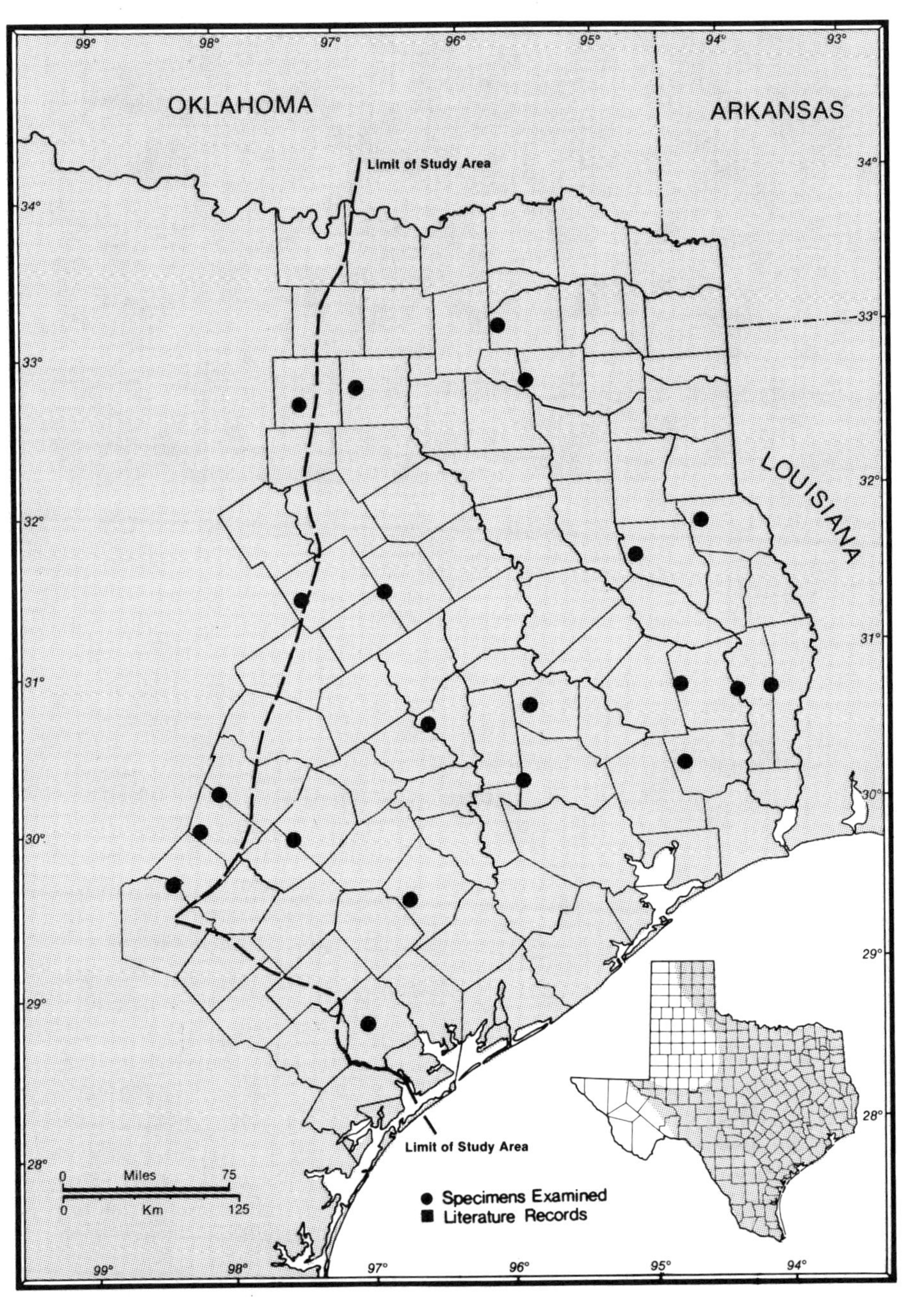

MAP 20. Distribution of the nine-banded armadillo, *Dasypus novemcinctus mexicanus*.

rows per animal and the more elaborate and complex are their burrows. A typical home (nesting) burrow consists of a tunnel 18 to 20 cm in diameter, about 1.2 to 7.3 m in length, with a slight enlargement for the nest at the end. Home burrows often have two and occasionally more tunnels leading to the outside, although only one is regularly used. There are usually more burrows than armadillos in any given area, and the accessory burrows may serve as food traps or temporary shelters.

The nest consists of a mass of leaves or grass which the armadillo stuffs into the nesting chamber and into which the animal forces its way to sleep. The nesting material may be half a bushel in volume, and is of such construction that the animal literally packs itself in insulation. Feces are not found in the nest, but they are occasionally found in the tunnels. The nest is extremely important to the survival of the armadillo at northern latitudes because the animal has very poor temperature control. At 22° C, it is uncomfortably cool and shivers continually. At colder temperatures it cannot survive long unless provided with adequate nesting material into which it can crawl. The animal does not hibernate and, while able to go for relatively long periods without eating, must seek food during all seasons of the year. While in the nest an armadillo can survive for some time unless the ground is frozen down to that level.

Population density estimates range from 0.05 to 3.04 individuals per ha. Home range size varies from 3.4 to 20.3 ha and may be markedly reduced by drought conditions. Armadillos are not very territorial as evidenced by greatly overlapping home ranges and a lack of intraspecific aggression.

Armadillos are essentially crepuscular or nocturnal, although on rainy or cloudy days they may search for food during daylight hours. They seem to react more to temperature than to light. Cold greatly hampers their movements, and they are seldom active in extremely cold weather. In the summer they seem to avoid the hottest part of the day, coming out near sundown, or immediately following rains or extreme cloudiness, if the temperature falls. Upon leaving their den they immediately begin to forage. Armadillos leave an easily recognized trail wherever they go, as their dragging tail leaves a plain and distinctive imprint similar to that of a rope.

Foraging patterns are typically erratic and random. The armadillo locates food exclusively by smell. It shuffles along, nose to the ground, and often ploughs a furrow in the litter of the forest floor, which constitutes one of its favorite haunts. It can locate grubs beneath 13 to 15 cm of earth, and digs a small, conical hole with its fore feet when a food item is found. A wheezing, grunting sound is often emitted while rooting and digging. During periods of foraging or traveling, an armadillo will periodically stop at intervals, rear on its haunches, and sniff the air while turning its head slowly from side to side. When not foraging, it walks with a shuffling gait or trots like a pig, and often shifts from one gait to another.

The diet of the armadillo is primarily, but not totally, insectivorous. Baker (1943) analyzed twenty-five stomachs of animals taken in Polk and

Trinity counties and found that better than 90 percent of the stomach contents were animal in nature. Insects constituted 77.4 percent and angleworms (Annelida) 13.6 percent of the bulk, while other animal food, including three vertebrate items, constituted only a small percentage. Vegetable matter made up only a small portion of the diet, with blackberries comprising 2.6 percent of the contents and grasses and roots being present in only trace amounts. Sand and mud were found in all stomachs and constituted 4.4 percent of the bulk. Kalmbach (1943) analyzed the contents of 169 stomachs and noted similar results.

Field observations made in Polk County (Newman and Baker, 1942) have also yielded evidence that the armadillo may at times prey upon young and helpless mammals. An armadillo was observed devouring three young cottontail rabbits. Evidence pointed to the fact that the rabbits had been killed and mutilated by thrusts of the armadillo's front feet and that actual eating was accomplished by continued chewing until the food was softened and torn enough to be swallowed.

Reproduction in the nine-banded armadillo is marked by two distinct and apparently unrelated phenomena: the long period of arrested development of the blastocyst prior to implantation (delayed implantation), and the phenomenon of specific polyembryony, which results in the normal formation of identical quadruplets. In normal years about half of the females become pregnant by the end of July, which is the beginning of the breeding season. At five to seven days the ovum forms a blastocyst and passes into the uterus. At this point development ceases, and the vesicle remains free in the uterus. Here it is constantly bathed in fluids secreted by the glandular lining of the uterus, which supplies enough nutrition and oxygen for survival. Implantation does not occur until November, about fourteen weeks after fertilization. During this process, the blastocyst divides into growth centers, each of which very shortly redivides to produce four embryonic growth centers attached by a common placenta to the uterus. Development of each of the embryos then proceeds normally, and the four young are born approximately four months later in March, although some females have been noted with new litters as early as February and as late as the latter part of May. Young are born fully formed and with eyes open. Within a few hours they are walking, and they begin to accompany the mother on foraging expeditions within a few weeks. The nursing period is probably less than two months, but the young may remain with the mother even after weaning until they are several months old. Normally the young born in one year mature during the winter and mate for the first time in the early summer of the following year.

This phenomenon of delayed implantation may, in part, account for the successful invasion of the armadillo into temperate regions. Without this characteristic of the reproductive cycle, the young would be born at the beginning of winter, when their chance of survival would be greatly reduced. Apparently, the reproductive cycle is easily affected by adverse environmental conditions, particularly drought conditions. This probably is due to the shortage of ground insects or the difficulty of obtaining these in sandy or hard dried soils.

Armadillos are believed to pair for each breeding season, and a male and a female may share a burrow during the season. Because of the bony carapace and ventral position of the genitalia, copulation occurs with the female lying on her back.

The armadillo's only serious predator appears to be man. Sperry (1941) examined stomach contents of 566 coyotes and found no armadillo remains. Kalmbach (1943) reported armadillo remains from stomach contents of one cougar. Vehicles seem to kill by far the greatest numbers. Armadillos are particularly prone to highway dangers because their habit of jumping upward when startled makes them vulnerable to the entire width of a vehicle.

The armadillo lives in the same general environment as the raccoon, opossum, and skunk, but, compared to these neighbors, is strikingly free of parasites. The only disease of clinical importance known to occur in armadillos is American human trypanosomiasis, or Chagas' disease. A leprosy-like disease has been reported in wild armadillos from Louisiana (Walsh et al., 1975; Weiser, 1975), but no one has documented association between armadillo contact and leprosy in humans (Filice et al., 1977).

The armadillo possesses a pronounced odor, objectionable to most persons, which has its origin in a pair of glands situated laterally and close to the anus. They are present in both sexes but are obscure except when protruded and functioning. Though a trace of this odor is evident at all times, it is most pronounced when the animal is excited or has been engaged in struggle.

Remarks. The common occurrence of this species in eastern Texas is a phenomenon that has developed largely since 1900. When Vernon Bailey published his *Biological Survey of Texas* in 1905, he mapped the distributional limits of the armadillo as between the Colorado and Guadalupe rivers with extralimital records from Colorado, Grimes, and Houston counties. By 1914 the armadillo had crossed the Brazos River and moved to the Trinity River, and along the coast had already reached the Louisiana line in Orange County. The northward and eastward range expansions continued over the next forty years, and by 1954 the armadillo was known from everywhere in eastern Texas except Red River and Lamar counties (Buchanan and Talmage, 1954). By 1958 it was known from these latter two counties (Buchanan, 1958), and today it is abundant everywhere in the region (Cleveland, 1970).

Apparently pioneering was most successful in a riparian habitat, and invasion was especially rapid parallel to rivers, which served as dispersal conduits. Average invasion rates have been calculated as from 4 to 10 km per year in the absence of obvious physical or climatic barriers (Humphrey, 1974). Possible reasons for the armadillo's northward expansion since the nineteenth century include progressive climatic changes, encroaching human civilization, overgrazing, and decimation of large carnivores.

References. Buchanan, 1957; W. B. Davis, 1974; Fitch et al., 1952; Hollister, 1925; Kalmbach, 1943; McBee and Baker, 1981; H. H. Newman, 1913; Strecker, 1926b; Taber, 1945; Talmage and Buchanan, 1945.

Order Lagomorpha

Lagomorphs have ever-growing incisors and a dentition superficially like that of rodents, but they are easily distinguished by their incisors. Lagomorphs have four instead of two upper incisors; there is a second, peglike pair immediately behind the front upper pair. Also, each incisor has enamel on both the posterior and the anterior surfaces instead of only the anterior surface, as in rodents. In lagomorphs, the maxillary tooth rows are farther apart than the mandibular rows, and only one molar row of the upper and the lower jaw are capable of opposition at the same time. The facial portion of the maxillary bone is incomplete. The body is well furred, and the tail is very short. Locomotion is by hopping or leaping, and the hind feet are longer than the front.

There are two families of lagomorphs, the Ochotonidae (pikas) and the Leporidae (hares and rabbits). Only the latter occurs in eastern Texas, and it is represented by two species of rabbits of the genus *Sylvilagus* and one species of hare of the genus *Lepus*. The young of hares (jack rabbits) are born precocious, furred, and with their eyes open; they have no nest prepared for them. Young rabbits (cottontails) are born blind, helpless, and hairless in a fur-lined nest.

1   Length of ear from notch more than 100 mm; tail with black dorsal stripe .... Black-tailed jack rabbit, *Lepus californicus*
Length of ear from notch less than 100 mm; tail lacking black dorsal stripe 2
2   Length of hind foot usually more than 100 mm; total length in adults near 500 mm; greatest length of skull over 80 mm; eye ring buffy .... Swamp rabbit, *Sylvilagus aquaticus*
Length of hind foot usually less than 100 mm; total length in adults near 400 mm; greatest length of skull less than 77 mm; eye ring white .... Eastern cottontail, *Sylvilagus floridanus*

Family Leporidae (Hares and Rabbits)

Eastern Cottontail
Sylvilagus floridanus (Allen)

Name. The generic name is derived from the Latin word *sylva*, meaning "a wood," and the Greek word *lagos*, meaning "hare." The specific epithet is a latinized word meaning "of Florida," referring to the place where the first specimen was collected and described.

Identification. The eastern cottontail is a moderately large rabbit with relatively short ears, large hind legs and feet, short front legs and feet, and a short, fluffy tail. The pelage is long and dense, brownish to grayish on the upper parts and white on the underside of the body and tail. Average external measurements are total length, 405 mm; tail,

Eastern cottontail, *Sylvilagus floridanus.*

52 mm; hind foot, 89 mm; ear, 57 mm. The dental formula is I 2/1, C 0/0, Pm 3/2, M 3/3 × 2 = 28.

This rabbit differs from the swamp rabbit (*S . aquaticus*) by its smaller hind foot (usually less than 100 mm instead of exceeding 100 mm, as in *aquaticus*) and by its slightly smaller skull. The postorbital process touches the skull toward the rear in both species, but in the cottontail it usually is not fused to the skull and a distinct slit remains, whereas in the swamp rabbit it usually is fused and only a small hole remains.

Subspecies. Only the one subspecies, *Sylvilagus floridanus alacer*, occurs in eastern Texas, and it was named by Bangs (*Proc. Biol. Soc. Washington*, 10:36, December 28, 1896) with type locality from Stilwell, Boston Mountains, Adair County, Oklahoma.

Distribution and habitat. The eastern cottontail ranges widely over most of Texas, being absent only from sections of the coastal marshes and the arid western regions (Map 21). It occurs throughout eastern Texas in all vegetational regions and in all habitats except the aquatic ones.

Optimum habitat for cottontails includes brush for escape and loafing cover and abundant grasses and herbs to act as a food source and a groundcover screen. They typically are found in open country, pastures, and grassy areas, although they occasionally occur in woodlands and swamps. Cottontails are found in all the early stages of second growth following timber harvest, but they are most abundant from about five to twelve years after the timber is cut. This period coincides roughly with the period of greatest variety and abundance of herbaceous plants. As the sapling pines and brushy hardwoods crowd out the herbaceous species foreshadowing the approach of the subclimax pine woods, cottontails give

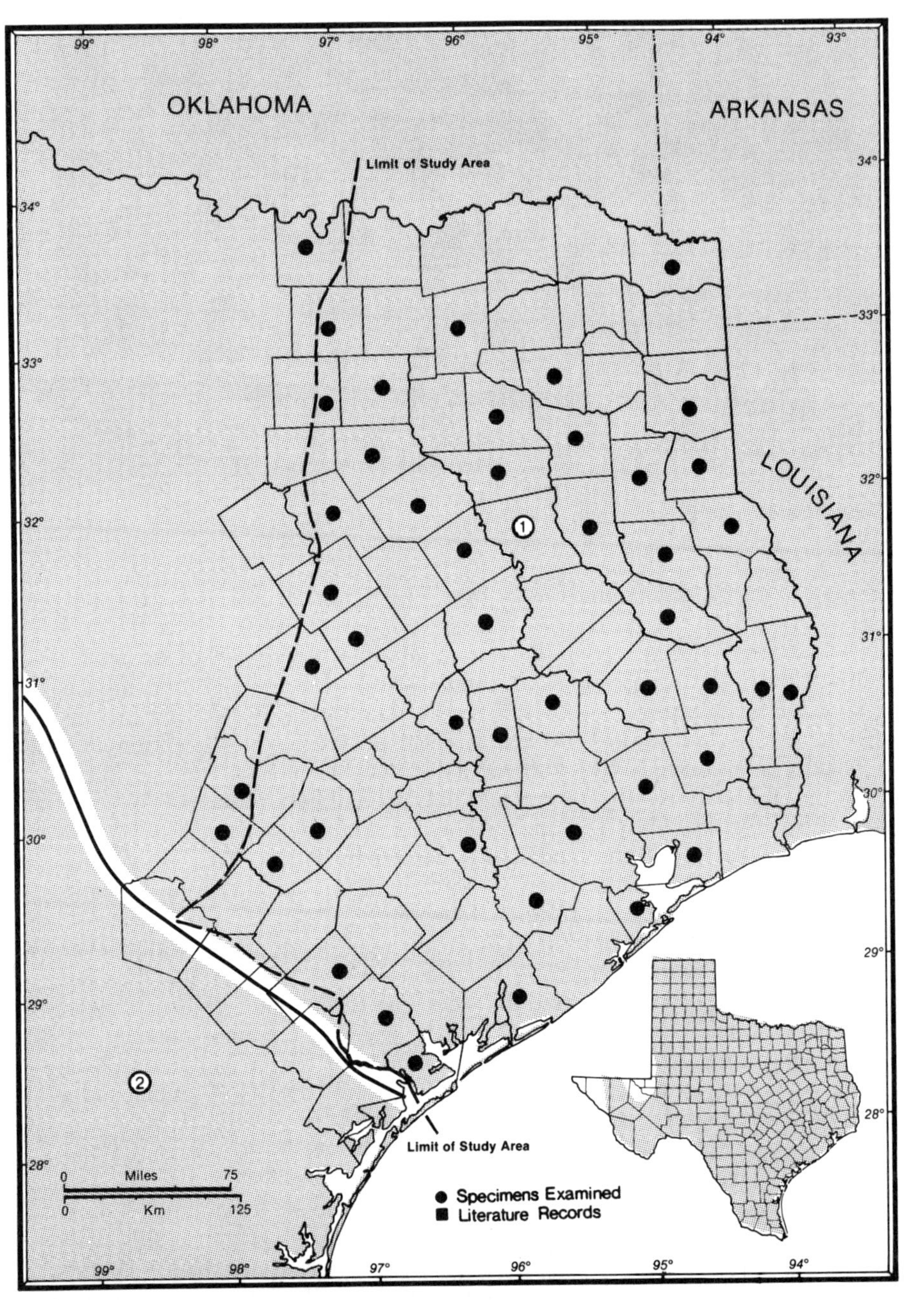

MAP 21.   Distribution of the eastern cottontail, *Sylvilagus floridanus*. 1. *S. f. ala-cer*. 2. *S. f. chapmani*.

way to swamp rabbits. The latter are usually more common than any other species in second-growth timber over twelve years old, although cottontails hold on persistently in spots where the forest growth is open enough to permit the growth of bluestem.

Grazing has an appreciable influence on the occurrence and distribution of these rabbits. When grazing is light or absent, cottontails are more numerous than at any other place. Cottontail habitat can be improved by interspersing old fields and briar thickets, by creating edge, and by establishing open food plots or by breaking up large, continuous parcels of monotypic habitat. Burning followed by grazing is destructive to habitat quality.

Life history. Cottontails live in nests constructed in slanting holes in the ground that average 125 mm in length, 104 mm in width, and 91 mm in depth. Nest holes usually have an outer lining of grass or herbaceous stems covering all sides, with a heavy, inner layer of belly or side fur from the female.

The home range size of eastern cottontails varies with season, sex, and the individual rabbit. Mean home ranges for adult males vary from about 0.95 ha to 2.8 ha; home ranges are smaller for adult females, averaging only 1 to 1.2 ha. The home range size of males increases with the onset of sexual activity. There is considerable home range overlap after the breeding season because cottontails do not maintain territories. These rabbits do not "hole up" for extended periods. Whether feeding or traveling in their home range, they travel along regular paths, producing trails or runways in the vegetation or under local brush piles.

Feeding habits of cottontails vary seasonally and with the succession of plants. They feed upon a variety of plants, preferring herbaceous species, such as clover and alfalfa, during the growing season and switching to woody species during the dormant season. They generally exhibit two pronounced feeding periods, an early effort about three or four hours after sunrise and a second one from sunset to one hour after. These times correlate with their greatest activity, which is at dawn and dusk.

Cottontails are well known for their coprophagous habits. They excrete two types of fecal pellets: hard, brown fecal pellets and soft, greenish food pellets. Hard pellets are the product of the final stages of digestion, and they comprise approximately 60 percent of the total fecal excretion. Soft pellets, which are produced in the caecum and provide vitamin B supplementation, are eaten directly from the anus before they touch the ground.

Evidence suggests that these rabbits breed year round in eastern Texas. Breeding activity probably varies between different populations and within the same population from year to year, depending on such environmental factors as temperature and rainfall. Severe weather delays the onset of breeding. Rainfall affects the amount of succulent vegetation available, which, in turn, may limit the breeding season. The mean gestation period is about twenty-eight days (range, twenty-five to thirty-five days). Females produce an average of three or four litters per year with an average of four young per litter. The potential productivity of adult females is about 9.4 young per female per year; for juvenile females, 6.2.

Young at birth are covered with fine hair, their eyes are tightly closed, and their legs are developed enough so that they can crawl into the nest. They open their eyes about six to seven days after birth and move away from the nest after twelve days. The average life span of these rabbits in the wild is about fifteen months; females have a greater longevity than males.

Cottontails are primary consumers and as such provide a staple food source for predatory animals. Mammalian predators include raccoons, ring-tailed cats, weasels, red and gray foxes, coyotes, bobcats, and feral cats. Avian predators include red-tailed hawks, red-shouldered hawks, marsh hawks, and golden eagles.

These rabbits are important as game animals in eastern Texas and serve as a supplemental food item for some people. However, because of their ubiquity they are not classified as game animals by state law.

References. Bothma and Teer, 1977; J. A. Chapman et al., 1980; Taylor and Lay, 1944.

Swamp Rabbit
Sylvilagus aquaticus (Bachman)

Name. The generic name *Sylvilagus* has the same derivation as that given previously for the eastern cottontail. The specific name *aquaticus* is Latin and means "found in water."

Identification. The swamp rabbit resembles the eastern cottontail (*S. floridanus*) but is appreciably larger and darker in coloration. Compared to *S. floridanus*, the overall coloration of *S. aquaticus* is yellowish brown, instead of grayish brown, with more black mottling on the dorsal pelage. An adult cottontail and a half-grown swamp rabbit are about the same size. The cottontail is a little larger and thinner and shows more white on its tail and buff in its coat than does a half-grown swamp rabbit. The latter will have longer legs and wider feet; the feet of the cottontail have a buff-orange color. The tips of the ear of the swamp rabbit are rounded as compared with the cottontail's more pointed ear tips. Average external measurements are total length, 511 mm; tail length, 71 mm; hind foot, 106 mm; ear, 71 mm. The dental formula is the same as that of all the members of this family in eastern Texas.

Subspecies. Two subspecies of *S. aquaticus* supposedly occur in eastern Texas: *S. a. aquaticus* in the wooded regions of the area and *S. a. littoralis* in the tidal marshes and coastal prairies. The latter is allegedly much darker and more reddish brown than *aquaticus*, especially on the rump, hind legs, and tops of all the feet. However, Lowery (1974) has demonstrated that the reddish brown coloration results from a ferruginous stain that the marsh-dwelling rabbits pick up from the terrain. Fur-

Swamp rabbit, *Sylvilagus aquaticus.*

thermore, he has shown that the reddish stain is easily removed by applying oxalic acid. Hence, the alleged redder brown coloration of the feet of the so-called *littoralis* is purely adventitious, and this subspecies is not worthy of recognition. Thus, all swamp rabbits from eastern Texas are referable to the nominate race, *S. a. aquaticus,* which was named by Bachman (*Jour. Acad. Nat. Sci. Philadelphia,* 7:319, 1837), with the type locality in the western part of Alabama.

Distribution and habitat. Swamp rabbits are abundant in the coastal marshes and hardwood bottomland swamps of eastern Texas (Map 22). Here they live among the tangled marsh vegetation and briar bushes as well as in the dense thickets of shrubs, trees, and vines bordering floodplains of rivers and creeks, which afford them excellent cover. In the forested pineywoods region, they are usually more common than any other lagomorph in second-growth timber over twelve years old. Farther inland in the post oak woodlands, they prefer fields of knee-high grass, interspersed with scrub oaks, in the ecotone area between the bottomlands and the prairie. They are virtually restricted to the floodplains of rivers and creeks in the blackland prairie region and are seldom found far from water.

Life history. Swamp rabbits have a definite affinity for water. They are known to swim across creeks and ponds or to run through shallow bodies of water. They frequently dive under water and also hide in water with just their nose breaking the surface. These rabbits will also seek refuge in hollow trees or burrows constructed by other mammals, such as the armadillo, when hard-pressed by predators.

Swamp rabbits build their nests in a slight depression in the ground

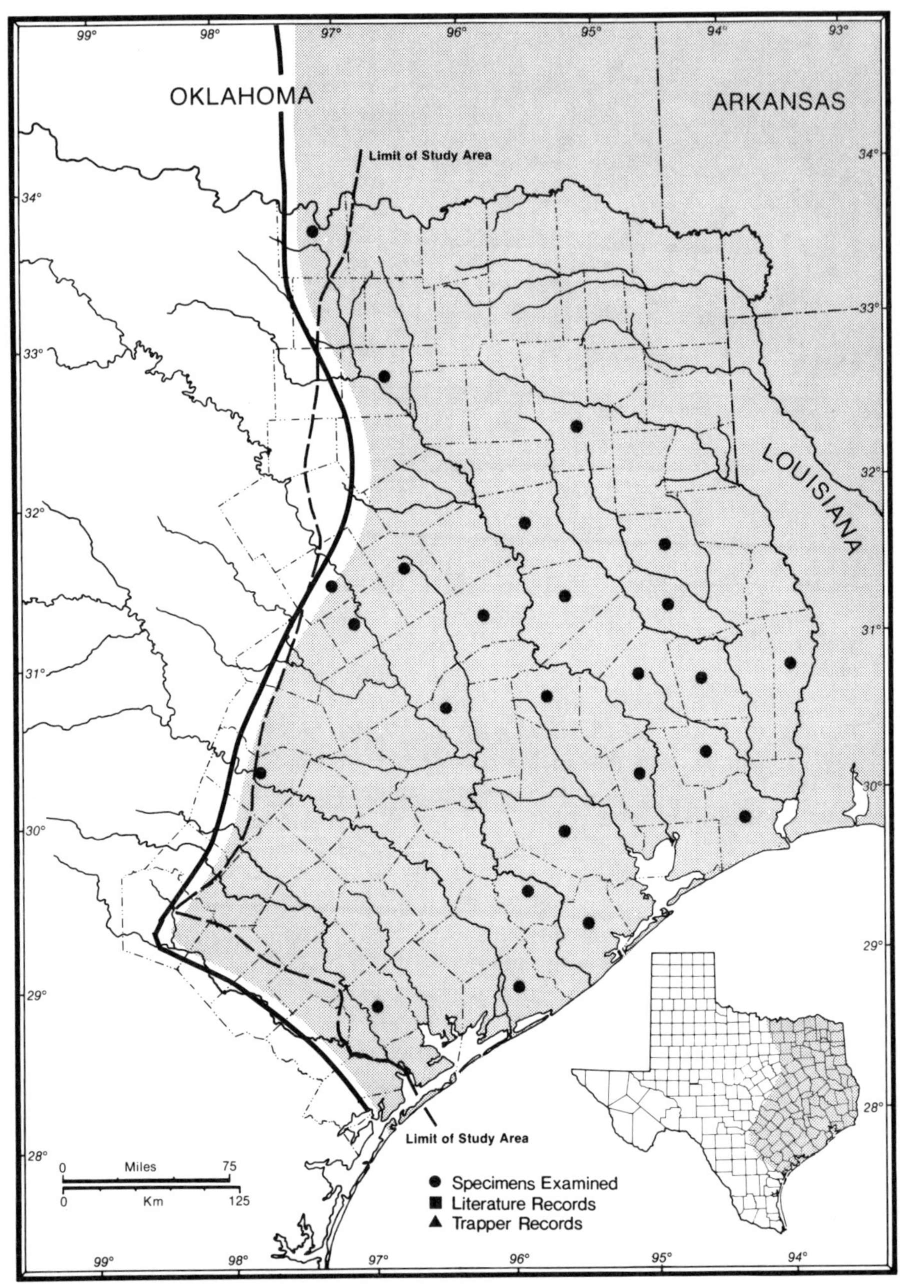

MAP 22. Distribution of the swamp rabbit, *Sylvilagus aquaticus aquaticus*.

and in a variety of ecological situations, including around fallen branches (Strecker and Williams, 1929), in old cypress stumps (R. D. Svihla, 1929), in weed patches (Goodpasture and Hoffmeister, 1952), and beneath brush piles (Hunt, 1959). Nests are composed of grasses or Spanish moss and are lined with rabbit fur. Females build nests about three days before the young are born; the fur is added to the nesting material just prior to birth.

Swamp rabbits appear to frequent a definite local range, averaging about 2.4 ha for females and 1.8 ha for males. They are mainly active at night or at dawn or dusk. During the day they do not use a hollow like a cottontail but usually rest on stumps or down logs that are surrounded by water.

Swamp rabbits feed on emergent vegetation, grasses, sedges, cane, tree seedlings, bark, and leaves. They are especially fond of cane and along the coast are referred to as "cane cutters." They often forage on cultivated crops, such as corn or sorghum, where the fields adjoin areas in which the rabbits live. In captivity they may eat an amount of food equivalent to about one-half of their weight each day.

A certain amount of breeding occurs throughout the year as gravid females have been found in each month except September, October, and December. The peak of breeding occurs in February and March and levels off from April to August. Breeding in the fall seems to correlate with the persistence of green vegetation in the bottomlands. It is also possible that older females breed during the first part of the new breeding season and that females born during the new season are responsible for the breeding that occurs in the late summer and fall. Prenatal litter size ranges from 1 to 5, with an average of 2.8. The gestation period is thirty-nine to forty days. There is a general positive association between the average litter size by month and the monthly percentage of females that are gravid during the same period. The young are born with the pelage well developed and the eyes closed. The eyes are fully opened and the animal is able to walk by the second or third day following birth.

The swamp rabbit has a habit of thumping the ground with its hind feet when it becomes alarmed. The only other noise that this rabbit is known to make in the wild is the scream that is often heard when a rabbit has been wounded and cannot move, or when one is seized by a hound or some predator. Known predators include alligators, gray foxes, coyotes, and horned owls, but many other animals probably prey on them as well. When these rabbits fight each other, they stand on their hind feet and use their teeth and the claws on their front feet to inflict wounds. They often jump off the ground, striking their opponent with the claws of their hind feet.

Optimum swamp rabbit habitat in eastern Texas is gradually shrinking with drainage of wetlands and clearing of hardwood forests. Unless steps are taken to prevent this type of habitat destruction, swamp rabbits will become increasingly rare in this region.

References. W. B. Davis, 1974; Hunt, 1959; Sealander, 1979; R. D. Svihla, 1929; Taylor and Lay, 1944; Terrel, 1972.

Black-tailed Jack Rabbit
Lepus californicus Gray

Name. Lepus is Latin for "hare" and *californicus* is a latinized word meaning "of California," which is where the first specimen was collected.

Identification. The jack rabbit may be distinguished from other lagomorphs in eastern Texas by its large, naked ears (usually more than 100 mm in length) and by its tail, which has a black dorsal stripe that extends onto the rump. Its skull may be distinguished from the skulls of the other two members of this family by the triangular and winglike supraorbital processes that stand out from the braincase and by the presence of many perforations on the base of the skull. The dental formula is the same as for the two rabbits in the region. Average external measurements are total length, 579 mm; tail, 66 mm; hind foot, 121 mm; ear, 125 mm.

Subspecies. Two subspecies occur in eastern Texas: *Lepus californicus melanotis* (True, *Proc. U.S. Nat. Mus.*, 7:601, November 29, 1884—type locality Independence, Montgomery County, Kansas) from the northern half of the region (north of a line positioned approximately thirty-one degrees latitude) and *L. c. merriami* (Mearns, *Proc. U.S. Nat. Mus.*, 18:444, May 23, 1896—type locality Fort Clark, Kinney County, Texas) from the southern portion.

Distribution and habitat. The jack rabbit is a species characteristic of the western United States that reaches its eastern distributional limits in eastern Texas. It is common and occurs throughout the blackland prairies and coastal prairies of eastern Texas, but it occurs only as disjunct populations in the oak-hickory and the pine-oak regions and is completely absent from the Big Thicket area (Map 23).

Jack rabbits have probably always been extremely common in the prairie-type communities that occur on black clay soil in the southern and western portions of eastern Texas. Here they occupy open plains, pastures, haylands, and cultivated areas, especially before the crops grow very high. Their occurrence in the pine-oak forested regions has been a recent event that in most places occurred only in the past forty to fifty years as a result of intensified timber-cutting and land-clearing programs in this area. When pine timber is clear-cut, jack rabbits move onto the cleared lands, especially if there has been some burning of slash to further open up the habitat. Much of this cleared land has subsequently been converted to pastureland for dairy cattle. These pastureland openings, although usually of small acreage (8 to 12 ha), are contiguous and extend westward in a dendritic pattern. They undoubtedly serve as avenues for the dispersal of jack rabbits in the central and southern parts of eastern Texas (except where the Big Thicket may act as an intervening barrier in the southern part) as well as to the north.

In the last twenty-five years many of these pastures have been either abandoned or reseeded to native species of southern pines. This change in land use has permitted plant succession to occur. Grasses such as bluestem, needlegrass, and redtop now dominate much of this land, and this

Black-tailed jack rabbit, *Lepus californicus.*

grassy type of habitat is suitable for jack rabbits. Jack rabbits remain only as long as the ground is open. Without proper management the burns become scrubby with oak sprouts and miscellaneous shrubs after three or four years, and the jack rabbits disappear.

Grazing has as appreciable influence on the occurrence and distribution of jack rabbits as well as cottontails. Where grazing is light or absent, cottontails are more numerous than at any other place. Up to a certain point jack rabbits benefit from grazing, tending to be scarce or absent when thick herbage, whether of grass or other species, covers the ground and cuts down visibility. Thus, as overgrazing removes the vegetation, jack rabbits tend to increase and cottontails decrease.

McCarley (1959d) suggests that jack rabbits have been introduced in the pine-oak regions of eastern Texas from time to time so that they could be coursed by greyhounds belonging to groups of sportsmen. Packard (1963) interviewed a number of individuals living in rural areas and contacted several groups of sportsmen in Nacogdoches and Angelina counties. None of the people interviewed by Packard were aware of introduced jack rabbits in those counties. Probably there have been some limited introductions, but I suspect that most of the jack rabbits in this region of eastern Texas immigrated there from the west and north.

Life history. Jack rabbits spend most of the day sleeping in a simple unlined hollow, or form, which they scratch in the ground. A typical form is from 25 to 46 cm in length, 10 to 15 cm wide, and up to 19 cm deep. Some are made in the open and others in dense vegetation; they may be used only once or many times over a period of days. Jack rabbits become active at twilight. They begin to feed about dusk or early evening and may forage well into the night. Occasionally, they have a short feeding period about daybreak.

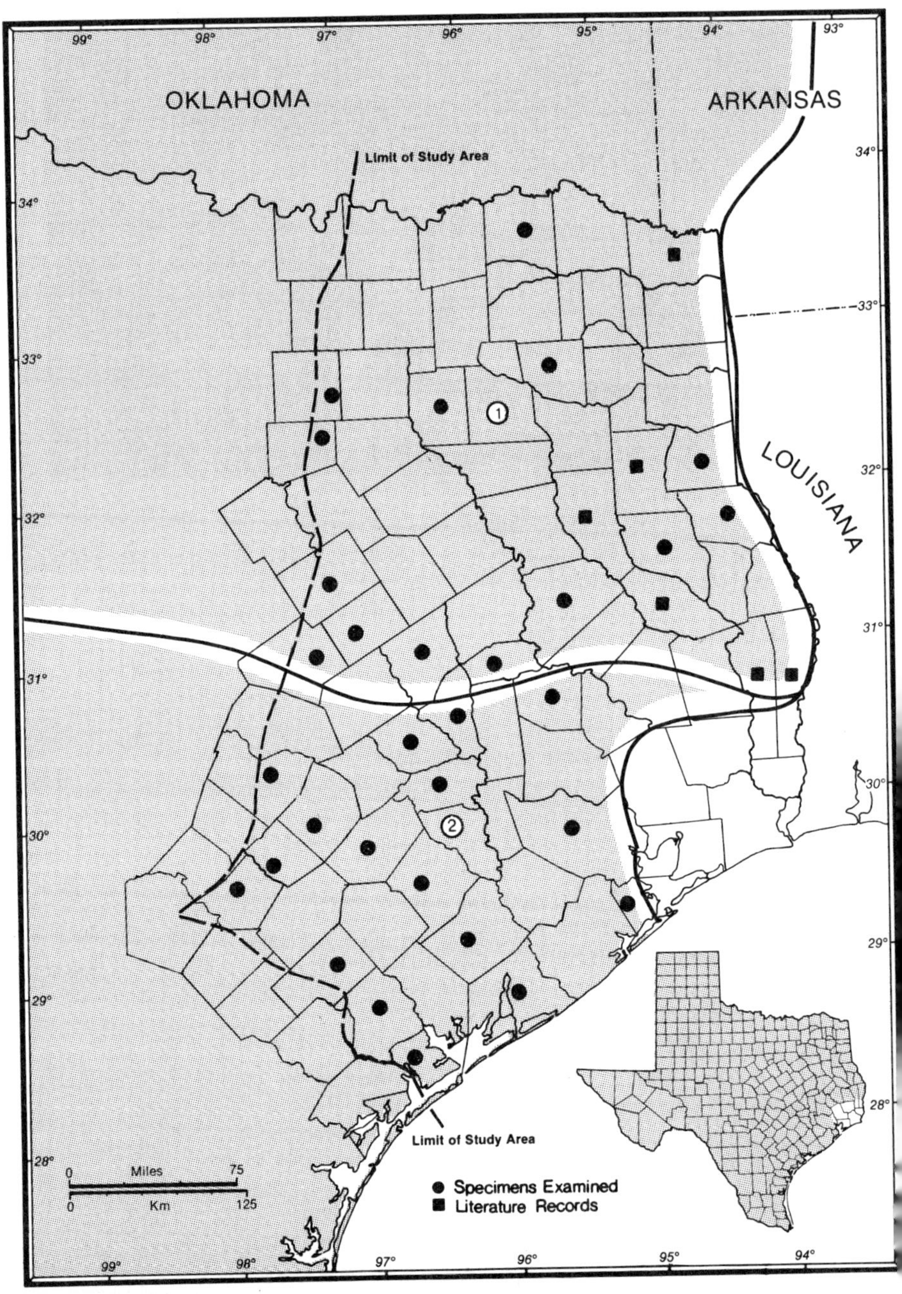

MAP 23. Distribution of the black-tailed jack rabbit, *Lepus californicus*. 1. *L. c. melanotis*. 2. *L. c. merriami*. The literature records are from Packard (1963).

Jack rabbits eat only vegetation. In spring and summer they prefer herbaceous plants and grasses, but they will also feed on various cultivated crops such as alfalfa, clover, and soybeans. In fall and winter, they eat assorted dry grasses and herbs, buds, twigs, bark, prickly pear, forage crops, and fruits. It has been estimated that 128 rabbits may eat as much as one cow.

Nothing is known of the reproductive biology of jack rabbits in eastern Texas. The following information is based on studies by Lechleitner (1959) of their breeding cycle in California. The primary season extends from January through August, but sporadic breeding may occur at all times of the year. The factors affecting the onset and maintenance of breeding are related to the annual cycle of rainfall and the subsequent greenness of the vegetation. The average number of embryos per female is one in January, four in April, and one in August. The gestation period ranges from forty-one to forty-seven days with a mean of forty-three days. Young females are capable of breeding at around eight months of age, but most do not do so until they are two years old. From these data it is apparent that jack rabbits have a much lower reproductive potential than cottontails or swamp rabbits. However, they appear to have a greater longevity. Lechleitner estimated that approximately 25 percent of the population he studied was over one year old. Individuals are known to live as long as eight years in the wild.

The young are born in a nest lined with fur especially built for them by the female. They weigh between 57 and 170 g at birth and are between 14 and 20 cm in total length. They are born well furred with their eyes open and are capable of taking a few steps. Young are independent of the female at one month, but they do not reach adult size until seven or eight months after birth.

Young and adult jack rabbits are favorite food items of several avian and mammalian predators, including hawks, owls, coyotes, foxes, badgers, and weasels. Snakes may also take a few young rabbits, but coyotes are probably their greatest enemy.

References. Lechleitner, 1959; McCarley, 1959d; Packard, 1963; Taylor and Lay, 1944.

Order Rodentia

The order Rodentia contains over 40 percent of all species of mammals. They are a remarkably successful group with a virtually cosmopolitan distribution. They have adapted to most habitats of the world's land areas and include terrestrial, fossorial, saltatorial, arboreal, gliding, and semiaquatic forms.

Rodents are remarkably uniform in structural characters. The upper and lower jaw have a single pair of continually growing incisors. Because only the anterior surfaces are covered with enamel, the incisors assume a characteristic beveled tip as a result of wear. The canines and anterior premolars are lacking, leaving a space (called a diastema) between the incisors and the cheek teeth.

Rodents are of considerable importance to man. On the negative side, those commensal with man damage grains stored in unprotected granaries. Others become pests by feeding extensively on agricultural crops, debarking trees in orchards or forests, and establishing burrows in areas where man does not want them (such as lawns and dikes). Some carry parasites that transmit diseases to which man is susceptible. On the positive side, rodents eat many noxious insects. A few such as the muskrat, beaver, and nutria are valuable fur animals, and squirrels provide us with an important hunting resource.

There are thirty-four species, representing seven families, of rodents in eastern Texas, making this the largest group of mammals in the area. Seven species are of peripheral or problematic occurrence, and these are treated in Chapter 5.

1   Tail paddle-shaped, broad, scaly, and naked . . . .
. . . . Family Castoridae (beaver, *Castor canadensis*)
Tail not so modified   2
2   External fur-lined cheek pouches   3
No external fur-lined cheek pouches   8
3   Front feet much larger than hind feet; ear short and inconspicuous; tail about one-third length of head and body . . . .
. . . . Family Geomyidae (pocket gophers)   4
Front feet much smaller than hind feet; ear conspicuous; tail
about as long as head and body . . . .
. . . . Family Heteromyidae (pocket mice)   6
4   Dorsal exposure of jugal longer than width of rostrum ventral
to infraorbital foramina; hind feet usually more than 30 mm;
karyotype with a diploid number of 72; X-chromosome acrocentric . . . . Plains pocket gopher, *Geomys bursarius*
Dorsal exposure of jugal shorter than width of rostrum ventral
to infraorbital foramina; hind feet usually less than 30 mm; karyotype with a diploid number of 70 or 74; X-chromosome
biarmed   5
5   Karyotype with a diploid number of 74 and a fundamental
number of 70; all autosomes acrocentric . . . .
. . . . Louisiana pocket gopher, *Geomys breviceps*
Karyotype with a diploid number of 70 and a fundamental
number of 72, 73, or 74; at least one pair of biarmed autosomes present . Attwater's pocket gopher, *Geomys attwateri*
6   Total length (of adults) more than 200 mm; hind feet more than
twice as long as front feet; auditory bullae greatly enlarged
. . . . Padre Island kangaroo rat, *Dipodomys compactus*
Total length (of adult) less than 200 mm; hind feet less than
twice as long as front feet; auditory bullae not greatly enlarged
. . . .   7

7   Pelage soft and silky; size small, with total length less than 150 mm . . . . Silky pocket mouse, *Perognathus flavus*
Pelage harsh, often bristly, never silky; size large, with total length more than 150 mm . . . .
. . . . Hispid pocket mouse, *Perognathus hispidus*

8   Size large, total length of adult more than 750 mm; mammary glands (nipples) located along each side of back; infraorbital canal larger than foramen magnum . . . .
. . . . Family Capromyidae (nutria, *Myocastor coypus*)
Size smaller, total length of adult less than 750 mm; mammary glands located on belly; infraorbital canal smaller than foramen magnum 9

9   Lower jaw with four cheek teeth on each side . . . .
. . . . Family Sciuridae 10
Lower jaw with three cheek teeth on each side 17

10   Lateral furred membrane on side of body connecting front and hind legs . . . . . . Southern flying squirrel, *Glaucomys volans*
No lateral furred membrane connecting front and hind legs . . 11

11   Upper parts striped or distinctly spotted or both; total length less than 350 mm 12
Upper parts not striped or distinctly spotted; total length of adults more than 350 mm 13

12   Upper parts with six continuous whitish stripes alternating with seven rows of whitish spots . . . .
. . . . Thirteen-lined ground squirrel, *Spermophilus tridecemlineatus*
Upper parts without alternating stripes and spots, having instead ten or more distinct rows of spots . . . .
. . . . Mexican ground squirrel, *Spermophilus mexicanus*

13   Tail less than one-third total length 14
Tail more than one-half total length 15

14   Incisor teeth white; maxillary tooth rows approximately parallel instead of convergent posteriorly . . . .
. . . . Woodchuck, *Marmota monax*
Incisor teeth yellow; maxillary tooth rows strongly convergent posteriorly . Black-tailed prairie dog, *Cynomys ludovicianus*

15   Belly reddish, orangish, or whitish; upper parts grayish and unspotted; zygomatic arches nearly parallel 16
Belly grayish; back mottled grayish with faint light spots; zygomatic arches convergent anteriorly . . . .
. . . . Rock squirrel, *Spermophilus variegatus*

16   Belly reddish, orangish, or buffy; tail bordered with fulvous-tipped hairs; hind foot usually greater than 65 mm . . . .
. . . . Fox squirrel, *Sciurus niger*
Belly whitish; tail bordered with white-tipped hairs; hind foot usually less than 65 mm . Gray squirrel, *Sciurus carolinensis*

17   Cusps of upper molars in two longitudinal rows; hairs on tail

conspicuous; tail either rounded or flattened laterally . . . . Family Cricetidae (New World rats and mice)   18
Cusps of lower molars in three longitudinal rows; hair on tail inconspicuous; tail rounded . . . . Family Muridae (Old World rats and mice)   33

18   Tail scaly; laterally flattened . . . Muskrat, *Ondatra zibethicus*
Tail not scaly, or if so, not laterally flattened   19

19   Mouse-sized; ears hidden in fur; tail short, less than 32 mm in length   20
Mouse- or rat-sized; ears conspicuous or only partially hidden in fur; tail greater than 32 mm in length   21

20   Pelage auburn in color; long guard hairs absent; females with four mammae . . . . Woodland vole, *Microtus pinetorum*
Pelage grayish to dark brown in color; long guard hairs present; females with six mammae . . . . Prairie vole, *Microtus ochrogaster*

21   Upper incisors with deep groove on anterior exposed face . . .   22
Upper incisors with smooth, ungrooved face   24

22   Tail much longer than head and body; color of upper parts usually rich golden brown . . . . Fulvous harvest mouse, *Reithrodontomys fulvescens*
Tail shorter than head and body; color of upper parts not a rich golden brown   23

23   Pelage rich brown in color . . . . Eastern harvest mouse, *Reithrodontomys humulis*
Pelage pale grayish in color, sometimes washed with fulvous . . . . Plains harvest mouse, *Reithrodontomys montanus*

24   Total length less than 200 mm in adults   25
Total length greater than 200 mm in adults   30

25   Pelage ochraceous in color . . . . Golden mouse, *Ochrotomys nuttalli*
Pelage not ochraceous in color   26

26   Total length less than 100 mm; tail length less than 35 mm; color blackish . . . . Pygmy mouse, *Baiomys taylori*
Total length more than 100 mm; tail length more than 35 mm; color not blackish   27

27   Tail much longer than head and body . . . . Encinal mouse, *Peromyscus pectoralis*
Tail as long as or much shorter than head and body   28

28   Tail sharply bicolored . . . . Deer mouse, *Peromyscus maniculatus*
Tail not sharply bicolored   29

29   Hind foot greater than 23 mm . . . . Cotton mouse, *Peromyscus gossypinus*
Hind foot less than 23 mm . . . . White-footed mouse, *Peromyscus leucopus*

30   Tail usually well-haired, annulations nearly or completely con-

cealed by hair; crown of molar teeth with enamel in triangular
folds (prisms) 31
Tail sparsely haired, annulations not concealed by hair, giving
scaly appearance; crowns of molar teeth with two rows of tu-
bercles or with traverse lophs 32

31   Upper parts brownish; interorbital constriction usually greater
than 6.8 mm; sphenopalatine vacuities relatively small
. . . . Eastern woodrat, *Neotoma floridana*
Upper parts gray, interorbital constriction usually less than
6.8 mm; sphenopalatine vacuities relatively large . . . .
. . . . Southern Plains woodrat, *Neotoma micropus*

32   Dorsal surface of hind foot white or light gray in color; cheek
teeth with two rows of cusps . . . .
. . . . Marsh rice rat, *Oryzomys palustris*
Dorsal surface of hind foot gray-brown in color; cheek teeth
with S-shaped transverse ridges of enamel (lophs) . . . .
. . . . Cotton rat, *Sigmodon hispidus*

33   Total length less than 250 mm; length of skull less than 20 mm
. . . . House mouse, *Mus musculus*
Total length more than 250 mm; length of skull more than 20
mm 34

34   Tail as long as or longer than head and body; temporal ridges
on each side of the parietals bowed outward . . . .
. . . . Roof rat, *Rattus rattus*
Tail shorter than head and body; temporal ridges on each side
of the parietals more or less parallel and not bowed outward
. . . . Norway rat, *Rattus norvegicus*

Family Sciuridae (Squirrels)

Members of the squirrel family in eastern Texas can be divided into
three groups: ground squirrels, tree squirrels, and flying squirrels. All
species have four toes on the front foot and five on the rear, and all have
hairy, somewhat bushy tails. With the exception of the flying squirrel,
which is nocturnal, these sciurids are diurnal in habits. One species,
the thirteen-lined ground squirrel, hibernates. Members of this family
are capable of vocalization, such as high-pitched whistling, barking, or
chattering.

Thirteen-lined Ground Squirrel
Spermophilus tridecemlineatus (Mitchill)

Name. The first part of the scientific name, *Spermophilus*, is derived from the Greek words *sperma*, meaning "seed," and *phileo*, meaning "loving," in allusion to the animal's principal food. The last part,
tridecemlineatus, is from the Latin words *tridecem*, meaning "thirteen,"
and *lineatus*, meaning "lined."

Thirteen-lined ground squirrel, *Spermophilus tridecemlineatus*.

Identification. This is a short-eared, short-tailed, thick-set little ground squirrel that is distinctive in possessing thirteen alternating dark and light stripes extending lengthwise from head to rump on the back and sides of the animal. The dark stripes contain a series of squarish, buffy spots; the light stripes are occasionally broken into spots. The underparts are white or soiled whitish. Average external measurements are total length, 257 mm; tail, 89 mm; hind foot, 36 mm; ear, 8 mm. The dental formula is I 1/1, C 0/0, Pm 2/1, M 3/3 $\times$ 2 = 22.

Subspecies. Spermophilus tridecemlineatus texensis is the only subspecies in eastern Texas and was named by Merriam (*Proc. Biol. Soc. Washington*, 12:71, March 24, 1898) with type locality at Gainesville, Cooke County, Texas.

Distribution and habitat. These ground squirrels, which are common on the Texas Panhandle, reach the eastern limits of their range in eastern Texas, where they occur principally in the grassland habitats of the blackland prairie region (Map 24). Golf courses, cemeteries, and parks apparently provide them with optimum ecological requirements. They have expanded their range eastward in recent times primarily as a result of the clearing of extensive areas of timber in the uplands of the oak-hickory belt. This trend has created favorable habitat for them in sandy soils of pastures, along fence rows, and on mowed borders of highways. They have been recorded as far east as Delta and Lamar counties in the north and as far east as Fort Bend, Colorado, and Washington counties in the southern part of eastern Texas. Ground squirrels are completely absent from the forested habitats of the pineywoods and Big Thicket, and they are uncommon in the coastal prairie.

Life history. McCarley (1966) conducted a remarkable study of a marked population of these ground squirrels on a golf course near Sher-

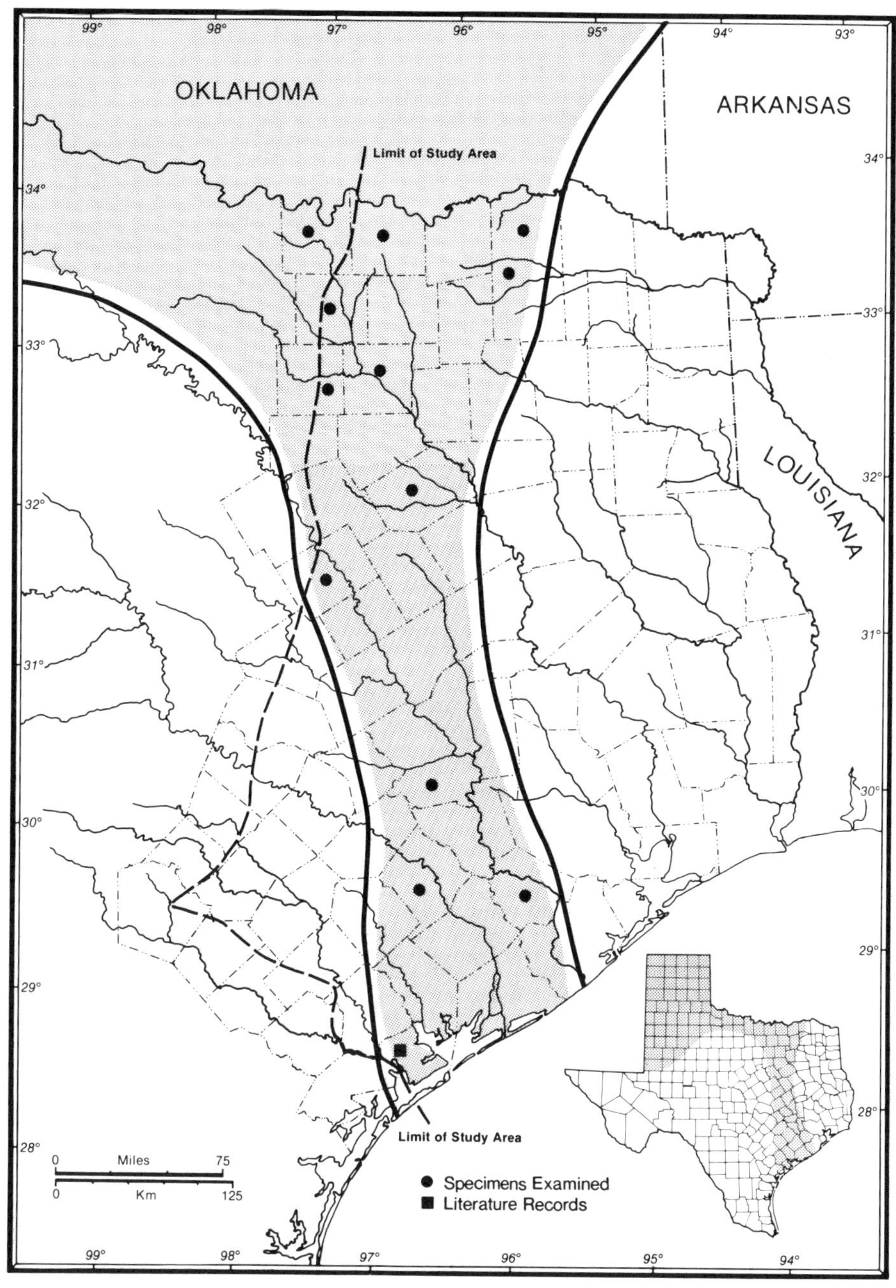

MAP 24. Distribution of the thirteen-lined ground squirrel, *Spermophilus tridecemlineatus texensis*. The literature record is from W. B. Davis (1974).

man in Grayson County. His life history account is undoubtedly typical for this species throughout eastern Texas and most of the following information is taken from his study.

The species occurs in colonies that exist as disjunct populations wherever herbaceous vegetation is at a suitable level. Population size, which on the golf course near Sherman averaged 131 individuals per year, reaches a maximum each year during the latter part of April after all squirrels emerge from hibernation (emergence from hibernation occurs between March 12 and April 5). Populations decline in July when animals begin entering hibernation, a process which continues until all adults are inactive in September. An annual hibernation cycle such as this allows the animals to avoid extremely high or extremely low temperatures and shortages of food.

These ground squirrels are strictly diurnal in their daily activities. Home ranges average 4.7 ha for males and 1.4 ha for females. Males remain close to their nest burrows after emerging from hibernation, then expand their home ranges to maximum size during the breeding season, and again restrict their movements in late June prior to entering hibernation. Females also show restricted movements after emergence, followed by home range expansion during pregnancy and lactation when litters are within the nest burrows. Once litters emerge, females again restrict their home ranges until after the young are weaned.

Ground squirrel activity during the day is dependent on local weather conditions. Generally, temperatures lower than 10° C inhibit squirrel activity. Surface winds in excess of 9 kmph also inhibit activity in the sense that squirrels remain close to the burrow entrances and do not forage far afield. Rain causes a cessation of all above-ground activity.

Thirteen-lined ground squirrels use three types of burrows: hiding, nesting, and hibernating. Hiding burrows lack nests, typically have a single entrance, and are shallow (about 0.15 m in maximum depth). Nesting burrows, which probably also serve as hibernating burrows, have grass nests, usually two or more entrances, and extend below the average frost depth of the soil. Each squirrel ordinarily has its own home burrow system containing several hiding and nesting burrows that it uses preferentially, but when alarmed it may use any convenient burrow within its area of activity. There can be a change of function of burrow systems from one year to another such that a hiding burrow one year might be used as a nest burrow the next year or vice versa. Simultaneous use of the same burrow by different squirrels is rare.

About 50 percent of the diet of these squirrels is composed of animal matter. Insects, particularly grasshoppers and lepidopterous larvae, are preferred foods, with grass and seeds comprising the remainder of the diet. These squirrels have been observed preying on other vertebrates, including young cottontail rabbits (*Sylvilagus floridanus*), six-lined race runners (*Cnemidophorus sexlineatus*), and loggerhead shrikes (*Lanius ludovicianus*).

Mating takes place above ground in April, May, and June. Litters are born in May, June, and July following a gestation period of twenty-seven or twenty-eight days. The breeding season lasts for about 9.5 weeks. Some females older than one year produce two litters per reproductive season. The size of litters emerging from the nest burrow ranges from an average of 4.9 for young females to 7.0 for old females. Young thirteen-lined ground squirrels are reddish-pink at birth. By day eight, the mottled, striped pattern characteristic of adults is evident. The eyes begin to open from twenty-one to thirty-one days after birth and are completely open after twenty-three to thirty-three days. Young are born toothless with small "gum buds." The teeth begin to erupt after seventeen days. Young ground squirrels remain in the nest burrow for a period of thirty-two days before emergence above ground.

Predation is apparently slight on these squirrels and is mainly confined to juveniles. The only known predators are bull snakes (*Pituophis melanoleucus*) and roadrunners (*Geococcyx californicus*).

Because this species tends to occur in colonies, there is a considerable amount of social interplay among individuals. Several behavior patterns center around auditory communication between and among females and juveniles. After a litter emerges from the burrow the female begins giving an alarm call or trill. This call is given by females whenever an intruder (predator or human) comes within 30 to 60 m of the litter or the nest burrow. The young react to the call by diving for the burrow entrance. A second call of adaptive value to survival of the young is the "peep" call, which is given by the young when they wander away from the nest burrow and become lost. This call, which is repeated every five to ten seconds, elicits a quick and positive response by the mother and enables her to locate the lost juvenile and lead it to the burrow entrance.

References. Bridgewater, 1966; Bridgewater and Penny, 1966; Desha, 1966; McCarley, 1966; Streubel and Fitzgerald, 1978.

Gray Squirrel
Sciurus carolinensis Gmelin

Name. Sciurus is Latin for squirrel and is derived from the Greek words *skia*, meaning "shadow," and *oura*, meaning "tail," which in literal translation means a creature that sits in the shadow of its tail. The name *carolinensis* is a latinized word meaning "of Carolina," in reference to the place where the species was first collected and described.

Identification. The gray squirrel is named for its color, which is usually gray on the back and sides, with whitish underparts. It is readily distinguished from the fox squirrel (*S. niger*) by its smaller size, by its basically grayish overall coloration, and by the fact that its underparts are almost always grayish or white, never reddish or orangish, as in the fox squirrel. Occasionally, gray squirrels may be black or white. True albinos, with pink eyes, have been found near Lufkin, Angelina County, and Caddo Lake, Harrison County (Goodrum, 1961). The average weight of a gray squirrel is about half that of a large eastern Texas fox squirrel. Aver-

Gray squirrel, *Sciurus carolinensis*.

age external measurements are total length, 448 mm; tail, 209 mm; hind foot, 60 mm; ear, 24 mm. The dental formula is I 1/1, C 0/0, Pm 2/1, M 3/3 × 2 = 22.

Subspecies. *Sciurus carolinensis carolinensis* is the only subspecies in eastern Texas and was named by Gmelin (*Systema Naturae*, 1:148, 1788) from "Carolina."

Distribution and habitat. The range of the Texas gray squirrel lies almost entirely in the eastern part of the state (Map 25). Hays County appears to be the western limit of the southern part of its range, and Fannin County is its western limit in the northern part of the state. Formerly, this squirrel occurred farther west, particularly in the northern portion of its range, but intensive land use has caused shrinkage of the range, resulting in a loss of good gray squirrel habitat and thus in fewer squirrels.

The largest concentrations of gray squirrels are found in the big hardwood timber in the bottomlands of the rivers and large creeks, in flatlands centering around Brazoria and Matagorda counties, and in the mixed hardwood pine areas of the Big Thicket. In particular, the sandy ridges (hammocks) that frequently occur in these bottomlands are favored. Hammocks, which generally include a mixture of several species of oak, sweetgum, blackgum, elm, red mulberry, magnolia, holly, ironwood, yaupon, beech, huckleberry, pecan, hickory, and some pine, supply squirrels with needed foods for all seasons and ample den cavities for escape cover, winter shelter, and brood-rearing. Tree stands must be dense enough to permit squirrels to travel from tree to tree, through the crowns, without descending to the ground. The presence of Spanish moss and several types of vines provide excellent escape cover. Gray squirrels are seldom found in the pine woods and upland forest.

Life history. Gray squirrels construct two types of nests. One is a

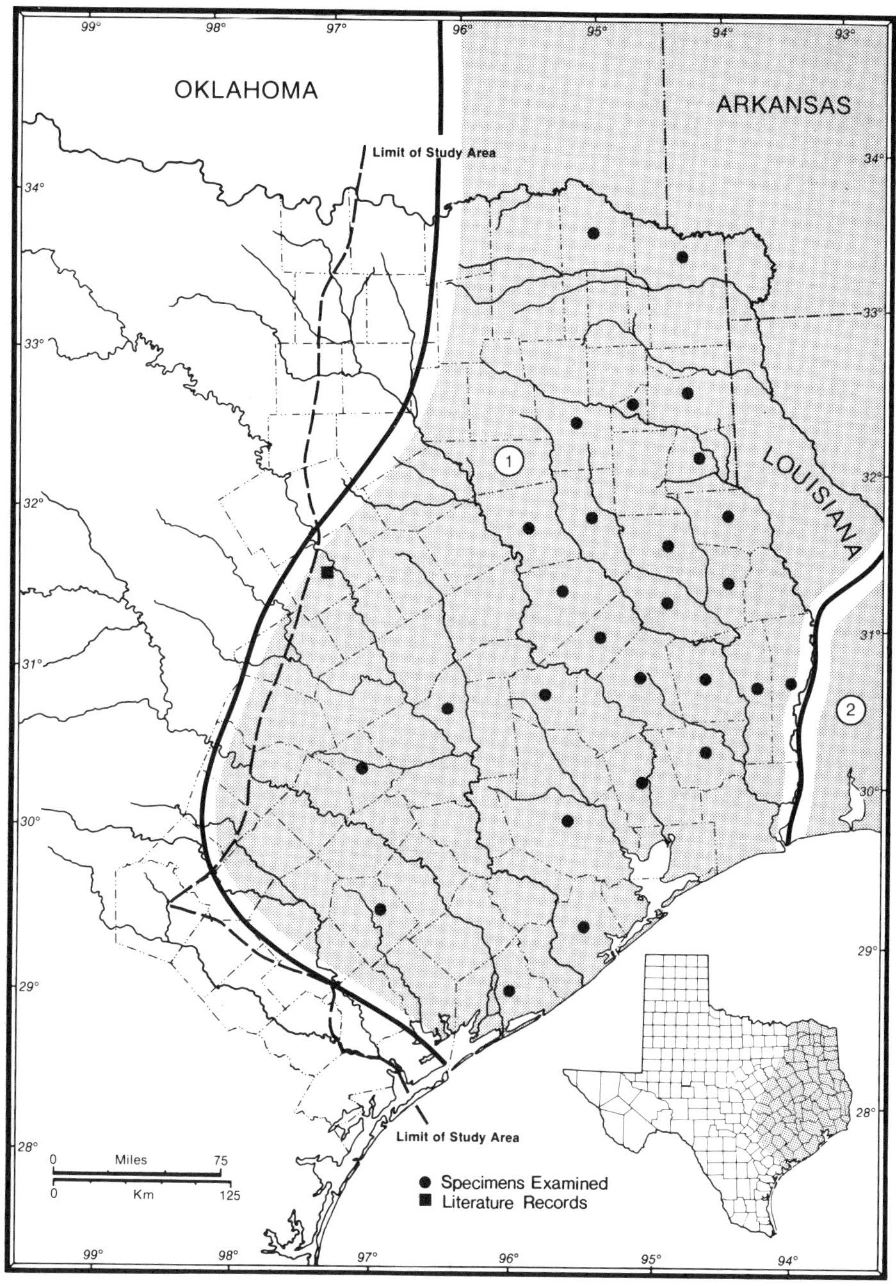

MAP 25. Distribution of the gray squirrel, *Sciurus carolinensis*. 1. *S . c . carolinensis*. 2. *S . c . fuliginosus*. The literature record is from W. B. Davis (1974).

den in a tree cavity, which is essential for winter shelter, escape cover, and rearing young. The other is an outside nest built of leaves and twigs that is used as temporary shelter and occasionally for winter shelter and brood-rearing. In late summer female squirrels often move their suckling brood from tree dens to leaf nests to take advantage of cooler quarters provided by the nest, but overall outside nests are definitely inferior to den cavities. Litters born and reared in nesting cavities have a significantly higher survival rate—up to 2.5 times as high—than those in leaf nests.

Nest-building activity begins in late June and early July. Adult as well as young squirrels participate, with each individual working on its own nest. Generally, there are about as many squirrels as there are nests in an area prior to the hunting season. Adult females with young will not tolerate other squirrels in the same den or den tree.

The home range of gray squirrels varies from 0.6 to 3.2 ha depending upon the age and sex of the animals and the population density. Populations develop social hierarchies or "pecking orders." The most dominant animals exhibit the largest home range; the least dominant, the smallest. Males characteristically range over larger areas than females. Adult squirrels, especially females, are sedentary and become firmly established in a selected home range.

Densities of gray squirrels fluctuate with changing yields of heavy-seeded mast, particularly acorns. The average gray squirrel density in eastern Texas is about 5 squirrels per ha for a protected river bottom area, 2 squirrels per ha in open river bottom habitat, and 1.2 squirrels per ha in open upland creek situations. If protected from hunting, squirrel populations will reach their maximum density in a given region within four to five years. When a good crop of young is produced, the entire population may contain 65 percent or more young squirrels.

Gray squirrels have two well-defined periods of activity, very early morning and late afternoon. They are comparatively inactive through the middle of the day except during the rutting period. Warm summer rains generally cause an increase in activity, whereas low temperature and wind cause a reduction in activity.

Gray squirrels exhibit two breeding seasons in eastern Texas, one in winter and one in summer. The winter peak is reached about the latter part of January and the summer peak in August. More young are usually produced during the winter breeding period than the summer. The young, which number from 1 to 4 (average 2.7) per litter, are born following a gestation period of about forty-two to forty-four days. The young are born helpless, without hair or teeth, and with their eyes and ears closed. Weaning is gradual and completed at about twelve weeks of age. Young gray squirrels remain in family groups for about 4.5 months.

Gray squirrels eat a variety of wild foods, but they have a special liking for acorns and nuts of various kinds. During the early spring they supplement this mast diet with buds, tender stems, and flowers of a wide variety of trees and shrubs. Animal matter in the form of larvae of many insects is also taken. Mushrooms are relished, and they are fed upon avidly during periods of wet weather when they sprout from the damp soil and rotten logs. Squirrels supplement their diet with different kinds of bone, including the antlers of deer, which supply them with needed calcium.

The extent of damage done to squirrels through natural predation is unknown. Hawks, snakes, gray fox, mink, ringtail cats, and bobcats are known to prey upon them, but seemingly predation is less important in limiting their numbers than are habitat changes and overhunting.

Gray squirrels have a nervous temperament, a characteristic that makes them a superior game animal because it betrays them to hunters. They are the most popular small game animal in eastern Texas, surpassing rabbits, quail, and doves. Gray squirrels can sustain heavy hunting pressure and long seasons, thereby providing much outdoor recreation. Consequently, sound management of their habitat is becoming an increasingly important responsibility. Their future will depend upon the acreage remaining in hardwood forests, the length of timber rotations, the species composition of hardwood stands, and the abundance of mast supplies and dens.

References. Baker, 1944a; Goodrum, 1937, 1938, 1940, 1961; Norton, 1981.

Fox Squirrel
Sciurus niger Linnaeus

Name. The derivation of the generic name *Sciurus* is the same as for the gray squirrel. The Latin name *niger* means "black" and refers to the black color phase, which is common in many individuals of this species from the southeastern United States.

Identification. The fox squirrel may be distinguished from the gray squirrel on the basis of pelage characteristics, as described in the account of the latter. In addition, these two squirrels differ in the coloration of the bones of the skull and other skeletal parts, which are reddish in the fox squirrel as opposed to creamy white in the gray squirrel. The skulls of the two species are similar, but there is a major difference in the dental formula, which in the fox squirrel is I 1/1, C 0/0, Pm 1/1, M 3/3 × 2 = 20. *S. niger* has only four cheek teeth on each side of the upper jaw, whereas in *S. carolinensis* a small, peglike upper premolar is added. Average external measurements are total length, 520 mm; tail, 237 mm; hind foot, 70 mm; ear, 27 mm.

Subspecies. In eastern Texas there is only one subspecies, *Sciurus niger ludovicianus.* It was named by Custis (*Philadelphia Med. Phys. Journ.*, 2:47, 1806) with type locality at Red River, Louisiana (restricted to Natchitoches Parish by Lowery and Davis, 1942).

Distribution and habitat. Fox squirrels occur wherever adequate timbered habitats exist in eastern Texas (Map 26), although they seemingly occur in greater densities in the mature oak-hickory woodlands of

Fox squirrel, *Sciurus niger*.

the central portion of the region. They are adapted to a wide variety of forest, woodlot, and parklike habitat, but they prefer upland creeks lined with hardwoods and well-drained bottomlands. Pristine upland conditions, such as a longleaf pine forest with almost no other tree species present and almost nonexistent understory, support relatively small numbers of these squirrels. In some places fox squirrels appear to be increasing in abundance at the expense of gray squirrels. The drainage of low bottomlands seems to result in a reduction of the number of gray squirrels and an increase in the number of fox squirrels. A population of about 1.4 squirrels per ha is about the average for good, unimproved fox squirrel habitat.

Life history. Den requirements of fox squirrels are similar to those of grays. They readily use cavities in trees, such as those excavated by woodpeckers, for escape cover, winter shelter, and rearing young. Leaf nests, constructed of layers of leaves, are also built in the tops of trees, but they are inferior to den cavities mainly due to the greater hazard of storm and predator damage. Known predators include owls, hawks, foxes, bobcats, and weasels.

Fox squirrels generally spend the entire year in the vicinity of a specific nest tree. Their home range is normally from 2 to 4 ha, depending upon the sex and age of the animal. Females have a smaller range than males. Fox squirrels do not defend their territories against others except within the immediate vicinity of dens or nests. They are apparently less gregarious than gray squirrels. They normally live alone, although pairs may stay together for a while at the beginning of the mating season. A litter may also stay with the female during the winter.

Fox squirrels have three main periods of daily activity. They come out just before sunrise and remain active for several hours. Then they either return to their nests or remain idle on a limb or other spot. They

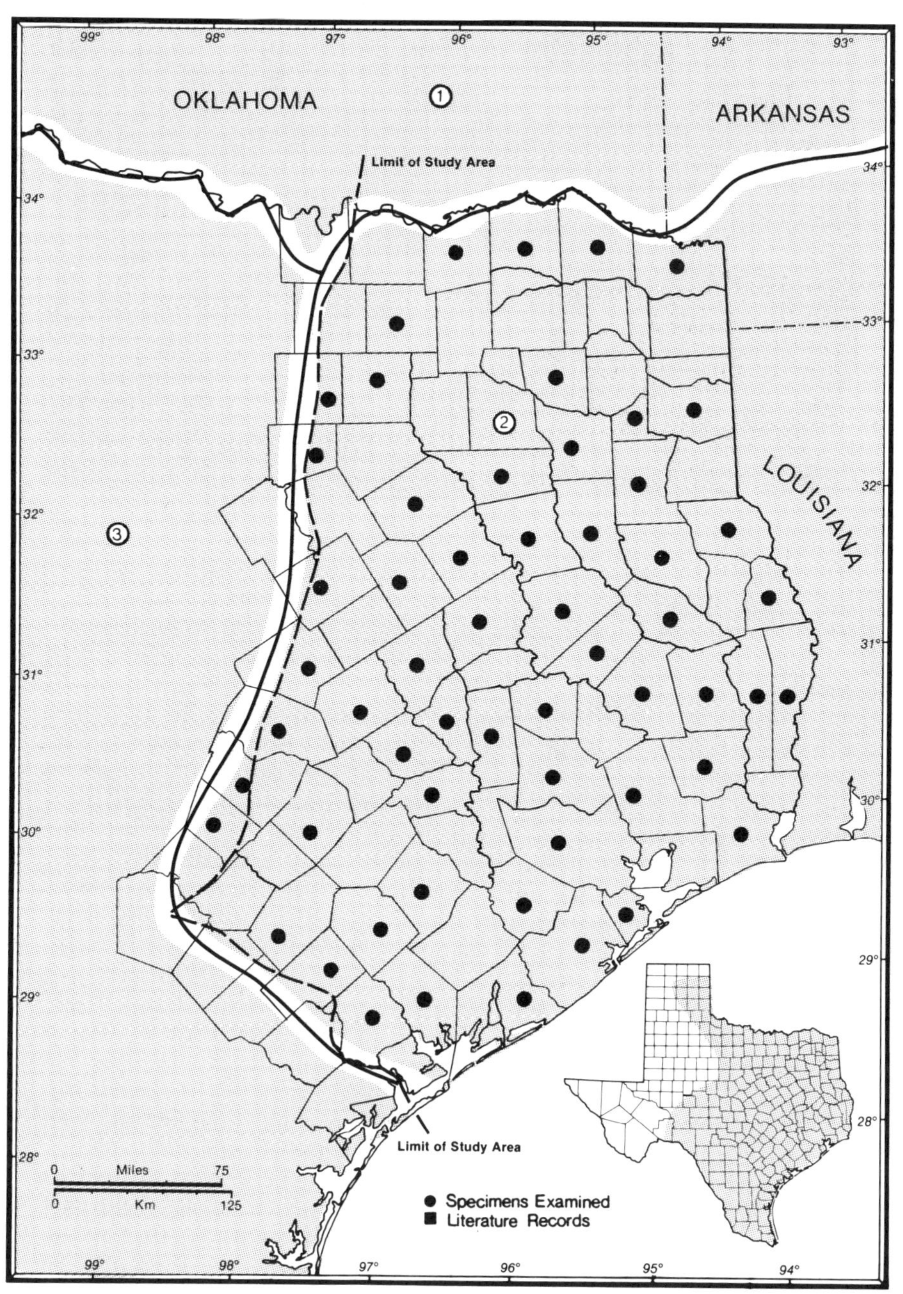

MAP 26. Distribution of the fox squirrel, *Sciurus niger*. 1. *S . n . rufiventer*. 2. *S . n . ludovicianus*. 3. *S . n . limitis*.

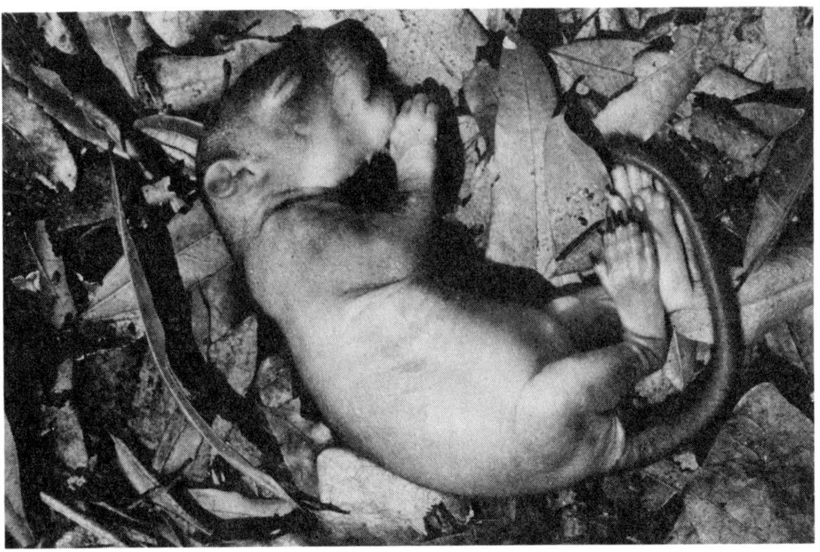

Newborn fox squirrel, *Sciurus niger*.

move about some during the middle of the day and then relax for several hours. In late afternoon they emerge and forage again before retiring to their nests. Thus, compared to gray squirrels, fox squirrels come out later, retire earlier, and are frequently more active in the middle of the day.

Two distinct breeding seasons are evident in eastern Texas, a light summer breeding season beginning in June and a heavier, winter breeding season beginning in December. Older females usually breed twice a year, whereas yearlings breed but once. The first young are dropped in July and February, respectively, following a gestation period of forty-five days. After the winter mating season all squirrels, especially the gravid females, seclude themselves to a marked degree. Fox squirrels give birth to their young approximately two weeks earlier than grays. Litter size is from two to four (average three) young per individual female.

Newborn young weigh about 14 g and are blind, nearly naked, and helpless. They develop rather slowly. Their eyes open in the fifth week, and they begin to climb about the nest tree after seven to eight weeks and to venture onto the ground at about ten weeks. By three months of age they lead a more or less independent existence; they reach sexual maturity from ten to eleven months. Fox squirrels may live from four to seven years in the wild.

Food habits of fox squirrels are essentially similar to grays except that they prefer a more varied diet of hard mast (especially acorns), soft fruits, pine seeds, and agricultural grains. They are also known to feed on the larvae, pupae, and adults of insects. Buds of many trees and fruits of osage orange are important in their winter diet. It has been estimated that a fox squirrel consumes approximately 680 g of mast (dry weight) per week, or approximately 18 kg in the period from September to March.

Apparently there is little or no social competition between individual fox and gray squirrels where they live in the same range, but they probably do compete for food and den location sites. There are never many fox or gray squirrels in areas where feral hogs (*Sus scrofa*) cause a loss of mast on the ground.

Fox squirrels are less popular with hunters than grays, but gainful hunting is sustained by smaller populations than would be huntable for grays. Because of their larger size, their preference for open parklike forests, and their daytime feeding habits (compared to the early-morning, late-evening preferences of grays), fox squirrels are easier to hunt than grays.

References. Baker, 1944a; W. B. Davis, 1974; Goodrum, 1937, 1938; Lowery, 1974; C. W. Schwartz and Schwartz, 1981.

Southern Flying Squirrel
Glaucomys volans (Linnaeus)

Name. The generic name *Glaucomys* is derived from the Greek words *glaukos*, meaning "gray," and *mys*, for "mouse." The specific name *volans* is the Latin word for "flying."

Identification. The flying squirrel may be distinguished from other squirrels in eastern Texas by its smaller size, flattened and bushy tail, and by the presence of a loose fold of fully haired skin (called a patagium), which connects the forelimbs and hindlimbs from wrist to ankle. The dorsal coloration is uniform drab or pinkish cinnamon compared to the creamy white of the venter. Average external measurements are total length, 219 mm; tail, 97 mm; hind foot, 29 mm; ear, 19 mm. The dental formula is I 1/1, C 0/0, Pm 2/1, M 3/3 × 2 = 22.

Subspecies. In eastern Texas there is only one subspecies, *Glaucomys volans texensis*, named by Howell (*Proc. Biol. Soc. Washington*, 28:110, May 27, 1915) with type locality 7 mi. NE Sour Lake, Hardin County, Texas.

Distribution and habitat. Flying squirrels occur throughout the timbered regions of eastern Texas, except for that portion south of the Colorado River, and in wooded areas along the streams of the coastal prairie (Map 27). They are found in both upland and lowland wooded habitats wherever deciduous forests occur, and their abundance seems to be controlled more by the quantity of hollow trees and limbs for nesting purposes and available food than by the tree species involved.

Life history. Flying squirrels prefer tree cavities as nesting sites, with woodpecker holes comprising an important percentage of the cavities. Entrances are usually 40 to 50 mm in diameter, which is large enough to admit flying squirrels but small enough to exclude larger tree squirrels, with which they may compete for nest sites. The inside of the nest is usually lined with finely divided inner bark, leaves, Spanish moss, or palmetto fibers. Nests average 4.5 to 6 m above the ground, but may be situated anywhere from 1.5 to 12 m or more in height. Two general

Southern flying squirrel, *Glaucomys volans*.

categories of nests are constructed: primary nests, those used more or less continuously, and secondary nests or retreats. There are usually several secondary nests, which serve variously as sheltering stations for feeding and defecating, as well as refuges should the primary nest be disturbed or destroyed.

Although exact estimates of population density are lacking for eastern Texas, estimates of two to five squirrels per ha in prime habitat are probably reasonable for this region. Home range size has not been exactly defined, but it probably varies from about 1.6 to 2 ha. Flying squirrels are strictly nocturnal, being more or less continuously active throughout the night during warm months (July to October); however, as ambient temperatures decrease in the winter (November to February), their activities become restricted, with peaks following sunset, sometimes around midnight, and before dawn. These squirrels are known for their homing abilities, and there is a record of one squirrel released 1.6 km from its home being found in the original location six days later.

Flying squirrels generally travel by gliding in a descending curve from one tree to another. These glides are normally 6 to 9 m in length, although more extensive glides have been reported. The remarkable agility in gliding is demonstrated by an ability to make 90 and 180 degree turns in avoiding obstacles. Flying squirrels also run along tree limbs and leap horizontally from limb to limb. Occasionally they run and hop on the ground while foraging for mast, but they seldom travel long distances.

Flying squirrels are among the most carnivorous of sciurid rodents, and they will consume not only insects and other invertebrates but also birds, eggs, nestlings, and carrion when available. Plant matter in their diet consists of a wide variety of items like nuts, seeds, berries, fruits, blossoms, buds, mushrooms, lichens, and bark.

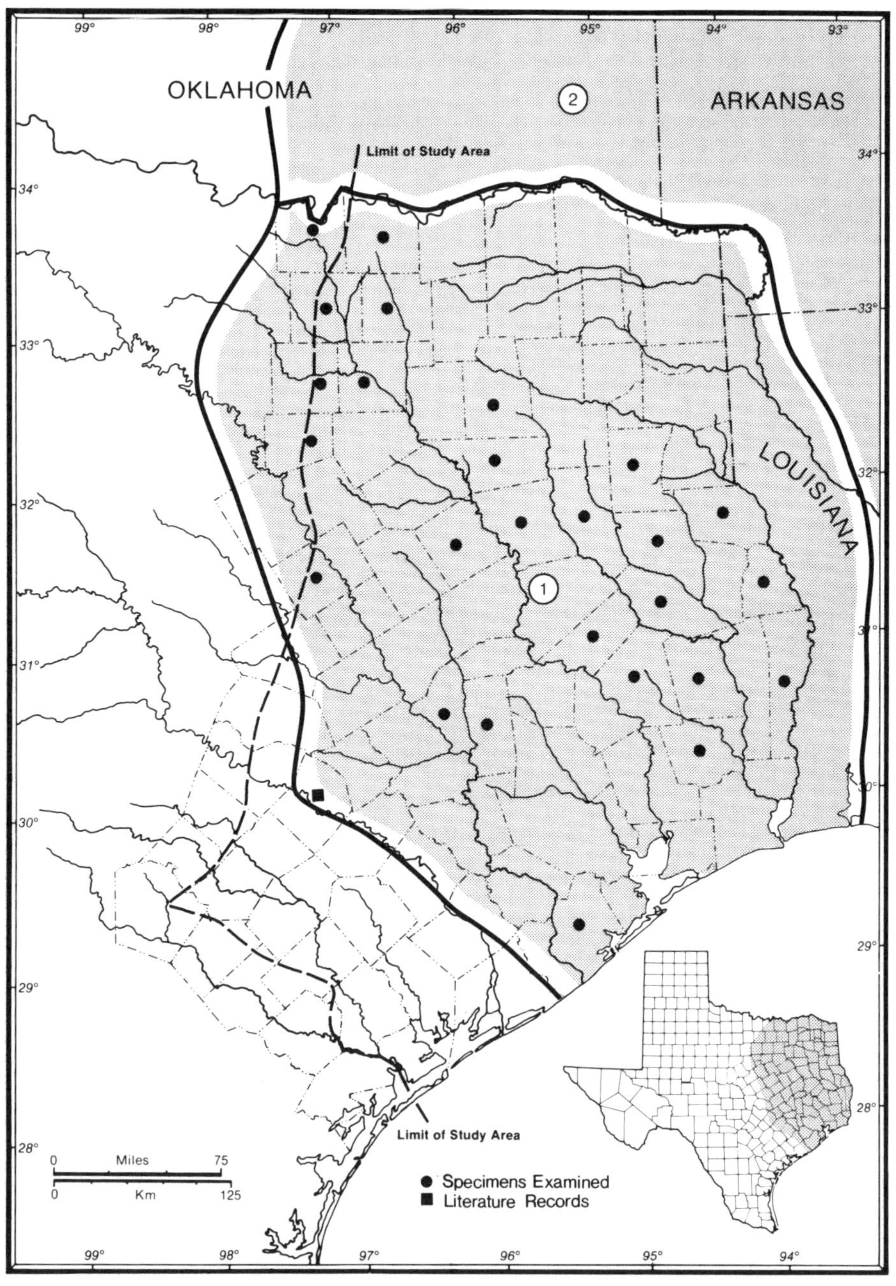

MAP 27. Distribution of the southern flying squirrel, *Glaucomys volans*. 1. *G. v. texensis*. 2. *G. v. saturatus*. The literature record is from W. B. Davis (1974).

The nocturnal habits of flying squirrels do not make them immune to predation. Owls and domestic cats are known mammalian predators, as is the rat snake (*Elaphe obsoleta*). Other potential predators include bobcats, raccoons, weasels, and hawks. Flying squirrels are relatively long-lived, living up to five years in the wild and up to ten years in captivity.

Flying squirrels have two breeding peaks, one in spring (April and May) and another in autumn (September and October). However, it is not known whether each female participates in both breeding periods. The male leaves the female before the young are born and may return later or select a different mate. The young, which generally number three to four and weigh only 3 to 5 g at birth, are born blind, deaf, practically hairless, and pink in color following a gestation period of forty days. The patagium is clearly evident as a transparent fold of skin in newborns. Young are weaned at approximately six to eight weeks and remain with the female if a second litter is not produced. Females take good care of the young and will actively defend them as well as retrieve them if they are, for some reason, removed from the nest.

Flying squirrels utter a variety of distinct calls, some of which seem to vary with age. The production of high-frequency sounds emitted during gliding may serve as a form of echolocation. Flying squirrels are much more gregarious than tree squirrels, and it is not surprising to sometimes find six to seven individuals roosting together in a single nest cavity. They form winter aggregations, presumably for purposes of thermoregulation, but it is not known whether these represent family groupings or whether extrafamilial individuals are included.

References. Dolan and Carter, 1977; Lowery, 1974; Muul, 1968; C. W. Schwartz and Schwartz, 1981; Sollberger, 1943.

Family Geomyidae (Pocket Gophers)

Pocket gophers are medium-sized burrowing rodents that spend most of their life below ground. They are characterized by a cylindrical, thick-set body that is heaviest anteriorly, especially about the head, and is covered by extremely short hair. There is no indication of a neck, and the thickest portion of the body is at the back part of the head, from which the body tapers gradually to the tail, widening a little across the thighs. Spacious, fur-lined cheek pouches, used for transporting food, lie wholly outside the mouth. The eyes are tiny and beadlike, and the ears are very rudimentary, represented only by a thickened ridge of skin. The tail is short, thickened, and naked, except for a few hairs at the base, and appears to possess some degree of tactile sensibility. Long, curved claws are present on the front feet for digging; the claws on the hind feet are much smaller. The dental formula is I 1/1, C 0/0, Pm 1/1, M 3/3 $\times$ 2 = 20.

Pocket gophers in eastern Texas have historically been grouped in one wide-ranging, morphologically variable species, *Geomys bursarius*, which is distributed over most of the Great Plains and south central

United States. However, recent studies by specialists trained in cytological and biochemical taxonomy have revealed that in actuality there are three species of pocket gophers in eastern Texas (designated *G. bursarius*, *G. breviceps*, and *G. attwateri*). These are considered cryptic species, meaning that they cannot be differentiated on the basis of observed morphological characteristics although they are genetically distinct (as determined by chromosomal and biochemical characteristics).

The ranges of the three cryptic species have been documented, and areas where their geographic ranges contact, called contact zones, are known (Honeycutt and Schmidly, 1979; Tucker and Schmidly, 1981). The Brazos River, which is one of the major waterways in Texas, is a significant factor affecting their distribution. This is strongly implied in the allopatry of *G. attwateri* and *G. breviceps* along the western and eastern banks of the Brazos River, respectively. Other rivers in eastern Texas do not appear to effectively limit the distribution of gophers. For example, the Navasota and San Jacinto rivers, located east of the Brazos River, have *G. breviceps* distributed along both the east and west banks; likewise, *G. attwateri* occupies both banks of the Colorado River in the south central part of eastern Texas.

Louisiana Pocket Gopher
Geomys breviceps Baird

Name. The word *Geomys* is from the Greek word roots *Geo*, meaning "earth," and *mys*, meaning "mouse." The specific name, *breviceps*, originates from the Latin roots *brevis*, meaning "short," and *ceps*, which is New Latin for "head."

Identification. Morphologically, this species may be distinguished from *G. bursarius* as described in the account of the latter, but there are no morphological features that will unambiguously distinguish it from *G. attwateri*. Pocket gophers of this species average smaller in cranial and external measurements than either *G. attwateri* or *G. breviceps* (Table 5).

The most important feature for identifying *breviceps* is its karyotype, which has a diploid number of 74 and a fundamental number of 72. The autosomal complement of the karyotype contains thirty-six pairs of size-graded acrocentric chromosomes (Fig. 2A). The X-chromosome is a medium-sized submetacentric, and the Y-chromosome is a small acrocentric. *G. breviceps* has four more chromosomes than *G. attwateri* and does not have any biarmed elements in the autosomal complement. Compared to *G. bursarius*, *breviceps* has two more chromosomes, and the X-chromosome is medium-sized and submetacentric instead of large and acrocentric.

Subspecies. Specimens from eastern Texas are referable to the subspecies *G. breviceps sagittalis*, which was named by Merriam (*North Amer. Fauna*, 8:134, January 31, 1895) with type locality at Clear Creek,

TABLE 5. Average and Extreme Measurements (in mm) of Three Species of *Geomys* in Eastern Texas.

Character	G. breviceps (74)	G. attwateri (71)	G. bursarius (65)
Total length	208	216.5	236
	(192–222)	(192–235)	(229–240)
Tail length	61.4	62.5	65
	(54–67)	(51–70)	(54–75)
Hind foot length	25.6	26.5	31
	(23–28)	(25–28)	(29.5–32)
Greatest skull length	38.2	40.6	42.3
	(34.0–41.7)	(37.1–44.6)	(39.3–46.0)
Length of rostrum	15.7	16.9	17.1
	(13.7–17.7)	(15.1–19.1)	(14.7–20.6)
Palatal length	21.8	23.8	24.0
	(19.3–24.0)	(21.0–27.8)	(22.2–26.6)
Mastoidal breadth	21.4	23.1	24.1
	(18.9–23.9)	(21.2–25.4)	(22.2–26.7)
Palatofrontal depth	13.6	14.3	14.7
	(12.4–15.0)	(12.8–15.7)	(13.8–16.3)

Galveston Bay, Harris County, Texas. Honeycutt and Schmidly (1979) recently completed a morphological review and assessment of subspecies of this species in Texas.

Distribution and habitat. This species has a continuous distribution east of the Brazos River in all vegetational regions where soils are suitable (Map 28). At a few places in Falls, Milam, and Burleson counties, major and minor land transfers (in the form of oxbow lakes) have occurred as a result of shifts in the course of the river, and these have effectively isolated portions of the once contiguous distribution of *breviceps* and placed them on the western side of the river.

Soils having a low content of clay and a high content of sand are preferred by these gophers. Typically, they require at least 10 cm of sandy topsoil in which to burrow and are absent from areas in which the topsoil is shallower. Moisture also seems to be correlated with the local presence or absence of pocket gophers, who seem to avoid soils with a high moisture content.

Life history. The pocket gopher is fossorial and spends virtually all its existence within a system of tunnels that are normally sealed to the surface with earthen plugs and marked on the surface of the ground by numerous mounds of excavated earth. The animal moves to or upon the surface only to deposit excavated soil, to disperse, to surface-feed on occasion, and perhaps to seek the opposite sex. The subterranean gallery system of the pocket gopher is essentially a "sealed system" containing a simplified environment. In addition to providing protection from predators,

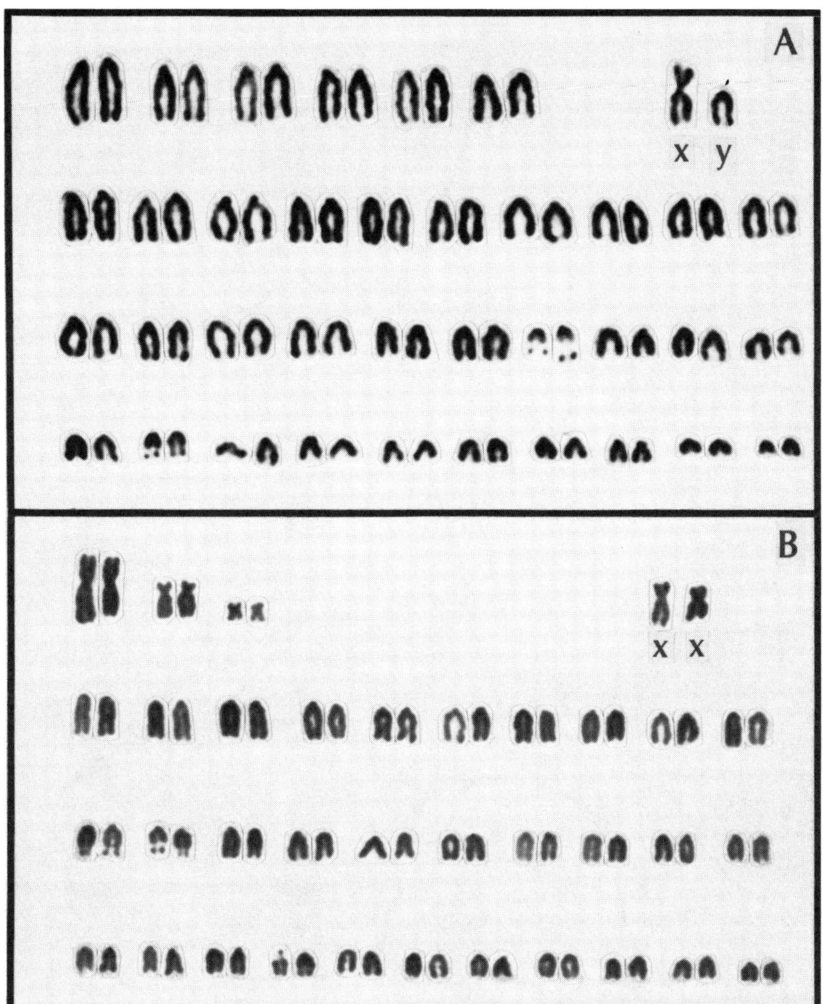

FIGURE 2. Karyotype of (A) *Geomys breviceps* (2N = 74; FN = 72) and (B) *Geomys attwateri* — race F (2N = 70, FN = 74). Karyotypes provided by Robert C. Dowler.

the burrow protects the gopher from climatic extremes, especially of temperature.

Surface mounds vary in size, but they may reach a diameter of 1.8 m and become heaped up 30 to 60 cm above ground. The soil-moving capabilities of gophers are staggering. For example, in Brazos County Buechner (1942) estimated that the amount of soil brought to the surface of the ground by gophers ranged from 0.51 m³ of dirt per ha on ungrazed land to 10.21 m³ per ha on overgrazed land.

Burrows occur, on the average, between 13 and 68 cm below the

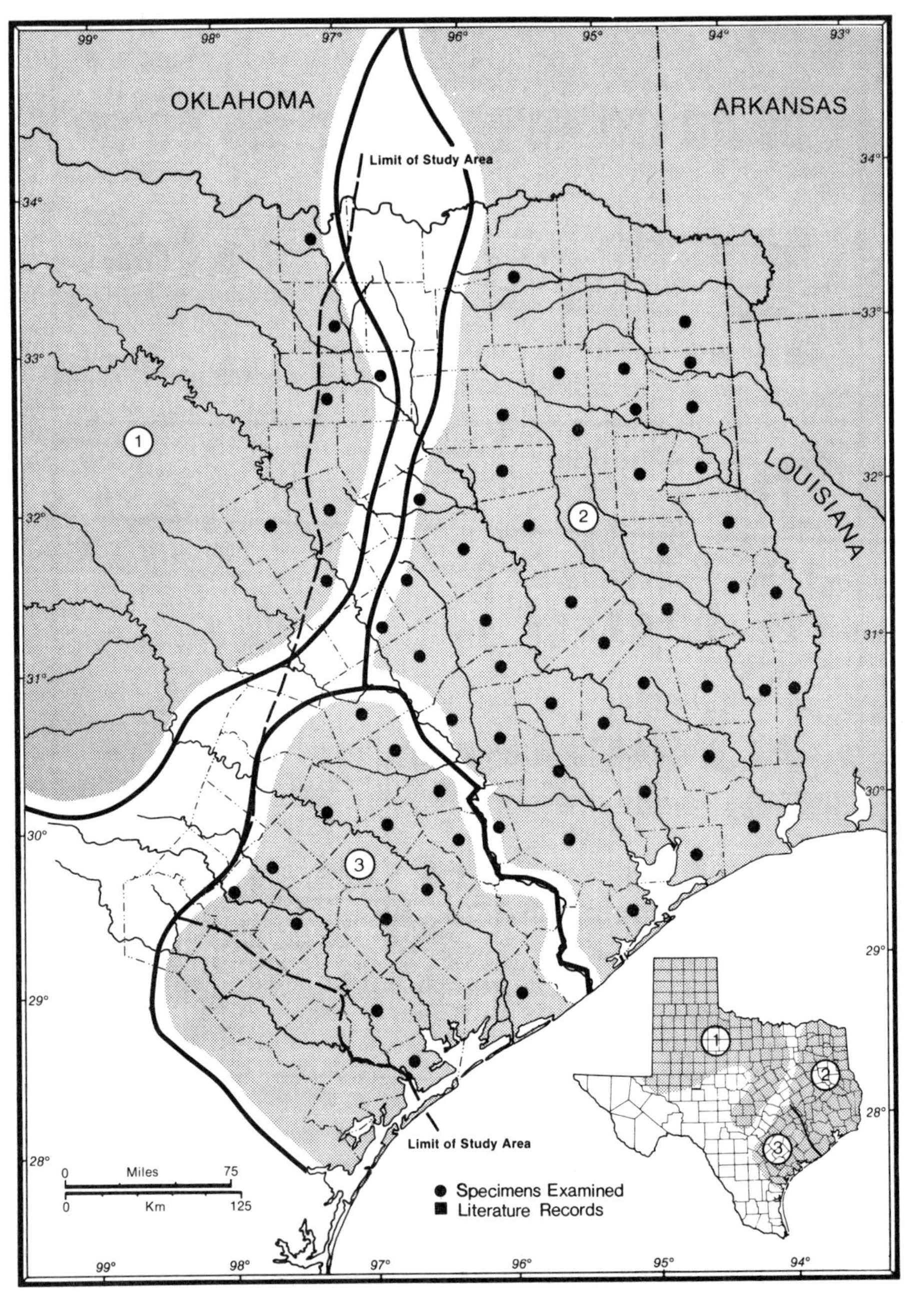

MAP 28. Distribution of three species of *Geomys*. 1. *Geomys bursarius*. 2. *G. breviceps*. 3. *G. attwateri*.

ground and have a mean diameter of between 6 and 9 cm. Burrow systems, which may extend as much as 55 to 180 m in length, are complex and dynamic and may contain several types of chambers, including latrines, food-storage places, and nest chambers. Feeding tunnels generally comprise more than 90 percent of the total system. Gophers are constantly digging new tunnels and plugging old ones as they search for better feeding areas and abandon poorer situations. Aside from the acquisition of food, gophers also continually "patrol" the burrow so that they can discover and repair any damage to the tunnel within a short time. The nest chamber, usually one per system, is deeper than the tunnel system and may extend as much as 64 cm below the surface. Gophers are normally very clean animals. The burrow has special tunnels for the disposal of feces, and these are plugged when filled.

Pocket gophers are solitary animals throughout most of their lives. Males appear to be intolerant of other males, and females are apparently intolerant of other females. The home ranges of males and females overlap to a considerable degree. This pattern indicates the ready access of the sexes to each other and suggests that there may be connections between burrow systems of males and females. During the breeding season territoriality breaks down, and it is not uncommon to find an adult male and female in the same burrow. Frequently the young are also present in the burrow to form a family group.

Gophers are active day and night, but they dig most energetically at night, early in the morning, or late in the evening. Soil temperature is a major factor in determining daily activity patterns. During the hot and dry months of late summer, gophers are more active in the forenoon than at night, and they move their activity to lower levels, where moisture and temperature are presumably more favorable. The upper tunnels are filled with dirt from the deeper diggings, and very few surface mounds are formed.

The vision of gophers is not acute. Animals released a few centimeters in front of their open burrow almost invariably begin to dig a new hole, apparently completely unaware of the nearby opening. The tactile sense, which is much more useful in the dark burrow than is vision, is highly developed, and the tail is especially useful as a tactile organ.

The density of gophers seems to vary with the type of soil and land use. In the Lufkin fine sandy loam near College Station in Brazos County densities vary between 1.66 and 3.34 gophers per ha, whereas in the Norfolk sandy soils of Van Zandt County densities of 16.8 gophers per ha have been recorded. Land that has been left idle for several years generally has fewer pocket gophers than land that has been moderately overgrazed.

Pocket gophers are strictly herbivorous. Their food is determined by the plants present near the nest and includes a great variety of succulent roots, underground stems, succulent stems of grasses and legumes, leaves of livestock forage plants, as well as small fruits (such as strawberries) and grains. Most plant food is encountered and ingested while the pocket gopher digs. However, some "grazing" of food along extant burrow walls probably occurs, and this may be an important means of obtaining food during the summer. The fur-lined cheek pouches are used to transport food and nesting material and are never used to carry dirt. Large pieces of food, which are not eaten immediately, are pushed into the pouch as far as possible. The excess is then bitten off and pushed into the pouch. The process of emptying the cheek pouches is accomplished by quick forward pushes of the forefeet along the pouches.

Cellulose-digesting bacteria have been found in the caecum and large intestine of *G. breviceps* (Boley and Kennerly, 1969). Microbial digestion, which is well known in ruminant herbivores, may be important to pocket gophers in winter, when food is least available, by allowing them to practice subterranean "grazing" on stored rhizomes. *G. breviceps* also reingests fecal pellets. This practice apparently increases the efficiency of food utilization and may lessen to some degree the amount of energy required for digging for food.

Pocket gophers are polygamous, and breeding is restricted to immediate neighbors. The annual reproductive cycle in eastern Texas shows seven consecutive months of breeding activity, from February until August. A peak in production occurs in June and July, and a lesser peak in April; no young are produced from September through January. Presumably copulation takes place in the burrow, but this fact is not known. There is evidence that females may produce two broods in rapid succession. The number of young per litter ranges from 1 to 6, with an average of about 2.6. The gestation period is four to five weeks; the lactation period is approximately five to six weeks, after which the young leave the parental burrow. Puberty is reached in females approximately three months after birth, and they may possibly reach sexual maturity and produce a litter before the end of the breeding season.

At birth, young gophers are no more than 5 cm long and have loose, wrinkled, pink skin. The eyes, ears, and cheek pouches are closed, and no teeth are visible. The incisors come through the gums a few days after birth. Weaning takes place at six weeks of age, and dispersal occurs shortly afterward, with the young digging a new tunnel system near their old home.

As long as they remain in their burrows, gophers are relatively safe from predators other than those which are specialized for digging, such as the badger and long-tailed weasel. However, when a gopher leaves the burrow it is then at the mercy of predators, and most of the predation losses probably occur on the surface. Known predators, other than those mentioned above, include coyotes, skunks, domestic cats, hawks and owls, and several kinds of burrowing snakes. As a result of the protection offered by the burrow, gophers are relatively more long-lived than most insectivores, rodents, and lagomorphs, living an average of one to two years in the wild.

References. Boley and Kennerly, 1969; Buechner, 1942; W. B. Davis, 1940b; W. B. Davis et al., 1938; English, 1932; Honeycutt and Schmidly, 1979; Kennerly, 1958; Tucker and Schmidly, 1981; Wilks, 1963; Wood, 1949, 1955a.

Attwater's Pocket Gopher
Geomys attwateri Merriam

Name. The derivation of the name *Geomys* is identical to that given in the previous account. The specific name *attwateri* is latinized from the last name of the collector, H. P. Attwater of San Antonio, who obtained nearly all of the first specimens of this species.

Identification. Morphologically, this species may be distinguished from *G. bursarius* as described in the account of the latter, but there are no morphological features that will unambiguously distinguish it from *G. breviceps*. It is intermediate in size between these two species, as reflected in external and cranial measurements (Table 5).

Its most distinguishing feature is the karyotype, which has a diploid number of 70 and a fundamental number of either 72 or 74. Two distinct karyotypes (designated chromosomal race F and chromosomal race G by Honeycutt and Schmidly, 1979) have been reported in this species. Race F (FN = 74) has an autosomal complement of thirty-one pairs of large to small acrocentrics, one pair of large submetacentrics, one pair of medium submetacentrics, and a pair of small metacentrics; the X-chromosome is a medium submetacentric, and the Y-chromosome is a small acrocentric (Fig. 2B). Race G (FN = 72) has an autosomal complement of thirty-two pairs of large to small acrocentrics, one pair of large submetacentrics, and a pair of small metacentrics; the X-chromosome is a medium submetacentric, the Y-chromosome, a small acrocentric. Individuals of both of these races as well as those with intermediate karyotypes (2N = 73) have been reported from the same population at several places within the range of this species in eastern Texas (Honeycutt and Schmidly, 1979; Tucker and Schmidly, 1981).

Subspecies. This species is monotypic, and subspecies are not recognized.

Distribution and habitat. This species ranges from the Brazos River in central eastern Texas south to southern Texas near the San Antonio River and along the coast as far south as Rockport in Aransas County (Map 28). Within its range, it occurs wherever soil conditions are suitable, with densities as high as 13.6 gophers per ha being recorded in some areas.

Life history. Most life history traits of this species are similar to those of *G. breviceps*, although the breeding season of the two species seems to differ. *G. attwateri* breeds from October through June with peaks in December-January and April-May. Apparently little if any breeding occurs during the summer months of July, August, and September. Females produce an average of 2.5 young per litter and at least two litters per year.

Remarks. Tucker and Schmidly (1981) found a zone of contact between *G. attwateri* and *G. breviceps* just west of the Brazos River in Burleson County. The contact zone is limited in size (1.2 by 0.7 km) and is located in an area of disturbed habitat comprised of rangeland, cultivated land, and the right-of-way along Farm Road 50, 24.1 km northwest of Texas A&M University. Of forty-two gophers collected in the contact

Attwater's pocket gopher, *Geomys attwateri*.

zone, 31 percent had an apparent F_1 karyotype intermediate between the two species (2N = 72, FN = 73). (F_1 individuals would result from the mating of a male and female of the two species.) However, no karyotypically detectable backcross or F_2 individuals were found except in the fetal state. (F_2 individuals would result from a mating between two F_1 hybrids; a backcross would involve the mating of an F_1 hybrid with either of the parental forms.)

The presence of pregnant F_1 hybrid females in the contact zone indicates that F_1 females are reproductively active and that fetal backcrosses or F_2 hybrids are present. The absence of any karyotypically identifiable adult F_2 hybrid individuals, however, indicates that backcrosses and F_2's may be, in some way, deficient. Postmating isolating mechanisms appear to be operating in the form of hybrid breakdown, in which F_1 hybrids are viable but produce deficient backcross or F_2 hybrid individuals that do not survive the fetal condition. Thus, it appears that *G. breviceps* and *G. attwateri* interact as species where they contact in Burleson County, which is the only known area of contact between them.

References. Kennerly, 1958; Tucker and Schmidly, 1981; Wilks, 1963.

Plains Pocket Gopher
Geomys bursarius (Shaw)

Name. *Geomys* is formed in the manner described for *G. breviceps*. The specific name *bursarius* is of Latin origin and means "pertaining to a pouch of skin."

Identification. This species is difficult to distinguish morphologically from *G. breviceps* and *G. attwateri*. The only consistent feature that I know for distinguishing *G. bursarius* from the other two species is the length of the jugal bone on the dorsal surface of the zygomatic arch compared to the width of the rostrum ventral to the infraorbital openings. In *G. bursarius*, the dorsal exposure of the jugal is longer than the width of the rostrum, whereas in *G. breviceps* and *G. attwateri* the dorsal exposure of the jugal is shorter than the width of the rostrum. This species averages larger in external and cranial measurements than the other two species of gophers in eastern Texas (Table 5).

The karyotype of *G. bursarius* (2N = 72, FN = 70) is similar to that of *G breviceps* except that it has two fewer acrocentric autosomes, and the X-chromosome is a small acrocentric instead of a medium-sized submetacentric. This is the only species of *Geomys* in eastern Texas that does not have a submetacentric X-chromosome.

Subspecies. In eastern Texas there is but the one subspecies, *Geomys bursarius major*, which was named by Davis (*Texas Agr. Exp. Station Bull.* 590, p. 32, October 23, 1940) with type locality 8 mi. W Clarendon, Donley County, Texas.

Distribution and habitat. Pocket gophers of this species in eastern Texas are limited in distribution to the Brazos River watershed in McLennan County and the Trinity River watershed in Tarrant and Denton counties (Map 28). It has a double-dendritic distribution, occupying the sandy, alluvial deposits along each side of the aforementioned rivers and their major tributaries. The term "double-dendritic" refers to occupancy of the alluvial soil strip along each side of a waterway that transects a region of soils unfavorable for occupancy (Kennerly, 1963). These alluvial strips tend to vary in width with size of the waterway, being narrower along upper reaches of drainage and broader along lower reaches of drainage. Densities of this species as high as six gophers per ha have been recorded in McLennan County.

Life history. The life history characteristics of this species do not appear to differ appreciably from those described for *G. breviceps*.

Remarks. *G. breviceps* and *G. bursarius* are largely allopatric, with contact zones along the Brazos River in Falls and McLennan counties in eastern Texas, and in the vicinity of Norman, Oklahoma. The hiatus between their ranges in northeastern Texas is a reflection of the absence of suitable soil types for gophers in the blackland prairies of this region. Zimmerman and Gayden (1981) and Bohlin and Zimmerman (1982) used the technique of electrophoresis to measure genetic distinctiveness between these two species in Texas and Oklahoma. These authors recorded a mean genetic distance between them on the order of magnitude reported for seven other species of *Geomys* (Penney and Zimmerman, 1976) and much lower than expected values for subspecific comparisons. Although an F_1 hybrid was reported at the Norman, Oklahoma, contact zone, no evidence of backcrossing was found at either contact zone. This evidence seems to indicate that the two forms are maintaining separate gene pools and should be recognized as distinct species (Bohlin and Zimmerman, 1982).

References. Kennerly, 1958, 1963, 1964.

Family Heteromyidae (Pocket Mice and Kangaroo Rats)

Heteromyid rodents are nocturnal, burrowing mammals with hind-limbs that are much larger than forelimbs and with external fur-lined cheek pouches that are used to carry food to storage. Members of this family are among the most characteristic rodents of arid habitats in the western United States, but they are virtually absent from forested and humid regions. Thus, of the thirteen species in this family that occur in Texas, only three (two species of pocket mice and one species of kangaroo rat) live in eastern Texas. The kangaroo rat is marginal in its occurrence and is discussed in Chapter 5.

Hispid Pocket Mouse
Perognathus hispidus Baird

Name. The name *Perognathus* came from two Greek words, *perg*, meaning "pouch," and *gnathus*, meaning "jaw." The second part of the name, *hispidus*, is Latin for "spiny or rough" and is in reference to the coarse pelage of this species.

Identification. Hispid pocket mice may be distinguished from other rodents in eastern Texas in possessing external, fur-lined cheek pouches and in having hindlimbs that are appreciably longer than the forelimbs. The ears are small and barely project beyond the fur. The tail, which is approximately as long as the head and body, is sharply bicolored, blackish above and whitish below. Coloration of the upper parts is olive buff with pure buff stripes along the sides; the underparts are white. Average external measurements are total length, 186 mm; tail, 92 mm; hind foot, 24 mm; ear, 10 mm. The dental formula is I 1/1, C 0/0, Pm 1/1, M 3/3 × 2 = 20. *P. hispidus* differs from *P. flavus*, the other pocket mouse in eastern Texas, as described in the account of the latter.

Subspecies. Perognathus hispidus hispidus is the only subspecies in eastern Texas and was named by Baird (*Rep. Expl. Surv. Railr. to Pacific*, 8:421, July 14, 1858) with type locality at Charco Escondido, Tamaulipas, Mexico.

Distribution and habitat. This mouse occurs over most of eastern Texas except for the extreme northern part along the Red River and the Big Thicket region in the southeastern part of the pine-oak forest (Map 29). It is not very common in coastal prairie habitats along the coast. *P. hispidus* is tolerant of a variety of vegetative complexes and soil types, but is probably most common in open fields in well-drained areas where sandy or other friable soils are covered with heavy stands of broomsedge and weeds in association with scattered stands of woody vegetation. In the pineywoods it has been recorded from sandy hillsides where the dominant vegetation consists of short-leaf pine and black locust.

Life history. Surprisingly little is known about the natural history of *P. hispidus* in eastern Texas or elsewhere. These pocket mice live in burrows dug into the ground to a depth of about 38 cm. Generally, two or

Hispid pocket mouse, *Perognathus hispidus.*

more entrances lead into the underground passages, but sometimes there is only one. Burrow openings are usually surrounded by dirt piles, and they are normally plugged during the day. An underground nest, composed of shredded grasses and weeds, is located somewhere in the passageway.

Wang and Hudson (1966) observed that individuals of this species maintained in the laboratory entered torpor at ambient temperatures between 0° and 23° C. However, the torpor was only a daily pattern, lasting less than twenty-four hours, and the animals could not tolerate body temperatures below 8° to 11° C. For these reasons, these authors concluded that it was inappropriate to classify this species as a true hibernator and/or estivator. Nevertheless, there is evidence that this species becomes inactive during the colder season of the year in some areas of eastern Texas. For example, during a one-year study of rodents on strip-mined lands in Freestone County, Waggoner (1975) found that hispid pocket mice were first trapped in March and that the last individuals were taken in October, with peak activity in July and August. No individuals were trapped from November through February. Physiologically, it is not known what happened to these mice during this period of inactivity.

Hispid pocket mice are rather sedentary mammals. Their mean home range has been estimated at 0.30 ha, with males having a slightly larger home range (0.34 ha) than females (0.24 ha). There is some indication, again from laboratory studies, that these mice are social and that several individuals may live together without showing aggression toward one another (Williams, 1968). Such social tendencies are unusual for pocket mice, which are generally considered antisocial.

The length of the breeding season of hispid pocket mice probably

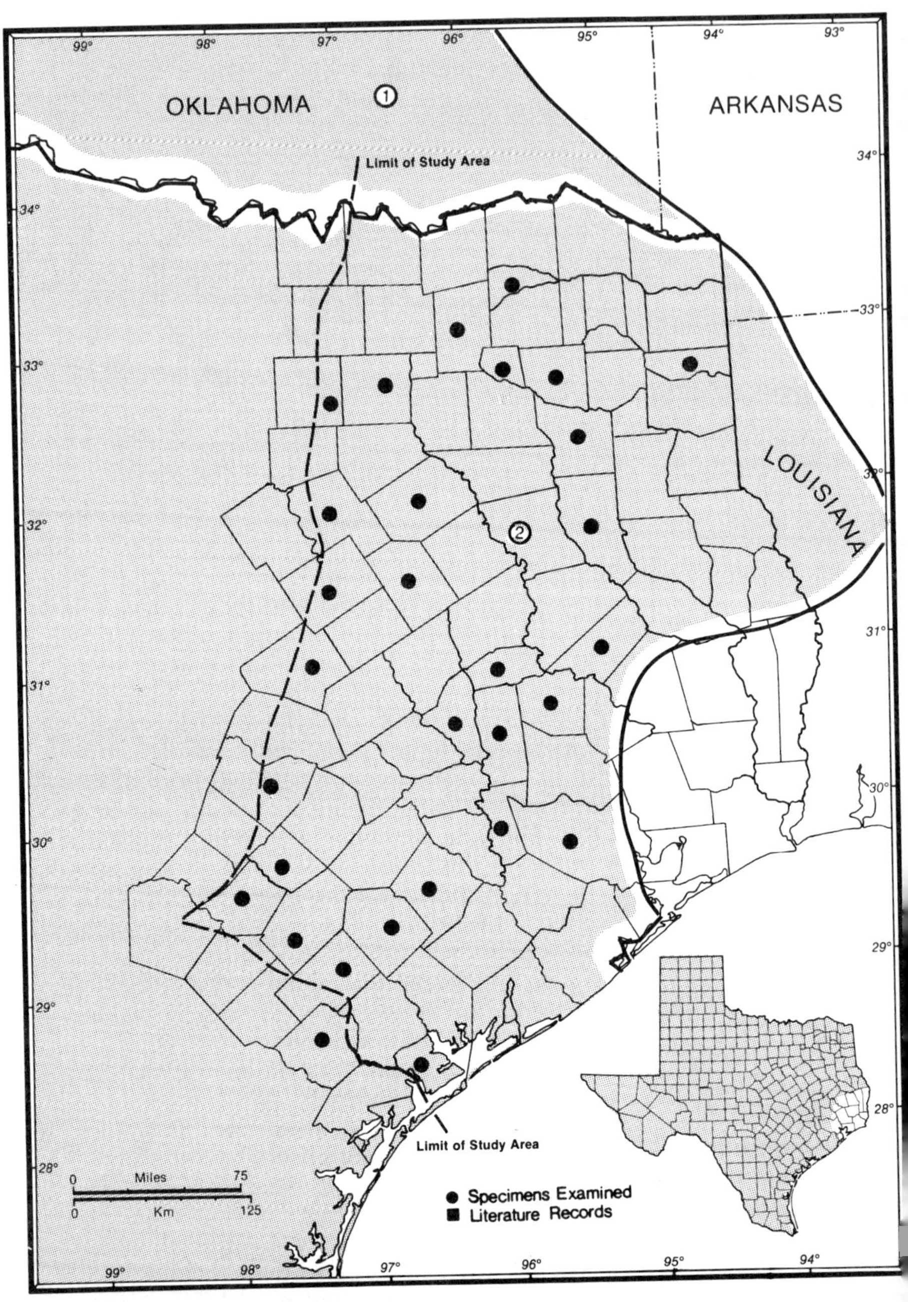

MAP 29. Distribution of the hispid pocket mouse, *Perognathus hispidus*. 1. *P. h. spilotus*. 2. *P. h. hispidus*.

varies with location. In the northern part of eastern Texas, breeding activity is confined to the months of June through August. In the southern part of the region, where winter conditions are milder, breeding may occur continuously. The number of young per litter varies from two to nine with an average of six.

These pocket mice are almost strictly vegetarians, feeding principally on the seeds of grasses and weeds. They are known to store great quantities of seeds in their burrows, which they transport from above ground in their cheek pouches.

Known predators include hawks, owls, coyotes, skunks, and snakes.

References. W. B. Davis, 1974; Glass, 1947; Lowery, 1974; McCarley, 1959d; Waggoner, 1975; Wang and Hudson, 1966; Williams, 1968.

Silky Pocket Mouse
Perognathus flavus Baird

Name. The derivation of the name *Perognathus* is identical to that given in the previous account. The name *flavus* is derived from the Latin word *flav*, which means "yellow" and is in obvious reference to the color of this small pocket mouse.

Identification. This is a small, silk-furred pocket mouse with short, rounded ears and a rather short, smooth tail. The prevailing color of the upper parts is a yellowish buff, darkest on the back, and with the hairs finely tipped with brownish, clouding the buff; the underparts are snowy white. *P. flavus* is easily distinguished from *P. hispidus* by its smaller size (total length 105 mm instead of 185 mm) and by the fact that its pelage is smooth and silky instead of rough and coarse. Average external measurements are total length, 105 mm; tail, 48 mm; hind foot, 15 mm; ear, 6 mm. The dental formula is identical to that of *P. hispidus*, the major difference in dentition being that in *hispidus* the front surface of each incisor has a longitudinal groove, whereas in *flavus* the front surface of the incisor is smooth.

Subspecies. Perognathus flavus merriami is the only subspecies in eastern Texas and was named by J. A. Allen (*Bull. Amer. Mus. Nat. Hist.*, 4:45, March 24, 1892) with type locality at Brownsville, Cameron County, Texas.

Distribution and habitat. This species, which is common in western and southern Texas, is uncommon in eastern Texas, where it has been recorded from the coastal prairie habitat of Jackson County and the blackland prairies in Travis, Johnson, and Tarrant counties (Map 30). Silky pocket mice are restricted to habitats where the soil is soft, presumably because of their limited digging ability, and where the vegetative understory is sparse and the groundcover is short. They avoid areas of tall, dense groundcover because it restricts their movement. In optimum habitat in southern Texas, population densities as high as 10.1 individuals per ha have been recorded (Chapman and Packard, 1974), but it is doubtful they are this common anywhere in eastern Texas.

Silky pocket mouse, *Perognathus flavus*.

Life history. An individual silky pocket mouse may maintain as many as five to seven burrows within its home range, including both home and refuge burrows. Pocket mice spend most of their time in home burrows, which generally have two or more entrances. An average tunnel in a home burrow descends almost vertically for 15 to 20 cm from the entrance, then lessens in grade until reaching a depth of 46 to 61 cm. Many burrows have blind side tunnels, which are used for deposition of fecal pellets. Home burrows typically possess enlarged nest chambers, which contain nests made of dried grass, seed husks, and finely broken weed twigs. Most home burrows possess separate food chambers in the form of enlarged, blind branches leading from the main tunnel. The other type of burrow, called a refuge burrow, is generally a blind tunnel used in storing food or for refuge or temporary shelter.

These mice have relatively small home ranges. Males seldom move beyond a radius of 38 m from their home burrows and females move even less (seldom farther than 29 m). Juveniles of both sexes travel farther than adults, suggesting they may disperse into marginal areas to a greater extent than do adults. There are some seasonal differences in movement patterns, with mice typically moving greater distances in the summer and fall than in winter. They become less active and are dormant at times during winter when weather conditions are extremely harsh.

The breeding season begins in early spring and continues until the late fall, extending from April to November. Some females may produce two or more litters, of three to six young each, per breeding season.

Pocket mice feed on a variety of seeds and plant parts depending upon seasonal availability. Undoubtedly, they prefer and select some

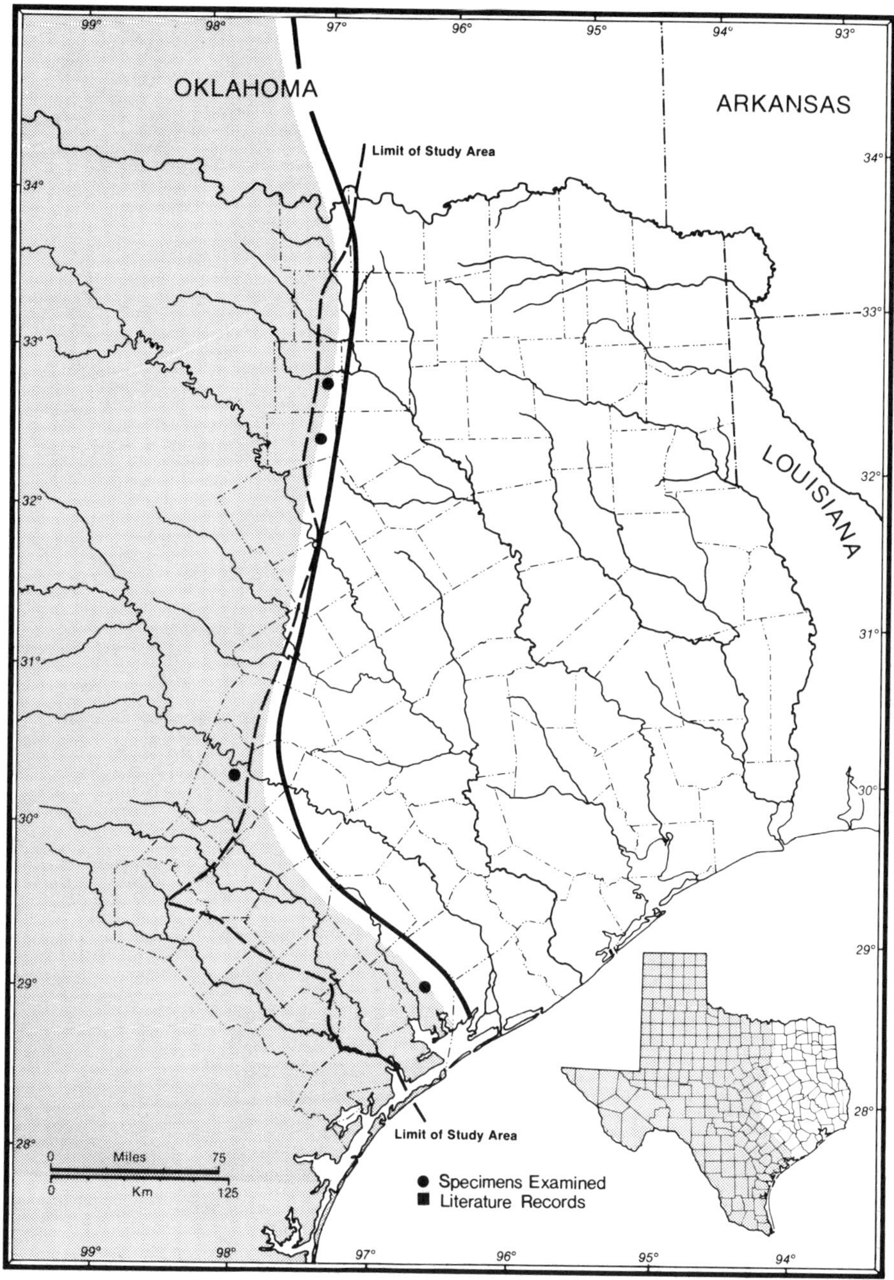

MAP 30. Distribution of the silky pocket mouse, *Perognathus flavus merriami*.

foods over others on the basis of palatability. Insects constitute a relatively minor portion of their diet.

Silky pocket mice are known to live for as long as three years in captivity on a diet of birdseed, without water or any other form of vegetation. They excrete a highly concentrated urine and prosper without surface moisture. Water is derived from the limited amount of vegetation and insect matter they eat.

Remarks. Until recently, two species of pocket mice (*P. flavus* and *P. merriami*) were recognized in Texas, with individuals from eastern Texas being assigned to *P. merriami.* Wilson (1973) studied cranial characters of both species from Texas and New Mexico and concluded that they were conspecific. W. B. Davis (1974), however, continues to treat them as distinct species. In examining specimens from the Trans-Pecos, Schmidly (1977) was unable to find any morphological features that consistently separated specimens of *flavus* and *merriami*, and he followed Wilson in regarding them as a single species. Using this arrangement, all specimens from the region of study are referable to *flavus*, which has nomenclatorial priority over *merriami.*

References. Chapman and Packard, 1974; W. B. Davis, 1974; Schmidly, 1977.

Family Castoridae (Beaver)

The beaver is the largest North American rodent. It occurs in favorable river systems from Texas to northern Canada and central Alaska. Long sought for its fur in North America, the beaver was an important reason for the early explorations of the western United States.

North American Beaver
Castor canadensis Kuhl

Name. The generic name *Castor* is from the Greek word *kastor*, which means "beaver." The second part of the scientific name, *canadensis*, is a latinized word meaning "of Canada."

Identification. The beaver is a large, robust, aquatic rodent with a broad, horizontally flattened, scaly tail and webbed hind feet. Both front and hind feet have five digits, all of which are clawed. The eyes have a nictitating membrane, the ears and nose are valvular, and the lips close behind the incisors. The upper parts are a rich reddish brown in winter pelage that becomes darker in summer; the belly is pale buff gray. Average external measurements are total length, 934 mm; tail, 303 mm; hind foot, 172 mm; ear, 29 mm. The dental formula is I 1/1, C 0/0, Pm 1/1, M 3/3 × 2 = 20. Beavers weigh about 15 kg.

Subspecies. The subspecies in eastern Texas is *Castor canadensis texensis*, which was named by V. Bailey (*N. Amer. Fauna*, 25:122, October 24, 1905) with type locality at Cummings Creek, Colorado County, Texas.

Distribution and habitat. Beavers are essentially aquatic and live in

Beaver, *Castor canadensis.*

ponds, streams, lakes, or rivers. They were once abundant in every suitable habitat in eastern Texas, but the great demand for them in the fur trade led to their virtual extirpation by the end of the nineteenth century. However, the last seventy-five years has witnessed a complete reversal in the situation as a result of the decline in the market value of beaver pelts and their reintroduction in places where they had been extirpated. Between 1939 and 1945 Texas Parks and Wildlife biologists introduced eighty-seven beaver trapped from the Llano River into the Brazos, Navasota, Angelina, Neches, Sabine, and Colorado river systems. The recovery of the beaver in eastern Texas, as a result of these measures, is evidenced by the fact that trappers reported taking them in almost three-fourths of the counties in the region between 1976 and 1981 (Map 31). Although large rivers and lakes offer suitable habitats in places where deep water and steep banks afford protection and housing sites, beaver seem to prefer smaller bodies of water, such as narrow creeks and tributaries leading into major rivers and small ponds.

Life history. With their ability to cut trees, beavers are known for constructing "lodges" surrounded by open water and watertight dams in fast-flowing streams. Because of the flat topography in most of eastern Texas, the waterways inhabited by beavers are usually slow-moving, sluggish streams or bayous. Consequently, the dams built are typically less massive than those built by beavers in other parts of the country. The beaver does not need the massive lodges or dens that beavers use in northern climates because streams in eastern Texas seldom freeze over, so there is no need for the storage of winter food.

More frequently beavers burrow into cut banks of streams or lakes and do not even build lodges or dams. In the Big Thicket area lodges are occasionally built where high banks are absent or where deep flooding is

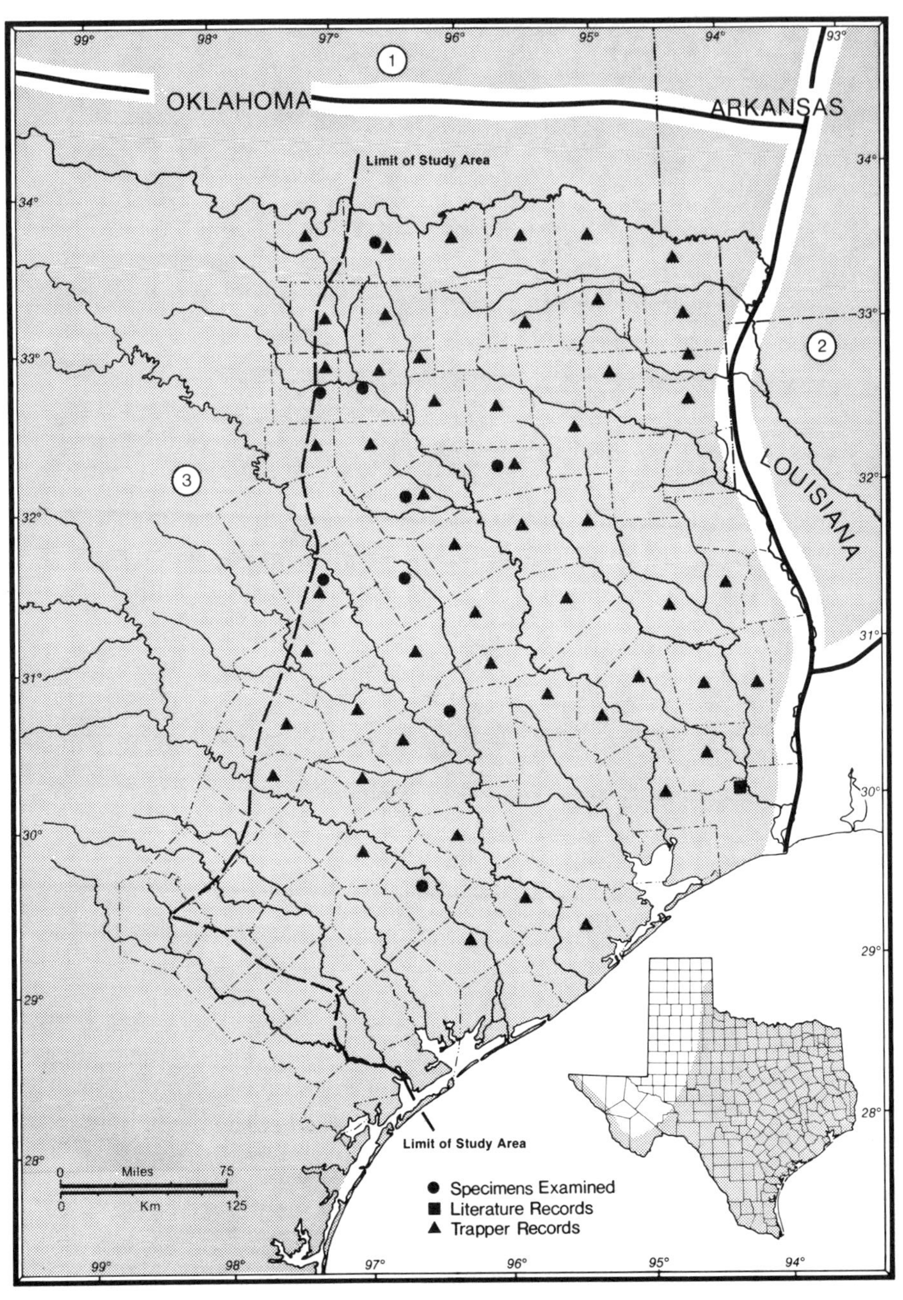

MAP 31. Distribution of the beaver, *Castor canadensis*. 1. *C . c . missouriensis*. 2. *C . c . carolinensis*. 3. *C . c . texensis*. The literature record is from Hall (1981).

frequent. Typically, a beaver burrow or den is built in a bank near deep water and has an entrance below the water line under some tree or root or overhanging bank. Over the chamber in the bank is a thin place to admit air. If the vent gives way, leaving the chamber dangerously exposed, the vent is repaired with a pile of interlacing sticks. The burrow usually contains only one chamber, which is about 61 cm high and 1.8 m across.

Beavers living in different places seem to show a preference for different species of plants. Frequently utilized woody plants in the poorly drained areas of southeastern Texas include loblolly pine, sweetgum, sweetbay, and ironwood. Farther west in the oak-hickory forests, cottonwood trees and willows are more important. Because beavers build few dams or lodges, fewer woody plants are felled than are barked, especially if the trees are larger than about 10 cm in diameter. Southern beaver feed much more extensively on land than those in northern states.

Beavers are prodigious workers, a talent which has given rise to such expressions as "busy as a beaver" or "an eager beaver." They are nocturnal and are most active from about 4:00 to 8:00 P.M. to 6:00 or 7:00 A.M. Most of their time is spent felling trees, cutting them into sections that can be manipulated, and dragging or floating them to their lodges or dams.

The fundamental unit of a beaver population is the colony, which typically consists of four to eight individuals occupying a pond or section of stream. A beaver family normally includes one adult male, one adult female, a one-year-old litter, and the succeeding litter. Young beavers disperse away from their "home" colony at about two years of age. Dispersal movements are usually less than 16 km.

Beavers are thought to be monogamous, with only one pregnant female per colony. They reproduce once a year, generally in January or February. Copulation usually takes place in the water, but may occur in a lodge or burrow. The gestation period is about 107 days, and the young are usually born in May or June. Mean litter size is generally between three and four. The kits are born fully furred, with eyes at least partially open and incisors erupted. They nurse for about six weeks, at which time they are weaned and begin to eat solid food. Kits typically stay with their parents until about two years of age.

Beavers eat a variety of leaves, twigs, and bark of woody plants that grow near water as well as many different kinds of herbaceous plants, especially aquatics. Sweetgum, cottonwood, and willow are cut heavily wherever beaver come in contact with them. Although beaver may cut pine for use in dams and lodges, they do not normally use it for food. During summer, they rely heavily on the roots and basal portions of herbaceous plants. An adult beaver may consume as much as 0.7 to 0.9 kg of food daily.

Movement in the water is primarily by the webbed hind feet, with the front feet remaining close to the body. Transverse motions of the tail are used intermittently, especially when swimming rapidly. One of the main sounds produced by the adult beaver is the loud slap of the tail on the surface of the water, which functions to warn other beavers of danger. On land, beavers usually walk, but they can gallop if frightened.

Adult beavers have few natural enemies in the water, with the possible exception of otters. While moving on land they occasionally fall prey to coyotes and possibly bobcats, but man is probably their most important predator. Alligators and mink prey on kits. Beavers are relatively long-lived for rodents. The longevity record for a wild beaver is twenty years, but few probably live beyond ten years.

Beavers can have considerable influence on the landscape as well as other animals living around them. Damming of streams by beavers affects fish populations both beneficially and adversely. Waterfowl populations may be greatly enhanced by the presence of beaver ponds. On the other hand, beavers may damage crops and valuable forest trees by their selective cutting of certain tree species and also by producing elevated water tables that drown many more plants. They may also hasten or impede forest succession adjacent to occupied ponds or streams, depending on local conditions.

References. Anonymous, 1939; Burr, 1946; W. B. Davis, 1940c, 1974; Jenkins and Busher, 1979; Lowery, 1974.

Family Cricetidae (New World Rats and Mice)

Almost one-third of the living kinds of rodents belong to this family,which includes a great variety of mouselike creatures such as rice rats, harvest mice, deer mice, golden mice, woodrats, pygmy mice, voles, and muskrats. These rodents exploit a variety of modes of life, including terrestrial, arboreal, semiaquatic, and fossorial habits.

Most cricetids retain a "standard" mouselike form, with a long tail and a generalized limb structure. They vary in size from roughly 10 g in weight and 100 mm in total length, as in the pygmy mouse (*Baiomys taylori*), to approximately 1,500 g and 600 mm, as in the muskrat (*Ondatra zibethicus*). The dental formula of all species is I 1/1, C 0/0, Pm 0/0, M 3/3 × 2 = 16.

There are sixteen species of this family living in eastern Texas, making this the single most diverse family of mammals in this region. Some of our most common and best-known mammals belong to this family.

Marsh Rice Rat
Oryzomys palustris (Harlan)

Name. The generic name *Oryzomys* is derived from two Greek words, *oryza*, meaning "rice," and *mys*, meaning "mouse," in reference to the rice-eating habits of this rodent. The specific name *palustris* is Latin for "marshy" and alludes to the preferred habitat of this species.

Identification. This is a small rat-sized rodent with a scantily haired and scaly tail that is about equal in length to the head and body combined. The ears are nearly buried in the coarse body hairs of the fur. The

Marsh rice rat, *Oryzomys palustris*.

upper parts are dark grayish and heavily interspersed with black; the underparts are grayish white. The tail is bicolored, brownish above and white below, and the hind feet are white. The marsh rice rat may be confused with the cotton rat (*Sigmodon hispidus*), from which it differs in having white instead of black feet. Average external measurements are total length, 243 mm; tail, 119 mm; hind foot, 28 mm; ear, 15 mm.

Subspecies. Oryzomys palustris texensis is the subspecies in eastern Texas. It was named by J. A. Allen (*Bull. Amer. Mus. Nat. Hist.*, 6:177, May 31, 1894) with type locality from Rockport, Aransas County, Texas.

Distribution and habitat. Rice rats are very common in the coastal prairie region, but they become less common to the west and northwest of this region (Map 32). They have been recorded as far north as Lamar and Red River counties on the Texas-Oklahoma border and as far west as Brazos County.

Rice rats have a clear preference for aquatic habitats, including marshes and swamps, grassy ditches, the edges of streams and lakes, and old fields where the soil is damp. They are seldom if ever found in dry fields or in well-drained woodlands far removed from water. In coastal regions, they occur in the tall grass that lines the banks along bayous and in the tidal marshes where the ground vegetation is not subject to periodic high tides and flooding. In the Big Thicket, I have trapped them in pine savanna wetlands, bottomland forests, baygall habitats, and briar thickets along the edges of fields, places where I often found them in association with cotton rats (*Sigmodon hispidus*) and fulvous harvest mice (*Reithrodontomys fulvescens*).

Life history. Rice rats live in globular nests, either built by the rats themselves or taken over from other animals and remodeled for their own use. In inland habitats, nests usually consist of a loosely woven ball of

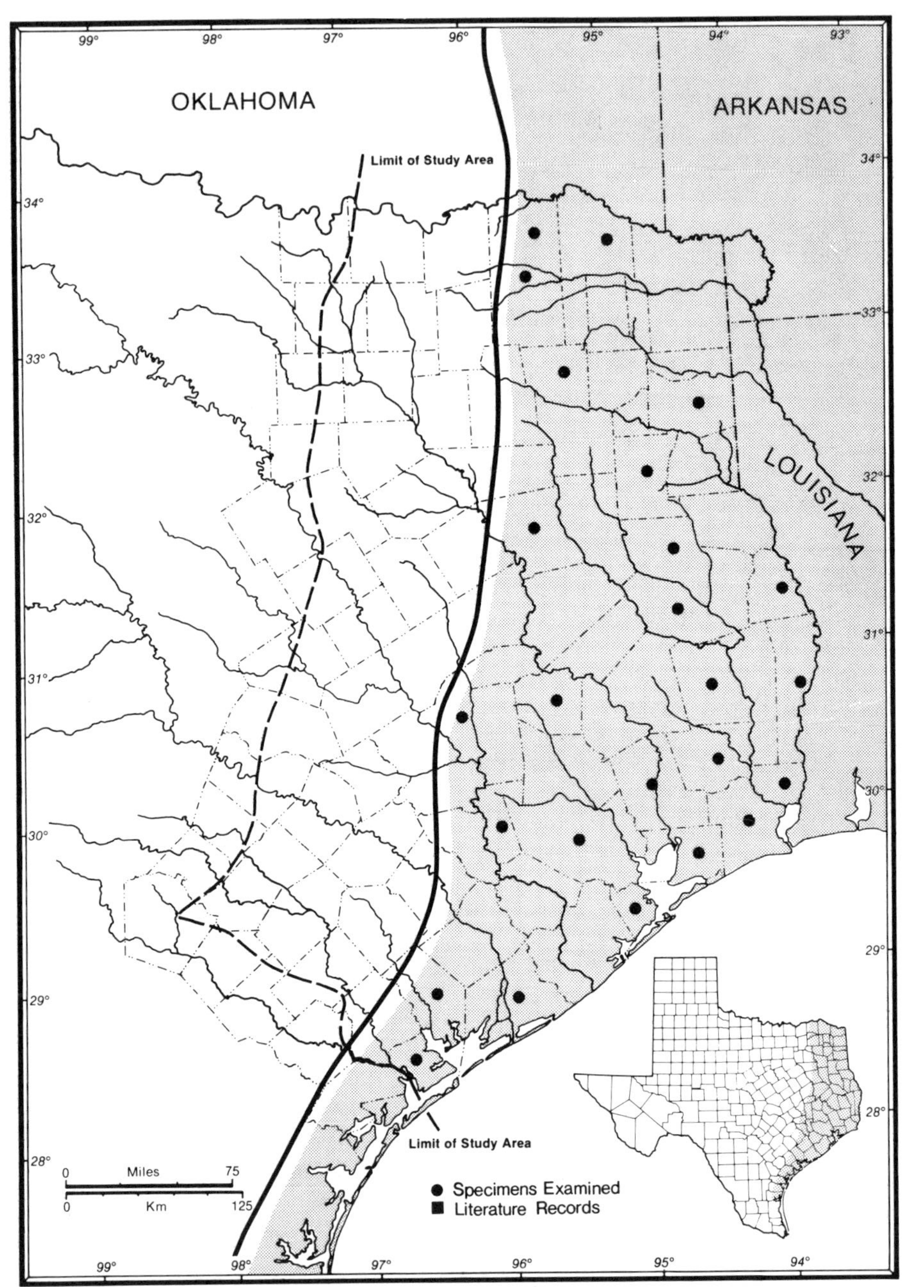

MAP 32. Distribution of the marsh rice rat, *Oryzomys palustris texensis*.

shredded leaves, about the size of a grapefruit, with an entrance in the side. They are typically placed at the end of a shallow burrow or in a shallow depression amid tangled vegetation. In coastal habitats, nests are rather elongate structures, about 50 to 70 mm wide and 125 to 150 mm long, composed of loosely interwoven grass and usually located on high ground, either in a hollow log, under pieces of driftwood, or suspended a meter or more above the water surface in tall dense stands of marsh grass or cattails. Rice rats are known to be communal during winter months, with several individuals sharing nests.

These semiaquatic rodents are active year round and do not hibernate. They move about primarily at night, with greater activity on cloudy and rainy nights. The average home range area for males is 0.32 ha; for females it is 0.20 ha (Negus et al., 1961). Considerable overlap of home ranges is evident, and there is a tendency, particularly along coastal marshlands, for home ranges to be oriented with their long axes roughly parallel to the shoreline, in correspondence to the parallel zonation of plant communities. When disturbed or frightened from their nests, rice rats are surprisingly agile and rapidly dart for cover. If continually pursued, they will not hesitate to dive into the water and swim rapidly and strongly underneath the water for some distance.

Population densities, which may range anywhere from 0.49 to 17.0 animals per ha, typically peak in summer and fall and decline sharply in late winter. The impact of climatic factors with changing food supply and the unsheltered nature of their habitat undoubtedly exerts a decisive influence on reproduction and mortality.

In eastern Texas, the breeding season may extend anywhere from nine months to year round. A single female may produce as many as five to six litters per year, although she may produce far fewer than the maximum number when subjected to inclement weather or food shortage. The gestation period is about twenty-five days, and females may undergo a postpartum heat, mating within ten hours after the birth of a litter. The number of young per litter is density-dependent, varying with contrasting phases of population growth (Negus et al., 1961). During periods of high population density, litter size averages 3.7 (range, 2 to 5); during periods of low density it averages 6 (range, 4 to 7).

The young are born blind, wrinkled, and covered with a sparse coating of fine, short hair on the legs and dorsum. They range in weight from 2.4 to 4.0 g. The eyes open on about the sixth day, by which time they are covered with a fine hair of brownish color on the upper surface of the body and white below. The young are weaned at eleven days and are driven out of the nest the following week. Rice rats become sexually mature between forty to forty-five days of age. An interesting aspect of their natural history is that an individual appears to grow substantially throughout its lifetime.

Food habits of rice rats are variable. Mostly, they feed on seeds and the succulent parts of various marsh grasses and sedges. However, at times during the year they apparently utilize a considerable amount of animal food, including insects, crustaceans, and bird eggs. During colder months, they also are known to eat fungus of the genus *Endogone*.

Apparently, population turnover is quite rapid for rice rats. The average life span for an individual is only about seven months. They are preyed upon heavily by hawks, owls, water snakes, and mink. Two of their main enemies in coastal marshes include the water moccasin (*Agkistrodon piscivorus*) and the barn owl (*Tyto alba*).

References. Birkenholz, 1963; Negus et al., 1961; Sharp, 1967; A. Svihla, 1931a.

Plains Harvest Mouse
Reithrodontomys montanus (Baird)

Name. The name *Reithrodontomys* is derived from three Greek words (*rheithron*, meaning "groove"; *odous*, meaning "tooth"; and *mys*, meaning "mouse") which translate as "groove-toothed mouse," in reference to the characteristic groove in each upper incisor. The second part of the name, *montanus*, is Latin for "pertaining to mountains" in reference to the type locality of this species, which is in the Rocky Mountains.

Identification. Harvest mice may be easily distinguished from other cricetine rodents by the groove on the anterior surface of each upper incisor. This species differs from the other two species of the genus in eastern Texas in having grayish brown coloration and a distinctly bicolored tail that is usually less than half the mouse's total length. *R. montanus* is most easily confused with *R. humulis*, from which it differs in features of the first two lower molars. In *R. humulis*, there is a distinct labial shelf or ridge, often with distinct cusplets, on the first two lower molars; this labial ridge is absent in *R. montanus*. Average external measurements of this species are total length, 114 mm; tail, 53 mm; hind foot, 15 mm; ear, 11 mm.

Subspecies. The subspecies in eastern Texas is *Reithrodontomys montanus griseus*, which was named by V. Bailey (*N. Amer. Fauna*, 25:106, October 24, 1905) with type locality from San Antonio, Bexar County, Texas.

Distribution and habitat. The plains harvest mouse is limited to the western portion of eastern Texas, where it has been recorded from eight counties (Tarrant, McLennan, Freestone, Robertson, Brazos, Madison, Williamson, and Travis) in the blackland prairie region (Map 33). Its preferred habitat is prairie communities in old fields where dense stands of bluestem grow on dark prairie soils. In Brazos and Madison counties, at the eastern edge of its range, *R. montanus* has occasionally been trapped in highway rights-of-way supporting a mixture of bluestem, bermudagrass, and Johnson grass (Wilkins and Schmidly, 1980), and the species could be expanding its range eastward in such habitats.

While studying small mammal communities on a lignite mining site in Freestone County, Waggoner (1978) trapped *R. montanus* in association with *R. humulis* on a reclaimed strip-mine area planted in crimson

Plains harvest mouse, *Reithrodontomys montanus.*

clover and sprigged in coastal bermudagrass. He obtained plains harvest mice in every month of the year save March at an average density of 1.3 animals per ha. In the same study, Waggoner took *montanus* and *humulis* as well as *R. fulvescens* in an abandoned field. The three species of *Reithrodontomys* seemed to prefer different habitat types in the old field, which contained three fairly distinct vegetational types: a bluestem meadow with heavy cover, a three-awn meadow with light cover, and an ecotone area between the two with moderate cover. *R. fulvescens* had no strong preference for any of the habitat types; *R. humulis* and *R. montanus*, on the other hand, preferred areas with light cover and avoided tall grass.

Life history. Virtually nothing is known of the life history of this small mouse in eastern Texas or elsewhere. It lives in nests composed of fine grass compacted into small balls and located in bunch grass, beneath the ground in burrows, or under boards and fallen logs. Home range estimates for three individuals captured several times over a fourteen-month period in Freestone County ranged from 0.23 to 0.84 ha (Waggoner, 1978). As far as known, its food consists of green parts and seeds of a variety of plants, including small grains.

Reproductive data, including extended testes, lactation, and embryo counts, seem to indicate that breeding in this species is carried out at any time of the year in eastern Texas. Males with scrotal testes have been collected in January and April. Pregnant females have been taken in January and October and lactating females in March. The gestation period is approximately twenty-one days; the number of young per litter ranges from two to five, averaging three. At birth the young are blind, naked, and weigh about 1 g. They are well haired in six days, their eyes open in eight days, and they are weaned in about fourteen days. They are as large as

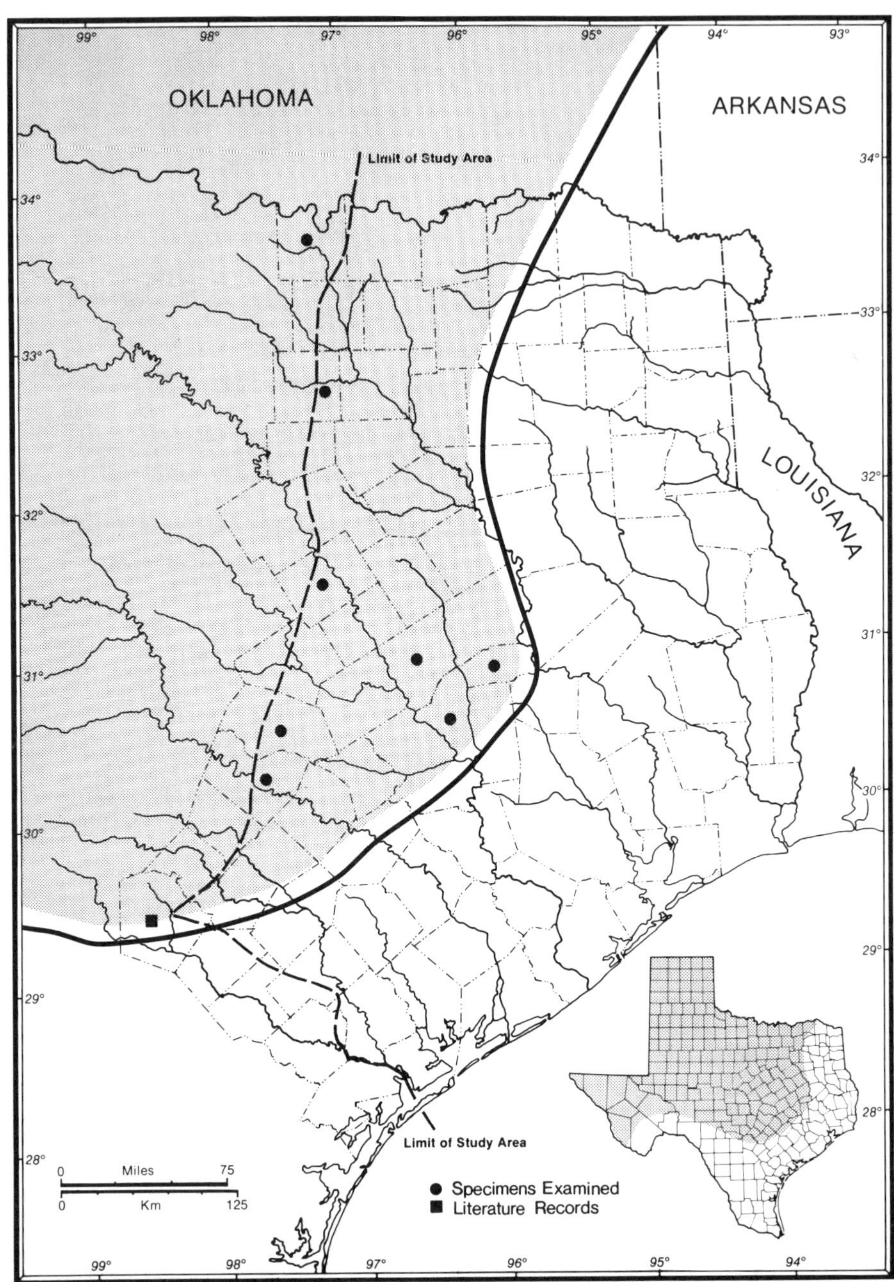

MAP 33. Distribution of the plains harvest mouse, *Reithrodontomys montanus griseus*. The literature record is from W. B. Davis (1974).

adults in five weeks and sexually mature in about two months.

References. W. B. Davis, 1974; Goertz, 1963; Waggoner, 1975, 1978; Wilkins and Schmidly, 1980.

Eastern Harvest Mouse
Reithrodontomys humulis (Audubon and Bachman)

Name. The derivation of the first part of the name, *Reithrodontomys*, is the same as that of the previous species. According to Lowery (1974:230), the specific name, *humulis*, should have been *humilis*, which is the Latin word for "small," since Audubon and Bachman, who originally named and described this species, referred to it as the "little harvest mouse." The use of *humulis*, which denotes the plant called hops, was probably a spelling error, since there is no indication that this was the meaning intended by Audubon and Bachman. However, subsequent workers have preserved the original orthography, and *humulis* is still used instead of *humilis*.

Identification. The eastern harvest mouse can be distinguished from the fulvous harvest mouse (*R. fulvescens*) by its diminutive size, duller coloration, and short tail (always less than 70 mm instead of considerably more). It is more easily confused with the plains harvest mouse (*R. montanus*), from which it differs in darker dorsal coloration and features of the lower molar teeth as described in the account of the latter. As in all harvest mice, the front face of each upper incisor has a lengthwise groove. Average external measurements are total length, 107 mm; tail, 47 mm; hind foot, 14 mm; ear, 10 mm.

Subspecies. Reithrodontomys humulis merriami is the subspecies in eastern Texas. It was named by J. A. Allen (*Bull. Amer. Mus. Nat. Hist.*, 7:119, May 21, 1895) with type locality from Austin Bayou, near Alvin, Brazoria County, Texas.

Distribution and habitat. The eastern harvest mouse has been recorded from nine counties (Bowie, Harrison, McLennan, Freestone, Nacogdoches, Hardin, Jefferson, Fort Bend, and Brazoria) scattered over the portion of eastern Texas east of the Brazos River (Map 34). *R. humulis* is found mainly in habitats dominated by grasses and other herbaceous plants characteristic of early vegetational succession, including places such as abandoned fields, weed-filled ditches, and briar thickets. In Nacogdoches County, it has been captured in grassy pastures containing a scattered growth of blackberry vines (McCarley and Bradshaw, 1953), and in an abandoned cultivated field covered with bermudagrass, partridge pea, woolly croton, and ragweed (Stephenson et al., 1963). Apparently, this tiny mouse is not common anywhere within its range in eastern Texas, as evidenced by the fact that only a single specimen, collected in a pine savanna wetland habitat, was obtained in over 31,000 trap nights in Big Thicket National Preserve (Schmidly et al., 1979).

R. humulis has been captured more commonly at two study plots situated on a lignite mining site in Freestone County than any other place in

Eastern harvest mouse, *Reithrodontomys humulis.*

eastern Texas. On a 1 ha plot that recently had been strip-mined and re-claimed in coastal bermudagrass and crimson clover, individuals were trapped in every month over a fourteen-month period except February; trapping success ranged from 1 to 6 (average, 1.9) individuals per 100 trap nights (Waggoner, 1978). The average catch was identical over a similar time period in an abandoned field covered with three-awn and bluestem at the same location, although individuals were not obtained from April through August or in October on this study plot. The catch for the re-maining months ranged from 1 to 7 (average, 3.5) individuals per 100 trap nights.

Life history. Eastern harvest mice are essentially nocturnal, al-though at times they may be active during daylight hours, particularly during cold weather. Increased daytime activity in this species may be correlated with "huddling behavior." During periods of cold weather, these mice huddle together in the nest at night to reduce heat loss from their bodies, and they feed in the daytime when it is warmer. Heat loss from an individual in a group of huddling mammals is less than heat loss from an isolated individual (Pearson, 1947).

R. humulis constructs nests of shredded grass and plant fibers that are placed on the ground in tangled herbage or above the ground in a clump of grass. The nest, which is about the size of a baseball, generally has a single entrance. These mice probably do not make definite runways for themselves, using instead those built by other rodents such as cotton rats (*Sigmodon hispidus*).

Little is known about the movements of these harvest mice. Home range estimates for two individuals captured several times in Freestone County averaged 0.38 ha (Waggoner, 1978), which is small compared to

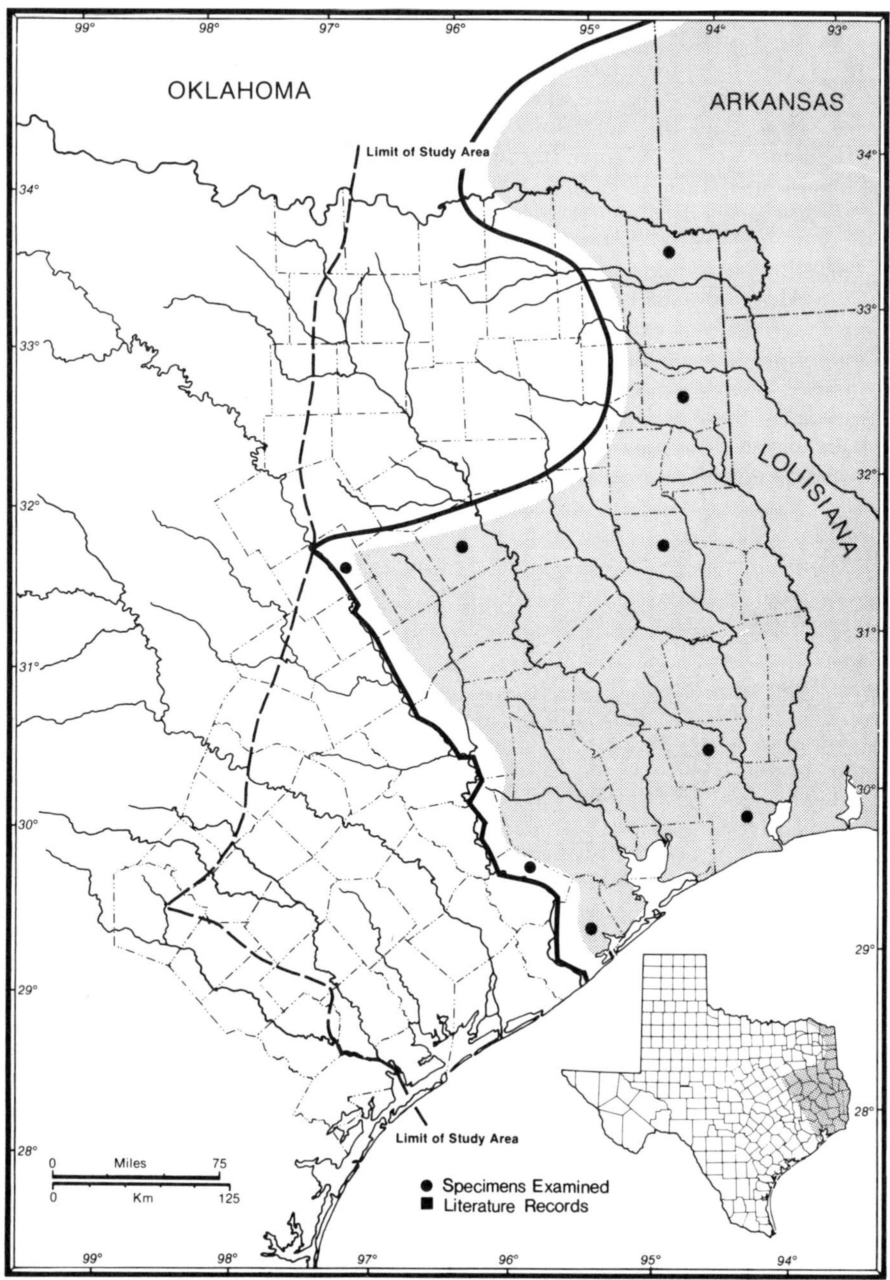

MAP 34. Distribution of the eastern harvest mouse, *Reithrodontomys humulis merriami.*

other species of harvest mice. Home ranges overlap broadly, indicating that territoriality is probably poorly developed.

Although breeding may occur throughout the year, most births take place between late spring and late fall. Litter sizes range from 1 to 8 (average, 3.4), and the gestation period is twenty-one to twenty-two days (Dunaway, 1968). At birth the young weigh approximately 1.2 g. The eyes do not open until seven to ten days, and weaning takes place between the second and fourth weeks. Young mice apparently stay in the nest until they are relatively large. They become sexually mature and are capable of breeding at about eleven to twelve weeks of age.

Mortality among young mice in the nest is relatively high; however, average life expectancy is relatively long after the mice leave the nest. One individual male remained on a study plot in Freestone County for eleven months (Waggoner, 1978). High nestling mortality, in combination with low reproductive potential, probably prevents the rapid buildup of populations and may, in part, explain why low density populations of this species exist in many places.

The food habits of the eastern harvest mouse are not well known. They seem to be mostly granivores, feeding almost wholly on seeds and grain, but they are known to eat grasshoppers and crickets in captivity.

References. Dunaway, 1968; Kaye, 1961a, 1961b; Layne, 1959; Lowery, 1974; Waggoner, 1978.

Fulvous Harvest Mouse
Reithrodontomys fulvescens Allen

Name. The specific name *fulvescens* is Latin for "reddish yellow," "tawny," or "gold colored" and refers to the coloration of the side of the body in this species. The derivation of the name *Reithrodontomys* is identical to the other two species of harvest mice in eastern Texas.

Identification. The fulvous harvest mouse is readily distinguished from other harvest mice in eastern Texas by its longer tail (in adults usually over 80 mm) and bright fulvous coloration on its sides. The upper parts are a golden brown, sometimes with a strong interspersion of black down the center of the dorsum; the underparts are white or pale buff. This mouse also resembles the house mouse (*Mus musculus*), but differs in having a shorter, less tapering tail and deeply grooved upper incisors. Average external measurements are total length, 156 mm; tail, 87 mm; hind foot, 20 mm; ear, 14 mm.

Subspecies. There are two subspecies in eastern Texas. *Reithrodontomys fulvescens aurantius* from the northern part of the region (above the Colorado River) was named by J. A. Allen (*Bull. Amer. Mus. Nat. Hist.*, 7:137, May 21, 1895) with type locality from Lafayette, Lafayette Parish, Louisiana. *Reithrodontomys fulvescens intermedius* from the southern part of the region (below the Colorado River) was also named by J. A. Allen (*Bull. Amer. Mus. Nat. Hist.*, 7:136, May 21, 1895) with type locality from Brownsville, Cameron County, Texas. The two subspecies

Fulvous harvest mouse, *Reithrodontomys fulvescens*, with newborn babies.

are similar in size and cranial characters but differ in coloration, with *aurantius* being darker and more rufescent than *intermedius* (Hooper, 1952).

Distribution and habitat. The fulvous harvest mouse is one of the most abundant and ubiquitous species of rodents in eastern Texas (Map 35). It is found principally in fallow fields or in ecotones between grasses and deciduous or coniferous forests; however, it also occurs in woodland communities where trees are spaced widely enough to permit growth of various grasses, vines, and shrubs. Optimal habitat in the coastal prairies includes fields dominated by sea myrtle and southern dewberry. In the pineywoods, it occurs predominately in grassland, pine-grass ecotone, and grass-brush habitat, and is significantly absent from pure pine areas. Preferred habitat in the Big Thicket includes pine savanna wetland, pine plantation grassland, and lower-slope hardwood-pine habitats. In the post oak woodlands, this species prefers old fields with a heavy cover of bluestem.

Specific ecological situations where fulvous harvest mice have been trapped include the following: Johnson grass in Smith and Brazos counties (Hooper, 1952); broomsedge, pinewood ecotones in Walker County (Taylor and Davis, 1947); bluestem fields in Brazos and Lavaca counties (Hooper, 1952); grassy prairie with heavy cover of bluestem and a low mat of other grasses in Jefferson County (Blair, 1941); marshy areas along edges of blackberry brush and weedy fence rows in Bowie County (Baker, 1942); unmowed highway rights-of-way and adjacent uncultivated fields in Brazos and Madison counties (Wilkins and Schmidly, 1980); and briar thickets between two cultivated fields in Walker County (Bailey, 1905).

Life history. Fulvous harvest mice nest in bushes, trees, and on the ground. Their nests are about the size of a baseball and are composed of shredded grass and weed stems with a single opening on one side. Arboreal nests are usually built 0.3 to 1.0 m above the ground and typically house a female with her litter or a pair of mice. Male and female fulvous harvest mice seem extremely tolerant of one another and multiple captures of males and females in the same trap are common in the field.

R. fulvescens are active year round and do not hibernate. They are nocturnal, with activity beginning abruptly after sunset, attaining its highest level at 9:00 P.M. and then steadily declining to zero by sunrise (Cameron et al., 1979a). Fulvous harvest mice are omnivorous, feeding on insects as well as the seeds and succulent parts of various grasses, sedges, and weeds. Kincaid and Cameron (1982) found that their diet consisted of 70 percent invertebrates and 28 percent monocot plants in coastal prairie habitats.

This species exhibits a bimodal annual density pattern, with peaks generally occurring during late summer and winter and troughs during autumn and spring. The late summer peak is generally much smaller than the winter peak. Population estimates have been calculated for four different ecological situations in eastern Texas: an abandoned field in Freestone County (Waggoner, 1978), a coastal prairie in Harris County (Cameron, 1977), a pine-grass ecotone area in Nacogdoches County (Packard,

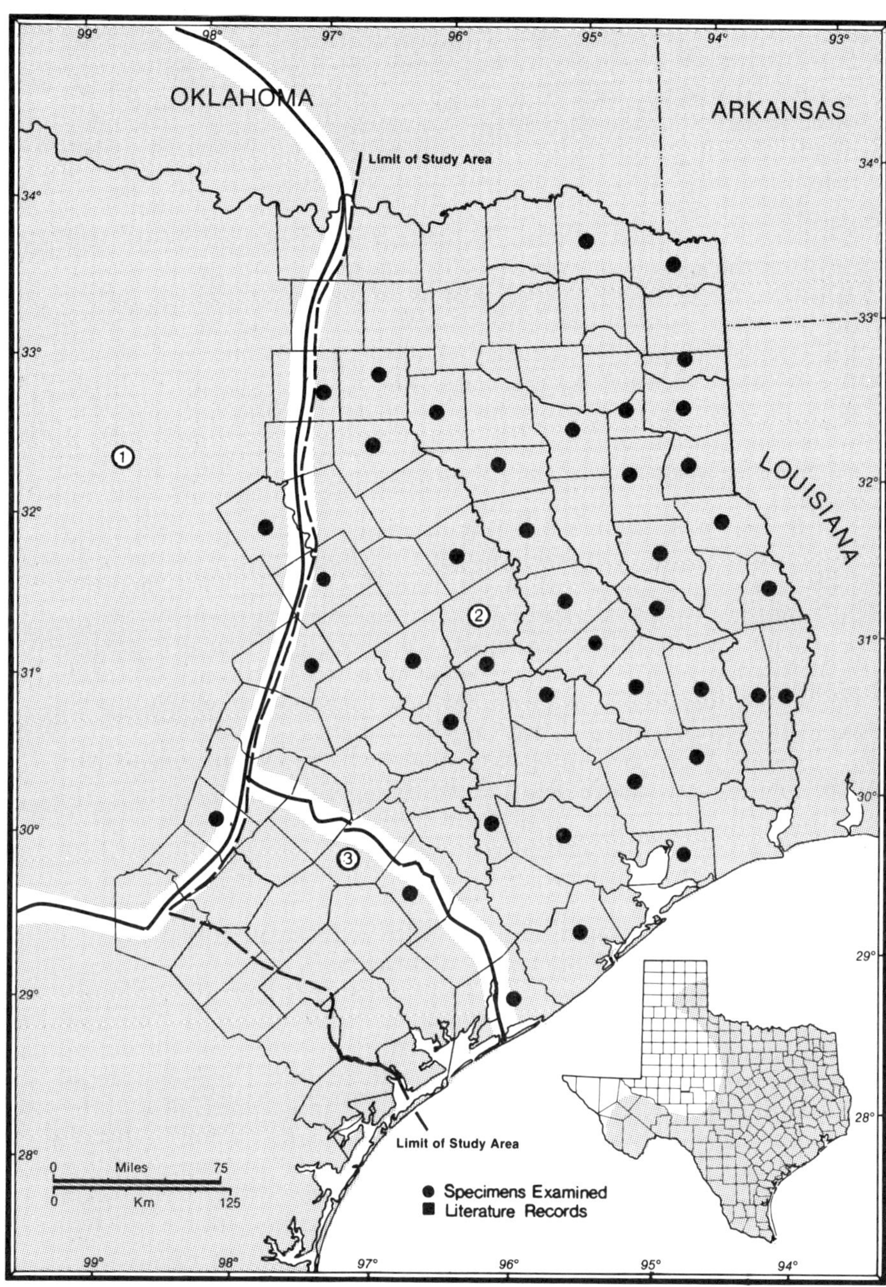

MAP 35. Distribution of the fulvous harvest mouse, *Reithrodontomys fulvescens*.
1. *R. f. laceyi.* 2. *R. f. aurantius.* 3. *R. f. intermedius.*

1968), and an old field in Brazos County (Wilkins and Schmidly, 1980). Seasonal density values for these four situations, respectively, were as follows (expressed in animals per ha): winter, 20.4, 28, 4, 6; spring, 13.3, 5.8, 0.7, 1; summer, 6.3, 11, 2, 1; fall, 8.7, 5.8, —, 3. Within-year seasonal changes in density patterns are probably cued by temperature trends. Density estimates correlate with the abundance of preferred habitat plants, which may be more important for nesting sites than for food.

Type of habitat seems to have some influence on demographic parameters of these harvest mice. In Nacogdoches County, Packard (1968) reported the movements of male and female *R. fulvescens* as approximately equal (0.19 ha for males; 0.24 ha for females); males and females did not show any decided degree of territorial behavior on the basis of home range overlap. Home ranges of fulvous harvest mice in Freestone County were almost twice the magnitude of those reported in Nacogdoches County, although values for males (0.42 ha) still averaged less than values for females (0.51 ha). Furthermore, there was little overlap in the home ranges of males, suggesting that they may be territorial (Waggoner, 1978).

R. fulvescens exhibits a density-dependent dispersal strategy that is synchronized with seasonally changing environmental conditions. Females appear to disperse early in life (juveniles and subadults), thereafter remaining philopatric to a particular area, whereas males maintain the potential for a wide range of movement throughout life. For males, and possibly females, an established population of these harvest mice appears to inhibit the immigration of its own species. Dispersal is probably a major regulatory mechanism of density for this species.

Although detailed histological studies of reproductive organs have not been made, available data indicate this species has a diestrous cycle. In Nacogdoches County (pineywood habitat), Packard (1968) reported spring (March) and summer (July) peaks in the breeding season with early summer (May-June) and winter (January) declines. In Harris County (coastal prairie habitat), Cameron (1977) reported that the breeding season extends from March to November with peaks in late spring (May and June) and early autumn (September and October).

The young, which range in number from two to four (average, three) are born after a gestation period of about twenty-one days. Young are born hairless, but within three to four days hair appears on the dorsum and becomes apparent on the venter by eleven days. The eyes open between nine and twelve days. Climbing ability is evident twelve to thirteen days following birth. Ability to climb is important to fulvous harvest mice because it allows them to utilize the vertical component of their habitat. Care of young by the female lasts approximately three weeks. Weaning occurs at thirteen to sixteen days, when young mice weigh from 3.0 to 3.5 g. There is some indication that females born during late spring or early summer probably produce their first litters as subadults in the winter.

Mean longevity for fulvous harvest mice is somewhere between two and three months (2.86 months according to Waggoner, 1978; 2.25 months according to Cameron, 1977). Males exhibit slightly higher survival rates than females (2.4 months compared to 2.2 according to Cameron, 1977). The longest period of survival for males is about fourteen to fifteen months, whereas for females it is eleven to twelve months (Cameron, 1977). Thus, population turnover occurs in about thirteen to fourteen months. Known predators of this species include hawks, owls, and several kinds of snakes (water moccasins and racers).

References. Cameron, 1977; Cameron et al., 1979a; Joule and Cameron, 1975; Kincaid and Cameron, 1982; Packard, 1968; Schmidly et al., 1979; Waggoner, 1978; Wilkins and Schmidly, 1980.

Deer Mouse
Peromyscus maniculatus (Waggoner)

Name. The etymology of the name *Peromyscus* is not clear (Lowery, 1974). The first part of the word could be derived from the Latin *pero*, meaning "pointed" and referring to the pointed shape of the head, or it could come from the Greek word *pera*, meaning "pouched" in reference to the internal cheek pouches. *Myscus*, the last part of the word, is derived from the Greek word *myskos* and means "little mouse." The second part of the scientific name, *maniculatus*, is derived from the Latin word *manicula*, meaning "small-handed" in reference to the size of the front feet.

Identification. This small, short-eared mouse has a tail that is decidedly shorter than its head and body. The tail is sharply bicolored, with a narrow, dark dorsal stripe and the remaining parts whitish. The general color of the upper parts is pale russet, lightly mixed with dusky on the sides and more heavily in the middle of the back; the underparts are creamy white, rather thinly overlaying pale plumbeous undercolor. *P. maniculatus* may be easily confused with *P. leucopus*, from which it differs in smaller external and cranial measurements (see Table 6) and in having a more sharply bicolored tail.

Subspecies. Two subspecies occur in eastern Texas. *P. m. pallescens* occurs from the Red River at the northern boundary of the region south to Bexar and Aransas counties at the southern boundary. It was named by J. A. Allen (*Bull. Amer. Mus. Nat. Hist.*, 8:238, November 21, 1896) with type locality from San Antonio, Bexar County, Texas. *P. m. ozarkiarum*, which is widely distributed in eastern Oklahoma and western Arkansas, barely occurs south of the Red River in eastern Texas in Cooke, Grayson, and Denton counties (Caire and Zimmerman, 1975). It was named by Black (*J. Mamm.*, 16:144, May 15, 1935) with type locality from 3 mi. S Winslow, Washington County, Arkansas. *P. m. ozarkiarum*, compared to *P. m. pallescens*, is darker in overall coloration and averages slightly larger in size. The two subspecies also differ karyotypically. The karyotype of *pallescens* has a diploid number of 48 and a fundamental number of 82; that of *ozarkiarum* has a diploid number of 48 and a fundamental number

TABLE 6. Average and Extreme External and Cranial Measurements (in mm) of Four Species of *Peromyscus* from Eastern Texas.

Character	*P. maniculatus* (16)	*P. leucopus* (24)	*P. gossypinus* (24)	*P. pectoralis* (12)
Total length	127.8	153.5	181.1	193.8
	(122–141)	(135–176)	(153–212)	(185–205)
Tail length	48.1	66.8	78.2	97.3
	(42–54)	(56–75)	(70–98)	(85–108)
Hind foot length	17.4	19.9	24.0	22.2
	(16–18)	(19–22)	(23–26)	(22–23)
Ear length	13.1	15.3	18.7	19.2
	(12–15)	(13–17)	(17–20)	(18–20)
Condylobasilar length	21.0	23.1	26.5	24.4
	(20.4–21.7)	(22.0–24.9)	(25.2–27.8)	(23.6–25.0)
Zygomatic breadth	12.0	13.3	14.9	13.7
	(11.6–12.4)	(12.8–14.2)	(13.8–15.6)	(13.1–14.4)
Length of rostrum	8.8	9.6	11.6	10.7
	(8.1–9.4)	(9.0–10.6)	(10.6–12.6)	(10.1–11.2)
Length of nasals	8.9	9.8	11.6	10.2
	(8.4–9.7)	(9.2–10.9)	(10.7–12.8)	(9.9–10.6)
Least interorbital constriction	3.8	4.1	4.6	4.3
	(3.5–4.0)	(3.8–4.4)	(4.4–4.8)	(4.1–4.6)
Mastoid breadth	10.2	10.9	12.0	11.4
	(9.6–10.6)	(10.2–11.4)	(11.4–12.4)	(11.0–11.8)
Length maxillary tooth row	3.4	3.5	3.9	4.1
	(3.2–3.7)	(3.2–3.8)	(3.7–4.2)	(4.0–4.3)
Depth of skull	8.6	9.2	10.3	9.4
	(8.0–9.2)	(8.8–9.6)	(9.8–10.8)	(9.1–9.7)

Deer mouse, *Peromyscus maniculatus*.

of 80 (Fig. 3; Caire and Zimmerman, 1975). The most obvious difference in morphology of chromosomes between the two subspecies is the number of acrocentric chromosomes. Animals with the *ozarkiarum* type have six pairs, and the *pallescens* type, five pairs.

Distribution and habitat. P. maniculatus occurs in the grassland communities of the blackland prairie region on both clay and sandy soils as well as in the open fields of the oak-hickory belt. The species has been recorded as far east as Red River, Van Zandt, Anderson, and Brazos counties and as far south as Bexar County (Map 36). It has also been recorded in Aransas County in the Gulf coastal plains in sandy areas supporting stands of scattered live oaks, low shrubs, and sparse grasses (Pettus, 1957). The deer mouse probably occurs in similar situations in the southern portion of eastern Texas, although no specimens have been obtained in this region.

The habitat preferences of the deer mouse include strictly open areas, such as weedy fields, highway and railroad rights-of-way, fence rows, pastures, and cropland. The species is absent from dense forests.

Life history. Probably more is known about the biology of this species than any other native North American rodent. However, the species is not very common in eastern Texas, and little is known of its habits in this area.

These mice typically live in underground burrows or brush piles where they construct globular nests out of dry grass and shredded weeds. They are generally solitary in their nesting habits, although they may live in pairs during the breeding season. Deer mice are nocturnal, with their customary activity period occurring during early evening and just before dawn. They spend the daytime in their nest sleeping intermittently, either curled into a ball, with the head tucked under the body, or curled on

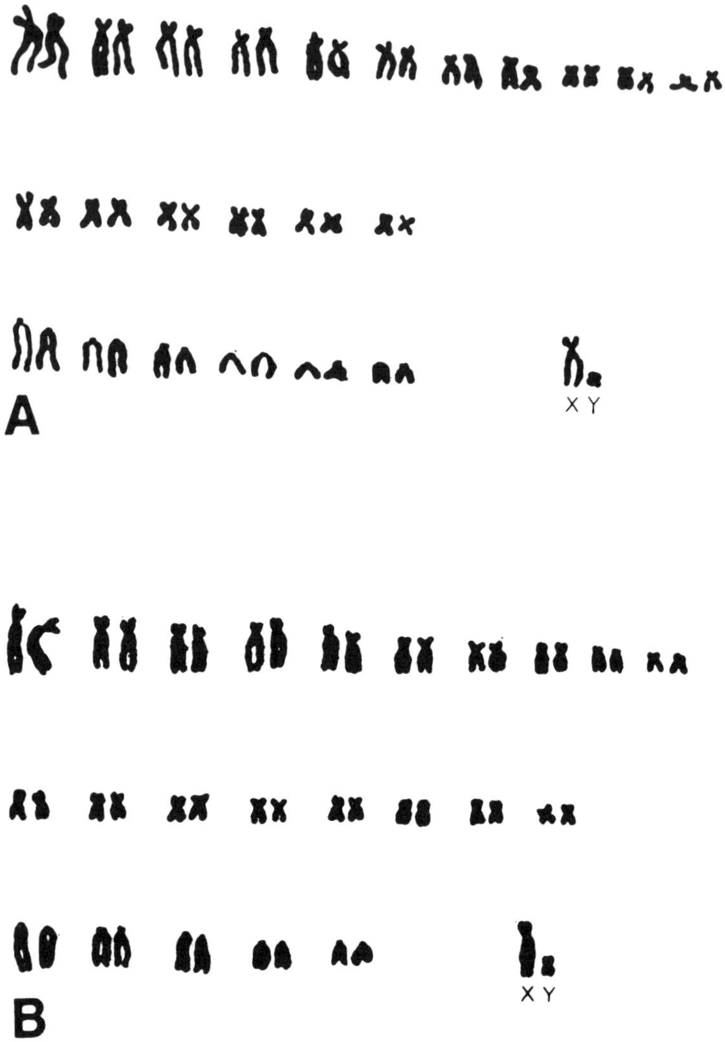

FIGURE 3. Karyotype of (A) *Peromyscus maniculatus ozarkiarum* (2N = 48; FN = 80) and (B) *Peromyscus maniculatus pallescens* (2N = 48; FN = 82). From Caire and Zimmerman (1975).

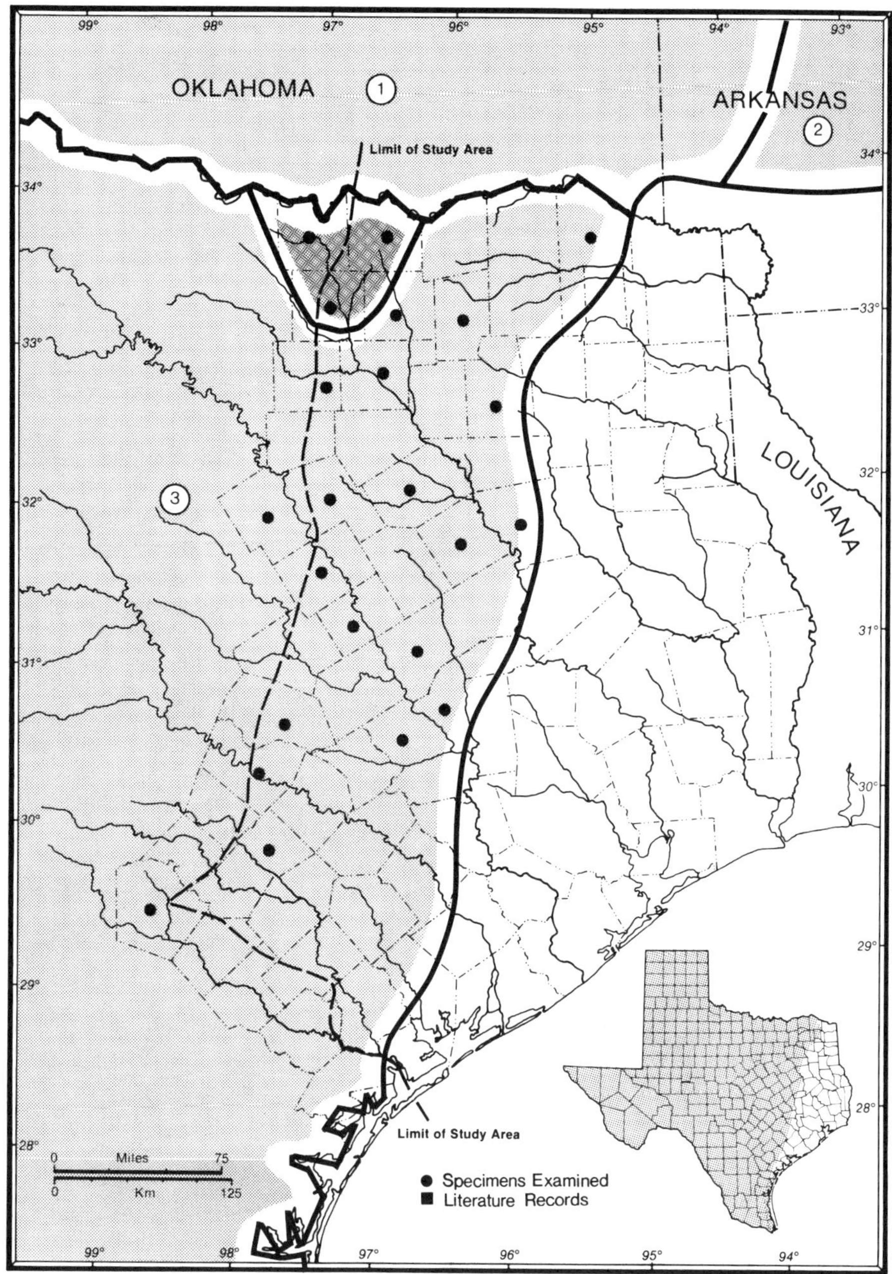

MAP 36. Distribution of the deer mouse, *Peromyscus maniculatus*. 1. *P. m. ozarkiarum*. 2. *P. m. bairdii*. 3. *P. m. pallescens*. The cross-hatched area indicates a region of sympatry between *P. m. ozarkiarum* and *P. m. pallescens*.

the sides. *P. maniculatus* does not hibernate, although in severe cold it may become torpid and hypothermic.

Waggoner (1975, 1978) commonly trapped deer mice on a reclaimed strip-mine area in Freestone County, and his study has produced the only available information concerning population dynamics of this species in eastern Texas. On a 1 ha study plot, he captured and marked (using a toe-clip method) fifty-five deer mice (twenty-five males, thirty females) that were recaptured 155 times over a fourteen-month period. Average population density was 10.2 animals per ha. Peak densities were reached in December (34 animals per ha), February (25), and March (24); lowest densities (ranging from 0 to 2 animals per ha) were from June through October. Periods of high population density correlated with the breeding season of this species. Survivorship rates were fairly low, with a complete population turnover occurring in less than six months. The size of home range averaged 0.44 ha, with that of females averaging slightly larger than that of males. Deer mice have good homing ability and will return to their home range even if removed distances of several kilometers.

The breeding season for this species extends from late fall through winter (November to March). During this period, Waggoner trapped scrotal males as well as pregnant and lactating females. The young, which typically average four per litter, are born after a gestation period of about twenty-four days. A single female may breed more than one time during the breeding season, producing several litters in rapid succession.

Births usually occur in daylight hours. The young are born pink, blind, and naked (except for vibrissae). Postnatal development is relatively fast. Hair becomes visible two to four days after birth, and the entire dorsum is well haired by one week. Within two weeks a full coat of short, sleek hair is in place. The teeth begin to erupt at about five days, and the eyes open around fourteen days. Weaning occurs at approximately eighteen days of age. The average time of first estrus is about seven weeks of age. Adult weight and body size is reached after about six weeks.

Deer mice feed on a variety of food items, including insects, nuts, wild seeds, domestic grains, fruits, leafy vegetation, worms, spiders, centipedes, millipedes, eggs and young of birds, and dead mice. There is some evidence that they store food during the fall in preparation for winter. Known predators include opossums, foxes, coyotes, weasels, skunks, minks, badgers, domestic cats, hawks, owls, and snakes.

Remarks. Caire and Zimmerman (1975) studied chromosomal variation in populations of this species from Texas and Oklahoma and found that the two subspecies in this region (*P. m. ozarkiarum* and *P. m. pallescens*) had different karyotypes. Animals with karyotypes characteristic of both subspecies were obtained in Denton, Grayson, and Cooke counties. Both types were found in the same habitat at two localities, and no chromosomal hybrids were found. Meiotic analysis of hybrids from laboratory crosses between the two subspecies indicated partial sterility. Thus, *P. m. ozarkiarum* and *P. m. pallescens* appear to act as good species in the portions of their range south of the Red River in eastern Texas. However, based on morphological evidence it appears that the two subspecies interbreed where their ranges contact in western Oklahoma. This situation, in which series of intergrading subspecies form an overlapping circle of sympatric, noninterbreeding populations, represents an example of "circular overlap," a phenomenon that is not uncommon in other parts of the range of *P. maniculatus* (Caire and Zimmerman, 1975).

References. W. B. Davis, 1974; C. W. Schwartz and Schwartz, 1981; Waggoner, 1975, 1978.

Cotton Mouse
Peromyscus gossypinus (Le Conte)

Name. The name *gossypinus* comes from two Latin words, *gossyp*, meaning "cotton tree," and *inus*, a suffix meaning "belong to." This and the common name were applied to the species by Le Conte, who found that the mice often used cotton for nest construction. The derivation of *Peromyscus*, the first part of the scientific name, is discussed in the previous account.

Identification. This medium-sized, heavy-bodied, white-footed mouse has a tail that is not sharply bicolored and shorter than the head and body. The upper parts are yellowish brown and contrast sharply with the sides, which are bright russet, and the underparts, which are creamy white. The hind foot is white, but the tarsal joint of the heel is dark like the leg. External and cranial measurements are given in Table 6.

Some authors (McCarley, 1959d; Lowery, 1974) have reported that *P. gossypinus* is difficult to distinguish from *P. leucopus*, the white-footed mouse. To the contrary, I find the two species relatively easy to distinguish in eastern Texas. *P. gossypinus* differs from *Peromyscus leucopus* in having larger hind feet (usually greater than 23 mm in *gossypinus*, less than 22 mm in *leucopus*); larger body length (greater than 95 mm in *gossypinus*, less than 95 mm in *leucopus*); larger condylobasilar length (greater than 25 mm in *gossypinus*, less than 25 mm in *leucopus*); larger skull depth (greater than 9.8 mm in *gossypinus*, less than 9.7 mm in *leucopus*); darker pelage color; and eight biarmed chromosomes rather than eleven. Although there is a small degree of size overlap between these two species, no noteworthy breakdown in reproductive isolation has been observed, and they do not appear to hybridize (see remarks section of *P. leucopus* account).

Subspecies. The only subspecies in eastern Texas is *Peromyscus gossypinus megacephalus*, which was named by Rhoads (*Proc. Acad. Nat. Sci. Philadelphia*, 46:254, October 1894) with type locality from Woodville, Jackson County, Alabama. St. Romain (1976) has recently reviewed geographic variation in this species in Louisiana and Texas.

Distribution and habitat. The cotton mouse, which is widely distributed over much of the southeastern United States, reaches the western limits of its range in eastern Texas, where it is the most common cri-

Cotton mouse, *Peromyscus gossypinus.*

cetine rodent in the woodlands of the pineywoods region. The western limit of its distribution is approximately along a line beginning with the confluence of the Brazos and Navasota rivers and extending north to the Red River (Map 37). The species occurs in greatest abundance in wooded areas subject to annual inundations by flood waters in the pine-oak and pine forest region. At the western margin of its range, in the oak-hickory belt, the cotton mouse has a more or less dendritic distribution pattern, coinciding with the location of rivers, streams, and other lowland areas. It also occurs sparingly in wooded areas along the streams of the coastal prairie regions.

Preferred habitats include flatland hardwood, flatland hardwood pine, and lower-slope hardwood-pine forests. This mouse also has been reported in mesic and hydric hammocks, swamps, palmetto thickets, stream floodplain forests, and mid-slope oak-pine habitats as well as in abandoned and intermittently used buildings. The only places where cotton mice live in upland habitats are where populations of this species also occur in the immediately adjacent lowlands. *P. leucopus* is the dominant species in most forested upland habitat.

Life history. These mice nest in and under logs, in stumps, and under brush piles and palmettos. Their nests are similar in size and construction to those of the white-footed mouse (*P. leucopus*). Cotton mice are strongly nocturnal and are seldom active during the day. Their home range averages 0.81 ha, with no significant difference between males and females (McCarley, 1959a).

McCarley (1954c) studied population fluctuations and composition of cotton mice in Nacogdoches County over a twenty-month period, and his observations are probably indicative of this species throughout eastern

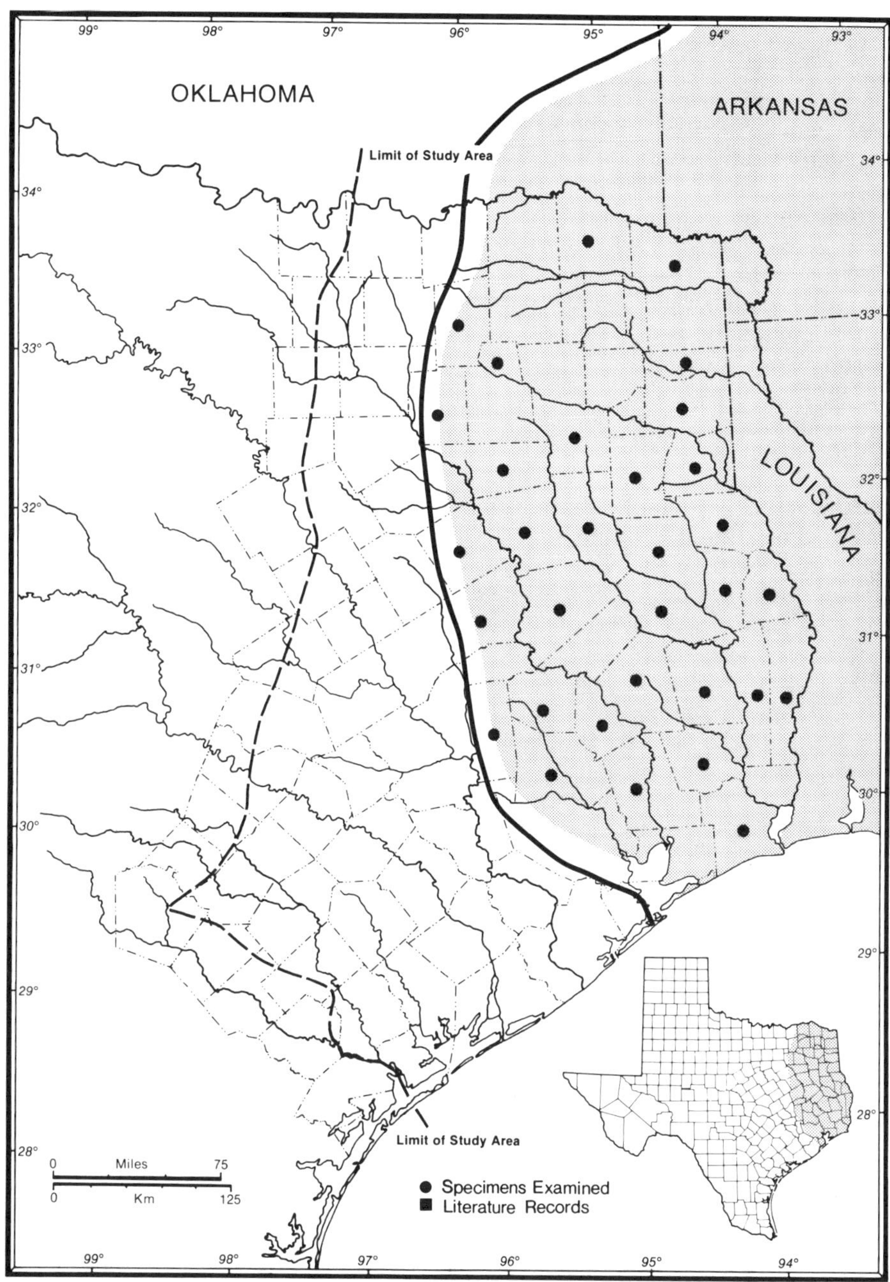

MAP 37. Distribution of the cotton mouse, *Peromyscus gossypinus megacephalus*.

Texas. *P. gossypinus* populations undergo changes in density that can be correlated, to a large extent, with breeding pattern and environmental factors such as weather and available food supply.

Populations typically reach their highest population density during the winter months. In McCarley's study, there was little difference in the population densities for the months of January (5.7 animals per ha), February (6.7 animals per ha), and March (5.9 animals per ha). During this time, juveniles and subadults made up about half of the population, which is consistent with the fact that most breeding takes place during the months of December and January. From April (4.4 animals per ha) until September (0.7 animals per ha) the population gradually declined in number; there were no juveniles in the population during July, August, and September, which is indicative of a cessation in breeding activity. During August and September the population remained essentially constant and was composed mostly of adults. In October the first evidence of population increase was shown by the appearance of juveniles, and this increase became even more apparent in November and December. The appearance of juveniles in the population in October is an indication that breeding started again in September.

Longevity of individuals in the field is generally short, and population turnover is rapid. The average cotton mouse lives no more than four to five months in the wild, with very few adults living through a year (McCarley, 1954c, 1959b). Natural predators include bobcats, foxes, feral house cats, owls, and snakes.

Some breeding takes place in every month of the year with the exception of the hot, dry summer months (June, July, and August), during which time reproduction is severely curtailed. Pournelle (1952) demonstrated in Florida that male *gossypinus* kept at temperatures from 31.7° C to 36.3° C were consistently not in breeding condition, whereas those individuals kept at 20.6° C to 28.9° C always had viable sperm in the epididymis and tubules. Peak breeding activity is in December and January, with other significant spells occurring in April and September. Females apparently produce litters in succession during the breeding season. Females remain in estrus for an average of 5.3 days (Pournelle, 1952). The gestation period ranges from twenty-three days (nonnursing females) to thirty days (nursing females). Litter size of ten pregnant females collected in the Big Thicket averaged 3.4 young and ranged from 1 to 6 (Schmidly et al., 1979).

Most litters are born during the morning. Young are born hairless (except for vibrissae), with the eyes closed and the incisors not erupted. By day five, fine hairs cover the dorsum, and by day seven the incisors have erupted. By day ten, animals are fully haired, and most individuals open their eyes between days twelve and fourteen. Weaning generally occurs by the third or fourth week.

Compared to the white-footed mouse (*P. leucopus*), which is predominately herbivorous, the cotton mouse is an omnivore. Animal matter constitutes over half of its diet, with favored items including snails, spiders, slugs, and various adult and larval insects. Seeds and other plant material comprise the remainder of the diet.

P. gossypinus is an adept climber and in laboratory situations shows a clear preference for elevated nesting sites. This species has been live-trapped as much as 4.6 m above the ground in hardwood trees and has also been found in abandoned gray squirrel nests. Their method of ascending a tree trunk is similar to that of gray squirrels. Cotton mice are also adept swimmers which, together with their climbing ability, is a useful adaptation in their preferred habitat. McCarley (1959b) studied the effects of flooding on populations of this species in Nacogdoches County. He found that short-term flooding (eight days duration) produced no detrimental effect on the mice present after the flood compared with those before the flood. Flooding for a three week period in a similar habitat produced a 70 percent decrease in the population. There was a remarkable tendency on the part of the mice to remain within their established home ranges during the flooding on both plots. The supposition is that, since these mice are at least partly arboreal, they lived in trees while the areas were flooded.

Little is known of the social behavior of these mice. Bradshaw (1965) noted that under caged conditions in the laboratory, cotton mice are extremely gregarious. They also seemed to be curious and readily willing to leave the nest. There is a higher agonistic interaction rate in *P. gossypinus* than in *P. leucopus*, and the former is usually dominant in interspecific encounters. This observation supports McCarley's (1963) contention that *P. gossypinus* may exclude *P. leucopus* from areas of optimum habitat.

Remarks. McCarley (1959a) described the effects of radiation on the population dynamics of cotton mice and golden mice (*Ochrotomys nuttalli*) in Nacogdoches County. The testes of male mice were treated with 500 r of x-irradiation, and the animals were released back to the population. Evidence obtained from subsequent study of the treated population indicated that the reproductive rate declined through a decrease in the number or size of litters. Life spans of presumed offspring of irradiated males were significantly shorter than life spans of presumed offspring of normal males, and the irradiated population exhibited a larger incidence of pelage color mutation.

References. Barnette, 1979; Bradshaw, 1965; Calhoun, 1941; McCarley, 1954a, 1954b, 1954c, 1959a, 1959b, 1963, 1964; Pournelle, 1952; Schmidly et al., 1979; R. J. Taylor and McCarley, 1963; Wolfe and Linzey, 1977.

White-footed Mouse
Peromyscus leucopus (Rafinesque)

Name. The etymology for the first part of the scientific name is the same as given in the previous two accounts. The name *leucopus* is derived from two Greek words, *leukon*, meaning "white," and *pous*, meaning "foot," in reference to the color of the feet of this species.

White-footed mouse, *Peromyscus leucopus*.

Identification. The tail of this medium-sized *Peromyscus* is shorter than the head and body, and its ears are small. The tail is indistinctly bicolored, darker above than below. In adults, the upper parts are dull grayish brown; the underparts and feet are pure white. This mouse may be confused with *P. gossypinus*, from which it differs as described in the account of the latter, and *P. maniculatus*, from which it differs by larger size; longer, more sparsely haired, and less sharply bicolored tail; and larger hind feet. External and cranial measurements are given in Table 6.

Subspecies. There is but one subspecies in eastern Texas, *Peromyscus leucopus leucopus*. It was named by Rafinesque (*Amer. Monthly Mag.*, 3:446, October 1818) with type locality from the pine barrens of Kentucky. W. B. Davis (1939) described the populations of this mouse in eastern Texas under the name *P. l. brevicaudus*. However, St. Romain (1975), in a review of geographic variation in populations of this species in Texas and Louisiana, has demonstrated that *brevicaudus* is a race not morphologically distinct from *P. l. leucopus*.

Distribution and habitat. The white-footed mouse occurs in most of the timbered regions of eastern Texas (Map 38), but it is most common in the oak-hickory belt of the post oak woodlands. It is one of the rarest small mammals in the upland pine-oak forests of the north central part of the region and is completely absent from the lowland pine-hardwood forests in the Big Thicket. In the coastal prairie and blackland prairie regions, *P. leucopus* occurs only along the forested margins of the streams.

Considerable field study of this species by Howard McCarley (1954b, 1963) revealed that in the pine-oak and pine forest regions these mice are restricted in their ecological distribution to upland wooded habitats. Occasionally, the ecological ranges of *P. leucopus* and *P. gossypinus* overlap, and in these areas they are generally separated ecologically, with *leuco-*

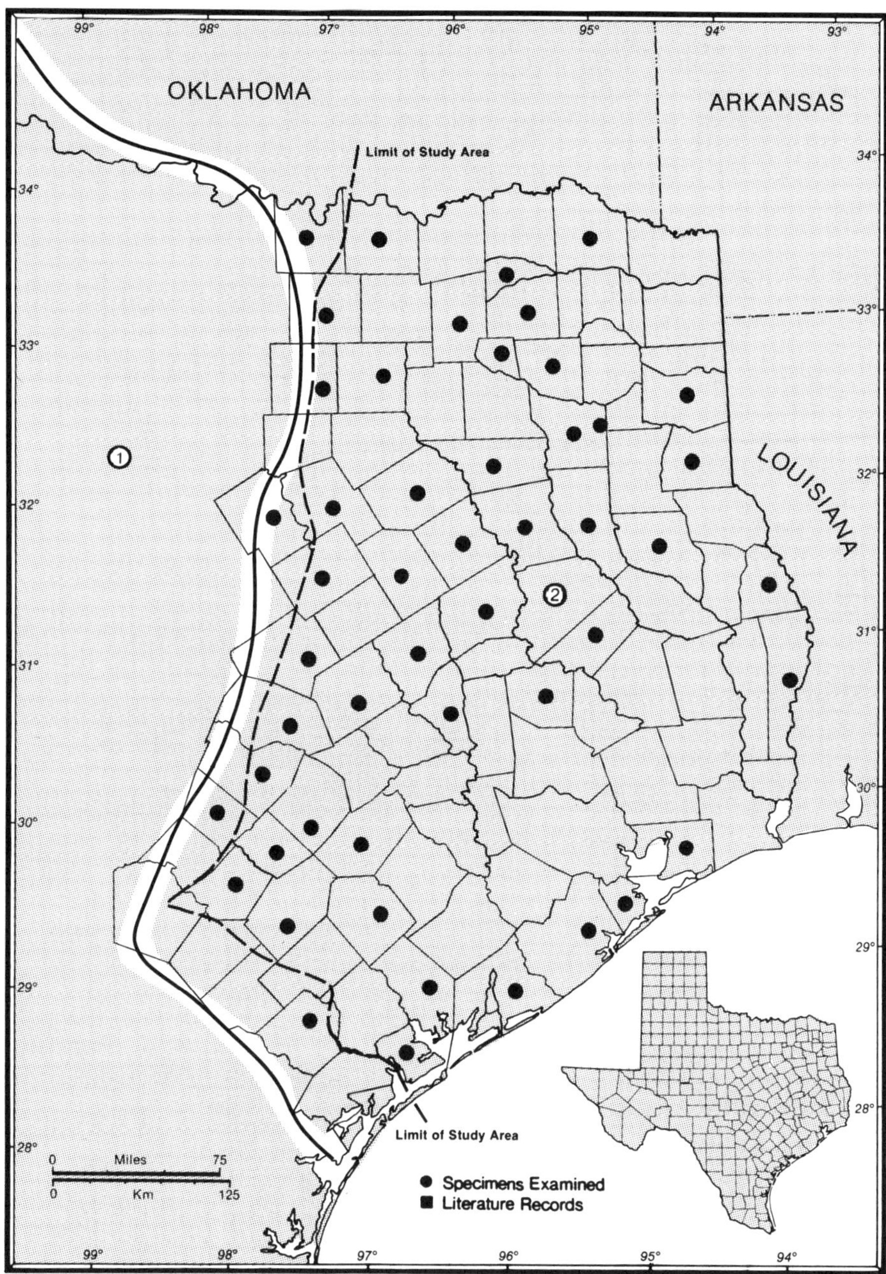

MAP 38. Distribution of the white-footed mouse, *Peromyscus leucopus*. 1. *P. l. texanus*. 2. *P. l. leucopus*.

pus occurring in upland situations and *gossypinus* in the lowlands. During periods of population highs the ecological ranges of the two species frequently overlap. However, *P. leucopus* is generally less abundant in sympatric areas than is *P. gossypinus*.

Life history. These mice build their nests in hollow trees, under logs, beneath stumps, around brush piles, in underground burrows, or in buildings. They may also occupy an old nest of a bird or squirrel. They do not make use of runways.

There is some evidence that this species makes extensive use of arboreal nesting sites. Taylor and McCarley (1963) designed some experiments to determine whether *P. leucopus* and *P. gossypinus* construct nests at different heights. Using an outdoor enclosure, containing both elevated and ground-level nest boxes, these authors noted an overwhelming preference for the elevated sites for both *leucopus* and *gossypinus* when tested individually. However, when tested together, *leucopus* continued to select the elevated sites, whereas *gossypinus* showed a preference for the ground-level boxes. These observations may be indicative of a species discrimination mechanism between these two species.

Little is known about the population dynamics of this species in eastern Texas. Waggoner (1975, 1978) found it to be the most common rodent in a woodland area of Freestone County. Population density averaged 3.5 animals per ha over a fourteen-month period, with peaks occurring in December, January, and February (average, 7 animals per ha). White-footed mice exhibited a large home range, with that of males averaging 1.6 ha compared to 0.7 ha for females; the average for both sexes was 1.2 ha. Mean longevity for individuals residing on the woodlot was only 1.7 months, indicating a high mortality rate, emigration rate, or both. Known predators include owls, foxes, weasels, feral house cats, and snakes.

White-footed mice breed year round, but most young are born in late fall and early winter. The young, which number between one and six (average four), are born after a gestation period of twenty-two to twenty-five days. They are born blind, helpless, and pink, weighing only about 2 g. They acquire hair on the dorsum after twenty-four hours, and the eyes open at about thirteen days. They are weaned at twenty-two to twenty-three days and become sexually mature at ten to eleven weeks of age.

Little is known about the behavior of these mice. Under laboratory conditions, individuals are gregarious and promiscuous (Bradshaw, 1965). Males frequently fight, and one individual typically dominates the others. Individuals are nervous and high-strung, always scurrying for cover and seldom leaving the nest.

In contrast to the food of cotton mice (*P. gossypinus*), that of *P. leucopus* is decidedly herbivorous. Favored foods include seeds, plant leaves and stalks, acorn and pecan nuts, and fungi. These mice may on occasion prey on insects, snails, and other invertebrates.

Remarks. McCarley (1954a) reported natural hybrids between *P. leucopus* and *P. gossypinus* from localities in Henderson and Nacogdoches counties. Two individuals were identified as hybrids on the basis that they were morphologically intermediate between the two species. Subsequently, Engstrom et al. (1982) demonstrated that the two individuals in question are actually not morphologically intermediate when similar age groups of the two species are compared. While this evidence in and of itself does not conclusively prove that the two species do not hybridize in eastern Texas, it does raise doubts about this supposition. The two species are interfertile and produce morphologically intermediate F_1 and backcross generations in the laboratory (Dice, 1937, 1940); however, when given the opportunity of assortive mating, no apparent hybrids are produced (Bradshaw, 1968). The mice apparently discriminate and prefer association with their own species.

References. Bradshaw, 1965, 1968; Calhoun, 1941; W. B. Davis, 1974; McCarley, 1954a, 1954b, 1959d, 1963; Waggoner, 1975, 1978.

Golden Mouse
Ochrotomys nuttalli (Harlan)

Name. The first part of the scientific name, *Ochrotomys*, is from two Greek words (*ochra* and *mys*) meaning "yellow-ochre or golden mouse." The last part is a latinized name meaning "of Nuttall" in commemoration of Thomas Nuttall (1786–1859), who was an early American naturalist.

Identification. This medium-sized mouse is very similar to the white-footed mouse (*Peromyscus leucopus*) and the cotton mouse (*Peromyscus gossypinus*) and is distinguished by its uniquely burnished to golden dorsal pelage coloration. The underparts are creamy white with an ochraceous wash, and the entire pelage is extremely dense and soft. Young golden mice are grayish brown and start to acquire their orange-brown color a few days after birth. Average external measurements are total length, 172 mm; tail, 80 mm; hind foot, 19 mm; ear, 17 mm.

Subspecies. Golden mice in eastern Texas are referable to the subspecies *Ochrotomys nuttalli lisae*, which was described by Packard (*Univ. Kansas Misc. Publ. Mus. Nat. Hist.*, 51:398, July 11, 1969) with type locality at the La Nana Creek bottoms in Nacogdoches, Nacogdoches County, Texas.

Distribution and habitat. This species is characteristic of the deciduous hardwood and pine stands of the southeastern United States. It reaches the western limits of its distribution in eastern Texas, where it has been recorded from nineteen different counties in the pine-oak and pine forest regions (Map 39). The golden mouse has been recorded as far west as Houston, Anderson, Wood, and Red River counties. It is absent from the coastal prairie region and from the oak-hickory forest.

Favored habitat includes heavily forested hardwood floodplain, upland pine-oak woodland, and hillsides with considerable lianas such as grapevine and honeysuckle. The main factor controlling its ecological distribution appears to be groundcover, particularly the amount of underbrush and vine entanglements. Densely thicketed underbrush is most often encountered where the upland forest meets the floodplain forest.

Golden mouse, *Ochrotomys nuttalli*.

Golden mice are scarce in floodplain situations with a complete overhead canopy of tall trees that shut out the sunlight from the forest floor and consequently reduce the amount of undergrowth.

Life history. Golden mice are relatively docile, semiarboreal rodents. Their prehensile tail is used as a balancing organ while climbing and moving in vines and trees. They wrap the tail around a branch or vine to stabilize themselves while resting. Using their tail, they may hang almost at right angles from a branch with only the hind feet assisting in support. Activity is mainly crepuscular and nocturnal.

Golden mice live in globular nests positioned in and under fallen logs or in trees and vines. Arboreal nests, which are used for both nurseries and feeding platforms, are constructed in entanglements of greenbriar, honeysuckle, or grapevines in various species of deciduous trees but not in coniferous trees (Packard and Garner, 1964). Most nests are located from 1.8 to 4.6 m above ground in trees ranging from 6.1 to 9.1 m high. Arboreal nesting is of adaptive value to golden mice because it allows them to avoid the detrimental effects of flooding. The average nest is 15 to 20 cm long, 10 to 12 cm wide, 10 to 20 cm high, and usually weighs between 10 and 30 g (Packard and Garner, 1964). An opening, about 25 mm in diameter and often partially closed, is present at one end of the nest. Nests consist of two distinct layers. The outer covering is mainly of deciduous leaves, grasses, or Spanish moss. The inner chamber is constructed of finely shredded bark, grasses, feathers, fur, cloth, and other similar materials.

Golden mice are gregarious in their social behavior, as evidenced by the fact that several individuals may occupy the same nest. McCarley (1959a) also noted a tendency for pairs to remain together during the breeding season. There is considerable overlap of home ranges of individ-

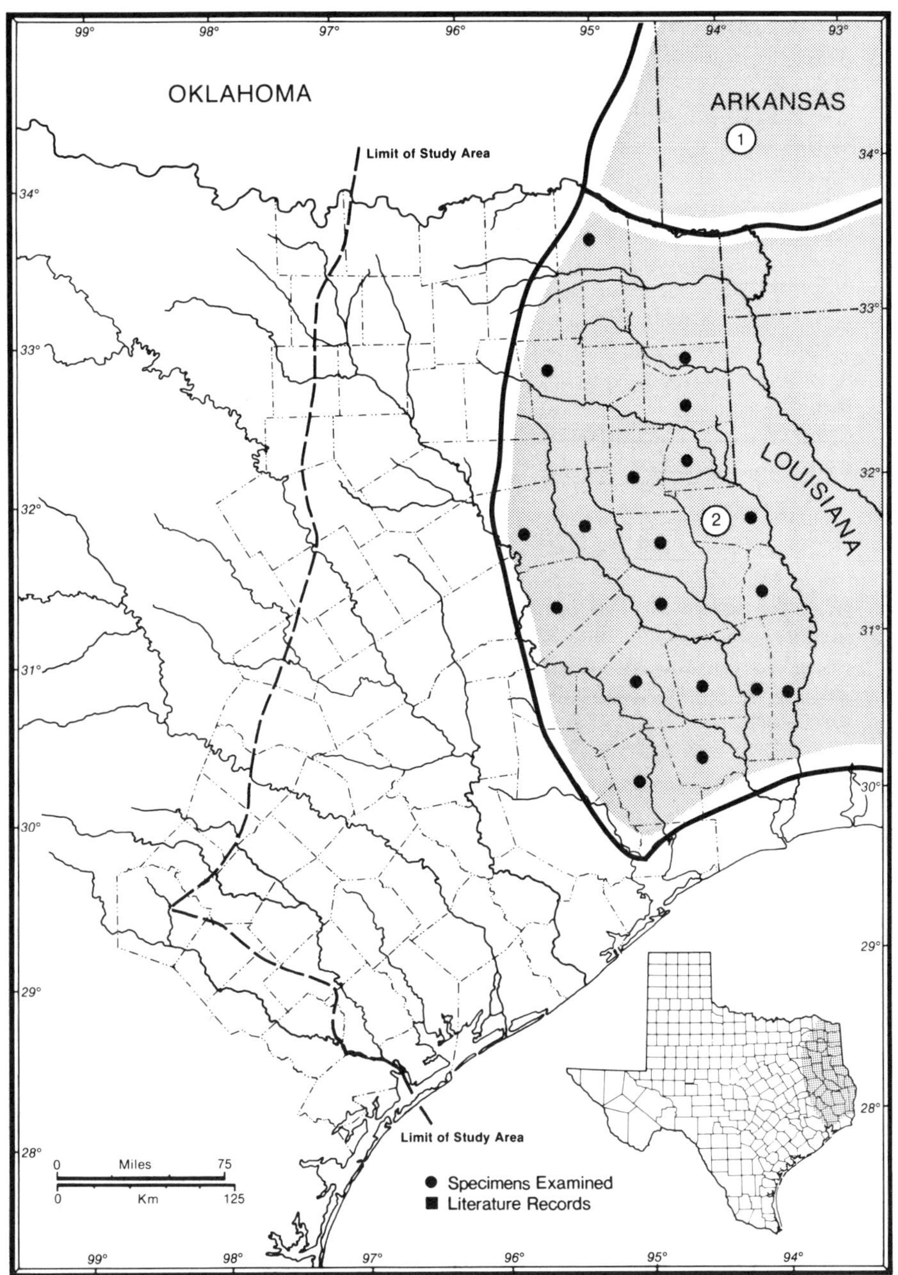

MAP 39. Distribution of the golden mouse, *Ochrotomys nuttalli*. 1. *O. n. flammeus*. 2. *O. n. lisae*.

uals, suggesting that territoriality is not well developed in this species.

McCarley (1958) studied the population dynamics of golden mice in Nacogdoches County. Population density ranged from none in summer to as many as 5.4 individuals per ha in early spring. Home range in the same area averaged 0.59 ha for males and 0.57 ha for females. Sex ratios in McCarley's study did not deviate from the expected 1:1. The average life span of this species was approximately 6.5 months, with the oldest animal, an adult male, living for 19 months in the study area. McCarley (1959b) noted that flooding caused a differential rate of mortality between *Peromyscus gossypinus* (less arboreal) and *O. nuttalli*. About 60 percent of a population of *P. gossypinus* remained after flooding, whereas 84 percent of the *O. nuttalli* population was still alive.

The breeding season begins in September and extends through winter and spring, with little reproduction during summer months. The peak breeding period is in winter (January and February). Adult females may produce as many as three litters annually. The young, ranging in number from two to five (average three), are born following a gestation period of twenty-five to thirty days. Golden mice have been observed copulating above ground on grapevines (Packard and Garner, 1964).

Newborn golden mice weigh about 2.7 g and are reddish with relatively smooth skin. The eyelids are sealed, as are the folded-over pinnae. By day seven, the dorsum is covered by a sleek, velvety, reddish brown pelage, and the young are identifiable as golden mice. The lower incisors erupt the gumline at day six, and the upper incisors between days seven and eight. The eyes open between days eleven to fourteen. Weaning begins about day seventeen or eighteen and is completed by day twenty-one. Adult size is attained between the eighth and tenth weeks, and reproductive maturity is reached after one or two months.

Invertebrates make up about 50 percent of their diet. They also eat a variety of seeds, including sumac, wild cherry, dogwood, greenbriar, poison ivy, and blackberry.

References. Goodpasture and Hoffmeister, 1954; Linzey and Packard, 1977; McCarley, 1958, 1959a, 1959b; Packard, 1969; Packard and Garner, 1964.

Northern Pygmy Mouse
Baiomys taylori (Thomas)

Name. The name *Baiomys* is derived from two Greek words, *baios*, meaning "little" or "insignificant," and *mys*, meaning "mouse," in reference to the diminutive size of this species. The name *taylori* is a latinized word meaning "of Taylor" and honors the person who collected the type specimen of this species.

Identification. This is the smallest of the cricetine mice in eastern Texas, with the exception of two harvest mice (*Reithrodontomys humulis* and *R. montanus*), both of which differ in having grooved upper incisors and longer tails. The color of the upper parts is grizzled and grayish; that

Northern pygmy mouse, *Baiomys taylori*.

of the underparts, smoke gray. The tail is sparsely haired and decidedly shorter than the head and body. The ears are small and slightly more rounded than in *Peromyscus*. Average external measurements are total length, 106 mm; tail, 44 mm; hind foot, 14 mm; ear, 11 mm.

Subspecies. Two subspecies occur in eastern Texas (Map 40). *Baiomys taylori subater* (named by V. Bailey, *North Amer. Fauna*, 25:102, October 24, 1905—type locality from Bernard Creek, near Columbia, Brazoria County, Texas) is from the coastal prairies in the southeastern part of the region (from Matagorda Bay west to Lavaca County, north to Brazos and Walker counties, and thence east to Hardin and Jefferson counties). *Baiomys taylori taylori* (named by Thomas, *Ann. Mag. Nat. Hist.*, 19:66, January 1887—type locality from San Diego, Duval County, Texas) is from the remainder of the region. The subspecies *subater* differs from *taylori* in having a blackish instead of grayish mid-dorsal region and slightly larger cranial measurements (Packard, 1960).

Distribution and habitat. This is a southern species, characteristic of the tropical lowlands in Mexico, that reaches its northern distributional limits in eastern Texas. Early records (Bailey, 1905) indicate that *Baiomys taylori* was restricted to the coastal prairie region of eastern Texas and the mesquite-chaparral regions of southern Texas. Since the early twentieth century, the species has apparently expanded its range northward by invading the oak-hickory association and the blackland prairies (Hunsaker et al., 1959), where it has been recorded as far north as Denton, Tarrant, and Dallas counties (Map 40). In the past ten years, the pygmy mouse has invaded typical Austroriparian habitat (pine-oak forest), as evidenced by a record from Harrison County on the Texas-Louisiana border (Baccus and Greer, 1971). This movement has been taking place along grassland corridors, opened by agriculture, through the oak-hickory forests.

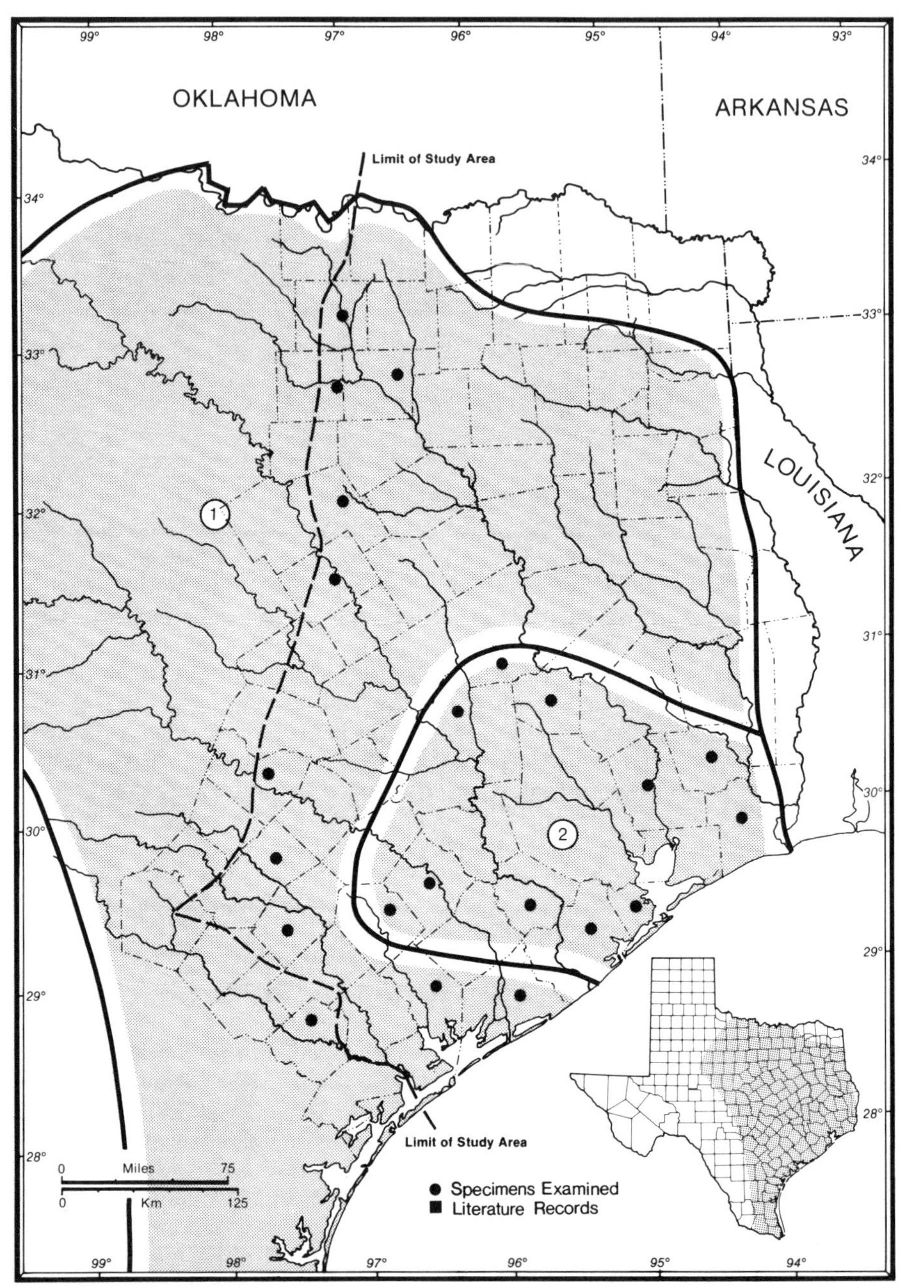

MAP 40. Distribution of the northern pygmy mouse, *Baiomys taylori.* 1. *B. t. taylori.* 2. *B. t. subater.*

These mice have a preference for grassy areas, and they are commonly found in old fields, pastures, and along railroad and highway rights-of-way, where they usually live in association with the cotton rat (*Sigmodon hispidus*). If other types of ground cover such as rocks, cactus, and fallen logs are available, the pygmy mouse may be found in areas where grass is relatively sparse. This species has been collected in the following specific ecological situations in eastern Texas: Dallas County, in a grassy area along the margin of a fallow field supporting a scattered cover of short brush and prickly pear (Hunsaker et al., 1959); Freestone County, an abandoned field (Waggoner, 1975); Brazos County, in old fields, pastures, cultivated fields, and both mowed and unmowed highway rights-of-way (Wilkins and Schmidly, 1977); Walker County, in broomsedge on the border of pine woods (Taylor and Davis, 1947); Jefferson County, in a small area of dense bluestem surrounding a pond on a low, moist coastal prairie (Blair, 1941); Galveston County, in grassy-covered runways of an orchard (Bailey, 1905); Fort Bend County, under a rich carpet of grass on the open prairie (ibid.); Travis County, in areas of mesquite brush with only sparse grass (Hunsaker et al., 1959); Gonzales County, in rocky ledges with a scattered cover of bluestem and in a marshy flat supporting cordgrass, willow, and common reed as well as in grassy meadows (ibid.); and in a deciduous forest near a swamp (Blair, 1952).

Life history. Pygmy mice live in nests placed in burrows in the ground, beneath fallen logs, among cactus pads, or in thick clumps of grass. The nest is typically a ball of finely shredded grass or cactus fibers with a central cavity and one or two openings. The nest cavity usually contains some fur. A network of runways or beaten paths, similar to but much smaller than those used by cotton rats (*Sigmodon hispidus*), leads away from the nest sites beneath the thick mat of dead grass.

The population dynamics of this species have been investigated along highway rights-of-way and adjacent old fields near College Station in Brazos County (Wilkins and Schmidly, 1980). In old fields, densities were remarkably stable, averaging two animals per ha in fall and spring and three per ha during winter and summer. Density was greatest in the unmowed highway right-of-way (fifteen per ha) during winter, when that of cotton rats was least. Pygmy mice were least abundant (one per ha) during summer at a time when cotton rat populations peaked. Intermediate densities were recorded during fall (eleven per ha) and spring (four per ha). The presence of high populations of cotton rats seems to depress populations of pygmy mice.

Pygmy mice are not very wide-ranging rodents. Home ranges of males average only 0.6 ha, and that of females is slightly less (0.4 ha). There appears to be some relationship between the density of cover and the size of an individual's home range, with home ranges being greater in areas of relatively heavy cover and smaller in the areas of less cover. There is considerable overlap in home ranges, both of males and females, suggesting a lack, or at least a low level, of territoriality in this species.

Population turnover is rapid, with an estimated mean minimum longevity of about five months (Raun and Wilks, 1964).

Pygmy mice breed throughout the year, with peaks in winter, spring, and late fall. Apparently there is no period of complete reproductive quiescence. Pregnant females carry an average of 2.6 embryos, ranging from 2 to 4. The gestation period is not more than twenty days. This litter size is relatively small for a rodent with a short ecological longevity; however, the frequency of breeding is apparently great enough to offset any negative effects of small litter size. There is no evidence as to the frequency of litter production in the field, but in the laboratory one pair of mice produced nine litters in 202 days, an average of one litter every 25 days, and another pair averaged a litter every 31 days (Blair, 1941). These data suggest that individuals are capable of breeding in rapid succession in the wild.

Young *Baiomys* are pink at birth, but become darkly pigmented within twenty-four hours. Shortly after birth they become attached to the mammae of the mother and are dragged about wherever she goes. If the young are forcibly detached, the male or female picks them up in the mouth and carries them into the nest, and they soon become reattached to the mammae. The young remain constantly attached to the mother until they are from eighteen to twenty-two days old. Apparently they are weaned at about the time they become detached. The eyes of the young open between the ages of twelve and fifteen days. Sexual maturity is reached at an average of about sixty days.

Pygmy mice are much less inclined to fight among themselves than are captive *Peromyscus*, and the males, unlike *Peromyscus* males, assist the females in caring for the young. Thus, social tolerence seems to be quite high in this species.

These mice are primarily herbivorous, eating such items as grass seeds and leaves, mesquite beans, and prickly pear cactus. However, animal food is apparently an integral part of their diet, and they are not strictly herbivorous. For example, they are known to readily eat snails (*Helicina orbiculata*) in captivity (C. Johnson, 1959). Similar observations of their carnivorous behavior were made by Pitts (1978), who kept twelve *B. taylori* in a terrarium for several months, during which time they were fed a diet of sunflower seeds, lettuce, carrots, and apples *ad libitum*. Despite the abundance of herbaceous food, pygmy mice killed and consumed small snakes (*Leptotyphlops dulcis* and *Tropidoclonion lineatum*) and insects of the families Tenebrionidae and Acrididae when these items were placed in the terrarium. Harvest mice (*Reithrodontomys*), in the same chamber with the *Baiomys*, neither killed nor ate the reptiles or insects.

Pygmy mice constitute one of the primary prey species for a variety of vertebrates. Snakes are probably their chief predators, particularly rattlesnakes (*Crotalus atrox*) and coachwhips (*Masticophis flagellum*). Mammalian predators include coyotes, raccoons, and striped skunks. Possible avian predators include several kinds of hawks and owls.

References. Blair, 1941; Packard, 1960; Raun and Wilks, 1964; Stickel and Stickel, 1949.

Hispid Cotton Rat
Sigmodon hispidus Say and Ord

Name. The generic name *Sigmodon* is derived from two Greek words, *sigma*, which is the Greek equivalent of the letter S, and *odus*, meaning "tooth"; these refer to the S-shaped enamel loops on the grinding surfaces of the cheek teeth. The last part of the name, *hispidus*, is the Latin word for "rough," in reference to the animal's coarse pelage.

Identification. This is a medium-sized rat with a coarse pelage of dark brownish to blackish hairs, interspersed with yellow or light tan hairs. The sides are only slightly paler, while the underparts are usually pale to dark grayish, sometimes faintly washed with buff. The overall pelage has a strong hispid and grizzled appearance, resulting from the abundance of large bristly hairs and blackish coloration. The feet are blackish, as is the scantily haired, indistinctly bicolored, somewhat scaly tail. The ears are not especially large, but they do extend well above the fur of the head and shoulders. Average external measurements are total length, 257 mm; tail, 99 mm; hind foot, 31 mm; ear, 19 mm.

Subspecies. There is but one subspecies in eastern Texas, *Sigmodon hispidus texianus*, which was named by Audubon and Bachman (*The viviparous quadrupeds of North America*, 3:229, 1853) with type locality from the Brazos River, Texas.

Distribution and habitat. The cotton rat occurs throughout eastern Texas in all vegetative regions (Map 41). During periods when conditions are especially favorable, it is probably present in greater numbers than any other mammal native to this region.

Optimum cotton rat habitat includes well-drained areas with lush, dense ground vegetation. Grass height and density are important components of their habitat. Tight stands of grass, such as broomsedge, bluestem, Johnson grass, and bermudagrass, seem to be preferred. In such situations a typical cotton rat "sign" consists of runways cleared beneath an overhanging layer of grass between the crowns at the ground surface. Areas with less dense grass stands are not as favored. However, in locations such as brush tangles and thick stands of tall weeds where an overhanging cover is provided, rats may be found in numbers. In such locations runways are less well defined but nonetheless present.

Typical habitat for cotton rats is found in a variety of ecological situations including uncultivated fields, meadows, along fence rows around the edges of plowed fields, along the grassy banks of streams and ditches, and along highway and railroad rights-of-way. In the oak-hickory, pine, and pine-oak regions these rats are largely confined to open fields, either cultivated or those which have grown up in grass and weeds, but where the successional stage is not advanced enough to include large woody vegetation. The species is widely distributed in areas of mixed grass and

Cotton rat, *Sigmodon hispidus*.

brush in the coastal prairie region, but it is not very common in the coastal marshes themselves. In the lowland areas of the Big Thicket, cotton rats are common in open, grassy habitats such as pine plantation grassland, pine savanna wetland, and clear-cut areas. They normally do not occur in stream or floodplain forests and only rarely occur in other woodland habitats.

Life history. More research has been conducted on the natural history of this species than any other small mammal occurring in eastern Texas. Recently, two review articles (Cleveland, 1979; Cameron and Spencer, 1981) have synthesized much of the literature concerning the natural history of this species, and they constitute the basis for much of the following account.

Cotton rats construct nests in shallow depressions or under a variety of natural or man-made objects, such as fallen logs, in abandoned holes, in rubbish heaps, and under pieces of tin in pastureland. Surface and burrow nests are made of woven grass and range from cup-shaped to hollow ball-shaped structures with a single entrance (Halloran, 1942).

The runway constitutes their basic "habitat unit." Runways consist of a network of interconnecting travelways about 5 to 8 cm wide. These runways are extensively used by other small mammals such as shrews, deer mice, harvest mice, pygmy mice, and house mice.

Cotton rats may be active at all hours of the day and night. In warmer months, they generally exhibit a crespuscular activity pattern with activity peaks at 7:00 P.M. and 9:00 A.M.; in colder months diurnal movement may be as extensive and frequent as nocturnal movement (Cameron et al., 1979a). It is difficult to describe their movement patterns because they are affected by a variety of factors, including population density, availability of cover, and reproductive stage. Nevertheless, the available

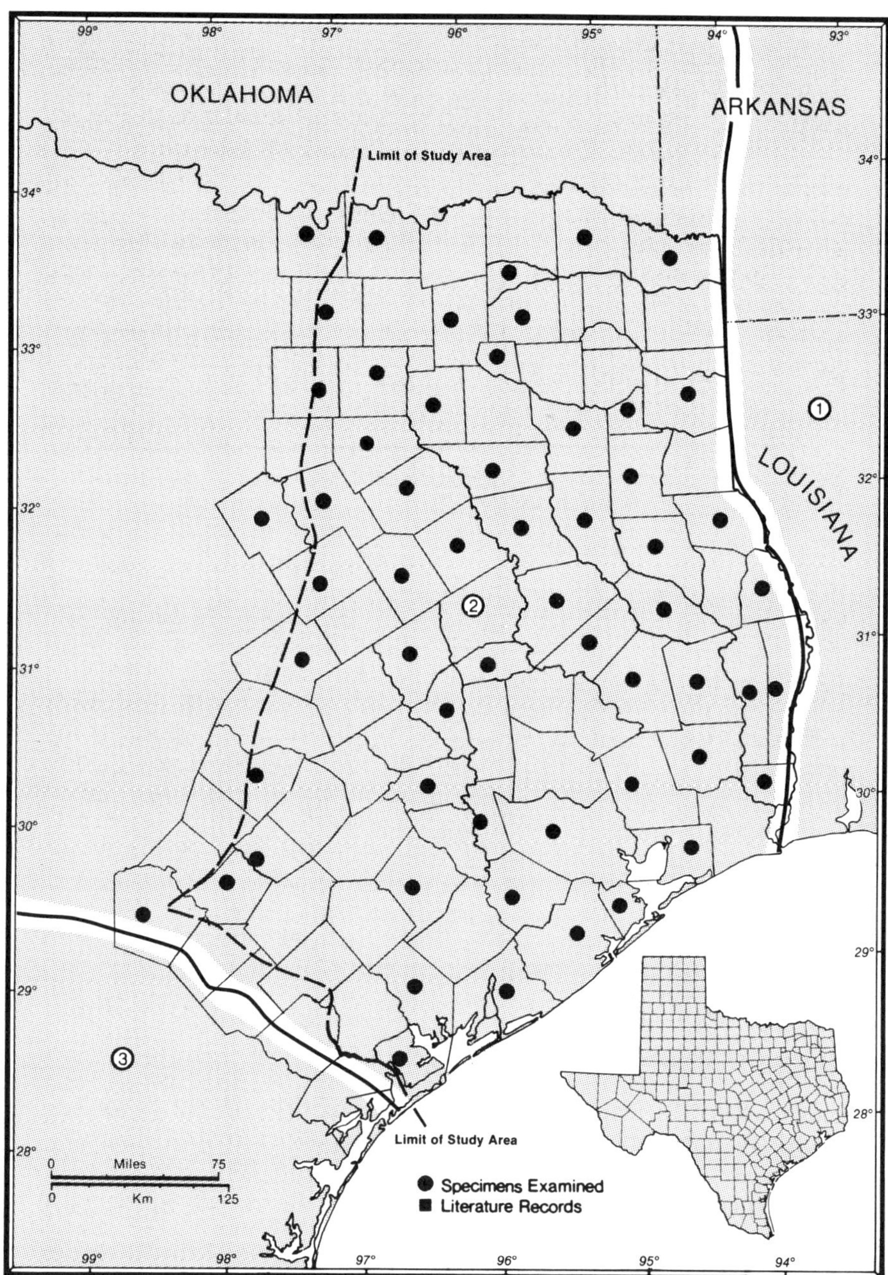

MAP 41. Distribution of the cotton rat, *Sigmodon hispidus*. 1. *S. h. hispidus*. 2. *S. h. texianus*. 3. *S. h. berlandieri*.

data suggest that these rodents are rather sedentary and do not move great distances. Cameron et al. (1979b) estimated the average daily movement of *Sigmodon* to be about 13 m, with males moving farther (17 m) than females (6.6 m). These authors also determined that adult males move farther than young adult males and that reproductive males move farther than nonreproductive males; there were no differences in movements among female groups. In addition to moving less than males, females also exhibited exclusive home ranges, suggesting that their requirements are satisfied with smaller, higher-quality home ranges.

Dispersal of *S. hispidus* is positively correlated with density (Joule and Cameron, 1975). Rather than representing a single or subset of age or sex classes, dispersers reflect a representative template of the resident population structure. This means that the sex ratio and age structure of dispersers are similar to those of the source population. The sex ratio of cotton rat populations approximates a 1:1 ratio. This rank-order templated dispersal strategy has the advantage of introducing a stabilized age structure into newly acquired habitat space.

Roads seem to be effective barriers to cotton rat movements (Joule and Cameron, 1974; Wilkins and Schmidly, 1977). Of the 1,572 *S. hispidus* marked in highway rights-of-way habitat around College Station in Brazos County, only 86 (5 percent) were known to cross pavements (Wilkins and Schmidly, 1977). At least twice as many cotton rats (60 individuals) crossed roadways in areas where right-of-way habitats were not mowed compared to areas that were mowed (26 individuals).

Cotton rat density patterns show within-year seasonal changes, probably cued by temperature trends, but the pattern seems to vary in different parts of the region. In coastal prairie habitat in Harris County, Cameron (1977) recorded a bimodal density response with spring and autumn peaks (9.4 per ha) and summer and winter lows (2.8 per ha). In abandoned fields in Brazos County, Wilkins and Schmidly (1980) reported maximum densities in fall (29 per ha) and early summer (24 per ha), with minimum densities in winter (11 per ha) and spring (9 per ha). Waggoner (1975) reported maximum densities in abandoned fields in Freestone County in the summer months of June (51 per ha) and July (54 per ha), with minimums in the winter months of January (6 per ha) and February (6 per ha).

There appears to be a strong correlation between population density of cotton rats and habitat quality, particularly the extent of vegetative cover. Wilkins (1977) found the mean annual density of cotton rats was almost three times higher in unmowed highway rights-of-way compared to those that had been mowed. Waggoner (1975) found cotton rats were the dominant rodent on an unreclaimed strip-mined area that had grown up in annual composites, weeds, and crimson clover until cattle were introduced onto the area, which resulted in a grazing away of heavy vegetation and a concomitant drop in the cotton rat population.

Populations of cotton rats are cyclical and subject to extreme fluctuations in density, somewhat comparable to population cycles of certain rabbits and rodents of more northern regions. Strecker (1929:216) stated that cotton rats in McLennan County were scarce in 1927, but that by June 1928, "Without going more than two or three yards from the road dividing the field and garden, it is possible for one to capture or kill a dozen or more of the rats in a few minutes time. . . ." A similar rise and decline in numbers of cotton rats during the summers of 1958, 1959, and 1960 was geographically widespread over much of eastern Texas (Haines, 1963). According to reports, the population built up rapidly in 1958 to a peak and then started to decline slowly. After the summer of 1959, a rapid die-off occurred. A variety of factors have been postulated by mammalogists to account for these "cyclic" fluctuations, including rainfall cycles, parasitism, and protracted periods of temperature extremes (Cleveland, 1979).

Complete population turnover occurs in cotton rat populations within nine to eleven months. The average longevity for individuals of this species is between 2.0 and 2.6 months, with females living slightly longer than males (Cameron, 1977; Waggoner, 1975). Longevity is most likely related to a combination of factors such as cover thickness, predator density, and parasite load. Cotton rats are a basic food for many predators including owls, hawks, snakes, coyotes, cats, and dogs, and predation undoubtedly plays a major role in mortality. Environmental stress, particularly temperature extremes, also is important. Prolonged low ambient temperatures, as well as unseasonal sudden changes in temperature, increase mortality.

Cotton rats support a variety of ectoparasites, encysted cestodes, and visceral trematodes, cestodes, and nematodes (Hugghins, 1951). Parasites have been suggested as a possible factor in large-scale population reduction in this species (Cleveland, 1979). *Sigmodon hispidus* also is a reservoir for a number of human diseases, including rabies, Chagas' disease, and Venezuelan equine encephalomyelitis (Cameron and Spencer, 1981).

Interspecific interactions have been reported between *S. hispidus* and other rodents in eastern Texas. Cotton rats compete with pygmy mice (*Baiomys taylori*) for favorable habitat and through aggression displace the latter into marginal areas (Raun and Wilks, 1964). However, Kincaid and Cameron (1982) have demonstrated that the effects of competition are minimal in the determination of resource utilization between cotton rats and fulvous harvest mice (*Reithrodontomys fulvescens*) in coastal prairie habitats.

Cotton rats breed throughout the year in eastern Texas, but they exhibit reproductive peaks during certain seasons, the timing of which varies geographically. Cameron (1977) reported reproductive peaks in fall and spring in coastal prairie habitat in Harris County. Wilkins and Schmidly (1977) noted peaks during spring and mid-summer among populations in Brazos County, and Waggoner (1975) recorded a similar pattern in a population inhabiting an old field in Freestone County. The young, which range in number between 2 and 7 (average, 4.8), are born following a gestation period of twenty-seven days. Females may undergo a postpartum mating between three and six hours after parturition.

Young are born with a sparse hair covering. They are vigorously active soon after birth and open their eyes within thirty-six hours. Female cotton rats make exceptionally fine mothers. Mothers generally will not kill their young even after they have been handled by humans. When picked up, the young emit frequent, high-pitched, one-note squeaks, which may attract an adult to within a few feet of the nest. Young cotton rats grow rapidly, gaining about 1 or 2 g per day (Waggoner, 1975). They can be weaned at ten to fifteen days of age. Although maximum body size is not reached until the sixth month, sexual maturity in cotton rats is achieved two months after birth. Females have been impregnated as early as thirty-eight days after birth by males of the same age. Few reach maximum size, since a majority do not live long enough.

Grass and grasslike plants available in the habitat are their preferred food. Inglis (1955) examined the stomach contents of twenty-eight cotton rats collected in Brazos County and found that 93 percent of the stomachs contained monocotyledon plants (Gramineae, Typhaceae), 39 percent contained forbs, and 36 percent contained insects. The most characteristic feeding technique is the harvesting of grass seeds by cutting culms into lengths and dragging them through overhanging vegetation into the runway. Food is cut with a diagonal slash of the incisors, held in the forefeet, and eaten. Often in locations with high cotton rat populations, plant stems are cut indiscriminately, with the greater mass of the vegetation left standing, held up by its own bulk. Insects are stripped of their wings, legs, and other appendages and eaten.

S. hispidus is a solitary species. The only prolonged social contact is between male and female, and the extent of this interaction depends on the female's reproductive status. Agonistic behavior is pronounced and is seemingly an important factor influencing social organization. Social behavior in this species is characterized by a relative dominance system in which males are dominant over females and adults are dominant over subadults. The development of behavioral traits in young cotton rats is so rapid that young can survive without maternal assistance at five days of age.

Homing behavior is well developed in cotton rats. Debusk and Kennerly (1975) found that homing occurred from distances of 100 m to 1,500 m with success decreasing with distance. Of 266 rats displaced, 112 successfully returned to their home area, with the highest proportion being those displaced up to 300 m. They concluded that cotton rats released up to 300 m away from their home areas were probably still on familiar grounds but that either navigation or random wandering were involved in instances of longer homing.

References. Cameron et al., 1979a, 1979b; Cameron and Spencer, 1981; Cleveland, 1979; Debusk and Kennerly, 1975; Haines, 1961, 1963, 1971; Halloran, 1942; Hugghins, 1951; Inglis, 1955; Joule and Cameron, 1974, 1975; Raun and Wilks, 1964; Schmidly and Wilkins, 1977; Strecker, 1929; Waggoner, 1975, 1978.

Eastern Woodrat
Neotoma floridana (Ord)

Name. Neotoma is derived from two Greek words, *neos*, meaning "new," and *tomos*, meaning "cut," in reference to a new kind of mammal with cutting teeth. The last part of the name, *floridana*, is a latinized word meaning "of Florida," which is the state where the species was first collected and described.

Identification. The eastern woodrat is a large rat with a relatively short, sparsely haired tail that is slightly less than half the total length. Its pelage is soft and smooth, its ears are exceptionally large and scantily haired, and its eyes are large and bulging. The vibrissae are long, frequently reaching the tips of the ears. The color above is blackish to reddish brown with an admixture of yellow on the sides and gray on the cheeks. The underparts are white or buffy, and the tail is distinctly bicolored, blackish above and grayish white below. The feet are white and comparatively small for a rat of its overall body size. Average external measurements are total length, 393 mm; tail, 182 mm; hind foot, 39 mm; ear, 29 mm.

Subspecies. There are three subspecies in eastern Texas. *Neotoma floridana illinoensis* is known only from Bowie County and was named by A. H. Howell (*Proc. Biol. Soc. Washington*, 23:28, March 23, 1910—type locality from Wolf Lake, Union County, Illinois). Woodrats from the oak-hickory, blackland prairie, and northern pine-oak regions are referable to *N. f. attwateri*, which was named by Mearns (*Proc. U.S. Nat. Mus.*, 19:721, July 30, 1897—with type locality from Lacey's Ranch, Turtle Creek, Kerr County, Texas). Those from the southern and central part of the pine-oak belt (including the Big Thicket) are referred to the subspecies *N. f. rubida*, which was named by Bangs (*Proc. Boston Soc. Nat. Hist.*, 28:185, March, 1898—with type locality from Gibson, Terrebonne Parish, Louisiana). Birney (1973) has recently reviewed geographic variation and the status of subspecies for this species.

Distribution and habitat. Eastern woodrats occur throughout the timbered regions of eastern Texas, including the oak-hickory, pine, and pine-oak belts as well as the timbered drainage systems of the blackland prairie and upper coastal prairie (Map 42). They do not occur in the coastal prairie proper. The Guadalupe River constitutes the known southern limits of their distribution.

N. floridana occupies a wide variety of habitats, including swamplands, forested uplands, mixed hammocks, and river bottom associations. They are partial to dense, riparian growth in hardwood bottomlands and are rare or absent in dry, wooded uplands and xeric, thornbrush situations. The most important factor in their habitat is the availability of cover together with materials and structural elements for construction of dwellings. Specimens have been obtained in a spectrum of ecological situations such as around woodpiles, brush piles, trash and refuse heaps, rock out-

Eastern woodrat, *Neotoma floridana*.

crops, flood drift, abandoned houses, and the root systems of uprooted trees.

Life history. Woodrats are well known for their habit of constructing surface houses or dens composed of piles of sticks, leaves, and all sorts of available debris. These houses may reach considerable size, ranging up to 2 m in height and 1 m in diameter. Worn pathways connect different houses, and midden heaps of dung, sticks, and refuse from the animal's feeding sometimes accumulate at den entrances. When building materials are unavailable for constructing houses, woodrats live in dens that are constructed underground in burrows or around the root system of uprooted trees. A well-built, well-situated house is of extreme importance to the survival of the occupant. It provides a stable internal environment and protects the occupant from weather extremes. Houses also protect woodrats from some of the predation pressure to which other species of rodents are exposed. A burrow has the serious disadvantage, compared to a house containing nests above ground level, of being subject to flooding, particularly in areas where surface and subsurface drainage is poor. Nests within dens are constructed of grass, leaves, and twigs.

Eastern woodrats are almost strictly nocturnal. They are active all year and do not hibernate, although they tend to remain in their nests during inclement weather. Little is known of their population dynamics in eastern Texas. Lay and Baker (1938) recorded a colony of fifty to sixty woodrats that lived along a 183 m section of a gully tributary associated with a wooded stream bank in Brazos County. In a woodland area in Freestone County, Waggoner (1978) reported an average density of 2 woodrats per ha over a thirteen-month period (range, 0 to 5 per ha). Woodrats have a potentially greater longevity than most other small mammals. In the wild they may attain an age of three or four years (Sealander, 1979).

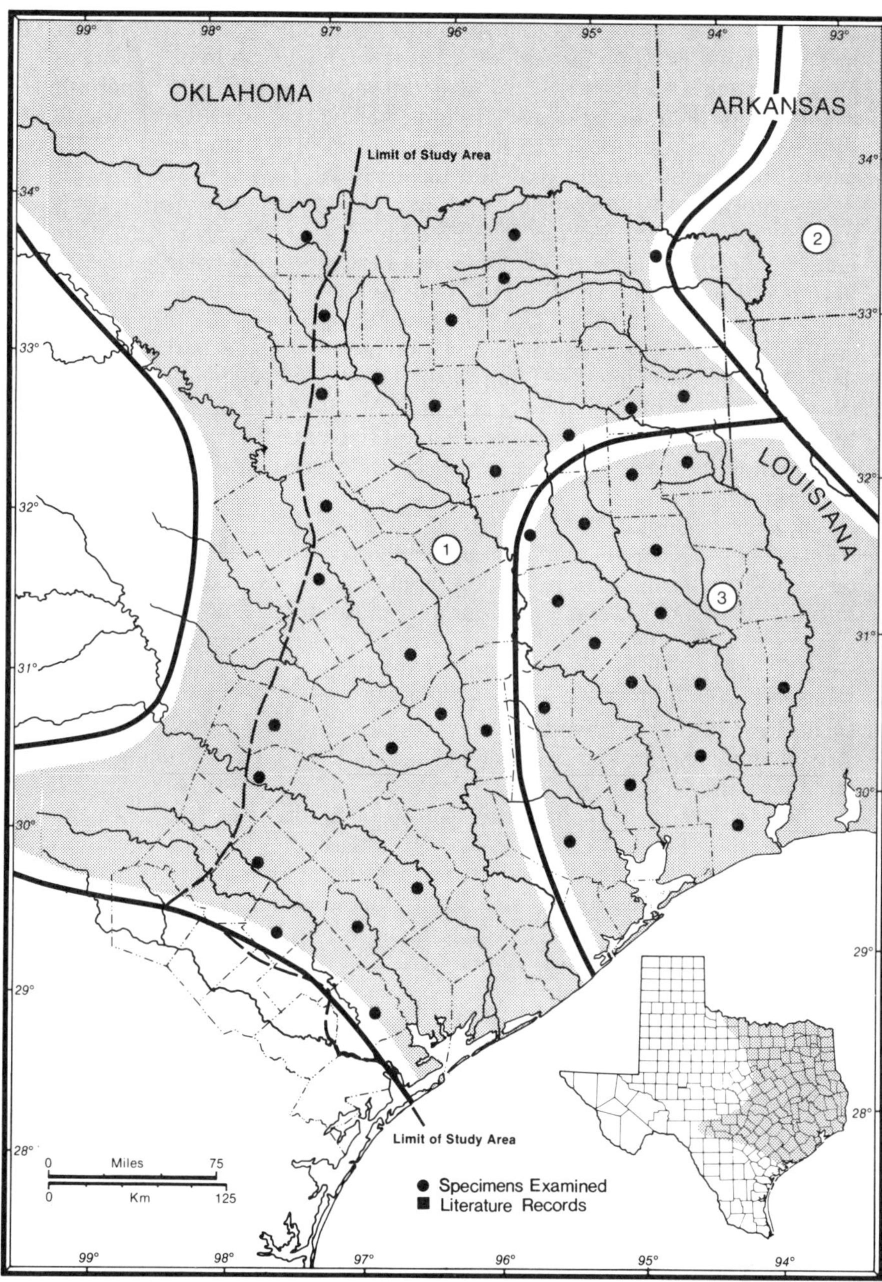

MAP 42. Distribution of the eastern woodrat, *Neotoma floridana*. 1. *N . f . attwateri*. 2. *S . f . illinoensis*. 3. *N . f . rubida*.

Eastern woodrats are rather sedentary in their movements (Tate, 1970). The average size of the home range, which is typically circular or linear in shape, is larger for males (382 m²) than females (218 m²). Females have a strong attachment to the den during the reproductive period, which limits their movements. Homing behavior is well developed in these rats. Rats released up to 400 m away from their home territory are known to return overnight (Lay and Baker, 1938).

N. floridana is polyestrous, and individual females may produce as many as three litters per year. The breeding season extends at least from January through July. Pregnant females or males with enlarged testes have been collected in the Big Thicket during January, March, April, and July (Schmidly et al., 1979). The young, which vary in number from 1 to 4 (average 2.5) are born following a gestation period of thirty to thirty-three days. Newborn woodrats are blind, deaf, naked, and weigh only 15 g. The eyes open at about fifteen days of age, and weaning takes place around the twentieth day. Woodrats do not reach adult size until they are about eight to nine months of age, and most females do not breed until they are about one year old.

Eastern woodrats demonstrate great adaptability in their feeding habits. They can thrive on almost any kind of available plant material and on occasion will eat snails and insects. Some of their favored items include nuts and leaves of water oak, walnut, and pecan trees; fruit and leaves of yaupon; cactus capsules and stems; various acorns; fruits and leaves of yaupon and hackberry; mushrooms; wild grapes; and juniper berries. Woodrats will climb trees and vines to feed, and there is evidence they cache food during the winter. They are also known to gnaw on bones strewn about the ground in order to sharpen their teeth and obtain certain minerals.

Known predators include carnivorous birds (owls and hawks), mammals (skunks, foxes, weasels, raccoons, and coyotes), and snakes (rattlesnakes and rat snakes). Woodrats serve as hosts for a great many parasites, including fleas, mites, and bot-fly larvae (*Cuterebra* sp.). I have trapped adult animals infested with as many as four bot-fly warbles; these are generally located on the woodrat's belly, in the mid-ventral region, or in the vicinity of the throat.

References. Birney, 1973; W. B. Davis, 1974; Lay and Baker, 1938; Lowery, 1974; McCarley, 1959d; Rainey, 1956; Schmidly et al., 1979; Strecker, 1929; Tate, 1970; Throckmorton, 1946; Waggoner, 1975, 1978.

Southern Plains Woodrat
Neotoma micropus Baird

Name. The derivation of the generic name *Neotoma* is explained in the previous account. The second part of the scientific name, *micropus*, is derived from the Greek words *mikros*, meaning "small" or "little," and *pous*, meaning "foot," in reference to the small foot of this species.

Identification. *N. micropus* is similar in general appearance to *N.*

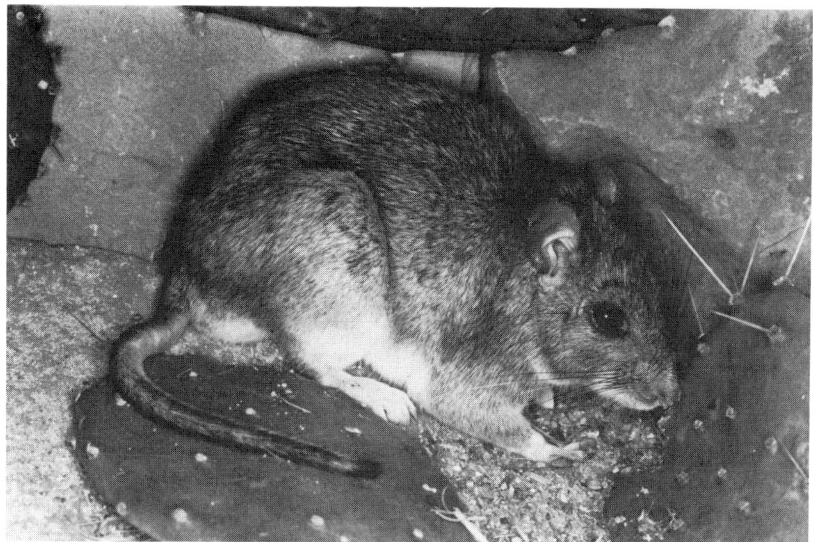

Southern plains woodrat, *Neotoma micropus*.

Young southern plains woodrat, *Neotoma micropus* (five days old).

floridana. Average external measurements are total length, 369 mm; tail, 158 mm; hind foot, 39 mm; ear, 30 mm. The primary means of distinguishing the two species over most of their range is the color of the upper parts. That of *micropus* is steely to slaty gray in contrast to the cinnamon or reddish brown color of *floridana*. However, a few specimens of *N. micropus* from South Texas and the southern part of eastern Texas are distinctly brownish and difficult to distinguish from *floridana* on the basis of color alone. Under such circumstances, it is necessary to resort to the following qualitative cranial features to distinguish the two species (See Fig. 4):

Neotoma floridana: skull large, elongated; sphenopalatine vacuities relatively small; palate lacking posterior median spine; forked anterior palatal spine; first molar with moderately developed anterointernal reentrant angle.

Neotoma micropus: skull generally similar to that of *N. floridana* but more robust and sculptured; sphenopalatine vacuities relatively large; palate usually with a posterior median projection; unforked anterior palatal spine; anterointernal reentrant angle of first molar relatively shallow.

Subspecies. Neotoma micropus micropus is the subspecies in eastern Texas. It was named by Baird (*Proc. Acad. Nat. Sci. Philadelphia*, 7:333, April 1855) with type locality from Charco Escondido, Tamaulipas, Mexico.

Distribution and habitat. This species occurs only at the extreme southern and western boundaries of eastern Texas (Map 43). It is known from Bexar, Guadalupe, Gonzales, and De Witt counties in the southern part of the region and from Johnson County in the western part.

Its favored habitat includes thickets of cacti, mesquite, and thornbush in xeric or semiarid areas. Mesquite and lotebush are the most common thornbush plants associated with its habitat. Generally, disturbed areas relieved of grazing pressure support dense prickly pear development and provide suitable cover.

Life history. Raun (1966) conducted a detailed natural history study of this species in San Patricio County, and most of the following information has been adopted from his account.

This woodrat lives in prickly pear patches, where it builds houses (middens) from such items as cactus pads, thornbrush sticks, and cowchips. A complex system of more or less radial runways leads away from the house and usually connects with a peripheral run encircling the cactus clump just inside the margin. The woodrat's orientation to this system is quite evident. Rarely will an individual leave a run. When it does, it appears confused and disoriented. Each woodrat occupies a single house more or less permanently throughout its adult history, although this seems more characteristic of females than of males. Woodrats are antisocial, and plural occupancy of houses is limited to females with litters.

Each individual occupies a home range centering around its house. Activity is almost exclusively nocturnal. The size and shape of the home range depends upon the extent of the home cactus and the distance between neighboring clumps. Males have larger home ranges (233 m²) than females (158 m²). Males also tend to wander farther and to undertake more frequent and longer exploratory trips outside the home range. *N. micropus* has a relatively long life span for a rodent, with females surviving longer than males on the average (13.6 compared to 11.6 months).

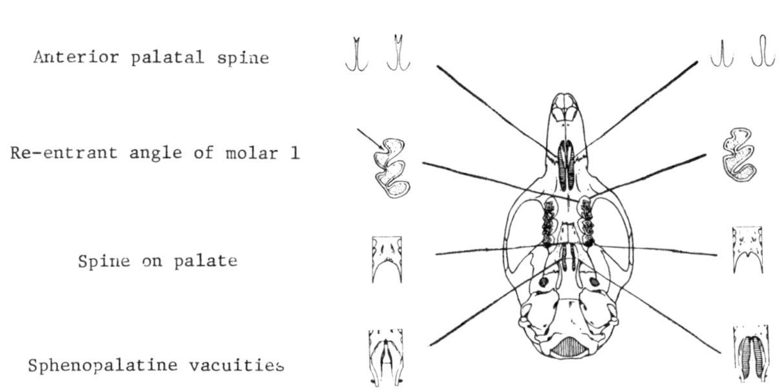

FIGURE 4. Woodrat skull showing method of distinguishing *Neotoma micropus* and *Neotoma floridana*.

Breeding occurs essentially year round, with no marked breeding season, although there is a slight indication of fall and spring peaks and a late summer low. The gestation period is less than thirty-three days. *N. micropus* is polyestrous, and individual females may produce from three to five litters per year. The average litter size is 2.25. Growth and development from birth to sexual maturity is retarded in comparison with most rodents, sexual maturity being reached in about the fifth or sixth month.

Coyotes and rattlesnakes are among the most important predators of this woodrat. *N. micropus* has evolved specialized behavior and physiological mechanisms to survive the predatory pressures that exist in thornbrush communities. Dense patches of cactus within which they construct middens provide protection from larger mammalian and avian predators; however, the cactus will not protect them from predation by rattlesnakes, which are abundant in these communities. Perez et al. (1978) investigated the resistance of *N. micropus* to rattlesnake venom and discovered that they are highly resistant to the venom (the LD_{50} of the venom for *N. micropus* was 140 times greater than that for laboratory mice).

Remarks. Hybridization, or possibly intergradation, has been reported between *N. micropus* and *N. floridana* where their ranges contact in Oklahoma and Colorado (Birney, 1973). Dalbey (1980) studied their distributional relationships and systematics in eastern Texas. In this region, the Guadalupe River separates most capture localities of the two species, with *N. floridana* occurring primarily on the north side of the river and *N. micropus* occurring strictly on the south side. At a locality along Cottle Creek (5.1 miles south of Gonzales) in Gonzales County, Dalbey (1980) found the two species living in parapatry within a distance of 100 m, which is well within the cruising range of males of both species. This locality, which is the only known place where *N. floridana* occurs

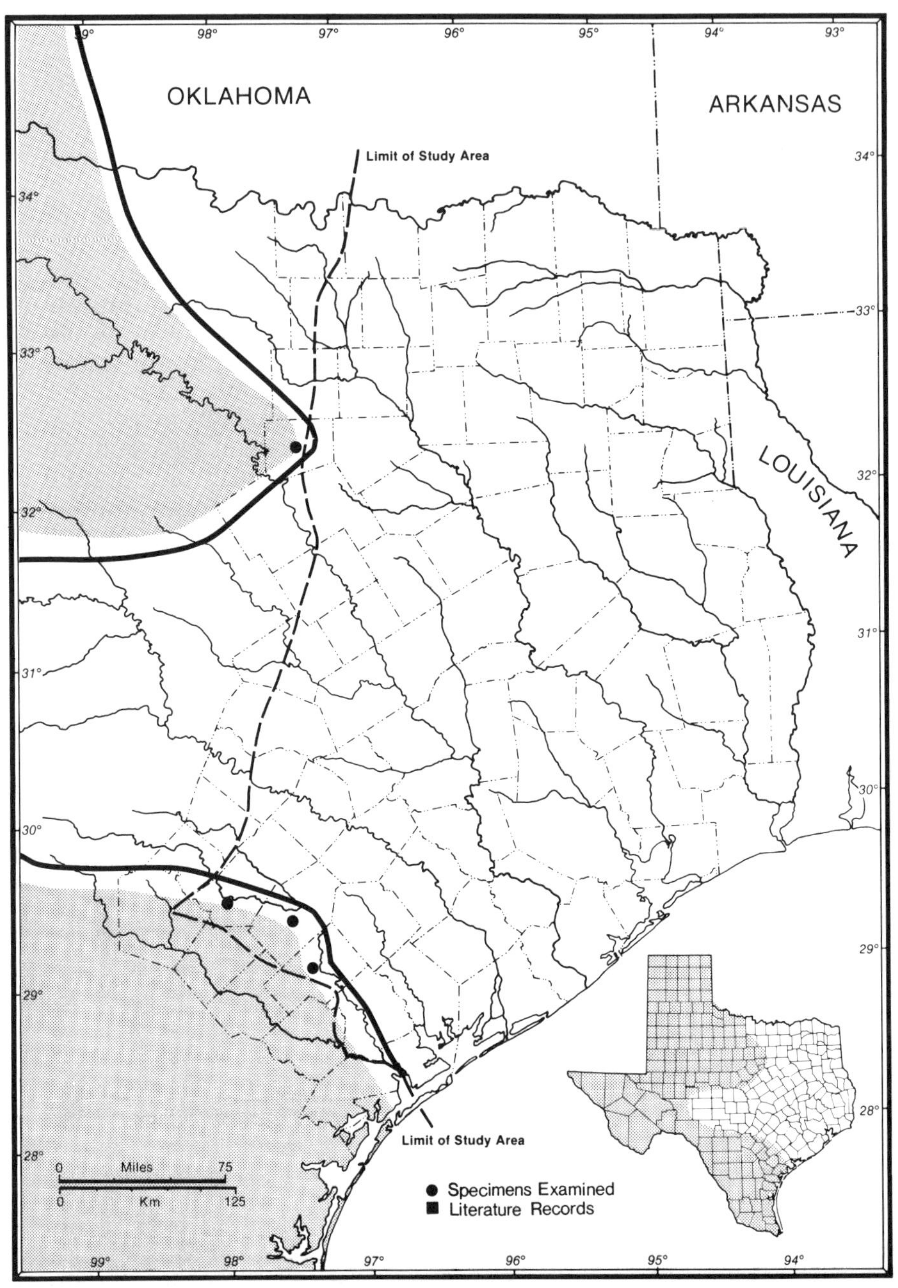

MAP 43. Distribution of the southern plains woodrat, *Neotoma micropus micropus*.

south of the Guadalupe River, is characterized by the close proximity of a bottomland woodland association, habitat favorable to *N. floridana*, with a mesquite-cactus association, habitat favorable to *N. micropus*. Dalbey (1980) speculates that there probably are other "contact areas" along the Guadalupe River where proximate riparian and thornbrush habitat types permit the two species to coexist at the same locality.

Dalbey (1980) compared specimens from the area of parapatry and other areas geographically intermediate to the distribution of the two species in eastern Texas to reference specimens from allopatric localities using a suite of quantitative and qualitative cranial characters. The results did not reveal the presence of a hybrid population at the parapatric locality. However, one specimen from the parapatric locality and two specimens from other nearby localities were morphologically intermediate to reference samples.

References. Dalbey, 1980; Raun, 1966.

Woodland Vole
Microtus pinetorum (Le Conte)

Name. The generic name *Microtus* is derived from two Greek words, *mikros*, meaning "small," and *otos*, meaning "ear," which collectively mean "small-eared." The second part of the name, *pinetorum*, is Latin for "of pine woods."

Identification. The woodland vole is a small mouse with an exceptionally short tail that is less than twice as long as the hind foot. The body is thick-set, the head is blunt, the legs are short, and the ears barely extend above the surrounding fur. The upper parts are reddish brown; the underparts are washed with buff or yellow. Average external measurements of this species are total length, 128 mm; tail, 21 mm; hind foot, 17 mm; and ear, 11 mm.

Subspecies. There are two subspecies in eastern Texas (Map 44). *Microtus pinetorum nemoralis* of the extreme northern part of the region was named by V. Bailey (*Proc. Biol. Soc. Washington*, 12:89, April 30, 1898) with type locality from Stilwell, Adair County, Oklahoma. *Microtus pinetorum auricularis* of the remainder of the area was also named by V. Bailey (ibid.) with type locality from Washington, Adams County, Mississippi. The former subspecies, compared to the latter, differs in its slightly larger size and duller coloration.

Distribution and habitat. Woodland voles occur in local isolated populations that occasionally reach large numbers, as evidenced by the occurrence of 173 skulls from 375 complete and 80 incomplete barn owl (*Tyto alba*) pellets from Panola County (Parmalee, 1954). Favored habitats include poorly drained, wet places in old fields with a dense growth of grasses and weeds growing on sandy soils and moist deciduous woodlands with a heavy layer of leaves and humus. These voles have been recorded in the following specific ecological situations in eastern Texas (Map 44): grassy marsh in Nacogdoches County (McCarley and Bradshaw, 1953);

Woodland vole, *Microtus pinetorum*.

edge of a swamp under a tangle of old grass and blackberry bushes in Marion County (Bailey, 1905); transition areas at the interface of old field communities with pine stands in Harrison and Smith counties (A. Cleveland and J. Baccus, personal communication); tall grassy field adjacent to Lake Whitney in Hill County (A. Cleveland, personal communication); and grassy habitats of highway rights-of-way in Harrison County (B. Wilson, personal communication).

Life history. Very little is known of the life history of this species in eastern Texas. These voles make burrows, from 8 to 10 cm in depth and about 2 to 5 cm in diameter, beneath the leaf litter or matted grass on the soil surface. Surface runways may be constructed in areas supporting a dense grass cover, but most of their activity is underground. They are mainly crepuscular or nocturnal and are rarely active in daylight. They do not hibernate. Their nests, which are from 15 to 18 cm in diameter with three or four openings, are made out of dead leaves and grasses and are usually located just below the ground surface or under the shallow roots of a stump. These voles live in colonies and seem to be quite social.

Woodland voles are highly sedentary, moving only short distances from their nests. Their home range seldom exceeds 0.10 to 0.13 ha. Like other cyclic rodents, numbers of these voles vary considerably from year to year. However, in suitable areas in the northern part of their range, they often reach incredibly high population densities. For example, in one orchard at Croton Falls, New York, Hamilton (1938) estimated the population as between 494 and 741 voles per ha. Given the scarcity of collecting records for this species, it seems highly unlikely that it ever reaches densities of that magnitude in eastern Texas.

The woodland vole, because of its subterranean habits, feeds largely upon succulent roots and tubers. Its semifossorial habits doubtless protect

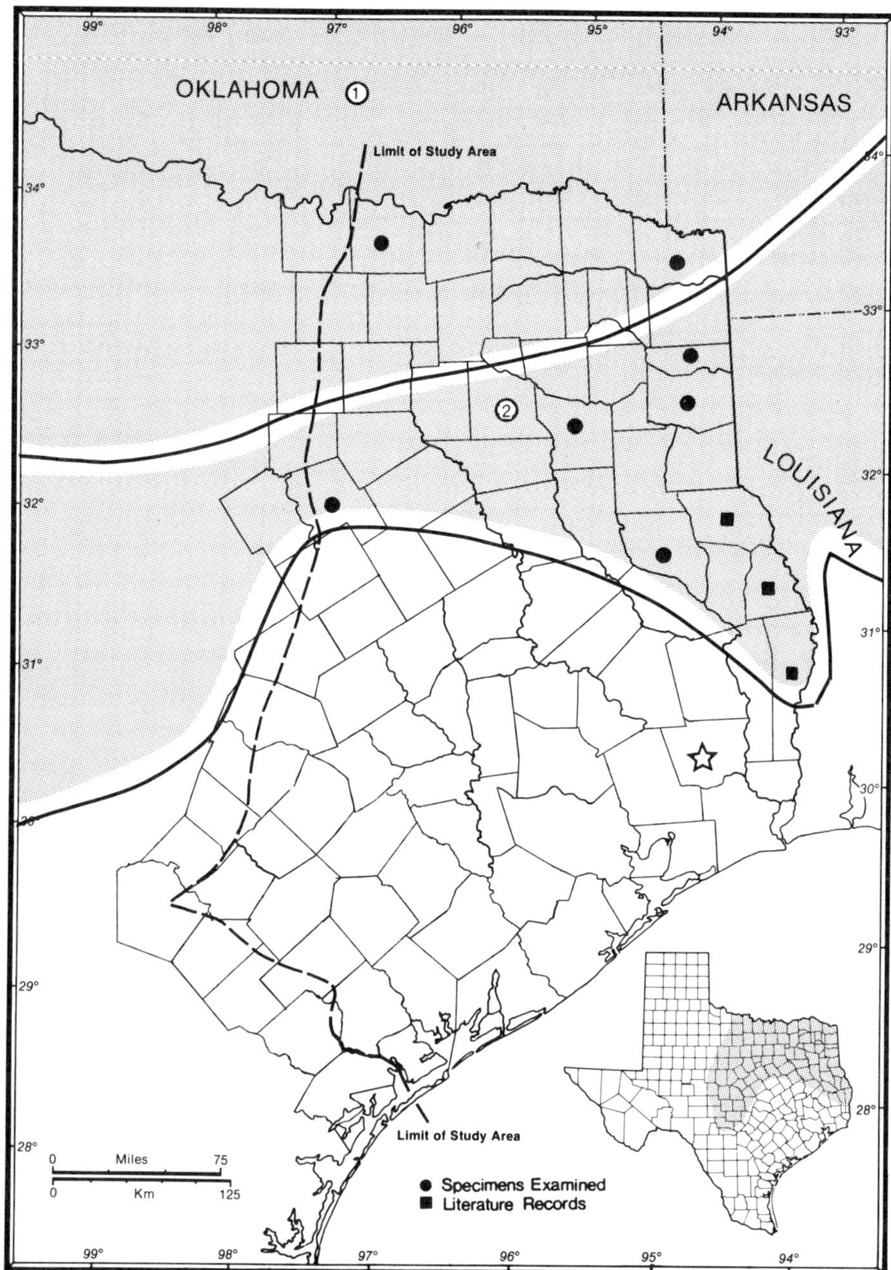

MAP 44. Distribution of the woodland vole, *Microtus pinetorum*. 1. *M. p. nemoralis*. 2. *M. p. auricularis*. The literature records are from Packard (1961). The star indicates the locality where the closely related species, the Prairie Vole (*Microtus ochrogaster ludovicianus*), has been taken.

it in some measure from predation. Known or suspected predators include barn owls, hawks, rat snakes, gray foxes, opossums, mink, and weasels.

Reproductive data recorded from specimen tags suggest a prolonged breeding period, perhaps lasting the year around. Pregnant females have been collected in March, June, and November. Lactating females have been taken in May, and juvenile woodland voles in January. Males with enlarged, swollen testes (thought to be indicative of breeding) have been trapped in June, October, and November. The number of embryos for four pregnant females was either two or three. The gestation period of the woodland vole is thought to be about twenty-four days. Woodland voles have a much lower reproductive potential than other species of voles, which is consistent with their ecology. They occupy a climate-moderating, predator-inhibiting burrow system that mitigates the effect of many natural controls to which other voles are subject.

References. Hamilton, 1938; Lowery, 1974; Schadler and Butterstein, 1979; Sealander, 1979; Smolen, 1981.

<h2 style="text-align:center">Muskrat
Ondatra zibethicus (Linnaeus)</h2>

Name. The generic name of the muskrat (*Ondatra*) is a French Canadian word for this animal of Iroquois Indian (=Huron) derivation (Davis and Lowery, 1940). The second part of the name, *zibethicus*, is the New Latin word for "musky odored," in reference to the characteristic odor of this species.

Identification. The muskrat is a large rodent (about the size of a small cat) with a tail slightly less than half its total length. Its ears are short, barely projecting above the surrounding fur and giving it the appearance of a large meadow vole. Its lips close behind its incisor teeth, permitting it to gnaw underwater. The fore feet have four clawed toes and a thumb with a nail; the hind foot possesses five clawed toes that are webbed at their bases. The scaly tail is vertically flattened, a feature that serves to distinguish a muskrat from an immature beaver, in which the tail is horizontally flattened, and from a nutria, in which the tail is rounded. The overall color is a rich, dark brown above; its grayish underparts, which lack guard hairs, shade to white on the throat. Average external measurements are total length, 544 mm; tail, 235 mm; hind foot, 78 mm; ear, 22 mm.

Subspecies. Two subspecies are tentatively recognized in eastern Texas. Specimens from the coastal marshes and adjacent Big Thicket are referable to *O. z. rivalicius*, which was named by Bangs (*Proc. Boston Soc. Nat. Hist.*, 26:541, July 31, 1895) with type locality from Burbride, Plaquemines Parish, Louisiana. According to Hall (1981), specimens from the remainder of eastern Texas belong to the subspecies *O. z. cinnamominus*, which was named by Hollister (*Proc. Biol. Soc. Washington*, 23:125, September 2, 1910) with type locality from Wakeeney, Trego

Muskrat, *Ondatra zibethicus* (photograph by Woodrow Goodpasture).

County, Kansas. *O. z. rivalicius*, compared to *O. z. cinnamominus*, is supposedly darker in coloration and slightly larger in size (Hollister, 1911). However, all of the localities of *cinnamominus* listed by Hall (1981) were taken from literature records, and, to my knowledge, he did not examine any specimens of this subspecies from eastern Texas. In fact, there is only a single specimen in collections from this region (see Appendix I, "Specimens Examined"). Thus, until more museum material is available, the recognition of two subspecies of the muskrat in eastern Texas must be considered tentative.

Distribution and habitat. The primary area of occurrence of the muskrat in eastern Texas is along the coastal prairie from the Texas-Louisiana border west to Harris and Brazoria counties. The species has also been reported by trappers from a scattered number of inland counties reaching as far north as Bowie County and as far west as Tarrant and Falls counties (Map 45).

Muskrats are primarily inhabitants of marshes. They also live in rice fields as well as along creeks, rivers, lakes, drainage ditches, and canals where necessary food and shelter are available. In inland areas, shallow freshwater marshes with clumps of cattails interspersed with bulrushes, sedges, and other marsh vegetation support the heaviest populations. In coastal areas, they are found in marshes ranging from fresh to saline, but the brackish marshes, characterized by smooth cordgrass, saltgrass, needlegrass rush, Olney bulrush, and saltmarsh bulrush, are favored.

Life history. In the near sea-level habitat of the coastal marshes, muskrats live in dome-shaped "lodges" or "beds" constructed out of marsh vegetation. These houses, which range in size from 1 to 2 m in diameter at the base and from 60 cm to 1 m in height, usually have two or more underwater openings. The essential purpose of den houses, which

Muskrat lodge.

are located above normal high tides, is to provide the animal a comparatively dry nest with an even temperature that is safe from predators. The usual number living together in one house is a pair of old adults and two to four young.

Muskrats are cooperative and diligent workers and construct a livable house within a couple of hours, and these are generally complete before the first young are born. The female leaves her young warmly packed in a ball of finely-shredded grass while she is out feeding or working on the house. During the time that the first litter is suckling, the male lives in a separate nest located in the opposite side of the house. Normally, about the time the first litter reaches kit stage, the second litter is born in a new nest that has been constructed in the same house. When the first litter reaches sexual maturity and the second litter reaches kit stage, the first litter is forcibly evicted by the original pair, to mate and repeat this same process. In a well-populated marsh, the young pairs will build their houses within 6 to 9 m of the original house.

Along stream banks, canals, and large levees and in deep peat soils, fewer houses are built and more of the muskrats live in burrows. Entrance to such burrows is usually by means of underwater openings. Dens are about 10 cm in diameter and 2 to 3 m in length and usually terminate in an enlarged nest chamber.

Muskrats are active year-round and do not hibernate. They are chiefly nocturnal animals, usually remaining in their beds from daylight through the afternoon. Individuals do travel considerably, but their home range depends to a certain extent upon the size and shape of the water area in which they live. Animals living in the center of a marsh usually occupy a circular area, whereas those along the shoreline live in a narrow area extending from bank burrows out several meters into deeper waters.

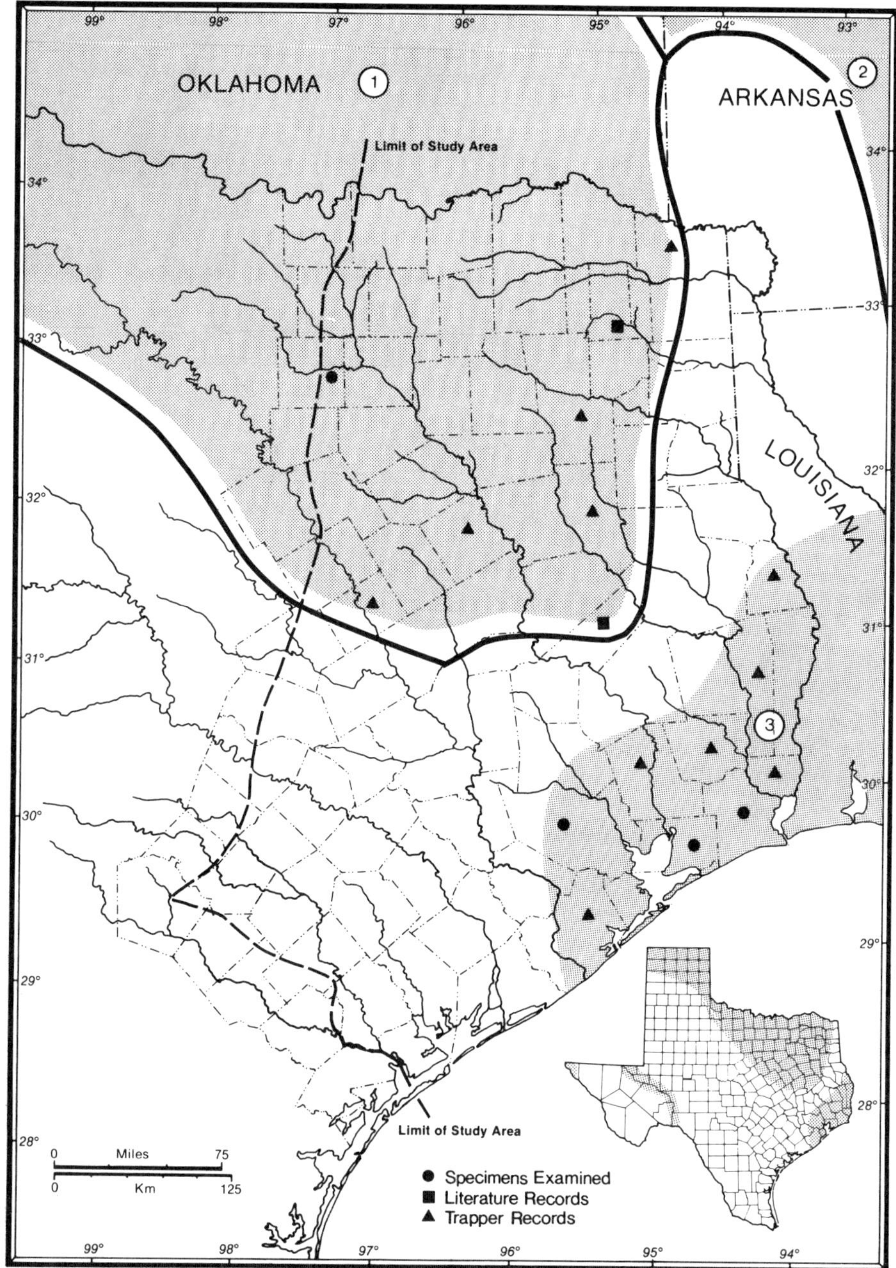

MAP 45. Distribution of the muskrat, *Ondatra zibethicus*. 1. *O. z. cinnamominus*. 2. *O. z. zibethicus*. 3. *O. z. rivalicius*. The literature records are from W. B. Davis (1974).

Muskrats living in rivers extend their range along the bank for a considerable distance and out into the river, even to the opposite bank in all but the very wide rivers.

Muskrats feed almost exclusively on vegetation. In selecting food items, they are largely opportunistic, taking what is most readily available. Among their favored items are cattail, smooth cordgrass, and salt-marsh bulrush, but they also consume a variety of other grasses, rushes, and sedges. Small amounts of animal life, mainly crustaceans and mollusks, constitute about 5 percent of their diet.

Muskrats breed year-round in the coastal marshes, with reproductive activity reaching its lowest levels during the colder winters (January) and in mid-summer (July and August). The highest degree of sexual activity is in November and March. The average embryo count for pregnant females is 4.1, and this is probably representative of the true average litter at birth (Lay, 1945). The gestation period is estimated to be from twenty-six to twenty-eight days. Several litters can be born in rapid succession since mating may immediately follow birth. A female generally produces five to six litters each year but is capable of having seven or eight. Females typically breed before they are one year of age, and some may breed as early as six months of age.

The young are born blind, almost naked, and weigh only about 21 g. The pelage develops rapidly, and by the end of the first week they are covered with a good coat of hair. The eyes open in fourteen to sixteen days, at which time they can dive and swim adeptly. They are weaned at about four weeks of age and reach sexual maturity at ten to twelve months.

With the high breeding potential of this species, it is inevitable that mortality is high. Only about one-third of the young live through their first winter. Marsh hawks, raccoons, and mink are common winter predators, and losses chargeable to water moccasins during the warmer months of the year are probably considerable. Losses by fighting among muskrats themselves may be large during periods of high population density.

Muskrat populations fluctuate considerably from year to year. Population peaks generally occur during wet years when the vegetation is lush and marshes are in optimum condition. Dense populations may result in vegetational "eat-outs," which destroy marsh habitat and start a "crash" in the muskrat population. Trapping is the most effective means of control in areas where muskrats are too numerous. Low muskrat production is typically a reflection of drought, hurricanes, floods, pollution, and other adverse factors affecting marsh productivity.

Remarks. Muskrats were, at one time, the economically most important fur-bearing mammal in eastern Texas, but this is no longer true. During the winter of 1936, muskrats produced a fur income of approximately $200,000 in Jefferson, Chambers, and Orange counties, and this constituted 54 percent of the total dollar value of the fur income (Lay, 1939). The estimated total value of the muskrat harvest for all of Texas for the 1972–73 trapping season was only $18,675, and this amount was less than 2 percent of the total fur income (figures from the Texas Parks and Wildlife Department). As a further comparison, the estimated total value of the muskrat harvest in Louisiana for the 1972–73 season was in excess of $1,400,000 (Lowery, 1974). This decline in the importance of the muskrat as a fur-bearing mammal is a reflection of a loss of habitat as a result of marsh deterioration and a concomitant decline in population production, variations in the market demand for muskrat fur, and the ascendancy of the nutria as an important fur-bearing mammal.

References. W. B. Davis, 1974; Lay, 1945; Lay and O'Neil, 1942; Lowery, 1974; O'Neal, 1949.

Family Muridae (Old World Rats and Mice)

This is the second largest family of rodents next to the family Cricetidae. Although murids occur virtually throughout the Old World, the only species that occur in the United States have been introduced by man. The introduced murids living in our country consist solely of the house mouse and the Norway and roof rats, and all three occur in eastern Texas. They differ from native cricetine rodents in having a more pointed nose, smaller eyes, and a naked tail with prominent annulations. The crowns of their cheek teeth possess three longitudinal rows of cusps as opposed to two rows in the cricetines. The dental formula of murid rodents is identical to that of cricetids (I 1/1, C 0/0, Pm 0/0, M 3/3 × 2 = 16).

Roof Rat
Rattus rattus (Linnaeus)

Name. Both parts of the scientific name of the roof rat are derived from the medieval Latin word *Rattus*, meaning "rat."

Identification. The roof rat is a medium-sized rat with a thin and coarse pelage, a long and pointed nose, narrow ears, and a long tail. Its tail is usually longer than its head and body, half naked, and scaly. Its color is variable, depending upon the subspecies. The roof rat can be confused only with the Norway rat (*Rattus norvegicus*), from which it differs as described in the account of the latter. Average external measurements of this species are total length, 385 mm; tail, 210 mm; hind foot, 36 mm; ear, 22 mm.

Subspecies. Three subspecies of the roof rat (*R. r. rattus*, *R. r. alexandrinus*, and *R. r. frugivorus*) have been introduced in North America (Hall, 1981). The subspecies differ markedly in color: *R. r. rattus* is wholly black; *R. r. alexandrinus* is grayish brown above and gray below; *R. r. frugivorus* is similar to *alexandrinus* except that it is white or yellowish below (Lowery, 1974). All three subspecies probably occur in eastern Texas; however, many intergrades exist among them, making it difficult to assign

Roof rat, *Rattus rattus.*

individual specimens to one subspecies or the other. Therefore, no attempt has been made to assign specimens to subspecies.

Distribution and habitat. Roof rats occur throughout eastern Texas in towns and on farms, although specimen records are available from only a few counties (Map 46). Roof rats live in close association with man and his structures. They may be found in grocery and drug stores, warehouses, theaters, and poultry stores and are very common in cotton gins and grain warehouses. On farms they live in barns and corn cribs, but few rats are ever found in farmhouses. Roof rats may live near the ground, but usually they frequent the rafters and crossbeams. They make typical runways along pipes, beams, or wires and up and down the rafters, which they frequently gnaw upon. In the corn cribs, the rats run along the horizontal boards and often leave a layer of grease and dirt; they also consume great quantities of corn and sorghum. Where they occur together with Norway rats, roof rats typically inhabit higher elevations of buildings, while the Norway rats select lower levels.

Life history. Reproduction in these rats may occur in any month of the year, but there appear to be peaks in January, February, and March and lows in July and August. Females carry an average of 6.8 embryos per litter, and the young are born following a twenty-one day gestation period. Compared to Norway rats, roof rats have fewer litters and fewer young per litter. At birth the young are naked, blind, and nearly helpless. They mature rather rapidly and are weaned in about three weeks. They are able to reproduce at approximately three months of age.

Roof rats are active mainly at night, but where there is a high density they may be seen in daylight. Their similarity in general habits to the Norway rat is discussed more fully in the next account.

References. D. E. Davis, 1947; W. B. Davis, 1974; Lowery, 1974.

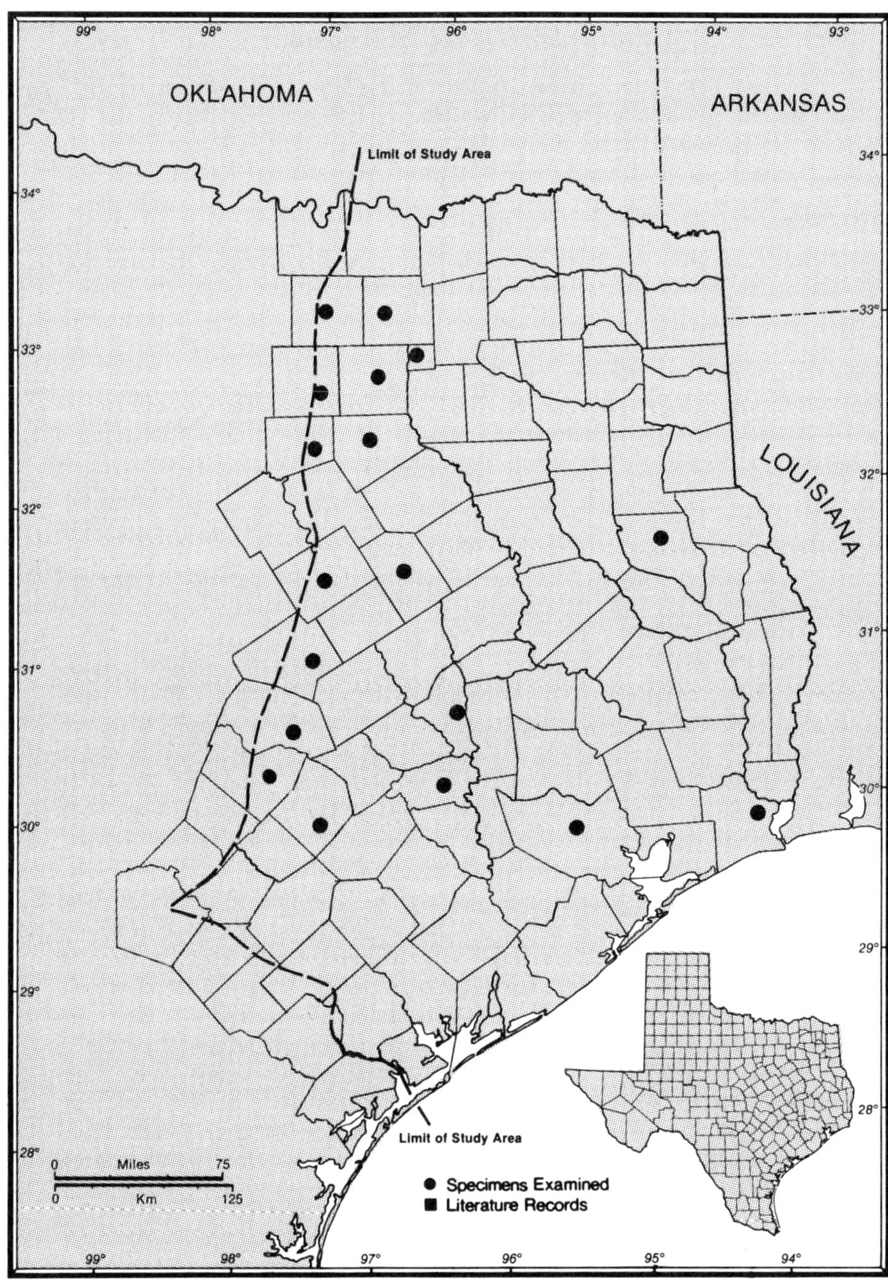

MAP 46. Distribution of the roof rat, *Rattus rattus*.

Norway Rat
Rattus norvegicus (Berkenhout)

Name. The generic name, *Rattus*, is the latinized rendition of "rat." The specific name, *norvegicus*, which is a latinized word meaning "of Norway," is actually a misnomer because the species is of Asiatic origin and the material for the original description came from England, not Norway (Lowery, 1974).

Identification. This rat is similar to the roof rat but can be distinguished externally by its tail, which is always shorter than its head and body; in *R. rattus* the tail is longer than the head and body. Its color is grayish brown above and pale gray or yellowish white below, and the hair is coarse. Average external measurements are total length, 440 mm; tail, 205 mm; hind foot, 37 mm; ear, 22 mm.

The only other species with which the Norway rat can be confused is the eastern woodrat (*Neotoma floridana*). The latter differs in having a finer, smooth pelage, larger and more protruding eyes, larger ears, a less elongated and pointed nose, a well-haired tail in which the rings or annulations are barely visible, much smaller feet, and underparts that are pure white and contrast sharply with the upper parts.

Subspecies. The Norway rat is monotypic and has no recognized subspecies.

Distribution and habitat. This rat is now probably resident in every town and city in eastern Texas as well as in some rural communities; however, it does not appear to be as widely distributed as the roof rat, especially in the southern part of the region (Map 47). For example, a survey of house rats in Lavaca County revealed that *R. norvegicus* was found in only one town, whereas *R. rattus* was present throughout the county in all towns and on all farms (D. E. Davis, 1947). The Norway rat lives both as a commensal, in close association with man and associated structures, and in the feral state, far removed from human dwellings where vegetation is tall and affords adequate protection. The marshy lands off Galveston Island, for example, offer ideal habitat for these rats, and they have been trapped among sedges and small thickets near houses (Baker and Lay, 1938). As a commensal, Norway rats live principally in basements, on the ground floor, or in burrows under sidewalks or outbuildings. They are most common in grain and poultry stores and around garbage dumps.

Life history. These rats build nests out of shredded grass, leaves, paper, cloth, or any other available material. Nests are generally well concealed in hollow walls, in ground tunnels, or under piles of rubbish. Their tunnels, which are about 1 m in length and about 6 or 7 cm in diameter, extend into the ground to depths of around 46 cm and usually contain an enlarged chamber for the nest. Rats establish definite pathways from nests to feeding places and use these habitually.

Although they will move about at any hour, night is their period of major activity, with peaks just after dark and just before daylight. Their home range seldom covers more than 30 m in its greatest dimension.

Norway rat, *Rattus norvegicus*.

They will cross alleys to enter adjacent buildings, but they typically do not cross streets or move from one city block to another. Around farms, Norway rats generally leave man's structures in spring and invade grain fields, pastures, and waste areas where they breed and feed.

These rats are social, living in colonies of ten to twelve individuals. The dominant individual is usually the largest and oldest male of this group. He achieves this status by aggressive behavior in driving others away from food and favorite nesting spots. The members of a colony derive both advantages and disadvantages from group affiliation. On the one hand, they may assist one another by cooperating to drive a strange rat away and protect their territory. On the other hand, when population levels are high, considerable competition may ensue among members of the group, resulting in physical combat, poor health, less successful breeding, and death.

Norway rats breed all during the year, but the heaviest production of young occurs in spring and fall with a slow-up in winter. They produce an average of five litters per year, and the number of young to a litter is generally between seven and eleven. The gestation period is somewhere between twenty-one and twenty-six days. It has been calculated that a captive pair of Norway rats and their subsequent young can produce more than 1,500 rats in a single year.

The young are born blind, naked, and helpless. Growth is rapid, with the eyes opening in fourteen to seventeen days and weaning occurring at about three weeks. Most of these rats begin to breed in their third or fourth month, but there are records of females only eight weeks old producing and raising a litter.

Norway rats feed on a variety of items, including both plant and ani-

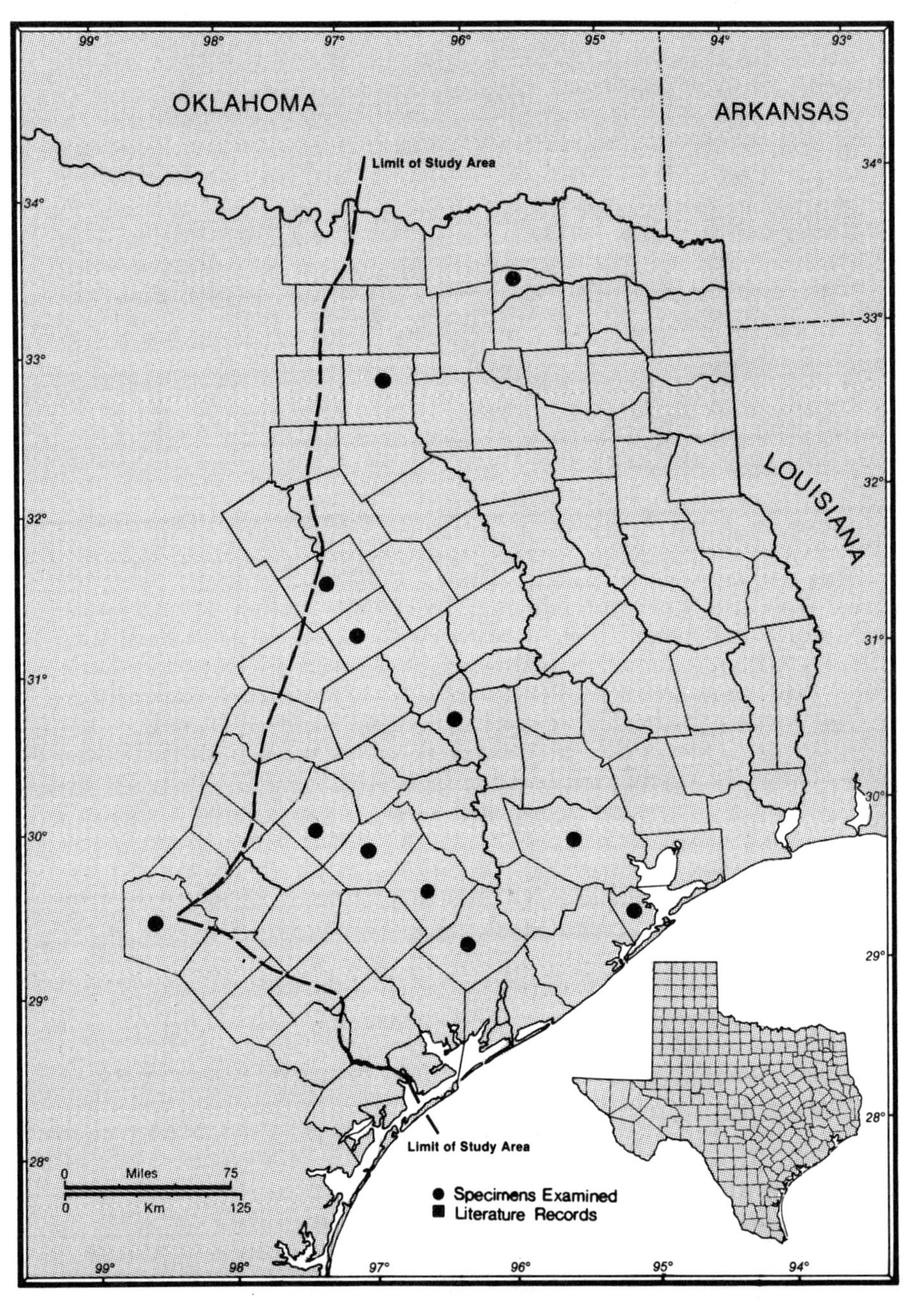

MAP 47. Distribution of the Norway rat, *Rattus norvegicus*.

mal matter. They eat all sorts of garbage, but various kinds of plant material, particularly grains, are their mainstay. Some of the animal foods they eat include eggs, milk, fish, and other animals. Animals known to be killed by these rats include chickens, young pigs, lambs, wild and domestic rabbits, rattlesnakes, and wild birds. There are even reports of several of these rats killing infant children. Norway rats will also prey on roof rats as well as their own young on occasion.

Population turnover is relatively rapid in this species. Only about 5 percent or less will live for more than a year. Some of their natural predators include house cats, dogs, skunks, weasels, foxes, mink, hawks, owls, and snakes. However, their worst enemy is probably another Norway rat. These rats can be extremely ferocious toward one another, and intraspecific fighting often leads to mortality for both adults and the young.

References. W. B. Davis, 1974; Lowery, 1974; C. W. Schwartz and Schwartz, 1981.

House Mouse
Mus musculus Linneaeus

Name. The first part of the scientific name, *Mus*, is Latin for "mouse." The second part, *musculus*, is Latin for "little mouse," in reference to the small size of this species.

Identification. The house mouse is a sleek little mouse with an elongated snout and a long, tapering tail that is naked and finely scaled. The eyes are small and bulging; the ears are large and scantily haired. The color of its upper parts is buffy brown; its underparts are buffy gray. The body fur is conspicuously short. Average external measurements are total length, 165 mm; tail, 98 mm; hind foot, 19 mm; ear, 12 mm.

The house mouse superficially resembles harvest mice (*Reithrodontomys*), deer mice (*Peromyscus*), golden mice (*Ochrotomys*), and pygmy mice (*Baiomys*), although it can be easily distinguished from these native rodents. From deer mice and harvest mice it differs by the absence of a sharp color contrast between the back and the belly; from golden mice by coloration; and from pygmy mice by larger size and coloration.

Subspecies. The subspecies in eastern Texas is *Mus musculus brevirostris*, which is widely distributed over the southern United States (E. Schwarz and H. K. Schwarz, 1943). It was named by Waterhouse (*Proc. Zool. Soc. London*, 1837, pt. 5, p. 19) with type locality from Maldonado, Uruguay.

Distribution and habitat. Although collecting records do not indicate it, house mice are found over all parts of eastern Texas (Map 48). They are commensal rodents, living in close association with man in houses and occupied or unoccupied buildings. However, they are not confined to man-made structures. Over much of the area they are feral and have become established in abandoned fields, fence rows, weedy roadsides, and cultivated fields. On recently reclaimed strip-mined lands in Freestone County, Waggoner (1975) found them living side by side

House mouse, *Mus musculus.*

with five species of native rodents at an average density of 1.2 individuals per ha of habitat. Similarly, Wilkins and Schmidly (1977) found house mice in association with as many as eight species of native rodents in old field, pasture, cultivated field, and highway right-of-way habitat in Brazos County. Baker and Lay (1938) trapped house mice on Galveston Island in sandy fields one mile or more from the nearest house. Colonies of their small burrows were found under piles of drift logs and clumps of cactus.

Life history. House mice live in nests placed in well-concealed places and constructed out of scraps of paper, shredded fabrics, grass, and feathers. In the field, they will use the runways of other small native mice such as deer mice and harvest mice. These mice are chiefly nocturnal and seldom move about during the daytime.

House mice are relatively sedentary and do not travel great distances. Waggoner (1975) found their average home range in the field was only 0.23 ha, which is considerably less than most native rodents. There is some indication that they undergo a seasonal movement from indoors to outdoors in spring and the reverse in fall.

House mice are gregarious and live in colonies. A family unit usually consists of a male and one or more females plus their offspring. The male is unusually aggressive and drives other males away from the family nest. Several families may live side by side, but the individuals of these families do not intermingle.

House mice are prolific breeders. Females may come into heat every four to six days, and breeding occurs throughout the year. However, the peak breeding season is from spring to late fall, and reproduction appears to be somewhat curtailed in colder months. A single female may produce as many as thirteen litters in a year, but the usual number is somewhere

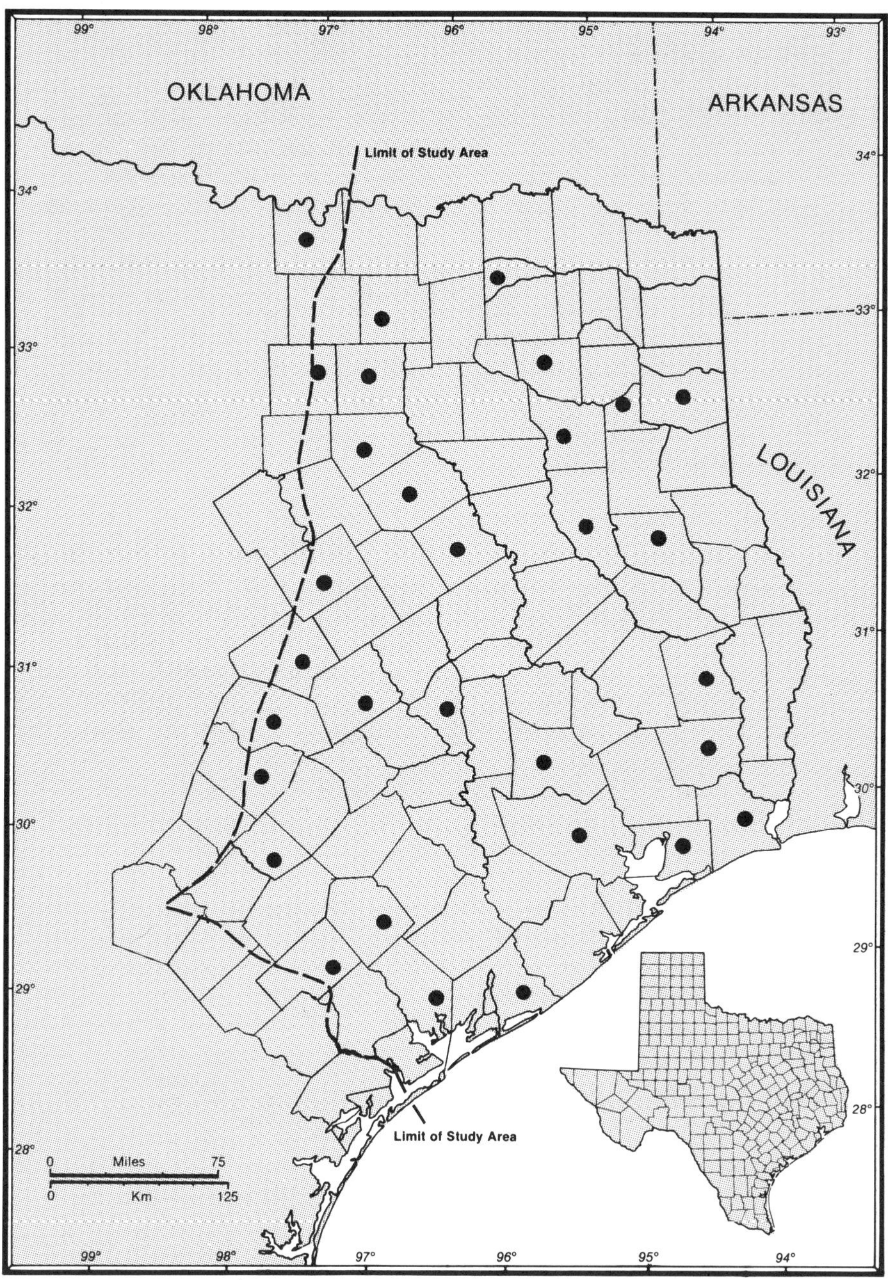

MAP 48. Distribution of the house mouse, *Mus musculus brevirostris.*

Newborn house mice, *Mus musculus*.

between five and ten. The young, which may number anywhere between two and thirteen (average five to six), are born following a gestation period of nineteen to twenty-one days.

The young are born blind, naked, and helpless, but development is rapid. Young mice have fur by ten days of age, and by fourteen days their eyes are open. They are weaned at three weeks of age, and by four weeks some females are capable of breeding, although the average age of sexual maturity is about six weeks.

House mice will feed on practically anything, but they prefer vegetable material, particularly grains. They will also eat insects and meat, if available, and they are particularly adept at catching houseflies and cockroaches. When especially hungry, they can cause considerable damage by chewing on books, boxes, and leather.

These mice are not especially long-lived. In the wild, they rarely live more than a year. Common predators include domestic cats, weasels, raccoons, snakes, owls, and shrikes.

References. Lowery, 1974; W. B. Davis, 1974; C. W. Schwarz and Schwarz, 1981.

Family Capromyidae (Capromyids)

This family, which includes the nutria and the hutias, is native to the West Indies and southern parts of South America. The nutria has been introduced widely in the southern United States and has thrived in certain areas, including eastern Texas, to the point that it has become both a serious pest and an asset. The nutria resembles the beaver in some of its habits.

Nutria
Myocastor coypus (Molina)

Name. The generic name *Myocastor* is derived from two Greek words, *mys*, meaning "mouse," and *kaster*, meaning "beaver," which translate as mouse beaver. The name *coypus* is the latinized form of *coypú*, a name in the language of the Araucanian Indians of Chile and Argentina for an aquatic mammal that was possibly this species.

Identification. The nutria is a large aquatic rodent resembling a beaver, but its tail is long, sparsely haired, and round, not paddle-shaped. Adults may reach a total length of 91 cm and weigh on the average between 9 and 11 kg, occasionally as much as 16 kg. The nutria differs from all our native rodents in that the mammary glands are located high on the back near the mid-line rather than on the abdomen. Its pelage consists of a dark, slaty underfur overlaid with long, glossy dark brown or yellowish brown guard hairs. The ears are short and barely extend beyond the surrounding fur. Average external measurements are total length, 917 mm; tail, 403 mm; hind foot, 140 mm; ear, 28 mm. The dental formula is I 1/1, C 0/0, Pm 1/1, M 3/3 × 2 = 20.

Subspecies. The original nutria introduced into Louisiana and Texas came from Argentina and are referable to the subspecies *Myocastor coypus bonariensis*. It was named by É. Geoffroy-Saint-Hilaire (*Ann. Mus. Hist. Nat.*, Paris, 6:82, 1805) with type locality Argentina.

Distribution and habitat. This semiaquatic rodent, which occurs natively in South America, represents a fairly recent addition to the fauna of eastern Texas. It was originally introduced into southern Louisiana in the vicinity of Avery Island in 1938. Since that time, through escape and help from man, the species has become established throughout eastern Texas (Map 49). Fur buyers reported as early as 1946 that a few nutria were trapped along the coast near Port Arthur, but there was no appreciable inland natural spread of this species. In that same year, individuals were released in Anderson and Houston counties about 241 km northwest of Port Arthur. The interest in introducing nutria in eastern Texas was triggered by their reputation for clearing aquatic plants from vegetation-choked lakes and farm ponds. Since their original introduction they have expanded their range throughout Texas except for the Trans-Pecos and High Plains regions of the state (Map 49). A survey of fur trappers from 1976 to 1981 revealed that nutria were obtained in all but nine counties in eastern Texas. Particularly large numbers were trapped in counties of the coastal prairie region.

Nutria occupy a wide variety of aquatic habitats, including swamps and marshes as well as the shores of rivers and lakes. Apparently they are equally at home in salt or fresh water. Population densities vary from one location to the next and from year to year, but they can become locally very abundant. For example, a mark-recapture study of a population on

Nutria, *Myocastor coypus.*

Blackcat Lake in Trinity County produced a population estimate of one nutria per 100 m of shoreline habitat (Simpson, 1980).

Life history. Although nutria can move about on land, they are adept swimmers and are more at home in the water. Nutria are often seen moving about in the daytime in coastal marshes, but their greatest activity is at night. Nutria can dig their own burrows in canal banks or levees, but they also use the old burrows of armadillos and muskrats. Burrows, which are approximately 20 to 23 cm in diameter and extend into the bank for a distance of about 1.2 m, are usually open at both ends with the entrance toward the river usually above water level. They will also build burrows under roots of trees exposed along the banks of rivers and streams. Not all nutria utilize burrows, constructing instead "beds" or "forms" beneath overhanging or collapsed marsh vegetation as places to rest, feed, and give birth to young. Their nests are made of reeds and sedges built up in large piles somewhat after the fashion of a swan's nest. These are built on land among the marsh vegetation and close to the water's edge.

Nutria are strict vegetarians and eat a wide variety of plants. Simpson (1980) studied their food habits in Trinity County and found the six most important food plants to be panic grasses, pondweeds, spikesedges, duckweeds, American waterlily, and rushes. Use of plants varied seasonally. Panic grasses were used more during spring and winter, whereas pondweeds were heavily used during summer and fall. Nutria normally eat about 1.1 to 1.6 kg of food per day, and they are capable of clearing an area of emergent vegetation, creating what is called an "eat-out." Nutria consume their food both on land and while floating in the water, but they normally do not forage great distances from water. They often amass large

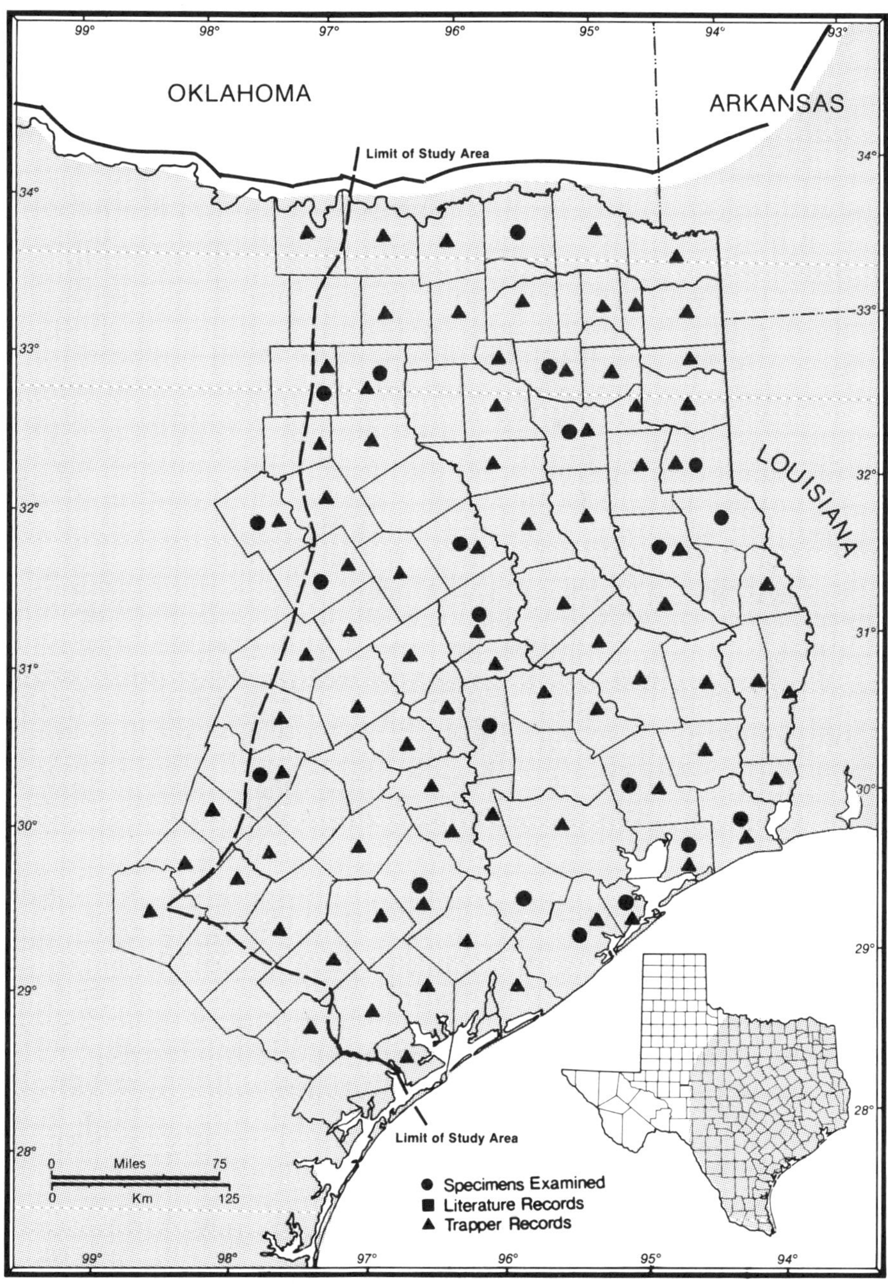

MAP 49. Distribution of the nutria, *Myocastor coypus bonariensis.*

quantities of vegetation into a platform, which they use as a place of feeding, resting, or as a toilet.

Nutria breed throughout the year. The number of young in a litter varies from 4 to 8, with the average being 5.2 (McKnown and Wilson, 1964). Female nutria experience a regular estrus cycle that is repeated in nonpregnant females approximately every twenty-three to twenty-eight days throughout the year (Ballard et al., 1966); they remain in this state for one to four days. Postpartum heat occurs in females within forty-eight hours after parturition, with normal cases ending in successful pregnancies.

At birth the young are fully furred, their eyes are open, and they are able to move about and feed upon vegetation within a few hours. They mature rapidly, increasing at the rate of about 0.5 kg per month during the first year. They reach sexual maturity at the age of four to five months before attaining adult size. With an adequate food supply and excellent habitat conditions, young nutria may breed when they are four months old, but normally they are close to eight months of age before mating. The maximum life span for nutrias kept in captivity is two years, but they almost certainly do not live this long in the wild.

Nutria are economically important mammals. On the positive side, they have value as fur producers and in the control of aquatic weeds and vegetation. From 1976 to 1981, fur trappers in eastern Texas harvested almost 129,000 nutria valued at approximately $1,030,000. On the negative side of the ledger, nutria can do great damage to dikes and levees as well as to rice crops. Furthermore, by overpopulating an area they may destroy vegetation that is valuable for such wildlife as waterfowl and muskrats.

References. W. B. Davis, 1956, 1958a; DeViney, 1964; Lowery, 1974; Petrides, 1950; Swank and Petrides, 1954.

Order Cetacea

Members of this order, which includes the whales and dolphins, are wholly aquatic and occur throughout the oceans and seas of the world. Cetaceans are characterized by a number of morphological features that distinguish them from terrestrial mammals. Their body is fusiform (torpedo-shaped), lacks external ears and sebaceous glands, is nearly hairless, and is insulated by thick blubber. Hind limbs are absent, and the forelimbs have been modified into flippers for use in steering and balancing. The flukes (tail fins) are horizontally flattened, and most forms have a dorsal fin.

Twenty-two cetaceans are known from the western Gulf of Mexico (see Schmidly [1981] for a list and discussion of each species). However, only one species, the Atlantic bottlenose dolphin (*Tursiops truncatus*), continually lives in the near-shore waters of the Texas coast, and, for this reason it is the only species discussed here. Other species in the western Gulf are off-shore, deep-water forms that only rarely venture into inshore waters.

Family Delphinidae (Dolphins and Small Whales)

Atlantic Bottlenose Dolphin
Tursiops truncatus (Montagu 1821)

Name. The first part of the scientific name, *Tursiops*, comes from the Latin word *tursio* for "a dolphinlike animal or porpoise." The second part, *truncatus*, is from the Latin word *truncus*, meaning "cut off," in reference to the relatively short beak of this species compared to that of other delphinids.

Identification. Atlantic bottlenose dolphins reach a length of about 3.7 m, though most individuals in the Gulf of Mexico are less than 2.7 m. They may weigh in excess of 650 kg. They are purplish gray to clear gray dorsally, and whitish ventrally except for the underside posterior to the vent, which is dark like the back; the sides are light gray. Their head tapers abruptly into a relatively short, robust snout with a groove or crease surrounding its base. The dorsal fin, located in the middle of the back, is moderately high and back-curved. The teeth, which are not differentiated into types, number between twenty-one and twenty-five and are about 8 mm in diameter.

Subspecies. Populations of the bottlenose dolphin in the Gulf of Mexico are referable to the nominate race *T. truncatus truncatus*, which also occurs in the western Atlantic (Hershkovitz, 1966). It was named by Montagu (*Mem. Wernerian Nat. Hist. Soc.*, 3:75, pl. 3, 1821) with type locality from Duncannon Pool, near Stoke Gabriel, approximately 5 mi. up River Dart, Devonshire, England.

Distribution and habitat. Bottlenose dolphins are common in the coastal waters of the Gulf of Mexico, including the coastline of eastern Texas. These dolphins primarily inhabit inshore waters. They are found in greatest numbers near passes connecting larger bays with the ocean, but are likewise present in back bays; there are reports of animals even ascending far up rivers. Bottlenose dolphins occur frequently just beyond the surf in the open ocean and occasionally wander much farther offshore, though they are seldom found in waters deeper than 50 m.

Life history. More is known about the life history of *Tursiops* than of any other marine mammal in the Gulf of Mexico, undoubtedly because of the species' inshore habits and propensity for stranding, as well as its popularity in marine shows and aquaria.

The general consensus of cetologists is that bottlenose dolphins in the Gulf are organized into local populations, each occupying a small region of the coast, and that some migration occurs to and from inshore and offshore areas and probably linearly along the coastline as well. There are

Bottlenosed dolphin, *Tursiops truncatus* (photograph by Susan Shane).

no estimates of the number of bottlenose dolphins inhabiting the Texas coast, but some estimates are available for specific regions. Using aerial survey techniques, Barham et al. (1979) censused dolphins in the bays and channels from Port Aransas northeast to Matagorda. Extrapolations of their counts produced a population estimate of 1,319 dolphins and a density estimate of 0.75 animals per km^2 for this area. These estimates are fairly high compared to other areas surveyed in the Gulf. However, these authors admitted to several sources of bias in their measurements and considered the estimates to be conservative.

Within a local area individual dolphins are organized into "pods" and "herds." A pod contains any number from a single individual to eight or nine dolphins actively associating with one another at any given time and generally performing the same behavior in close proximity of less than 1 or 2 m apart. Pod composition seems to be versatile and unpredictable, ranging from temporary, changeable bonds and encounters to long-term, enduring relationships among certain individuals. Several pods of varying size that actively associate with one another and form a cohesive unit within an area of 100 to 200 m constitute a herd. Herds often include discrete subgroups of adults, juveniles, and females with calves. Herd sizes vary considerably from one area to another. They tend to be larger in deeper, open-water areas than in shallow embankments, lagoons, and marshlands.

Dolphins have been recorded swimming at speeds up to 36 km per hour, but a swimming speed of about 20 km per hour is more common. They are constantly in motion and continuously traveling. They come to the surface regularly to breathe, mate, and play. The rest of their time is spent beneath the surface feeding. During short dives, which usually last less than thirty seconds, a dolphin surfaces, blows, and then dives after exposing only its blowhole and fin. During long dives, which last over thirty seconds, the dolphin arches its back after breathing and exposes its tail stock while diving. Occasionally a dolphin will raise its flukes vertically into the air as it performs a long dive.

Dolphin herds typically move in patterns described as "on parade" or "en masse." In "porpoise parades," pods of three to five dolphins string themselves out in a long, narrow line, often 1 to 2 km in length. Pod distances remain constant as the line, which may include from twenty to forty dolphins, slowly progresses forward in goal-oriented movement. A second movement type and herd configuration involves entire herds that move "en masse" and are assembled in dynamic, fluid pods that are less structured and progress more as a single large unit of intermingling pods. This type of organization is most often observed in conjunction with feeding and mating.

Daily movement patterns of bottlenose dolphins vary from seemingly aimless, random milling to rapid, goal-oriented travel. Daily movements are significantly influenced by tidal flow in channels and the outer parts of the bay systems, with dolphins consistently moving against the ebb tide and sometimes against the flood tide. Countercurrent movement may be related to feeding because dolphins may be able to catch fish more easily when fish are swimmming with or being carried by the current. Tidal flow does not seem to be significantly related to dolphin movements in the upper parts of the bay systems, where time of day is more significant. Dolphins typically show a pattern of moving northward early in the day, all directions at midday, and southward late in the day.

Most of the available information concerning the movements of individual dolphins has come from studies of naturally or mechanically tagged individuals in local herds. Two such studies, one by Shane (1980) and another by Gruber (1981), have been conducted in the Aransas and Matagorda bay systems, respectively, of the Texas coast. Both studies relied heavily on observations made from small boats of "naturally tagged" dolphins with uniquely marked dorsal fins. Seasonal occurrence patterns were similar in both bay systems. Dolphin abundance declined from summer to fall, rose in winter, and declined again in the spring. Individual dolphins were variously identified as summer residents, winter residents, or year-round residents of the bay systems.

It has been suggested that *Tursiops* may have two or more home ranges connected by traveling ranges (Caldwell and Caldwell, 1972). In this context, there has been one recorded incident of a significant movement of one of the naturally tagged dolphins, named Thick Fin, from one bay system to the other. Shane (1980) sighted Thick Fin near Port Aransas during the fall and winter of 1976 and 1977. Gruber (1981) sighted the same dolphin in June of 1979 near Port O'Connor, which is 100 km northeast of Port Aransas.

Most of the knowledge concerning the reproductive biology of *Tursiops* comes from the study of captive animals. Males mature at lengths of 2.4 to 2.6 m or at ten to thirteen years; females mature at lengths ranging from 2.2 to 2.4 m or at five to twelve years. Gestation lasts about twelve months, and the calving interval is either two or three years, with a lactation period of up to eighteen months. Calving and mating occur throughout the year with a peak in late spring. Reported birth lengths are from 98 to 126 cm and weights from 9.1 to 11.4 kg. A female has been estimated to give birth to about eight calves in her lifetime. During birth the fetus emerges flukes first. As soon as the fetus is extruded, the female suddenly whirls around to face the infant, and this action snaps the umbilical cord. The infant dolphin, which is born with its eyes open and no teeth, swims expertly and moves immediately to the surface to breathe. Should it show any hesitancy in doing so, it is raised to the surface by the mother for its first breath of air. The whole birth process seldom takes more than twenty minutes, but stillbirths are common.

The percentage of calves in a population is indicative of a population's reproductive viability. Along the Texas coast, calves constitute from 4 percent (winter) to 13 percent (spring) of the population. These percentages indicate a healthy population if the calving interval is three years, but below maximum productivity if the calving interval is two years.

Bottlenose dolphins feed on a wide variety of fishes and mollusks. They are very flexible in their feeding tastes and take whichever species is most abundant. In the bays of Texas, a large part of their food consists of mullet (*Mugil cephalus*), which is a fish of no commercial importance (Gunter, 1942). Considering the fact that these dolphins are relatively limited in their ranges and have rather short-term movements, plasticity in food habits is probably important for survival.

Seven recurrent feeding patterns have been recorded in the northern Gulf: (1) foraging behind working shrimp boats and eating organisms disturbed by the nets; (2) feeding on trash fish dumped from the decks of shrimp boats; (3) feeding on fish attracted to nonworking shrimpers; (4) herding schools of fish by encircling and charging the school or feeding on the stragglers; (5) sweeping schools of small bait fish into shallow water ahead of a line of dolphins charging into the school or feeding on stragglers; (6) crowding small fish onto shoals or mud banks at the base of grass flats, driving fish completely out of the water and then sliding onto banks to retrieve them; and (7) individual feeding (Leatherwood, 1975). Bottlenose dolphins have a strong attraction to shrimp boats, and this association has a profound influence on their feeding ecology. Dolphins have exploited the shrimping operation because for every kilogram of shrimp, 4 kg to as many as 10 kg of unwanted fish and other organisms are incidentally captured and later discarded. Dolphins utilize these discarded fish as a food resource, which correlates nicely with their flexible feeding habits.

Bottlenose dolphins are known for their acrobatic feats. They are commonly seen swimming in the bow wave of boats as well as engaging in a variety of leaps out of the water. Tail slapping, which occurs when a dolphin forcefully slaps its flukes against the surface of the water and causes a resounding noise, is another characteristic. One of their most remarkable feats is tail walking, which involves a dolphin raising its body out of the water vertically until only the flukes are submerged. It then flexes its flukes and moves backward briefly.

Numerous instances of cooperation among dolphins have been recorded. Calves may be left with "babysitters" when the adult leaves the surface to feed. Adult animals have been observed supporting an injured companion at the surface so that it may continue to breathe until it has recovered. "Scouting behavior," in which a dolphin leaves the herd to make echolocation runs on barriers and then returns, thereby guiding the school, has also been observed.

These animals produce a variety of sounds that take the form of whistles, barks, moans, and squeaking doors; these are as yet incompletely understood. Echolocation ability in *Tursiops* is well known and is used in locating food, identifying objects, and, in some cases, maintaining orientation in shallow water.

Bottlenose dolphins have relatively large brains that weigh up to 1,700 g, compared to 1,450 g for man. This has fostered speculation that these animals are exceptionally intelligent and that in the future man may be able to establish some form of two-way communication with dolphins (Lilly, 1958, 1961).

References. Gruber, 1981; Gunter, 1942, 1954; Lowery, 1974; Schmidly, 1981; Schmidly and Melcher, 1974; Shane, 1977, 1980.

Order Carnivora

The distinguishing characters of carnivores are their small incisors, greatly enlarged canines, and, generally, shearing or crushing cheek teeth. Their fundamental adaptations relate to their role as predators, and the order includes a variety of species of different shapes and sizes that are adapted to dealing with prey ranging in size from small insects to large buffalo. Plant foods make an important contribution to the diet of many carnivores, and there are even a few that have become secondarily almost pure vegetarians.

Adaptation within the order has resulted in diversification into a number of distinct lineages—the families—each within its own characteristics related to its particular habitat and general mode of life and its particular food and method of obtaining it (Ewer, 1973). Five families of carnivores are found in eastern Texas; they are the Ursidae (bears, now extinct), Procyonidae (raccoons and ringtails), Mustelidae (otters, badgers, skunks, mink, and weasels), Canidae (dogs and foxes), and Felidae (cats).

Fur trapping is an important industry in eastern Texas, and many of the carnivores are important to the fur trade.

1   Total number of teeth thirty-two or fewer; catlike; claws retractile   2
     Total number of teeth thirty-two or more; not catlike; claws usually not retractile   6
2   Tail less than half the length of body and shorter than hind foot; total number of teeth, twenty-eight; two upper premolars . . . . Bobcat, *Felis rufus*.
     Tail more than half the length of body and longer than hind foot; total number of teeth thirty; three upper premolars . . .   3
3   Total length more than 1,400 mm; weight more than 45 kg; greatest length of skull more than 158 mm   4
     Total length less than 1,400 mm; weight less than 45 kg; greatest length of skull less than 158 mm   5
4   Upper parts concolor in adults, not spotted . . . .
     . . . . Mountain lion, *Felis concolor*.
     Upper parts profusely spotted at all ages Jaguar, *Felis onca*.
5   Total length more than 800 mm; skull longer than 105 mm; last upper premolar longer than 12.7 mm Ocelot, *Felis pardalis*.
     Total length less than 800 mm; skull less than 105 mm; last upper premolar shorter than 12.7 mm . . . .
     . . . . Domestic cat, *Felis catus*.
6   Hind foot with four toes   7
     Hind foot with five toes   11
7   Total length more than 1,050 mm; hind foot length more than 170 mm; condylobasal length more than 150 mm; weight more than 8.2 kg   8

Total length less than 1,050 mm; hind foot length less than 170 mm; condylobasal length less than 150 mm; weight less than 8.2 kg 10

8   Dorsal profile of skull showing relatively bulging forehead; upper incisors usually (but not always) with spaces between teeth; ratio of palatal width to length of upper molar toothrow less than 2.7 .... Domestic dog, *Canis familiaris*. Dorsal profile of skull relatively straight; upper incisors always close set and even; ratio of palatal width to length of upper molar toothrow 3.1 or more 9

9   Hind foot less than 200 mm; nose pad less than 25 mm in width; condylobasal length usually less than 190 mm .... Coyote, *Canis latrans*. Hind foot more than 200 mm; nose pad more than 25 mm in width; condylobasal length usually more than 210 mm .... Red wolf, *Canis rufus*.

10   Tail with black stripe on upper side; hind foot usually more than 140 mm; temporal ridges large, beaded, and converging posteriorly in a U-shape .... Gray fox, *Urocyon cinereoargenteus*. Tip of tail white; upper parts yellowish or reddish, feet and lower part of legs black; temporal ridges not large and beaded, and not converging in a U-shape posteriorly .... Red fox, *Vulpes vulpes*.

11   Tail considerably shorter than hind foot; total number of teeth forty-two; total length 1,200 mm or more .... Black bear, *Ursus americanus*. Tail longer than hind foot; total number of teeth forty or fewer; total length less than 1,200 mm 12

12   Total number of teeth, forty; tail with conspicuous rings; scent glands not well developed .... 13 Total number of teeth, thirty-two to thirty-six; tail not ringed; scent glands well developed 14

13   Black facial mask; tail less than half length of head and body .... Raccoon, *Procyon lotor*. No black facial mask; tail more than half length of head and body .... Ringtail, *Bassariscus astutus*.

14   Dorsal coloration black but interrupted with prominent white markings; underparts blackish; bony palate ending about even with teeth .... 15 Dorsal coloration brown or grayish brown; underparts orangish yellow or light brown; bony palate extending well behind teeth 17

15   Total number of teeth, thirty-two; back with single broad white stripe from head to tail; nose pad large and flexible .... Hog-nosed skunk, *Conepatus mesoleucus*. Total number of teeth, thirty-four; back normally with two or

more white stripes; nose pad normal 16
16   White markings on back consisting of four or more broken
white stripes; white spot in center of forehead ....
.... Eastern spotted skunk, *Spilogale putorius*.
White markings on back forming continuous, bifurcate stripes;
no white spot in center of forehead ....
.... Striped skunk, *Mephitis mephitis*.
17   Feet webbed; tail long, heavy, tapering; ears short; total number of teeth, thirty-six; total length 1 m or more ....
.... River otter, *Lutra canadensis*.
Feet not webbed; total number of teeth, thirty-four; total
length less than 1 m 18
18   Body stout; fur lax and long; dorsal coloration silvery brown
with prominent white stripe extending over head nearly to
base of tail; bony palate more than half the length of the skull
.... Badger, *Taxidea taxus*.
Body slender; fur relatively short; dorsal coloration brown or
yellowish brown and without stripe; bony palate less than half
the length of the skull 19
19   Color chocolate brown to black; head without black and white
markings; tail black tipped; hind foot more than 50 mm
.... Mink, *Mustela vison*.
Color yellowish brown; head usually with black and white
markings; tail not black-tipped; hind foot less than 50 mm
.... Long-tailed weasel, *Mustela frenata*.

Family Canidae (Dogs and Relatives)

Members of this family, which are easily recognized by their doglike
features, are adapted to swift running on relatively open terrain. They
live mainly, but not exclusively, on flesh and possess crushing molar teeth
suitable for dealing with vegetable food. There are four species of this
family still present in eastern Texas, but one (the red wolf, *Canis rufus*) is
highly endangered and threatened with extinction. A fifth species, the
gray wolf (*Canis lupus*), was present in the western part of the region until about 1850, but it did not adapt well to civilization and has been eliminated from the fauna (see Chapter 5).

Coyote
Canis latrans Say

Name. The first part of the scientific name, *Canis*, is the Latin word
for "dog." The second part of the name, *latrans*, means "barking" or
"howling" in Latin. The word *coyote* means "barking dog" and is taken
from the Aztec word *coyotl*.

Identification. The coyote is a long-legged, long-muzzled, doglike
carnivore with a bushy tail and long, pointed ears. In general appearance,

Coyote, *Canis latrans.*

it is somewhat like a rather large grayish collie or a small, pale yellowish German shepherd. The color of the back is a grizzled gray or buff overlaid with black; the muzzle, ears, and outer sides of the legs are yellowish buff; the underparts are a light buff. The skull is moderately low, rather slender, and elongate, with a long and moderately narrow rostrum, heavy postorbital processes, and a well-developed and prominent sagittal ridge. Average external measurements are total length, 1,249 mm; tail, 382 mm; hind foot, 205 mm; ear, 111 mm. The dental formula is I 3/3, C 1/1, Pm 4/4, M 2/3 × 2 = 42.

In eastern Texas, the coyote may be difficult to distinguish from the red wolf (*Canis rufus*) and certain breeds of dogs (*Canis familiaris*). Hybrids have been reported between the coyote and the red wolf as well as between each of these species and the domestic dog. Some common characteristics that may be used to distinguish the coyote from the red wolf are given in Table 7. Howard (1949) suggests a way to distinguish the coyote from the dog that is about 95 percent reliable. It involves the calculation of the ratio of palatal width (between the inner margins of the alveoli of the upper first molars) to length of the upper molar tooth row (from the anterior margin of the alveolus of the first premolar to the posterior margin of the last molar alveolus). If the tooth row is 3.1 times the palatal width, the specimen is a coyote; if the ratio is less than 2.7, the specimen is a dog.

Subspecies. Coyotes from eastern Texas are referable to the subspecies *C. latrans frustror*, which was named by Woodhouse (*Proc. Acad. Nat. Sci. Philadelphia*, 5:147, June 30, 1851) with type locality near the present town of Perkins, Payne County, Oklahoma.

Distribution and habitat. In older faunal accounts, such as Bailey (1905), coyotes were not recorded from eastern Texas, but red wolves

TABLE 7. Characteristics Useful in Distinguishing Coyotes from Red Wolves.

	Coyote	Red Wolf
Weight (kg)	9.5–16	16.3–34.5
Total length (mm)	1,000–1,300	1,300–1,600
Ear length (mm)	106.2 (88.9–114.3)	127.2 (114.3–139.7)
Width of nose pad (mm)	less than 25	more than 25
Length of skull (mm)	174–216 (males) 173–204 (females)	218–261 (males) 210–247 (females)
Tracks (back of heel pad to end of longest claw, in mm)	66 (57–72)	102 (89–127)
Legs	shorter and wider	longer and slenderer
Muzzle and head	normally narrow	normally broad
Muzzle coloration	white area around lips narrow and sharply demarcated	white area around lips extends up sides of muzzle
Position of tail when running	low	horizontal

Note: Adapted from Lowery (1974), Paradiso and Nowak (1971), and W. B. Davis (1974).

were present and fairly common. Subsequently, over the past seventy-five years, red wolves have been practically eliminated from the region, and coyotes are now common in most areas (Map 50). They occur in all vegetational regions, although their distribution is not uniform. Generally, they occupy areas where the woody vegetation is broken by open or cultivated fields and in brushy situations that have invaded hardwood forests as a result of cutting or burning. Coyotes will also use marshlands and fields interspersed with thickets. The distributional changes of red wolves and coyotes coincide with intensive lumbering and agricultural practices, to which red wolves have apparently not been able to adapt. Coyotes, on the other hand, have been able to utilize the changing habitat and have ecologically replaced red wolves as primary predators.

Life history. Coyotes are opportunistic predators that eat a wide variety of food, and this dietary versatility has undoubtedly been important to their success. Percentage estimates of the stomach contents of 168 coyote collected in Arkansas are as follows: poultry, 34; persimmons, 23; insects, 11; rodents, 9; songbirds, 8; cattle, 7; rabbits, 7; deer, 5; woodchucks, 4; goats, 4; and watermelons, 4 (Gipson, 1974). Considerable seasonal variation is evident in their diet, with carrion of large game animals such as deer being important in winter, and various rodents and fruits increasing in importance in the spring, summer, and fall.

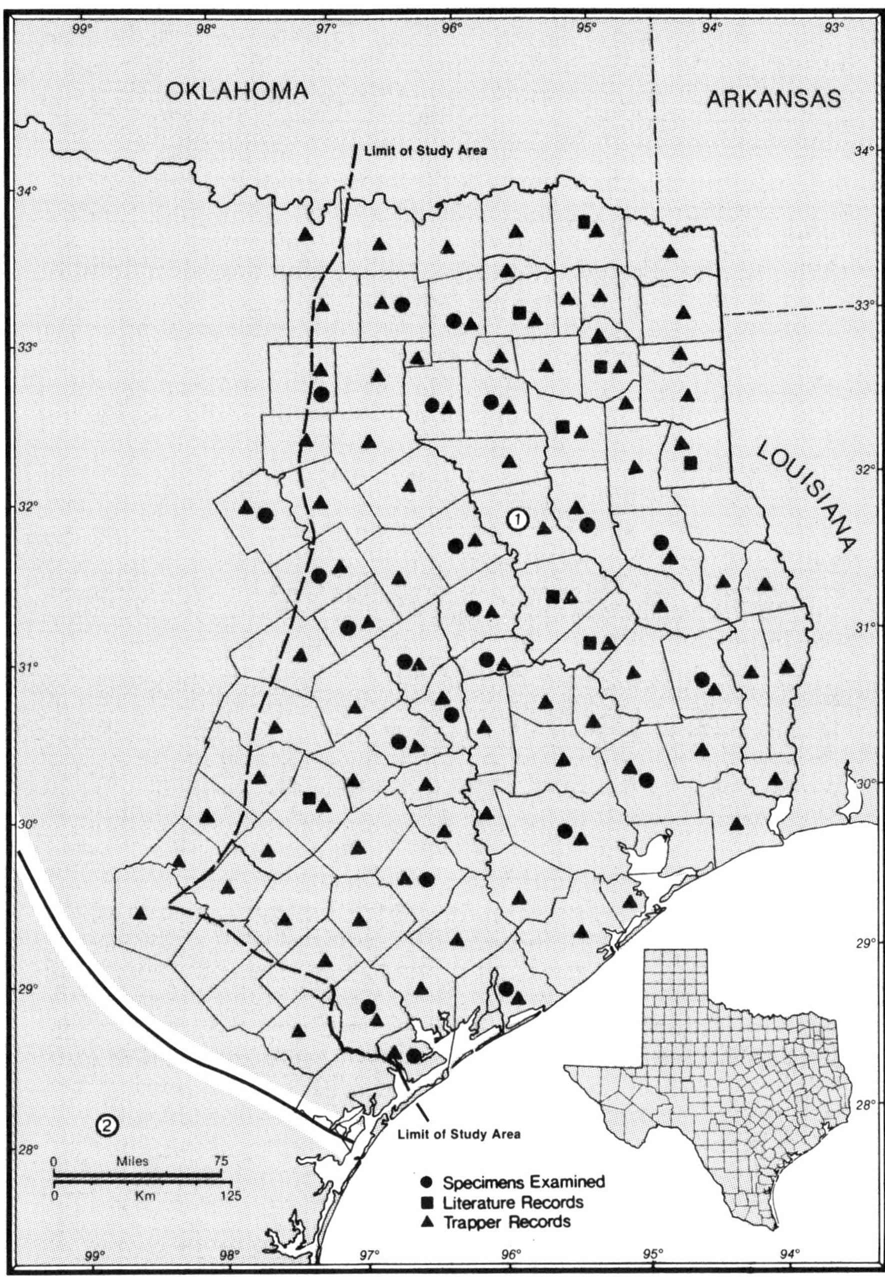

MAP 50. Distribution of the coyote, *Canis latrans*. 1. *C . l. frustror.* 2. *C . l. tex-ensis*. The literature records are from W. B. Davis (1974).

The basic social unit of coyotes is the family, which revolves around a reproductive female. A coyote family has its inception in mid-winter when a female comes into heat (estrus) and attracts one or more sexually active males. All the unattached males within an attractive female's territory join the parade and follow that female for days. Copulation is frequent and probably involves more than a single male. As the breeding season progresses, other bitches in the area become attractive, and one by one the male followers of the earlier female drift to new females until a single male is left with that particular female. The female and her selected mate spend the last few days of her estrus period alone, and it is during this time that ovulation and copulation resulting in pregnancy occur. The pair, consisting of a pregnant female and compatible male, establish a territory and prepare a den for their family. Coyote mates maintain a close social bond throughout the year. They hunt and sleep together, but in late pregnancy the male frequently hunts alone and brings food to his mate.

Nonfamily coyotes include bachelor males, nonreproductive females, and near-mature young. They may live alone or form a loose association with one another for purposes of companionship or killing prey so that they can survive until the next breeding season. Two to six such animals may band together loosely to form coyote "packs." One animal in this group is usually dominant, but the cohesion of the pack is only temporary.

The percentage of females that breed during a given year varies depending on local conditions. Yearling males and females are capable of breeding, but yearlings normally breed later than older females and contribute less to the population. Normal litter size is from two to twelve, averaging about six. Litter size may be affected by population density and rodent populations, averaging slightly higher when population densities are low and rodent populations are high. The gestation period is approximately sixty-three days. The female is monoestrous, showing one period of heat per year, usually between January and March.

Newborn coyotes weigh 200 to 250 g, depending on the litter size. They are born blind and helpless, usually in an excavated den located along brush-covered slopes, steep banks, thickets, hollow logs, or rock ledges. Dens of other animals may also be used. Dens are usually about 0.3 m in diameter and from 1.5 to 7.5 m long. Some females build a grass or leaf-lined nest in the den, whereas others deposit the young on the bare floor. Some females remove fur from their bellies for bedding, much as rabbits do, and in the process completely bare their nipples. The pups are nourished strictly by milk for the first ten days. Their eyes open on the tenth day, at which time they can move about somewhat. Their incisors appear on the twelfth day and the canines at the sixteenth day. They can walk by twenty days, and they can run by six weeks of age. At twelve to fifteen days of age, the adults start to supplementary feed the pups by regurgitation. Pups begin to eat solid food, such as mice, at four to six weeks when their "milk teeth" are functional. Lactation is progressively reduced after two months.

The months of May, June, and July are the basic training period for pups. They learn progressively to accept regurgitated food from their parents, to climb in and out of the den, to catch insects, and finally to hunt and catch larger prey. The den is abandoned by late June or early July, at which time the family begins to wander. Some pups may leave the family unit in August, but many of the family units remain intact for several months. November and December are the primary months when the young disperse.

Coyotes are primarily nocturnal animals. In forested areas their principal activity peak is at sunset, with a minor peak at daybreak; there may be some daytime activity in summer. In more open habitats, they are inactive during daylight and active from shortly before sunset until one to two hours after sunrise. Their daily movement patterns include travels within a territory or home range. Home ranges of males vary from 20.8 to 41.6 km^2; females, from 8 to 9.6 km^2 (Gipson and Sealander, 1972). The home ranges of males overlap considerably, but those of females do not, implying that females are territorial. Coyotes generally increase their home ranges during the adolescent, prebreeding, and breeding seasons. The density of coyote populations varies with local conditions, although it has been suggested that a density of 0.2 to 0.4 animals per km^2 is realistic over much of their range.

In the wild few coyotes live more than six to eight years. Losses are due mainly to predation, parasites and disease, and man. Mortality is particularly high for pups, who are vulnerable to hawks, owls, eagles, mountain lions, and even other coyotes. Hunting and trapping accounts for many adult deaths. Over a five-year period from 1976–77 to 1980–81, it is estimated that 102,920 coyotes were trapped in eastern Texas, producing a total income of $1,830,549 to trappers (Table 2).

Although dogs and coyotes are mortal enemies for ten months of the year, there is virtual compatibility between sexes of the two species during the breeding season. Male coyotes may mate with a domestic bitch, or domestic bitches may be lured into the coyote domain during their estrous periods and become "wild dogs." Likewise, a male dog may desert domestication, mate with a coyote bitch, and remain with her while she is in heat. Coyote-dog hybrids, called "coy-dogs," occur throughout the range of the coyote, including eastern Texas, and many of these retain coyote behavioral patterns. However, the breeding season of hybrids is random, and most of them are unable to breed back into the coyote population (Mengel, 1971).

Coyotes communicate with one another by calling and scent-marking. They are among the most vocal of all North American wild mammals, and they emit three distinct calls (squeaks, howl calls, and distress calls). The wavering calls of coyotes on clear nights serve primarily for announcing the position and hunting success of the caller. These coyote "songs"

Dead coyotes hung on a fence near Bay City, Matagorda County.

are more frequent during the breeding season than at other times of the year. Visiting coyotes also urinate or defecate on "scent posts," which may be a post, stump, bush, rock, dried cow dung, or a bare spot. A visiting animal may go many meters upwind to investigate a scent post and leave his mark. Whether these actions represent a territorial claim or a warning device to other coyotes or simply indicate the presence of an individual is not known.

References. Andelt and Gipson, 1979; Andelt et al., 1979; Bekoff, 1977; Gier, 1975; McCarley, 1962; Paradiso, 1968.

Red Wolf
Canis rufus Audubon and Bachman

Name. The derivation of the generic name *Canis* is the same as for the previous account. The second part of the name, *rufus*, is from the Latin word meaning "red" or "reddish."

Identification. The pure, rangy, long-legged red wolf is smaller than the gray wolf, but definitely larger and more robust than the coyote. Its legs are strikingly long and slender, adapting the animal for long-distance running and for coursing in open country. The general profile and more massive head, broader muzzle, and wide nose pad distinguish its wolflike appearance from the more pointed foxlike head of the coyote. The dull, yellowish brown (tawny) coloration resembles that of the coyote, but the red wolf has a much lighter cinnamon color around the muzzle and the eyes. Occasionally, individuals of a "black phase" are found. Compared with the coyote, the skull of the red wolf is always larger with a more pronounced sagittal crest, the postorbital constriction is relatively narrower

Red wolf, *Canis rufus* (photograph by Curtis Carley).

and more elongated, and the braincase is relatively smaller and more heavily ossified.

McCarley and Carley (1979) developed the following standards for the smallest acceptable external and cranial measurements (in mm) for wild adult red wolves (males listed first followed by females): skull length, 215, 210; zygomatic breadth, 110, 110; total length, 1,346, 1,295; hind foot length, 229, 222; ear length, 120.6, 114.3; shoulder height, 658.8, 673.1. The largest specimens of *C. latrans* are decidedly smaller in all of these measurements.

Subspecies. The two subspecies in eastern Texas are *Canis rufus rufus* of the western part of the region, named by Audubon and Bachman (*The vivaparous quadrupeds of North America*, 2:240, 1851), with type locality designated by Goldman (*J. Mamm.*, 18:45) as 15 mi. W Austin, Travis County, Texas; and *Canis rufus gregoryi* of the southeastern part of the region, named by Goldman (*J. Mamm.*, 18:44, February 11, 1937), with the type locality from Mack's Bayou, 3 mi. E Tensas River, 18 mi. SW Tallulah, Madison Parish, Louisiana.

Distribution and habitat. The red wolf, now an endangered species, once inhabited the pine forests, bottomland hardwood forests, swamps, and coastal prairies and marshes of eastern Texas and extended some distance up the wooded river valleys and through the broken woodlands onto the Edwards Plateau in central Texas. Today, its range has been so greatly reduced that only small populations occur on the coastal prairies and marshes of southeastern Texas (Map 51). Management areas have been established in Liberty, Chambers, and Jefferson counties, where red wolves may still exist.

The genetic integrity of red wolves has been seriously threatened by hybridization with coyotes. In the past, the ranges of these species proba-

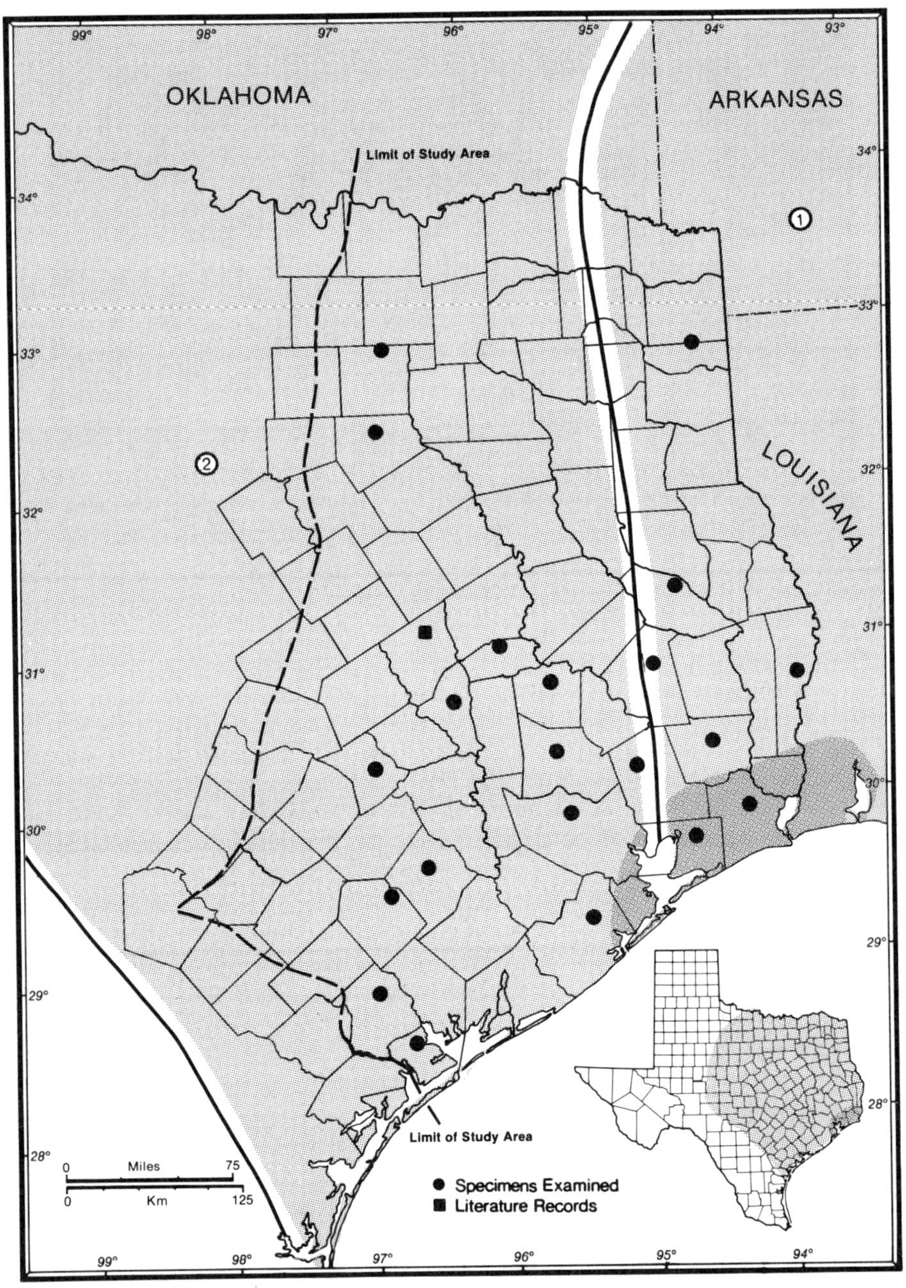

MAP 51. Distribution of the red wolf, *Canis rufus*. 1. *C. r. gregoryi*. 2. *C. r. rufus*. Today the red wolf is extinct over the area, with the possible exception of the heavily shaded region. The literature record is from W. B. Davis (1974).

bly did not overlap—the coyote was largely confined to the grassland prairies and the red wolf to forests. However, when the habitats of the two species were altered, coyotes moved into the forest lands, and extensive hybridization occurred (Paradiso and Nowak, 1972). This hybridization supposedly started on the Edwards Plateau in the period from 1890 to 1906. This "hybrid swarm" subsequently began to move eastward and by 1932 to 1942 had become established in parts of eastern Texas. By 1963 to 1969, hybrids were established throughout the wooded regions of eastern Texas, and pure red wolves remained in the coastal prairie habitats in Liberty, Chambers, and Jefferson counties.

McCarley and Carley (1979) studied the wild canid population on the coastal prairie of southeastern Texas. Their study was based on howl response surveys in which animals were identified by vocalization and from capture methods whereby animals were caught, examined, and identified. Their data indicated that the canid population in the coastal prairie was composed of pure red wolves, pure coyotes, and a wide spectrum of intermediate-type canids (presumed red wolf and coyote hybrids). These three canid types were geographically intermixed, with red wolves in the minority. From 1974 to 1977 the canid population remained stable in number, but red wolves declined as coyotes increased. By May 1977 a few red wolves were possibly present in southern Jefferson County. McCarley and Carley (1979) concluded that the decimation of the red wolf in southeastern Texas was primarily the result of interbreeding with coyotes and resulting hybrids, a process that began on the coastal prairie no later than the middle 1960s.

Man played a major role in bringing about the decline of the red wolf. Among the detrimental factors attributable to man are the cutting over of forest habitat, construction of wolf-proof fences, extensive hunting by ranchers and farmers, the bounty system, and state and federal control operations. All of these factors seemed to reach a peak by the 1930s. These factors, together with the expansion of the Houston metropolis, have virtually eliminated the last remaining red wolf populations.

Life history. Red wolves are more sociable toward one another than are coyotes. It is not unusual to find three or more individuals traveling together as a group, and it appears that they maintain a group structure throughout the year. Male red wolves are reported to range over an area of about 72 km^2, whereas the range of females averages smaller (40 to 50 km^2). Roads, canals, flooded rice fields, and bayous constitute barriers to their travels, and large canals and bayous may isolate family groups to some extent. Red wolves are predominantly nocturnal, with the highest levels of activity from 8:00 P.M. to midnight. Sometimes they bed down at night in the middle of a herd of cattle. In daylight, they rest in weedy fields, or grass or brush pastures.

Breeding occurs in January and February, and the pups are born in March and April. The gestation period is about sixty to sixty-three days. Litter sizes in captivity have ranged from 2 to 6 pups, with an average of 3.85 per litter. Red wolves rear their young in dens located in hollow logs, stumps, road culverts, sand knolls, and banks of canals, ditches and reservoirs. The den entrance is normally concealed from view by berry vines, wild roses, brush piles, or trees. Both parents participate in rearing the young, and yearlings from the last mating are often seen in the vicinity of the den.

The major prey species of the red wolf are nutria, swamp rabbits, and cottontail rabbits. Other common prey species include rice rats, cotton rats, and muskrats. Cattle and newborn calves may sometimes be killed and eaten, but red wolves are not serious livestock predators.

Red wolves produce a variety of sounds, including howls, whimpers, growls, and barks. It is possible to differentiate red wolves from coyotes in the field on the basis of voice characteristics. The coyote call has a peculiarly sharp rise in pitch that the wolf call lacks. Red wolf howls begin on a low note, rise smoothly, and end on a slightly lower note.

Causes of mortality for the red wolf include man, parasites, diseases, and accidents. Many pups acquire hookworms, which weakens them so that they cannot keep up with their parents. Heartworms are found in almost all adults because of their constant exposure to the mosquito vectors. Cases have been reported in animals three years of age and older in which the heart valves could not close because of the heavy infestation of heartworms. Animals with extensive parasite loads cannot tolerate stress situations, and many die from incidents that would be of little or no consequence to animals with a lesser degree of parasitism. However, in spite of their susceptibility to diseases and parasites, man is still the greatest enemy of *C. rufus*, and deliberate killing appears to have been one of the major factors in the decline of the species. Red wolves are unquestionably easier to trap and poison than coyotes. They are like coyotes in that they are conditioned to man's presence, but red wolves do not possess the cunning and caution of coyotes.

Remarks. With the passage of the Endangered Species Act of 1973 (Public Law 93–205; 87 Stat. 884), the red wolf was selected for priority treatment. At that time an expanded program to save the species was initiated by the U.S. Fish and Wildlife Service in cooperation with the Louisiana Wildlife and Fisheries Commission and the Texas Parks and Wildlife Department. By 1975, it was concluded that it was no longer feasible to preserve the red wolf gene pool in its limited range in Texas and Louisiana, and it was decided to locate and capture as many red wolves as possible in an attempt to preserve the species in captivity. In November 1973, the Red Wolf Captive Breeding Program was established through the Metropolitan Park Board of Tacoma at the Point Defiance Zoological Gardens in Tacoma, Washington. Presently there are about thirty wild-caught adult red wolves in the breeding program. The first litters of pups were born at the zoo in May 1977.

Red Wolf Recovery Program field activities were concluded in September 1980 due to the impracticality of capturing the few wolves that remained. For all practical purposes, the red wolf then became extinct. The Red Wolf Captive Breeding Program continues to certify wild-caught wolves and has produced certified red wolf offspring that are available for reestablishment attempts and transfer to qualified zoological gardens. Although red wolf genetic material can be maintained in captivity, the continued existence of the species in the wild depends on reestablishment in its historic range where it will be subjected to natural selective factors and display natural behavioral traits under the direction of a self-imposed social structure (Carley, 1979).

References. Carley, 1979; McCarley, 1978; McCarley and Carley, 1979; Paradiso, 1965; Paradiso and Nowak, 1971, 1972; Pimlott and Joslin, 1968; Riley and McBride, 1972, 1975; Russell and Shaw, 1971.

Red Fox
Vulpes vulpes (Linnaeus)

Name. The name *Vulpes* comes from the Latin word for "fox." The common name refers to the reddish yellow color of the body. Many authors still refer to this species by its former name, *V. fulva.*

Identification. This small fox is one of the most handsome of the wild canids. It may be easily recognized by its coloration, which is pale yellowish red to deep reddish brown on the back and sides, blending to lighter shades and even white on the undersides. The ears and lower legs are black; the tail is bushy and reddish yellow except for the terminal portion, which is black, tipped with white. Average external measurements are total length, 975 mm; tail, 310 mm; hind foot, 151 mm; ear, 85 mm. The dental formula is I 3/3, C 1/1, Pm 4/4, M 2/3 $\times$ 2 = 42.

Subspecies. Vulpes vulpes fulva is the only subspecies in eastern Texas and was named by Desmarest (*Mallogie*, 1:203, 1820), with the type from Virginia.

Distribution and habitat. Red foxes are not native to eastern Texas. They were introduced into the area by fox hunting clubs so that they could be run with dogs. Apparently, the first introductions occurred around 1895 (V. Bailey, 1905). Today, red foxes occur throughout the northern two-thirds of the region (Map 52), but they do not seem to be very common anywhere. Over a five-year period beginning with the 1976–77 trapping season and ending with the 1980–81 season, trappers harvested an estimated 8,479 red foxes, and almost 60 percent of these were taken in the pineywoods region (Table 2).

Their favored habitat is mixed pine-oak wooded uplands interspersed with farms and pastures. Vegetative types containing brush and a ground-cover of grasses and sedges also are heavily used. Thus, they seem to select diverse areas that support a mixture of vegetative components and avoid large homogenous tracts of any single type.

Life history. Red foxes are social. The family unit is composed of the male and the female (called the vixen) plus their young of the year.

Adult foxes are thought to remain in the same area for life. The size of the home range varies with terrain, complexity of the habitat, and food supply. In addition, the area of use changes daily and seasonally. Within

Red fox, *Vulpes vulpes*.

their home range, which may constitute several square kilometers in area, foxes travel from 1.6 to 4.8 km per night. The home ranges of fox families typically do not overlap.

Red foxes are most active at night, with a tendency toward crepuscular activity. Activity peaks typically correspond with peaks in prey activity. They often travel the same routes, which may become worn into trails.

The major food items of foxes are small rodents, rabbits, wild fruits and berries, and insects. They are opportunistic feeders and take any acceptable food in proportion to its availability. While hunting for mice, the fox stands motionless with tail arched stiffly to the rear, ears erect, listening and watching intently. The capture or attempted capture is executed by a leap in which the stiffened forelegs are brought down sharply. There may be frantic striking with the feet and searching with the nose as the intended victim attempts to escape.

Female red foxes are monoestrous and presumably monogamous, reputedly remaining mated for life. Males and females pair off and mate from late December to January or February. Females have a very short period of heat that lasts only two to four days. The young, which may number anywhere from one to ten (average, four to six), are born in March or April following a gestation period of about fifty-three days.

The female establishes the den site for the young in late winter, but both parents live together while raising the young. Foxes either dig their own dens or utilize those of other burrowing animals. Dens are preferably located in loose soils on well-drained sites near or within vegetative cover. Sometimes two litters may occupy one den. Vixens are also known to move litters into dens already occupied by separate litters, and the pups of one litter may occasionally become mixed with other litters.

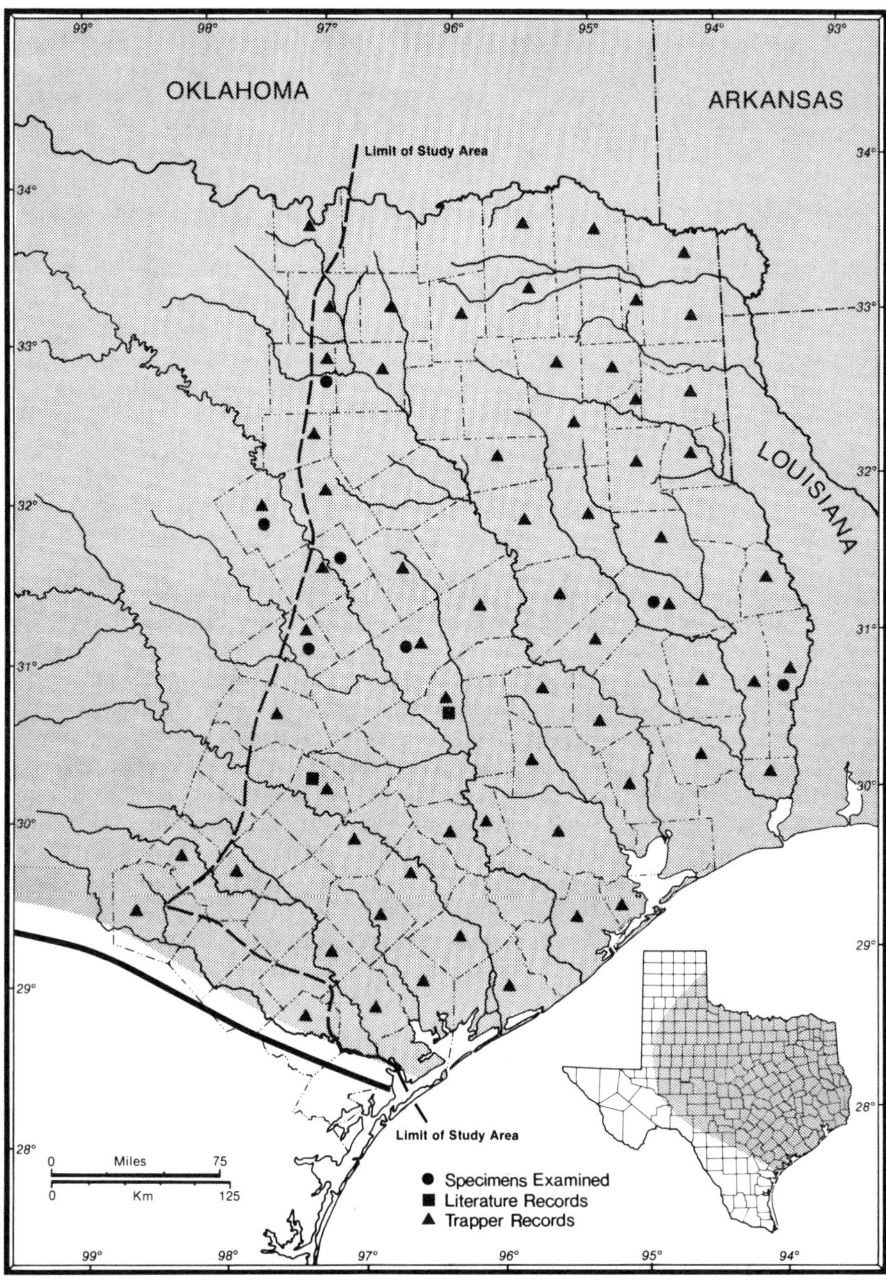

MAP 52. Distribution of the red fox, *Vulpes vulpes fulva*. The literature records are from W. B. Davis (1974).

Pups first open their eyes at nine days of age, appear outside of the den at about one month, and are weaned at eight to ten weeks. Both parents may bring solid food to the den for the pups. As the pups become more mobile, their ties to the den sites weaken, and the center of activity changes to some location, called a "rallying station," within the home range. The family unit remains together as a unit until early fall, when the young are full grown and dispersal occurs. After dispersal, foxes remain more or less solitary until they pair and travel together for several days during the mating season.

The average life span of a pup in the wild is less than one year, and few foxes live beyond the age of three to four years, particularly in areas where they are hunted and trapped heavily. Man and domestic dogs are their major predators, although pups may be lost to great horned owls and other predators. Red foxes are susceptible to a variety of diseases, including rabies, distemper, and infectious canine hepatitis.

References. Ables, 1969, 1975; Errington and Berry, 1937; C. W. Schwartz and Schwartz, 1981; Sheldon, 1950.

Gray Fox
Urocyon cinereoargenteus (Schreber)

Name. The first part of the name, *Urocyon*, comes from two Greek words (*oura*, meaning "tail," and *kyon*, meaning "dog") that translate as "tailed dog." The second part of the name, *cinereoargenteus*, comes from the Latin words *cinereus*, meaning "ash-colored" or "gray," and *argentum*, meaning "silver," in reference to the color of this fox.

Identification. This is a medium-sized fox that appears dark gray over most of its body except for the reddish or rusty lateral coloration, the white throat, and the black stripe along the dorsum of the tail. The tail does not have a white tip, as in the red fox. Average external measurements are total length, 932 mm; tail, 331 mm; hind foot, 136 mm; ear, 62 mm. The dental formula is the same as for the red fox.

Subspecies. Urocyon cinereoargenteus floridanus is the subspecies in eastern Texas and was named by Rhoads (*Proc. Acad. Nat. Sci. Philadelphia*, 47:42, April 9, 1895), with type locality from Tarpon Springs, Hillsboro County, Florida.

Distribution and habitat. Gray foxes are widely distributed throughout all the vegetational regions of eastern Texas (Map 53). They apparently occur in about equal abundance in both upland and bottomland communities and to a somewhat lesser extent on the coastal prairie and in the blackland prairies. According to Wood (1954), they are the commonest large predator of the oak-hickory belt.

Urocyon apparently benefits from "edge effects" created by man. It seems to prefer the borders of woodlands that result from the common practice of clearing small, irregular areas for croplands or pastures. It also does well around human habitations, being almost equally at home on the outskirts of cities and in less disturbed habitats.

Gray fox, *Urocyon cinereoargenteus*.

Life history. Gray foxes are social animals, with the primary unit being the family, which consists of an adult male and female plus a number of juveniles. Family aggregations appear to remain spatially segregated, suggesting that the species is probably territorial. Foxes use scent posts to mark territories by leaving urine and scats on or next to prominent objects within the natural habitat or along travel routes.

Gray foxes are most active at night, although they occasionally move about during the early morning and late afternoon. While traveling from one location to another, they frequently follow an old road or some open trail. Otherwise, they forage through thickets of dense underbrush in an erratic pattern that includes many abrupt turns and reversals of direction. Adult females move a mean distance of about 600 m in their nightly forays; adult males move about 475 m.

These foxes use a variety of places for denning sites, such as scrap or brush piles, space under old houses, holes in rocky outcroppings, cavities in hollow trees, and occasionally underground burrows dug by other animals or the foxes themselves. Dens in hollow trees may be as high as 9.1 m above the ground. Den sites are commonly located in dense cover and not very far from water.

Gray foxes are adept climbers, which is unusual for canids. Taylor (1943) raised five young foxes and found that within a month after they left the nest box the pups could climb a vertical trunk. Foxes climb trees to escape predators, feed on birds, or to rest and sun. They use their rounded claws to ascend the tree trunk in a fashion like that of bears, and they are capable of leaping from branch to branch like a cat.

Gray foxes are opportunistic consumers. The principal components of their diet vary seasonally, but the most important items, listed in order

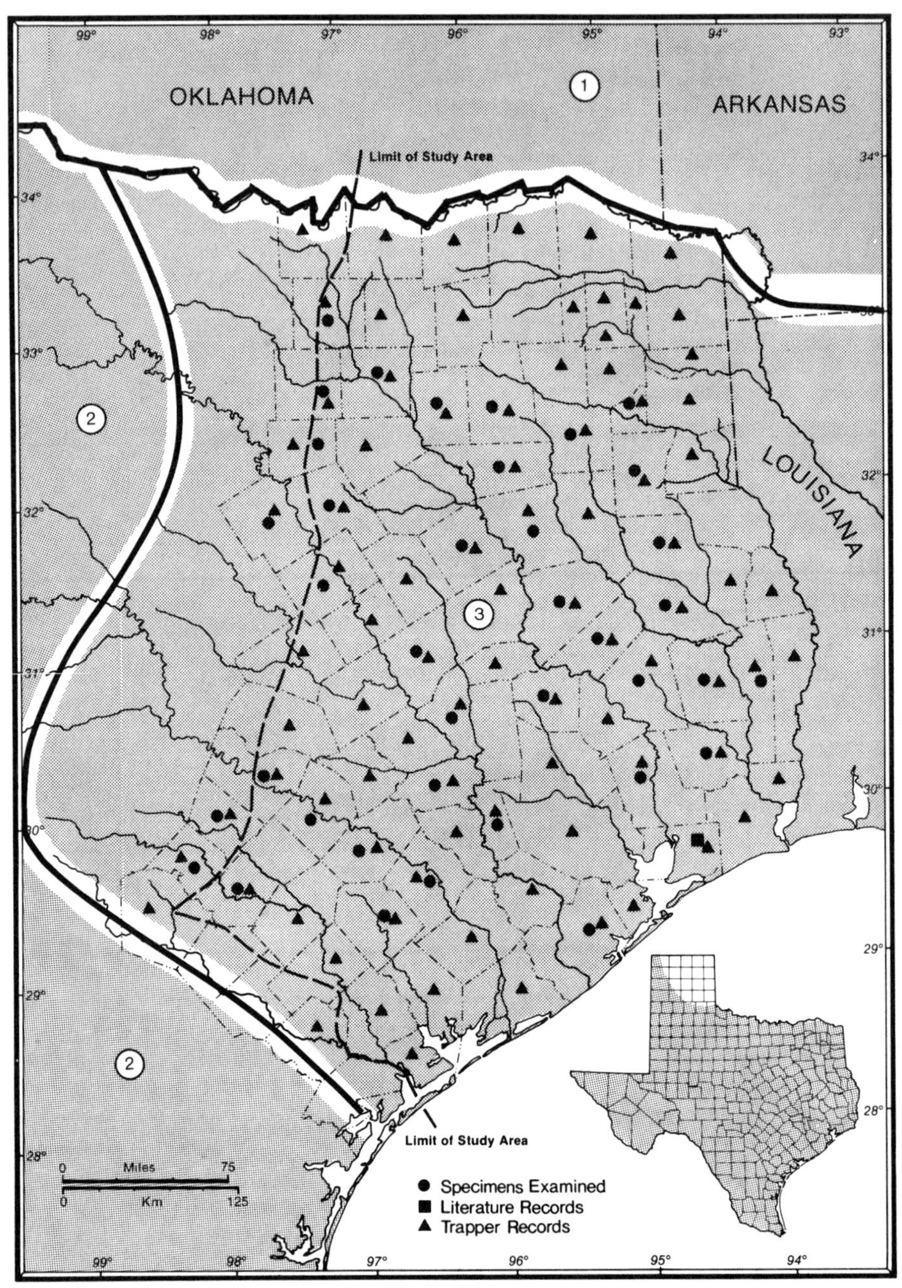

MAP 53. Distribution of the gray fox, *Urocyon cinereoargenteus*. 1. *U. c. ocythous*. 2. *U. c. scottii*. 3. *U. c. floridanus*. The literature record is from W. B. Davis (1974).

of decreasing importance, are small mammals, birds, plants, and insects (Wood, 1954). They eat a variety of small mammals, including white-footed mice, eastern woodrats, cotton rats, pocket mice, harvest mice, and cottontail rabbits, with the latter being the most important item in their diet. They eat a variety of passerine birds, but seem particularly fond of robins, spotted towhees, and mourning doves. Persimmons are their most important plant food, although they also eat yaupon and deciduous holly berries, acorns, and grasses. Insects are relatively unimportant in the diet.

Urocyon is thought to be monogamous, with the pair bond remaining intact throughout the year. The breeding season probably extends over several months from December to early March, with peaks from late January to early February. There is only one litter per year, and the range in litter size is about two to six, averaging four. Most female gray fox breed in their first season, and the majority of young are produced by one-year-old females. The exact gestation period is not known, but it is assumed to be about fifty-three days.

Gray foxes are thought to live from six to ten years in the wild. Major factors causing mortality include predation, diseases, and man. Large hawks occasionally take pups, and adults may be eaten by golden eagles, coyotes, and bobcats. Rabies also appears to be a density-dependent control mechanism in fox populations.

The gray fox is among the five most important fur-bearing mammals in eastern Texas (see Table 2). Over five trapping seasons from 1976–77 to 1980–81 an estimated 46,488 individuals were harvested, and these produced an income of approximately $1,390,000.

References. McCarley, 1959d; Trapp and Hallberg, 1975; Wood, 1954, 1959.

Family Procyonidae (Raccoons and Relatives)

Procyonids occupy much of the temperate and tropical parts of the New World, from southern Canada through much of South America. Only two species, the raccoon (*Procyon lotor*) and the ringtail (*Bassariscus astutus*), occur in eastern Texas, and the former is the most important fur-bearing mammal in this region.

Ringtail
Bassariscus astutus (Lichtenstein)

Name. The first part of the scientific name comes from the Greek word *bassaris*, for "fox," and the diminutive suffix *iskos*, meaning "little." The second part of the name, *astutus*, is a Latin word meaning "adroit," "clever," or "cunning."

Identification. The ringtail is a cat-sized carnivore with the face of a fox, prominent white rings around its eyes, and a long, bushy tail that has about fourteen to sixteen alternating black and white rings and a black tip.

Ringtail, *Bassariscus astutus*.

Its upper parts are light buff overcast with black and dark brownish over-hairs; the underparts are grayish white. The tail is approximately the same length as the head and body, and the black and white rings give it a striking resemblance to the tail of a raccoon. The ringtail differs from the raccoon in lacking a black facial mask. Average external measurements are total length, 734 mm; tail, 374 mm; hind foot, 70 mm; ear, 44 mm. The dental formula is I 3/3, C 1/1, Pm 4/4, M 2/2 × 2 = 40.

Subspecies. Bassariscus astutus flavus is the subspecies in eastern Texas and was named by Rhoads (*Proc. Acad. Nat. Sci., Philadelphia,* 45:417, January 30, 1894), with type locality from an unknown place in Texas.

Distribution and habitat. Ringtails occur throughout eastern Texas in all vegetational regions, but they are not very common east of the Trinity River (Map 54). They live in wooded areas, usually close to water, and they den in hollow trees and logs. In the Edwards Plateau and Trans-Pecos regions, where they are much more common than in eastern Texas, ringtails are denizens of rocky, brushy country.

Life history. These catlike, agile little carnivores are almost strictly nocturnal and active mainly during the middle of night. They are as much at home in a tree as a gray squirrel and are notably quick in running, jumping, and climbing. Their hind feet can be rotated externally at least 180 degrees, permitting them to run rapidly down a tree trunk or steep rock head first instead of having to back down the way a domestic cat does. Ability to rotate the hind feet also gives the ringtail dexterity in grasping objects with them.

Ringtails normally den alone, although members of a family group (a female and her kittens) may den close together. Den selection is informal,

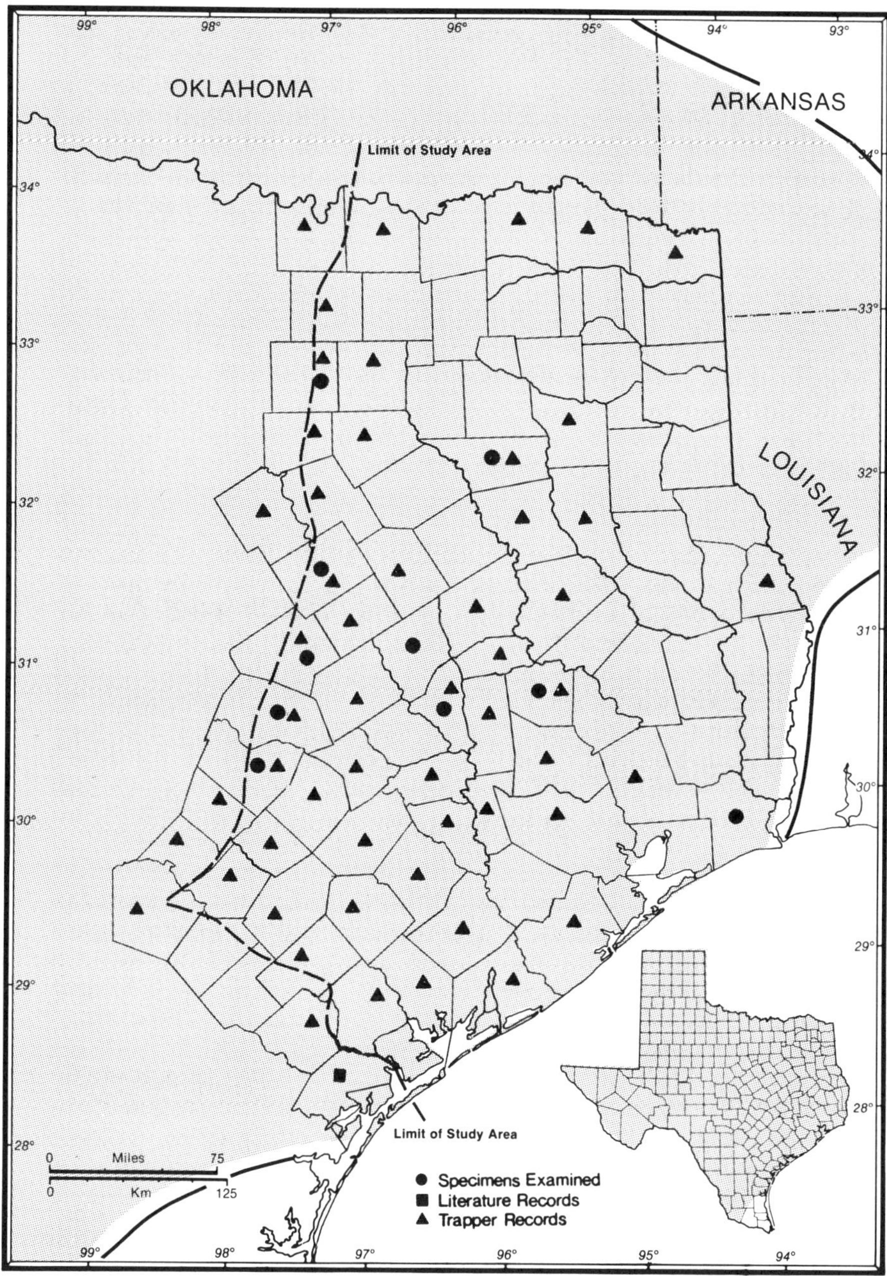

MAP 54. Distribution of the ringtail, *Bassariscus astutus flavus*. The literature record is from Hall (1981).

and dens are normally not modified by ringtails. Favored den situations include rock caves, hollow trees and logs, and brush piles. Females seem to prefer rock dens, whereas males tend to select dens in hollow trees and brush piles.

Ringtails have rather sizeable home ranges. Those of females average about 20 ha and males about 43 ha. Home ranges of females are non-overlapping, although they are overlapped by those of one or more males. Home ranges of males do not overlap. The overlap of a female's home range by one or more males enhances the possibility of the female being bred.

Breeding occurs from mid-March to mid-April. The young, which number from two to four, are born from mid-May to mid-June. Newborn young are small, pink, fuzzy, helpless creatures with closed eyes and ears, blunt muzzles, no teeth, small pinnae, and pigmented bands on their tail; they squeak and have awkward crawling, wriggling gaits. The eyes open thirty-one to thirty-four days after birth, by which time the young are fully furred. The kits will eat meat when seven weeks old, and they are weaned in August at about eight weeks of age, at which time they begin to forage with their parents. They begin to den independently about the end of September, but associate with their mother until at least the onset of winter. They exhibit the first signs of sexual activity when only thirteen weeks of age, and by nineteen weeks they are of adult appearance and behavior. Siblings associate regularly in their mother's home range until the onset of their first breeding period.

Ringtails emit a barking and a mating call. The barking sound is made by both sexes whenever they become frightened or agitated. The sound intensifies nearly to a growl when a ringtail is further disturbed. When females come into heat, they emit a series of loud chirping calls. This seems to serve as a signal to the male that the female is ready to copulate.

Ringtails eat a wide range of both plant and animal food (Wood, 1954). Small mammals form the largest part of the diet (62 percent of the volume), and fruits represent 28 percent. Small birds are third in importance (7 percent), with the remainder consisting, in descending order of importance, of insects, invertebrates other than insects, and cold-blooded vertebrates. The three most important species of mammals in the diet are cotton rats, cottontail rabbits, and white-footed mice. Among the birds consumed, cardinals, flickers, and robins are important. Common plants eaten include yaupon berries, acorns, hackberries, honeylocust, mulberries, and persimmons.

When frightened, ringtails tend to seek out a narrow, crevicelike retreat and wedge themselves in the most inaccessible portion. Also, while playing or exploring new places and objects, captive ringtails demonstrate their fondness for tight places by crawling into any space that will accommodate their bodies.

Remarks. The ringtail is the most important fur-bearing mammal on the Edwards Plateau (Cohen, 1982), but its importance is considerably less in eastern Texas. It ranked eighth out of fifteen species in terms of numbers harvested and economic value from 1976–77 to 1980–81 (Table 2). The average price of a ringtail pelt during this period was $6.50. Trapper records indicate that the ringtail was harvested more frequently in the blackland prairie and coastal prairie and marshes than in the pineywoods or post oak woodlands.

References. E. P. Bailey, 1974; Blair, 1949; Richardson, 1942; W. P. Taylor, 1954; Toweill, 1976; Trapp, 1977; Wood, 1954.

Raccoon
Procyon lotor (Linnaeus)

Name. The generic name *Procyon* is derived from two Greek words (*pro,* meaning "before," and *cyon,* meaning "dog"), in reference to the close relationship of raccoons to the primitive carnivore stock that gave rise to dogs and bears (Lowery, 1974). The specific epithet *lotor* comes from the Latin word *lutor,* meaning "washed," in reference to the food-washing behavior commonly observed in raccoons living in zoos.

Identification. Raccoons are rather stocky, short-legged, grayish to blackish carnivores with a pointed nose, a black facial mask, a bushy tail encircled by five or seven black rings, and large, flat-footed feet with naked soles. The "bandit" mask and ringed tail are the main characteristics. The pelage of the raccoon has a grizzled appearance, varying from iron grayish to blackish and with a brownish tinge on the nape of the neck. Average external measurements are total length, 728 mm; tail, 217 mm; hind foot, 111 mm; ear, 60 mm. The dental formula is identical to that of the ringtail.

Subspecies. The subspecies in eastern Texas is *Procyon lotor fuscipes.* Mearns (*Proc. Biol. Soc. Washington,* 27:63, March 20, 1914) named it, with type locality from Las Moras Creek, Fort Clark, Kinney County, Texas.

Distribution and habitat. Raccoons are among the most common fur-bearing mammals in eastern Texas, and they occur in all vegetational regions (Map 55). They prefer hardwood-timbered habitats and are especially abundant along the larger streams, where wide floodplains and adjacent sloping uplands support mature stands of oak timber together with other hardwoods. They also occur in a variety of other habitats, including bottomland swamps, marshes, around lakes or ponds surrounded by narrow stands of trees, farmlands (especially those with cornfields), and heavily wooded residential areas in cities. They are seldom found far from water, which has an important influence upon their distribution.

Life history. Raccoons live in dens located primarily in trees or rock ledges. However, the absence of suitable natural den sites does not seem to limit them, as they commonly use barns, attics, and other available buildings. In Trinity County, they have been observed denning in artificial nest boxes constructed for wood ducks (Baker and Newman, 1942). Raccoons are also known to share the same ground dens used by striped

Raccoon, *Procyon lotor*.

skunks and opossums, though not necessarily at the same time.

Raccoons are nocturnal and typically spend the day in their den. Activity begins around sunset and ceases around sunrise, lasting about nine hours. Raccoons do not hibernate, but during cold winter periods they may remain in the den for several days and live off their body fat reserves. Raccoon movement patterns vary seasonally and with a variety of conditions, such as habitat type, population density, and reproductive condition. Home ranges are typically larger in prairies and marshes than in wooded or suburban residential areas. Raccoons move less and use smaller home ranges when population density is high. Home ranges also change gradually from year to year.

Adults seemingly prefer to lead solitary lives, although they often travel in groups of two or more individuals. Indirect observations of raccoons by means of radiotelemetry suggest that males may be territorial in relation to other males but not to females, and that females are not territorial. Associations of adult males and females are largely restricted to the breeding season.

Raccoons eat a wide range of both plant and animal food. They are selective when food is abundant, but eat whatever is available when it is scarce. Plant food, particularly acorns and the fruits of yaupon and deciduous holly, make up over 50 percent of the annual diet. Insects, especially grasshoppers, are second in importance, followed in descending order by mammals (cottontails and cotton rats), invertebrates other than insects (crayfish and crabs), cold-blooded vertebrates (copperheads and water snakes), and birds (cardinals, blackbirds, sparrows, and meadowlarks). In forested habitat along the Neches River in Polk, Trinity, and Angelina counties, Baker and Wilke (1945) found that raccoons concentrate in timbered river bottoms during winter and spring, feeding largely on

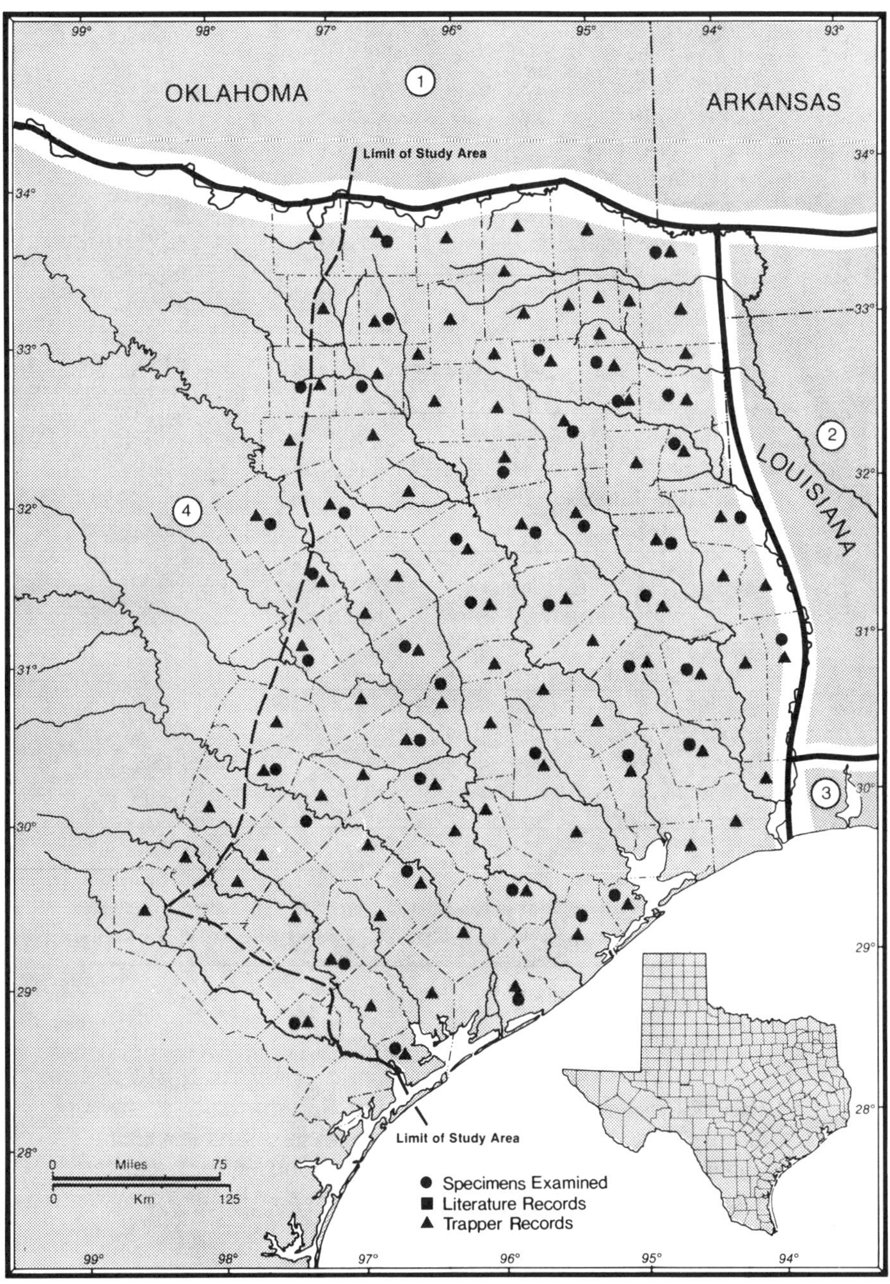

MAP 55. Distribution of the raccoon, *Procyon lotor*. 1. *P. l. hirtus*. 2. *P. l. varius*. 3. *P. l. megalodous*. 4. *P. l. fuscipes*.

acorns and crayfish. In the summer and autumn the populations disperse through the uplands as well as bottomlands in search of seasonal foods.

The mating season begins in February and continues through August, but a higher percentage of females mate in March than in any other month, and most of the young are born in April or May (Wood, 1955b). The gestation period is about sixty-three days. The number of young per litter varies from 2 to 4 with an average of 2.8. Males and females may breed in their first year or not until their second year.

Young raccoons are well haired at birth and have dark skin with no rings on their tail, and the eyes and ears are closed. The eyes open between the eighteenth and twenty-third day. Females have the prominent or sole role in caring for the young. Weaning of the young occurs between the age of seven to twelve weeks. The young run either ahead of or behind their mother while on forays during weaning and gradually begin to den without her just prior to winter. However, families den together again as the winter becomes more severe, and most young do not disperse from their natal area until the year after their birth.

Most raccoons in the wild live less than 5 years (the average is somewhere between 1.8 and 3.1 years). Their major predator is man, particularly hunters and trappers. Predators that occasionally eat them include bobcats, foxes, coyotes, and owls. Other factors causing mortality include food shortages, disease, parasitism, and physiological stress arising from high population densities.

Few attempts have been made to assess population densities of raccoons in eastern Texas. Wood (1952) estimated one raccoon per 3.8 ha in post oak woodland habitat, and Inglis et al. (1974) estimated densities from 1.2 to 6.0 animals per km² of pineywood habitat on a site in Newton County. Population densities probably fluctuate, increasing rapidly or slowly over a number of years and then decreasing.

Raccoons carry a variety of diseases that can be communicated to humans, including leptospirosis, rabies, Chagas' disease, and tularemia. In the southern United States, both leptospirosis and tularemia have their largest reservoirs in raccoon populations, and the pathogens causing these diseases are transmissible through direct contact with raccoons or by means of water contaminated with raccoon urine or feces.

Remarks. Raccoons, as the most valuable furbearer in eastern Texas, are of considerable economic importance to trappers. In five trapping seasons from 1976–77 to 1980–81, it is estimated that 1.2 million raccoons were harvested in eastern Texas, and these produced an estimated income of almost $21 million (Table 2). This monetary return accounts for about 70 percent of the total income of trappers during this period. Harvest levels and economic return were slightly higher in the pineywoods and post oak woodland regions than in the coastal prairies and marshes and blackland prairies.

References. Baker and Newman, 1942; Baker and Wilke, 1945; Lotze and Anderson, 1979; Wood, 1955b.

Family Mustelidae (Weasels and Relatives)

Mustelids are typically small to medium-sized, long-bodied carnivores with short limbs and "pushed-in" faces. Anal glands (musk glands) are present and, in some species, developed to a remarkable degree. In eastern Texas the family is represented by six genera and seven species.

Long-tailed Weasel
Mustela frenata Lichtenstein

Name. The generic name *Mustela* is a Latin word that means "weasel." The specific epithet *frenata* comes from the Latin word *frenum*, meaning "bridle."

Identification. This weasel is a long, slender animal with short legs, a long tail, and small, rounded ears. The pelage is brownish above and yellowish or yellow white below. The animal has a white chin, a dark brown face and ears, and a black tip on the tail. One of the subspecies occurring in eastern Texas has distinctive white facial markings between the eyes. In northern parts of its range, this species turns white, except for the black-tipped tail, in winter; in eastern Texas it does not change to white, but rather to a lighter color of brown. Average external measurements are total length, 430 mm; tail, 125 mm, hind foot, 42 mm; ear, 21 mm. The dental formula is I 3/3, C 1/1, Pm 3/3, M 1/2 × 2 = 34.

Subspecies. In eastern Texas there are three subspecies: *Mustela frenata primulina* Jackson (*Proc. Biol. Soc. Washington*, 26:123, May 21, 1913) in the extreme northern part of the region (Hopkins and Cass counties), with type locality from 5 mi. NE Avilla, Jasper County, Missouri; *Mustela frenata texensis* Hall (*Carnegie Inst. Washington Publ.*, 473:99, November 20, 1936) in the western part (McLennan County), with type locality at Kerr County, Texas; and *Mustela frenata arthuri* Hall (*Proc. Biol. Soc. Washington*, 40:193, December 2, 1927) from the remainder of the region, with type locality from Remy, St. James Parish, Louisiana. *M. f. texensis* differs from the other two subspecies in possessing white facial markings; *arthuri* is distinguished from *primulina* by several subtle features of the skull (Hall, 1951).

Distribution and habitat. These weasels are widely distributed in eastern Texas, but they are extremely rare and have been recorded in only a few counties (Map 56). Most of the localities are in the oak-hickory and pine-oak vegetation regions. Weasels are inconspicuous inhabitants of the blackland and coastal prairies, apparently never occurring in large numbers.

M. frenata occupies a variety of habitats, including brushlands, fence rows, upland woods, forest edges, and bottomland hardwoods. They usually live close to water and occasionally under a house or barn in close proximity to man. In April 1979 a specimen was collected in Nacogdoches County inside a house that had been vacant for two months. The new res-

Long-tailed weasel, *Mustela frenata*.

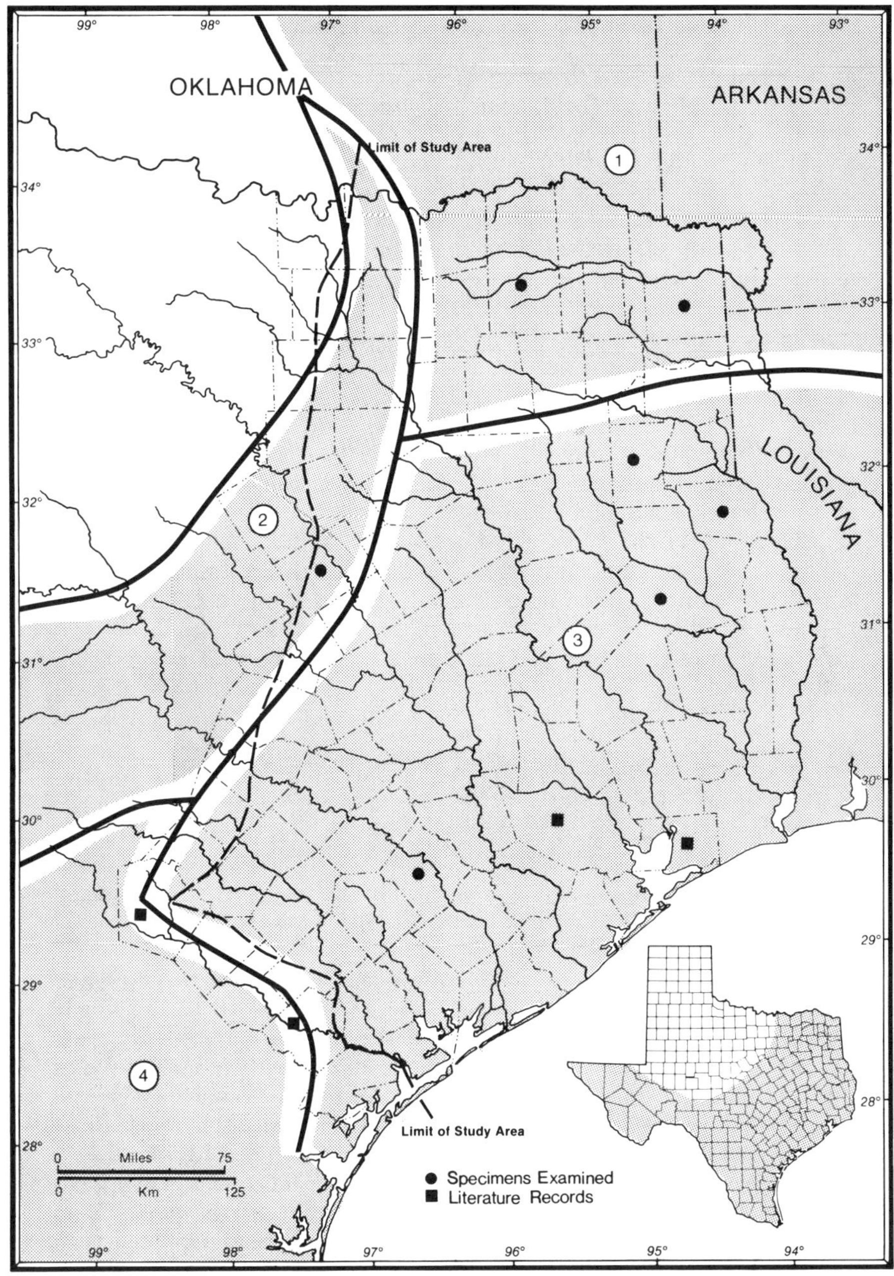

MAP 56. Distribution of the long-tail weasel, *Mustela frenata*. 1. *M.f. primulina*. 2. *M.f. texensis*. 3. *M.f. arthuri*. 4. *M.f. frenata*. The literature records are from W. B. Davis (1974).

idents of the house saw the animal run out of the fireplace and tapped it on the head with a yardstick, after which it threw off a scent that forced evacuation of the room for thirty minutes. The house was situated on blocks and located about 360 m from woods and water (Dan Lay, personal communication).

Life history. Long-tailed weasels typically nest in a rotten log or hollow stump, under tree roots, or in a hole in the ground. The nest is made of grass and leaves and is lined with rodent and rabbit fur. Depending upon the condition of their habitat, they may have one or several homes. Weasels are active both in the daytime and at night, but more so after dark. They are active the year around and show no tendency to "hole up" or hibernate during winter. They range over a fairly large hunting circuit (about 3 km in length and 1.5 km in width), which may take them from seven to twelve days to cover. Their nightly forays usually cover only a portion of their home range. When running, weasels arch their back up in a fashion reminiscent of a measuring worm.

The bulk of their diet is composed of small mammals, including moles, shrews, ground squirrels, tree squirrels, flying squirrels, pocket gophers, woodrats, cotton rats, deer mice, harvest mice, and small cottontails. Occasionally, they will eat small birds, reptiles, amphibians, and insects. Most of their prey are killed by a bite on the back of the head, with the body and legs of the weasel hugging the back of the victim. Weasels often kill more than they need, in which case the surplus is stored for future use.

Weasels are polygamous and breed mainly in July or August. Implantation is delayed for several months, and the embryos resulting from the mating do not become active until early spring, when they develop to full term in less than twenty-seven days after becoming implanted. The single litter, which may number up to nine young (five to seven is normal), is produced in April or May. The gestation period varies from 205 to 337 days (average, 279 days).

Newborns are blind, nearly helpless, and covered with fine white hair. The eyes open at thirty-six days, at which time they are already weaned and feeding on solid food. There is some indication that the male may aid in rearing the young. The young remain with the female until they are fully grown. The scent glands begin to function at six weeks of age. Sexual maturity and adult size are reached in females at about three months, but not in males until twelve months.

Known predators include rattlesnakes, water moccasins, foxes, bobcats, house cats, and dogs. While it lasts, the scent of this species is almost as powerful as that of a skunk and no doubt serves the animal as an excellent defensive weapon.

References. Baker, 1944b; W. B. Davis, 1961; Hall, 1951; Lowery, 1974; McCarley, 1959d; C. W. Schwartz and Schwartz, 1981; Sealander, 1979; Strecker, 1924.

Mink
Mustela vison Schreber

Name. The origin of the name *Mustela* is the same as given in the previous account. The specific epithet *vison* is a New Latin word that means "mink."

Identification. The mink is considerably longer and heavier-bodied than a weasel, and its color is decidedly darker, being a fairly uniform dark brown above and below except for white blotches on the chin and throat. The entire pelage is denser and glossier than that of a weasel, and the tail is longer and bushier. Anal glands are well developed. Average external measurements are total length, 575 mm; tail, 191 mm; hind foot, 68 mm; ear, 21 mm. Females are 10 percent or more smaller than males and about half as heavy. The dental formula is the same as that of the long-tailed weasel.

Subspecies. Mustela vison mink is the subspecies in eastern Texas and was named by Peale and Palisot de Beauvois (*A scientific and descriptive catalogue of Peale's museum*, Philadelphia, p. 39, 1796), with the type locality Maryland.

Distribution and habitat. Mink occur throughout eastern Texas (Map 57), but they are not very common south of the Guadalupe River. They are never found far from water and are especially numerous in coastal swamps and marshes, along wooded rivers and streams, and along the edges of lakes. Inland, mink seem to prefer the floodplain habitats along major rivers except during winter flood stages, at which time they disperse along small streams. Halloran (1941) studied mink on a ranch adjacent to the Navasota River in Brazos County. He noted that when the river was in flood stages mink were found on the creeks as much as 8 km from the river. When the water level dropped, the mink left the small streams altogether and were again found on the main river.

Life history. Mink are decidedly semiaquatic mammals. Their thick underfur prevents water from penetrating to the skin, and the toes of the hind feet are slightly webbed. They swim well enough to catch fish, and they can remain submerged for considerable periods of time.

Mink live in dens located near water in such places as a natural rock crevice or a cavity among rocks at the base of a bridge or dam, under roots of a tree, in a hole in the banks of a stream, in debris piled along streams, or in muskrat homes. Their nest, which is about 30 cm in diameter and may have several entrances, is lined with grass, feathers, fur, or any other soft material available.

Mink are active all year and do not hibernate. They are chiefly nocturnal, but often come out at dawn or dusk and less frequently during the day. They are not social animals and live alone except during the season when the young are being raised. Males travel greater distances and move more frequently than females. Movements up to 4.8 km in diameter have been recorded for males (Mitchell, 1961). It may take them sev-

Mink, *Mustela vison* (photograph by W. D. Zehr).

eral days to cover this area, during which time they use a series of temporary homes. The territories of males overlap, and several males may use
various dens in succession. Females usually occupy only one home site
during the year.

Mink produce one litter each year in the spring. Males are polygamous, but they generally stay with the last female bred to assist in rearing the young. Mating occurs from January to March. Delayed implantation is exhibited, with parturition occurring about thirty days after
implantation. The total gestation period ranges from forty to seventy-five
days (average, fifty-one days). A typical litter contains three to four kits,
but litters of more than ten have been recorded.

Kits are about 100 mm long at birth and weigh about 6 g. They are
born blind, helpless, and covered with a coat of fine, short, silvery white
hair. The coat color changes to reddish brown in about fourteen days, and
the eyes open at thirty-seven days. The young leave the nest for the first
time at seven weeks and are weaned at eight or nine weeks. Adults take
kits on foraging trips when they are about six to eight weeks of age and
occasionally carry them on their backs in the water. The family stays together until the end of August, when they split up. Mink reach adult size
in five months and attain sexual maturity at about ten months of age.

Mink are intermediate in their feeding habits between terrestrial
weasels and aquatic otters. Their diet varies seasonally; crayfish and some
mammals and frogs make up most of the summer diet, and small mammals are the major food item in winter. Mammals eaten by mink include
shrews, moles, bats, rats and mice, squirrels, and young muskrats.

Mink seldom live more than 1.5 to 2 years in the wild. They have few
enemies other than man, but young animals may fall victim to bobcats,

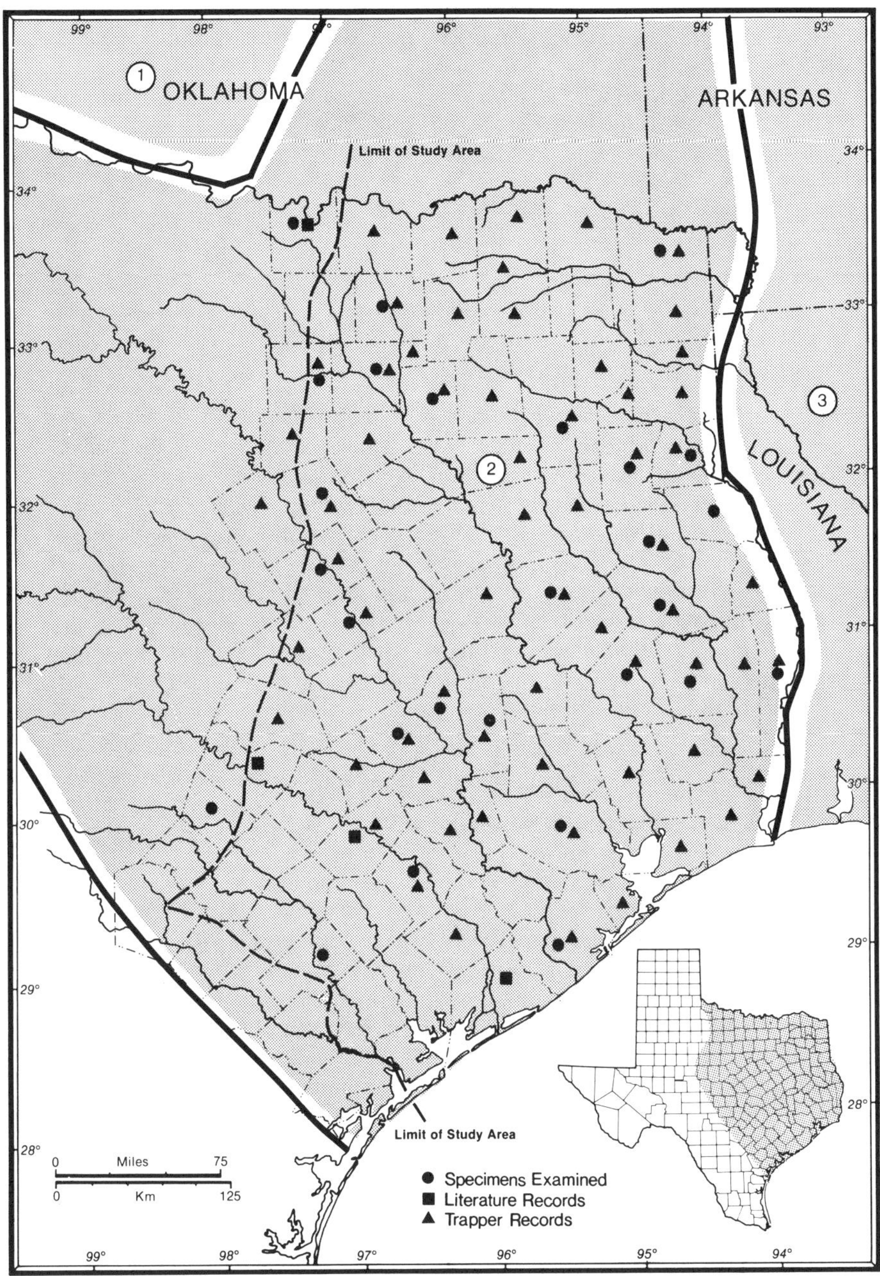

MAP 57. Distribution of the mink, *Mustela vison*. 1. *M . v . letifera*. 2. *M . v . mink*. 3. *M . v . vulgivaga*. The literature records are from W. B. Davis (1974).

coyotes, dogs, foxes, owls, and alligators in coastal marshes.

Remarks. The mink is one of the principal fur-bearing mammals in the eastern United States but not in eastern Texas, where they rank tenth in numbers of individuals harvested and economic value to trappers (Table 2). Harvest levels are highest in the pineywoods and lowest in the post oak woodlands. The average price paid for a pelt from 1976–77 to 1980–81 was $12.80 for a male and $6.60 for a female.

References. Barbour and Davis, 1974; Halloran, 1941; Lowery, 1974; Mitchell, 1961; C. W. Schwartz and Schwartz, 1981; A. Svihla, 1931b.

Badger
Taxidea taxus (Schreber)

Name. The first part of the scientific name, *Taxidea*, is of Latin and Greek origin and means "badgerlike." The second part of the name, *taxus*, is the New Latin word for "badger."

Identification. The badger is a short-legged, squat, robust animal with a short, bushy tail; long, curved fore claws; and shovellike hind claws. The shaggy pelage has silvery gray upper parts with a tinge of brown; the underparts are yellowish white. A white stripe extends from the nose over the head either midway over the body or all the way to the base of the tail. The face has "badges"—patches of black surrounded by white pelage. Average external measurements are total length, 695 mm; tail, 115 mm; hind foot, 103 mm; ear, 49 mm. The dental formula is I 3/3, C 1/1, Pm 3/3, M 1/2 × 2 = 34.

Subspecies. The subspecies in eastern Texas is *Taxidea taxus berlandieri* and was named by Baird (Mammals, in *Repts.*, *Expl. Surv. Railr. to Pacific*, 8:205, July 14, 1858), with type locality from Llano Estacado, Texas, near the border of New Mexico.

Distribution and habitat. Although the badger is fairly common in the western and southern portions of the state, it has only recently been recorded in eastern Texas (Map 58). On September 19, 1975, I identified and photographed an adult male badger taken by a trapper in the Navasota River bottom. The specimen was obtained using a steel trap scented with coyote dung and set next to a creek in a yaupon-oak-brier thicket about five miles east of Carlos in Grimes County. A second specimen was taken on July 31, 1980, near Paris in Lamar County. In addition to these two verified records, trappers responding to a Texas Parks and Wildlife questionnaire reported capturing badgers in seven additional counties (Hunt, Anderson, Cherokee, Travis, Guadalupe, Gonzales, and Matagorda). From these records, it appears that the badger represents another example of a western species that has recently expanded its range eastward as a result of land-clearing operations.

The badger prefers open country, such as prairies and plains, in areas with loose, sandy soils. Rocky soils and heavily wooded areas are avoided.

Life history. Since no one has critically studied the badger in east-

Badger, *Taxidea taxus.*

ern Texas, the life history and habits presented here are the results of studies made elsewhere. Badgers are active both day and night, and they are extremely fossorial. They dig burrows for dens, escape, and predation. Their burrows are quite conspicuous and usually include a pile of dirt thrown by the animal. Burrows are typically shallow and narrow, except during the breeding season, when they are dug deeper. Badgers are both sedentary and wide-ranging in their movements, depending upon the season. One radio-tracked female exhibited an overall home range of 850 ha, which varied from 725 ha in summer to 53 ha in autumn, and to only 2 ha in winter (Sargeant and Warner, 1972).

Badgers are ordinarily solitary except during the mating season. They breed in summer and early autumn. Males are probably polygamous and mate with more than one female. Implantation is delayed until between December and February, and the young are not born until March or April. Litter size ranges from one to five, averaging about three. Young are lightly furred and blind at birth. The eyes open at four weeks, and weaning occurs at about eight weeks of age, when the young are half grown. The young remain with their mother until late fall, when the family scatters.

Badgers are mainly carnivores, and they are especially fond of rodents such as ground squirrels, pocket gophers, and mice as well as cottontail rabbits. They will also eat fish, snakes, lizards, and various insects and arthropods (including grasshoppers, beetles, and scorpions). Their diet includes only traces of plant material.

Badgers have few natural enemies other than man. Some predation occurs by coyotes and golden eagles. Badgers present a ferocious appearance to enemies by emitting a variety of aggressive sounds like hisses, grunts, growls, and snarls.

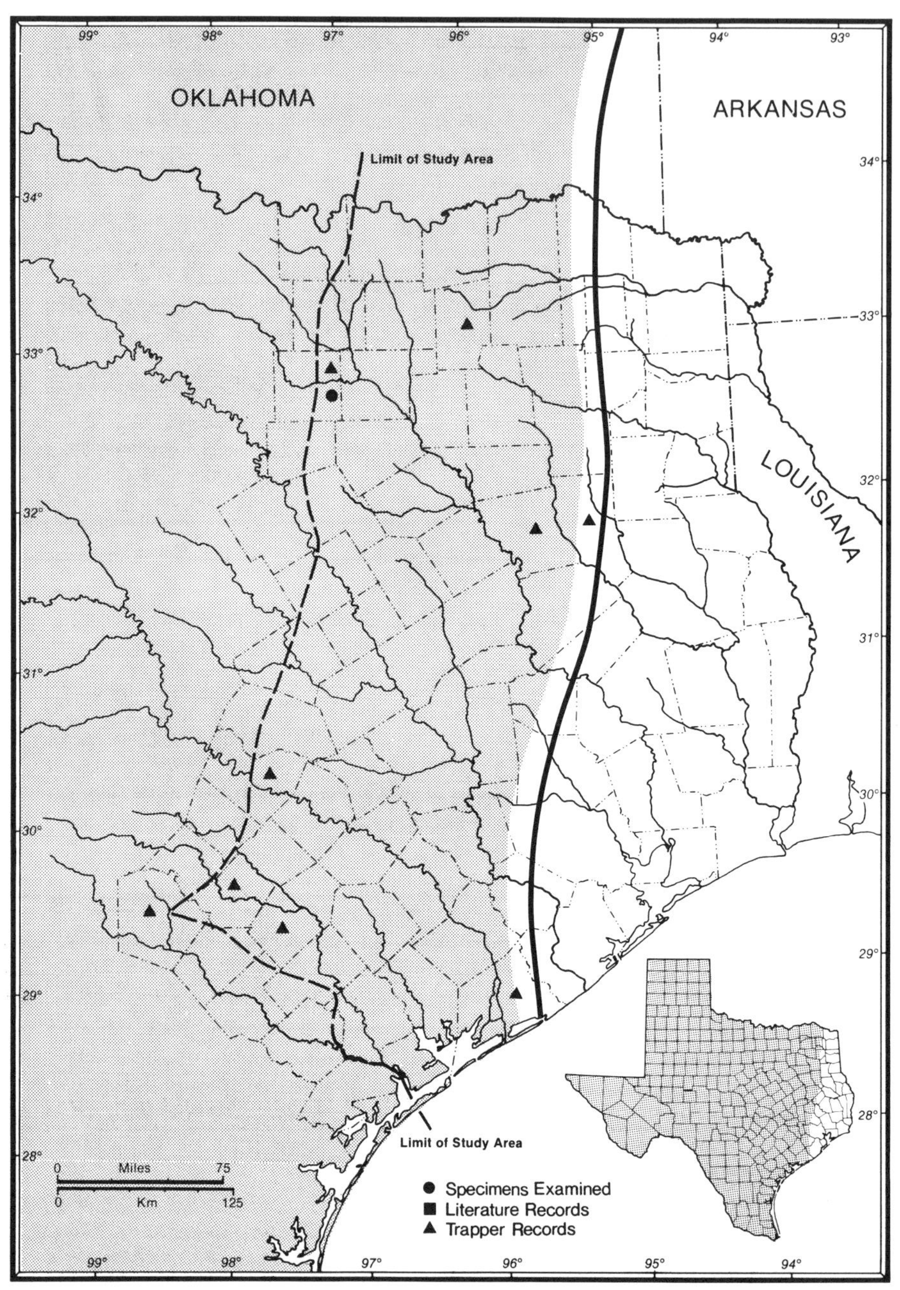

MAP 58.   Distribution of the badger, *Taxidea taxus berlandieri.*

Remarks. Badgers are not abundant enough to be economically significant in eastern Texas. An estimated 628 pelts were obtained by trappers between 1976 and 1981, and these produced a total income of only $3,684.

References. V. Bailey, 1905; W. B. Davis, 1946, 1974; W. B. Davis and Robertson, 1944; Long, 1972, 1973; Sargeant and Warner, 1972; C. W. Schwartz and Schwartz, 1981.

Eastern Spotted Skunk
Spilogale putorius (Linnaeus)

Name. The generic name *Spilogale* comes from two Greek words, *spilos* (meaning "spot") and *gale* (meaning "polecat" or "weasel"), which collectively mean "spotted weasel." The second part of the name, *putorius*, comes from the Latin word *putor*, which means "stench" or "foul smell," in reference to the odor of the glandular secretions of this animal.

Identification. This small, relatively slender skunk has a long, bushy tail that is white at the tip. Its pelage is black, except for the four white stripes on the back and the two on the sides, which are broken near the middle of the back into large "spots." A large white spot is present between the eyes. Average external measurements are total length, 442 mm; tail, 161 mm; hind foot, 42 mm; and ear, 22 mm. The dental formula is I 3/3, C 1/1, Pm 3/3, M 1/2 × 2 = 34.

Subspecies. Spilogale putorius interrupta is the subspecies in eastern Texas. It was named by Rafinesque (*Annals of Nature*, 1:3, 1820) from the upper Missouri River. Specimens from the coastal prairies are considered to be intergrades between *S. p. interrupta* and *S. p. putorius*, which is widely distributed over the eastern United States (Van Gelder, 1959). The character that is usually used to distinguish *interrupta* from *putorius* is the reduced amount of white on the body and, in particular, the totally black tail.

Distribution and habitat. The distribution of this species based on specimens collected and deposited in collections is entirely in the western portion of the study area (west of the Trinity River). However, when trapper reports are considered the species' distribution includes all of eastern Texas except for the extreme northeastern portion (Map 59).

Spotted skunks occur in a variety of ecological situations, including open fields, prairies, croplands, fence rows, farmyards, forest edges, and woodlands. They seem to prefer brush, wooded areas, and tall-grass prairies. In areas where they are common, they have a tendency to live around farmyards and often den under or in buildings.

Life history. Spotted skunks den in a variety of situations, including cracks and crevices among rocks, hollow logs, haystacks, woodpiles, shallow depressions beneath tree roots, brush, or stone piles, and junk heaps. They also will use dens abandoned by other animals, such as the armadillo. Several skunks may use the same den site during the nonbreeding season.

Eastern spotted skunk, *Spilogale putorius*.

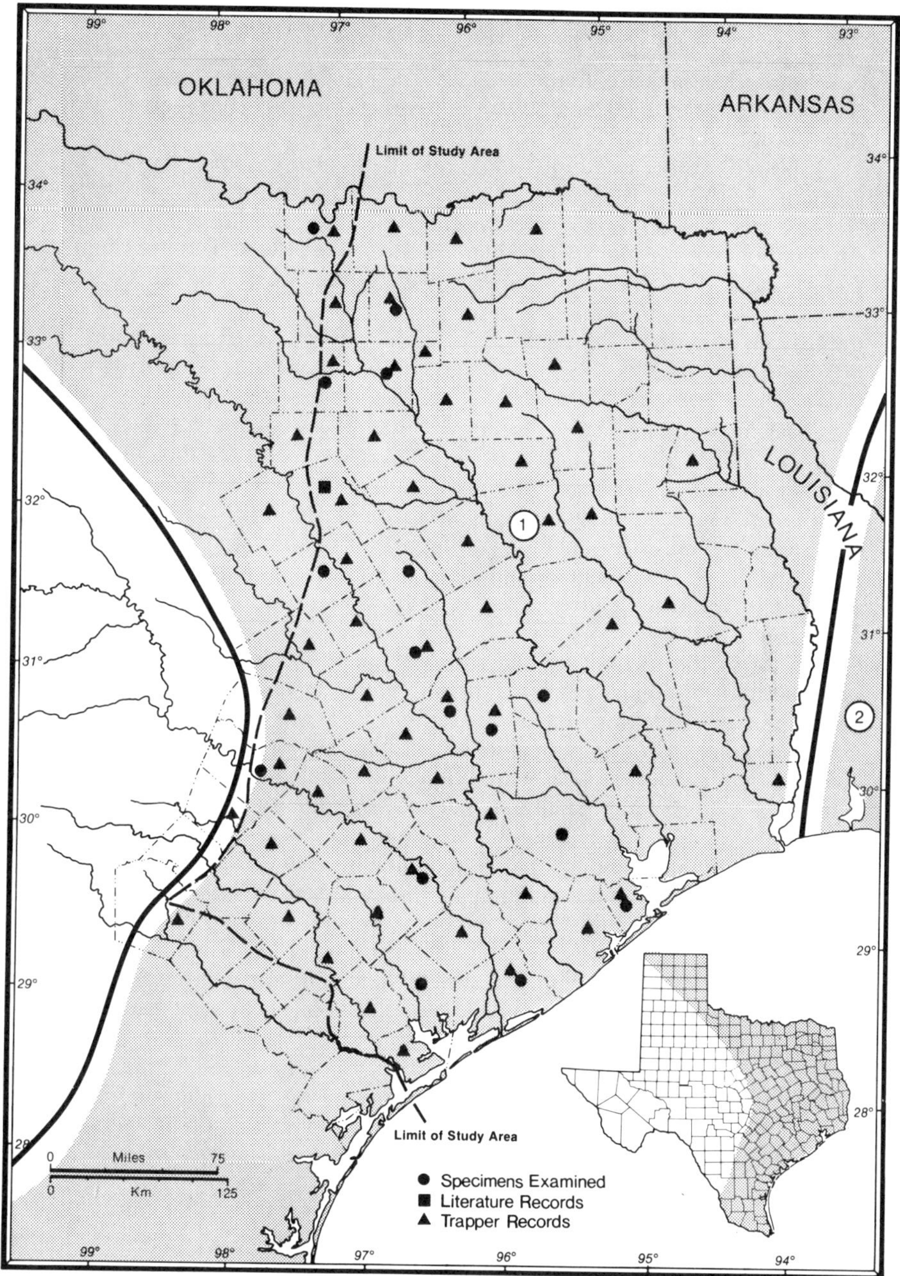

MAP 59. Distribution of the eastern spotted skunk, *Spilogale putorius*. 1. *S. p. interrupta*. 2. *S. p. putorius*. The literature record is from W. B. Davis (1974).

Spotted skunks are almost entirely nocturnal and are seldom seen in the daytime. They are less active in mid-winter than at other seasons, but they do not hibernate.

Spotted skunks are omnivorous animals. They seem to prefer insects, particularly during the summer and fall. Small mammals (cottontails, Norway rats, and field mice) are a regular and important item in the diet, especially in winter and spring. Plant material (mostly fruit) is consumed when readily available in summer and fall. Grain, such as corn, is eaten frequently when other foods are difficult to procure. Birds appear infrequently in the diet. *Spilogale* is an agile climber capable of running up and down a tree like a squirrel, and this enables it to feed on fruit and bird eggs.

Mating occurs in March and April. Some males become fertile in January, but most do not attain this state until March. Females come into heat, at about the same age, in March, and by the end of April nearly all females are bred. Some females possibly mate again in July or August and produce a second litter. The gestation period is estimated to be fifty to sixty-five days, and no known period of delayed implantation exists. The number of young in a litter may range from two to nine, but the usual litter consists of four to five young.

At birth the newborns, which weigh about 9 g, are blind, helpless, covered with fine hair, and have distinct white and black markings. The eyes open at thirty to thirty-two days, and they can walk and play after thirty-six days. They are capable of musking by forty-six days and are weaned by fifty-four days, at which time they are half grown. They reach adult size at three months and are sexually mature at nine to ten months of age.

Their enemies, other than man, include domestic dogs, coyotes, foxes, domestic cats, bobcats, and owls. Their defensive behavior consists of a rapid series of handstands, which serve as a warning device to aggressors. If approached too closely, they drop to all fours in a horseshoe-shaped stance, lift their tail, and direct their anus and head toward the potential aggressor. The foul-smelling musk can be accurately discharged for a distance of 4 or 5 m.

Remarks. Spotted skunks are not very important fur-bearing mammals. They rank fourteenth out of fifteen species in terms of numbers harvested and economic importance (Table 2). The value of a pelt averaged $4.55 from 1976–77 to 1980–81, which is low considering the unpleasantness of preparing the skin.

References. Crabb, 1941, 1944; W. B. Davis, 1974; Manaro, 1961; Mead, 1968; Van Gelder, 1959.

Striped Skunk
Mephitis mephitis (Schreber)

Name. The name *Mephitis* is a Latin word that means "noxious exhalation," "bad odor," or "stench," in obvious reference to the ineffably offensive odor of the secretions of the anal glands.

Striped skunk, *Mephitis mephitis*.

Identification. This is a medium-sized, stout-bodied skunk with two white stripes on the back. These stripes join each other in the neck region, extend forward onto the head, and continue backward as separate stripes on each side of the tail. The tip of the tail is black. Two large scent glands at the base of the tail produce the characteristic skunk musk. The ears are short and rounded and the eyes are small. Their feet have five toes, and the front one is armed with long claws. The fur is long, coarse, and oily. There is often considerable variation in the stripe pattern, as reflected in the so-called narrow-striped, short-striped, broad-striped, and black skunk color phases. Average external measurements are total length, 640 mm; tail, 285 mm; hind foot, 65 mm; ear, 26 mm. Males are usually larger than females. The dental formula is I 3/3, C 1/1, Pm 3/3, M 1/2 × 2 = 34.

Subspecies. The subspecies in eastern Texas is *Mephitis mephitis mesomelas* and was named by Lichtenstein (*Darstellung neuer oder wenig bekannter Säugethiere . . .* , pl. 45, fig. 2, 1832), with the type from Louisiana.

Distribution and habitat. The striped skunk is one of the commonest medium-sized mammals in eastern Texas. It occurs in all vegetational regions (Map 60), but is commonest in the oak-hickory belt of the post oak woodlands and the blackland and coastal prairies. It is rather scarce in the pine forest regions. This species seems to prefer woodland or brushy areas and associated farmlands, broken by cultivated fields that are usually near permanent water.

Life history. Striped skunks are largely nocturnal in habit, seldom venturing forth until late in the day and retiring to their dens early in the morning. Under ordinary circumstances they remain within 1.6 to 3.2 km of the den during their nightly forages. Although not true hibernators, skunks store quantities of body fat in winter, and with the advent of cold weather they may become dormant in underground nests for short periods of time.

Striped skunks construct their homes wherever a convenient place is found. In the blackland prairie country their favorite denning site is under a clump of prickly pear cactus. Striped skunks will also build their dens in natural cavities along the edge of a stream. When natural denning sites are absent, they may utilize the burrows of armadillos, badgers, foxes, and other animals or establish themselves under deserted houses or barns.

Skunks are gregarious, living in families from the time the young are old enough to walk until they are able to fend for themselves. The mother, occasionally accompanied by the male, may often be seen feeding with her brood. The members of the family separate in the fall, but winter aggregations of as many as seven to ten individuals, either adults or a mixture of adults and young, have been reported in well-situated dens.

Female striped skunks are in estrus from late February through March. Occasionally they may breed as late as the middle of June, but

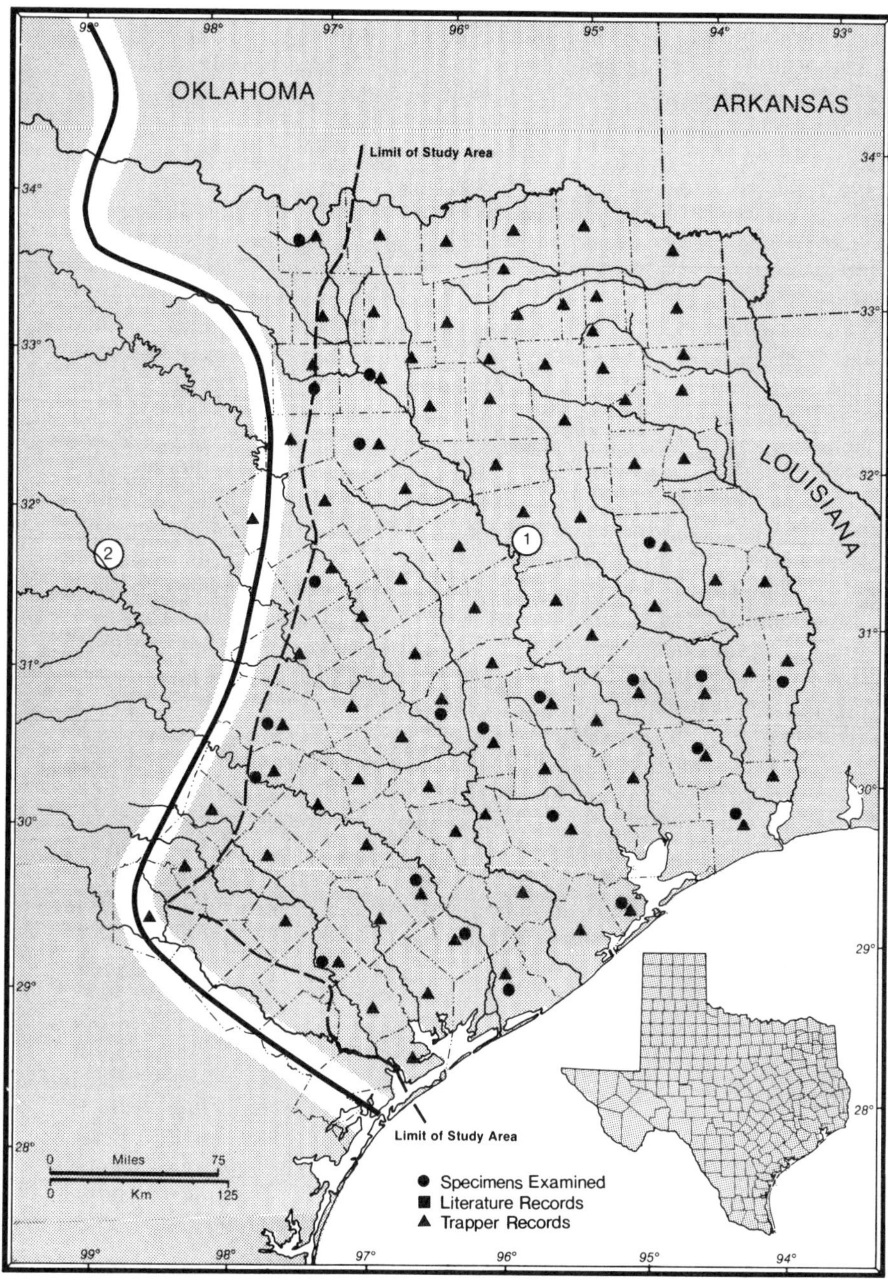

MAP 60. Distribution of the striped skunk, *Mephitis mephitis.* 1. *M. m. meso-melas.* 2. *M. m. varians.*

this is an exception and probably occurs only when the female has lost an earlier litter. Males are in prime breeding condition throughout February and March. Most young are born during the first part of May following a gestation period of sixty-two to seventy-five days. Litter size ranges from three to nine and averages about five.

Young striped skunks are born with short hair, a distinct stripe pattern, closed eyes, and closed ear canals. Their mean weight is about 21 g. The eyes and ears open after about thirty days, at which time they are also able to musk. They are weaned at eight to ten weeks; once babies are able to leave their dens, they follow their mother about as she forages for food. Dispersal of family units takes place during late summer and autumn.

Striped skunks are omnivorous like the opossum. Their favorite foods are insects, especially grasshoppers, beetles, and crickets, followed by birds, mammals, and plants. Depending upon the season, insects may constitute anywhere from 52 to 96 percent of their diet. They are also fond of nestling birds and eggs. Field mice, young rabbits, and small reptiles are other sources of food. Freshwater clams are often dug for in the loose sands along the banks of a stream, and once it acquires the habit, a skunk can become a persistent visitor to chicken houses and apiaries, causing considerable damage.

Skunks have few natural enemies. Owls, hawks, coyotes, bobcats, foxes, and dogs may occasionally take one, but most predators are repulsed by the odor of their musk. Striped skunks are highly susceptible to being struck by vehicles, and road-killed animals are commonly seen along highways throughout eastern Texas. Individuals seldom live more than two years in the wild.

When disturbed or startled, skunks utter a peculiar purring sound and often growl when attacked by man. They typically express their anger by rising upon their hind feet, lurching forward, stamping both front feet, and at the same time clicking their teeth. The expelling of musk generally follows this behavior. Cuyler (1924) has described the musk and the manner in which it is thrown in detail, and portions of his explanation of his account with skunks around Austin are worthy of direct quotation:

> The musk is contained with two egg-shaped bags varying in size with that of the individual. . . . From each sac a duct leads into the rectum, opening near the anus. When the skunk is about to emit a charge, the walls of the anus are relaxed and turned back, leaving exposed to the outside the opening of the ducts leading from the musk sacs. By a contraction of the walls of these sacs, the fluid is forced out in two streams. . . . It is astonishing to note the accuracy with which the stream of musk is directed. The writer was on one occasion sprayed with musk at a distance of twenty feet. . . .
>
> There seems to be some doubt in the minds of the layman or even the naturalist, as to when, and under what conditions, a skunk discharges its musk. The writer has had considerable experience along this line. In hunting skunks, dogs trained for the purpose are

used in order that the animals may be taken alive. When caught, they should be grasped by the tail if possible, which is not difficult when they are bayed on the ground; but if they are driven into a hole or up a tree, they are caught wherever a hold is to be had. When held up by the tail the skunk will invariably discharge its musk under the slightest provocation. . . . It makes no difference whether or not its hind feet are touching the ground or braced against any object. During the past winter, the writer was particularly desirous of procuring some female skunks. A hunt was planned, and much to the party's delight, a skunk was bayed a few minutes after starting. Being anxious to determine the sex of the animal, I lifted it by the tail to the level of my eyes and turned a flashlight upon it. This startled the animal and it discharged, with remarkable accuracy, a stream of musk into my eyes. . . .

When caught in a trap, a skunk will cover the trap with musk until it finds that the trap is not affected. As soon as the trapper comes within sight, the formidable end is turned toward him, and if he goes close enough, he is sure to receive some of the spray. I once caught a large male in a steel trap by its right hind leg. I picked up the chain leading from the trap, and held the animal level with my eyes so as to determine the sex. While examining it, it discharged a stream into my eyes. This skunk had three feet in the air and one in the trap.

While dying violently, as when its neck is broken or it is stabbed in the heart, the animal always exhausts the supply of musk before the heart stops beating. The fluid does not come out in a steady flow as by a continuous contraction of the walls of the musk bag, but is forced out as normally, that is, in jets. This may be done with the animal lying on its back and its four feet pawing the air. . . .

The skunk's musk affects dogs variously. Some vomit and groan as if in great distress, but the spell lasts for a few minutes only. I have often caught as many as fifteen skunks in one night with the same pair of dogs. Other dogs, when they are covered with the musk, get down on their knees and rub head and shoulders on the ground, wallow over and over in the grass or leaves. Still others the liquid does not affect except for the eyes watering, in which case they paw and rub their eyes.

Persons, like dogs, are affected variously by the odor of the musk. Very few people that I know, however, are actually nauseated by the scent, but a few are made so ill that they are forced to lie down and recuperate before the hunt can proceed. I suppose, however, that if many of those who are not made ill by the odor were to get it as concentrated as do the dogs that bay them, they would become sickened also. To some, particularly to women, the musk gives the sensation of drowsiness and oppression, even though it does not produce nausea. Most people, in fact the majority, the musk smell does not affect at all, although to them the odor is very disagreeable.

To a very few the smell seems to act rather as a stimulant.

. . . I have encountered the prevalent belief that a discharge of musk into the eyes causes blindness. The belief is erroneous. . . . I know of a number of persons who have had the liquid discharged into their eyes with no ill results whatever. I have had my eyes filled with it many times and my eyes are perfect. The liquid causes the eyes to burn excruciatingly and the tears flow rather freely for a few minutes. The flow of tears might be offered as an explanation of the fact that some persons say they see more clearly after the experience. If the eyes are wiped or washed, they soon stop smarting, and the vision is as good as ever. Many old trappers and hunters say that a few drops of the musk in the wash water in which a person bathes his face will keep the eye-sight clear. . . .

Old trappers go so far as to contend that skunk musk is good for a headache. On this point I cannot speak from experience, never suffering from this malady, but in one hunting party that I conducted there was a young lady who started on the hunt with a frightful headache, which disappeared after the capture of an unusually active skunk.

Realizing the difficulty of distinguishing between the taste and the smell of such a substance as the musk of a skunk, I hesitate to discuss the taste of the musk. However, the fluid has a characteristic taste as well as odor. A friend of mine, a member of the zoology staff of the University of Texas, was assisting me at an operation on an unusually vicious skunk. I was holding the animal and for some reason let go the tail, while my friend, quite off his guard, with his mouth open in a hearty laugh, received a full charge of musk squarely in his mouth. Now Mr. H. differs from the writer in that he is in full possession of all his senses including taste and smell. He states that the musk itself tastes like the concentrated odor of the liquid. It has a sweetish tang and flavor resembling that of analin oil. The musk does not burn the lining of the mouth but has the same puckering effect as gasoline. . . .

There are many ways of partially eliminating the odor of the skunk from one's skin but there are very few means which are sufficiently strong to kill the odor immediately. In fact it is nearly impossible to deodorize the skin or clothing permanently by a single cleansing, but some methods are capable of reducing the odor to the point where close examination is necessary to detect it. The hands even after many washings may seem free from the skunk odor which is brought out again when the hands are warmed over the fire.

Gasoline or ammonia will take off the smell thoroughly enough to make the odor inoffensive or even unrecognizable after the first washing. A few drops of crude carbolic acid in a pan of water together with a drop or two of oil of wintergreen will also eliminate the smell for the most part. To bury the clothes for a certain length of time and to let them soak in running water are old methods of cleansing, said to be effective. The ordinary treatment of soap and water has little effect upon the odor, removing only the strong, fresh smell.

A footnote to the article written by Cuyler reads as follows: "For the purposes of this study the writer, Mr. Cuyler, is eminently endowed (?) by nature, for he has completely lost his sense of smell."

Remarks. Striped skunks are commonly obtained by trappers, but because of the low value of their pelt they are not an important fur producer in eastern Texas. From 1976–77 to 1980–81 they ranked ninth out of fifteen species in terms of individuals harvested and economic value (see Table 2). The average price paid for a pelt during this period was $1.95.

References. Cuyler, 1924; W. B. Davis, 1951b; McCarley, 1959d; Patton, 1974; Storm, 1972; Verts, 1967; Wood, 1954.

Hog-nosed Skunk
Conepatus mesoleucus (Lichtenstein)

Name. The generic name *Conepatus* comes from the Mexican word *conepatl*, in reference to the burrowing habits of this species (Coues 1877). The specific epithet *mesoleucus* comes from two Greek words, *mesos*, meaning "middle," and *leukos*, meaning "white," in obvious reference to the broad white stripe that is characteristic of this species.

Identification. This large skunk has a long, naked nose, very long claws, a brownish black body, and a solid white stripe that begins on top of its head and extends the entire length of the body. The tail is white all over, with a few scattered black hairs beneath, and is shorter in proportion to the body length than the tails of other skunks in eastern Texas. Average external measurements are total length, 625 mm; tail, 257 mm; hind foot, 78 mm; ear, 27 mm. Females average smaller than males. The dental formula is I 3/3, C 1/1, Pm 2/3, M 1/2 × 2 = 32.

Subspecies. Two subspecies occur in eastern Texas. *Conepatus mesoleucus mearnsi* occurs along the western and southern boundary of the region and was named by Merriam (*Proc. Biol. Soc. Washington*, 15:163, August 6, 1902), with the type locality from Mason, Mason County, Texas. Specimens from the Big Thicket area belong to a separate subspecies, *C. m. telmalestes*, which was named by V. Bailey (*N. Amer. Fauna*, 25:203, October 24, 1905), with the type locality from 7 mi. NE Sour Lake, Hardin County, Texas. Compared to *mearnsi*, *telmalestes* has a slenderer skull and strikingly smaller upper and lower carnassials (V. Bailey, 1905:203).

Distribution and habitat. The hog-nosed skunk reaches the eastern limits of its distribution in the study area. The range of *C. m. telmalestes* is apparently disjunct by about 200 km from the main portion of the species range to the west (Map 61). The closest recorded localities for *C. m. mearnsi* are Waco, Austin, and San Antonio. The only record from the southern portion of eastern Texas is from near Cuero in DeWitt County.

Hog-nosed skunk, *Conepatus mesoleucus* (photograph by Woodrow Goodpasture).

Both subspecies of the hog-nosed skunk are extremely rare in eastern Texas, and nothing is known of their habitat. The species is generally associated over a wide area with the rugged canyon country of foothills and mountainous regions (Schmidly, 1977). Thus, the occurrence of a relict population in the most humid and densely timbered region of Texas is of particular interest.

Life history. Hog-nosed skunks, unlike striped skunks, are seldom found around human constructions. They are better adapted for rough, rocky terrain than are other skunks. They use their long claws and piglike

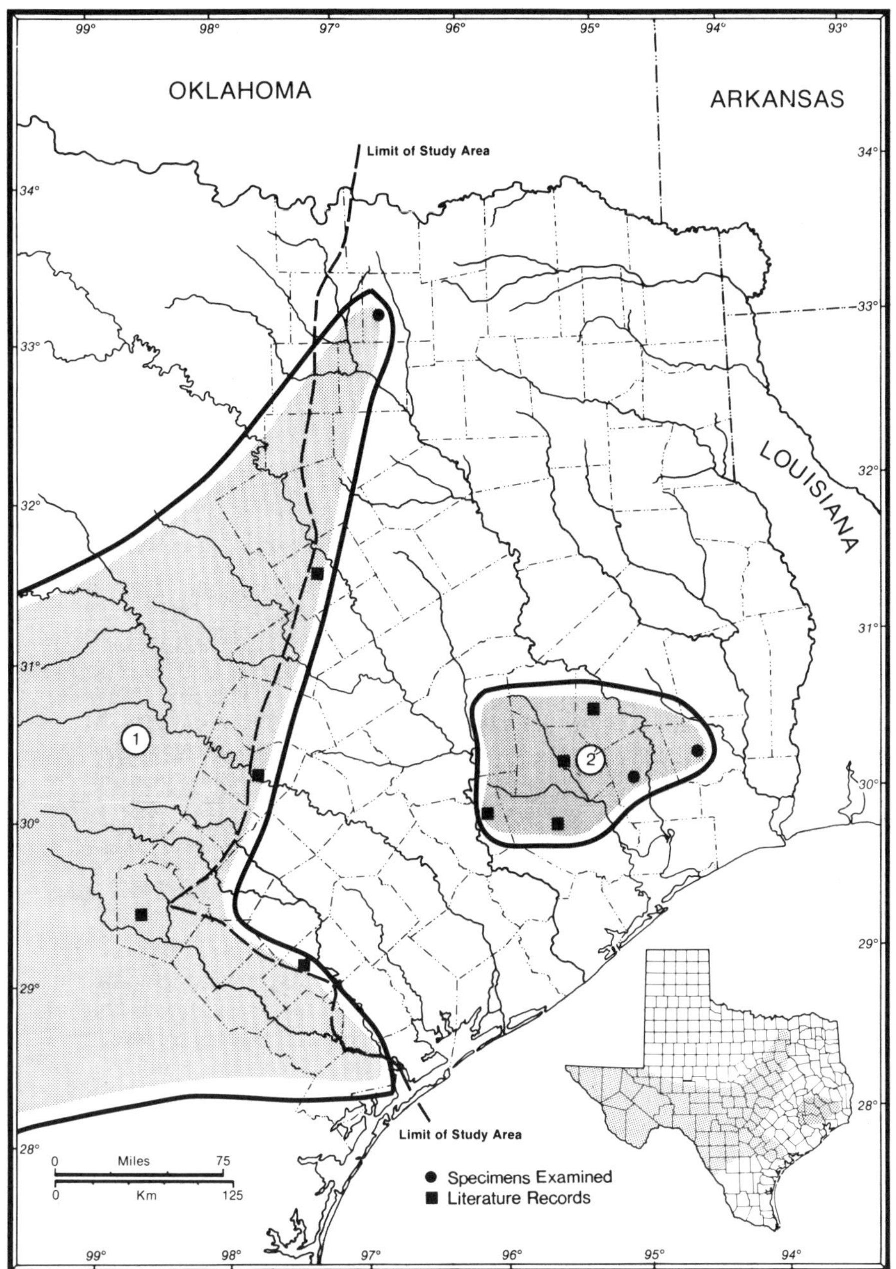

MAP 61. Distribution of the hog-nosed skunk, *Conepatus mesoleucus*. 1. *C. m. mearnsi*. 2. *C. m. telmalestes*. The literature records are from W. B. Davis (1974), Hall and Kelson (1959), and Raun and Wilks (1961).

nose to dig for insects, and their presence in an area is easily detected by their diggings, which resemble the rootings of a pig.

Although largely nocturnal, they are not strictly so and occasionally may be seen feeding during the heat of the day. They are seldom as abundant as striped skunks in any part of their range. As mentioned previously, these skunks prefer rocky situations when available because of the numerous cracks and hollows that can serve as den sites. Not only do the skunks winter in such dens, but they also use them as nurseries for their young. Unlike the striped skunk, this species is more or less unsocial. Usually only one individual lives in a den.

Hog-nosed skunks are primarily insectivorous, but they will eat vegetation in season as well as spiders, snails, small mammals, and reptiles. Mating occurs in late February, and the young are born in late April or early May following a gestation period of approximately two months. Litter size ranges from two to four (average, three) and is limited because each female has only three pair of mammae, compared to six or seven pair in the striped skunk. Nothing has been recorded on the growth and development of the young.

Because hog-nosed skunks are not abundant, they are not important as a fur producer in eastern Texas. Their pelt is inferior in quality and never commands as high a price as that of striped skunks.

Remarks. V. Bailey (1905:205) was the first to report the isolated population of *C. m. telmalestes* in the Big Thicket region in Liberty and Hardin counties. He obtained eight specimens and commented, "At Saratoga, Kountze, and Cleveland the white-backed skunk is said to be the commonest species, and under a trapper's shed at a ranch on Tarkington Prairie in November, 1904, I saw eight or ten of their skins hanging up to dry with a smaller number of skins of *Mephitis mesomelas.*" The implication of Bailey's statement is that *Conepatus* may have been more common than *Mephitis* in the Big Thicket around the turn of the century. No other specimens of this skunk were obtained or reported until March 5, 1960, when Raun and Wilks (1961) picked up a specimen dead on the road in Waller County. W. B. Davis (1945) assumed that the Big Thicket population had been wiped out, but McCarley (1959d) believed that, on the basis of conversations with individuals familiar with the region, *Conepatus* was extant but very rare in some sections of the Big Thicket.

During my three years of field work in Big Thicket National Preserve, I did not find any evidence that the hog-nosed skunk occurs on any of the units of the preserve. No individuals were observed or trapped, and none of the skunks found dead along the highways were of the hog-nosed type. However, several individuals who actively trap in the Big Thicket told me they occasionally trap hog-nosed or what they call "white-backed" skunks. For this reason, I mailed a questionnaire to all licensed trappers in the four-county area of the preserve (Hardin, Tyler, Polk, and Liberty) with a specific question relating to the type of skunks (striped or hog-nosed) harvested. The survey instrument included pictures of striped and hog-nosed skunks, and each respondent was asked to list the number of each type harvested. Thirty trappers, or 8 percent of the individuals who responded to the questionnaire, reported taking a total of eighty-eight hog-nosed skunks. This harvest was about one-third of the number of striped skunks harvested and more than five times greater than the number of spotted skunks taken.

Based on the trapper survey it seems likely that hog-nosed skunks are still extant in the Big Thicket. However, it is also possible that some trappers are confusing hog-nosed skunks with striped skunks, which have extremely broad dorsal stripes. Patton (1974) demonstrated that varying amounts of white are found on striped skunks and that in some geographic areas hog-nosed skunks have evolved a pattern similar to that of striped skunks. Final verification of the existence of hog-nosed skunks in the Big Thicket will require voucher specimens.

References. V. Bailey, 1905; W. B. Davis, 1945, 1951b; McCarley, 1959d; Patton, 1974; Raun and Wilks, 1961; Schmidly, 1977; Strecker, 1924.

River Otter
Lutra canadensis (Schreber)

Name. The generic name *Lutra* is derived from the Latin word meaning "otter." The specific epithet *canadensis* is a combination of the country Canada and the Latin word *ensis*, meaning "belonging to," in reference to the country from which the species was first described.

Identification. This long-bodied, short-legged, semiaquatic mustelid cannot be confused with any other mammal in eastern Texas. Included among its distinctive features are its sleek, dark brown pelage with dense, oily underfur overlaid by glossy guard hairs; its short, thick neck and flattened head; its long, heavy tail, which is flat on the bottom, thick at the base, and tapered toward the tip; and its five fully webbed toes on each foot. The underparts are paler than the upper parts; the muzzle and throat are silvery gray. Average external measurements are total length, 1,090 mm; tail, 405 mm; hind foot, 120 mm; ear, 25 mm. Weight is about 9.4 kg. Females are slightly smaller and lighter than males. The dental formula is I 3/3, C 1/1, Pm 4/3, M 1/2 × 2 = 36.

Subspecies. Otters from eastern Texas are referable to the subspecies *Lutra canadensis lataxina*, which was named by F. Cuvier (*Dictionnaire des sciences naturelles* . . . , 27:242, 1823) with the type from South Carolina. Specimens from Texas and Louisiana were formerly included within the range of *L. c. texensis* (type locality 20 mi. W Angelina, Brazoria County), but this subspecies was recently placed in synonomy under *lataxina* (Van Zyll de Jong, 1972).

Distribution and habitat. Otters occur in the marshes, freshwater swamps, and permanent streams and tributaries throughout eastern Texas (Map 62). They occupy a variety of aquatic situations because they are very mobile and capable of changing habitats at any time. Ideal habitat is a deep-water swamp, which supplies both food and shelter, adjacent to a

River otter, *Lutra canadensis*.

large, log-filled, fish-producing lake, which furnishes additional food and abundant water for swimming or play. Otters seemingly prefer clear to muddy waters.

Historical reports indicate that otters were common throughout the region around the turn of the century, especially in the Big Thicket area of Liberty and Hardin counties (V. Bailey, 1905). Reports of their presence were also made along the Red River at Texarkana, along the Neches and San Jacinto rivers near Beaumont and Conroe, from Palacio Creek in Matagorda County, and on the Colorado River near Austin. Seton (1926) referred to a specimen collected in Colorado County, and Peterson (1946) reported that otters occurred in Brazos County until about 1932.

In recent years concern has been voiced about the disappearance of otters in many portions of their range as a result of habitat loss and heavy trapping pressure. In response to this concern, Brownlee (1977) of the Texas Parks and Wildlife Department prepared a special report on the status of the otter in Texas. Information presented in the Brownlee report indicates that otters still occur in the Sulphur, Cypress, Sabine, Neches, Neches-Trinity, Trinity–San Jacinto, and San Jacinto watersheds as well as the eastern quarter of the Red River watershed. They are especially abundant in San Augustine, Hardin, Chambers, and Orange counties. The Brownlee report suggests that otters are more plentiful than in earlier years because increased freshwater impoundments have created additional suitable habitat.

Life history. Most otters locate their dens in excavations close to water under tree roots, rock piles, logs, or thickets. The hollow bases of cypress trees and tupelo gums are especially popular. Occasionally, they will take over beaver lodges or muskrat dens for their own use after killing

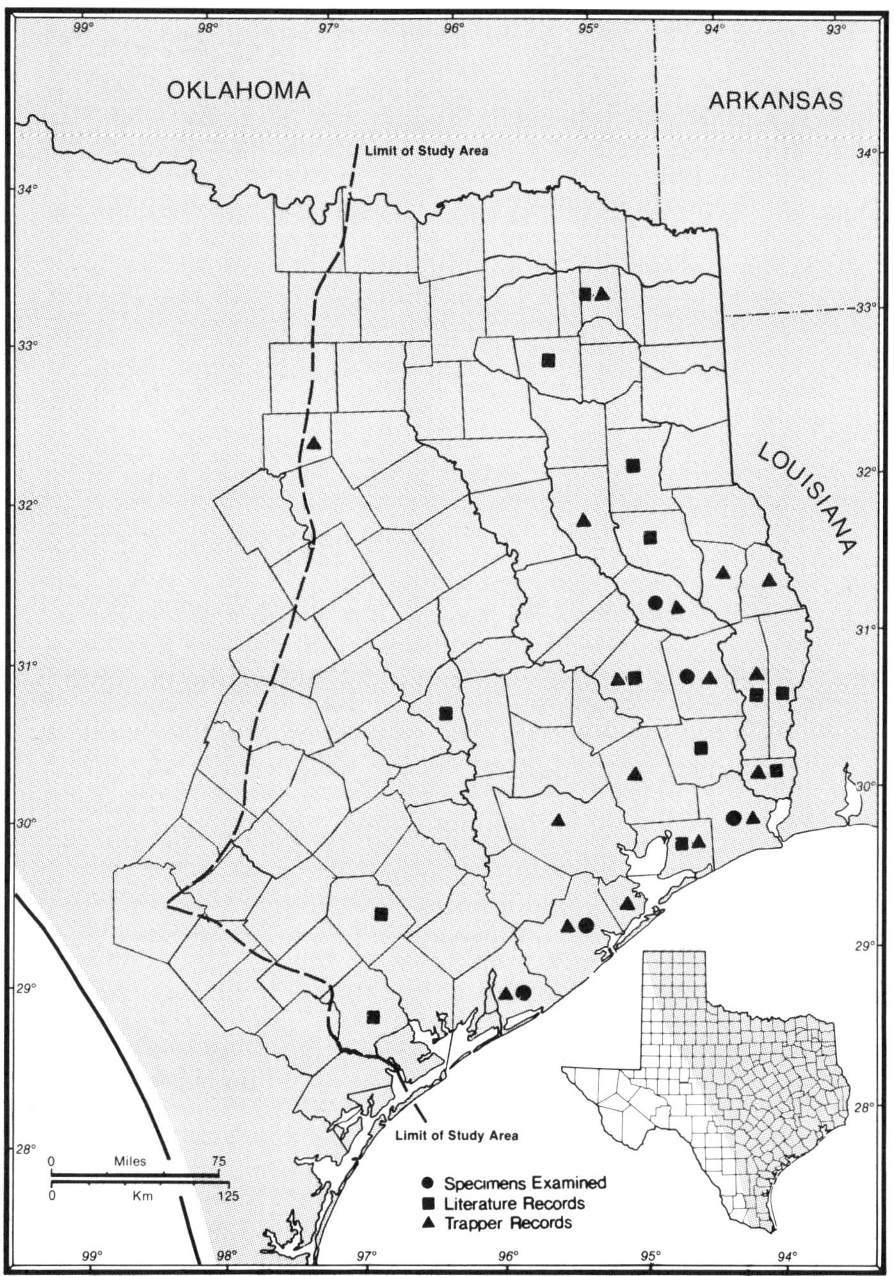

MAP 62. Distribution of the river otter, *Lutra canadensis lataxina*. The literature records are from W. B. Davis (1974).

the occupants. A typical den consists of a hole leading into a bank, with the entrance below water level. The tunnel leads to a chamber located above this level containing a nest constructed out of dry grass, leaves, and moss. Another side chamber is used as a toilet, and there are usually one or more openings to the exterior for passage and ventilation. Otters may occupy two dens, one as a temporary resting den and the other as a permanent nesting den.

Otters are active mostly at twilight or during the night. They do not hibernate and seem to be more active during the winter. They typically range over a distance of 5 to 16 km in a season and from 80 to 96 km in the course of a year, but movements may be considerably less (13 to 19 km in a year) in the warmer, food-rich coastal marshes.

Otters are among the most sociable and friendliest of mammals. They are very playful even as adults. Play is usually focused around water and seems to accompany almost every activity they engage in. They take particular delight in sliding down mud banks into the water. Groups of as many as fifteen to thirty otters have been seen playing or eating together without friction. Throughout much of the year they are family-oriented, but ties weaken in the breeding season and individuals set out on their own.

Otters are not specific in their food habits. Their main diet consists of fish, crustaceans, molluscs, amphibians, reptiles, invertebrates, birds, and mammals. One of their choicest morsels is crayfish, and where they are abundant an otter will consume a tremendous number in a year's time. The fish they eat are largely small, nongame species. They will also eat aquatic plants such as pond weeds and roots. Otters typically search for food by swimming along the bottom, poking their nose and front paws into cracks beneath rocks, rooting around submerged logs, and digging in the mud.

Marking or scenting behavior is common to mustelids, and otters are no exception. They set up scent stations near the mouths of dens, at places where they roll in grass to dry off, near slides or runways, or at any commonly used place. Scent is deposited on any small elevation, such as a clump of earth, a small bush, a stone, or a tuft of grass. Scenting with both urine and feces occurs throughout the year and is of vital importance during the breeding season.

Virtually nothing is known about the reproductive biology of otters in eastern Texas. They probably breed in the fall, but males generally do not mate until they are five years of age, and females rarely breed before two years. Males typically engage in fierce combat during the mating season, and they are believed to be solitary except when accompanying estrous females. Estrus lasts forty to forty-five days, and the female is receptive to the male at about six-day intervals. Mating usually occurs in the water. Delayed implantation results in the gestation period extending to as much as 270 days. Litter size varies from one to five, with two about average. Females may mate again as soon as twenty days following birth, which means that otters may remain continuously pregnant once they reach sexual maturity.

Newborns are about 275 mm in total length and weigh about 130 g. They are fully furred, but the eyes are closed and none of the teeth are erupted. Their eyes open at twenty-two to thirty-five days, and they are weaned at eighteen weeks. The adult waterproof pelage appears after about three months. The mother will usually not allow the father or anyone else to come near the cubs until they are at least six months old. Males as well as females are usually kind to the young.

Otters are long-lived animals that are capable of living from fifteen to twenty years in captivity. Other than man they have few natural enemies. There are unverified reports of coyotes killing young otters and speculation that other carnivores and large birds of prey, as well as alligators, may kill them.

Remarks. Even though their pelts command a high price (average price, $35.20 from 1976–77 to 1980–81), otters are not a major fur-bearing mammal in eastern Texas because so few pelts are harvested. The Texas Parks and Wildlife Department trapper survey revealed that otters were taken in approximately equal numbers in the pineywoods, coastal prairies and marshes, and post oak woodland areas, but none were obtained in the blackland prairies (Table 2).

References. Dresner, 1982; Liers, 1951; Van Zyll de Jong, 1972; Yeager, 1938.

Family Felidae (Cats)

Of all the carnivores, the cats are the most proficient killers. Their jaws are short, and the canine teeth are highly specialized for delivering a lethal bite. Some species regularly kill prey as large as or considerably larger than themselves. Their usual hunting method involves preliminary stalking and a quick final rush. Members of this family are cosmopolitan in distribution. In eastern Texas the family is represented by four species. However, two of the species (the ocelot, *Felis pardalis*, and the jaguar, *Felis onca*) no longer occur in the area, and a third (the mountain lion, *Felis concolor*) is represented only by an occasional transient individual. Chapter 5 contains a discussion of each of these species.

Bobcat
Felis rufus (Schreber)

Name. The generic name *Felis* is the Latin word for "cat." The specific epithet *rufus* comes from the Latin word meaning "red" or "reddish," in reference to the general body color.

Identification. The bobcat is a medium-sized, short-tailed cat with pointed ears that have tufts of black hairs, about 25 mm in length, at their tips. It is rather long-legged and rangy in appearance, and its general

Bobcat, *Felis rufus*.

color is yellowish to reddish brown. Although its markings are variable, the upper parts are generally spotted and often have one or two black stripes along the back with lateral bands over the shoulders, whereas the underparts are white with black spots. Average external measurements, for males, are total length, 870 mm; tail, 146 mm; hind foot, 171 mm. For females these measurements are 772 mm, 144 mm, and 158 mm, respectively. The dental formula is I 3/3, C 1/1, Pm 2/2, M 1/1 × 2 = 28.

Subspecies. Based on a recent study of geographic variation in bobcats from the south central United States (Read, 1981), there is only one subspecies in eastern Texas, *Felis rufus texensis* J. A. Allen (*Bull. Amer. Mus. Nat. Hist.*, 7:188, June 20, 1895), with type locality in the vicinity of Castroville, on the headwaters of the Medina River, Medina County, Texas.

Distribution and habitat. Bobcats are locally common throughout the timbered regions of eastern Texas (Map 63). They are not as common in the coastal prairies or blackland prairies, except along the timbered floodplains of the major streams. Their preferred habitats are heavily wooded uplands and bottomland forests, especially second-growth timber, with considerable underbrush; timbered swamps; and semiopen farmland.

Life history. Little has been learned about the bobcat in Texas because of its stealth, nocturnal habits, remote habitat, and relative scarcity. They are mainly active at night, but may begin hunting long before sundown. During the day they stay in a rest shelter located in a thicket, a standing or fallen hollow tree, or in a crevice in a rocky cliff. They are active year round and do not hibernate.

It has been estimated that bobcats travel from 3.2 to 8.0 km each night in their hunting forays, but the exact size of their home range varies

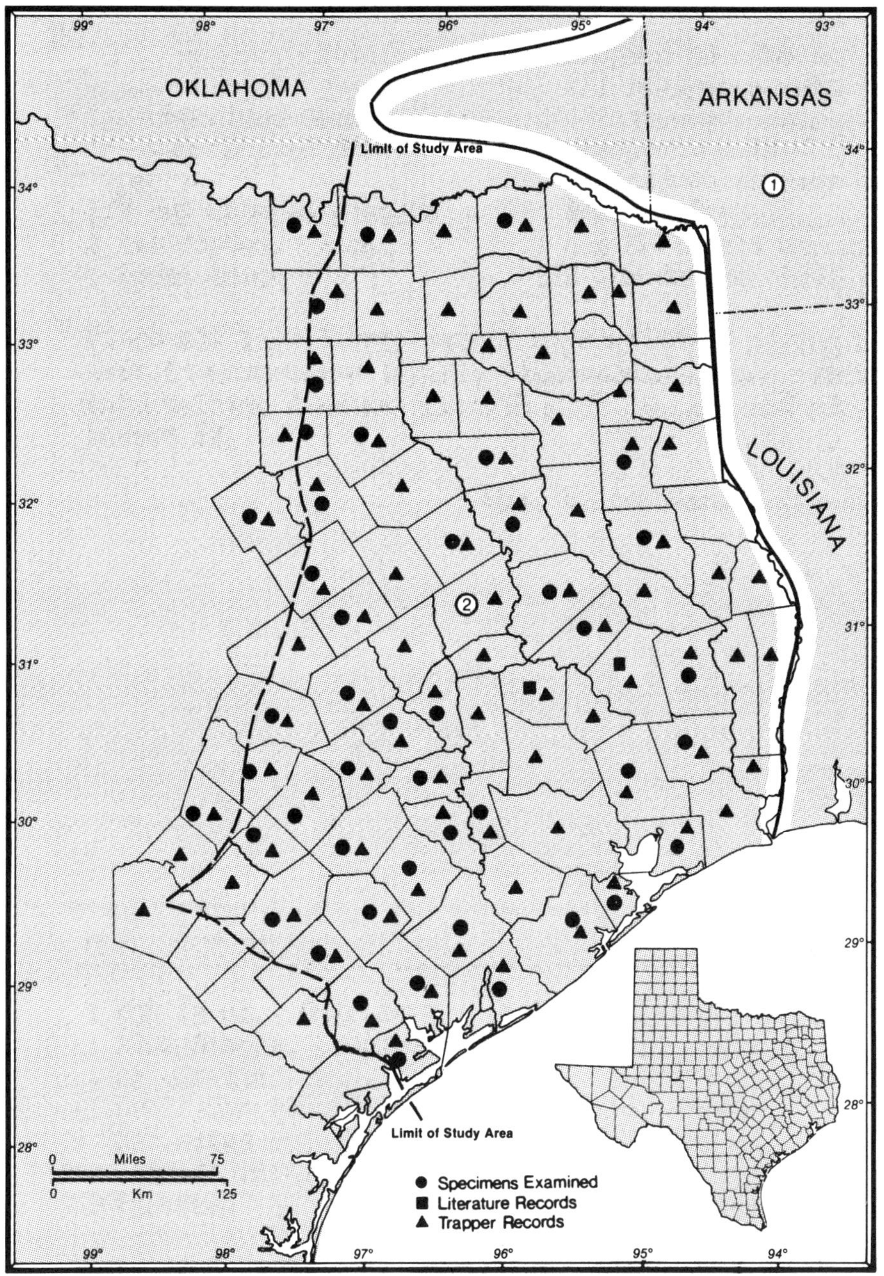

MAP 63. Distribution of the Bobcat, *Felis rufus*. 1. *F. r. floridanus*. 2. *F. r. texensis*. The literature records are from W. B. Davis (1974).

depending upon the availability of prey, the extent to which they are hunted, and season of the year. Bobcats frequently hunt from roads and railroads. They depend on their keen sense of eyesight, smell, and hearing to detect prey, and hunting skill is strongly related to experience. Their usual method of procuring prey is to sneak up and pounce upon it, but sometimes they lie in wait on the edge of a game trail until something comes along.

Bobcats are primarily carnivorous in their diet, but occasionally they eat grass. Rabbits are by far their most important food, followed by squirrels (fox squirrels, gray squirrels, flying squirrels), and rats and mice (cotton rats, woodrats, deer mice, voles, and harvest mice). Other minor items in their diet include opossums, raccoons, skunks, birds, and snakes. Deer, mostly carrion, is sometimes consumed in autumn and winter following deer hunting season.

Breeding activity reaches a peak in February and March, but some breeding may occur as early as November and as late as July (Blankenship, 1979). The major months of parturition are April and May, but young may be born as early as January and as late as September. The litter, which ranges in size from 1 to 5 (average, 2.7), is born following a gestation period of about sixty-two days. Nutrition plays an important role in the reproductive process of bobcats. At times of nutritional stress, reproductive activities may be reduced, or abortion and absorption of the embryo may occur.

The young are born well furred and spotted, but with their eyes closed, in a denning nest constructed out of dead leaves, grass, and moss. They are weaned at about two months of age and generally are able to fend for themselves by six months. Family ties are not generally broken until the female mates and becomes pregnant again. Females do not breed during their first year, but they may mate successfully between their first and second years and continue doing so until they are at least eight or nine years of age.

Bobcats are fairly long-lived animals. Individuals twelve to thirteen years of age have been reported in the wild, and a significant portion of the population may be older than six years. Mortality is high among juveniles, then decreases to a low level at five years, and then gradually increases again. Humans and dogs are their most important predators, but foxes, coyotes, and great horned owls probably feed on the young.

Remarks. Until recently bobcat pelts have not been in great demand in the fur trade, but the ban on importation of various species of cats from abroad has greatly increased the demand for fur of native cats (Sealander, 1979). The average price paid for a bobcat pelt between 1976–77 and 1980–81 in eastern Texas was $67.80. During this time approximately 27,000 bobcats were harvested, and these produced an income of almost $2 million (see Table 2). Only the raccoon and coyote produced a greater dollar return to trappers; however, for these species it took several times the number of pelts, compared to the bobcat, to generate this income.

References. Blankenship, 1979; Fritts and Sealander, 1978a, 1979b; Marshall and Jenkins, 1966; Pollack, 1951; Rollings, 1945.

Order Artiodactyla

The ungulates, or hoofed animals, are separated into two large orders, the Perissodactyla and the Artiodactyla. The Artiodactyla include the piglike animals, bison, antelopes, and deerlike forms, as well as both domestic and wild cattle, sheep, and goats. The limbs of these ungulates are paraxonic, with the plane of symmetry passing between the third and fourth digits of each foot, which are similar in size and equally share the main bulk of the animal's weight. The other digits are greatly reduced or diminished. Some members of this order have a complex, four-chambered stomach that permits them to chew a cud, and horns or antlers are present in many species.

The order Artiodactyla was once represented in eastern Texas by four families and four species: Family Tayassuidae (collared peccary), Family Antilocapridae (pronghorn antelope), Family Bovidae (bison), and Family Cervidae (white-tailed deer). Today, all but the white-tailed deer have been extirpated in the region (see Chapter 5 for a discussion of these). Another species (the wild hog), belonging to the family Suidae, occurs in a feral or semiferal state within the region. Other domesticated artiodactyls in eastern Texas include cattle, sheep, and goats, but these species do not occur in the feral state.

A closely related order, the Perissodactyla, includes the horselike mammals, tapirs, and rhinoceroses. These ungulates have a mesaxonic limb structure in which a large central digit carries the bulk of the animal's weight and smaller lateral digits may or may not be present. There are no wild representatives of this order in eastern Texas, but it does contain our domestic horses, asses, and mules (see Chapter 6 for a discussion of these and other domesticated species).

Because one often finds a skull of a horse, cow, sheep, goat, or pig in a pasture or even in a wooded area, the following key includes both the native and domesticated species of ungulates (Artiodactyla and Perissodactyla) that live in eastern Texas.

1	Upper incisors present; never with horns or antlers	2
	Upper incisors absent; horns or antlers usually present in males, less often present in females	4
2	Eye socket not enclosed by solid bony ring; canines large relative to other teeth	3
	Eye socket enclosed by solid bony ring; canines small when present . . . . Horse (*Equus caballus*)	
3	Upper canines straight; two pairs of upper incisors; six pairs of upper cheek teeth; three pedal digits . . . . Collared peccary (*Dicotyles tajacu*)	
	Upper canines curve either outward, upward, or both; three pairs of upper incisors; seven pairs of upper cheek teeth; four pedal digits . . . . Wild hog (*Sus scrofa*)	
4	Total length of skull (not including horns or antlers if present) more than 35 cm	5

Total length of skull less than 35 cm 6
5   Orbital rim protruding; premaxillary bone not in contact with
nasal bone .... Bison (*Bison bison*)
Orbital rim less protruding; premaxillary bone in contact with
nasal bone .... Cow (*Bos taurus*)
6   Antlers or antler pedicels present; skull narrow in orbital region; in dorsal view zygomatic arches usually visible behind
orbits .... White-tailed deer (*Odocoileus virginianus*)
Horns or horn cores present; skull broad in orbital region; in
dorsal view zygomatic arches not visible 7
7   Orbits high on skull; horn forked; one or two large foramina in
frontal bone at base of horn cores ....
.... Pronghorn (*Antilocapra americana*)
Orbits not so high on skull; horns not forked; no foramina in
frontal at base of horn cores 8
8   Deep depression in skull bones (lachrymal bones) immediately in front of eye sockets; horns curved down and out ....
.... Sheep (*Ovis aries*)
No deep depression in skull bones immediately in front of eye
sockets; horns parallel and directed back ....
.... Goat (*Capra hircus*)

Family Cervidae (Deer and Relatives)

White-tailed Deer
Odocoileus virginianus Zimmerman

Name. The first part of the scientific name, *Odocoileus*, comes from the Greek words *odon*, meaning "tooth," and *koilas*, meaning "hollow," in probable reference to the depressions in the crown of the molar teeth. The second part of the name, *virginianus*, is a latinized word meaning "of Virginia," the place where the species was first described.

Identification. The white-tailed deer is a moderately sized deer that may be easily recognized by its long, spindly legs, hoofed toes, a moderately short tail that is white beneath, and the presence of antlers in males during part of the year. Antlers have erect, unbranched tines, arising from a main base. In winter the upper parts are grayish brown but in summer they become decidedly reddish; the underparts are white. The range in external measurements typically is total length, 137–198 cm; tail, 152–292 mm; hind foot 457–520 mm; ear, 139–228 mm. The weight of males ranges from 30 to 70 kg. The dental formula is I 0/3, C 0/1, Pm 3/3, M 3/3 × 2 = 32. Upper canine teeth occur rarely.

Subspecies. Because a great number of deer have been transplanted into eastern Texas from the central and southern portions of the state over the past fifty years, the present-day populations do not reflect the pattern of geographic variation that once prevailed under natural conditions. Genetically, white-tailed deer in eastern Texas today represent a conglomer-

Male white-tailed deer, *Odocoileus virginianus.*

Female white-tailed deer, *Odocoileus virginianus.*

ate of hybrids between several geographic races. For this reason, I am recognizing subspecies based on samples of natural populations collected prior to the extensive transplantation of deer that began in the 1930s.

Three subspecies originally occurred in eastern Texas (Map 64). *Odocoileus virginianus macroura* occurred in the northeastern part of the region and was named by Rafinesque (*Amer. Monthly Mag.*, 1:436,

1817), with type from plains of Kansas River, upper Mississippi Valley. *Odocoileus virginianus mcilhennyi* occurred in the low-lying coastal section of southeastern Texas and was named by F. W. Miller (*J. Mamm.*, 9:57, February 9, 1928), with type locality from near Avery Island, Iberia Parish, Louisiana. *Odocoileus virginianus texana* occurred over the remainder of the region and was named by Mearns (*Proc. Biol. Soc. Washington*, 12:23, January 27, 1898), with type locality from Fort Clark, Kinney County, Texas. Native deer of the subspecies *O. v. macilhennyi* and *O. v. macroura* were eliminated in eastern Texas because of overhunting, and individuals of the subspecies *O. v. texana* from central or southern Texas were restocked into their former range.

Distribution and habitat. White-tailed deer range from relatively common to absent in eastern Texas, depending on the locality. They occur in all vegetational regions (Map 64), ranging from the low-lying coastal marshes in the southeast to the blackland prairies in the west, but they are found in larger numbers in timbered areas. Bottomland hardwoods are the best habitats for deer, followed by short-leaf–loblolly pine–hardwood, upland hardwood, and long-leaf–slash pine forest types. The pattern and distribution of the timber in a given area influences their presence and abundance to a great extent because deer utilize the borders or edges more than the dense uniform stands of timber.

The estimated white-tailed deer population in the ecological regions of eastern Texas over an eight-year period is given in Table 8. Based on these estimates, the overall condition of this deer population appears to be healthy. This situation is due in large measure to the excellent management practices conducted by the highly trained wildlife biologists and technicians of the Texas Parks and Wildlife Department. The following assessment of the status of the deer populations in each of the four major ecological areas of eastern Texas has been adapted from Harwell and Gore (1982).

Deer populations in the pineywoods are increasing, particularly in the southern part of the area. In localities with protection from illegal hunting, deer herds respond positively, and moderately high populations exist. From 1974 to 1981 deer numbers increased by 92 percent (Table 8). However, on a long-term basis, clear-cutting, even-aged forestry practices and "pure pine" management are detrimental to deer herds. Additionally, considerable loss of prime bottomland habitat has resulted from creation of large water impoundments throughout the area.

A rather static deer population exists in the coastal prairies and marshes, where deer are concentrated in limited areas in a heterogeneous pattern. Heaviest deer populations occur in small areas of Brazoria, Fort Bend, Matagorda, Victoria, Jackson, and Calhoun counties.

The deer herd in the post oak woodlands has declined sharply over the past twenty years. Some local populations declined from populations of over 200 deer per 400 ha (1 deer per 2 ha) to 50 deer per 400 ha (1 deer per 8 ha). This decline in numbers has been especially obvious in Brazos, Grimes, and Robertson counties, with substantial declines in Burleson,

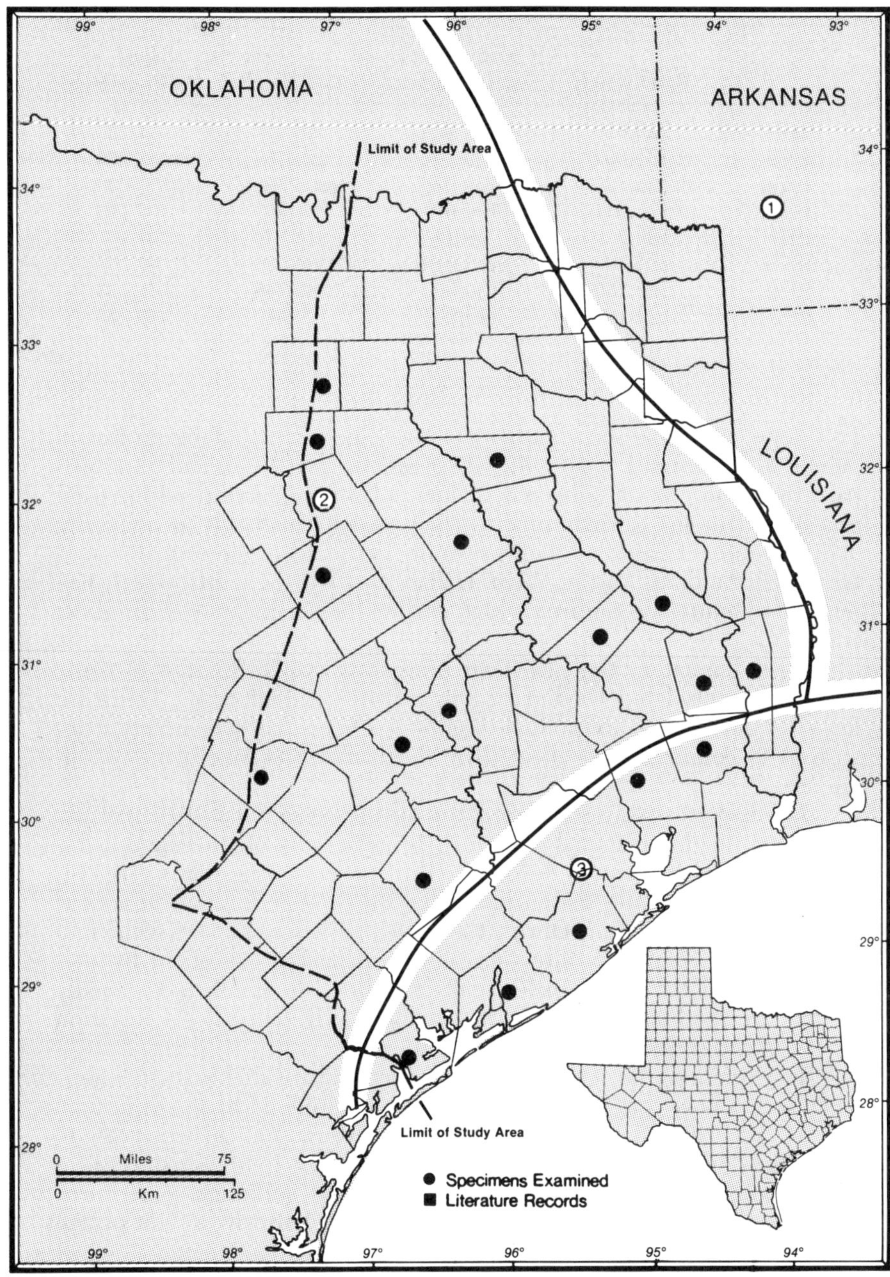

MAP 64. Distribution of the white-tailed deer, *Odocoileus virginianus*. 1. *O. v. macroura*. 2. *O. v. texana*. 3. *O. v. mcilhennyi*.

TABLE 8. Estimated White-tailed Deer Populations in Texas, 1974–81

	Pineywoods	Coastal Prairies and Marshes	Post Oak Woodlands	Blackland Prairies
1974	129,820	96,924	288,273	4,233
1975	131,094	99,740	226,767	3,759
1976	150,720	103,970	266,338	3,890
1977	177,041	104,694	256,369	5,179
1978	188,760	98,141	313,720	10,467
1979	211,790	103,518	302,220	11,102
1980	249,380	130,000	337,748	7,725
1981	249,155	115,977	279,020	5,820

Source: Harwell and Gore (1982).

Freestone, and Madison counties. The decline is attributable to loss of habitat due to intensive agricultural operations (grainfields and improved pastures). There has also been a decline in habitat quality resulting from excessive deer and cattle numbers. The post oak woodlands are a favorite of deer hunters because of their proximity to the major metropolitan centers of San Antonio, Austin, Waco, Dallas–Fort Worth, and Houston. The number of hunters in the area is high despite the decline in deer numbers (Table 3).

Deer habitat in the blackland prairies is usually limited to some drainages and isolated wooded areas in transition habitat types. There are few deer in the area, and suitable habitat has been almost completely destroyed in counties most affected by the Dallas-Fort Worth metropolitan area.

Life history. More is known of the life history of the deer than of any other free-ranging mammal in eastern Texas because of its economic importance and the attention devoted to this species by the state's game biologists. The breeding season lasts from September through February, with a peak in November. During the breeding season, females come into heat at twenty-eight-day intervals, and the heat lasts for about twenty-four hours. The young, which usually number one or two (occasionally triplets are produced), are born in May and early June after a gestation period of about seven months.

The young are born with their eyes open and are able to stand feebly. They weigh between 1.8 and 3.2 kg, measure from 43 to 48 cm in total length, and exhibit a characteristic spotting pattern. Young fawns begin to follow the doe at about three to four weeks, at which time they start to eat solid food. Weaning typically begins at this time, although some fawns nurse until they are six months old. The spotting pattern on their pelage disappears after the first molt, when they are four to five months of age. About one-third of the young females become sexually mature at six to eight months of age and will breed in the first year of life; the remaining young breed between one and two years of age.

Deer reach the prime of life between 2.5 and 7.5 years of age, and some individuals may live as long as 15 years. However, in heavily hunted areas it is rare for an individual to live more than 2.5 years and exceptional for one to live as long as 7 years. Predation by free-running dogs and bobcats accounts for 6 and 2 percent, respectively, of the annual mortality. This compares with 63 percent through legal gun harvest and 20 percent through illegal hunting. Other potential predators include wolves and mountain lions, and natural disease also causes many deaths.

The principal foods of deer are browse (leaves and twigs of woody plants), fruits (especially oaks, yaupon, American beautyberry, black tupelo, and hawthorn), succulent herbage (grasses, sedges, ferns), mushrooms, and agricultural crops (peas, melons, soybeans, corn). Browse accounts for about half of the diet, but preference of different items varies by season. The diet is limited to what is available within the travel range of the deer. A deer will move to seasonal supplies of acorns and other fruit, but it generally will not move out of its established territory.

White-tailed deer are relatively sedentary during most of their life. They are decidedly territorial and have a relatively small home range and cruising radius. Alexander (1968) studied deer movements in northeastern Texas and found that captured animals only moved an average of 1.9 km from the point of their initial capture. However, when persistently hunted or chased, deer are apt to move beyond the limits of their home range. Also, a buck in quest of a mate may travel far during the rutting season. Deer are most active just before sunset and immediately after sunrise. They generally bed down in the middle of the day, but they may feed well into the night.

The paired antlers of bucks arise from a short base on the frontal bone (called the pedicel), and they are entirely bony. The antlers are shed annually, usually in later winter, and begin growing again shortly thereafter. Their annual growth cycle is primarily under the control of testicular and pituitary hormones and is closely correlated with the breeding season and reproductive cycle (Wislocki, 1942, 1943). Pituitary secretions, activated by increasing day length in the spring, initiate antler growth in April or May and at the same time stimulate testicular growth. While the antlers are growing, they are covered by a protective layer of skin called "velvet," which provides them with blood vessels and nerves. In the fall, a hormone secreted by the testes (androgen) inhibits the action of the pituitary antler-growth hormone, and this causes the velvet to dry up and be lost. At this time the animals rub and thrash their antlers against vegetation, and also use them in combat during the ensuing rutting season. In winter, pituitary stimulation of the testes declines as day length is reduced and androgen secretion declines. The antlers then become weak at the base and are dropped sometime between late December and mid-February. For several months in late winter, before reinitiation of antler growth, the males are antlerless.

References. Alexander, 1968; Lay, 1965, 1967, 1969; Stransky, 1969.

5

Extirpated Species and Those of Incidental, Marginal, or Problematic Occurrence

In addition to the sixty-three species of mammals already described, there are others that have occurred, might occur, or marginally occur in eastern Texas. Included are some species that at one time inhabited the region but, for one reason or another, have been extirpated. Other species, not yet found in eastern Texas, may in fact live there. A third group includes species that are not native to the region but that have been purposely released or have escaped from confinement. Finally, some species that live in neighboring regions may occasionally wander into eastern Texas, or they occur adjacent to but not significantly inside of the boundary of the region. Following are brief descriptions and assessments for eighteen species that fit into these categories.

Order Soricomorpha

Family Soricidae

Southwestern Short-tailed Shrew
Blarina hylophaga Elliot

This species is remarkably similar morphologicaly to *B. carolinensis*, from which it differs as described in the account of the latter (see page 43). Although it has not yet been recorded in eastern Texas, it has been taken immediately to the south (Aransas County, Texas) and east (Caddo Parish, Louisiana) of this region (George et al., 1981). *B. hylophaga* seems to live primarily in dark, damp, or wet localities in wooded areas or fields covered with heavy, woody growth. It occurs less often in grassy cover, where the least shrew (*Cryptotis parva*) predominates. In Aransas County, these shrews were captured in a mixed live oak-grassland association, with a thick litter layer and standing dead grasses providing most of the ground-cover (Brown, 1977). Nothing is known of the life history of this species, but it is probably very similar to that of its close relative, *B. carolinensis*.

Desert Shrew
Notiosorex crawfordi (Coues)

This is a small shrew with a short, well-haired tail that is less than one-third of the total length. The ears are more conspicuous than in ei-

Desert shrew, *Notiosorex crawfordi*.

ther *Blarina* or *Cryptotis*. Average external measurements are total length, 86 mm; tail, 29 mm; hind foot, 10 mm; ear, 8 mm.

Although this species has not been recorded from eastern Texas, it has been taken at San Antonio, which is just a few kilometers from the study region. Desert shrews frequently live in the dens of the southern plains woodrat (*Neotoma micropus*), which is a common species in the southern portion of eastern Texas.

Order Chiroptera

Family Vespertilionidae

Cave Myotis
Myotis velifer (J. A. Allen)

This bat is one of the larger members of the genus *Myotis*. It is characterized by its stubby-nosed appearance, dull brown coloration, short ears, and large hind feet. Average external measurements are total length, 98 mm; tail, 44 mm; hind foot, 11 mm; ear, 16 mm.

This species is abundant in the cave country of central Texas and in the band of gypsum caves in the Texas Panhandle. It reaches the western limits of its range along the Balcones Escarpment, where specimens have been recorded in six counties (Dallas, McLennan, Williamson, Travis, Hays, and Bexar). The range of the species extends only a few kilometers east of the western boundary of the study region, and the few individuals that have been recorded probably represent strays that wandered from

Cave myotis, *Myotis velifer* (photograph by Roger W. Barbour).

caves on the nearby Edwards Plateau and found a temporary roosting place in old, abandoned buildings.

Order Rodentia

Family Sciuridae

Woodchuck
Marmota monax (Linneaus)

This is a large, heavy-bodied rodent with a short, blunt snout; a short, bushy tail; short, rounded ears; and short, powerful legs with long, slightly curved claws on the toes. The fur is grayish yellow to reddish brown and grizzled as a result of white tips on the long, coarse guard hairs. Average external measurements are total length, 567 mm; tail, 178 mm; hind foot, 83 mm; ear, 34 mm.

The only record of this species in Texas is the capture of an adult female in a burrow system under a shed near a house 4 mi. S Kennedale, Tarrant County. The specimen, which was obtained in October 1964, is preserved in the mammal collection of the Fort Worth Museum of Science. According to the curator of the mammal collection, the owner of the house did not know where the animal had come from. Tarrant County is about 386 km west of the known range of the woodchuck in southeastern Arkansas. Considering the circumstances, I suspect that the animal was brought into the county and released.

Woodchuck, *Marmota monax* (photograph by Roger W. Barbour).

Mexican Ground Squirrel
Spermophilus mexicanus (Erxleben)

This ground squirrel is distinctive in possessing a brownish dorsum with nine rows of squarish white dorsal spots. The tail is moderately bushy and about two-fifths of the total length. The ears are short and rounded. *S. mexicanus* is easily distinguished from *S. tridecemlineatus* by its spotted instead of striped upper parts. Average external measurements are total length, 291 mm; tail, 116 mm; hind foot, 40 mm; ear, 9 mm.

Although this species has not been recorded within the boundaries of the study region, it is known from San Antonio and the breaks of the Balcones Escarpment and likely occurs in the extreme southwestern portion of eastern Texas. Mexican ground squirrels inhabit brushy or grassy areas, and they are frequently associated with cactus and mesquite flats.

Rock Squirrel
Spermophilus variegatus (Erxleben)

The rock squirrel is a large ground squirrel with grayish upper parts resulting from a variegated or mottled pattern of black and white fur. The upper parts of some individuals are completely black. The tail is bushy and the same color as the back. Average external measurements are total length, 457 mm; tail, 206 mm; hind foot, 76 mm; ear, 29 mm.

Rock squirrels are common on the Edwards Plateau and Trans-Pecos portions of Texas and reach their distributional limits along the lower seg-

Mexican ground squirrel, *Spermophilus mexicanus*.

Rock squirrel, *Spermophilus variegatus*.

ment of the Balcones Escarpment. Specimens have been obtained in the city limits of Austin, Travis County, and Waco, McLennan County, which are just inside the western boundary of the study region. There may also be other places where this species barely infringes into eastern Texas. Rock squirrels are usually associated with rocky outcrops, where they seek refuge and make their dens.

Black-tailed prairie dog, *Cynomys ludovicianus.*

Black-tailed Prairie Dog
Cynomys ludovicianus (Ord)

Prairie dogs are thick-bodied, short-legged, short-tailed, ground-dwelling squirrels with small ears. They are light reddish brown in coloration; the tip and underside of the tail are black. Average external measurements are total length, 367 mm; tail, 95 mm; hind foot, 61 mm; ear, 14 mm.

Prairie dogs are common in the short-grass prairie habitats of northern and western Texas. They do not occur naturally in eastern Texas, but a few individuals were introduced several decades ago into a mesquite-grassland area between Arlington and Fort Worth. These individuals survived and successfully established a breeding population that remains in the area today.

Family Heteromyidae

Padre Island Kangaroo Rat
Dipodomys compactus True

The long tail (well haired at the end), long hind legs and feet, small front feet, fur-lined cheek pouches, and large, owllike eyes serve to distinguish kangaroo rats from other rodents. The general yellowish brown color with pure white underparts, a white stripe over each hip, and a conspicuous white patch behind each ear also are distinctive. Average external measurements are total length, 222 mm; tail, 117 mm; hind foot, 35 mm; ear, 8 mm.

Padre Island kangaroo rat, *Dipodomys compactus*.

D. compactus occurs throughout the eastern two-thirds of the South Texas mainland and the adjacent barrier islands (Baumgardner and Schmidly, 1981). This species is known in eastern Texas on the basis of a single specimen collected near Nixon in Gonzales County, which is situated just north of the southern boundary of the study region. The specimen was obtained in a post oak–blackjack oak association in deep sandy soils (Raun, 1959).

Family Cricetidae

Encinal Mouse
Peromyscus pectoralis Osgood

This mouse is a medium-sized, long-tailed *Peromyscus* with white fur over the tarsal joint on each hind foot. Its tail is longer than its head and body (a trait that readily distinguishes it from the other species of the genus in eastern Texas), scantily haired, and not sharply bicolored. The upper parts are grayish brown; the underparts and feet are white. Average external measurements are total length, 194 mm; tail, 97 mm; hind foot, 22 mm; ear, 19 mm.

P. pectoralis occurs in the Trans-Pecos, Edwards Plateau, and north central regions of Texas. It reaches the western limits of its range along the Balcones Escarpment, where it has been recorded in several counties from Bexar County northward to McLennan County. This species has been recorded along rocky outcroppings near Austin and Waco, inside the western boundary of eastern Texas where the Colorado and Brazos rivers cut through the Balcones Escarpment. The encinal mouse is a saxicolous

Encinal mouse, *Peromyscus pectoralis.*

species, showing a decided preference for rocky situations and brushy habitats (Schmidly, 1974).

Prairie Vole
Microtus ochrogaster (V. Bailey)

The prairie vole is a small mouse with an exceptionally short tail that is less than twice as long as the hind foot. As in other microtines, the body is thick-set, the head is blunt, the legs are short, and the ears barely extend above the surrounding fur. The upper parts are usually grizzled gray, but varying from chestnut brown to nearly black; the underparts are whitish or washed with buff or yellow. The prairie vole may be confused with the woodland vole, from which it is distinguished as described in the account of the latter (page 205). Average external measurements are total length, 136 mm; tail, 32 mm; hind foot, 18 mm; ear, 10 mm.

This species is known from eastern Texas on the basis of a single specimen secured in the coastal prairie at Sour Lake on July 16, 1902. It was caught in a brush patch at the edge of the prairie in company with the cotton rat, *Sigmodon hispidus* (V. Bailey, 1905: 119). Bailey commented on the specimen obtained at Sour Lake as well as on his capture of the species in Louisiana as follows: "The prairie about Sour Lake is very similar to that just east of Lake Charles, La., where I found these little voles fairly numerous, living in the peculiar, flat mounds that are scattered over the low, damp prairie, and making their runways through the grass from one to another." Subsequent attempts to collect this species have been unsuccessful; consequently, its status in eastern Texas is in doubt. The fact that a large number (over 200) of mammals were trapped within a 5 km

Prairie vole, *Microtus ochrogaster*.

radius of Sour Lake in the last seventy-five years, none of which were prairie voles, suggests that this species is probably now extinct in eastern Texas.

Order Carnivora

Family Canidae

Gray Wolf
Canis lupus Linnaeus

The wolf, or lobo, as it is often called, resembles the coyote in general appearance but is much larger and about twice as heavy.

The gray wolf was a common resident of the grasslands in western and central Texas in the early 1800s, and apparently its range extended as far east as Waco in McLennan County. According to Strecker (1926a:6), "Gray wolves may never have been very common permanent residents of McLennan County, but in late fall and winter, small packs followed the great herds of buffalo and deer from northwestern Texas and remained here for several months. It was probably only a small minority that remained throughout the year. Old settlers refer to packs of from five to eight wolves which they considered small family groups." Today this species is absent from the state except for a few individuals that cross from Mexico into the Trans-Pecos region of Texas.

Gray wolf, *Canis lupus.*

Family Ursidae

Black Bear
Ursus americanus Pallus

The black bear is a large, bulky, flat-footed animal with long, dense, and glossy black hair. Its tail is exceedingly short and conspicuous, its facial profile is rather blunt, its eyes are small, and its nose pad is broad with large nostrils. It has five toes with short, curved claws on both front and hind feet. Black bears weigh between 90.8 and 272.4 kg.

No native bears are extant in eastern Texas today. They were regarded as extremely rare by V. Bailey (1905) at the beginning of the twentieth century. They disappeared first from the western, northern, and southern parts of the region during the period from 1850 to 1890. They were exterminated from their last strongholds of swamps and thickets in southeastern Texas during the period from 1900 to 1940, with the possible exception of a few individuals in the Big Thicket in Hardin County and in the dense woodlands of Matagorda County, where bears were sighted in 1943 and 1940, respectively (Anonymous, 1945).

There have been some recent reports of the black bear, but these are based on individuals that have wandered from release sites in Louisiana. In the summers of 1964 through 1967 agents of the Louisiana Wildlife and Fisheries Commission trapped 161 black bears in Cook County, Minnesota, transported them to Louisiana, and released them as part of a restocking program (Lowery, 1974). The Big Thicket Museum in Saratoga,

Black bear, *Ursus americanus.*

Hardin County, contains the remains of a black bear shot May 20, 1973, at a locality eight miles north of Silsbee. According to museum records, the animal wandered across the Louisiana border from a preserve there. The bear was over two years old and measured 1,588 mm in length.

The extermination of bears can be attributed largely to hunting. Hunting was motivated by the desire to seek recreation, to obtain fresh meat, and to protect livestock, particularly the free-ranging "pineywoods rooter" hogs. In many areas of eastern Texas, residents would not tolerate bears because of their depredations upon hogs, even though in most localities these hogs were of little or no consequence in the economy of the residents. Local residents also obtained several useful products from the animals. The flesh, especially the hams, were highly prized as food. The grease that was a liquid at normal temperature was often stored in deer-hide pouches. The grease would remain "sweet" indefinitely and was a valuable ingredient for the preparation of food. Thick fat from the sides of the bear was cut into thin slabs and dried. These slabs, when cooked, were known as "fish."

Family Felidae

Jaguar
Felis onca True

This large, powerful cat is easily distinguished by its massive size (total length, 162 to 224 cm; weight, 64 to 114 kg) and its beautiful golden buff, black-spotted coat. Many of the spots are in the form of blotches of irregular shape or rosettes, each of the latter with a small spot in the center.

Jaguar, *Felis onca*.

According to V. Bailey (1905:163–66), the jaguar was once common over southern Texas and occupied nearly the whole of the eastern part of the state to Louisiana and north to the Red River. Localities mentioned, based mostly on reports only and not on specimens, included "Brazos River, Texas"; Jasper; Neches River near Beaumont; and the timber south of Conroe. Apparently the last verified records were from 1902, when one was killed south of Jasper, and 1904, when a jaguar was shot in Mills County, which is only 153 km west of McLennan County on the western border of eastern Texas.

Ocelot
Felis pardalis Baird

The ocelot is a medium-sized spotted and blotched cat with a moderately long tail. It is about the size of a bobcat, but its spots are much larger, its tail much longer, and its pelage shorter than a bobcat's. The upper parts are grayish or buff, heavily marked with blackish spots, small rings, blotches, and short bars; the underparts are white spotted with black. The tail is spotted and ringed with black.

Small leopards, probably ocelots, were reported in the Big Thicket by early Spanish explorers and trappers who wrote that the skins of the animal "constitute the greater part of the annual haul." According to Strecker (1924:9), they also occurred in the Brazos bottoms near Waco and were purchased by fur traders there. Even as late as the early 1900s (V. Bailey, 1905:166), ocelots were "still reported as very rare about Beaumont and Jasper, near the eastern line of the state, and farther north, near Waskom and Long Lake." Baker (1956) interviewed George Walker (born before 1860) of Lufkin, who remembered that ocelots (called "tiger cats" by locals) were found in Polk and Hardin counties. Today, ocelots are

Ocelot, *Felis pardalis*.

confined to extreme South Texas. Hunting, settlement, and timber cutting probably contributed to their disappearance in eastern Texas.

Mountain Lion, Puma, Cougar, Panther
Felis concolor Linnaeus

The mountain lion is a large, long-tailed cat (total length, 178 to 213 cm; weight, 36 to 50 kg) in which the color of the upper parts in adults is uniformly light brown or grayish buff and not spotted. The underparts are whitish, and the tip of the tail and the backs of the ears are dusky black. No documented observation of a melanistic cougar is known from North America, but reports of so-called "black panthers" are very common in eastern Texas.

The puma probably occurred throughout this region prior to settlement by the white man. However, since the end of the nineteenth century, they have consistently been eliminated over most of the region. By 1905, V. Bailey reported that cougars were extremely rare. Individuals had been killed around this time in the swamps not far from Jefferson (Marion County) in the northeastern part and Sour Lake (Hardin County) in the Big Thicket. Old residents also recalled the presence of cougars in Tyler and San Augustine counties before 1900 (Baker, 1956). Verified sightings were made along the Neches River in Angelina County in 1917 and again in 1927 (Baker, 1956). Panthers, which were common in the Brazos bottoms of McLennan County in the mid-1800s, had become extremely rare in this area by 1926 (Strecker, 1926a). In the 1950s there were persistent reports of their presence in Leon and Brazos counties in the oak-hickory forest (McCarley, 1959d). To my knowledge, the last report of a mountain lion that was verified by the actual killing of a specimen was in Colorado County in 1948 (Baker, 1949). Today, although a few individuals occasionally stray into the area from the Rio Grande area by way of the brush country bordering the Gulf Coast, it is unlikely that they remain and become established as breeding residents.

Order Artiodactyla

Family Tayassuidae

Collared Peccary or Javelina
Dicotyles tajacu (Linnaeus)

This small wild pig has straight, daggerlike canines, a short tail, and a light stripe or collar encircling its shoulders. It has four hoofed toes on the front feet, but only three on the hind feet. The pelage is harsh and grizzled black or grayish in color; a distinct black "mane" extends from the crown to the rump.

The peccary formerly occurred throughout the lower part of eastern Texas from the southern boundary of the region northward to the Brazos River valley. Today, they are restricted to western Texas and the brush country south of San Antonio (W. B. Davis, 1974), although a few scat-

Mountain lion, *Felis concolor*.

Collared peccary, *Dicotyles tajacu.*

tered populations probably still exist along the southern boundary of the study region. At one time, peccaries were exceedingly abundant in the brakes along the Brazos River near Waco in McLennan County (Strecker, 1926a) and Bryan–College Station in Brazos County (Peterson, 1946). Early writers tell of hunting javelinas along the San Bernard River in Brazoria County, where they frequented the dense growths of palmetto and cane (Anonymous, 1945). On November 4, 1981, a student in the anthropology department at Texas A&M University picked up the carcass of a dead javelina on Highway 21 in Brazos County. The animal, which was a very old, adult female, was probably someone's pet that either was released or escaped.

Family Antilocapridae

Pronghorn
Antilocapra americana (Ord)

The pronghorn is a small, deerlike mammal with forked or branched horns that are shed and replaced annually. The horns reach beyond the tip of the ears in males; in females they are shorter and seldom pronged. Conspicuous white patches are present on the sides and rump, and two white bands extend across the throat. The general color is tan, with white rump and underparts and black markings on the neck and face.

Major George B. Erath, one of the pioneers of Waco, says in his memoirs that in the early to middle 1800s it was common to encounter small herds of antelopes in the region now comprised by McLennan,

Pronghorn, *Antilocapra americana*.

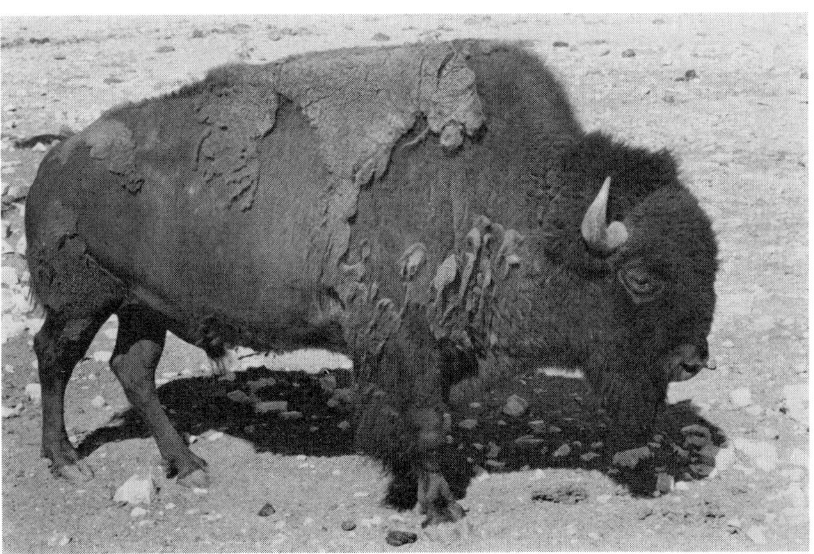

Bison, *Bison bison*.

Falls, and Robertson counties, but he asserts that this animal was never found in this section in as great numbers as in the High Plains region of Texas (Strecker, 1927).

Family Bovidae

Bison
Bison bison (Linnaeus)

The bison is a large, cowlike animal with a high hump over the shoulders and long, dense, wooly hair about the head, neck, shoulders, and forelegs. The general coat color is dark brown.

Bison once ranged over almost the whole of eastern Texas, except for the densely wooded Big Thicket, and they were probably numerous in the coastal prairies and in the post oak woodlands, which were covered with woods and open prairies. They were apparently abundant in the northern part of Brazos County in 1822 (Peterson, 1946) as well as in the northern and western sections of McLennan County (Strecker, 1926a). They became extinct in these areas very soon after white man occupied the land.

6
Domesticated Mammals

THIS treatise would not be complete without mention of the domesticated species that live in close association with man. Some of these mammals are of considerable economic importance, providing man with meat and other food products. Others are valued as pets and provide man with companionship and protection. Sometimes individual domestic animals, through lack of human care, successfully take up a wild existence. At least three species (feral cats and dogs and the wild hog) occur in the feral or semiferal state at many places in eastern Texas, and they may have profound impact on habitats and wildlife in these areas.

Order Carnivora

Family Canidae

Domestic Dog
Canis familiaris Linnaeus

Domestic dogs are numerous in eastern Texas, including feral residents, free-ranging pets, and strays. The distinction between these three categories is a matter of degree (Nesbitt, 1975). A free-ranging pet might become stray and perhaps finally feral. A feral dog is a wild animal. Even if owned at one time, the dog will no longer freely approach humans and usually shows strong fear of them. Such a dog is fully capable of surviving in nature and reproducing without aid from man. German shepherds, Doberman pinschers, and collies are the types of dog that most often become feral (Nesbitt, 1975). The situation is further complicated by the fact that feral dogs can mate with coyotes and produce fertile offspring, which are called "coy-dogs." In the past dogs and coyotes also interbred with red wolves. Thus, positive identification of specimens is sometimes difficult. The skull of a domestic dog (Fig. 5) is very similar to that of coyotes and red wolves. A reliable means of distinguishing the skulls of coyotes and dogs is given in Chapter 4 in the account of the coyote.

Feral and free-roaming dogs feed mainly on garbage, carrion, and small mammals. They can do great damage to wildlife and should be eliminated whenever possible. Particularly vulnerable are white-tailed deer, which are sometimes run to exhaustion by packs of these hounds. While conducting track count surveys to census carnivores in Big Thicket National Preserve, Norton (1981) obtained track counts of domestic dogs

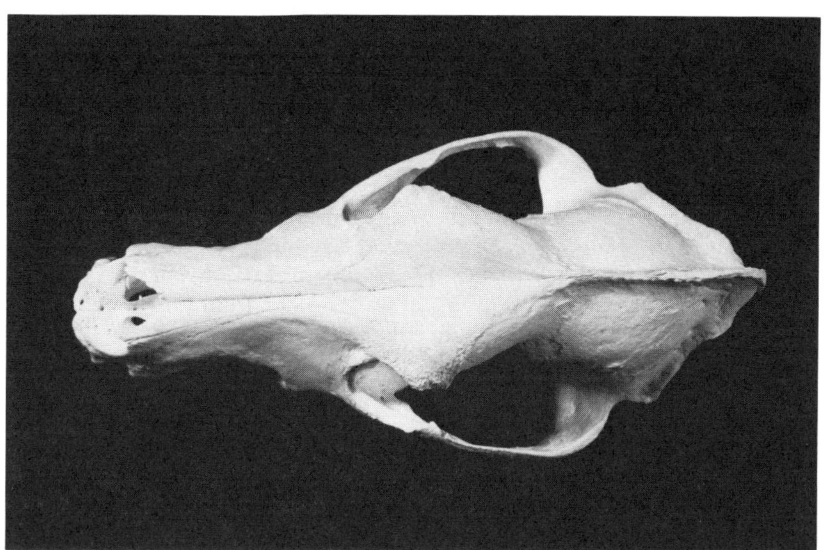

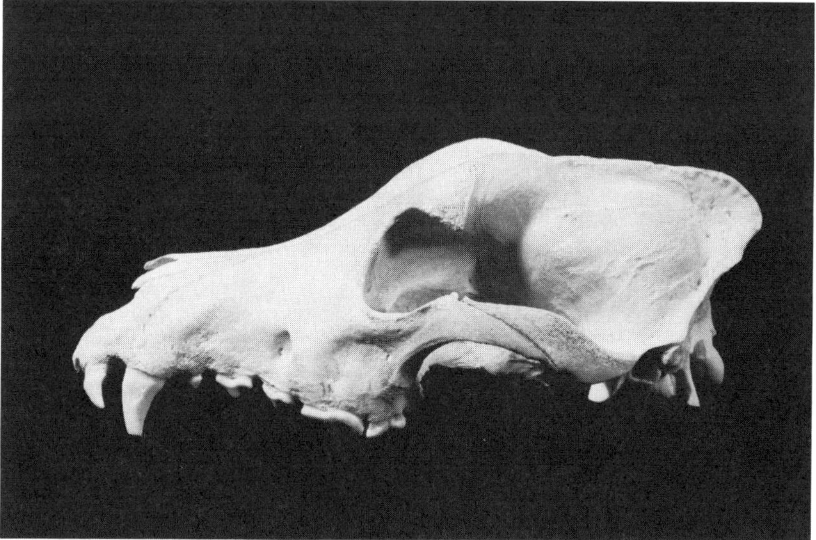

FIGURE 5. Skull of the domestic dog, *Canis familiaris*.

that were higher than those values for several kinds of native mammals and recorded several instances of dogs chasing deer. Dogs were commonly used in the late 1800s to hunt bears, and they played a significant role in the extinction of this species in eastern Texas.

Family Felidae

Domestic Cat
Felis catus Linnaeus

The skull of the domestic cat (Fig. 6) can be easily told from those of native cats of the genus *Felis* by its smaller size, and it differs further from that of the bobcat (*Felis rufus*) in possessing an extra premolar on each side of the upper jaw. Externally, feral cats differ from bobcats in their long tail, smaller size, and variable coloration. Hybrids between bobcats and domestic cats have been produced in captivity, but they are sterile, and there are only a few authentic records of such hybrids occurring in the wild (Sealander, 1979).

Feral cats or "tabbies" that are allowed outside the house are great decimators of wildlife, particularly of songbirds and small rodents. People who release unwanted cats in the wild often do irreparable damage to wildlife populations in these areas. Parmalee (1953) collected thirty-three feral cats in Brazos, Robertson, and neighboring counties of the post oak woodlands and found the following items, listed in order of decreasing abundance, in their stomachs: insects (principally grasshoppers and black crickets), cotton rats, cottontail rabbits, house mice, hispid pocket mice, deer mice, domestic chickens, bobwhite quail, red-winged blackbirds, rough green snakes, fence lizards, racerunners, and little brown skinks.

Order Artiodactyla

Family Suidae

Wild Hog
Sus scrofa Linnaeus

The European wild boar was domesticated by man approximately eight thousand years ago (Springer, 1975). Races of this species have remained as a game species in much of its original range (Europe, Asia, North Africa, Sumatra, and Java), and the species was first introduced into the United States in the late 1800s and early 1900s (Rue, 1968). The wild hog's domestic counterpart also has worldwide distribution, and in areas where suitable habitat is available free-ranging animals often become feral. Feral hogs have been present in the United States since the first settlers brought them to Florida in 1539 (Hanson and Karstad, 1959).

European wild hogs have several distinguishing characteristics that set them apart from domestic or feral hogs. Among these are brown to blackish brown color, with grizzled guard hairs, a mane of hair (8 to 16 cm long) running dorsally from the neck to the rump, a straight heavily tufted tail, and ears covered with hair (Springer, 1975). Characteristics of feral hogs are varied, depending upon the breed of the ancestral stock. When

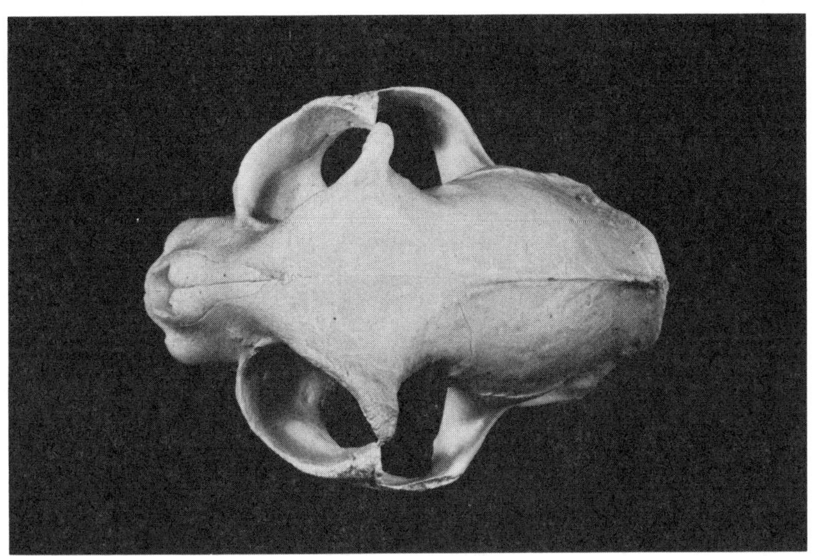

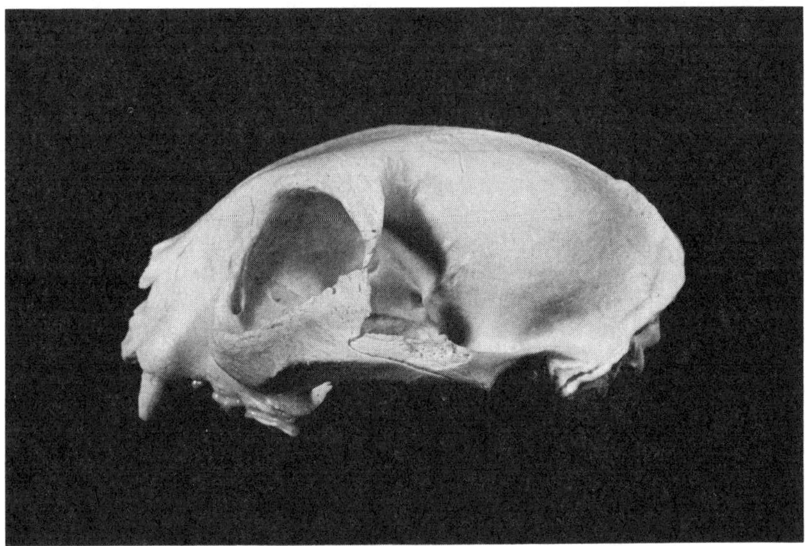

Figure 6. Skull of the domestic cat, *Felis catus*.

liberated together, European wild hogs and feral hogs interbreed readily, with the traits of European wild hogs apparently being more dominant.

There is a sizeable population of feral hogs, European wild hogs, and European × feral hog hybrids in Texas, with estimates of their total number ranging between 500,000 and 1,000,000 animals (Jackson, 1964; Ramsey, 1968). Free-ranging hogs occur throughout much of the coastal plain and timbered country of eastern Texas, although populations are slowly

Wild hog, *Sus scrofa* (photograph by Greg K. Yarrow).

declining, as is the amount of available free range. Largely unprotected by landowners, hogs are indiscriminantly harvested without any significant attempts at management. Good feral hog habitat in timbered areas consists of diverse forests with some openings. The presence of a good litter layer to support soil invertebrates and/or the presence of ground vegetation affording green forage, roots, and tubers is desirable. Hogs are also fond of marsh and grass-sedge flats in coastal areas, particularly if wild grapes are common. During hot summer months, "wallows," or depressions dug in the mud by wild hogs, are much in evidence near marshes or standing water, such as along roadside ditches.

Springer (1975) studied the food habits of wild hogs on the Texas coast and found that they eat a variety of items, including fruits, roots, mushrooms and invertebrates, depending upon the season. The major foods in the spring were herbage, roots, invertebrates, and mushrooms. Summer foods were dominated by fruits, roots, invertebrates, and vertebrates. Fruits, invertebrates, and herbage were most common in fall and winter diets. Herbage eaten by wild hogs was mainly water hyssop, pennywort, frog fruit, spadeleaf, onion, and various grasses. The most important roots eaten by wild hogs were bulrush, cattail, flatsedges, and spikesedges. Fruits and seeds such as grapes, acorns, and cultivated sorghum were dominant as preferred foods. Animal matter ingested by wild hogs included earthworms, marsh fly larvae, leopard frogs, snakes, and rodents.

Wild hogs can have detectable influences on wildlife and plant communities as well as domestic crops and livestock (Benke, 1973). Extensive disturbance of vegetation and soil occurs as a result of their rooting habits. The disturbed area may cause a shift in plant succession on the immediate site. Wild hogs also compete, to some degree, with several species of wildlife for certain foods, particularly mast.

Feral hogs generally breed year round; litters range from 1 to 7, averaging 1.9 per sow (Hanson and Karstad, 1959). An average of one to three suckling pigs usually accompanies brood sows. The heat period is approximately forty-eight hours, and the average gestation period is 115 days (Henry, 1968).

Family Bovidae

Domestic Cow
Bos taurus Linnaeus

Some farm areas in eastern Texas are not grazed by cattle, and much of the land is exceedingly low in carrying capacity. However, heavy concentrations of stock on more favorable areas may create overstocking. Overgrazing often results in the removal of the original palatable grasses and herbs and their replacement by less desirable varieties.

The chief influence of the cow on wildlife is indirectly through the modification or removal of essential food and cover plants, with all the consequences of this process in soil erosion, flooding, and lessened productiveness. Creek-bottom vegetation is especially attractive and valuable to livestock. Stocking should be adjusted so that these restricted areas of special attractiveness are not overgrazed. The improvement of bottomland pastures will permit a marked increase in their carrying capacity and perhaps will better serve the cattle in eastern Texas today without the detrimental effects of less well-regulated grazing.

The skull of a cow (Fig. 7) possesses a pair of permanent horns in both sexes that are not shed annually, as are the antlers of a deer. The horns are formed around a bony core arising from the frontal bones. Some breeds, such as the polled cattle, are hornless. Upper incisor teeth and canine teeth are absent.

Domestic Sheep
Ovis aries Linnaeus

The number of sheep in eastern Texas is not large. There are none in the pineywoods and coastal prairies, and only a few in the post oak woodlands. The majority of sheep in the region are in the blackland prairies. If sheep, and particularly goats, are brought into eastern Texas in large numbers, wildlife conservation will be increasingly difficult because sheep compete directly with wildlife for food. They are outstanding consumers of herbaceous plants, some of which are important foods for seed-eating birds and mammals, and they consume some browse as well. The skull of the domestic sheep (Fig. 8) is easily recognized by the strongly convex roof of the cranium and the depression in front of the eye socket.

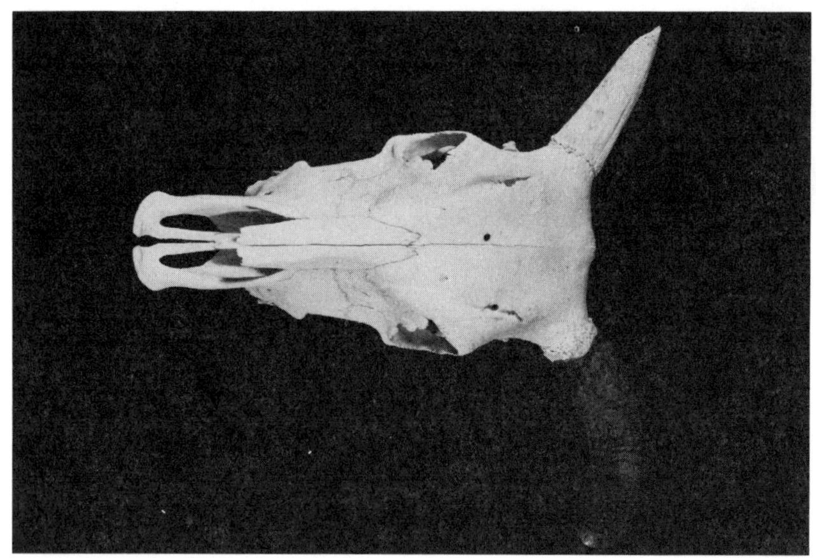

Figure 7. Skull of the domestic cow, *Bos taurus*.

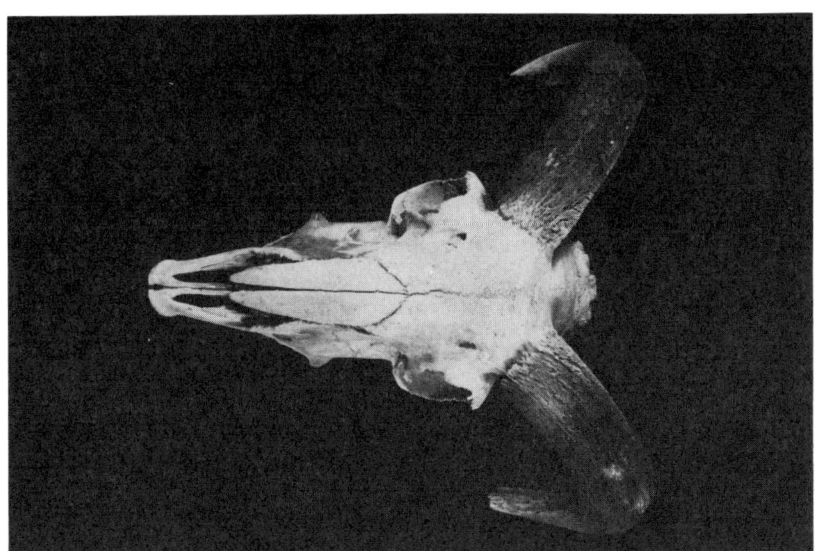

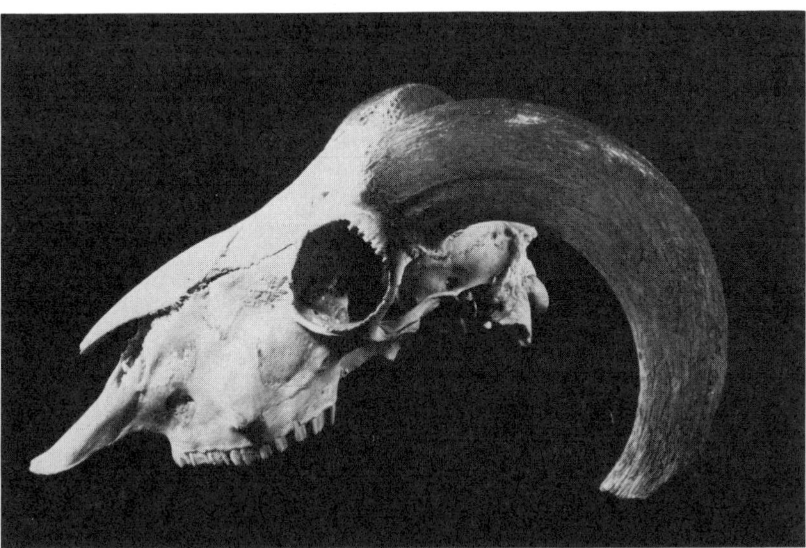

FIGURE 8. Skull of the domestic sheep, *Ovis aires*.

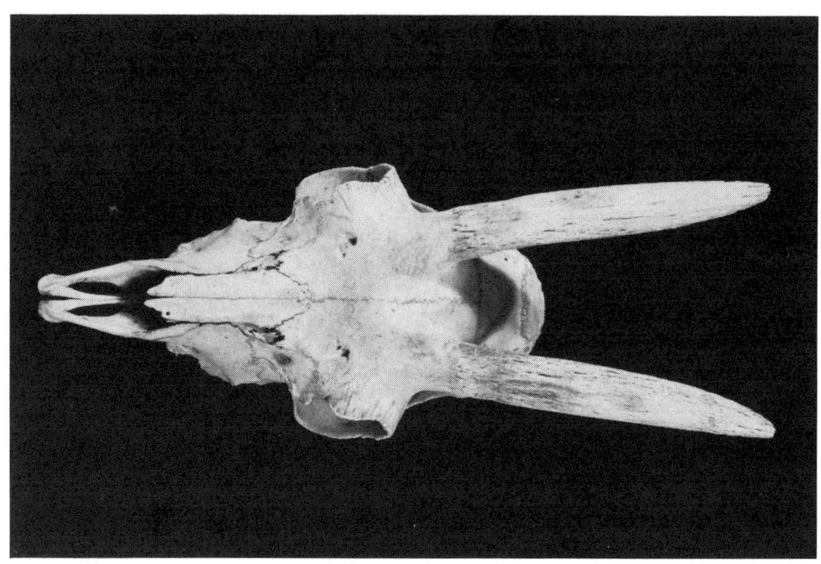

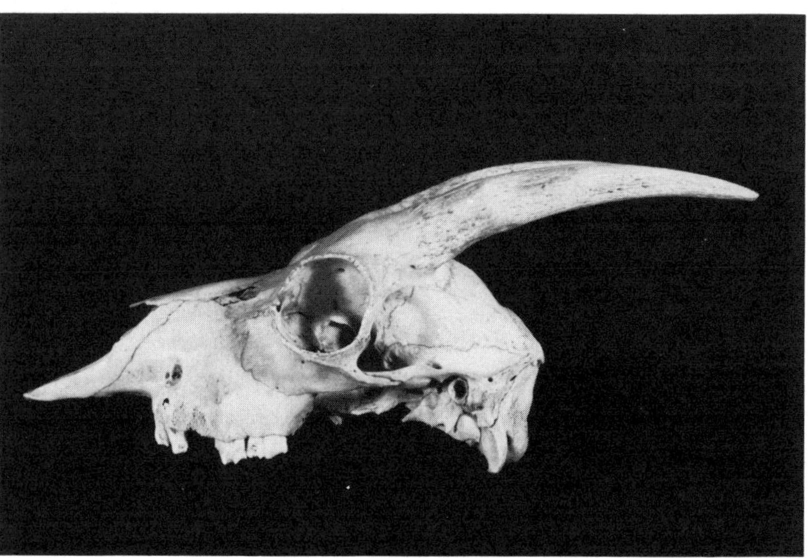

Figure 9. Skull of the domestic goat, *Capra hircus*.

Domestic Goat
Capra hircus Linnaeus

There are very few goats in eastern Texas, and these are primarily in the blackland prairie region. The effects of goats on native vegetation and wildlife are profound. They compete directly with deer and directly or indirectly with every form of wildlife that uses pasture vegetation either for food or shelter. Where they are used in the forest farming that is primary in eastern Texas, they should be carefully controlled through fencing and concentrated on areas designed for pasture improvement. The skull of a goat (Fig. 9) lacks the depressions in front of the eye sockets characteristic of sheep, and the horns are parallel and directed back instead of curved down and out, as in the sheep.

Order Perissodactyla

Family Equiidae

Horse
Equus caballus Linnaeus

Ass
Equus hemionus Linnaeus

Mule
Equus caballus × *Equus hemionus*

Horselike animals are not sufficiently numerous to exercise any major effects on the vegetation, or on the wildlife, except perhaps in limited localities where intensive pasturing may be practiced. The skull (Fig. 10) is easily recognized by the presence of upper incisors and the solid bony ring that surrounds the eye socket.

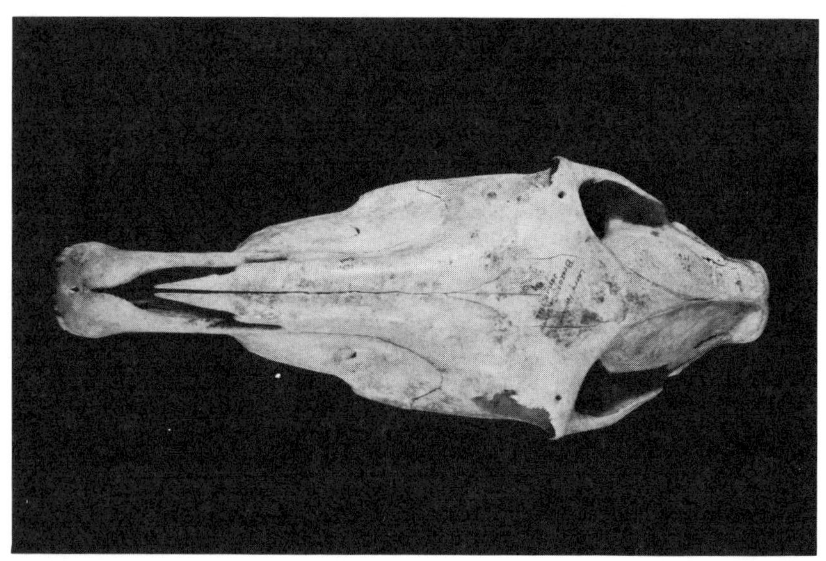

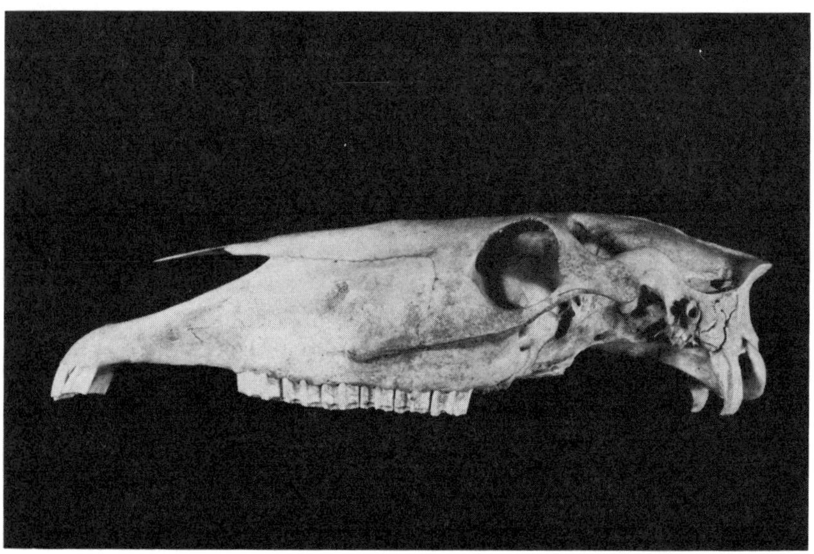

Figure 10. Skull of the horse, *Equus caballus*.

Appendix I
Specimens Examined

THIS study was based on the holdings of the following institutions with important collections of eastern Texas mammals, as listed by their abbreviations:

AUSCO   Austin College, Sherman, Texas
BUSM   Strecker Museum, Baylor University, Waco, Texas
DMNHT   Dallas Museum of Natural History
FWMSH   Fort Worth Museum of Science and History
KU   Museum of Natural History, University of Kansas, Lawrence
LSUMZ   Museum of Zoology, Louisiana State University, Baton Rouge
MVZ   Museum of Vertebrate Zoology, University of California, Berkeley
NTSU   North Texas State University, Denton
SFAVC   Stephen F. Austin State University, Nacogdoches, Texas
SWTS   Southwest Texas State University, San Marcos
TCWC   Texas Cooperative Wildlife Collection, Texas A&M University
TNHC   Texas Natural History Collection, Texas Memorial Museum, University of Texas at Austin
TTU   The Museum, Texas Tech University, Lubbock
TWC   Texas Wesleyan College, Fort Worth
UIMNH   Museum of Natural History, University of Illinois, Urbana
UMMZ   Museum of Zoology, University of Michigan, Ann Arbor
USNM   United States National Museum of Natural History, including the former U.S. Biological Surveys Collections, Washington, D.C.
UTAVC   University of Texas at Arlington

Didelphis virginiana virginiana (160). *Anderson Co.*: 4 mi. SW Tennessee Colony, FM Rd. 645, 1 (TNHC); 20 mi. NW Palestine, Engling Wildlife Refuge, 1 (TNHC); 3.5 mi. SE Elkart, 1 (SFAVC). *Angelina Co.*: 23 mi. SE Nacogdoches, 1 (SFAVC). *Austin Co.*: 5 mi. N Bellville, 1 (TCWC). *Bowie Co.*: 4.4 mi. S, 5.1 mi. W Texarkana, 1 (TTU). *Brazos Co.*: 2 mi. NW Bryan, 1 (TCWC); 4 mi. W Bryan, 1 (TCWC); Bryan, 1 (TCWC); 7 mi. W College Station, 1 (TCWC); 5 mi. W College Station, 1 (TCWC); 2 mi. W College Station, 1 (TCWC); 0.75 mi. W College Station, 1 (TCWC); College Station, 4 (TCWC); Texas A&M University, College Station, 1 (TCWC), 1 (UIMNH); 2.5 mi. S College Station, 7 (TTU); 5 mi. SW College Station, 1 (TCWC). *Burleson Co.*: 6 mi. E Caldwell, 1 (TCWC). *Calhoun Co.*: Port Lavaca, 1 (USNM). *Colorado Co.*: 6 mi. N Eagle Lake, 1 (TCWC); 3 mi. NW Altair, 1 (TCWC). *Cooke Co.*: Gainesville, 2 (USNM). *Dallas Co.*: NE Dallas, 1 (UTAVC); Dallas, 1 (DMNHT); 4.5 mi. SW Dallas, 2 (UTAVC). *De Witt Co.*: 10 mi. W Cuero, 1 (TCWC). *Falls Co.*: 7 mi. S Asa, FM Rd. 434, 1 (BUSM). *Freestone Co.*: no specific locality, 1 (TWC). *Galveston Co.*: Virginia Point, 1 (USNM). *Gregg Co.*: Kilgore, 1 (SFAVC). *Grimes Co.*: 4 mi. N Carlos, 1 (TCWC). *Hardin Co.*: 8.3 mi. N, 2.4 mi. E Silsbee, 1 (TCWC); Sour Lake, 5 (USNM). *Harris Co.*: 2.5 mi. N Hockley, 3 (TCWC); 4 mi. N Huffman, 1 (TCWC); 12 mi. N Baytown, 1 (TNHC). *Hays Co.*: 9.4 mi. W San Marcos, 1 (TNHC). *Henderson Co.*: 6 mi. W Athens, 1 (TCWC); 0.5 mi. S Athens, 1 (SFAVC). *Jackson Co.*: 10 mi. S Lolita, 1 (BUSM). *Jefferson Co.*: Beaumont, 1 (MVZ). *Lavaca Co.*: 15 mi. S Hallettsville, 1

(TCWC); 0.5 mi. W Sweet Home, 1 (TCWC). *Liberty Co.*: 28 mi. E Conroe, 1 (TNHC); Tarkington, 2 (USNM); Liberty, 1 (USNM); 2.5 mi. N, 3.8 mi. E Moss Hill, 1 (TCWC). *Limestone Co.*: 4 mi. N Groesbeck, 1 (TCWC). *McLennan Co.*: Mosheim, 1 (BUSM); Mother Neff State Park, 1 (BUSM); 0.5 mi. W jct. Hwy. 185 and FM Rd. 1637, 1 (BUSM); 3 mi. W Lake Waco Dam, 1 (BUSM); 2 mi. N Woodway, 1 (BUSM); Waco, 10 (BUSM); 3.5 mi. SW Mart, 1 (BUSM); 5 mi. S Waco, 1 (BUSM); 6.1 mi. S Waco, 1 (BUSM). *Nacogdoches Co.*: La Nana Creek, Nacogdoches, 1 (SFAVC); Stephen F. Austin University, Nacogdoches, 12 (SFAVC); Nacogdoches, 4 (SFAVC); Bonita Creek, Nacogdoches, 1 (SFAVC); 11 mi. E Nacogdoches, 1 (SFAVC); 1 mi. S Nacogdoches, 1 (SFAVC); 7 mi. SE Nacogdoches, 1 (SFAVC); 8 mi. S Nacogdoches, 1 (SFAVC); 9 mi. S Nacogdoches, 1 (SFAVC); 10 mi. S Nacogdoches, 1 (SFAVC); 11 mi. SW Nacogdoches, 1 (SFAVC); 4 mi. E Starr, 1 (SFAVC). *Orange Co.*: no specific locality, 1 (SFAVC). *Panola Co.*: near Carthage, 1 (SFAVC). *Polk Co.*: 1 mi. S Neches River, 3 mi. E Hwy. 59, 1 (SFAVC); 10 mi. E Livingston, 1 (USNM). *Shelby Co.*: 14 mi. SE Center, 1 (SFAVC). *Smith Co.*: 3 mi. E Tyler, 1 (SFAVC); 1.5 mi. W Arp, 1 (SFAVC). *Tarrant Co.*: 3 mi. E Keller, 1 (TCWC); Fort Worth, 2 (DMNHT), 5 (FWMSH), 1 (TWC), 4 (UTAVC); 7 mi. SE Fort Worth, 1 (TWC); 9 mi. S Fort Worth, 1 (TWC); 18 mi. SE Fort Worth, 1 (UTAVC); 2 mi. SSE Lake Arlington Dam, 1 (UTAVC); Arlington, 1 (UTAVC). *Travis Co.*: 7.7 mi. W Bee Cave, 1 (TNHC); 11 mi. NW Austin, Balcones Research Center, 1 (TNHC); 7 mi. W Austin, 1 (TNHC); University of Texas, 1 (TNHC); Municipal Golf Course, Austin, 1 (TNHC); Hemphill Park, Austin, 1 (TNHC); Austin, 2 (TNHC); 32 mi. E Austin, 1 (TNHC); 7.6 mi. S Austin, 1 (TNHC). *Trinity Co.*: 1.3 mi. E Trinity, 1 (TCWC). *Tyler Co.*: 3.6 mi. S, 2.9 mi. W Town Bluff, 1 (TCWC); 0.6 mi. N, 0.7 mi. W Spurger, 2 (TCWC). *Walker Co.*: 7 mi. WNW Huntsville, 1 (TCWC); 17 mi. SW Huntsville, 3 (TCWC). *Washington Co.*: Long Point, 1 (USNM); 10 mi. W Brenham, 2 (TCWC); 11.5 mi. SW Brenham, 2 (TCWC). *Williamson Co.*: 10.3 mi. NW Taylor, 1 (TNHC).

Blarina carolinensis carolinensis (40). *Bowie Co.*: Sulphur River, 1 (BUSM); Anderson Creek, N of Simms, 1 (FWMSH). *Denton Co.*: 2 mi. N Roanoke, 1 (UTAVC). *Gregg Co.*: Kilgore, 1 (SFAVC). *Harrison Co.*: 15 mi. NE Marshall, 1 (TNHC), 1 (SFAVC); 1 mi. N jct. IH 20 and Hwy. 31, 1 (DMNHT). *Henderson Co.*: Malakoff, 1 (SFAVC). *Nacogdochess Co.*: 5 mi. W Nacogdoches, 1 (SFAVC); Nacogdoches, 2 (TTU), 3 (SFAVC); Bonita Creek, Nacogdoches, 1 (SFAVC); La Nana Creek, Nacogdoches, 4 (SFAVC); 1 mi. E Nacogdoches, 7 (TNHC), 1 (SFAVC); 3 mi. E Nacogdoches, 1 (SFAVC); 7 mi. SE Nacogdoches, 1 (SFAVC); Stephen F. Austin College Farm, Nacogdoches, 1 (SFAVC); 12 mi. S, 2 mi. W Nacogdoches, 1 (SFAVC); 15 mi. SW Nacogdoches, 1 (SFAVC); 2 mi. W. Etiole, 1 (SFAVC). *Red River Co.*: 14 mi. NE Clarksville, 4 (DMNHT). *Rusk Co.*: 1.6 mi. NE New London, 1 (SFAVC). *Shelby Co.*: 8 mi. E Shelbyville, 1 (TNHC); near Sabine River, East Hampton Scenic Area, Sabine National Forest, 1 (FWMSH)

Blarina carolinensis minima (87). *Hardin Co.*: 3.25 mi. E, 2 mi. S Village Mills, 1 (TCWC); 10.9 mi. N, 2.6 mi. E Silsbee, 1 (TCWC); 0.9 mi. N, 4.5 mi. E Saratoga, 6 (TCWC); 0.8 mi. N, 2.6 mi. E Saratoga, 6 (TCWC); Rosier Park, Saratoga, 3 (TCWC); 4.6 mi. E Saratoga, Hwy. 770, 1 (TCWC); 8 mi. NE Sour Lake, 1 (USNM); 7 mi. NE Sour Lake, 1 (USNM). *Harris Co.*: Bayou Bend, Houston, 1 (TCWC). *Liberty Co.*: 2.5 mi. N, 3.8 mi. E Moss Hill, 2 (TCWC). *Newton Co.*: 11.5 mi. N Burkeville, 1 (TCWC); 11.4 mi. N Burkeville, 4 (TCWC); 10.5 mi. N Burkeville, 1 (TCWC); 10.4 mi. N Burkeville, 1 (TCWC); 10 mi. N Burkeville, 2 (TCWC); 9.9 mi. N Burkeville, 1 (TCWC); 9.5 mi. N Burkeville, 1 (TCWC); 9.4 mi. N Burkeville, 2 (TCWC); 9.3 mi. N Burkeville, 4 (TCWC); 9.2

mi. N Burkeville, 2 (TCWC); 9 mi. N. Burkeville, 4 (TCWC); 7.4 mi. N Burkeville, 1 (TCWC); 7.3 mi. N Burkeville, 1 (TCWC). *Polk Co.*: 2.2 mi. W, 1.4 mi. N Dallardsville, 3 (TCWC); 2 mi. E, 1.7 mi. S Camp Ruby, 1 (TCWC). *Sabine Co.*: 1 mi. W Hemphill, 2 (TTU); Big Sandy Creek, 1 (DMNHT). *San Jacinto Co.*: 3 mi. NW Shepard, 1 (TCWC). *Tyler Co.*: 3.1 mi. N, 2.5 mi. W Spurger, 8 (TCWC); 1.7 mi. N, 1.6 mi. W Spurger, 3 (TCWC); 1.2 mi. N, 1.9 mi. W Spurger, 1 (TCWC); 1.9 mi. S, 1.5 mi. E Town Bluff, 1 (TCWC); 4.2 mi. S, 1.6 mi. W Warren, 5 (TCWC); 4.2 mi. S, 1.2 mi. W Warren, 1 (TCWC); 4.3 mi. S, 1.4 mi. W Warren, 1 (TCWC); 4.3 mi. S, 1 mi. W Warren, 1 (TCWC); 4.8 mi. S, 1.2 mi. W Warren, 1 (TCWC); 4.5 mi. S, 0.5 mi. W Warren, 6 (TCWC); 4.6 mi. SE Warren, 1 (TCWC). *Victoria Co.*: Victoria, 1 (USNM). *Walker Co.*: 2 mi. E Huntsville, 1 (TCWC).

Cryptotis parva parva (192). *Bell Co.*: 1.5 mi. S Killeen, 1 (TCWC). *Bowie Co.*: 1 mi. NE Simms, 1 (TCWC). *Brazoria Co.*: 2 mi. NW Sweeny, 1 (TCWC). *Brazos Co.*: 5 mi. NW Bryan, 1 (TCWC); Bryan, 2 (KU); 2 mi. S Bryan, 1 (TCWC); 4 mi. NW College Station, 1 (TCWC); 0.25 mi. N College Station, 1 (TCWC); 2 mi. W College Station, 2 (KU); 1 mi. W College Station, 6 (TCWC); College Station, 22 (TCWC), 2 (KU), 1 (UIMNH); Easterwood Airport Lake, College Station, 1 (TCWC); 3 mi. E College Station, 2 (TCWC); 3 mi. SW College Station, 1 (TCWC); 3.5 mi. SW College Station, 1 (TCWC); 7 mi. SW College Station, 1 (TCWC); 5 mi. W Wellborn, 1 (TCWC). *Cooke Co.*: Gainesville, 1 (USNM); Camp Howze, 1 (MVZ). *Dallas Co.*: White Rock Lake, 1 (DMNHT); Mountain Creek Lake, 3 (UTAVC); Dallas, 2 (DMNHT). *Denton Co.*: 2.5 mi. N Roanoke, 1 (UTAVC). *Falls Co.*: 7 mi. E Marlin, 1 (BUSM). *Fort Bend Co.*: Richmond, 1 (USNM). *Gonzales Co.*: 5 mi. S Luling, 3 (TNHC). *Grimes Co.*: 4 mi. N Carlos, 1 (TCWC). *Guadalupe Co.*: 0.5 mi. S Prairie Lea, 1 (TNHC). *Hardin Co.*: 2.5 mi. W Sour Lake, 2 (UIMNH); 0.5 mi. E Sour Lake, 1 (UIMNH); 5.5 mi. E Sour Lake, 3 (UIMNH). *Harris Co.*: 6 mi. N Baytown, 1 (TCWC). *Harrison Co.*: 5 mi. E Marshall, Hwy. 80, 1 (BUSM). *Houston Co.*: 5 mi. W Grapeland, 1 (SFAVC). *Hunt Co.*: Sabine River bottom, Lake Tawakoni, 1 (FWMSH). *Jackson Co.*: 2 mi. S Lolita, 1 (TCWC); 2 mi. S Lolita, 1 (TCWC); 2 mi. S Lolita, 1 (TCWC). *Jefferson Co.*: 1 mi. SW Sabine Pass, 1 (TNHC). *Matagorda Co.*: 1 mi. W Palacios, 2 (TCWC). *McLennan Co.*: 7 mi. N Valley View, 1 (BUSM); 2.5 mi. SW Ross, 1 (BUSM); Waco, 1 (BUSM); Tehuacan Creek, Waco, 2 (BUSM); Lake Creek Reservoir, 8 mi. S Waco, 2 (BUSM); 10 mi. S Waco, 1 (BUSM). *Nacogdoches Co.*: 2 mi. E Garrison, 1 (SFAVC); Appleby, 1 (SFAVC); La Nana Creek, Nacogdoches, 1 (SFAVC); 1 mi. E La Nana Creek, 2 (TTU); 2 mi. NE Nacogdoches, 1 (SFAVC); 7 mi. W Nacogdoches, 1 (SFAVC); 1 mi. W Nacogdoches, 1 (SFAVC); Nacogdoches, 14 (SFAVC); Stephen F. Austin University, Nacogdoches, 1 (SFAVC), 4 (TTU); 1 mi. E Nacogdoches, 1 (SFAVC); 4 mi. E Nacogdoches, 4 (SFAVC); 7 mi. S Nacogdoches, 1 (SFAVC); 8 mi. S Nacogdoches, 1 (SFAVC); 10 mi. S Nacogdoches, 4 (SFAVC); 14 mi. SW Nacogdoches, 4 (SFAVC). *Panola Co.*: 5 mi. SE Long Branch, 1 (SFAVC). *Red River Co.*: 5.5 mi. S Boxelder, 1 (DMNHT). *Robertson Co.*: 3 mi. W Hearne, 2 (TCWC); 7 mi. SE Hearne, 2 (TWC). *Rusk Co.*: 6 mi. W Henderson, 1 (SFAVC). *Sabine Co.*: 1 mi. W Hemphill, 1 (TTU); Big Sandy Creek, Hwy. 87, 2 (DMNHT). *San Augustine Co.*: 9 mi. S Broaddus, 7 mi. N Zaralla, Hwy. 147, 1 (FWMSH). *Shelby Co.*: Shelbyville, 1 (SFAVC). *Smith Co.*: 20 mi. NE Tyler, 1 (SWTS); 3 mi. SW Flint, 1 (SFAVC). *Tarrant Co.*: Keller, 4 mi. N jct. Hwy. 377 and Loop 820, 1 (UTAVC); Hurst, 2 (FWMSH); Fort Worth, 10 (FWMSH); Convair Recreation Area, Fort Worth, 1 (FWMSH); Arlington, 1 (TCWC), 7 (UTAVC), 1 (FWMSH); 2.75 mi. E Clear Fork of the Trinity River, Hwy. 377, 1 (FWMSH). *Travis Co.*: 9 mi. NW Austin, 2

(TNHC); 8 mi. NW Austin, 1 (TNHC); Austin, 1 (MVZ); 9 mi. E Austin, 1 (TNHC). *Tyler Co.*: 1.9 mi. W, 1.2 mi. N Spurger, 3 (TCWC); 4.5 mi. S, 0.5 mi. W Warren, 5 (TCWC). *Victoria Co.*: Victoria, 2 (USNM); 14 mi. SE Victoria, 3 (TCWC). *Walker Co.*: 6 mi. S Huntsville, 1 (TCWC). *Waller Co.*: Hempstead, 1 (USNM). *Washington Co.*: Independence, 1 (TCWC); Brenham, 1 (TCWC). *Williamson Co.*: 2 mi. S Taylor, 1 (TNHC).

Scalopus aquaticus alleni (23). *Bastrop Co.*: 2 mi. W Bastrop, 1 (TCWC). *Burleson Co.*: 0.4 mi. S Somerville, Hwy. 36, 1 (TCWC). *Colorado Co.*: 6 mi. N Eagle Lake, 1 (TCWC). *Falls Co.*: Gurley, 1 (BUSM). *Lavaca Co.*: 4 mi. S Hallettsville, 1 (TCWC); 5 mi. S Hallettsville, 1 (TCWC); 8 mi. S Hallettsville, 1 (TCWC); 2 mi. E Yoakum, 1 (TCWC); 33 mi. N Victoria, Hwy. 77, 1 (TCWC). *Milam Co.*: 3 mi. NE Gause, 1 (TCWC); 1.8 mi. NE Gause, 2 (TCWC); 7.4 mi. W Gause, 1 (TCWC); 6.2 mi. W Gause, 1 (TCWC); 1 mi. E Gause, 1 (TCWC); 7.2 mi. S Gause, 1 (TCWC); 3 mi. E Milano, 1 (TCWC); 4 mi. E Milano, 1 (TCWC); 5 mi. E Milano, 1 (TCWC); 1 mi. S Rockdale, FM Rd. 487, 1 (TCWC); 7.5 mi. S Rockdale, 1 (TCWC). *Travis Co.*: University of Texas, Austin, 2 (TNHC).

Scalopus aquaticus aereus (57). *Angelina Co.*: 3 mi. W Lufkin, 1 (SFAVC); Huntington City, 1 (SFAVC); 1 mi. N Diboll, 1 (TCWC). *Bowie Co.*: 3 mi. N New Boston, 1 (TCWC); Texarkana, 1 (TCWC), 1 (SFAVC). *Hardin Co.*: 3.5 mi. E, 1.7 mi. N Village Mills, 1 (TCWC); 9 mi. NE Sour Lake, 1 (USNM); 8 mi. NE Sour Lake, 9 (USNM); 7 mi. NE Sour Lake, 6 (USNM); Sour Lake, 14 (USNM). *Harrison Co.*: 3 mi. SE Hallsville, 2 (SFAVC). *Jasper Co.*: 8 mi. W, 1.4 mi. N Jasper, 1 (TCWC); 8.6 mi. W Jasper, 1 (TCWC); 8 mi. W Jasper, 2 (TCWC). *Newton Co.*: 7.4 mi. N Burkeville, 2 (TCWC); 7.2 mi. N Burkeville, 1 (TCWC); 7 mi. N Burkeville, 1 (TCWC); 6.8 mi. N Burkeville, 1 (TCWC); 30 mi. N Orange, Angelina Wildlife Management Area, 1 (TCWC). *Panola Co.*: Carthage, 1 (SFAVC). *Rusk Co.*: 1 mi. N Henderson, 1 (SFAVC); 12 mi. S Henderson, 2 (TCWC). *Sabine Co.*: 12 mi. W Hemphill, 1 (SFAVC). *Shelby Co.*: Joaquin, 1 (USNM), 1 (USNM); 5 mi. W Timpson, 1 (SFAVC).

Scalopus aquaticus cryptus (189). *Anderson Co.*: Frankston, 1 (SFAVC); Engling Wildlife Management Area, 3 (TCWC); 20 mi. S Athens, 1 (SFAVC); 20 mi. NW Palestine, 6 (TNHC); 5 mi. SE Slocum, 1 (SFAVC); Elkhart, 1 (SFAVC). *Brazos Co.*: 5 mi. N Bryan, 1 (TCWC); 3 mi. N Bryan, 1 (TCWC); Bryan, 7 (TCWC); 2.5 mi. S Bryan, 1 (MVZ); 0.5 mi. N College Station, 1 (TCWC); 0.25 mi. N College Station, 1 (TCWC); 2 mi. W College Station, 2 (TCWC); 1 mi. W College Station, 1 (TCWC), 1 (KU); College Station, 14 (TCWC), 1 (UMMZ); 1.5 mi. SW College Station, 1 (TCWC); 3 mi. SW College Station, 1 (TCWC). *Cherokee Co.*: 1 mi. N Rusk, 1 (SFAVC); 0.5 mi. N Maydelle, 1 (SFAVC); 0.25 mi. N Maydelle, 1 (SFAVC); 2 mi. S Maydelle, 1 (SFAVC); 7 mi. S Maydelle, 1 (SFAVC). *Dallas Co.*: Dallas, 1 (DMNHT). *Denton Co.*: 6.5 mi. W Lewisville, 2 (DMNHT). *Grayson Co.*: near Dennison, 1 (TCWC). *Grimes Co.*: Carlos, 1 (TCWC). *Harris Co.*: 2.5 mi. N Hockley, 1 (TCWC). *Henderson Co.*: Cedar Creek Lake, 1 (DMNHT); 10 mi. S Athens, 1 (SFAVC). *Hill Co.*: Willis Camp, 5 mi. NW jct. FM Rd. 933 and FM Rd. 2114, 2 (TCWC); 2.1 mi. N Waco, jct. FM Rd. 933 and FM Rd. 2114, 1 (TCWC); jct. FM Rd. 933 and FM Rd. 2114, Spivey Crossing, 2 (TCWC); 5 mi. NW jct. FM Rd. 933 and FM Rd. 2114, Spivey Crossing, 1 (TCWC). *Houston Co.*: 3 mi. W Ratcliff, 1 (SFAVC); 2 mi. W Ratcliff, 1 (SFAVC); 0.18 mi. S Kenard, 1 (SFAVC). *Leon Co.*: 13 mi. E Centerville, 1 (TCWC). *McLennan Co.*: Waco, 10 (BUSM). *Montgomery Co.*: 2 mi. N Conroe, 3 (TCWC); 1 mi. N Conroe, 4 (TCWC); 10 mi. W Conroe, 1 (UMMZ); 2 mi. S Conroe, 2 (TCWC); 10 mi. S Conroe, 29 (TCWC); 1.6 mi. E Decker Prairie, 1 (TCWC). *Nacogdoches Co.*: 10 mi. ENE Nacogdoches, 2 (SFAVC); 5 mi. NE Nacogdoches, 3 (SFAVC); 4 mi. NW

Nacogdoches, 1 (TTU); 3 mi. N Nacogdoches, 1 (SFAVC); 2.5 mi. NW Nacogdoches, 1 (SFAVC); 2.5 mi. W Nacogdoches, 1 (SFAVC); Nacogdoches, 2 (SFAVC); Stephen F. Austin Experimental Forest, 1 (SFAVC); 10 mi. S Nacogdoches, 1 (SFAVC). *Polk Co.*: 2 mi. E, 1.7 mi. S Camp Ruby, 1 (TCWC); 2 mi. W Sheppard, 1 (BUSM). *Robertson Co.*: 1 mi. S Hearne, 2 (TCWC). *Smith Co.*: Lindale, 1 (BUSM); 18 mi. E Tyler, 1 (SFAVC). *Tarrant Co.*: 3 mi. SE Roanoke, 1 (DMNHT); Keller, 1 (UTAVC); Haltom City, 1 (FWMSH); Arlington, 5 (UTAVC); Fort Worth, 10 (FWMSH); Benbrook, 1 (TWC); Burleson, 1 (TWC). *Trinity Co.*: 4 mi. NE Trinity, 1 (TCWC); 7 mi. E Trinity, 1 (TCWC); 1 mi. E Sebastopol, 4 (TCWC). *Tyler Co.*: 3 mi. E Chester, 1 (TCWC); 4.25 mi. E, 2 mi. S Town Bluff, 1 (TCWC); 11 mi. W Woodville, 2 (TCWC); 5 mi. W Woodville, 1 (TCWC); 9.7 mi. N Spurger, 1 (TCWC); 9.5 mi. N Spurger, 1 (TCWC); 6.8 mi. N Spurger, 1 (TCWC); 1.8 mi. N, 2.6 mi. W Spurger, 2 (TCWC). *Upshur Co.*: Gilmer, 1 (TCWC). *Van Zandt Co.*: 5 mi. N Grand Saline, 2 (TTU); 3.5 mi. N Canton, 1 (TCWC); 8 mi. W Canton, 1 (DMNHT); 3 mi. E Canton, 1 (TCWC). *Walker Co.*: 17 mi. WNW Huntsville, 1 (TCWC); 10 mi. NW Huntsville, 1 (TCWC); 15 mi. S Huntsville, 1 (TCWC). *Wood Co.*: 4 mi. S Winnsboro, 6 (TCWC); 1 mi. W Mineola, 1 (TTU); 2 mi. S Hawkins, 1 (TCWC).

Myotis austroriparius austroriparius (24). *Bowie Co.*: New Boston, 1 (TTU). *Hardin Co.*: 11.2 mi. N, 2.3 mi. E Silsbee, 1 (TCWC); 10.9 mi. N, 2.3 mi. E Silsbee, 1 (TCWC); 9 mi. N, 1.3 mi. E Silsbee, 1 (TCWC). *Liberty Co.*: 2.5 mi. N, 3.8 mi. E Moss Hill, 1 (TCWC). *Newton Co.*: 12 mi. N Burkeville, 7 (TCWC); 11.5 mi. N Burkeville, 2 (TCWC); 8.5 mi. N Burkeville, 2 (TCWC). *Panola Co.*: 8 mi. SW Gary, 1 (TCWC). *Tyler Co.*: 1.1 mi. S, 1 mi. W Town Bluff, 3 (TCWC); 2 mi. S, 1.5 mi. W Town Bluff, 1 (TCWC); 3.6 mi. S, 2.9 mi. W Town Bluff, 1 (TCWC); 0.6 mi. N, 0.7 mi. W Spurger, 2 (TCWC).

Myotis velifer incautus (32). *Bexar Co.*: San Antonio, 1 (USNM). *Comal Co.*: New Braunfels, 1 (USNM); Bracken Cave, 6 (TCWC). *McLennan Co.*: Baylor University, Waco, 1 (BUSM). *Travis Co.*: 1 mi. NW Austin, 1 (TNHC); Austin, 5 (TNHC); 5 mi. E University of Texas, Austin, 1 (TNHC); 7 mi. SW University of Texas, Austin, 1 (TNHC). *Williamson Co.*: 2.5 mi. NW McNeil, 9 (TNHC); 3 mi. N Georgetown, 1 (TNHC); 3 mi. W Georgetown, 3 (TNHC); 2 mi. SW Georgetown, 1 (TNHC); 3 mi. SW Georgetown, 1 (TNHC).

Lasionycteris noctivagans noctivagans (5). *Galveston Co.*: Galveston, 1 (TCWC). *Polk Co.*: 2 mi. E, 1.7 mi. S Camp Ruby, 1 (TCWC). *Tyler Co.*: 3.6 mi. S, 2.9 mi. W Town Bluff, 2 (TCWC); 4.2 mi. S, 0.8 mi. W Warren, 1 (TCWC).

Pipistrellus subflavus subflavus (44). *Anderson Co.*: Long Lake, 3 (USNM). *Comal Co.*: 10 mi. NE New Braunfels, 1 (TCWC). *Dallas Co.*: Irving, 1 (UTAVC). *Galveston Co.*: Clear Creek , 1 (USNM). *Hardin Co.*: 11 mi. N, 2.3 mi. E Silsbee, 1 (TCWC). *Harris Co.*: 4 mi. N Huffman, 1 (TCWC). *Nacogdoches Co.*: 4 mi. SW Garrison, 5 (SFAVC); 10 mi. E Cushing, 1 (SFAVC); 1 mi. S Cushing, 1 (SFAVC); Nacogdoches, 1 (SFAVC); Nacogdoches, 1 (SFAVC); 15 mi. E Nacogdoches, 1 (SFAVC). *Newton Co.*: 12 mi. N Burkeville, 2 (TCWC); 11.5 mi. N Burkeville, 1 (TCWC); 9.3 mi. N Burkeville, 1 (TCWC); 8.5 mi. N Burkeville, 1 (TCWC). *Panola Co.*: Lake Mervaul, 1 (SFAVC); 4 mi. SW Gary, 2 (SFAVC). *Polk Co.*: 4 mi. E Livingston, 2 (TCWC); 3 mi. S Livingston, 1 (TCWC). *Shelby Co.*: 3 mi. N Timpson, 1 (SFAVC); cave between Timpson and Gray, 1 (SFAVC); 15 mi. N Center, 1 (TTU); 14 mi. N Center, 3 (SFAVC); Neville Cave, 8 mi. S Center, 2 (UIMNH). *Tarrant Co.*: University of Texas, Arlington, 1 (UTAVC). *Travis Co.*: 3 mi. W Austin, 1 (TNHC). *Tyler Co.*: 2 mi. S, 1.5 mi. W Town Bluff, 3 (TCWC); 3.6 mi. S, 2.4 mi. W Town Bluff, 1 (TCWC). *Walker Co.*: 11 mi. NW New Waverly, 1 (TNHC). *Williamson Co.*: 6 mi. W Round Rock, 1 (TNHC).

Eptesicus fuscus fuscus (38). *Hardin Co.*: 11 mi. N, 2.3 mi. E Silsbee, 1 (TCWC); Grady, 1 (USNM); 7 mi. NE Sour Lake, 1 (USNM). *Marion Co.*: Jefferson, 1 (USNM). *McLennan Co.*: Waco, 1 (BUSM). *Nacogdoches Co.*: Nacogdoches, 1 (SFAVC); Stephen F. Austin University, Nacogdoches, 4 (SFAVC), 1 (TTU). *San Jacinto Co.*: jct. FM Rd. 945 and E San Jacinto River, 1 (TTU); 5 mi. NW Cleveland, 2 (TTU). *Trinity Co.*: Pine Oak, 1 (TCWC); Trinity, 1 (USNM), 1 (TCWC). *Tyler Co.*: 1.1 mi. S, 1 mi. W Town Bluff, 1 (TCWC); 2 mi. S, 1.5 mi. W Town Bluff, 1 (TCWC); 3.8 mi. N, 1.9 mi. W Spurger, 2 (TCWC); 0.6 mi. N, 0.7 mi. W Spurger, 2 (TCWC). *Upshur Co.*: Gilmer, 13 (TCWC). *Walker Co.*: 2 mi. SW Huntsville, 2 (TCWC).

Lasiurus borealis borealis (286). *Angelina Co.*: 23 mi. S Nacogdoches, 1 (TTU); 5 mi. N Lufkin, 1 (SFAVC); 1 mi. S Lufkin, 1 (SFAVC). *Bexar Co.*: Somerset, 1 (TNHC). *Bowie Co.*: 8 mi. N New Boston, 1 (TCWC). *Brazos Co.*: Bryan, 4 (TCWC); 4 mi. W College Station, 1 (TCWC); College Station, 11 (TCWC); 6.5 mi. SW College Station, 1 (TCWC); 6.5 mi. SE College Station, 4 (TCWC). *Cherokee Co.*: Maydelle, 1 (SFAVC); 3 mi. W Forest, 2 (SFAVC), 1 (TTU). *Dallas Co.*: Dallas, 1 (USNM), 1 (UTAVC), 5 (DMNHT). *Galveston Co.*: Bolivar Peninsula, 7.5 mi. NE Ferry Landing, 1 (TNHC). *Hardin Co.*: 11 mi. N, 2.3 mi. E Silsbee, 1 (TCWC); 7 mi. NE Sour Lake, 1 (USNM); Sour Lake, 2 (USNM). *Harris Co.*: Westfield, 1 (SFAVC); Houston, 5 (TCWC). *Houston Co.*: 6.3 mi. N Ratcliff, 2 (UTAVC). *Jasper Co.*: Bouton Lake, 1 (UTAVC). *Jefferson Co.*: Port Arthur, 6 (SFAVC), 6 (TTU). *Lamar Co.*: Arthur City, 3 (USNM); Paris, 3 (USNM). *Liberty Co.*: Tarkington, 1 (USNM); 20 mi. NW Liberty, 1 (USNM); 12 mi. N Dayton, 3 (TTU). *Marion Co.*: Jefferson, 2 (USNM). *McLennan Co.*: Lake Waco, 1 (BUSM); Waco, 6 (BUSM). *Montgomery Co.*: 20 mi. SW Huntsville, 2 (TNHC). *Nacogdoches Co.*: Martinsville, 1 (SFAVC); Nacogdoches, 2 (SFAVC), 5 (TTU), 1 (TNHC); Stephen F. Austin University, Nacogdoches, 5 (SFAVC); Stephen F. Austin Experimental Forest, 2 (TTU); 6 mi. E Nacogdoches, 1 (SFAVC); Sam Rayburn Reservoir, 1 (SFAVC). *Newton Co.*: 11.5 mi. N Burkeville, 2 (TCWC); 8.5 mi. N Burkeville, 4 (TCWC); 7.5 mi. N Burkeville, 1 (TCWC); 7 mi. N Burkeville, 1 (TCWC); Newton, 1 (TTU). *Panola Co.*: 7.5 mi. ENE Carthage, 4 (TCWC); 6 mi. E Carthage, 1 (SFAVC). *Polk Co.*: 2 mi. E, 1.7 mi. S Camp Ruby, 1 (TCWC); 4 mi. W, 0.3 mi. S Dallardsville, 1 (TCWC). *Red River Co.*: Clarksville, 1 (USNM). *Rusk Co.*: 1.6 mi. NE New London, 2 (SFAVC); 6 mi. E Mt. Enterprise, 1 (SFAVC). *San Jacinto Co.*: San Jacinto River, FM Rd. 945, 32 (TTU); 5 mi. NW Cleveland, 10 (TTU). *Shelby Co.*: Choice, 1 (LSUMZ). *Smith Co.*: Tyler, 1 (TCWC). *Tarrant Co.*: Hurst, 1 (UTAVC); Fort Worth, 67 (FWMSH), 1 (TNHC), 1 (TWC); River Oaks, Fort Worth, 1 (DMNHT); Halton City, Fort Worth, 4 (FWMSH); Arlington, 8 (FWMSH), 7 (UTAVC), 2 (TCWC). *Travis Co.*: Austin, 2 (TNHC). *Trinity Co.*: Trinity, 1 (USNM), 1 (TCWC); 1.3 mi. E Trinity, 1 (TCWC). *Tyler Co.*: 1.1 mi. S, 1 mi. W Town Bluff, 2 (TCWC); 2 mi. S, 1.5 mi. W Town Bluff, 1 (TCWC); 3.6 mi. S, 2.9 mi. W Town Bluff, 3 (TCWC); 3.8 mi. N, 1.9 mi. W Spurger, 7 (TCWC); 0.6 mi. N, 0.7 mi. W Spurger, 5 (TCWC). *Van Zandt Co.*: 1 mi. SW Grand Saline, 1 (TTU). *Victoria Co.*: Victoria, 1 (USNM). *Walker Co.*: 2 mi. NE Huntsville, 1 (TCWC); 16 mi. SW Huntsville, 1 (TCWC).

Lasiurus seminolus seminolus (102). *Cherokee Co.*: 3 mi. W Forest, 1 (SFAVC). *Grimes Co.*: 5 mi. E Richards, 1 (TCWC). *Hardin Co.*: 8.6 mi. N, 3.8 mi. E Silsbee, 1 (TCWC). *Harris Co.*: Katy, 1 (FWMSH); Houston, 10 (LSUMZ), 4 (TCWC). *Houston Co.*: 6.3 mi. N Ratcliff, 1 (UTAVC). *Jefferson Co.*: 11.7 mi. W Sabine Pass, Hwy. 87, 1 (TCWC). *Liberty Co.*: 12 mi. N Dayton, 2 (TTU). *Nacogdoches Co.*: Nacogdoches, 6 (SFAVC); Stephen F. Austin University, Nacogdoches, 1 (TTU), 2 (SFAVC); 9.5 mi. SW Nacogdoches, 1 (TNHC). *Newton Co.*:

11.5 mi. N Burkeville, 6 (TCWC); 8.5 mi. N Burkeville, 1 (TCWC). *Panola Co.*:
7.5 mi. ENE Carthage, 1 (TCWC). *Polk Co.*: 1 mi. S Neches River, 3 mi. E Hwy.
59, 2 (SFAVC); 2 mi. E, 1.7 mi. S Camp Ruby, 1 (TCWC); 4 mi. E Livingston, 1
(TCWC); 3 mi. S Livingston, 4 (TCWC); 2 mi. NNW Segno, 2 (TCWC). *Rusk Co.*:
6 mi. E Mt. Enterprise, 1 (SFAVC). *Sabine Co.*: 5 mi. N Geneva, 1 (TCWC); 0.5
mi. N Geneva, 1 (TCWC); Hemphill, 1 (SFAVC). *San Augustine Co.*: Angelina
National Forest, near Broaddus, 1 (FWMSH). *San Jacinto Co.*: San Jacinto River,
FM Rd. 945, 10 (TTU); 5 mi. NW Cleveland, 15 (TTU). *Shelby Co.*: 4 mi. S Joaquin, 1 (SFAVC); 2.3 mi. SE Patroon, 1 (TCWC). *Trinity Co.*: 3 mi. E Upland, 1
(TCWC); Trinity, 1 (USNM), 1 (TCWC). *Tyler Co.*: 1.1 mi. W, 1 mi. S Town
Bluff, 1 (TCWC); 2 mi. S, 1.5 mi. W Town Bluff, 2 (TCWC); 2.8 mi. S, 2.8 mi. W
Town Bluff, 1 (TCWC); 3.6 mi. S, 2.9 mi. W Town Bluff, 8 (TCWC); 3.8 mi. N, 1.9
mi. W Spurger, 2 (TCWC); 0.6 mi. N, 0.7 mi. W Spurger, 2 (TCWC); 4.3 mi. S,
4.5 mi. E Warren, 1 (TCWC).

Lasiurus cinereus cinereus (8). *Galveston Co.*: 5 mi. E Bolivar Peninsula, 1
(TCWC). *Hardin Co.*: 10.9 mi. N, 2.3 mi. E Silsbee, 1 (TCWC). *Jasper Co.*: 10
mi. E Jasper, Sherwood Forest Ranch, 1 (TCWC). *San Jacinto Co.*: 5 mi. NW
Cleveland, 1 (TTU). *Tarrant Co.*: Arlington, 1 (UTAVC). *Travis Co.*: Austin, 1
(TCWC). *Tyler Co.*: 3.6 mi. S, 2.9 mi. W Town Bluff, 2 (TCWC).

Lasiurus intermedius floridanus (11). *Brazos Co.*: 8 mi. SW College Station,
1 (TCWC). *Colorado Co.*: Eagle Lake, 1 (TCWC). *Fort Bend Co.*: 2 mi. S. Dewalt, 1 (TTU). *Harris Co.*: 4 mi. N. Huffman, 1 (TCWC); Houston, 1 (KU), 2
(TCWC), 2 (MVZ). *Madison Co.*: Bedias Creek, Madison and Walker County
line, 1 (SFAVC). *Travis Co.*: Austin, 1 (TNHC).

Nycticeius humeralis humeralis (260). *Anderson Co.*: Engling Wildlife Man-
agement Area, 18.5 mi. NW Palestine, 1 (TCWC). *Bowie Co.*: 8 mi. N New
Boston, 1 (TCWC); Texarkana, 3 (USNM). *Brazos Co.*: 2 mi. SE Bryan, 1
(TCWC); 3 mi. S Bryan, 1 (TCWC); College Station, 5 (TCWC); 8 mi. SE College
Station, 1 (TCWC). *Cherokee Co.*: 1 mi. E Alto, 1 (SFAVC); 3 mi. W Forest, 3
(SFAVC). *Fort Bend Co.*: 3 mi. S Dewalt, 1 (LSUMZ). *Grimes Co.*: 5 mi. S Rich-
ards, 1 (TCWC). *Hardin Co.*: 11 mi. N, 2.3 mi. E Silsbee, 1 (TCWC). *Harris Co.*:
Houston, 10 (LSUMZ), 1 (USNM). *Henderson Co.*: Camp Blue Star, 1 (TNHC).
Jasper Co.: Jasper, 1 (USNM). *Jefferson Co.*: 11.7 mi. W Sabine Pass, Hwy. 87, 1
(TCWC). *Lamar Co.*: Arthur City, 1 (USNM); Paris, 3 (USNM). *Liberty Co.*: 12
mi. N Dayton, 2 (TTU). *Marion Co.*: Jefferson, 1 (USNM). *Montgomery Co.*: 5
mi. E Richards, 1 (TCWC). *Nacogdoches Co.*: 1 mi. N Nacogdoches, 1 (SFAVC);
Nacogdoches, 56 (SFAVC), 33 (TTU); Stephen F. Austin University, Nacogdoches,
31 (SFAVC), 1 (TTU), 1 (DMNHT); 0.5 mi. E Nacogdoches, 1 (SFAVC); 1 mi. E
Nacogdoches, 1 (SFAVC); 9.5 mi. SW Nacogdoches, 1 (TNHC); 11 mi. SW Nacogdoches, 1 (TTU). *Newton Co.*: 12 mi. N Burkeville, 1 (TCWC); 11.5 mi. N Burkeville, 2 (TCWC); 9.3 mi. N Burkeville, 1 (TCWC); 9.2 mi. N Burkeville, 3
(TCWC); 8.5 mi. N Burkeville, 1 (TCWC); 7.5 mi. N Burkeville, 1 (TCWC). *Pan-
ola Co.*: 7.5 mi. ENE Carthage, 1 (TCWC); 6 mi. E Mt. Enterprise, 1 (TCWC).
Polk Co.: 5.5 mi. W Dallardsville, 4.2 mi. NNW Segno, 2 (TCWC); 4 mi. W, 0.3
mi. S Dallardsville, 4 (TCWC). *Red River Co.*: no specific locality, 1 (DMNHT).
Rusk Co.: 1.6 mi. NE New London, 6 (SFAVC). *Sabine Co.*: 5 mi. N Geneva, 1
(TCWC); Pineland, 1 (TCWC). *San Jacinto Co.*: San Jacinto River, FM Rd. 945,
10 (TTU); 5 mi. NW Cleveland, 15 (TTU). *Shelby Co.*: 4 mi. S Joaquin, 1
(SFAVC); Shelbyville, 2 (SFAVC); 2.3 mi. SE Patroon, 1 (SFAVC). *Trinity Co.*: 4
mi. W Trinity, 4 (TCWC); Trinity, 3 (USNM), 5 (TCWC). *Tyler Co.*: 1.1 mi. S, 1
mi. W Town Bluff, 1 (TCWC); 3.6 mi. S, 2.9 mi. W Town Bluff, 8 (TCWC); 3.8 mi.
N, 1.9 mi. W Spurger, 3 (TCWC); 0.6 mi. N, 0.7 mi. W Spurger, 9 (TCWC); 2.6

mi. S, 3.9 mi. E Warren, 1 (TCWC). *Victoria Co.*: Victoria, 2 (USNM).

Plecotus rafinesquii macrotis (46). *Hardin Co.*: 7 mi. SE Silsbee, 1 (TCWC). *Harrison Co.*: 27 mi. W Jefferson, 1 (SFAVC). *Marion Co.*: no specific locality, 1 (SFAVC). *Nacogdoches Co.*: Nacogdoches, 14 (SFAVC); 10 mi. S Nacogdoches, 2 (SFAVC); 10 mi. SE Nacogdoches, 5 (TCWC), 5 (SFAVC); 12 mi. S Nacogdoches, 2 (SFAVC); 15 mi. SE Nacogdoches, 2 (SFAVC). *Newton Co.*: 10.3 mi. N Burkeville, 1 (TCWC); 10 mi. N Burkeville, 1 (TCWC); 9.5 mi. N Burkeville, 1 (TCWC); 7 mi. N Burkeville, 1 (TCWC); 6 mi. N Burkeville, 1 (TCWC). *Polk Co.*: 1 mi. S Neches River, 3 mi. E Hwy. 59, 3 (SFAVC), 2 (TCWC). *Sabine Co.*: 3 mi. NE Milan, 3 (SFAVC).

Tadarida brasiliensis cynocephala (229). *Angelina Co.*: Lufkin, 2 (SFAVC). *Cherokee Co.*: Alto, 1 (SFAVC). *Harris Co.*: Houston, 20 (TCWC). *Nacogdoches Co.*: Stephen F. Austin University, Nacogdoches, 3 (TTU), 20 (SFAVC); Nacogdoches, 13 (TTU), 59 (SFAVC); 11 mi. SW Nacogdoches, 1 (TTU). *Polk Co.*: Corrigan, 1 (SFAVC). *Sabine Co.*: 1 mi. N Hemphill, 1 (SFAVC); Pineland, 107 (TCWC). *San Augustine Co.*: 10 mi. S Center, 1 (SFAVC).

Tadarida brasiliensis mexicana (193). *Anderson Co.*: Palestine, 12 (TCWC). *Bexar Co.*: 10 mi. S San Antonio, 5 (MVZ). *Brazos Co.*: College Station, 29 (TCWC). *Calhoun Co.*: Indianola, 1 (USNM). *Comal Co.*: Bracken Cave, 10 mi. SW New Braunfels, 75 (TCWC). *Grimes Co.*: Navasota, 22 (TCWC). *Lavaca Co.*: Hallettsville, 1 (TCWC). *McLennan Co.*: Waco, 8 (BUSM); Baylor University, Waco, 1 (BUSM). *Tarrant Co.*: 12 mi. NW Grapevine, 2 (DMNHT); Fort Worth, 26 (FWMSH), 1 (TWC). *Travis Co.*: 20.5 mi. NW Austin, 1 (TNHC); Austin, 1 (TNHC), 2 (USNM); University of Texas, Austin, 3 (TNHC); Mansfield Dam, Lake Travis, 2 (TNHC). *Victoria Co.*: Victoria, 1 (USNM).

Dasypus novemcinctus mexicanus (49). *Bastrop Co.*: 15 mi. W Bastrop, 2 (MVZ). *Brazos Co.*: 10 mi. S Bryan, 1 (TCWC); 4 mi. E College Station, 1 (MVZ); 9 mi. SW College Station, 1 (TCWC). *Colorado Co.*: Rock Island, 1 (MVZ). *Comal Co.*: near New Braunfels, 1 (USNM). *Dallas Co.*: no specific locality, 1 (DMNHT). *Hardin Co.*: 11.3 mi. N, 3.3 mi. E Silsbee, 1 (TCWC); 9.4 mi. N, 2.3 mi. E Silsbee, 1 (TCWC). *Hays Co.*: 2 mi. E Wimberley, 1 (TNHC); 4 mi. W Kyle, 2 (TCWC). *Hopkins Co.*: 1.6 mi. W Birthright, 1 (TWC). *Jasper Co.*: near Lake Bouton, 1 (UTAVC). *Limestone Co.*: 4 mi. N Groesbeck, 1 (TCWC); 3 mi. S Kosse, 1 (KU). *McLennan Co.*: Waco, 2 (BUSM); Baylor University, Waco, 1 (BUSM). *Montgomery Co.*: 20 mi. SW Huntsville, 2 (TNHC); 3 mi. SSW Montgomery, 2 (TNHC). *Nacogdoches Co.*: Nacogdoches, 1 (TTU); Stephen F. Austin Experimental Forest, 1 (TTU). *Newton Co.*: 11.5 mi. N Burkeville, 1 (TCWC). *Shelby Co.*: Center, 1 (TTU). *Tarrant Co.*: Fort Worth, 6 (FWMSH); Arlington, Trinity River, 1 (UTAVC); Benbrook, 1 (DMNHT); Benbrook city limits, Hwy. 377, 3 mi. S Castleberry, 1 (DMNHT). *Travis Co.*: San Gabriel River, 1 mi. N bridge on Burnet highway, 2 (TNHC); 22 mi. NW Austin, 1 (TNHC); 3 mi. NW Austin, 1 (TNHC); 10 mi. E Austin, 1 (TNHC). *Tyler Co.*: 1.8 mi. W, 1.2 mi. N Spurger, 2 (TCWC). *Victoria Co.*: Victoria, 1 (USNM). *Walker Co.*: 17 mi. SW Huntsville, 2 (TCWC); 11 mi. NW New Waverly, 1 (TNHC). *Wood Co.*: 3 mi. SE Quitman, 1 (TCWC).

Sylvilagus floridanus alacer (148). *Angelina Co.*: 1 mi. SW Lufkin, 1 (SFAVC). *Austin Co.*: 8 mi. SW Bellville, 3 (TCWC). *Bastrop Co.*: 15 mi. W Bastrop, 1 (MVZ). *Bell Co.*: 3 mi. E Temple, 1 (TCWC); 6 mi. E Temple, 1 (TNHC). *Bowie Co.*: 5 mi. N Texarkana, 1 (TTU); Texarkana, 1 (USNM). *Brazos Co.*: 5 mi. E Benchley, 1 (UIMNH); 3 mi. S Bryan, 1 (TCWC); 3 mi. W College Station, 1 (TCWC); 3 mi. S College Station, 1 (TCWC); 10 mi. SE College Station, 2 (TCWC). *Caldwell Co.*: Lockhart, 1 (TCWC). *Calhoun Co.*: Indianola, 1

(USNM); 7 mi. SW Port Lavaca, 1 (USNM). *Chambers Co.*: 8 mi. S Winnie, 1 (FWMSH). *Cherokee Co.*: 4 mi. NE Sacul, 1 (SFAVC); 24 mi. W Nacogdoches, 1 (SFAVC). *Cooke Co.*: Gainesville, 5 (USNM); Camp Howze, 1 (MVZ). *Dallas Co.*: 5 mi. NW Irving, 1 (UTAVC); 1 mi. N Grand Prairie, 2 (UTAVC); County Line Rd., Trinity River, 1 (UTAVC). *Denton Co.*: 4 mi. SW Justin, 1 (FWMSH). *De Witt Co.*: 15 mi. NW Yoakum, 1 (USNM); 8 mi. SW Cuero, 1 (USNM). *Ellis Co.*: Ennis, 1 (TCWC). *Falls Co.*: Gurley, 4 (USNM). *Fort Bend Co.*: Richmond, 1 (USNM); 3 mi. W Guy, 1 (TCWC). *Freestone Co.*: no specific locality, 1 (TWC). *Galveston Co.*: Virginia Point, 1 (USNM). *Grimes Co.*: 4 mi. N Carlos, 1 (TCWC); 1 mi. W Montgomery Co. line, 1 (TCWC). *Hardin Co.*: 13 mi. NE Sour Lake, 4 (USNM). *Harris Co.*: 2.5 mi. N Hockley, 1 (TCWC); 4 mi. N Huffman, 1 (TCWC). *Harrison Co.*: 5 mi. E Marshall, 1 (BUSM). *Hays Co.*: 1 mi. N Buda, 1 (TNHC). *Henderson Co.*: 3 mi. SE Eustace, 1 (SFAVC); 25 mi. W Tool, 1 (SFAVC). *Hill Co.*: 6.5 mi. NW Mt. Calm, 1 (BUSM). *Hunt Co.*: 16 mi. N Greenville, 1 (TCWC). *Jasper Co.*: Jasper, 1 (USNM). *Leon Co.*: 7 mi. W Normangee, 1 (UIMNH). *Liberty Co.*: 12 mi. E Liberty, 1 (SFAVC). *Matagorda Co.*: Matagorda, 6 (USNM). *McLennan Co.*: Lake Waco, Waco, 1 (BUSM); Baylor Camp, 10 mi. W Waco, 2 (BUSM); Waco, 3 (BUSM); 4.7 mi. E Waco, 1 (BUSM); 15 mi. E Waco, 1 (BUSM); 6.5 mi. S Waco, 1 (BUSM); 5 mi. SE Waco, 1 (BUSM); 1 mi. N Mart Lake, 2 (BUSM); New Mart Lake, 1 (BUSM). *Nacogdoches Co.*: 3 mi. N Nacogdoches, 1 (SFAVC); 2 mi. NNE Nacogdoches, 1 (SFAVC); 5 mi. NE Nacogdoches, 1 (SFAVC); Nacogdoches, 8 (SFAVC); 10 mi. E Nacogdoches, 1 (SFAVC); 11 mi. E Nacogdoches, 1 (SFAVC); 5 mi. SW Nacogdoches, 3 (TTU); 1 mi. SW Nacogdoches, 1 (SFAVC); 11 mi. SW Nacogdoches, 3 (TTU); 3.5 mi. S Nacogdoches, 1 (SFAVC); 12.5 mi. SE Nacogdoches, Stephen F. Austin Experimental Forest, 3 (SFAVC); 2 mi. W Etiole, 1 (SFAVC). *Navarro Co.*: 2 mi. E Eureka, 1 (TCWC). *Newton Co.*: 6 mi. NW Newton, 1 (TTU). *Panola Co.*: 3 mi. S Carthage, 1 (SFAVC). *Polk Co.*: 2.2 mi. W, 1.4 mi. N Dallardsville, 1 (TCWC). *Rusk Co.*: 3 mi. S Henderson, 1 (SFAVC). *Shelby Co.*: Joaquin, 1 (USNM); Timpson, 2 (SFAVC). *Smith Co.*: 5 mi. E Tyler, 2 (SFAVC). *Tarrant Co.*: Carswell Air Force Base, White Settlement, 1 (FWMSH); 7 mi. NE Fort Worth, 1 (TWC); Fort Worth, 6 (FWMSH); 7 mi. SE Fort Worth, 1 (TWC); Arlington, 4 (UTAVC); 3 mi. SE Benbrook, 1 (UTAVC); Sycamore Creek, 2 (USNM). *Travis Co.*: Balcones Research Center, Austin, 1 (TNHC); 10 mi. SW Austin, 1 (TNHC). *Tyler Co.*: 2.8 mi. S, 2.8 mi. W Town Bluff, 1 (TCWC); 1.5 mi. N jct. Hwy. 69 and FM Rd. 1013, near Hillister, 1 (TCWC); 2.8 mi. N, 2.7 mi. W Spurger, 1 (TCWC); 2.1 mi. N, 2.7 mi. W Spurger, 1 (TCWC). *Van Zandt Co.*: 0.5 mi. N Grand Saline, 1 (TTU). *Victoria Co.*: Victoria, 3 (USNM); 6 mi. S Victoria, 1 (TCWC). *Walker Co.*: 2 mi. SW Huntsville, 1 (TCWC); 20 mi. SW Huntsville, 2 (TCWC). *Wood Co.*: 3 mi. SE Quitman, 4 (TCWC).

Sylvilagus aquaticus aquaticus (67). *Anderson Co.*: 20 mi. NW Palestine, 2 (TNHC). *Angelina Co.*: 3 mi. NW Zavalla, Hwy. 69, 1 (UTAVC); 2 mi. NNE Zavalla, 1 (UTAVC). *Brazoria Co.*: Barnard Creek, 12 mi. W Columbia, 2 (USNM). *Brazos Co.*: Bryan, 1 (TCWC); 6 mi. E Bryan, 1 (TCWC); 16 mi. E Bryan, 1 (UIMNH); 10 mi. NE College Station, 1 (TCWC); 5 mi. E College Station, 1 (UIMNH); 8.5 mi. E College Station, 1 (MVZ); 9 mi. SW College Station, 1 (TCWC); 10 mi. S College Station, 1 (TCWC); 10 mi. SE College Station, 5 (MVZ), 5 (TCWC). *Cooke Co.*: no specific locality, 1 (USNM). *Dallas Co.*: no specific locality, 1 (DMNHT). *Falls Co.*: Gurley, 1 (USNM). *Fort Bend Co.*: Richmond, 1 (USNM). *Hardin Co.*: 30 mi. SE Livingston, 1 (TCWC); 10.9 mi. N, 3.9 mi. E Silsbee, 1 (TCWC); 0.6 mi. E pumping station, Lower Neches Valley Authority, 1 (TCWC); 13 mi. NE Sour Lake, 2 (USNM); 7 mi. NE Sour Lake, 1

(USNM). *Harris Co.*: Hockley, 2 (TCWC); 5 mi. SE Baytown, 1 (SFAVC). *Houston Co.*: Antioch, 1 (USNM). *Jefferson Co.*: Beaumont, 1 (MVZ). *Leon Co.*: 7 mi. W Normangee, 1 (UIMNH). *Liberty Co.*: 12 mi. E Liberty, 1 (SFAVC); 6.5 mi. N Dayton, 2 (SFAVC), 1 (TTU). *Limestone Co.*: 4 mi. N Groesbeck, 1 (TCWC). *Matagorda Co.*: Selkirk Island, Matagorda, 1 (USNM). *McLennan Co.*: Waco, 1 (BUSM); 5 mi. E Waco, 1 (BUSM). *Nacogdoches Co.*: 3 mi. S Nacogdoches, 1 (SFAVC); 10 mi. SW Nacogdoches, 1 (SFAVC); 11 mi. SW Nacogdoches, 1 (TTU). *Newton Co.*: 9.7 mi. N Burkeville, 1 (TCWC); 9.5 mi. N Burkeville, 1 (TCWC). *Polk Co.*: 1.8 mi. E, 1.3 mi. S Camp Ruby, 1 (TCWC); 5.8 mi. N Dallardsville, FM Rd. 1276, 1 (TCWC); 4.9 mi. N Dallardsville FM Rd. 1276, 2 (TCWC); Dallardsville, 1 (TCWC). *Smith Co.*: Lake Tyler, 1 (SFAVC); Troup, 1 (USNM). *Travis Co.*: 5 mi. S Austin, 1 (TNHC). *Tyler Co.*: 3.1 mi. N, 2.5 mi. W Spurger, 1 (TCWC); 2.8 mi. N, 2.7 mi. W Spurger, 1 (TCWC); 2.1 mi. N, 2.6 mi. E Spurger, 1 (TCWC). *Victoria Co.*: Victoria, 1 (USNM). *Walker Co.*: 14 mi. SW Trinity, 1 (TCWC); 10 mi. SE Huntsville, 1 (TCWC).

Lepus californicus melanotis (19). *Bell Co.*: 3 mi. N Temple, 1 (BUSM). *Falls Co.*: Lott, 4 (USNM). *Houston Co.*: Antioch, 1 (USNM). *Johnson Co.*: 4.5 mi. SW Godley, 1 (BUSM); Rio Vista, 1 (FWMSH). *Kaufman Co.*: 1.5 mi. N Mabank, 1 (SFAVC). *Lamar Co.*: 16 mi. E Paris, 1 (SFAVC). *Madison Co.*: no specific locality, 1 (SFAVC). *McLennan Co.*: 3 mi. E Waco, 1 (BUSM); Golindo, 1 (USNM). *Nacogdoches Co.*: 3 mi. N Nacogdoches, 1 (SFAVC). *Panola Co.*: 3.5 mi. W Carthage, 1 (SFAVC). *Robertson Co.*: 6 mi. NE Benchley, 1 (UIMNH). *Shelby Co.*: 5 mi. SW Center, 1 (SFAVC). *Tarrant Co.*: Saginaw, 1 (USNM); no specific locality, 2 (DMNHT), 2 (FWMSH). *Wood Co.*: 10 mi. S Mineola, 1 (SFAVC).

Lepus californicus merriami (52). *Bastrop Co.*: 18 mi. W Giddings, Hwy. 290, 1 (TNHC). *Brazos Co.*: 2 mi. W Edge, 2 (TCWC); 5 mi. E Benchley, 1 (UIMNH); 8 mi. W College Station, 1 (TCWC). *Burleson Co.*: 8 mi. W College Station, 1 (TCWC). *Caldwell Co.*: Lockhart, 1 (TCWC). *Calhoun Co.*: 7 mi. SW Port Lavaca, 1 (USNM). *Colorado Co.*: Eagle Lake, 1 (USNM); 12 mi. SW Eagle Lake, 1 (TCWC). *De Witt Co.*: 8 mi. NW Cuero, 1 (TCWC); Cuero, 5 (USNM). *Fayette Co.*: 3 mi. NE Walhalla, 1 (TCWC). *Galveston Co.*: Texas City, 1 (SFAVC). *Guadalupe Co.*: Seguin, 1 (USNM). *Harris Co.*: Houston, 9 (USNM); 3 mi. NE Webster, 2 (TCWC). *Matagorda Co.*: Matagorda, 2 (USNM). *Travis Co.*: Austin, 1 (USNM). *Victoria Co.*: Victoria, 5 (USNM); Guadalupe, 1 (USNM). *Walker Co.*: 17 mi. WNW Huntsville, 1 (TCWC). *Washington Co.*: no specific locality, 1 (USNM). *Wharton Co.*: East Bernard, 11 (USNM).

Marmota monax monax (1). *Tarrant Co.*: 4 mi. S Kennedale, 1 (FWMSH).

Spermophilus tridecemlineatus texensis (59). *Colorado Co.*: 7 mi. N Eagle Lake, 2 (TCWC). *Cooke Co.*: Gainesville, 4 (USNM). *Dallas Co.*: Farmers Branch, 1 (UTAVC); White Rock Lake, 1 (DMNHT); Grand Prairie, 1 (TCWC). *Delta Co.*: 1 mi. N Klondike, 1 (TWC). *Denton Co.*: Lake Dallas, 1 (DMNHT). *Fort Bend Co.*: Richmond, 4 (USNM). *Grayson Co.*: 4 mi. S Dennison, 10 (MVZ). *Lamar Co.*: 7 mi. N Paris, 3 (TWC). *McLennan Co.*: Municipal Golf Course, Waco, 1 (BUSM). *Navarro Co.*: 5 mi. N Corsicana, 1 (TCWC). *Tarrant Co.*: Fort Worth, 12 (FWMSH), 2 (UTAVC); 3 mi. W Arlington, 1 (TWC); Arlington, 5 (TWC), 1 (UTAVC); Lake Arlington Municipal Golf Course, 7 (UTAVC). *Washington Co.*: Brenham, 1 (TNHC).

Spermophilus mexicanus parvidens (6). *Bexar Co.*: 10 mi. S San Antonio, 1 (TNHC). *Travis Co.*: Austin city limits, 1 (TNHC); Zilker Park, Austin, 3 (TNHC). *Williamson Co.*: 2.3 mi. N Sweden, (TNHC).

Spermophilus variegatus buckleyi (7). *McLennan Co.*: Airport Park, 6 mi. N Waco, 1 (BUSM). *Travis Co.*: 16 mi. NW Austin, 1 (USNM); 5.2 mi. NW Hwy. 71,

1 (TCWC); 0.5 mi. NE Miller Dam, Lake Austin, 1 (MVZ); Austin, 1 (TNHC); Bull Creek, 1 (USNM); 5 mi. SW Austin, 1 (TNHC).

Cynomys ludovicianus ludovicianus (4). *Tarrant Co.*: 0.25 mi. W jct. Loop 820 and Hwy. 287, 1 (TWC); SE Fort Worth, 1 (UTAVC); 1.6 mi. S, 3 mi. W Lake Arlington Dam, 1 (UTAVC); 4 mi. SE Fort Worth, 1 (TWC).

Sciurus carolinensis carolinensis (109). *Anderson Co.*: Long Lake, 1 (USNM). *Angelina Co.*: 10 mi. S Etiole, 1 (SFAVC); 2 mi. N Lufkin, 1 (SFAVC); 7 mi. NE Huntington, 1 (SFAVC). *Bowie Co.*: 5 mi. N Texarkana, 1 (TTU). *Brazoria Co.*: 5 mi. W Lake Jackson, 2 (TNHC); Barnard Creek, 12 mi. NW Columbia, 5 (USNM); Columbia, 1 (USNM); 6 mi. SW Brazoria, 2 (SFAVC); Velasco, 1 (USNM). *Brazos Co.*: 17.5 mi. NE Bryan, 1 (TCWC). *Cherokee Co.*: Hwy. 21 at Neches River, 1 (SFAVC); 8 mi. W Alto, 1 (SFAVC); 2 mi. W Alto, 1 (SFAVC). *Cooke Co.*: Gainesville, 1 (USNM). *Gregg Co.*: Longview, 1 (UTAVC); 7 mi. S Longview, 1 (SFAVC). *Hardin Co.*: Kountze, 1 (USNM); 9 mi. N Silsbee, 1 (TCWC); 7 mi. N Silsbee, 1 (TCWC); Sour Lake, 4 (USNM); Goat Island, Pine Island Bayou, 1 (TCWC). *Harris Co.*: 3 mi. NE Webster, 1 (TCWC). *Harrison Co.*: Marshall, 2 (SFAVC). *Houston Co.*: 5 mi. N Ratcliff, 1 (SFAVC). *Jasper Co.*: 10 mi. S Zavalla, 1 (SFAVC); Jasper, 3 (USNM). *Lavaca Co.*: 21 mi. SE Hallettsville, 1 (TCWC). *Lee Co.*: Giddings, 1 (TCWC). *Liberty Co.*: 20 mi. N Liberty, 1 (SFAVC); 8 mi. N Liberty, 1 (TCWC); Liberty, 1 (USNM). *Matagorda Co.*: Selkirk Island, Matagorda, 1 (USNM). *Nacogdoches Co.*: Douglass, 1 (SFAVC); 15 mi. N Nacogdoches, 1 (SFAVC); 11 mi. N Nacogdoches, 1 (SFAVC); 12.3 mi. NNW Nacogdoches, 1 (SFAVC); 18 mi. W Nacogdoches, 1 (SFAVC); 12 mi. W Nacogdoches, 1 (SFAVC); 2 mi. W Nacogdoches, 1 (SFAVC); Nacogdoches, 2 (SFAVC); 7 mi. E Nacogdoches, 1 (SFAVC); 8 mi. S Nacogdoches, 1 (SFAVC); 10 mi. S Nacogdoches, 1 (SFAVC); 12 mi. S Nacogdoches, 2 (SFAVC); Angelina River, S of Nacogdoches, 1 (SFAVC); Stephen F. Austin Experimental Forest, 10 mi. SW Nacogdoches, 2 (SFAVC); 3 mi. SE Nacogdoches, 1 (SFAVC); 0.5 mi. E Angelina River bridge, Hwy. 7, 1 (SFAVC). *Newton Co.*: 9.6 mi. N Burkeville, 1 (TCWC); E bank Sabine River, 1 (SFAVC). *Panola Co.*: 10 mi. N Carthage, 1 (SFAVC). *Polk Co.*: 1 mi. S Neches River, 3 mi. E Hwy. 59, 1 (SFAVC); 9 mi. E Corrigan, 1 (SFAVC); 5.8 mi. N Dallardsville, FM Rd. 1276, 1 (TCWC); 4.6 mi. NW Dallardsville, 2 (TCWC); 5.2 mi. W Dallardsville, 5 mi. N Segno, 1 (TCWC); 2.5 mi. E Segno, 1 (TCWC); 1 mi. S Segno, 1 (SFAVC); 6.5 mi. SW Segno, 1 (TCWC). *Red River Co.*: 18 mi. N Clarksville, 1 (TCWC); SE Boxelder, 2 (DMNHT). *San Augustine Co.*: 26 mi. E Nacogdoches, 1 (SFAVC). *Shelby Co.*: Joaquin, 6 (USNM); 15 mi. SW Center, 1 (SFAVC); 10 mi. E Shelbyville, 1 (SFAVC). *Smith Co.*: Troup, 2 (USNM). *Trinity Co.*: 8 mi. S Apple Springs, Neches River, 1 (TCWC). *Tyler Co.*: 6 mi. E Chester, 1 (SFAVC); 1.8 mi. W, 1.5 mi. S Town Bluff, 1 (TCWC); 2 mi. SW Dam B Reservoir, B. A. Steinhagen Lake, 3 (TCWC). *Walker Co.*: 12 mi. SW Trinity, 2 (TCWC); 13 mi. SW Trinity, 1 (TCWC); 14 mi. SW Trinity, 5 (TCWC); 16 mi. SW Trinity, 1 (TCWC); 17 mi. SW Trinity, 1 (TCWC); 18 mi. SW Trinity, 1 (TCWC). *Washington Co.*: no specific locality, 2 (USNM).

Sciurus niger ludovicianus (380). *Anderson Co.*: Engling Wildlife Preserve, 18.5 mi. NW Palestine, 2 (TNHC); Palestine, 1 (TCWC); 11 mi. SW Elkhart, 1 (SFAVC). *Angelina Co.*: 23 mi. S Nacogdoches, 1 (SFAVC); 10 mi. W Lufkin, 1 (SFAVC); 3 mi. W, 2 mi. S Lufkin, 1 (SFAVC); 12 mi. S Lufkin, 1 (SFAVC); Neches River, 1 (KU). *Bastrop Co.*: 5 mi. S Elgin, 1 (TNHC); 2 mi. N Bastrop, 1 (TNHC); 15 mi. W Bastrop, 1 (MVZ); 12 mi. W Bastrop, 1 (TNHC); 1 mi. S Bastrop, 1 (TNHC). *Bell Co.*: Belton Lake, 1 (TCWC), 1 (TNHC). *Bowie Co.*: 4 mi. N New Boston, 1 (TCWC). *Brazoria Co.*: 6 mi. SW Brazoria, 1 (SFAVC). *Brazos*

Co.: 6 mi. SE Bryan, 1 (MVZ); 2 mi. N College Station, 1 (TCWC); College Station, 1 (TCWC); Texas A&M University, College Station, 1 (TCWC); 3 mi. E College Station, 1 (TCWC); 10 mi. S College Station, 1 (TCWC); 9 mi. SW College Station, 1 (TCWC); 3 mi. SW College Station, 1 (TCWC); 15 mi. SE College Station, 1 (TCWC); 16 mi. SE College Station, 1 (TCWC). *Burleson Co.*: 5 mi. N Caldwell, 1 (TCWC); 3 mi. NW Caldwell, 1 (TCWC); 4 mi. SW Caldwell, 1 (TCWC); 8 mi. SW Caldwell, 1 (TCWC); Lake Somerville, 1 (TCWC). *Cherokee Co.*: W Jacksonville, Hwy. 175, 1 (SFAVC); Jacksonville, 1 (SFAVC); 5 mi. W Sacul, 1 (TTU); 15 mi. W Rusk, 1 (SFAVC); 26 mi. E Elkhart, 1 (SFAVC). *Collin Co.*: Plano, 1 (TNHC). *Colorado Co.*: 3 mi. N Sheridan, 2 (TCWC). *Cooke Co.*: Gainesville, 4 (USNM). *Dallas Co.*: Irving, 1 (UTAVC), 1 (DMNHT); Dallas, 7 (DMNHT), 5 (UTAVC); 10 mi. SW Dallas, 1 (UTAVC); 1 mi. N Grand Prairie, 1 (UTAVC); Duncanville, 2 (UTAVC). *De Witt Co.*: 15 mi. NW Yoakum, 1 (TCWC). *Fannin Co.*: 4 mi. N, 2 mi. E Ravenna, 1 (BUSM). *Fort Bend Co.*: W Guy, 2 (TCWC). *Freestone Co.*: 1.5 mi. E Kirvin, 1 (UTAVC); 15 mi. S Fairfield, 1 (SFAVC); 3 mi. W Teague, 1 (TCWC). *Galveston Co.*: La Marque, 1 (TCWC). *Gonzales Co.*: 2 mi. N Ottine, 1 (TNHC). *Gregg Co.*: 10 mi. W Longview, 1 (TCWC); 3 mi. S Longview, 2 (TCWC). *Grimes Co.*: 4 mi. E Kurten, 2 (TCWC); 16 mi. E College Station, 2 (TCWC); 2 mi. N Shiro, 1 (TCWC); Navasota, 1 (USNM); 3 mi. E Plantersville, 1 (TCWC). *Hardin Co.*: 13 mi. NE Sour Lake, 1 (USNM); Sour Lake, 2 (USNM); 13 mi. SE Sour Lake, 1 (USNM). *Harris Co.*: 7 mi. E Tomball, 2 (TCWC); Crosby, 1 (TCWC); 2 mi. NE Sheldon, 1 (TCWC); 6 mi. E Katy, 2 (TCWC); 20 mi. SE Houston, 1 (SFAVC); Webster, 1 (TCWC). *Harrison Co.*: Karnack, 1 (SFAVC); 13 mi. S Marshall, 1 (SFAVC); 12 mi. SE Longview, 1 (SFAVC). *Hays Co.*: 4 mi. W Dripping Springs, 1 (TNHC); Blanco River, 4 mi. W Kyle, 1 (TCWC). *Henderson Co.*: 3 mi. S Brownsboro, 0.25 mi. W Tool, 1 (SFAVC); 6 mi. NE Athens, 1 (TCWC); 5 mi. SW Malakoff, 1 (SFAVC); 5 mi. E Athens, 1 (BUSM); 1 mi. SE Malakoff, 1 (SFAVC). *Houston Co.*: 7 mi. E Crockett, 1 (SFAVC). *Jackson Co.*: 1 mi. E Francitas, 2 (TCWC). *Jasper Co.*: 4 mi. W Jasper, 1 (TCWC); 15 mi. E Jasper, 1 (SFAVC); Kirbyville, 1 (USNM). *Jefferson Co.*: 13 mi. SE Sour Lake, 1 (USNM); E Thicket, S Norma, 1 (TCWC). *Johnson Co.*: Wilson Creek, 2 (UTAVC). *Lamar Co.*: Arthur City, 13 (USNM); 10 mi. S Paris, 1 (TCWC). *Lavaca Co.*: 23 mi. S Hallettsville, 1 (TCWC). *Lee Co.*: Giddings, 1 (TCWC). *Leon Co.*: Normangee, 1 (TCWC). *Liberty Co.*: Cleveland, 1 (SFAVC), 1 (USNM); 5 mi. W Hardin, 1 (SFAVC); 2.9 mi. N, 3.9 mi. E Moss Hill, 1 (TCWC). *Limestone Co.*: 0.5 mi. N Navasota River, Groesbeck, 2 (TCWC). *Matagorda Co.*: Matagorda, 4 (USNM). *McLennan Co.*: 2 mi. above mouth of N Bosque River, 1 (BUSM); Bosque River, 1 (BUSM); Lake Waco, 1 (BUSM); Chalk Bluff, 7 mi. N Waco, 1 (BUSM); 1.8 mi. NW Waco, FM Rd. 1637, 1 (BUSM); Waco, 6 (BUSM), 1 (MVZ); Baylor University, Waco, 2 (BUSM); 1.3 mi. S Waco, 1 (BUSM). *Milam Co.*: 1 mi. SE Cameron, 1 (TCWC); Milano, 2 (BUSM). *Montgomery Co.*: Sam Houston National Forest, 1 (TCWC). *Nacogdoches Co.*: 2 mi. W Douglas, 1 (SFAVC); 15 mi. N Nacogdoches, 1 (TTU); 10 mi. NW Nacogdoches, 1 (SFAVC); 10 mi. NE Nacogdoches, 1 (SFAVC); 5 mi. NW Nacogdoches, 1 (SFAVC); 1 mi. NW Nacogdoches, 1 (SFAVC); 15 mi. W Nacogdoches, 1 (SFAVC); 12 mi. W Nacogdoches, 1 (SFAVC); 10 mi. W Nacogdoches, 1 (SFAVC); 8 mi. W Nacogdoches, 1 (SFAVC); 5 mi. W Nacogdoches, 1 (SFAVC); 2 mi. W Nacogdoches, 1 (SFAVC); Nacogdoches, 16 (SFAVC); Stephen F. Austin University, Nacogdoches, 1 (SFAVC); 1 mi. E Nacogdoches, 1 (SFAVC); 4 mi. E Nacogdoches, 1 (SFAVC); 7 mi. E Nacogdoches, 2 (SFAVC); 4 mi. S Nacogdoches, 1 (SFAVC); 4.5 mi. SE Nacogdoches, 1 (SFAVC); 5 mi. SW Nacogdoches, 1 (SFAVC); 6 mi. SW Nacogdoches, 1 (SFAVC); 6 mi. S Nacogdoches, 1 (SFAVC); 9.5 mi. S Nacogdoches, 1 (SFAVC); 10 mi. SW Nacogdoches, 1 (SFAVC); Stephen F. Austin Experimental Forest, 10 mi. SW Nacogdoches, 1 (SFAVC); 10 mi. SE Nacogdoches, 3 (SFAVC); 13 mi. S Nacogdoches, 1 (SFAVC). *Navarro Co.*: 5 mi. S Kerens, 1 (SFAVC). *Newton Co.*: 9.5 mi. N Burkeville, 1 (TCWC); 7.5 mi. N Burkeville, 1 (TCWC); 2.3 mi. N Burkeville, 1 (TCWC); 3 mi. S Farrsville, 1 (SFAVC); 15 mi. E Jasper, 1 (SFAVC); Newton, 2 (USNM); 12 mi. E Buna, 1 (TNHC); 30 mi. S Sabine River, 2 (USNM). *Polk Co.*: Livingston, 1 (SFAVC); 5.4 mi. N Dallardsville, FM Rd. 1276, 1 (TCWC); 1 mi. N Dallardsville, 1 (SFAVC); 1 mi. W Dallardsville, 1 (SFAVC); 4 mi. W Segno, 1 (TCWC). *Red River Co.*: 2 mi. N White Rock, FM Rd. 1158, 1 (DMNHT); Boxelder, 1 (DMNHT). *Robertson Co.*: 8 mi. N Franklin, 1 (TCWC); 6 mi. E Hearne, 1 (TCWC); 6 mi. E Benchley, 1 (SFAVC). *Rusk Co.*: 20 mi. SE Henderson, 2 (TCWC); 5 mi. W Laneville, 1 (SFAVC); 2.2 mi. N New London, 2 (SFAVC). *Sabine Co.*: 5 mi. S Hemphill, 1 (SFAVC). *Shelby Co.*: Joaquin, 1 (USNM); 5 mi. W Timpson, 1 (SFAVC); Timpson, 1 (SFAVC); 5 mi. S Center, 1 (SFAVC); 14 mi. S Center, 1 (SFAVC); 24 mi. SE Center, 1 (SFAVC). *Smith Co.*: 10 mi. NW Tyler, 1 (SFAVC); Tyler, 1 (SFAVC); 0.5 mi. E Smith County Courthouse, 1 (SFAVC); 3 mi. SW Flint, 1 (SFAVC); Troup, 1 (USNM). *Tarrant Co.*: 3 mi. NE Keller, 1 (TWC); near Lake Worth, 1 (UTAVC); Richland Hills, 1 (TWC); Fort Worth, 5 (UTAVC), 4 (TWC), 26 (FWMSH), 2 (DMNHT); Panther Recreation Area, 4 (FWMSH); 7 mi. SE Fort Worth, 1 (TWC); Arlington, 23 (UTAVC). *Travis Co.*: 11 mi. NW Austin, 1 (TNHC); 5 mi. N Austin, 1 (TNHC); 14 mi. W Austin, 1 (TNHC); Austin, 19 (TNHC); 4 mi. E Austin, 1 (TNHC); 2 mi. SW Austin, 1 (TNHC); 3 mi. S Austin, 1 (TNHC). *Trinity Co.*: 8 mi. S Apple Springs, 1 (TCWC); Trinity, 2 (TCWC); 3 mi. E Trinity, 1 (TCWC); 12 mi. E Trinity, 3 (TCWC); 3 mi. SW Trinity, 1 (TCWC). *Tyler Co.*: 6 mi. E Chester, 1 (SFAVC); 2.5 mi. E Warren, FM Rd. 143, 1 (TCWC). *Victoria Co.*: Guadalupe, 1 (USNM); San Antonio River, 6 (USNM). *Walker Co.*: 18 mi. SW Trinity, 1 (TCWC); 17 mi. SW Trinity, 1 (TCWC); 15 mi. SW Trinity, 1 (TCWC); 14 mi. SW Trinity, 2 (TCWC); 3 mi. E Riverside, 2 (TCWC); 11 mi. SSW Huntsville, 1 (TCWC); 15 mi. S Huntsville, 1 (SFAVC). *Washington Co.*: Washington, 1 (USNM); 13 mi. W Brenham, 1 (TCWC). *Williamson Co.*: 2 mi. W Jarrell, 1 (BUSM). *Wood Co.*: 3 mi. SE Quitman, 5 (TCWC).

Glaucomys volans texensis (81). *Anderson Co.*: 23 mi. NW Palestine, 8 (TCWC); 5 mi. SE Slocum, 1 (SFAVC). *Angelina Co.*: 20 mi. SW Nacogdoches, 2 (TNHC). *Brazoria Co.*: Lake Jackson, 1 (SFAVC). *Brazos Co.*: 3 mi. W Bryan, 1 (TCWC); 0.5 mi. N College Station, 2 (TCWC); College Station, 2 (TCWC). *Cherokee Co.*: Rusk, 1 (SFAVC); 2 mi. S Alto, 1 (SFAVC). *Collin Co.*: McKinney, 1 (DMNHT). *Cooke Co.*: Gainesville, 3 (USNM). *Dallas Co.*: White Rock Creek, Dallas, 1 (UMMZ). *Denton Co.*: Roanoke Rd., 1 (FWMSH). *Freestone Co.*: 11 mi. NE Palestine, 1 (BUSM). *Grayson Co.*: 12 mi. N Pottsboro, 1 (MVZ). *Grimes Co.*: 5 mi. E Kurten, 1 (TCWC). *Hardin Co.*: 3.25 mi. E, 2 mi. S Village Mills, 1 (TCWC); 1.8 mi. S, 2.9 mi. E Village Mills, 1 (TCWC); 2.7 mi. S, 3.2 mi. E Village Mills, 1 (TCWC); Rosier Park, Saratoga, 1 (TCWC). *Henderson Co.*: 5 mi. S Brownsboro, 1 (SFAVC); 1 mi. SE Malakoff, 1 (KU), 1 (SFAVC). *Johnson Co.*: Lilian, 1 (FWMSH). *McLennan Co.*: Bosque River, near Cameron Park, Waco, 1 (BUSM); Waco, 1 (BUSM). *Nacogdoches Co.*: 1 mi. N Nacogdoches, 1 (SFAVC); Nacogdoches, 8 (SFAVC), 1 (TTU); La Nana Creek, 1 mi. E Stephen F. Austin University, Nacogdoches, 1 (TTU); 2 mi. E Nacogdoches, 3 (TTU); 6 mi. E Nacogdoches, 1 (TNHC); 9 mi. E Nacogdoches, 1 (SFAVC); 11 mi. E Nacogdoches, 1 (SFAVC); 1 mi. S Nacogdoches, 1 (TNHC); 10 mi. SW Nacogdoches, 2 (SFAVC); 14 mi. SW Nacogdoches, 1 (SFAVC); 20 mi. SW Nacogdoches, 1 (TNHC). *Newton Co.*: 9.5 mi. N Burkeville, 1 (TCWC); 7.5 mi. N Burkeville, 1 (TCWC); Bleakwood, 1 (TCWC). *Polk Co.*: 1 mi. S Neches River, 3 mi. E Hwy. 59, 1 (SFAVC); 4 mi. S Livingston, 1 (SFAVC); 5.8 mi. N Dallardsville, 1 (TCWC). *Rusk Co.*: 2.5 mi. N New London, 1 (SFAVC). *Sabine Co.*: 1 mi. W Hemphill, 1 (SFAVC). *Shelby Co.*: 11 mi. E Center, 2 (TTU). *Tarrant Co.*: Rush Creek, 1 mi. SE Lake Arlington Dam, 1 (UTAVC). *Trinity Co.*: 1 mi. N Trinity, 1 (TCWC); CCC Camp, Trinity, 1 (TCWC). *Tyler Co.*: Colmesniel, 1 (USNM); 0.5 mi. N, 3.2 mi. E Warren, 1 (TCWC); 3.2 mi. E Warren, 1 (TCWC); 4.3 mi. SE Warren, 2 (TCWC); 6 mi. S, 3.9 mi. E Warren, 1 (TCWC); 6 mi. S, 4.3 mi. E Warren, 1 (TCWC). *Van Zandt Co.*: no specific locality, 1 (DMNHT).

Perognathus hispidus hispidus (110). *Bell Co.*: 3 mi. N Satin, 1 (BUSM). *Brazos Co.*: Fish Lake, 1 (TCWC); 0.5 mi. N College Station, 1 (UIMNH); 2.5 mi. W College Station, 1 (TCWC); 2 mi. W College Station, 1 (TCWC); College Station, 2 (TCWC), 2 (MVZ); 10 mi. E College Station, 1 (TCWC); College Station, 0.5 mi. S Hwy. 60 on FM Rd. 2818, 2 (TCWC); 3 mi. S College Station, 3 (KU); 7 mi. S, 4 mi. W College Station, 1 (TCWC); 7 mi. SW College Station, 3 (TCWC); 1 mi. NE Millican, 1 (TCWC). *Caldwell Co.*: 3 mi. NE Lytton Springs, 1 (TCWC). *Calhoun Co.*: Port O'Connor, 1 (USNM). *Cherokee Co.*: 8 mi. NW Maydelle, 1 (TNHC). *Colorado Co.*: 9 mi. E Eagle Lake, 1 (TCWC). *Cooke Co.*: Gainesville, 8 (USNM). *Dallas Co.*: Dallas, 1 (DMNHT); Mountain Creek Lake, 1 (DMNHT). *Delta Co.*: 3 mi. SW Klondike, 1 (TWC). *De Witt Co.*: Cuero, 3 (USNM). *Goliad Co.*: 8 mi. NE Goliad, 3 (TNHC); 8 mi. E Goliad, 1 (TNHC). *Gonzales Co.*: Palmetto State Park, 1 (TNHC). *Grimes Co.*: 0.75 mi. E Bedias, 1 (USNM). *Guadalupe Co.*: Seguin, 6 (USNM). *Harris Co.*: 2.5 mi. W Hockley, 1 (TCWC). *Hill Co.*: Spivey Crossing, 5 mi. NW jct. FM Rd. 933 and FM Rd. 2114, 1 (TCWC). *Hunt Co.*: 3 mi. SE Quinlan, 2 (DMNHT). *Lavaca Co.*: 2.4 mi. S Hallettsville, 1 (TCWC); 4 mi. SW Sweet Home, 1 (TCWC). *Limestone Co.*: Mexia, 1 (SFAVC). *Madison Co.*: 1 mi. S jct. Hwy. 21 and Hwy. 45, 1 (TCWC). *Marion Co.*: Jefferson, 1 (USNM). *McLennan Co.*: 2.5 mi. SW Ross, 3 (BUSM); Cameron Park, Waco, 1 (BUSM); Waco, 1 (BUSM); 11 mi. S Waco, 1 (BUSM). *Nacogdoches Co.*: 12 mi. N Nacogdoches, 1 (SFAVC); 1 mi. NW Nacogdoches, 1 (SFAVC); 2 mi. W Nacogdoches, 1 (SFAVC); 1 mi. W Nacogdoches, 1 (SFAVC); Nacogdoches, 1 (SFAVC); 1 mi. E Nacogdoches, 2 (SFAVC), 1 (TNHC); 1 mi. SW Nacogdoches, Stephen F. Austin Experimental Forest, 1 (SFAVC). *Navarro Co.*: 10 mi. W Corsicana, 1 (SFAVC). *Rains Co.*: 5.5 mi. E Rains County Courthouse, Emory, 1 (KU). *Smith Co.*: 4 mi. N Tyler, 1 (TCWC). *Tarrant Co.*: 3 mi. SE Roanoke, 3 (DMNHT); Saginaw, 1 (USNM); Hurst, 1 (FWMSH); Fort Worth, 2 (UTAVC); 7 mi. SW Benbrook, 1 (TWC). *Travis Co.*: 9 mi. NW Austin, 1 (TNHC); 6 mi. E Austin, 2 (TNHC). *Trinity Co.*: 9 mi. W Trinity, 1 (TCWC). *Walker Co.*: 1 mi. SW Huntsville, 1 (TCWC). *Waller Co.*: Hempstead, 2 (USNM). *Wood Co.*: 8 mi. W Quitman, 1 (TWC).

Perognathus flavus merriami (5). *Jackson Co.*: 1 mi. E Francitas, 1 (TCWC). *Johnson Co.*: 10 mi. W Cleburne, 1 (TWC); 8 mi. SW Cleburne, 1 (TWC). *Tarrant Co.*: Benbrook, 1 (FWMSH). *Travis Co.*: Austin, 1 (USNM).

Geomys breviceps sagittalis (480). *Anderson Co.*: 20 mi. NW Palestine, 26 (TNHC); 1 mi. W Palestine, 1 (TCWC); Palestine, 1 (TCWC). *Angelina Co.*: 13 mi. W Lufkin, 1 (SWTS); 1 mi. S Zavalla on Hwy. 63, 2 mi. W on dirt road, 3 (DMNHT). *Brazos Co.*: 3 mi. E Kurten, 1 (TCWC); Bryan, 1 (TCWC), 2 (UMMZ); 1 mi. NW College Station, 1 (UIMNH); Fish Lake, 1 (UMMZ); Texas A&M University, College Station, 8 (TCWC), 5 (UIMNH); College Station, 5 (UMMZ); 2 (TCWC); 2 mi. SE College Station, 1 (TCWC); 3 mi. SW College Station, 1 (TCWC); 4 mi. SE College Station, 1 (TCWC); 6.2 mi. S College Station, 1 (TCWC); 7 mi. SW College Station, 2 (TCWC); 7 mi. S College Station, 1

(TCWC); 16 mi. S College Station, 1 (TCWC); 0.2 mi. E Brazos River bridge, Hwy. 21, 1 (TCWC); 0.7 mi. E Brazos River bridge, Hwy. 21, 1 (TCWC); 7 mi. E Brazos River bridge, Hwy. 21, 1 (TCWC). *Burleson Co.:* 1.5 mi. S jct. Hwy. 21 and Hwy. 50, 5 (TCWC); 2 mi. S jct. Hwy. 21 and Hwy. 50, 24 (TCWC); 2 mi. S jct. Hwy. 21 and Hwy. 50, 6 (TCWC); 2.3 mi. S jct. Hwy. 21 and Hwy. 50, 12 (TCWC); 3.8 mi. NW Grant, Hwy. 50, 1 (TCWC); 3.6 mi. NW Grant, Hwy. 50, 6 (TCWC); 2.8 mi. NW Grant, Hwy. 50, 1 (TCWC); 2.5 mi. NW Grant, Hwy. 50, 1 (TCWC); 2.3 mi. NW Grant, Hwy. 50, 1 (TCWC); 2.1 mi. NW Grant, Hwy. 50, 1 (TCWC); 0.8 mi. NW Grant, Hwy. 50, 1 (TCWC); 0.7 mi. NW Grant, Hwy. 50, 1 (TCWC); 0.6 mi. NW Grant, Hwy. 50, 1 (TCWC); 0.1 mi. SE Grant, Hwy. 50, 1 (TCWC); 1.4 mi. SE Grant, Hwy. 50, 1 (TCWC); 3.1 mi. SE Grant, near Brazos River, 1 (TCWC); 3.4 mi. SE Grant, near Brazos River, 1 (TCWC); 3.8 mi. SE Grant, Hwy. 50, 1 (TCWC); 3.25 mi. ENE Tunis, 1 (TCWC); 17 mi. E Caldwell, W bank Brazos River, near Koppes Bridge, 2 (TCWC); 2.6 mi. SW FM Rd. 166, 1 (TCWC); 6.9 mi. NW jct. Hwy. 50/60, 1 (TCWC); 6.7 mi. NW jct. Hwy. 50/60, 2 (TCWC); 0.4 mi. SE jct. Hwy. 50/60, 1 (TCWC); 6.1 mi. N Clay, near Brazos River, 1 (TCWC); 3.2 mi. NE Clay, 1 (TCWC); 3 mi. NE Clay, 3 (TCWC); 2.4 mi. NE Clay, 1 (TCWC). *Cass Co.:* 2 mi. N Atlanta, 1 (DMNHT). *Chambers Co.:* 4.7 mi. N Anahuac, 1 (TTU). *Delta Co.:* 1.3 mi. E Charleston, 1 (TWC). *Falls Co.:* 3.4 km. S Satin, 2 (NTSU); 2.5 mi. NE Chilton, 1 (TCWC); 11.3 km. E Chilton, 25 (NTSU); 0.4 mi. E Chilton, Hwy. 7, 1 (TCWC); 7.3 km. NW Marlin, 2 (NTSU); 7.3 km. W Marlin, 2 (NTSU); 10.1 km. WSW Marlin, 3 (NTSU); 4.8 km. SSW Marlin, 19 (NTSU); 2.8 mi. SW Marlin, FM Rd. 712, 1 (TCWC); 3.1 mi. SW Marlin, FM Rd. 712, 1 (TCWC); 12.3 mi. SE Marlin, Hwy. 6, 1 (TCWC); 7.6 km. W Reagan, 7 (NTSU); 1.9 mi. SE Reagan, Hwy. 6, 2 (TCWC); 9.7 km. SW Reagan, 24 (NTSU); 0.5 mi. E Highbank, FM Rd. 413, 1 (TCWC); 1 mi. N Eloise, FM Rd. 1373, 1 (TCWC); 0.8 mi. N Wilderville, FM Rd. 2027, 1 (TCWC); 2.3 mi. E Wilderville, FM Rd. 413, 1 (TCWC); 2.6 mi. E Wilderville, 1 (TCWC); 3.8 mi. E Wilderville, FM Rd. 413, 1 (TCWC); 0.6 mi. S Wilderville, FM Rd. 2027, 1 (TCWC); 0.7 mi. S Wilderville, 1 (TCWC); 4.4 mi. N Cedar Springs, FM Rd. 2027, 1 (TCWC); 2.15 mi. N Cedar Springs, 1 (TCWC); 2.6 km. E Cedar Springs, 8 (NTSU); 0.3 mi. S Cedar Springs, 1 (TCWC); 0.3 mi. S Cedar Springs, FM Rd. 2027, 1 (TCWC); 1.7 mi. S Cedar Springs, FM Rd. 2027, 1 (TCWC). *Freestone Co.:* Fairfield, 1 (TCWC). *Galveston Co.:* 2 mi. N Texas City, 2 (TCWC); 1 mi. N Texas City, 4 (TCWC); 1.4 mi. S, 2.3 mi. W Hitchcock, 2 (TTU). *Grimes Co.:* 2 mi. E Shiro, 1 (TCWC); 0.5 mi. E Carlos, 1 (TTU); 2 mi. E Carlos, Hwy. 30, 1:(TCWC). *Hardin Co.:* 5 mi. N Kountze, 2 (TCWC); Silsbee, 1 (TTU). *Harris Co.:* 4 mi. N Huffman, 1 (TCWC); 3 mi. N Mason's Bay, La Porte, 1 (TCWC); 3 mi. NE Webster, 1 (TCWC). *Harrison Co.:* Karnack, 1 (TCWC). *Henderson Co.:* 4 mi. S Malakoff, 2 (DMNHT); 5 mi. S Malakoff, 1 (DMNHT). *Jasper Co.:* 15 mi. N Jasper, 1 (TCWC); 5 mi. S, 1.1 mi. E Jasper, 3 (TTU); 2.2 mi. N Buna, 1 (TTU); 7 mi. SW Buna, 1 (TCWC). *Jefferson Co.:* 7 mi. SW Fannett, 3 (TCWC). *Leon Co.:* 13 mi. E Centerville, 1 (TCWC); 7 mi. N Normangee, 2 (TCWC). *Liberty Co.:* 2 mi. E Liberty, 4 (TCWC). *Limestone Co.:* Mexia State Park, 1 (DMNHT). *Madison Co.:* 17 mi. NE Madisonville, 2 (DMNHT); near North Zulch, 1 (BUSM). *Marion Co.:* mi. W Jefferson, 3 (UIMNH); 12.5 mi. NE Marshall, 1 (TWC). *Milam Co.:* 2.3 mi. S Wilderville, 1 (TCWC); 2.4 mi. S Wilderville, Hwy. 413, 1 (TCWC); 2.6 mi. S Wilderville, 1 (TCWC); 2 mi. E Maysfield, Hwy. 190, 1 (TCWC); 6.8 mi. E Maysfield, 2 (TCWC); 1.2 mi. SE Branchville, Hwy. 190, 1 (TCWC); 2.1 mi. SE Branchville, near Brazos River, 1 (TCWC); 3.8 mi. SE Branchville, Hwy. 190, 1 (TCWC). *Montgomery Co.:* 5 mi. W Conroe, 1 (TCWC); 2 mi. S Conroe, 3 (TCWC); 5 mi. S Conroe, 1 (TCWC); 1.6 mi. E Decker Prairie,

3 (TCWC); 2 mi. E Decker Prairie, 1 (TCWC); 7 mi. E Tomball, 1 (TCWC). *Nacogdoches Co.*: 12 mi. E Nacogdoches, Hwy. 21, 1 (FWMSH); 5 mi. S Nacogdoches, 1 (TCWC); 11 mi. SW Nacogdoches, 1 (TCWC). *Newton Co.*: 12 mi. NE Burkeville, 1 (TCWC); Newton, 5 (TCWC); 13 mi. NE Kirbyville, 1 (TCWC); 3 mi. NE Kirbyville, 1 (TCWC). *Panola Co.*: 4 mi. NE Carthage, 2 (TCWC). *Polk Co.*: 3 mi. W Livingston, 2 (TCWC). *Red River Co.*: 2.4 km. NW Manchester, 50 (NTSU). *Robertson Co.*: 1 mi. W Bremond, 2 (TCWC); 3.6 mi. SW Bremond, 1 (TCWC); 0.3 mi. S Eloise, FM Rd. 1373, 1 (TCWC); 3.4 mi. N, 2 mi. W Calvert, 7 (TTU); 2.3 mi. N, 1.6 mi. W Calvert, 1 (TTU); 2.3 mi. N Calvert, Hwy. 6, 2 (TCWC); 0.5 mi. N Calvert, Hwy. 6, 2 (TCWC); 5 mi. SW Calvert, 1 (TCWC); 7 mi. S Calvert, FM Rd. 1644, 1 (TCWC); 8 mi. S Calvert, FM Rd. 1644, 1 (TCWC); 7 mi. NW Hearne, 1 (TCWC); 7 mi. N, 1 mi. W Hearne, 1 (TCWC); 4 mi. NE Hearne, 1 (TCWC); 4 mi. NE Hearne, Hwy. 79, 1 (TCWC); 5 mi. W Hearne, 1 (TCWC); 5 mi. W Hearne, Hwy. 190, 1 (TCWC); 4 mi. W Hearne, 1 (TCWC). *Rusk Co.*: 12 mi. S Hendrickson, 1 (TCWC). *Sabine Co.*: Hwy. 21, 2 mi. E Milam, 1 (FWMSH); 3 mi. N Bronson, 1 (TCWC); 2 mi. N Bronson, 1 (TCWC); 8 mi. W Hemphill, 1 (TCWC); 7 mi. W Hemphill, 1 (TCWC). *San Augustine Co.*: 8 mi. S San Augustine, 1 (TCWC). *San Jacinto Co.*: 2 mi. W Evergreen, 1 (TCWC); 3 mi. SW Evergreen, 1 (TCWC); Shepherd, 4 (TTU); 2 mi. S Shepherd, 2 (TTU). *Shelby Co.*: 7 mi. S Center, 1 (TCWC); 10 mi. S Center, 1 (TCWC). *Smith Co.*: 1 km. N Mt. Sylvan, 3 (NTSU); 10 km. NNW Tyler, 12 (NTSU). *Trinity Co.*: 13.5 mi. S, 3.5 mi. W Grove, 2 (TTU); Trinity, 1 (TTU). *Tyler Co.*: 8.05 km. E Colmesneil, 10 (NTSU); 17 mi. S Woodville, 3 (TCWC). *Upshur Co.*: 7 mi. W Gilmer, 2 (TCWC); 1 mi. W Gilmer, 1 (TCWC). *Van Zandt Co.*: 3.5 mi. SE Fruitvale, 1 (DMNHT). *Walker Co.*: 17 mi. W on Huntsville-Bedias Rd., 1 (TCWC); 6 mi. S Huntsville, 1 (TCWC). *Waller Co.*: Pine Island, 1 (BUSM). *Wood Co.*: 4 mi. S Winnsboro, 2 (TCWC); Timberlake Farm, 3 mi. E, 1.6 mi. S Quitman, 3 (BUSM).

Geomys attwateri attwateri (292). *Austin Co.*: 2 mi. NE Bellville, 3 (TCWC). *Bastrop Co.*: 1 mi. S Elgin, 1 (TNHC); 26 mi. E Austin, 2 (TNHC); 28 mi. E Austin, 1 (TNHC); 10 mi. NE Bastrop, 1 (TNHC); Bastrop State Park, 3 (TNHC); 5 mi. E Bastrop, 1 (TNHC), 3 (TCWC); 7 mi. E Bastrop, 1 (TNHC); 10 mi. E Bastrop, 2 (TCWC); 3 mi. E Cedar Creek, 4 (TNHC). *Burleson Co.*: 0.5 mi. SW jct. Brazos River and Hwy. 21, 3 (TCWC); 1 mi. S Hwy. 21 on Hwy. 50, 17 (TCWC); 1.5 mi. S Hwy. 21 on Hwy. 50, 2 (TCWC); 2 mi. S Hwy. 21 on Hwy. 50, 37 (TCWC); 2 mi. S Hwy. 21 on Hwy. 50, Moelhman's Slough, 15 (TCWC); 2 mi. S Hwy. 21 on Hwy. 50, Moelhman's Slough, 6 (TCWC); 2.3 mi. S Hwy. 21 on Hwy. 50, 12 (TCWC); 4.8 mi. N Tunis, 10 (TCWC); 4.7 mi. N Tunis, 2 (TCWC); 4.5 mi. N Tunis, 9 (TCWC); 4 mi. N Tunis, 1 (TCWC); 3.75 mi. N Tunis, 1 (TCWC); 3.2 mi. NNE Tunis, 1 (TCWC); 3 mi. NE Tunis, 3 (TCWC); 3.25 mi. ENE Tunis, 1 (TCWC); 5 mi. SE Tunis, 1 (TCWC); 13 mi. NE Caldwell, Hwy. 50, 3 (TCWC); 7.4 mi. N Caldwell, Hwy. 36, 1 (TCWC); 3.3 mi. N Caldwell, Hwy. 36, 1 (TCWC); 3 mi. N Hwy. 36, Caldwell, 2 (TCWC); 12 mi. E Caldwell, 6 (TCWC); 17 mi. E Caldwell, 3 (TCWC); 8 mi. SW Caldwell, 5 (TCWC); 8 mi. SW Caldwell, 1 (TCWC); 2.6 mi. SW FM Rd. 166, 1 (TCWC); 7 mi. NW jct. Hwy. 50/60, 1 (TCWC); 6.9 mi. NW jct. Hwy. 50/60, 1 (TCWC); 6.7 mi. NW Hwy. 50/60, 7 (TCWC); 5.9 mi. NW jct. Hwy. 50/60, 1 (TCWC); 3.25 mi. NE jct. Hwy. 50/60, 2 (TCWC); 2.3 mi. NE jct. Hwy. 60/50, 1 (TCWC); 0.4 mi. SE jct. Hwy. 50/60, 1 (TCWC); 9 mi. SE jct. Hwy. 50/60, 2 (TCWC); 0.1 mi. E Snook, 1 (TCWC); 0.2 mi. E Snook, Hwy. 60, 1 (TCWC); 3.2 mi. NE Clay, 1 (TCWC); 3 mi. NE Clay, 1 (TCWC); 3 mi. NE Clay, 2 (TCWC); 2.4 mi. NE Clay, 3 (TCWC); 1.3 mi. NE Clay, 1 (TCWC); 0.3 mi. N, 0.7 mi. W Clay, 2 (TCWC); 5 mi. SW Old Dime Box,

1 (TCWC); 8.1 mi. SE Gause, 1 (TCWC); 14.4 mi. SE Gause, 1 (TCWC). *Caldwell Co.*: 4 mi. SE Luling, 3 (TNHC). *Calhoun Co.*: 7 mi. S, 1 mi. E Port Lavaca, 1 (TCWC); Port O'Connor, 2 (TCWC). *Colorado Co.*: Eagle Lake, 2 (TCWC). *Falls Co.*: 2.9 mi. NE Chilton, 1 (TCWC); 0.7 mi. E Chilton, 2 (TCWC); 5.7 mi. W Marlin, 1 (TCWC); 2.9 mi. SW Marlin, 1 (TCWC); 3.4 mi. WSW Marlin, 1 (TCWC); 12.3 mi. SE Marlin, Hwy. 6, 2 (TCWC); 1 mi. SE Reagan, 1 (TCWC); 1.9 mi. SE Reagan, Hwy. 6, 2 (TCWC); 4.7 mi. N Cedar Springs, 1 (TCWC); 2.15 mi. N Cedar Springs, 1 (TCWC); 1.8 mi. S Cedar Springs, 1 (TCWC); 3 mi. S Cedar Springs, 1 (TCWC); 0.6 mi. E Highbank, 1 (TCWC); 0.8 mi. N Wilderville, 1 (TCWC); 2.6 mi. E Wilderville, 1 (TCWC); 3.8 mi. E Wilderville, 1 (TCWC); 4.5 mi. E Wilderville, 1 (TCWC); 0.7 mi. S Wilderville, 1 (TCWC); 2 mi. NW Bremond, 1 (TCWC). *Fayette Co.*: 6 mi. N La Grange, 2 (TCWC); La Grange, 2 (TCWC). *Gonzales Co.*: Palmetto State Park, 1 (UTAVC); 1 mi. N Nixon, 2 (TCWC). *Guadalupe Co.*: 12 mi. S Seguin, 5 (TCWC). *Lavaca Co.*: 12 mi. SW Hallettsville, 1 (TCWC). *Matagorda Co.*: 5.5 mi. W Palacios, 1 (TCWC). *Milam Co.*: 2.3 mi. S Wilderville, 1 (TCWC); 2.6 mi. S Wilderville, 1 (TCWC); 2 mi. E Maysfield, Hwy. 190, 1 (TCWC); 6.8 mi. E Maysfield, Hwy. 190, 1 (TCWC); 1 mi. SE Cameron, 1 (TCWC); 4.1 mi. SE Cameron, Hwy. 36, 1 (TCWC); 9.1 mi. SE Cameron, Hwy. 36, 1 (TCWC); 3 mi. NE Gause, 1 (TCWC); 6.3 mi. W Gause, Hwy. 79, 2 (TCWC); 4.4 mi. W Gause, Hwy. 79, 1 (TCWC); 1 mi. W Gause, Hwy. 79, 1 (TCWC); Gause, Hwy. 79, 1 (TCWC); 1.7 mi. E Gause, Hwy. 79, 1 (TCWC); 3 mi. E Gause, 1 (TCWC); 3.8 mi. E Gause, Hwy. 79, 1 (TCWC); 1.7 mi. S Gause, 1 (TCWC); 1.9 mi. S Gause, 1 (TCWC); 2.3 mi. SE Gause, 1 (TCWC); 2.4 mi. SE Gause, 1 (TCWC); 2.6 mi. S Gause, 1 (TCWC); 2.7 mi. SE Gause, 1 (TCWC); 3 mi. S Gause, 1 (TCWC); 3 mi. SE Gause, 1 (TCWC); 3.4 mi. S Gause, 1 (TCWC); 4 mi. S Gause, 1 (TCWC); 4.4 mi. SE Gause, 1 (TCWC); 4.9 mi. SE Gause, 1 (TCWC); 5.4 mi. SE Gause, 2 (TCWC); 5.7 mi. SE Gause, 1 (TCWC); 6.4 mi. SE Gause, 1 (TCWC); 2.8 mi. S Milano, Hwy. 36, 1 (TCWC); 1 mi. S Rockdale, FM Rd. 487, 1 (TCWC); 7.5 mi. S Rockdale, 1 (TCWC); 2.1 mi. E Aloca Lake, FM Rd. 2116, 1 (TCWC); 2 mi. NW Brazos River bridge, Hwy. 190, 1 (TCWC); 0.1 mi. W Brazos River, Hwy. 190, 1 (TCWC); 6 mi. S Hearne, Hwy. 79, 2 (TCWC). *Victoria Co.*: 4 mi. E Victoria, Hwy. 89, 1 (TCWC); 3 mi. SW Victoria, 4 (TCWC); 6 mi. S Victoria, 1 (TCWC). *Washington Co.*: 1 mi. N Brenham, 3 (TCWC); 13 mi. W Brenham, 1 (TCWC); 13 mi. W Brenham, 1 (TCWC).

Geomys bursarius major (399). *Bosque Co.*: 1 mi. SE Smith's Bend, FM Rd. 2114, 1 (TCWC). *Cooke Co.*: 5.5 mi. SE Gainesville, 1 (TTU). *Dallas Co.*: Martin Farm, 5 (DMNHT). *Denton Co.*: 4 km. N jct. Hwy. 380 and Hwy. 377, 14 (NTSU); 2.4 km. W Spur 428 and FM Rd. 428, 17 (NTSU); jct. Hwy. 380 and FM 720, 14 (NTSU); 12 mi. W Denton, 1 (UTAVC); 6.5 mi. W Lewisville, 1 (DMNHT); near Lewisville, 1 (DMNHT). *Hill Co.*: 21 mi. NW Waco, FM Rd. 933, 2 (TCWC); Willis Camp, 5 mi. SW jct. FM Rd. 2114 and FM Rd. 933, 2 (TCWC); Willis Camp, 5.8 mi. SW Aguilla, 2 (TCWC). *McLennan Co.*: 2.05 mi. N Gholson, 1 (TCWC); 0.4 mi. N Gholson, 1 (TCWC); Gholson Rd., 1 (UTAVC); 5 mi. NE Bosqueville, 1 (TCWC); 4.5 mi. NE Bosqueville, 1 (TCWC); 1.8 mi. NE Bosqueville, 1 (TCWC); 1.3 mi. E Bosqueville, 1 (TCWC); 3.3 mi. SE Bosqueville, 1 (TCWC); 3.6 mi. ESE Bosqueville, 1 (TCWC); Connally Jr. High, 7.1 mi. N Waco, 1 (BUSM); Waco, 12 (BUSM), 134 (UTAVC), 59 (NTSU), 7 (TCWC); Baylor University, Waco, 1 (BUSM); 0.2 mi. S Waco, FM Rd. 434, 1 (TCWC); 1 mi. S Waco, 18 (TTU); FM Rd. 434, 1 mi. S Waco, 2 (BUSM); 1 mi. SE Waco, FM Rd. 434, 1 (TCWC); 2 mi. SE Waco, 1 (TCWC); 3 mi. S Baylor University, Waco, 1 (BUSM); 4.5 mi. SE Waco, 1 (TCWC); 4.8 mi. SE Waco, 1 (TCWC); 6 mi. S Waco, 6 (TCWC); 7 mi. S Waco, 2 (UTAVC); 1.1 km. ENE jct. Hwy. 81 and FM

Rd. 434, 10 (NTSU); 8.1 km. SE jct. Hwy. 81 and FM Rd. 434, 16 (NTSU); Brazos River, 1 (BUSM); Brazos River bottom near Waco, 3 (BUSM); 8.5 km. WNW Riesel, 5 (NTSU); 3.3 mi. NNE Downsville, 1 (TCWC); 4.8 km. N Downsville, 4 (NTSU); 3 mi. NE Downsville, 1 (TCWC); 2.25 mi. ESE Downsville, 1 (TCWC); 2.5 mi. SE Downsville, 1 (TCWC); 5 km. NE Asa, 5 (NTSU). *Tarrant Co.:* 3 mi. SW Roanoke, 1 (DMNHT); Foy's Farm, 3 mi. SE Roanoke, 4 (DMNHT); 3 mi. E Keller, 1 (TCWC); Hurst, 5 (FWMSH); Arlington, 16 (UTAVC); University of Texas, Arlington, 2 (UTAVC); Fort Worth, 1 (UTAVC), 1 (FWMSH); 15 mi. SE Fort Worth, 1 (TWC); 17 mi. SE Fort Worth, 1 (TWC); Mansfield, Hwy. 157, 1 (UTAVC).

Castor canadensis texensis (18). *Brazos Co.:* 8 mi. NW Bryan, 1 (TCWC); 10 mi. NW College Station, 1 (TCWC); 5 mi. W College Station, 1 (TCWC); 8 mi. SW College Station, 1 (TCWC). *Colorado Co.:* Cummings Creek, 2 (USNM). *Dallas Co.:* White Rock Lake, 1 (DMNHT); Elm Fork of the Trinity River, near Irving, 1 (DMNHT); Elm Fork Nature Area, 1 (DMNHT); Bachman Lake, 1 (DMNHT). *Grayson Co.:* Tucker's Cove, Lake Texoma, 1 (TCWC). *Henderson Co.:* no specific locality, 1 (SFAVC). *Limestone Co.:* Riddle Ranch, 2 mi. SW Shiloh, 1 (BUSM). *McLennan Co.:* 5 mi. N Waco, 1 (BUSM); Waco, 1 (BUSM); 7 mi. E Waco, 1 (BUSM). *Navarro Co.:* no specific locality, 1 (SFAVC). *Tarrant Co.:* SE Grapevine Lake, Sandy Point, 1 (UTAVC).

Oryzomys palustris texensis (277). *Anderson Co.:* Frankston, 1 (SFAVC); Engling Wildlife Management Area, 6 mi. SE Cayuga, 1 (BUSM). *Angelina Co.:* 12 mi. W Lufkin, 4 (TCWC). *Brazos Co.:* 0.5 mi. N IH 6, E bypass on FM Rd. 158, 1 (TCWC); Bryan, 1 (TCWC); 7 mi. S, 4 mi. W College Station, 1 (TCWC). *Calhoun Co.:* Port Lavaca, 4 (USNM); 4 mi. E Port Lavaca, 3 (TCWC); 6.5 mi. S, 1.25 mi. E Port Lavaca, 3 (TCWC); 7 mi. S, 1 mi. E Port Lavaca, 93 (TCWC). *Chambers Co.:* 3 mi. NE Cedar Bayou, FM Rd. 565, 1 (TNHC); 3 mi. NE Cedar, 2 (TNHC). *Delta Co.:* 1 mi. S Liberty Grove, 1 (TWC); Klondike, 1 (TWC). *Galveston Co.:* Virginia Point, 1 (USNM); Texas City, 4 (TTU); 1 mi. W Hitchcock, 1 (TTU); 9 mi. W Galveston, 1 (TNHC). *Hardin Co.:* 3.25 mi. E, 2 mi. S Village Mills, 1 (TCWC); Rosier Park, Saratoga, 1 (TCWC); 4.6 mi. E Saratoga, 1 (TCWC); 4.6 mi. E Saratoga, Hwy. 770, 1 (TCWC); Honey Island, 1 (TTU); 5.5 mi. NW Sour Lake, 11 (UIMNH); 1.5 mi. N Sour Lake, 1 (UIMNH); Sour Lake, 4 (UIMNH), 1 (TTU); 0.5 mi. E Sour Lake, 12 (UIMNH). *Harris Co.:* 22 mi. N Houston, 1 (SFAVC); Armand Bayou, 1 (TCWC); 3 mi. NE Webster, 2 (TCWC); 1 mi. S Webster, 1 (TTU). *Harrison Co.:* 7 mi. S Hallsville, 5 (SWTS). *Jackson Co.:* 2 mi. S Lolita, 1 (TCWC). *Jefferson Co.:* 5 mi. W Beaumont, 9 (TNHC); Beaumont, 6 (TCWC), 5 (TNHC); 3.5 mi. N Nome, 6 (UIMNH); La Belle, 2 (TTU); 7 mi. N Winnie, 6 (TCWC); J. D. Murphree Wildlife Management Area, 1 (TCWC); Sabine, 1 (USNM); Sea Rim State Park, 8 mi. S Sabine, 4 (TCWC). *Lamar Co.:* Paris, 10 (UIMNH). *Liberty Co.:* 2.5 mi. N, 3.5 mi. E Moss Hill, 1 (TCWC); 2.5 mi. N, 3.8 mi. E Moss Hill, 2 (TCWC). *Matagorda Co.:* 10 mi. N Bay City, 9 (TCWC); 4 mi. W Palacios, 1 (TCWC); Selkirk Island, Matagorda, 1 (USNM); Matagorda, 6 (USNM); Matagorda Peninsula, near Matagorda, 1 (USNM). *Nacogdoches Co.:* 2 mi. NE Nacogdoches, 1 (SFAVC); 1 mi. W Nacogdoches, 1 (SFAVC); Nacogdoches, 4 (SFAVC); 1 mi. E Nacogdoches, 2 (SFAVC); 9.5 mi. SW Nacogdoches, 1 (TNHC). *Newton Co.:* 9.8 mi. N Burkeville, 1 (TCWC); 6.6 mi. N Burkeville, 3 (TCWC). *Orange Co.:* Orange, 1 (UIMNH). *Red River Co.:* Lennox Ranch, Cuthand, 2 (UTAVC). *Rusk Co.:* 2.2 mi. N New London, 1 (SFAVC); 2 mi. NE New London, 1 (SFAVC). *Sabine Co.:* Big Sandy Creek, Hwy. 87, 4 (DMNHT). *Tyler Co.:* 3.1 mi. N, 2.6 mi. W Spurger, 1 (TCWC); 3.1 mi. N, 2.5 mi. W Spurger, 2 (TCWC); 1.7 mi. N, 1.6 mi. W Spurger,

1 (TCWC); 4.3 mi. S, 0.4 mi. W Warren, 2 (TCWC); 4.5 mi. S, 0.5 mi. W Warren, 5 (TCWC). *Walker Co.*: Huntsville, 1 (TCWC). *Waller Co.*: 1 mi. N Katy, 1 (BUSM); Katy, 1 (BUSM). *Wood Co.*: 3 mi. E, 1.6 mi. S Quitman, 1 (BUSM).

Reithrodontomys montanus griseus (40). *Brazos Co.*: 1 mi. NE College Station, 2 (TCWC); 0.5 mi. N jct. Hwy. 60 and 158, 1 (TCWC); College Station, 1 (TCWC); 0.2 mi. S College Station, 1 (TCWC); 0.25 mi. S College Station, 2 (TCWC); 2 mi. SE College Station, 2 (TCWC). *Cooke Co.*: Gainesville, 2 (USNM). *Madison Co.*: 0.5 mi. S jct. Hwy. 21 and IH 45, 1 (TCWC); 1 mi. S jct. Hwy. 21 and IH 45, 1 (TCWC). *McLennan Co.*: 1 mi. S West, 1 (BUSM); 2.5 mi. SW Ross, 1 (BUSM); Waco, 1 (BUSM); 5 mi. SW Waco, 1 (BUSM). *Robertson Co.*: 3 mi. W Hearne, 1 (TCWC); 2 mi. W Hearne, 9 (TCWC). *Tarrant Co.*: Hurst, 2 (FWMSH); Fort Worth, 4 (FWMSH); jct. Hwy. 377 and FM Rd. 2376, 1 (FWMSH); Hwy. 157 between Arlington and Watsonville, 1 (UTAVC). *Travis Co.*: 6 mi. S Round Rock, 1 (TNHC); 8 mi. NW Austin, 2 (TNHC); 2 mi. N Austin, 1 (TNHC). *Williamson Co.*: near Taylor, 1 (TNHC).

Reithrodontomys humulis merriami (26). *Angelina Co.*: 1 mi. N Lufkin, 2 (SFAVC). *Bowie Co.*: 1 mi. S New Boston, 1 (TTU), 1 (SFAVC). *Brazoria Co.*: Austin Bayou, near Alvin, 9 (USNM), 1 (AMNH). *Fort Bend Co.*: Richmond, 2 (USNM). *Freestone Co.*: Fairfield, 2 (TCWC). *Hardin Co.*: 0.9 mi. N, 4.5 mi. E Saratoga, 1 (TCWC). *Harrison Co.*: 1 mi. N jct. IH 20 and Hwy. 31, 2 (DMNHT). *Jefferson Co.*: La Belle, 1 (UMMZ). *McLennan Co.*: Waco, 1 (BUSM). *Nacogdoches Co.*: Nacogdoches, 1 (TTU); 1 mi. E Nacogdoches, 1 (TNHC); 2 mi. E Nacogdoches, 1 (TNHC).

Reithrodontomys fulvescens aurantius (501). *Anderson Co.*: 20 mi. NW Palestine, 4 (TCWC), 14 (TNHC). *Angelina Co.*: 13 mi. W Lufkin, 1 (SWTS); Lufkin, 1 (SFAVC). *Bell Co.*: 8.4 mi. S, 2.2 mi. E Killeen, 3 (BUSM). *Bosque Co.*: 7 mi. N jct. Hwy 56 and Hwy. 22, 1 (DMNHT). *Bowie Co.*: 4 mi. SW Dekalb, 6 (TCWC); Texarkana, 1 (USNM); 1 mi. NE Simms, 1 (TCWC). *Brazoria Co.*: Barnard Creek, W of Columbia, 6 (USNM); Velasco, 10 (USNM). *Brazos Co.*: Bryan, 1 (TCWC); 4 mi. E Bryan, 1 (TCWC); 4 mi. NE College Station, 1 (TCWC); 3 mi. N Texas A&M University, College Station, 1 (TCWC); 1 mi. NW Texas A&M University, 1 (TCWC); 1 mi. N College Station, 1 (TCWC); 0.5 mi. NW College Station, 1 (UIMNH), 1 (MVZ); 4 mi. W College Station, 1 (TCWC); 3 mi. W College Station, 3 (TCWC); Texas A&M Range Area, 9 (TCWC); College Station, 7 (TCWC); 0.2 mi. S College Station, 1 (TCWC); 1 mi. S College Station, 3 (TCWC); 2 mi. SE College Station, 1 (TCWC); 3 mi. SW College Station, 3 (TCWC); 3 mi. SE College Station, 2 (TCWC); 4 mi. SE College Station, 1 (TCWC); 6 mi. SW College Station, 1 (TCWC); 7 mi. SW College Station, 2 (TCWC); 7 mi. S, 4 mi. W College Station, 2 (TCWC); 7.5 mi. S Wellborn, 1 (TCWC). *Chambers Co.*: 7 mi. N Winnie, 3 (TCWC). *Colorado Co.*: 6 mi. N Eagle Lake, 1 (TCWC). *Dallas Co.*: 4 mi. NW Irving, 1 (UTAVC); Audubon Wildlife Refuge, Mt. Creek Lake, 1 (UTAVC). *Ellis Co.*: 6 mi. NW Rosser, 1 (SFAVC). *Freestone Co.*: 2 mi. N Fairfield, 1 (TCWC). *Gregg Co.*: 3 mi. N Longview, 1 (TCWC). *Hardin Co.*: 7.7 mi. N Silsbee, 1 (TCWC); 7.7 mi. N, 0.1 mi. E Silsbee, 4 (TCWC); 0.9 mi. N, 4.5 mi. E Saratoga, 1 (TCWC); 0.9 mi. N, 5 mi. E Saratoga, 4 (TCWC); Rosier Park, Saratoga, 4 (TCWC); 0.5 mi. SE Saratoga, Hwy. 770, 1 (UTAVC); 5.5 mi. NW Sour Lake, 1 (UIMNH); 2.5 mi. W Sour Lake, 1 (UIMNH); Sour Lake, 11 (USNM), 3 (UIMNH); 0.5 mi. S Sour Lake, 3 (UIMNH). *Harris Co.*: Pasadena, 4 (TCWC); 1 mi. S Webster, 4 (TTU). *Harrison Co.*: 3 mi. S Karnack, 1 (SWTS); 12.5 mi. NE Marshall, 1 (TWC); 5 mi. NE Marshall, 1 (SWTS); 5 mi. W Marshall, 1 (SWTS); 6 mi. E Hallsville, 1 (SFAVC); 1 mi. N jct. IH 20 and Hwy. 31, 24 (DMNHT); 5 mi. SSW jct. IH 20 and Hwy. 43, 1 (DMNHT). *Hender-*

son Co.: E Chandler, 1 (SFAVC); 3 mi. S Brownsboro, 2 (SFAVC); 1 mi. E Malakoff, 2 (SFAVC). *Houston Co.*: 3 mi. E Crockett, 1 (SFAVC). *Jasper Co.*: Kirbyville, 4 (USNM). *Jefferson Co.*: 5 mi. W Beaumont, 2 (TNHC); Beaumont, 2 (TNHC); 5 mi. SW Beaumont, 2 (TNHC); La Belle, 2 (UMMZ); 7 mi. S La Belle, 1 (UMMZ). *Kaufman Co.*: 1 mi. W Rosser, 1 (SFAVC). *Liberty Co.*: 2.5 mi. N, 3.8 mi. E Moss Hill, 4 (TCWC); 2.5 mi. N, 4.3 mi. E Moss Hill, 1 (TCWC); 12 mi. S Liberty, 3 (SFAVC). *Madison Co.*: 0.5 mi. S jct. Hwy. 21 and IH 45, 4 (TCWC). *Marion Co.*: Lake O' the Pines, 1 (DMNHT). *Matagorda Co.*: 10 mi. N Bay City, 10 (TCWC); Elliot's, 1 (USNM); 1 mi. W Palacios, 6 ft., 1 (TCWC); Matagorda, 7 (USNM); Matagorda Island, 5 (USNM). *McLennan Co.*: 2.5 mi. SW Ross, 2 (BUSM); 3.2 mi. N Axtell, 1 (BUSM); Waco, 7 (BUSM); 5 mi. S Waco, 5 (BUSM); 6 mi. SW Waco, 1 (BUSM). *Nacogdoches Co.*: 2 mi. E Garrison, 3 (SFAVC); 13 mi. ENE Nacogdoches, 2 (SFAVC); 11 mi. NE Nacogdoches, 1 (SFAVC); 5 mi. NNE Nacogdoches, 2 (SFAVC); 5 mi. N Nacogdoches, 1 (SFAVC); 3 mi. NW Nacogdoches, 1 (SFAVC); 3 mi. NE Nacogdoches, 1 (SFAVC); 1 mi. N Nacogdoches, 2 (SFAVC); 1 mi. ENE Nacogdoches, 2 (SFAVC); 1 mi. W Nacogdoches, 4 (SFAVC); Nacogdoches, 2 (USNM), 5 (TTU), 31 (SFAVC); Stephen F. Austin University Farm, Nacogdoches, 3 (SFAVC); La Nana Creek, Nacogdoches, 12 (SFAVC); Bonita Creek, Nacogdoches, 1 (SFAVC); La Mar Creek, Nacogdoches, 1 (SFAVC); sewage plant, Nacogdoches, 1 (SFAVC); 0.5 mi. E Nacogdoches, 1 (SFAVC); 1 mi. E Nacogdoches, 4 (SFAVC); 0.8 mi. S, 1 mi. E Nacogdoches, 1 (SFAVC); 1 mi. SE Nacogdoches, 2 (SFAVC); 2 mi. S, 1 mi. E Nacogdoches, 1 (SFAVC); 5 mi. SE Nacogdoches, 4 (SFAVC); 8 mi. SW Nacogdoches, 2 (SFAVC); 8 mi. S Nacogdoches, 1 (SFAVC); 9 mi. SW Nacogdoches, 1 (SFAVC); 9 mi. S Nacogdoches, 1 (TNHC); 9.5 mi. SW Nacogdoches, 10 (TNHC); 10 mi. SW Nacogdoches, Stephen F. Austin Experimental Forest, 3 (SFAVC); 14 mi. SW Nacogdoches, 2 (SFAVC). *Newton Co.*: 10.5 mi. N Burkeville, 3 (TCWC); 15 mi. NE Buna, 4 (TNHC). *Panola Co.*: 3 mi. SE Long Branch, 2 (SFAVC); 5 mi. SE Long Branch, 2 (SFAVC); 6 mi. SE Long Branch, 2 (SFAVC). *Polk Co.*: 5.8 mi. N Dallardsville, 1 (TCWC); 5.4 mi. N Dallardsville, 2 (TCWC); 2 mi. SE Goodrich, Trinity River, 1 (SFAVC); 1.8 mi. S Segno, FM Rd. 943, 2 (TCWC). *Red River Co.*: Pecan Farm, 14 mi. NE Clarksville, 2 (DMNHT). *Robertson Co.*: 2 mi. W Hearne, 1 (TCWC). *Rusk Co.*: 2 mi. E Old London, 3 (SFAVC). *Sabine Co.*: Big Sandy Creek, Hwy. 87, 22 (DMNHT). *Shelby Co.*: Joaquin, 7 (USNM); Shelbyville, 1 (SFAVC). *Smith Co.*: 12 mi. NW Kilgore, 1 (SFAVC); 20 mi. NE Tyler, 4 (SWTS); 6 mi. N Tyler, 1 (SFAVC); 4 mi. N Tyler, 2 (TCWC); 18 mi. E Tyler, 1 (SFAVC). *Tarrant Co.*: Fort Worth, 1 (TWC), 1 (FWMSH), 2 (UTAVC); Arlington, 1 (UTAVC); Benbrook, 1 (UTAVC), 3 (FWMSH). *Trinity Co.*: Trinity, 2 (TCWC). *Tyler Co.*: 0.5 mi. S, 2.3 mi. W Town Bluff, 6 (TCWC); 2.8 mi. S, 1.8 mi. W Town Bluff, 1 (TCWC); 3.6 mi. S, 2.9 mi. W Town Bluff, 5 (TCWC); 3.1 mi. N, 2.6 mi. W Spurger, 2 (TCWC); 3.1 mi. N, 2.5 mi. W Spurger, 3 (TCWC); 1.7 mi. N, 1.6 mi. W Spurger, 4 (TCWC); 1.2 mi. N, 1.9 mi. W Spurger, 9 (TCWC); 0.5 mi. N, 3.2 mi. E Warren, 2 (TCWC); 0.7 mi. S, 2.8 mi. E Warren, 3 (TCWC); 2.6 mi. S, 3.9 mi. E Warren, 4 (TCWC); 4.2 mi. S, 0.8 mi. W Warren, 8 (TCWC); 4.3 mi. S, 1.1 mi. E Warren, 3 (TCWC); 4.3 mi. S, 1.4 mi. W Warren, 2 (TCWC); 4.5 mi. S, 0.5 mi. W Warren, 7 (TCWC); 4.6 mi. S, 1 mi. W Warren, 1 (TCWC); 4.8 mi. S, 0.7 mi. W Warren, 4 (TCWC). *Walker Co.*: 20 mi. W Huntsville, 1 (TCWC); 2 mi. E Huntsville, 3 (TCWC); 1 mi. SW Huntsville, 6 (TCWC). *Waller Co.*: Hempstead, 8 (USNM).

Reithrodontomys fulvescens intermedius (22). *Caldwell Co.*: 3 mi. NE Lytton Springs, 4 (TCWC). *Calhoun Co.*: 7 mi. S, 1 mi. E Port Lavaca, 4 (TCWC); 5 mi. W Port O'Connor, 10 ft., 2 (TCWC). *Gonzales Co.*: Palmetto State Park, 4 (TNHC), 1 (SWTS); 4 mi. S Gonzales, 1 (SWTS). *Hays Co.*: Blanco River, 4 mi.

NE San Marcos, 1 (TCWC). *Jackson Co.*: 1 mi. N Edna, 1 (TCWC); E Carancahua Creek, 3 (USNM). *Lavaca Co.*: 14 mi. WSW Hallettsville, 1 (TCWC).

Peromyscus maniculatus ozarkiarum (15). *Cooke Co.*: 1 mi. S Sivells Bend, 2 (NTSU); 5 mi. SSE Moss Lake, 1 (NTSU). *Denton Co.*: 3 mi. NNW Denton, 1 (NTSU). *Grayson Co.*: 2 mi. N Tioga, 2 (NTSU); 2.8 mi. W, 5 mi. N Pilot Point, 2 (NTSU); 2.8 mi. W, 1.5 mi. N Pilot Point, 1 (NTSU); 0.5 mi. W Pilot Point, 5 (NTSU); 3 mi. S Pilot Point, 1 (NTSU).

Peromyscus maniculatus pallescens (150). *Anderson Co.*: Engling Wildlife Management Area, 20 mi. NW Palestine, 1 (TCWC); 10 mi. NW Palestine, 1 (BUSM). *Bexar Co.*: San Antonio, 5 (NTSU); 4.5 mi. E Sayers, 1 (KU). *Bosque Co.*: 7.4 mi. N Walnut Springs, 1 (BUSM). *Brazos Co.*: 0.5 mi. N jct. Hwy. 6 and FM Rd. 159, 2 (TCWC); 4 mi. W College Station, 1 (TCWC); College Station, 2 (TCWC); 2.5 mi. S College Station, 2 (TTU). *Burleson Co.*: 20 mi. ESE Caldwell, 1 (TCWC). *Caldwell Co.*: 2 mi. S Lockhart, 13 (NTSU). *Collin Co.*: 4 mi. N Wylie, 6 (DMNHT). *Cooke Co.*: Gainesville, 1 (USNM); 3 mi. S Gainesville, 3 (NTSU); 6 mi. S Gainesville, 1 (NTSU); Camp Houze, 1 (MVZ). *Dallas Co.*: 3.9 mi. N jct. Hwy. 183 and County Line Rd., 1 (UTAVC); jct. NW Hwy. and E Richardson Rd., 1 (DMNHT); White Rock Lake, 1 (DMNHT); 0.5 mi. E Mesquite, 2 (NTSU); Mt. Creek Lake, 1 (DMNHT). *Denton Co.*: 3 mi. S Pilot Point, 1 (NTSU); 8 mi. N Bolivar, 5 (NTSU); 2 mi. S Bolivar, 2 (NTSU); 1.7 mi. NW Denton, 1 (NTSU); 1 mi. NE Denton, 1 (NTSU); Denton, 7 (NTSU); 4.5 mi. SW Denton, 1 (NTSU); 12 mi. S Denton, 1 (NTSU); Little Elm, 1 (NTSU); Argyle, 2 (NTSU); 2 mi. NE Roanoke, 5 (UTAVC). *Falls Co.*: 6.5 mi. E Marlin, 2 (BUSM). *Freestone Co.*: 1.8 mi. N Fairfield, 1 (TCWC). *Grayson Co.*: Pottsboro, 1 (MVZ). *Hill Co.*: 3.4 mi. E, 1.6 mi. W Hillsboro, 1 (TCWC). *Hunt Co.*: 2 mi. S Commerce, 1 (DMNHT). *McLennan Co.*: 24 mi. NE Waco, 1 (BUSM); 7 mi. NE Waco, 1 (BUSM); 5 mi. W Waco, 2 (BUSM); Lake Waco, 1 (BUSM); Waco, 1 (BUSM); Bellmead, 1 (BUSM); 4.7 mi. E Waco, 1 (BUSM); Trading House Creek Lake, 6.8 mi. E Waco, 3 (BUSM); 1.3 mi. S Crawford, 1 (BUSM); 4.8 mi. SW Waco, 1 (BUSM). *Navarro Co.*: 10 mi. W Corsicana, 4 (SFAVC); 8 mi. W Corsicana, 3 (SFAVC); 5 mi. S Corsicana, 3 (NTSU); 6 mi. S Richland, 2 (NTSU). *Orange Co.*: 10 mi. E Vidor, 1 (TCWC). *Red River Co.*: 14 mi. NE Clarksville, 4 (DMNHT). *Robertson Co.*: 2 mi. W Hearne, 20 (TCWC). *Tarrant Co.*: Blackland, Hwy. 157, 1 (UTAVC); White Lake Hills, 1 (TWC); 12 mi. NE Fort Worth, 1 (TNHC); Fort Worth, 1 (TCWC); Panther Recreation Area, 12 mi. S Fort Worth, 1 (FWMSH); 16.5 mi. SW Fort Worth, 1 (TWC); Arlington, 5 mi. S jct. IH 20 and Matlock Rd., 1 (UTAVC); SE Lake Arlington, 1 (FWMSH). *Travis Co.*: 10 mi. N Austin, 1 (TNHC); 9 mi. NW Austin, 2 (TNHC); Balcones Research Center, Austin, 2 (TNHC); 4 mi. E Austin, 1 (TNHC); 6 mi. E Austin, 1 (TNHC). *Van Zandt Co.*: 4.5 mi. SE Grand Saline, 2 (TCWC). *Williamson Co.*: 2 mi. S Taylor, 2 (TNHC).

Peromyscus leucopus leucopus (346). *Anderson Co.*: 20 mi. NW Palestine, 5 (TNHC); 20 mi. SW Palestine, 6 (TNHC). *Bastrop Co.*: 3 mi. E, 1 mi. S Bastrop, 1 (SWTS). *Bell Co.*: 8.4 mi. S, 2.4 mi. E Killeen, 1 (BUSM). *Bosque Co.*: no specific locality, 1 (BUSM). *Brazoria Co.*: Austin Bayou, near Alvin, 2 (USNM); 5 mi. SW Brazoria, 2 (SWTS); Velasco, 8 (USNM). *Brazos Co.*: 2.5 mi. N Edge, 2 (UMMZ); 2 mi. NE Edge, 1 (UMMZ); 2 mi. S Edge, 2 (TCWC); 6 mi. NW Kurten, 2 (TCWC); 6 mi. N Bryan, 1 (TNHC); 5 mi. W Bryan, 1 (UIMNH); 9 mi. E Bryan, 1 (TCWC), 1 (UMMZ); 0.5 mi. N jct. Hwy. 6 and Hwy. 158, 1 (TCWC); near Koppe's Bridge, 1 (UMMZ); 7 mi. W College Station, 2 (UMMZ); 3 mi. W College Station, 5 (TCWC); 3 mi. W College Station, Fish Lake, 1 (UMMZ); 2 mi. W College Station, 2 (TCWC); 1 mi. W College Station, 3 (TCWC); College Station, 2 (TCWC), 1 (UIMNH), 2 (USNM), 2 (UMMZ); Texas A&M University, College Station, 1 (TCWC); 10 mi. E College Station, 1 (TCWC); 0.25 mi. S Fish Lake, College Station, 1 (TCWC); 2 mi. SW College Station, 2 (TCWC); 3 mi. SW College Station, 3 (TCWC); 3 mi. S College Station, 1 (TCWC); 3 mi. SE College Station, 2 (TCWC); 6 mi. SW College Station, 1 (UMMZ), 1 (TCWC); 6 mi. SE College Station, 4 (TCWC); 7 mi. SW College Station, 7 (TCWC), 2 (UMMZ); 8 mi. SW College Station, 1 (TCWC). *Caldwell Co.*: 3 mi. NE Lytton Springs, 2 (TCWC). *Calhoun Co.*: Port O'Connor, 1 (USNM). *Chambers Co.*: 3 mi. NE Cedar Bayou, FM Rd. 565, 1 (TNHC). *Cherokee Co.*: Douglass, 1 (BUSM); 2.3 mi. E Linwood, Hwy. 21, 1 (BUSM). *Cooke Co.*: Gainesville, 3 (USNM). *Dallas Co.*: Irving, Trinity River, 1 (UTAVC). *Delta Co.*: 1 mi. E Liberty Grove, 1 (TWC); 3 mi. SW Delta, 2 (TWC); 3 mi. SW Klondike, 1 (TWC). *Denton Co.*: Denton, 68 (UMMZ). *Fayette Co.*: 11 mi. S, 3 mi. E Smithville, 2 (SWTS). *Freestone Co.*: 10 mi. NE Fairfield, 3 (TCWC); 9 mi. NE Fairfield, 1 (TCWC). *Galveston Co.*: Arcadia, 1 (USNM). *Goliad Co.*: 8 mi. NE Goliad, 1 (TNHC). *Gonzales Co.*: Palmetto State Park, 9 (TNHC); Soejice Peat Bog, 1 (TNHC); 5 mi. S Gonzales, 2 (SWTS); 6 mi. S Gonzales, 1 (SWTS). *Grayson Co.*: Sherman, 1 (MVZ). *Guadalupe Co.*: 0.5 mi. SW Martindale, 2 (SWTS). *Harrison Co.*: 15 mi. NE Marshall, 2 (TNHC); 5 mi. NE Marshall, 1 (SWTS); Marshall, 1 (SWTS). *Hays Co.*: 2 mi. E San Marcos, 1 (SWTS). *Henderson Co.*: 2 mi. NE Malakoff, 5 (SFAVC); 1 mi. NE Malakoff, 2 (TNHC); 2 mi. E Malakoff, 1 (SFAVC); 1.5 mi. SE Malakoff, 1 (TNHC); 2 mi. S Malakoff, 1 (TNHC), 2 (SFAVC). *Hill Co.*: 3.4 mi. S, 1.6 mi. W Hillsboro, 1 (TCWC); 5.8 mi. S, 3.4 mi. W Hillsboro, 8 (TCWC). *Hopkins Co.*: 5 mi. N Peerless, 1 (TWC). *Hunt Co.*: 3 mi. SE Quinlan, 3 (DMNHT); 8.5 mi. SE Quincan, 3 (UTAVC). *Jackson Co.*: 7 mi. S El Dorado, 1 (TCWC). *Lavaca Co.*: 12 mi. N Hallettsville, 2 (TCWC); 8 mi. N Hallettsville, 1 (TCWC); 3 mi. W Hallettsville, 3 (TCWC); 16 mi. SE Hallettsville, 1 (TCWC). *Leon Co.*: 13 mi. SE Centerville, 1 (SFAVC); 2 mi. E Flynn, 1 (TCWC). *Limestone Co.*: 5.5 mi. S Groesbeck, 1 (BUSM). *Matagorda Co.*: 10 mi. N Bay City, 11 (TCWC); Elliot, 1 (USNM); Matagorda, 3 (USNM); Matagorda Peninsula, 1 (USNM); Selkirk Island, 8 mi. above mouth Colorado River, 1 (USNM). *McLennan Co.*: near Trading House Creek, 1 (BUSM); Tehaucana Creek, Waco, 1 (BUSM); 7 mi. N Valley View, FM Rd. 2490, 1 (BUSM); Baylor Camp, 10 mi. W Waco, 1 (BUSM); 8 mi. W Waco, 1 (BUSM); 4 mi. W Waco, 1 (BUSM); Waco, 3 (BUSM); 4.8 mi. SW Waco, 1 (BUSM); 14 mi. S Waco, 1 (BUSM). *Milam Co.*: 1 mi. SE Cameron, 2 (TCWC). *Nacogdoches Co.*: 2 mi. N Trawick, 1 (SFAVC); 15 mi. NW Nacogdoches, 10 (TNHC); 12 mi. NW Nacogdoches, 2 (SFAVC); 1.5 mi. NE Nacogdoches, 1 (SFAVC); Nacogdoches, 1 (SFAVC); La Nana Creek, Nacogdoches, 2 (SFAVC); 1 mi. E Nacogdoches, 1 (TNHC); 14 mi. E Nacogdoches, 1 (SFAVC); 13 mi. SW Nacogdoches, 1 (SFAVC). *Navarro Co.*: 10.3 mi. E Corsicana, 1 (BUSM). *Newton Co.*: 10 mi. N Burkeville, 2 (TCWC); 15 mi. NE Buna, 10 (TNHC). *Panola Co.*: 5 mi. SE Long Branch, 2 (SFAVC); 8 mi. SE Long Branch, 1 (SFAVC). *Rains Co.*: 1 mi. N Hogansville, 1 (TWC). *Red River Co.*: 14 mi. NE Clarksville, 5 (DMNHT); 5.5 mi. S Boxelder, 2 (DMNHT). *Robertson Co.*: 2 mi. NW Hearne, 1 (TCWC); 2 mi. W Hearne, 1 (TCWC); 1 mi. S Hearne, 1 (TCWC). *Sabine Co.*: 4 mi. N, 1 mi. E Milam, 1 (SWTS). *Smith Co.*: 3 mi. N Loop 323, Tyler, 1 (TCWC). *Tarrant Co.*: Fort Worth, 1 (TWC); S Forest Hills, 1.3 mi. S Loop 820, 1 (UTAVC); Arlington, 5 mi. S jct. IH 20 and Matlock Rd., 1 (UTAVC); Benbrook, 1 (USNM); Kennedale, 1 (TWC). *Travis Co.*: 10 mi. NW Austin, 1 (TNHC); 7 mi. W Austin, 1 (TNHC); 5 mi. E Austin, 1 (TNHC); 5 mi. E University of Texas, Austin, 1 (TNHC); 5 mi. SE Austin, 1 (TNHC). *Trinity Co.*: Trinity, 2 (TCWC); 5 mi. S Trinity, 2 (TCWC). *Walker Co.*: 15 mi. NE Huntsville,

1 (TCWC); 1.5 mi. NE Huntsville, 1 (USNM); 20 mi. W Huntsville, 2 (USNM), 6 (TCWC); Huntsville, 2 (TCWC); 7 mi. E Huntsville, 1 (TCWC). *Williamson Co.*: 11 mi. E Bertram, 1 (TNHC); 2 mi. S Taylor, 1 (TNHC). *Wood Co.*: 3 mi. SE Quitman, 1 (DMNHT); 15 mi. NE Hawkins, 1 (BUSM).

Peromyscus gossypinus megacephalus (801). *Anderson Co.*: Engling Wildlife Management Area, 2 (TCWC); 20 mi. NW Palestine, 14 (TNHC); 18.5 mi. NW Palestine, 1 (TNHC); 10 mi. S Palestine, 1 (SFAVC); Long Lake, 1 (USNM). *Angelina Co.*: 20 mi. SW Nacogdoches, 5 (SFAVC), 10 (TNHC); 13 mi. W Lufkin, 6 (SWTS); 11.5 mi. W Lufkin, 1 (SWTS); 10 mi. W Lufkin, 1 (SWTS); Lufkin, 1 (TNHC); 13 mi. W, 2 mi. S Lufkin, 1 (SWTS); 5 mi. S Lufkin, 1 (SFAVC). *Bowie Co.*: 0.5 mi. S New Boston, 1 (DMNHT); Texarkana, 1 (USNM). *Cherokee Co.*: 1 mi. S Ponta, 2 (SFAVC); 8 mi. NW Maydelle, 1 (TNHC); 1.5 mi. SW Maydelle, 2 (SFAVC); 4 mi. S Maydelle, 2 (SFAVC); 7 mi. SW Maydelle, 1 (TNHC); 8 mi. SW Maydelle, 1 (SFAVC); 9 mi. S Maydelle, 1 (SFAVC); Angelina River, 4.3 mi. W Douglas, 1 (BUSM); 7 mi. SW Alto, 4 (SFAVC), 1 (TNHC); 7 mi. S Alto, 1 (SFAVC). *Freestone Co.*: 10 mi. NE Fairfield, 1 (TCWC). *Grimes Co.*: 17 mi. E Bryan, 2 (TCWC). *Hardin Co.*: 1.8 mi. S, 2.4 mi. E Village Mills, 1 (TCWC); 1.8 mi. S, 2.9 mi. E Village Mills, 6 (TCWC); 3.25 mi. E, 2 mi. S Village Mills, 6 (TCWC); Honey Island, 3 (TTU); 11 mi. N, 2.3 mi. E Silsbee, 3 (TCWC); 11 mi. N, 2.8 mi. E Silsbee, 3 (TCWC); 10.9 mi. N, 1.8 mi. E Silsbee, 10 (TCWC); 10.9 mi. N, 2.3 mi. E Silsbee, 3 (TCWC); 9.4 mi. N, 1.8 mi. E Silsbee, 6 (TCWC); 9 mi. N, 0.8 mi. E Silsbee, 3 (TCWC); 9 mi. N, 1.3 mi. E Silsbee, 10 (TCWC); 7.7 mi. N Silsbee, 1 (TCWC); 7.7 mi. N, 0.1 mi. E Silsbee, 3 (TCWC); 0.9 mi. N, 5 mi. E Saratoga, 2 (TCWC); 0.8 mi. N, 2.6 mi. E Saratoga, 5 (TCWC); Rosier Park, Saratoga, 5 (TCWC); 4.6 mi. E Saratoga, Hwy. 770, 30 (TCWC); 13 mi. NE Sour Lake, 2 (USNM); Sour Lake, 9 (USNM). *Harrison Co.*: 3.5 mi. W Karnack, 3 (SWTS); Caddo Lake State Park, 3 (TNHC); 2 mi. S Karnack, 1 (TWC); 16 mi. NE Marshall, 2 (TNHC); 15 mi. NE Marshall, 5 (TNHC); 12.5 mi. NE Marshall, 1 (TWC); 5 mi. ENE Marshall, 1 (SWTS). *Henderson Co.*: 6 mi. NE Brownsboro, 5 (TNHC); 1 mi. NE Malakoff, 1 (TNHC); 2 mi. S Malakoff, 4 (SFAVC); 2 mi. SE Malakoff, 3 (SFAVC), 1 (KU); 9 mi. NW Trinidad, 6 (SFAVC). *Houston Co.*: 5.7 mi. N Ratcliff, 5 (UTAVC); 2 mi. W Ratcliff, 1 (SFAVC); 15 mi. NE Crockett, 3 (TNHC). *Hunt Co.*: Sabine River bottom, Lake Tawakoni, 3 (FWMSH). *Jasper Co.*: Jasper, 3 (USNM). *Jefferson Co.*: Lower Neches Valley Authority pump station, Pine Island Bayou, 1 (TCWC). *Kaufman Co.*: 1 mi. W Rosser, 1 (SFAVC). *Leon Co.*: 13 mi. SE Centerville, 2 (SFAVC). *Liberty Co.*: 6.5 mi. N Dayton, 1 (SFAVC); 12 mi. S Liberty, 1 (SFAVC); 3.1 mi. N, 3.8 mi. E Moss Hill, 19 (TCWC); 3.1 mi. N, 3.9 mi. E Moss Hill, 6 (TCWC); 3.1 mi. N, 4.3 mi. E Moss Hill, 23 (TCWC); 2.9 mi. N, 3.9 mi. E Moss Hill, 38 (TCWC); 2.5 mi. N, 3.8 mi. E Moss Hill, 34 (TCWC); 2.5 mi. N, 3.9 mi. E Moss Hill, 5 (TCWC); 2.5 mi. N, 4.3 mi. E Moss Hill, 25 (TCWC). *Marion Co.*: Jefferson, 1 (USNM). *Montgomery Co.*: 20 mi. SSW Huntsville, 1 (TNHC). *Nacogdoches Co.*: 17 mi. NW Nacogdoches, 1 (TNHC); 11 mi. NE Nacogdoches, 1 (SFAVC); 5 mi. NNE Nacogdoches, 1 (SFAVC); 1 mi. N Nacogdoches, 1 (SFAVC); 1 mi. NE Nacogdoches, 1 (TNHC); 6 mi. W Nacogdoches, 2 (TNHC); 4 mi. N Nacogdoches, 3 (SFAVC); 2 mi. W Nacogdoches, 1 (SFAVC); La Nana Creek, Nacogdoches, 1 (TTU), 16 (SFAVC); Nacogdoches, 17 (SFAVC); Stephen F. Austin University Farm, Nacogdoches, 2 (SFAVC); 1 mi. E Nacogdoches, 8 (SFAVC); 1 mi. E Nacogdoches, 4 (SFAVC), 34 (TNHC); 2 mi. E Nacogdoches, 1 (SFAVC); 5 mi. E Nacogdoches, 1 (SFAVC); 10 mi. E Nacogdoches, 1 (SFAVC); 8 mi. S Nacogdoches, 1 (SFAVC); 8.75 mi. SW Nacogdoches, 1 (SFAVC); 9.5 mi. SW Nacogdoches, 5 (TNHC), 1 (SFAVC); 12 mi. SW Nacogdoches, 17 (SFAVC), 2 (TNHC), 2 (TTU); Stephen F. Austin Experimental Farm, 2 (SFAVC); 13 mi. SW Nacogdoches, 2 (SFAVC); 14 mi. SW Nacogdoches, 1 (SFAVC); 20 mi. SW Nacogdoches, 10 (TNHC); Boggy Creek Marina, Sam Rayburn Reservoir, 1 (SFAVC). *Newton Co.*: 10 mi. N Burkeville, 2 (TCWC); 6.5 mi. N Burkeville, 3 (TCWC); 10 mi. E Burkeville, 2 (SFAVC); 7 mi. NW Newton, 1 (TTU); 6 mi. NW Newton, 3 (TTU); 15 mi. NE Buna, 12 (TNHC). *Panola Co.*: 2 mi. E Long Branch, 2 (SFAVC); 2 mi. SE Long Branch, 2 (SFAVC); 5 mi. SE Long Branch, 3 (SFAVC); 8 mi. SE Long Branch, 1 (SFAVC). *Polk Co.*: 14 mi. N Camden, 9 (TCWC), 2 (KU); 1 mi. S Livingston, 2 (TNHC); 0.7 mi. E, 0.6 mi. S Camp Ruby, 1 (TCWC); 2 mi. E, 1.7 mi. S Camp Ruby, 2 (TCWC); 5.8 mi. N Dallardsville on FM Rd. 1276, 3 (TCWC); 5.4 mi. N Dallardsville on FM Rd. 1276, 11 (TCWC); 4.9 mi. N Dallardsville on FM Rd. 1276, 9 (TCWC); 4.8 mi. N Dallardsville on FM Rd. 1276, 1 (TCWC); 2.2 mi. W, 1.4 mi. N Dallardsville, 3 (TCWC); 2 mi. W, 0.8 mi. N Dallardsville, 5 (TCWC); 4.8 mi. SW Dallardsville, 1.6 mi. NNW Segno, 1 (TCWC). *Rains Co.*: Sabine River bottom, below Iron Bridge Dam, 1 (FWMSH). *Red River Co.*: 18 mi. N Clarksville, 2 (TCWC); 14 mi. NE Clarksville, 3 (DMNHT); 5.5 mi. S Boxelder, 11 (DMNHT). *Rusk Co.*: NW bank Cherokee Lake, 3 (TCWC). *Sabine Co.*: 4 mi. W, 1 mi. E Milam, 5 (SWTS); 5 mi. S Milam, 1 (TNHC); Big Sandy Creek on Hwy. 87, 18 (DMNHT); Magasco, 1 (SFAVC). *San Augustine Co.*: 12 mi. SW San Augustine, 1 (SFAVC); 1 mi. NE Broaddus, 1 (SFAVC); 3 mi. S Broaddus, 1 (DMNHT). *San Jacinto Co.*: 3 mi. SE Coldsprings, 1 (TCWC); 7 mi. S Coldsprings, 1 (TCWC). *Shelby Co.*: Shelbyville, 1 (SFAVC); 8 mi. E Shelbyville, 1 (TNHC); 20 mi. E Shelbyville, Toledo Bend, 1 (TWC). *Smith Co.*: 3 mi. N Loop 323, Tyler, 1 (TCWC); 6 mi. SE Chandler, 15 (SFAVC). *Tyler Co.*: 2.3 mi. W, 0.5 mi. S Town Bluff, 1 (TCWC); 1.7 mi. S, 1.8 mi. W Town Bluff, 7 (TCWC); 1.9 mi. S, 2.9 mi. W Town Bluff, 16 (TCWC); 1.8 mi. W, 2.8 mi. S Town Bluff, 6 (TCWC); 3.6 mi. S, 2.9 mi. W Town Bluff, 26 (TCWC); 3.1 mi. N, 2.6 mi. W Spurger, 9 (TCWC); 3.1 mi. N, 2.5 mi. W Spurger, 3 (TCWC); 2.8 mi. N, 2.7 mi. W Spurger, 1 (TCWC); 2.1 mi. N, 2.5 mi. E Spurger, 1 (TCWC); 2 mi. N, 2.5 mi. E Spurger, 1 (TCWC); 1.8 mi. N, 2.6 mi. W Spurger, 4 (TCWC); 1.7 mi. N, 1.6 mi. W Spurger, 11 (TCWC); 0.5 mi. N, 3.2 mi. E Warren, 1 (TCWC); 3.2 mi. E Warren, 4 (TCWC); 3.9 mi. E Warren, 6 (TCWC); 0.6 mi. S, 3.9 mi. E Warren, 3 (TCWC); 2.7 mi. E, 2 mi. S Warren, 1 (TCWC); 3.3 mi. SE Warren, 1 (TCWC); 4.2 mi. S, 1.6 mi. W Warren, 7 (TCWC); 4.3 mi. S, 1.4 mi. W Warren, 4 (TCWC); 4.6 mi. SE Warren, 3 (TCWC); 5.5 mi. SE Warren, 4 (TCWC). *Walker Co.*: 7 mi. WNW Huntsville, 1 (TCWC); 7 mi. E Huntsville, 3 (TCWC); 6 mi. S Huntsville, 1 (TCWC); 20 mi. SSW Huntsville, 1 (TNHC).

Peromyscus pectoralis laceianus (41). *Bosque Co.*: 10 mi. W of Meridian, 1 (BUSM). *Hays Co.*: 7 mi. ESE Wimberly, Fern Banks Spring, 1 (TCWC); San Marcos, 3 (UMMZ). *Travis Co.*: 18 mi. NW Austin, 1 (UIMNH); 8 mi. NW Austin, 1 (UIMNH); 1.2 mi. N Mt. Bonnell, Austin, 5 (TNHC); 5 mi. W Austin, 1 (TNHC); Austin, 6 (UMMZ); Miller Dam, Lake Austin, 4 (TNHC), 3 (MVZ); Lake Austin, 6 (MVZ); 4 mi. SW Austin, 3 (UMMZ), 5 (TNHC). *Williamson Co.*: 3 mi. NW McNeil, 1 (TNHC).

Ochrotomys nuttalli lisae (207). *Anderson Co.*: 20 mi. NW Palestine, 1 (SFAVC), 5 (TNHC). *Angelina Co.*: 20 mi. SW Nacogdoches, 3 (SFAVC); Lufkin, 1 (SFAVC). *Cherokee Co.*: 2 mi. N Rusk, 1 (SFAVC); Rusk, 1 (SFAVC); 5 mi. E Rusk, 1 (SFAVC); 3 mi. SE Rusk, 1 (SFAVC). *Hardin Co.*: 1.8 mi. S, 2.9 mi. E Village Mills, 2 (TCWC); 6 mi. S, 4.3 mi. E Warren, 1 (TCWC); 11 mi. N, 2.8 mi. E Silsbee, 1 (TCWC); Rosier Park, Saratoga, 11 (TCWC); 4.6 mi. E Saratoga, Hwy. 770, 3 (TCWC). *Harrison Co.*: 16 mi. NE Marshall, 1 (TNHC); 15 mi. NE Marshall, 1 (SFAVC); 8 mi. E Longview, 1 (SFAVC); 1 mi. N jct. IH 20 and Hwy. 31, 2 (DMNHT). *Houston Co.*: 5.7 mi. N Ratcliff, 1 (UTAVC). *Jasper Co.*: Angelina National Forest, Bouton Lake, 4 (UTAVC). *Liberty Co.*: 3.1 mi. N, 3.8 mi. E Moss Hill, 1 (TCWC); 3.1 mi. N, 4.3 mi. E Moss Hill, 2 (TCWC); 2.9 mi. N, 3.9 mi. E Moss Hill, 5 (TCWC); 2.5 mi. N, 3.8 mi. E Moss Hill, 3 (TCWC); 2.5 mi. N, 4.3 mi. E Moss Hill, 2 (TCWC). *Marion Co.*: Lake of the Pines, 5 (DMNHT). *Nacogdoches Co.*: 3 mi. N Nacogdoches, 1 (SFAVC); 1.5 mi. NE Nacogdoches, 1 (SFAVC); 6 mi. W Nacogdoches, 1 (SFAVC); 4 mi. W Nacogdoches, 1 (SFAVC); Nacogdoches, 2 (UMMZ), 10 (SFAVC); La Nana Creek, Nacogdoches, 12 (SFAVC); Bonita Creek, Nacogdoches, 1 (SFAVC); Stephen F. Austin Experimental Forest, 8 (SFAVC); 1 mi. E Nacogdoches, 7 (SFAVC); 2 mi. S Nacogdoches, 1 (SFAVC); 9.5 mi. SW Nacogdoches, 4 (TNHC); 10 mi. SW Nacogdoches, 1 (SFAVC); 14 mi. SW Nacogdoches, 1 (SFAVC); 12 mi. N Lufkin, 1 (TCWC). *Newton Co.*: 10.5 mi. N Burkeville, 1 (TCWC). *Panola Co.*: 4 mi. SE Long Branch, 1 (SFAVC). *Polk Co.*: 5.8 mi. N Dallardsville, 3 (TCWC); 5.4 mi. N Dallardsville, FM Rd. 1276, 6 (TCWC); 4.9 mi. N Dallardsville, FM Rd. 1276, 2 (TCWC); 4.8 mi. SW Dallardsville, FM Rd. 1276, 1.6 mi. NNW Segno, 4 (TCWC); 3.8 mi. S Segno, FM Rd. 943, 1 (TCWC); Menard Creek, lower end FM Rd. 943, 1 (TCWC); Big Sandy Creek, 1 (TCWC). *Red River Co.*: 14 mi. NE Clarksville, 6 (DMNHT). *Rusk Co.*: 2 mi. E Old London, 2 (SFAVC). *Sabine Co.*: Big Sandy Creek, Hwy. 87, 1 (DMNHT). *Shelby Co.*: Joaquin, 1 (USNM). *Tyler Co.*: 1.9 mi. S, 1.5 mi. E Town Bluff, 5 (TCWC); 1.8 mi. W, 2.8 mi. S Town Bluff, 10 (TCWC); 3.1 mi. N, 2.6 mi. W Spurger, 1 (TCWC); 3.1 mi. N, 2.5 mi. W Spurger, 2 (TCWC); 1.7 mi. N, 1.6 mi. W Spurger, 3 (TCWC); 3.2 mi. E Warren, 2 (TCWC); 3.9 mi. E Warren, 9 (TCWC); 0.6 mi. S, 3.9 mi. E Warren, 2 (TCWC); 4.3 mi. S, 1.1 mi. W Warren, 2 (TCWC); 4.3 mi. S, 1.4 mi. W Warren, 2 (TCWC); 4.3 mi. SE Warren, 10 (TCWC); 4.6 mi. SE Warren, 4 (TCWC); 5.5 mi. SE Warren, 4 (TCWC); 5.6 mi. SE Warren, 3 (TCWC); 5.8 mi. S, 4.3 mi. E Warren, 2 (TCWC). *Wood Co.*: 2 mi. SW Little Hope, 1 (BUSM); 1.6 mi. S, 3 mi. E Quitman, 1 (BUSM); 3 mi. SE Quitman, 1 (DMNHT); 3 mi. E, 6 mi. S Quitman, 1 (BUSM).

Baiomys taylori subater (156). *Brazoria Co.*: Austin Bayou, near Alvin, 2 (USNM); Barnard Creek, W of Columbia, 7 (USNM). *Brazos Co.*: Bryan, 1 (TCWC); 4 mi. NW College Station, 1 (TCWC); 0.5 mi. NW College Station, 1 (MVZ), 3 (TCWC); 3 mi. W College Station, 1 (TCWC); 1 mi. W College Station, 1 (TTU), 2 (TCWC); College Station, jct. Hwy. 6 and Hwy. 30, 1 (TCWC); 1 mi. SW College Station, 1 (TCWC); 1 mi. S College Station, 2 (TCWC); 2 mi. S College Station, 1 (TCWC); 3 mi. SW College Station, 1 (TCWC); 7 mi. SW College Station, 1 (TCWC). *Colorado Co.*: 10 mi. N Eagle Lake, 1 (TCWC); 7 mi. N Eagle Lake, 1 (TCWC). *Fort Bend Co.*: Richmond, 4 (USNM). *Galveston Co.*: Texas City, 2 (SFAVC); Virginia Point, 1 (USNM). *Hardin Co.*: 1.5 mi. N Sour Lake, 1 (UIMNH); 2.5 mi. W Sour Lake, 20 (UIMNH); Sour Lake, 1 (USNM). *Jefferson Co.*: La Belle, 65 (UMMZ); La Belle, near Fannett, 2 (TTU); 7 mi. S La Belle, 12 (KU). *Lavaca Co.*: 4 mi. W Hallettsville, 2 (TCWC); 1 mi. SW Hallettsville, 3 (TCWC); 13.7 mi. WSW Hallettsville, 2 (TCWC). *Liberty Co.*: Hardin, 1 (TNHC). *Madison Co.*: 0.5 mi. S jct. Hwy. 21 and IH 45, 3 (TCWC); 1 mi. S jct. Hwy. 21 and IH 45, 3 (TCWC). *Walker Co.*: 19 mi. NW Huntsville, 5 (TTU); Huntsville, 1 (TCWC).

Baiomys taylori taylori (81). *Caldwell Co.*: 3 mi. NE Lytton Springs, 1 (TCWC). *Cooke Co.*: near Gainesville, 2 (USNM). *Dallas Co.*: near Lancaster, 3 (DMNHT). *Goliad Co.*: 8 mi. NE Goliad, 1 (TNHC). *Gonzales Co.*: Palmetto State Park, 2 (TNHC); 5 mi. SE Gonzales, 1 (SWTS); 7 mi. SE Luling, 2 (TNHC). *Hill Co.*: 3.4 mi. S, 1.6 mi. W Hillboro, 1 (TCWC). *Jackson Co.*: 3 mi. S Lolita, 20 ft., 1 (TCWC). *Matagorda Co.*: 10 mi. N Bay City, 6 (TCWC); Matagorda, 4 mi.

W Palacios, 2 ft., 2 (TCWC); Matagorda Peninsula, 7 (USNM). *McLennan Co.*: 2.5 mi. SW Ross, 3 (BUSM); 4.8 mi. SW Waco, 2 (BUSM); Troy, 1 (BUSM). *Tarrant Co.*: Benbrook Lake, 2 (UTAVC). *Travis Co.*: 15 mi. N Austin, 1 (TNHC); 8 mi. NW Austin, 2 (TNHC); 5 mi. N Austin, 2 (TNHC); Austin, 2 (TNHC); 4 mi. E Austin, 6 (TNHC); 5 mi. E Austin, 3 (TNHC); 6 mi. E Austin, 23 (TNHC); 7 mi. E Austin, 1 (TNHC).

Sigmodon hispidus texianus (934). *Anderson Co.*: 10 mi. SW Elkhart, 1 (SFAVC). *Angelina Co.*: 20 mi. SW Nacogdoches, 1 (SFAVC); Lufkin, 3 (SFAVC). *Bell Co.*: 1 mi. W Killeen, 3 (BUSM). *Bexar Co.*: 1.47 mi. W San Antonio River, San Antonio, 2 (UIMNH). *Bosque Co.*: 7.7 mi. W, 8.5 mi. N Waco, 1 (BUSM); Wallet Bend Park, Lake Whitney, 1 (DMNHT). *Bowie Co.*: 4 mi. SW DeKalb, 9 (TCWC). *Brazoria Co.*: 1.5 mi. W, 1.5 mi. SW Columbia, 2 (KU); Velasco, 1 (USNM); 3 mi. E Surfside, 2 (UTAVC); Freeport Beach, 5 mi. S Freeport, 6 (UTAVC). *Brazos Co.*: Bryan, 4 (UMMZ), 5 (TCWC); Bryan, 0.2 mi. S jct. Reliance Rd. and Hwy. 6 bypass, 1 (TCWC); 1 mi. S Bryan, 1 (UMMZ); 1.5 mi. S Bryan, 2 (UMMZ); 4.5 mi. SE Bryan, 2 (BUSM); 2 mi. N College Station, 2 (TCWC); 1 mi. N College Station, 5 (TNHC); 1 mi. N Texas A&M University, College Station, 1 (TCWC); 0.75 mi. N FM Rd. 60, 2 (TCWC); 0.5 mi. NW College Station, 3 (TCWC); 0.25 mi. NW College Station, 2 (UMMZ); 5 mi. W Texas A&M University, 1 (TCWC); 4 mi. SW College Station, 1 (TCWC); 3 mi. W College Station, Fish Lake, 1 (UMMZ); 3 mi. W College Station, 1 (UIMNH); 1 mi. W College Station, 1 (TCWC); College Station, 11 (UMMZ), 8 (UIMNH), 24 (TCWC); Texas A&M University Range Area, College Station, 6 (TCWC); 3 mi. E College Station, 2 (TCWC); 0.2 mi. S College Station, 1 (TCWC); 0.5 mi. S College Station, 1 (UMMZ); College Station, 0.6 mi. S jct. FM Rd. 2818 and Hwy. 60, 4 (TCWC); 1 mi. S College Station, 6 (TCWC); 1.2 mi. S College Station, 2 (TCWC); 2 mi. S College Station, 1 (UMMZ), 4 (TCWC); 3 mi. SW College Station, 1 (UIMNH); 3 mi. S College Station, 2 (TCWC); 4 mi. S College Station, 4 (TCWC); 6 mi. SE College Station, 1 (TCWC); 7 mi. SW College Staion, 7 (TCWC); 7 mi. S, 4 mi. W College Station, 3 (TCWC); 7 mi. S College Station, 1 (TCWC). *Caldwell Co.*: 3 mi. NE Lytton Springs, 1 (TCWC). *Calhoun Co.*: Port Lavaca, 6 (USNM); 4 mi. E Port Lavaca, 1 (TCWC); 7 mi. S, 1 mi. E Port Lavaca, 29 (TCWC); 1 mi. S, 3.5 mi. W Port O'Connor, 4 (TCWC); 7 mi. S, 1 mi. E Port O'Connor, 1 (TCWC). *Chambers Co.*: 6 mi. SE Mt. Belview, 2 (TNHC); 3 mi. NE Cedar Bayou, 2 (TNHC); Anahuac National Wildlife Refuge, 1 (TCWC). *Cherokee Co.*: 1.5 mi. S Gallatin, 1 (SFAVC); 1.5 mi. N Maydelle, 1 (SFAVC); 2 mi. N Maydelle, 1 (SFAVC); Alto, 1 (TWC). *Colorado Co.*: 6 mi. NNW Eagle Lake, 3 (TCWC). *Cooke Co.*: near Gainesville, 11 (USNM); Camp Howze, 8 (MVZ). *Dallas Co.*: Carrollton, 2 (UTAVC); 2 mi. W Farmers Branch, 4 (UTAVC); N of White Rock Lake, 7 (DMNHT); MKT railroad trestle over White Rock Creek, 1 (DMNHT); 3.9 mi. N Hwy. 183 on County Line Rd., 3 (UTAVC); Dallas, 8 (DMNHT), 2 (UTAVC); NW of Mt. Creek Lake, 1 (DMNHT); Audubon Reserve, Mt. Creek Lake, 7 (UTAVC); 3 mi. WSW Dallas, Mt. Creek Lake, 1 (TNHC); S Mt. Creek Lake, 1 (UTAVC); 1 mi. W DeSoto, 1 (UTAVC). *Delta Co.*: 0.5 mi. S Liberty Grove, 1 (TWC). *Denton Co.*: 1 mi. N, 2.7 mi. W Krum, 1 (TCWC); 1 mi. N Krum, 2 (TCWC). *Ellis Co.*: Ennis, 350 ft., 4 (TCWC). *Fort Bend Co.*: Richmond, 4 (USNM). *Freestone Co.*: 1.8 mi. NE Fairfield, 1 (TCWC); Big Brown Reservoir, 10 mi. E Fairfield, 1 (UTAVC). *Galveston Co.*: 1 mi. N Texas City, 5 (TCWC), 4 (MVZ); 0.5 mi. S Dickinson Bayou bridge, Texas City, 15 (TTU); 9 mi. W Galveston, 1 (TNHC). *Grayson Co.*: Sherman, 9 (MVZ). *Gregg Co.*: 8 mi. NW Longview, 1 (SFAVC); 5 mi. E Kilgore, 2 (TNHC). *Guadalupe Co.*: Seguin, 1 (USNM). *Hardin Co.*: 4.3 mi. S, 1.4 mi. W Warren, 1 (TCWC); 4.3 mi. S, 1.1 mi.

W Warren, 1 (TCWC); 6 mi. S, 4.3 mi. E Warren, 1 (TCWC); 7.7 mi. N Silsbee, 3 (TCWC); 0.9 mi. N, 5 mi. E Saratoga, 2 (TCWC); Rosier Park, Saratoga, 1 (TCWC); 1.5 mi. N Sour Lake, 1 (UIMNH); Sour Lake, 7 (USNM), 2 (UIMNH). *Harris Co.*: Houston, 2 (SFAVC), 4 (KU); 1.7 mi. S jct. Hwy. 80 and Voss Rd., Houston, 4 (KU); 2 mi. SE Houston, 1 (TCWC); 25 mi. SE Houston, 2 (MVZ); 1 mi. S Pasadena, 1 (TCWC); 3 mi. N Mason Bay, La Porte, 1 (TCWC); 3 mi. N Webster, 2 (TCWC). *Harrison Co.*: 8 mi. E Longview, 1 (SFAVC). *Henderson Co.*: 2 mi. NE Malakoff, 1 (SFAVC); 1 mi. NE Malakoff, 5 (SFAVC); 0.5 mi. NE Malakoff, 1 (SFAVC). *Hill Co.*: Spivey Crossing, 5 mi. NW jct. FM Rd. 933 and FM Rd. 2114, 2 (TCWC); 14 mi. W Hillsboro, 5 (TWC); 3.4 mi. E, 1.6 mi. W Hillsboro, 5 (TCWC); 3.4 mi. S, 5.1 mi. W Hillsboro, 2 (TCWC); 3.4 mi. S, 1.6 mi. W Hillsboro, 6 (TCWC); 4.5 mi. S, 5.8 mi. W Hillsboro, 1 (TCWC); 6 mi. S, 4.2 mi. W Hillsboro, 2 (TCWC); 8.3 mi. SW Hillsboro, 1 (TCWC); 8.9 mi. SW Hillsboro, 1 (TCWC). *Hopkins Co.*: 5 mi. N Peerless, 1 (TWC). *Houston Co.*: no specific locality, 1 (SFAVC). *Hunt Co.*: Lake Tawakoni, 1 (FWMSH). *Jackson Co.*: 1 mi. N Edna, 1 (TCWC). *Jasper Co.*: Kirbyville, 23 (USNM). *Jefferson Co.*: Lower Neches Valley Authority pumping station, Pine Island Bayou, 3 (TCWC); 5 mi. W Beaumont, 1 (TNHC); Beaumont, 1 (TCWC), 3 (UMMZ), 1 (MVZ), 1 (TNHC); 3 mi. S Beaumont, 2 (MVZ); 3.7 mi. N Nome, 2 (UIMNH); 3.5 mi. N Nome, 5 (UIMNH); Sabine, 1 (USNM). *Kaufman Co.*: no specific locality, 2 (DMNHT). *Liberty Co.*: 2.5 mi. N, 3.8 mi. E Moss Hill, 2 (TCWC). *Limestone Co.*: 2.1 mi. SE jct. Hwy. 14, and Springfield Rd., 1 (BUSM); 2 mi. S Shiloh, 2 (BUSM). *Madison Co.*: Madisonville, 0.5 mi. S jct. Hwy. 21 and IH 45, 3 (TCWC); Madisonville, 1 mi. S jct. Hwy. 21 and IH 45, 2 (TCWC). *Matagorda Co.*: 10 mi. N Bay City, 7 (TCWC); Matagorda, 20 (USNM). *McLennan Co.*: 2.5 mi. SW Ross, 2 (BUSM); Bellmead, 1 (BUSM); Lake Waco, 1 (UTAVC); Baylor Camp, 10 mi. NW Waco, 1 (BUSM); 6.5 mi. NW Waco, 2 (BUSM); 5 mi. N Waco, 1 (BUSM); Baylor Camp, 15 mi. W Waco, 1 (BUSM); Baylor Camp, 10 mi. W Waco, 5 (BUSM); 8 mi. W Waco, 3 (BUSM); 6 mi. W Waco, 1 (BUSM); Veterans Administration hospital, 2 mi. W Waco, 2 (BUSM); Veterans Administration hospital, 3 mi SW Waco, 1 (BUSM); Waco, 15 (BUSM), 1 (MVZ); Baylor University Natural Science Area, Waco, 2 (BUSM); 0.5 mi. S Baylor Camp, Waco, 1 (BUSM); 1 mi. S Waco, 1 (BUSM); 4.5 mi. SW Waco, 1 (BUSM); 4.8 mi. SW Waco, 5 (BUSM); 5 mi. S Waco, 5 (BUSM), 3 (UTAVC); Bagby, 5 mi. SE Waco, 1 (BUSM); 5.5 mi. S Waco, 1 (BUSM); 0.4 mi. W Robinson, 1 (BUSM). *Nacogdoches Co.*: 7 mi. NW Nacogdoches, 1 (SFAVC); 3 mi. NW Nacogdoches, 1 (SFAVC); 1 mi. NE Nacogdoches, 1 (SFAVC); 1 mi. W Nacogdoches, 1 (SFAVC); Nacogdoches, 22 (SFAVC); Stephen F. Austin College Farm, Nacogdoches, 1 (SFAVC); Stephen F. Austin University, Nacogdoches, 1 (TTU); 2 mi. E Nacogdoches, 1 (SFAVC); Stephen F. Austin Experimental Forest, 11 mi. SW Nacogdoches, 3 (SFAVC). *Navarro Co.*: 4 mi. W Kerens, 1 (SFAVC). *Newton Co.*: 9.5 mi. N Burkeville, 1 (TCWC); 6.5 mi. N Burkeville, 1 (TCWC). *Orange Co.*: Orange, 2 (UIMNH). *Polk Co.*: 6.5 mi. N Dallardsville, 1 (TCWC); 1.8 mi. S Segno, FM Rd. 943, 6 (TCWC); 3.8 mi. S Segno, FM Rd. 943, 6 (TCWC). *Rains Co.*: 5.5 mi. E Rains County Courthouse, Emory, 1 (KU). *Red River Co.*: Cuthand, 16 (UTAVC). *Robertson Co.*: 2 mi. W Hearne, 1 (TCWC); 2 mi. W, 1.5 mi. S Hearne, 1 (TCWC). *Rusk Co.*: 1.7 mi. N Old London, 3 (SFAVC); 2 mi. SW Old London, 1 (SFAVC). *Sabine Co.*: Big Sandy Creek, Hwy. 87, 6 (DMNHT). *Shelby Co.*: Shelbyville, 1 (SFAVC). *Smith Co.*: 6.5 mi. W Tyler, 1 (SFAVC); Tyler, 1 (TCWC). *Tarrant Co.*: Hurst, 4 (FWMSH), 1 (UTAVC); 3 mi. W Arlington, 2 (TWC); 1 mi. W Arlington, 2 (TWC); Arlington, 35 (UTAVC), 3 (TCWC); Poly Webb Rd., between Arlington and Watsonville, 4 (UTAVC); 4 mi. S Arlington, FM Rd. 157, 2 (UTAVC); 4 mi. S

Arlington, 2 (UTAVC); 7 mi. SW Arlington, 3 (TWC); 10 mi. S Arlington, 3 (UTAVC); 12 mi. NE Fort Worth, 1 (TNHC); 7 mi. W Fort Worth, 2 (UTAVC); 1 mi. W Fort Worth, 2 (UTAVC); Fort Worth, 3 (TCWC), 38 (FWMSH), 3 (TNHC), 8 (TWC), 56 (UTAVC); Village Creek sewage plant, 3 (UTAVC); Grapevine, jct. Hwy. 114 and FM Rd. 157, 1 (UTAVC); 10 mi. E Fort Worth, 1 (TWC); 5 mi. S Fort Worth, 1 (UMMZ); Benbrook Lake, 2 (UTAVC); 7 mi. SW Benbrook, 7 (TWC); 3 mi. SE Roanoke, 2 (DMNHT); Crestwood, 6 (FWMSH); 2 mi. E Webb, 1 (UTAVC); 4 mi. N Mansfield, 1 (TWC); Hwy. 157, N Mansfield, 2 (UTAVC); Mansfield, 1 (UTAVC). *Travis Co.*: 9 mi. NW Austin, 2 (TNHC); 1 mi. NW Austin, 2 (TCWC); Austin, 1 (TNHC); University of Texas, Austin, 1 (TNHC); Lake Austin, 3 (MVZ); 4 mi. E Austin, 5 (TNHC); 5 mi. E Austin, 21 (TNHC); 6 mi. E Austin, 22 (TNHC); 7 mi. E Austin, 1 (TNHC); 6 mi. E Lockhart, 1 (TCWC). *Trinity Co.*: 3 mi. E Trinity, 1 (TCWC). *Tyler Co.*: 0.5 mi. S, 2.3 mi. W Town Bluff, 16 (TCWC); 3.6 mi. S, 2.9 mi. W Town Bluff, 2 (TCWC); 2 mi. N, 2.2 mi. E Spurger, 1 (TCWC); 1.8 mi. N, 2.6 mi. W Spurger, 1 (TCWC); 1.9 mi. W, 1.2 mi. N Spurger, 14 (TCWC); 2.6 mi. S, 3.9 mi. E Warren, 1 (TCWC); 4.2 mi. S, 0.8 mi. W Warren, 2 (TCWC); 4.3 mi. S, 1.1 mi. E Warren, 2 (TCWC); 4.8 mi. S, 0.7 mi. W Warren, 1 (TCWC); 5.8 mi. S, 1.1 mi. E Warren, 2 (TCWC). *Walker Co.*: 3 mi. E Riverside, 1 (TCWC); 20 mi. W Huntsville, 1 (TCWC); Huntsville, 4 (TCWC); 1 mi. S Huntsville, 1 (TCWC). *Waller Co.*: Hempstead, 5 (USNM). *Washington Co.*: Long Point, 2 (USNM).

   Neotoma floridana attwateri (112). *Brazos Co.*: 3 mi. W Bryan, 1 (TCWC); 6 mi. SE Bryan, 3 (MVZ); 7 mi. W College Station, 1 (TCWC); 3 mi. W College Station, 1 (TCWC); 2 mi. W College Station, 1 (TCWC); Texas A&M University Range Area, College Station, 5 (TCWC); College Station, 1 (TCWC); 1 mi. E College Station, 1 (TCWC); 12 mi. E College Station, 1 (TCWC); 2 mi. SW College Station, 1 (TCWC); 3 mi. SW College Station, 4 (TCWC); 3 mi. S College Station, 2 (TCWC); 3 mi. SE College Station, 4 (TCWC); 4 mi. SW College Station, 1 (TCWC); 5 mi. SE College Station, 1 (TCWC); 7 mi. SW College Station, 2 (TCWC); 10 mi. SE College Station, 1 (TCWC). *Burleson Co.*: S side Somerville Lake, 1 (TCWC). *Caldwell Co.*: 3 mi. N Lytton Springs, 2 (SWTS); 3 mi. NE Lytton, 2 (TCWC); 5 mi. SW Lockhart, 5 (SWTS); 7 mi. SW Lockhart, 1 (SWTS); 8 mi. SW Lockhart, 1 (SWTS); 3 mi. S Martindale, 1 (SWTS); 1 mi. E Stairtown, 1 (SWTS); 2 mi. E Stairtown, 1 (SWTS). *Colorado Co.*: 11 mi. W Altair, 1 (TCWC). *Cooke Co.*: Marysville, 2 (USNM); Gainesville, 3 (USNM); Camp Howze, 1 (MVZ). *Dallas Co.*: White Rock Lake, 1 (DMNHT); Irving, 1 (DMNHT); Dallas, 1 (DMNHT). *Delta Co.*: 3 mi. W Delta, 1 (TWC); 3 mi. SW Delta, 1 (TWC); 1 mi. E Liberty Grove, 1 (TWC). *Denton Co.*: no specific locality, 1 (DMNHT). *Gonzales Co.*: Palmetto State Park, 1 (TNHC); 2 mi. W jct. Hwy. 183 and FM Rd. 3282, 1 (SWTS); 7 mi. E Gonzales, 3 (SWTS); 7 mi. ESE Gonzales, 4 (SWTS); 5.1 mi. S Gonzales, 2 (SWTS). *Gregg Co.*: 3.2 mi. E Gladewater, 1 (TTU). *Grimes Co.*: 4 mi. N Carlos, 1 (TCWC); Navasota, 3 (USNM). *Harrison Co.*: 7 mi. NE Longview, 1 (SFAVC). *Henderson Co.*: 12 mi. SE Athens, 2 (SFAVC); 2 mi. NE Malakoff, 3 (SFAVC). *Hill Co.*: Spivey Crossing, 3 mi. NW jct. FM Rd. 933 and FM Rd. 2114, 1 (TCWC). *Hunt Co.*: 16 mi. N Greenville, 1 (TCWC). *Kaufman Co.*: no specific locality, 1 (DMNHT). *Lamar Co.*: 21 mi. W Paris, 1 (SFAVC). *Lavaca Co.*: 3 mi. W Hallettsville, 1 (TCWC); 14 mi. WSW Hallettsville, 1 (TCWC); 14 mi. SW Hallettsville, 2 (SWTS); 0.5 mi. W Sweet Home, 1 (TCWC). *McLennan Co.*: 2.5 mi. SW Ross, 1 (BUSM); 8.5 mi. N Waco, 1 (BUSM). *Robertson Co.*: 2 mi. W Hearne, 2 (TCWC). *Smith Co.*: 4 mi. S Tyler, 1 (TCWC). *Tarrant Co.*: Keller, 1 (TWC); 1.5 mi. E jct. Hwy. 157 and Arlington Rd., 1 (UTAVC); Lake Worth, 1 (FWMSH); Fort Worth, 1 (FWMSH); 3 mi. SE Roanoke, 1

(DMNHT); Bear Creek, 3 mi. upstream from Benbrook Lake, 2 (FWMSH). *Travis Co.*: 7 mi. W Austin, 1 (TNHC); Austin, 1 (USNM). *Victoria Co.*: Victoria, 5 (USNM). *Williamson Co.*: 3 mi. N McNeil, 1 (TNHC).

Neotoma floridana illinoensis (3). *Bowie Co.*: 8 mi. N New Boston, 1 (TCWC); Bowie Lake, Texarkana, 1 (USNM); Texarkana, 1 (USNM).

Neotoma floridana rubida (164). *Anderson Co.*: Engling Wildlife Management Area, 6 mi. SE Cayuga, 1 (BUSM); 20 mi. NW Palestine, 1 (TCWC); 5.5 mi. SE Slocum, 1 (SFAVC). *Angelina Co.*: Diboll, 1 (SFAVC). *Cherokee Co.*: 3 mi. SW Maydelle, 1 (SFAVC); 3 mi. S Maydelle, 1 (SFAVC); 0.5 mi. N Forest, 1 (SFAVC); 3 mi. W Forest, 1 (SFAVC); 3 mi. SW Forest, 1 (SFAVC). *Hardin Co.*: Kountze, 2 (USNM); 11 mi. N, 2.8 mi. E Silsbee, 1 (TCWC); 10.9 mi. N, 1.8 mi. E Silsbee, 2 (TCWC); 10.9 mi. N, 2.3 mi. E Silsbee, 3 (TCWC); 9.4 mi. N, 1.8 mi. E Silsbee, 1 (TCWC); 9 mi. N, 0.8 mi. E Silsbee, 3 (TCWC); 9 mi. N, 1.3 mi. E Silsbee, 1 (TCWC); 7.7 mi. N Silsbee, 2 (TCWC); 0.8 mi. N, 2.6 mi. E Saratoga, 2 (TCWC); Rosier Park, Saratoga, 1 (TCWC); 4.6 mi. E Saratoga, Hwy. 770, 16 (TCWC); 7 mi. NE Sour Lake, 8 (USNM); 8 mi. NE Sour Lake, 11 (USNM); Sour Lake, 3 (USNM). *Harris Co.*: 22 mi. N Houston, 1 (SFAVC). *Houston Co.*: 6.3 mi. N Ratcliff, 1 (UTAVC). *Jefferson Co.*: Beaumont, 5 (UMMZ). *Liberty Co.*: 2.5 mi. N, 3.8 mi. N Moss Hill, 9 (TCWC); 3.1 mi. N, 3.8 mi. E Moss Hill, 4 (TCWC); 3.1 mi. N, 3.9 mi. E Moss Hill, 3 (TCWC); 3.1 mi. N, 4.3 mi. E Moss Hill, 2 (TCWC); 2.9 mi. N, 3.9 mi. E Moss Hill, 4 (TCWC); 2.5 mi. N, 4.3 mi. E Moss Hill, 4 (TCWC). *Nacogdoches Co.*: 2 mi. NW Nacogdoches, 1 (SFAVC); Nacogdoches, 8 (SFAVC); Bonita Creek, Nacogdoches, 1 (SFAVC); La Nana Creek, Nacogdoches, 1 (SFAVC); 0.75 mi. E Nacogdoches, 1 (TTU); 1 mi. E Stephen F. Austin University, Nacogdoches, 1 (TTU); 1 mi. E Nacogdoches, 1 (SFAVC); 3 mi. E Nacogdoches, 1 (SFAVC); 5 mi. S Nacogdoches, 1 (SFAVC); 7 mi. S Nacogdoches, 1 (SFAVC); 8 mi. S Nacogdoches, 1 (SFAVC); 10 mi. SW Nacogdoches, 2 (SFAVC). *Newton Co.*: 10.5 mi. N Burkeville, 1 (TCWC); 9.3 mi. N Burkeville, 1 (TCWC). *Panola Co.*: 5 mi. W Carthage, 1 (SFAVC). *Polk Co.*: 14 mi. N Camden, 4 (TCWC); 12 mi. W Camden, 1 (TCWC); 4.9 mi. N Dallardsville, 1 (TCWC); 4.8 mi. N Dallardsville, 1 (TCWC). *Rusk Co.*: 12 mi. S Henderson, 1 (TCWC). *Trinity Co.*: 1 mi. E Trinity, 1 (TCWC). *Tyler Co.*: 2.3 mi. W, 0.5 mi. S Town Bluff, 3 (TCWC); 1.6 mi. S, 2.2 mi. W Town Bluff, 1 (TCWC); 1.7 mi. S, 1.8 mi. E Town Bluff, 1 (TCWC); 1.9 mi. S, 1.5 mi. E Town Bluff, 1 (TCWC); 2.8 mi. S, 1.8 mi. W Town Bluff, 1 (TCWC); 3.6 mi. S, 2.9 mi. W Town Bluff, 8 (TCWC); 1.2 mi. N, 1.9 mi. W Spurger, 1 (TCWC); 1.7 mi. N, 1.6 mi. W Spurger, 4 (TCWC); 2.1 mi. N, 2.6 mi. E Spurger, 1 (TCWC); 3.1 mi. N, 2.6 mi. W Spurger, 4 (TCWC); 3.1 mi. N, 2.5 mi. W Spurger, 5 (TCWC); 0.5 mi. N, 3.2 mi. E Warren, 1 (TCWC); 3.3 mi. E Warren, 3 (TCWC); 5.5 mi. SE Warren, 1 (TCWC). *Walker Co.*: 7 mi. WNW Huntsville, 1 (TCWC); Huntsville, 1 (TCWC); 4 mi. E Huntsville, 2 (TCWC); 1 mi. S Huntsville, 1 (TCWC); 2 mi. SW Huntsville, 1 (TCWC); 11 mi. NW New Waverly, 1 (TNHC).

Microtus ochrogaster ludovicianus (1). *Hardin Co.*: Sour Lake, 1 (USNM).

Microtus pinetorum nemoralis (4). *Bowie Co.*: 3 mi. N Leary, FM Rd. 2253, 1 (UTAVC); 2 mi. W Bassett, 2 (TNHC). *Grayson Co.*: no specific locality, 1 (SFAVC).

Microtus pinetorum auricularis (68). *Harrison Co.*: 1 mi. E Marshall, 9 (SWTS); 3 mi. E Marshall, 5 (SWTS); 2 mi. SE Marshall, 2 (SWTS); 4 mi. SE Marshall, 7 (SWTS); 7 mi. SSE Hallsville, 1 (SWTS); 1 mi. N jct. IH 20 and Hwy. 31, 10 (DMNHT). *Hill Co.*: 14 mi. W Hillsboro, 1 (TWC). *Marion Co.*: Jefferson, 2 (USNM). *Nacogdoches Co.*: La Nana Creek, 1 mi. E Nacogdoches, 5 (SFAVC), 3 (TNHC); La Nana Creek, 1.5 mi. E Nacogdoches, 1 (TTU); Nacogdoches,

4 (SFAVC). *Panola Co.*: Carthage, 10 (TCWC). *Smith Co.*: 20 mi. NE Tyler, 6 (SWTS). *Wood Co.*: Mann Lake #1, 1 (TNHC); 0.9 mi. W Little Hope, 1 (FWMSH).

Ondatra zibethicus cinnamominus (1). *Tarrant Co.*: Fort Worth, 1 (UTAVC).

Ondatra zibethicus rivalicius (9). *Chambers Co.*: 5 mi. S Stowell, 2 (TCWC). *Harris Co.*: 2 mi. SW Pasadena, 2 (TCWC). *Jefferson Co.*: Brakes Bayou, Beaumont, 1 (TNHC); Port Arthur, 2 (SFAVC); J. D. Murphree Wildlife Management Area, 1 (TCWC); 10 mi. SW Port Arthur, 1 (TCWC).

Rattus rattus (104). *Bastrop Co.*: 1306 Farm St., Bastrop, 1 (TCWC); Bastrop, 3 (TCWC). *Bell Co.*: 5 mi. W Temple, 1 (TCWC); 8 mi. SW Belton, 2 (TCWC). *Brazos Co.*: Bryan, 1 (TCWC); 2 mi. N College Station, 2 (TCWC); 1 mi. NW College Station, 1 (TCWC); 1 mi. W College Station, 2 (TCWC); 1 mi. W College Station, 1 (TCWC); College Station, 5 (TCWC); Texas A&M University campus, College Station, 2 (TCWC); 5 mi. E College Station, 1 (TCWC); 13 mi. S College Station, 2 (TCWC). *Collin Co.*: Spurlin Farm, 5 mi. SE Frisco, 1 (BUSM). *Dallas Co.*: Carrollton, 1 (DMNHT); 2 mi. W Farmers Branch, 1 (UTAVC); Dallas, 2 (DMNHT), 7 (UTAVC); Southern Methodist University, Dallas, 1 (DMNHT); DeSoto, 1 (UTAVC). *Ellis Co.*: 4 mi. NW Ennis, 1 (TCWC); Ennis, 1 (TCWC). *Denton Co.*: Justin, 1 (FWMSH). *Harris Co.*: 12 mi. N Baytown, 1 (TNHC). *Jefferson Co.*: 7 mi. N Winnie, 1 (TCWC). *Johnson Co.*: 22 mi. S Fort Worth, 2 (FWMSH); 6 mi. SE Mansfield, 2 (UTAVC). *Limestone Co.*: FM Rd. 1245, 45 mi. E Waco, 1 (BUSM). *McLennan Co.*: 2.5 mi. SW Ross, 1 (BUSM); 30 mi. W Waco, 1 (BUSM); 10 mi. W Waco, 2 (BUSM); Waco, 3 (BUSM); 5.8 mi. S Waco, 1 (BUSM); 10 mi. S Waco, 1 (BUSM). *Nacogdoches Co.*: Stephen F. Austin University, Nacogdoches, 1 (TTU). *Rockwall Co.*: Wiley, 1 (DMNHT). *Tarrant Co.*: Saginaw, 1 (TWC); Hurst, 4 (FWMSH); Arlington, 3 (UTAVC), 2 (TWC); University of Texas, Arlington, 6 (UTAVC); SW Arlington, 2 (UTAVC); Fort Worth, 5 (TWC), 9 (FWMSH); Arlington Heights, Fort Worth, 1 (FWMSH); 1.5 mi. E jct. IH 20 and Collin St., 1 (UTAVC). *Travis Co.*: 1 mi. NW Austin, 1 (TNHC); Austin, 4 (TNHC), 1 (USNM); University of Texas, Austin, 1 (TNHC); 5 mi. E Austin, 1 (TNHC). *Washington Co.*: Brenham, 1 (TNHC). *Bell-Williamson Co.*: Barlett, 1 (TCWC).

Rattus norvegicus (28). *Bastrop Co.*: Bastrop, 2 (TCWC). *Bexar Co.*: San Antonio, 1 (TNHC). *Brazos Co.*: Texas A&M University, College Station, 3 (TCWC). *Colorado Co.*: 2 mi. E Eagle Lake, 1 (TCWC). *Dallas Co.*: Richardson, 1 (UTAVC); Southern Methodist University, Dallas, 1 (DMNHT). *Delta Co.*: 1 mi. W Klondike, 1 (TWC). *Falls Co.*: 12 mi. E Marlin, 3 (BUSM). *Fayette Co.*: La Grange, 1 (TCWC). *Galveston Co.*: Galveston, 1 (TCWC). *Harris Co.*: Houston, 1 (USNM); 12 mi. N Baytown, 1 (TNHC); 3 mi. N Mason's Bay, La Porte, 1 (TCWC). *McLennan Co.*: Waco, 9 (BUSM). *Wharton Co.*: 7 mi. S El Campo, 1 (USNM).

Mus musculus brevirostris (170). *Bell Co.*: 3 mi. E Temple, 2 (TCWC). *Brazos Co.*: Bryan, 3 (TCWC); College Station, 5 (TCWC); 2 mi. E College Station, 1 (TCWC); Peach Creek, 13 mi. S College Station, 1 (TCWC). *Caldwell Co.*: 0.5 mi. S Mendoza, 1 (BUSM). *Chambers Co.*: 9 mi. E Double Bayou, 1 (USNM). *Cherokee Co.*: 4 mi. W Rusk, 1 (TCWC), 1 (TNHC). *Collin Co.*: no specific locality, 1 (DMNHT). *Cooke Co.*: Gainesville, 6 (USNM). *Dallas Co.*: 3.2 mi. W Farmers Branch, 1 (TCWC); 2 mi. W Farmers Branch, 3 (UTAVC); White Rock Creek, Dallas, 1 (DMNHT); 4 mi. N Irving, 1 (UTAVC); 3.9 mi. N Hwy. 183, 2 (UTAVC); Dallas, 6 (DMNHT); near Mt. Creek Lake, 1 (UTAVC). *Delta Co.*: 1 mi. S Liberty Grove, 1 (TWC). *De Witt Co.*: 5 mi. WSW Thomaston, 2 (TNHC). *Ellis Co.*: S Ennis, 3 (TCWC). *Freestone Co.*: 4 mi. W Teague, 1 (TCWC). *Gregg*

Co.: 5 mi. E Kilgore on FM Rd. 1249, 1 (TNHC). *Hardin Co.*: 11 mi. N, 2.8 mi. E Silsbee, 1 (TCWC). *Harris Co.*: 4 mi. N Huffman, 2 (TCWC); Houston, 1 (USNM), 1 (TNHC); 3 mi. NE Webster, 1 (TCWC). *Harrison Co.*: 3 mi. N Longview, 1 (TCWC). *Jackson Co.*: Lolita, 1 (TCWC). *Jefferson Co.*: 4.5 mi. NW Beaumont, 1 (TNHC); 5 mi. W Beaumont, 1 (TNHC). *Lavaca Co.*: 14 mi. S Hallettsville, 1 (TCWC). *Matagorda Co.*: Palacios, 1 (TCWC). *McLennan Co.*: 2.5 mi. SW Ross, 1 (BUSM); 5 mi. N Valley View, Fm Rd. 2490, 1 (BUSM); Waco, 11 (BUSM); Baylor University, Waco, 3 (BUSM); 8 mi. E Waco, Hwy. 6, 1 (BUSM); 1 mi. S Waco, 1 (BUSM); 2.6 mi. S Waco, 2 (BUSM); 4 mi. SW Waco, Hwy. 6, 1 (BUSM); 4.8 mi. SW Waco, 1 (BUSM); 10 mi. S Waco, 1 (BUSM); Crawford, 1 (BUSM). *Milam Co.*: Rockdale, 2 (TCWC). *Montgomery Co.*: 4 mi. S Montgomery, 1 (TCWC). *Nacogdoches Co.*: 9.5 mi. SW Nacogdoches, 1 (TNHC). *Navarro Co.*: Silver City Community, Purdon, 1 (TCWC). *Smith Co.*: Flint Community, 10 mi. S Tyler, 1 (TCWC). *Tarrant Co.*: Arlington, 13 (UTAVC); Fort Worth, 5 (FWMSH), 1 (TWC); 3 mi. E Fort Worth, 1 (TWC); 8 mi. S Fort Worth, 1 (TWC); Benbrook Lake, 2(FWMSH). *Travis Co.*: 9 mi. NW Austin, 1 (TNHC); Austin, 1 (TNHC); Balcones Research Center, Austin, 1 (TNHC); 4 mi. E Austin, 5 (TNHC); 6 mi. E Austin, 37 (TNHC); 7 mi. E Austin, 7 (TNHC); 10 mi. E Austin, 1 (TNHC). *Tyler Co.*: 3.6 mi. S, 2.9 mi. W Town Bluff, 1 (TCWC); 1.9 mi. N Spurger, 1 (TCWC); 5.5 mi. SE Warren, 1 (TCWC). *Williamson Co.*: 2 mi. S Taylor, 1 (TNHC). *Wood Co.*: 4 mi. W Mineola, 2 (TCWC).

Myocastor coypus bonariensis (40). *Bosque Co.*: 2 mi. E Valley Mills, 1 (BUSM). *Brazoria Co.*: 6 mi. S Danbury, 1 (SFAVC); 35 mi. S Danbury, 1 (SFAVC). *Chambers Co.*: 9 mi. E Double Bayou, 2 (USNM). *Colorado Co.*: Eagle Lake, 1 (UIMNH). *Dallas Co.*: Carrollton, 1 (UTAVC); White Rock Lake, 1 (DMNHT); 4.5 mi. SSE Lancaster, 1 (UTAVC). *Fort Bend Co.*: 4 mi. SE Sugarland, 1 (TNHC). *Freestone Co.*: 1 mi. W Teague, 3 (BUSM). *Galveston Co.*: NE shore Galveston Bay, 1 (BUSM); 2 mi. SW Crystal Beach, 1 (SFAVC). *Grimes Co.*: 5 mi. W Shiro, 2 (SFAVC). *Jefferson Co.*: 15 mi. SE Beaumont, 1 (SFAVC); J. D. Murphree Wildlife Management Area, Port Arthur, 1 (SFAVC). *Lamar Co.*: 5 mi. N Paris, 1 (SFAVC). *Leon Co.*: Normangee Lake, 2 (USNM). *Liberty Co.*: 16 mi. E Cleveland, 1 (SFAVC). *McLennan Co.*: Waco, 1 (BUSM); Mart, 1 (BUSM). *Nacogdoches Co.*: 1 mi. N Garrison, 1 (SFAVC); 1 mi. E Nacogdoches, 1 (SFAVC); 4 mi. SE Nacogdoches, 1 (SFAVC); Stephen F. Austin Experimental Forest, 1 (SFAVC). *Newton Co.*: 12 mi. N Burkeville, 1 (TCWC); Newton, 1 (TTU). *Panola Co.*: 12 mi. NE Carthage, 1 (SFAVC). *Rusk Co.*: 3 mi. E Henderson, 1 (SFAVC). *Shelby Co.*: 3 mi. N Timpson, 2 (SFAVC). *Smith Co.*: Lake Palestine, 1 (SFAVC). *Tarrant Co.*: Arlington, 2 (FWMSH). *Travis Co.*: Barton Creek, Austin, 1 (TNHC). *Wood Co.*: 5 mi. S Winnsboro, 1 (UTAVC).

Canis latrans frustror (54). *Bosque Co.*: 45 mi. N Waco, 1 (BUSM). *Brazos Co.*: 7 mi. W College Station, 2 (TCWC); 6 mi. S College Station, 1 (TCWC). *Burleson Co.*: 9 mi. W Caldwell, 1 (TCWC). *Calhoun Co.*: Port Lavaca, 2 (USNM). *Cherokee Co.*: 5 mi. N Rusk, 1 (SFAVC). *Collin Co.*: near McKinney, 2 (TCWC). *Colorado Co.*: Frelsburg, 1 (USNM). *Falls Co.*: Marlin, 1 (DMNHT). *Freestone Co.*: 14.4 mi. N Teague, FM Rd. 1451, 1 (BUSM). *Harris Co.*: 8 mi. W Humble, 1 (USNM); Humble, 1 (USNM); Genoa, 2 (USNM); 7 mi. E Genoa, 1 (USNM). *Hunt Co.*: Greenville, 1 (USNM); near Greenville, 1 (TCWC). *Kaufman Co.*: 8 mi. W Terrell, 1 (TCWC). *Leon Co.*: 4 mi. NW Marquez, 3 (TCWC); 6 mi. S Marquez, 1 (TCWC); 5 mi. W Flynn, 1 (TCWC). *Liberty Co.*: Dayton, 2 (USNM). *Madison Co.*: 5 mi. W Madisonville, 1 (USNM), 1 (TCWC); 11 mi. SE Madisonville, 2 (USNM). *Matagorda Co.*: 3 mi. W Palacios, 1 (TCWC). *McLennan Co.*: Waco, 1 (BUSM). *Nacogdoches Co.*: Cushing, 2 (SFAVC); 2 mi. E Cushing, 1 (SFAVC); 7 mi. E Nacogdoches, 1 (TTU). *Robertson Co.*: between Hearne and Wheelock, 1 (TCWC). *Tarrant Co.*: Eagle Mt. area, 3 (FWMSH). *Tyler Co.*: 1.8 mi. N, 2.6 mi. W Spurger, 1 (TCWC); 2 mi. S FM Rd. 1746, 1 mi. N FM Rd. 2992, 1 (TCWC); 12 mi. E Hwy. 69, 5 mi. N Hwy. 256, 1 (TCWC). *Van Zandt Co.*: no specific locality, 2 (TCWC). *Victoria Co.*: Bloomington, 6 (USNM); 6 mi. S Bloomington, 1 (USNM).

Canis rufus rufus (68). *Brazoria Co.*: 9 mi. NE Angleton, 2 (USNM); Angleton, 4 (USNM); 12 mi. E, 9 mi. E Angleton, 9 (USNM); SE Angleton, 1 (USNM); Columbia, 1 (USNM); 5–10 mi. SSW Brazoria, 1 (USNM); Clemens Farm, 1 (USNM). *Brazos Co.*: Bryan, 1 (USNM). *Calhoun Co.*: Port Lavaca, 2 (USNM); Port O'Connor, 4 (USNM). *Colorado Co.*: Frelsburg, 1 (USNM); 6 mi. SW Columbus, 1 (UMMZ); Bucksnag Prairie, 1 (TCWC); Bussek Ranch, border Colorado and Lavaca cos., 1 (TCWC). *Dallas Co.*: no specific locality, 5 (DMNHT). *Ellis Co.*: Midlothian, 1 (DMNHT). *Harris Co.*: near Humble, 1 (USNM); 3 mi. S Hockley, 2 (USNM); Genoa, 1 (USNM); 5 mi. SE Genoa, 1 (USNM). *Lavaca Co.*: 15 mi. W Hallettsville, 1 (TCWC). *Lee Co.*: 5 mi. N Giddings, 1 (TCWC). *Liberty Co.*: 0.5 mi. N Rye, 2 (USNM); Cleveland, 1 (USNM); 6 mi. N Dayton, 2 (USNM); Dayton, 2 (USNM); Tarkington, 1 (USNM). *Madison Co.*: Madisonville, 2 (USNM). *Montgomery Co.*: Security, 3 (USNM); Magnolia, 1 (USNM); Porter, 1 (USNM). *Victoria Co.*: 9.5 mi. S Inez, 1 (TCWC); 6 mi. S Welder Ranch, Bloomington, 6 (USNM). *Walker Co.*: 11 mi. SE Madisonville, 2 (USNM); New Waverly, 1 (USNM).

Canis rufus gregoryi (21). *Angelina Co.*: Diboll, 1 (UMMZ). *Chambers Co.*: Mont Belvieu, 1 (USNM); 3 mi. E Mont Belvieu, 1 (USNM); Monroe City, 1 (USNM); Stowell, 1 (USNM); Double Bayou, 4 (USNM); Logan Ranch, 3 (USNM). *Hardin Co.*: Kountze, 2 (USNM). *Jefferson Co.*: Pipkin's Ranch, 1 (USNM). *Marion Co.*: Jefferson, 1 (USNM). *Newton Co.*: Rock Creek, 1 (USNM). *Polk Co.*: N Polk Co., 1 (USNM); near Wakefield, 2 (USNM); Segno, 1 (USNM).

Vulpes vulpes fulva (12). *Angelina Co.*: 3 mi. NW Huntington, 1 (SFAVC). *Bell Co.*: 3 mi. SW Seaton, 1 (BUSM). *Bosque Co.*: FM Rd. 203, 3 (DMNHT); SE Glen Rose, 1 (DMNHT). *McLennan Co.*: Hallsburg, 12 mi. E Waco, 1 (BUSM). *Newton Co.*: Devil's Pocket Community, 25 mi. S Newton, 1 (TCWC). *Robertson Co.*: 2.5 mi. NE Benchley, 1 (TCWC). *Tarrant Co.*: Hurst, near Trinity River, 2 (UTAVC); Greer Island Refuge, Fort Worth, 1 (FWMSH).

Urocyon cinereoargenteus floridanus (86). *Anderson Co.*: 3.5 mi. SE Elkhart, 1 (SFAVC). *Angelina Co.*: Lufkin, 1 (SFAVC). *Bastrop Co.*: 9 mi. W Manheim, 1 (TCWC); 15 mi. W Bastrop, 1 (MVZ). *Bosque Co.*: FM Rd. 203 SE Glen Rose, 10 (DMNHT); Fisk Ranch, 3 mi. W Valley Mills, 1 (BUSM); farm near Mosheim, 2 (BUSM). *Brazoria Co.*: FM Rd. between Sweeny and Old Ocean, 1 (SFAVC). *Brazos Co.*: Kurten, 1 (TCWC); College Station, 1 (TCWC). *Colorado Co.*: 10 mi. SE Weimer, 1 (TNHC). *Comal Co.*: 9 mi. N New Braunfels, 1 (TCWC). *Dallas Co.*: Kiest Park, 1 (DMNHT). *Denton Co.*: 1.5 mi. E Bartonsville, 1 (UTAVC). *Fayette Co.*: 6 mi. N La Grange, Hwy. 77, 1 (TCWC). *Freestone Co.*: no specific locality, 1 (TNHC). *Gregg Co.*: 4 mi. N Kilgore, 1 (SFAVC). *Guadalupe Co.*: 6.5 mi. S Seguin, 1 (TCWC). *Hardin Co.*: 7 mi. NE Sour Lake, 1 (USNM); Sour Lake, 1 (USNM). *Hays Co.*: 1 mi. S Dripping Springs, 1 (TNHC). *Henderson Co.*: 15 mi. S Mabank, 1 (SFAVC). *Hill Co.*: Lake Whitney, Chisolm Trail State Park, 1 (FWMSH). *Houston Co.*: San Pedro, near Eagle Pass, 1 (USNM). *Jasper Co.*: 10 mi. S Jasper, 1 (TCWC). *Johnson Co.*: 1.5 mi. W Lilian, 2 (FWMSH). *Kaufman Co.*: 4 mi. W Mabank, 1 (SFAVC). *Lavaca Co.*: Fitch Ranch, 15 mi. SW Hallettsville, 2 (TCWC). *Liberty Co.*: Cleveland, 2 (USNM); 6 mi. E Cleveland, 2 (USNM); Tarkington, 1 (USNM). *McLennan Co.*: 2.5 mi. N

Crawford, 1 (BUSM); near Mart, 1 (BUSM). *Nacogdoches Co.*: Appleby, 1 (SFAVC); 4.5 mi. N Nacogdoches, 1 (SFAVC); 2 mi. W Nacogdoches, 1 (SFAVC); Nacogdoches, 1 (SFAVC); 2 mi. S Nacogdoches, 1 (SFAVC); 9.5 mi. SW Nacogdoches, 1 (TNHC); 12.5 mi. SW Nacogdoches, 1 (SFAVC); 20 mi. SE Nacogdoches, 1 (TTU), 1 (SFAVC); Chireno, 1 (TTU). *Polk Co.*: near Moscow, 2 (TCWC). *Robertson Co.*: 4 mi. W Wheelock, 1 (TCWC). *Rusk Co.*: 2 mi. S Henderson, 1 (SFAVC); 4 mi. S Henderson, 1 (SFAVC). *Smith Co.*: Tyler, 1 (SFAVC). *Tarrant Co.*: 2 mi. N Trinity River, Hwy. 157, 1 (UTAVC); Lake Arlington, 2 (UTAVC); N Arlington, 1 (UTAVC); NE Arlington, jct. Hwy. 80 and Hwy. 360, 1 (UTAVC); Lake Worth, 1 (FWMSH); inter. Magic Mile Rd. and road to Six Flags, 1 (UTAVC); Benbrook, 1 (FWMSH); no specific locality, 2 (DMNHT). *Travis Co.*: 3 mi. ESE Del Valle, 1 (MVZ). *Trinity Co.*: 11 mi. W Trinity, 1 (TCWC). *Tyler Co.*: 9 mi. E Hwy. 69, 5 mi. N Hwy. 190, 2 (TCWC); 4 mi. W Hwy. 92, 2 mi. S FM Rd. 1746, 3 (TCWC); 6 mi. S Woodville, 3 (TCWC). *Van Zandt Co.*: IH 20 at Myrtle Springs, 1 (DMNHT). *Walker Co.*: 17 mi. WNW Huntsville, 1 (TCWC). *Waller Co.*: 5 mi. N Hempstead, 1 (TCWC). *Washington Co.*: 11.5 mi. NW Brenham, 1 (TCWC).

Ursus americanus luteolus (24). *Fort Bend Co.*: 21 mi. NW Angleton, 7 (USNM). *Hardin Co.*: Kountze, 8 (USNM); 8 mi. N Silsbee, 1 (BTM); Sour Lake, 2 (USNM). *Liberty Co.*: Dayton, 2 (USNM). *Wharton Co.*: Wharton, 1 (USNM). *Matagorda/Brazoria Cos.*: 19 mi. E Bay City, 3 (USNM).

Bassariscus astutus flavus (20). *Bell Co.*: 9 mi. SE Killeen, 1 (BUSM). *Brazos Co.*: 2 mi. N Edge, 1 (TCWC); 4 mi. S Wellborn, 1 (TCWC). *Comal Co.*: 5 mi. S Spring Branch, 1 (BUSM). *Henderson Co.*: 4 mi. W Athens, 1 (SFAVC). *Jefferson Co.*: no specific locality, 1 (TNHC). *McLennan Co.*: 3 mi. SW Ross, 1 (BUSM); 2 mi. E McGregor, 1 (BUSM). *Robertson Co.*: 4 mi. W Wheelock, 1 (TCWC). *Tarrant Co.*: Azle, 3 (FWMSH); Fort Worth, 1 (FWMSH). *Travis Co.*: 5 mi. W Austin, 1 (TNHC); Austin, 1 (USNM); 10 mi. SW Austin, 1 (TNHC). *Walker Co.*: 4 mi. NE Riverside, 1 (SFAVC). *Williamson Co.*: 4 mi. NW Florence, 1 (BUSM); 17 mi. W Jarrell, 1 (BUSM); near Georgetown, 1 (BUSM).

Procyon lotor fuscipes (140). *Anderson Co.*: 14 mi. W Jacksonville, 1 (SFAVC); 10 mi. SW Elkhart, 1 (SFAVC). *Angelina Co.*: 3 mi. NE Huntington, 1 (SFAVC). *Bastrop Co.*: 15 mi. W Bastrop, 1 (MVZ). *Bell Co.*: 6 mi. E Temple, 1 (TCWC); 8 mi. E Belton, 1 (TCWC); 12 mi. S Belton, 1 (BUSM). *Bosque Co.*: 4.5 mi. NW Clifton, 1 (BUSM); 2 mi. E Valley Mills, 1 (BUSM). *Bowie Co.*: 5 mi. N Texarkana, 1 (TTU); Texarkana, 2 (USNM). *Brazoria Co.*: 22 mi. NW Angleton, 1 (USNM); Angleton, 1 (USNM); Columbia, 1 (USNM); 2 mi. W Lake Jackson, 1 (SFAVC). *Brazos Co.*: 3 mi. W College Station, 2 (TCWC); 2 mi. SW College Station, 1 (TCWC). *Burleson Co.*: no specific locality, 1 (DMNHT). *Calhoun Co.*: Port Lavaca, 1 (USNM). *Cherokee Co.*: 11.5 mi. W Alto, 1 (SFAVC). *Collin Co.*: Wylie, 1 (DMNHT). *Colorado Co.*: 3 mi. W Altair, 1 (TCWC); 2 mi. W Altair, 1 (TCWC). *Dallas Co.*: Carrollton, 1 (UTAVC); 4 mi. W Irving, 1 (UTAVC); Dallas, 4 (DMNHT), 1 (UTAVC); DeSoto, 1 (UTAVC). *De Witt Co.*: 8 mi. NW Cuero, 1 (TCWC). *Fort Bend Co.*: 4 mi. SE Sugarland, 3 (TNHC). *Freestone Co.*: 12 mi. NW Fairfield, 1 (TCWC); 15 mi. S Fairfield, 1 (SFAVC). *Galveston Co.*: Dickinson Bayou, opposite Galveston, 1 (USNM). *Goliad Co.*: 17 mi. S Goliad, 1 (TNHC). *Grayson Co.*: Sherman, 1 (MVZ). *Gregg Co.*: 4 mi. N Kilgore, 1 (SFAVC). *Hardin Co.*: Kountze, 1 (USNM); 11 mi. N, 2.8 mi. E Silsbee, 1 (TCWC); Sour Lake, 4 (USNM). *Harrison Co.*: 3 mi. E Marshall, 1 (SFAVC). *Henderson Co.*: 4 mi. N Athens, 1 (SFAVC); 2 mi. SE Malakoff, 1 (SFAVC). *Hill Co.*: 7.2 mi. NE Mertens, 1 (UMMZ). *Houston Co.*: Grapeland, 4 (SFAVC). *Leon Co.*: 20 mi. S Oakwood, 1 (BUSM). *Liberty Co.*: 5 mi. W Hardin, 2 (SFAVC); Liberty, 1

(USNM). *Matagorda Co.*: Matagorda, 3 (USNM); Matagorda Island, 1 (TNHC). *McLennan Co.*: 4 mi. N China Springs, 1 (BUSM); Waco, 1 (BUSM); 2.6 mi. S Waco, 1 (BUSM); 3 mi. S Waco, 1 (BUSM); 1.8 mi. S Crawford, 1 (BUSM); 5 mi. ENE Satin, 1 (BUSM). *Montgomery Co.*: 4 mi. S Montgomery, 1 (TCWC). *Nacogdoches Co.*: 2 mi. S Appleby, 1 (SFAVC); 13 mi. NW Nacogdoches, 1 (SFAVC); 8 mi. N Nacogdoches, 1 (SFAVC); 4 mi. NE Nacogdoches, 1 (SFAVC); 12 mi. W, 2 mi. N Nacogdoches, 1 (SFAVC); 11 mi. W Nacogdoches, 3 (SFAVC); 4 mi. W Nacogdoches, 1 (SFAVC); Nacogdoches, 3 (SFAVC); Stephen F. Austin Experimental Forest, 1 (TCWC), 2 (SFAVC); 8 mi. S Nacogdoches, 1 (SFAVC); 12 mi. S Nacogdoches, 1 (SFAVC); 15 mi. N Lufkin, 1 (KU); Lake Alazan, 1 (SFAVC). *Newton Co.*: 9.5 mi. N Burkeville, 1 (TCWC); 7 mi. N Burkeville, 1 (TCWC); Alligator Lake, 9 (TTU). *Panola Co.*: 8 mi. SW Clayton, 1 (SFAVC). *Polk Co.*: 25 mi. ESE Livingston, 1 (TCWC); 1 mi. S Segno, 1 (SFAVC). *Robertson Co.*: Davis Ranch, 1 (UTAVC). *Shelby Co.*: 30 mi. NE Nacogdoches, 1 (SFAVC); 14 mi. SE Center, 1 (SFAVC); 22 mi. SE Center, 1 (SFAVC). *Smith Co.*: 10 mi. NE Tyler, 1 (TNHC); Tyler, 1 (SFAVC). *Tarrant Co.*: W Lake Arlington, 1 (UTAVC); Arlington, 1 (UTAVC); near Lake Worth, 1 (UTAVC); Fort Worth, 2 (FWMSH); Trinity River, Fort Worth, 1 (FWMSH); Trinity Park, Fort Worth, 1 (FWMSH); 2 mi. E Fort Worth, 1 (UTAVC); 2 mi. W Crowley, 1 (FWMSH). *Travis Co.*: 7 mi. N Austin, 1 (TNHC); 1.2 mi. NW Austin, 1 (TNHC); Austin, 1 (TNHC); Colorado River, Austin, 1 (TNHC); 7 mi. E Austin, 1 (TNHC). *Tyler Co.*: 7 mi. E Hwy. 69, 2 mi. S Hwy. 190, 1 (TCWC); 2 mi. N FM Rd. 1746, 3 mi. S Hwy. 190, 1 (TCWC); 2 mi. S FM Rd. 1746, 1 mi. N FM Rd. 2992, 4 (TCWC); 3.2 mi. E Warren, 1 (TCWC). *Upshur Co.*: 9.7 mi. W Gilmer, Hwy. 154, 1 (FWMSH). *Washington Co.*: 10.5 mi. W Brenham, 2 (TCWC). *Wood Co.*: 3.5 mi. SE Quitman, 2 (TCWC); 3.5 mi. SE Mineola, Butler Lake, 2 (TTU), 1 (SFAVC).

Mustela frenata texensis (2). *McLennan Co.*: Erath, 1 (BUSM); Fish Pond, 5 mi. N Waco, 1 (BUSM).

Mustela frenata primulina (3). *Cass Co.*: 5 mi. W Linden, 1 (TTU). *Hopkins Co.*: 10 mi. S Sulphur Springs, 1 (KU), 1 (MVZ).

Mustela frenata arthuri (6). *Angelina Co.*: 12 mi. S Lufkin, 1 (SFAVC). *Colorado Co.*: 12 mi. N Eagle Lake, 1 (TCWC); 5 mi. W Eagle Lake, 1 (TCWC); 3 mi. S Garwood, 1 (MVZ). *Rusk Co.*: 2.8 mi. S Mt. Enterprise, 1 (SFAVC). *Shelby Co.*: Timpson, 1 (TTU).

Mustela vison mink (49). *Angelina Co.*: 3 mi. W, 2 mi. N Lufkin, 1 (SFAVC). *Bowie Co.*: 10 mi. NW Texarkana, 5 (USNM). *Brazos Co.*: 2 mi. W Edge, 1 (TCWC); College Station, 1 (TCWC); 2 mi. ESE College Station, 1 (TCWC). *Burleson Co.*: 12 mi. SW College Station, 1 (TCWC); 5 mi. NE Snook, 2 (TCWC); 10.5 mi. NNW Clay, Hwy. 50, 1 (TCWC). *Collin Co.*: approx. 2 mi. from Dallas Co. line, 1 (DMNHT). *Colorado Co.*: 6 mi. N Eagle Lake, 2 (TCWC); Eagle Lake, 1 (DMNHT). *Cooke Co.*: Gainesville, 4 (USNM). *Dallas Co.*: FM Rd. 1382, 0.5 mi. W Camp Wisdom Rd., 1 (UTAVC); no specific locality, 1 (DMNHT). *De Witt Co.*: 9 mi. NW Cuero, 1 (TCWC). *Falls Co.*: 2 mi. E Marlin, 1 (TCWC). *Grimes Co.*: 6 mi. S Iola, 1 (TCWC); Navasota, 2 (USNM). *Harris Co.*: no specific locality, 1 (USNM). *Hays Co.*: San Marcos State Fish Hatchery, 1 (TNHC). *Hill Co.*: 2 mi. S Abbott, 1 (TCWC). *Houston Co.*: Antioch, 1 (USNM). *Kaufman Co.*: 5 mi. NE Kaufman, Kaufman Lake, 1 (DMNHT). *Matagorda Co.*: Matagorda, 1 (USNM). *McLennan Co.*: Waco, 2 (BUSM); 7 mi. S Waco, FM Rd. 1695, 1 (BUSM). *Nacogdoches Co.*: 5 mi. E Nacogdoches, 1 (TTU). *Newton Co.*: Big Caw Creek, 1 (TTU). *Panola Co.*: 5 mi. NW Carthage, 1 (SFAVC); 5 mi. E Carthage, 1 (SFAVC); 6 mi. SE Long Branch, 1 (SFAVC). *Polk Co.*: near Moscow, 1 (TCWC); 25 mi. ESE Livingston, 1 (TCWC). *Rusk Co.*: Tatum, 1 (SFAVC). *Shelby Co.*: no specific locality, 1 (TTU). *Smith Co.*: 2 mi. N Tyler, 1 (SFAVC). *Tarrant Co.*: Fort Worth, 1 (FWMSH). *Tyler Co.*: Rockland, 2 (USNM).

Taxidea taxus berlandieri (1). *Tarrant Co.*: between Watanga and Richland Hills, tributary of Big Fossil Creek, 1 (FWMSH).

Spilogale putorius interrupta (36). *Brazos Co.*: 2 mi. NE Bryan, 1 (TCWC); Bryan, College Station, 5 (TCWC); College Station, 2 (TCWC), 1 (MVZ). *Collin Co.*: Wylie, 1 (DMNHT). *Colorado Co.*: 6 mi. N Eagle Lake, 1 (TCWC). *Cooke Co.*: no specific locality, 1 (USNM). *Dallas Co.*: 5 mi. W Dallas, 1 (DMNHT). *Galveston Co.*: 1 mi. N Texas City, 1 (MVZ); Virginia Point, 2 (USNM). *Grimes Co.*: Navasota, 2 (USNM). *Harris Co.*: 2.5 mi. N Hockley, 1 (TCWC). *Jackson Co.*: Edna, 1 (USNM). *Limestone Co.*: 3 mi. S Groesbeck, 1 (TCWC). *Matagorda Co.*: Elliot Crossing, 1 (USNM); Matagorda Bay, Indianola, 1 (USNM). *McLennan Co.*: Bosque Hills, 5 mi. N Waco, 1 (BUSM); Waco, 2 (BUSM). *Robertson Co.*: 2 mi. W, 1 mi. S Hearne, 1 (TCWC); 2 mi. SE Hearne, 1 (TNHC). *Tarrant Co.*: 9 mi. W Grapevine, 1 (DMNHT); NW Arlington, 1 (UTAVC); Arlington, 1 (FWMSH); Fort Worth, 2 (FWMSH); 7 mi. SE Fort Worth, 1 (TWC). *Travis Co.*: 8 mi. E Austin, 1 (TNHC). *Walker Co.*: 6 mi. E Huntsville, 1 (TCWC).

Mephitis mephitis mesomelas (70). *Brazos Co.*: 1 mi. N College Station, 1 (TCWC); College Station, 3 (TCWC), 1 (UMMZ), 3 (MVZ); Texas A&M University Campus, College Station, 2 (TCWC). *Colorado Co.*: 9 mi. W Eagle Lake, 1 (TCWC). *Cooke Co.*: Gainesville, 2 (USNM). *Dallas Co.*: North Lake, 1 (UTAVC); 3 mi. S North Lake, 1 (UTAVC); 3 mi. W Farmers Branch, 2 (UTAVC); NW Irving, near DFW Regional Airport, 1 (UTAVC). *De Witt Co.*: 8 mi. NW Cuero, 1 (TCWC). *Ellis Co.*: 34 mi. S Dallas, Lake Bardwell, 1 (TCWC). *Galveston Co.*: Virginia Point, 1 (USNM). *Grimes Co.*: 4 mi. N Carlos, 1 (TCWC); Navasota, 1 (USNM). *Hardin Co.*: Sour Lake, 1 (USNM). *Harris Co.*: 5 mi. NE Webster, 1 (TCWC). *Jefferson Co.*: 7 mi. SW Sabine Pass, Hwy. 87, 1 (TNHC). *Matagorda Co.*: Matagorda, 4 (USNM); 9 mi. S Indianola, 11 (USNM). *McLennan Co.*: Lake Waco, 1 (BUSM); Waco, 3 (BUSM). *Nacogdoches Co.*: 5 mi. N Nacogdoches, 1 (SFAVC); 6 mi. ENE Nacogdoches, 3 (SFAVC); 10 mi. E Nacogdoches, 1 (SFAVC); 14 mi. E Nacogdoches, 1 (SFAVC). *Newton Co.*: 3 mi. E Newton, 1 (TTU). *Polk Co.*: 4.1 mi. S, 0.3 mi. W Camp Ruby, 1 (TCWC). *Tarrant Co.*: Keller, 1 (TWC); Eagle Mt. Lake, 1 (FWMSH); Trinity River, N Arlington, 1 (UTAVC); Arlington, 1 (UTAVC); 1 mi. SW Arlington, 1 (UTAVC); 22 mi. SE Fort Worth, Hwy. 287, 1 (UTAVC). *Travis Co.*: Austin, 2 (TNHC). *Tyler Co.*: 9 mi. E Hwy. 69, 3 mi. N Hwy. 190, 1 (TCWC); 1.5 mi. N FM Rd. 2992, 2 mi. S FM Rd. 1746, 2 (TCWC); 4.3 mi. S, 0.4 mi. W Warren, 1 (TCWC). *Walker Co.*: Huntsville, 1 (TCWC); 6 mi. E Huntsville, 1 (TCWC). *Wharton Co.*: Hungerford, 1 (TCWC). *Williamson Co.*: 2 mi. S Taylor, 1 (TNHC).

Conepatus mesoleucus mearnsi (1). *Collin Co.*: Watson Farm, 1 (DMNHT).

Conepatus mesoleucus telmalestes (12). *Hardin Co.*: Sour Lake, 6 (USNM). *Liberty Co.*: Cleveland, 5 (USNM); Tarkington Prairie, near Cleveland, 1 (USNM).

Lutra canadensis lataxina (9). *Angelina Co.*: 8 mi. W Lufkin, 1 (TCWC); 25 mi. SW Nacogdoches, 1 (TCWC). *Brazoria Co.*: 20 mi. W Angleton, 4 (USNM). *Jefferson Co.*: 7 mi. SW Port Arthur, 1 (TCWC). *Matagorda Co.*: 18 mi. E Bay City, 1 (USNM). *Tyler Co.*: 4.5 mi. E Hillister, 1 (TCWC).

Felis concolor stanleyana (1). *Colorado Co.*: 15 mi. S Rock Island, 1 (KU).

Felis pardalis albescens (5). *Brazoria Co.*: 17 mi. NW Angleton, 1 (USNM); NW Angleton, 1 (USNM); 18 mi. W Angleton, 1 (USNM). *Falls Co.*: Cow Bayou, near Mooreville, 1 (BUSM). *Matagorda Co.*: 18 mi. E Bay City, 1 (USNM).

Felis rufus texensis (141). *Anderson Co.*: 7.5 mi. SE Slocum, 1 (SFAVC).

Austin Co.: 5 mi. SW Bellville, 1 (TCWC). *Bastrop Co.*: no specific locality, 10 (TCWC). *Bosque Co.*: FM Rd. 203, SE Glen Rose, 6 (DMNHT); 3 mi. past Iredell on Bosque River, 1 (BUSM). *Brazoria Co.*: 19 mi. NW Angleton, 2 (USNM); 2 mi. N Clute, 1 (SFAVC). *Brazos Co.*: 4 mi. W College Station, 1 (TCWC); 6 mi. SE College Station, 1 (TCWC); Wellborn, 2 (TCWC). *Burleson Co.*: no specific locality, 7 (TCWC). *Caldwell Co.*: no specific locality, 1 (TCWC). *Calhoun Co.*: Port Lavaca, 1 (USNM); Port O'Connor, 1 (USNM). *Chambers Co.*: no specific locality, 3 (USNM). *Colorado Co.*: 6 mi. S Columbus, 1 (TCWC); San Mar Ranch, 1 (TCWC). *Cooke Co.*: no specific locality, 1 (USNM). *Denton Co.*: no specific locality, 2 (TCWC). *De Witt Co.*: no specific locality, 1 (TCWC). *Ellis Co.*: no specific locality, 1 (TCWC). *Falls Co.*: no specific locality, 4 (TCWC). *Fayette Co.*: no specific locality, 5 (TCWC). *Freestone Co.*: Wortham, 1 (BUSM). *Galveston Co.*: Dickinson Bayou, opposite Galveston, 1 (USNM). *Gonzales Co.*: no specific locality, 2 (TCWC). *Grayson Co.*: Sherman, 1 (MVZ); no specific locality, 3 (TCWC). *Hardin Co.*: Kountze, 1 (USNM); Saratoga, 1 (USNM); Sour Lake, 6 (USNM). *Hays Co.*: no specific locality, 1 (USNM), 1 (TCWC). *Henderson Co.*: 4 mi. W Athens, 1 (SFAVC). *Hill Co.*: no specific locality, 1 (TCWC). *Houston Co.*: Antioch, 1 (USNM). *Jackson Co.*: no specific locality, 10 (TCWC). *Johnson Co.*: near Cresson, 1 (FWMSH). *Lamar Co.*: no specific locality, 1 (TCWC). *Lavaca Co.*: no specific locality, 2 (TCWC). *Lee Co.*: no specific locality, 3 (TCWC). *Liberty Co.*: 12 mi. N Cleveland, 4 (USNM); Tarkington, 2 (USNM); 20 mi. NW Liberty, 1 (USNM); Liberty, 1 (USNM). *Matagorda Co.*: Matagorda, 1 (USNM). *McLennan Co.*: 6 mi. NE Waco, 1 (BUSM); Waco, 1 (BUSM); near Mart, 1 (BUSM); Lorena, 1 (BUSM). *Milam Co.*: no specific locality, 9 (TCWC). *Nacogdoches Co.*: 5 mi. S Etiole, 1 (SFAVC). *Rusk Co.*: 5 mi. S Mt. Enterprise, 1 (SFAVC). *Tarrant Co.*: NW Carswell, 1 (FWMSH). *Travis Co.*: no specific locality, 3 (TCWC). *Trinity Co.*: 34 mi. SW Nacogdoches, 1 (TTU). *Tyler Co.*: 2 mi. N FM Rd. 1746, 3 mi. S Hwy. 190, 1 (TCWC); 7.5 mi. S Woodville, 1 (TCWC). *Victoria Co.*: no specific locality, 4 (TCWC). *Waller Co.*: Spring Creek, 1 (USNM). *Washington Co.*: no specific locality, 1 (TCWC), 1 (USNM). *Wharton Co.*: no specific locality, 5 (TCWC). *Williamson Co.*: no specific locality, 5 (TCWC).

Dicotyles tajacu angulatus (3). *Brazoria Co.*: Velasco, 1 (USNM). *Brazos Co.*: .01 mi. W Smetana turnoff, Hwy. 21, 1 (TCWC). *McLennan Co.*: Waco, 1 (BUSM).

Odocoileus virginianus mcilhennyi (15). *Brazoria Co.*: Angleton, 1 (USNM). *Calhoun Co.*: St. Joe Island, 1 (TCWC). *Hardin Co.*: Kountze, 2 (USNM); Sour Lake, 5 (USNM). *Liberty Co.*: Tarkington Prairie, 1 (USNM); 6 mi. E Cleveland, 3 (USNM). *Matagorda Co.*: Bay City, 2 (USNM).

Odocoileus virginianus texana (18). *Angelina Co.*: 11 mi. W Lufkin, 1 (TCWC). *Brazos Co.*: 17 mi. SE Hearne, 1 (TCWC). *Burleson Co.*: Dime Box, 1 (USNM). *Colorado Co.*: Columbus, 1 (TCWC); 20 mi. W Eagle Lake, 1 (TCWC); Eagle Lake, 1 (TCWC); 4 mi. W Altair, 1 (TCWC). *Freestone Co.*: 3 mi. E Kirvin Carter Ranch, 1 (UTAVC). *Henderson Co.*: no specific locality, 1 (SFAVC). *Jasper Co.*: Jasper, 2 (USNM). *Johnson Co.*: 15 mi. SE Rio Vista, 1 (UTAVC). *McLennan Co.*: Waco, 1 (BUSM); Mart, 1 (BUSM). *Tarrant Co.*: no specific locality, 1 (DMNHT). *Travis Co.*: 11 mi. W Austin, 1 (TCWC). *Trinity Co.*: 16 mi. W Lufkin, 1 (TCWC). *Tyler Co.*: 1.7 mi. S, 1.8 mi. E Town Bluff, 1 (TCWC).

Bison bison bison (3). *Calhoun Co.*: 12 mi. SW Port Lavaca, 1 (BUSM). *McLennan Co.*: Waco, 2 (BUSM).

Appendix II
Plants Named in the Text

THE following list (arranged alphabetically by vernacular names) gives the scientific name for all plants referred to in this book. When authors did not list complete scientific names, species designations could not be assigned. Most vernacular and scientific names were taken from F. W. Gould (1975, 1978).

Alfalfa	*Medicago sativa*
American Beautyberry	*Callicarpa americana*
American Elm	*Ulmus americana*
American Waterlily	*Nymphaea odorata*
Arrowhead	*Sagittaria* spp.
Beech	*Fagus grandifolia*
Bermudagrass	*Cynodon*
Big Bluestem	*Andropogon gerardi*
Big Cordgrass	*Spartina cynosuroides*
Birch	*Betula nigra*
Blackberry	*Rubus louisianus*
Black Gum	*Nyssa sylvatica*
Black Hickory	*Carya texana*
Black Locust	*Robinia pseudo-acacia*
Black Tupelo	*Nyssa sylvatica*
Black Walnut	*Juglans nigra*
Black Willow	*Salix nigra*
Blackjack Oak	*Quercus marilandica*
Bluejack Oak	*Quercus incana*
Bluestem	*Andropogon* spp.
Brier	*Smilax* spp.
Broomsedge	*Andropogon virginicus*
Brownseed Paspalum	*Paspalum plicatulum*
Buffalograss	*Buchloë dactyloides*
Bulrush	*Scirpus* spp.
Bushy Bluestem	*Andropogon glomeratus*
California Bulrush	*Scirpus californicus*
Cane	*Arundinaria gigantea*
Carpetgrass	*Axonopus* spp.
Carrot	*Daucus* spp.
Cattail	*Typha* spp.
Clover	*Trifolium* spp.
Coastal Bermudagrass	*Cynodon dactylon*
Coastal Sacahuista	*Spartina spartinae*
Common Reed	*Phragmites communis*
Cordgrass	*Spartina* spp.
Corn	*Zea mays*
Cottonwood	*Populus deltoides*
Crimson Clover	*Trifolium incarnatum*

Cypress	*Cupressus*
Dallisgrass	*Paspalum dilatatum*
Deciduous Holly (Possumhaw)	*Ilex decidua*
Dewberry	*Rubus* spp.
Dogwood	*Cornus* spp.
Duckweed	*Lemna* spp.
Eastern Red Cedar	*Juniperus virginiana*
Elm	*Ulmus* spp.
Flatsedge	*Cyperus* spp.
French Mulberry	*Callicarpa americana*
Frog Fruit	*Phyla incisa*
Gallberry holly	*Ilex coriacea*
Grapevine	*Vitus* spp.
Greenbriar	*Smilax* spp.
Gulfdune Paspalum	*Paspalum monostachyum*
Hackberry	*Celtis* spp.
Hairy Grama	*Bouteloua hirsuta*
Hawthorn	*Crataegus* spp.
Hickory	*Carya* spp.
Holly	*Ilex* spp.
Honeylocust	*Gleditsia* spp.
Honeysuckle	*Lonicera* spp.
Huckleberry	*Vaccinium* spp.
Indiangrass	*Sorghastrum* spp.
Ironwood	*Ostrya virginiana*
Jamaica Sawgrass	*Cladium jamaicense*
Johnson Grass	*Sorghum halapense*
Juniper	*Juniperus* spp.
Laurel Oak	*Quercus laurifolia*
Lettuce	*Lactuga* spp.
Little Bluestem	*Schizachyrium scoparium*
Live Oak	*Quercus virginiana*
Loblolly Pine	*Pinus taeda*
Long-leaf Pine	*Pinus palustris*
Lotebush	*Condalia obtusifolia*
Lovegrass	*Eragrostis* spp.
Magnolia	*Magnolia* spp.
Marsh Grass	*Spartina* spp.
Marshhay Cordgrass	*Spartina patens*
Mesquite	*Prosopis glandulosa*
Mulberry	*Morus* spp.
Needlegrass	*Stipa* spp.
Needlegrass Rush	*Juncus roemerianus*
Oak	*Quercus* spp.
Olney Bulrush	*Scirpus olneyi*
Onion	*Allium* spp.
Osage Orange	*Maclura pomifera*
Overcup Oak	*Quercus lyrata*
Palmetto	*Sabal minor*
Panicum	*Panicum* spp.
Panic Grass	*Panicum* spp.
Partridge Pea	*Cassia fasciculata*

Pecan	*Carya illinoinensis*
Pennywort	*Hydrocotyle* spp.
Persimmon	*Diospyros* spp.
Pine	*Pinus* spp.
Poison Ivy	*Rhus toxicodendron*
Pondweed	*Potamogeton* spp.
Post Oak	*Quercus stellata*
Prickly Pear	*Opuntia* spp.
Purple Threeawn	*Aristida purpurea*
Ragweed	*Ambrosia* spp.
Rattail Smutgrass	*Sporobolus indicus*
Red Bay	*Persea borbonia*
Red Mulberry	*Morus rubra*
Red Oak	*Quercus falcata*
Redtop	*Tridens flavus*
Roemer's Threeawn	*Aristida roemeriana*
Rush	*Juncus* spp.
Saltgrass	*Distichlis spicata*
Saltmarsh Bulrush	*Scirpus robustus*
Sassafras	*Sassafras albidum*
Sea myrtle	*Baccharis halimifolia*
Coastal Saltgrass	*Distichlis spicata*
Short-leaf Pine	*Pinus echinata*
Sideoats Grama	*Bouteloua curtipendula*
Silver Bluestem	*Bothriochloa saccharoides*
Slash Pine	*Pinus elliottii*
Slender Bluestem	*Schizachyrium tenerum*
Smooth Cordgrass	*Spartina alterniflora*
Sorghum	*Sorghum bicolor*
Southern Dewberry	*Rubus trivialis*
Soybeans	*Glycine* spp.
Spadeleaf	*Centella asiatica*
Spanish Moss	*Tillandsia usneoides*
Spikesedge	*Eleocharis* spp.
Squarestem Spike Sedge	*Eleocharis quadrangulata*
Sumac	*Rhus* spp.
Sunflower	*Helianthus* spp.
Swamp Chestnut Oak	*Quercus prinus*
Sweetbay	*Magnolia virginiana*
Sweetgum	*Liquidambar styraciflua*
Switchgrass	*Panicum virgatum*
Sycamore	*Platanus occidentalis*
Tall Dropseed	*Sporobolus asper*
Texas Grama	*Bouteloua rigidiseta*
Texas Wintergrass	*Stipa leucotricha*
Threeawn	*Aristida* spp.
Titi	*Cyrilla racemiflora*
Tupelo Gum	*Nyssa aquatica*
Vaseygrass	*Paspalum urvillei*
Walnut	*Jugulans* spp.
Water Hyssop	*Bacopa* spp.
Water Oak	*Quercus nigra*

Wax Myrtle	*Myrica* spp.
White Oak	*Quercus alba*
Wild Cherry	*Prunus serotina*
Wild Grape	*Vitis* spp.
Willow	*Salix* spp.
Willow Oak	*Quercus phellos*
Winged Elm	*Ulmus alata*
Woolly Croton	*Croton capitatus*
Yaupon	*Ilex vomitoria*

Appendix III
Conversion Table

U.S. Customary to Metric		Metric to U.S. Customary	
LENGTH			
To convert	*Multiply by*	*To convert*	*Multiply by*
inch to millimeter	25.4	millimeter to inch	0.039
inch to centimeter	2.54	centimeter to inch	0.394
foot to meter	0.305	meter to foot	3.281
yard to meter	0.914	meter to yard	1.094
mile to kilometer	1.609	kilometer to mile	0.621
AREA			
square foot to square meter	0.093	square meter to square foot	10.764
square yard to square meter	0.836	square meter to square yard	1.196
square mile to square kilometer	2.590	square kilometer to square mile	0.386
acre to hectare	0.405	hectare to acre	2.471
square mile to hectare	258.999	hectare to square mile	0.004
VOLUME			
cubic yard to cubic meter	0.765	cubic meter to cubic yard	1.308
gallon to liter	3.785	liter to gallon	0.264
WEIGHT			
ounce to gram	28.350	gram to ounce	0.035
pound to kilogram	0.454	kilogram to pound	2.205
TEMPERATURE			
Fahrenheit (°F) to Celsius (°C) $= °F - 32/1.8$		Celsius (°C) to Fahrenheit (°F) $= °C \times 1.8 + 32$	

Glossary

ACROCENTRIC. Designation for a chromosome with the centromere at or near one of the ends.

AGONISTIC BEHAVIOR. Fighting or combative behavior.

ALLOPATRIC. Of populations or species occupying mutually exclusive, but usually adjacent, geographical areas.

ALTRICIAL. Pertaining to young born in a very underdeveloped condition, requiring extended development and parental care. Opposite to precocial.

ALLUVIAL. Pertaining to the soil, sand, and gravel deposited by a running watercourse where it issues from a canyon or gorge onto an open plain.

ALVEOLUS (pl. ALVEOLI). Sockets in the jaw bone that receive the root or roots of teeth.

ANAL GLAND. A gland located near the anus.

ANGULAR PROCESS. The posteroventral projection of the mandible, located ventrally to the coronoid process and mandibular condyle.

ANNULATIONS. Rings, such as the rows of scales visible beneath the hair on the tail of certain mice.

ARBOREAL. Pertaining to mammals that spend all or most of their life living in trees.

ARTHROPOD. Segmented animals (including crustaceans, insects, and arachnids) with a chitinous exoskeleton and segmental appendages.

AUDITORY BULLA. The bony capsules, one on each side of the skull, enclosing the middle ears.

AUSTRORIPARIAN BIOTIC PROVINCE. One of the seven biotic provinces in Texas (Blair, 1950), encompassing the pine and hardwood forests of the eastern Gulf coastal plain.

AUTOSOME. Any chromosome other than a sex chromosome.

BACKCROSS. A cross between a hybrid and one of its parents.

BAYGALL. A plant community found in southeastern Texas wherever groundwater survaces at the base of slopes or in mound-and-swale areas, with dominant plants of titi, gallbery holly, sweet bay, red bay, and black gum.

BICOLORED. Of two, contrasting colors.

BIFURCATE. To divide or fork into two branches.

BIOME. A complex biotic community covering a large geographic area and characterized by the distinctive life forms of important climax species.

BIOTIC PROVINCE. A community occupying an area where similarity of climate, physiography, and soil leads to the recurrence of similar combinations of organisms.

BLASTOCYST. An early embryo consisting of 8 to 16 cells that is characteristic of placental mammals.

BRAINCASE. That portion of the skull (posterior to the rostrum) enclosing the brain.

BROWSE. Twigs, shoots, and leaves that are consumed by livestock and other grazing animals.

CACHE. In reference to a mammal that collects and stores food.

CALCAR. A cartilaginous rod that projects from the ankle in many bats and serves to support the interfemoral membrane.

CANINE TOOTH. One of the four basic kinds of teeth found in mammals. The anteriormost tooth rooted in the maxillary and its lower counterpart in the dentary.

CARAPACE. The bony shell of an armadillo.

CARNIVOROUS. Feeding primarily on meat.

CARRION. Dead and putrefying flesh that some animals feed upon.

CENTROMERE. A special region of a chromosome to which the spindle fiber is attached during cell division.

CESTODE. Parasitic tapeworms of the Class Cestoda, Phylum Platyhelminthes.

CHAGAS' DISEASE. An acute and chronic protozoan disease of man caused by the hemoflagellate *Trypanosoma cruzi*. Also known as trypanosomiasis.

CHROMOSOME. A deeply staining DNA-containing threadlike structure in the nucleus of a cell which carries the linearly arranged genetic units.

CIRCULAR OVERLAP. A phenomenon whereby a chain of contiguous and intergrading populations (or subspecies) curves back until the terminal links overlap with each other and behave like good (non-interbreeding) species.

CONCOLOR. Of uniform coloration.

CONDYLOBASAL LENGTH. A measurement of the skull taken from the front of the base of the incisor teeth to the back of the rounded condyles that border the large opening (foramen magnum) at the back of the skull.

COPROPHAGOUS. Feeding on dung or excrement.

COPULATION. The sexual union of male and female reproductive organs, resulting in insemination of sperm from the male into the female.

CORONOID PROCESS. The dorsalmost projection on the posterior of the mandible.

CREPUSCULAR. Pertaining to activity during the twilight periods of dusk and dawn.

CRETACEOUS. The latest geological period of the Mesozoic Era, between 136 and 65 million years ago.

CURSORIAL. Pertaining to a mammal adapted for running.

CUSP. A point, projection or bump on the masticating surface of a tooth.

DELAYED FERTILIZATION. The condition in some bats whereby mating occurs in late summer or early fall but fertilization does not occur until the following spring.

DELAYED IMPLANTATION. Situation found in several mammals whereby the embedding of the embryo into the lining of the uterus and consequent growth is delayed for several months.

DEMOGRAPHY. The statistical study of populations with respect to natality, mortality, migratory movements, age, sex, and other factors.

DENDRITIC DISTRIBUTION. Having a distribution that is like the branches of a tree as opposed to being evenly distributed over a broad area.

DENTAL FORMULA. A convenient way of expressing the number and arrangement of mammalian teeth; e.g., I 3/3, C 1/1, Pm 4/4, M 3/3 × 2 = 44. See page xiii.

DENTARY. One of the two bones that comprise the mandible (lower jaw) of mammals.

DIASTEMA. A space between teeth, such as the space between incisors and premolars in rodents.

DIESTROUS. Pertaining to mammals that have two estrous cycles each year.

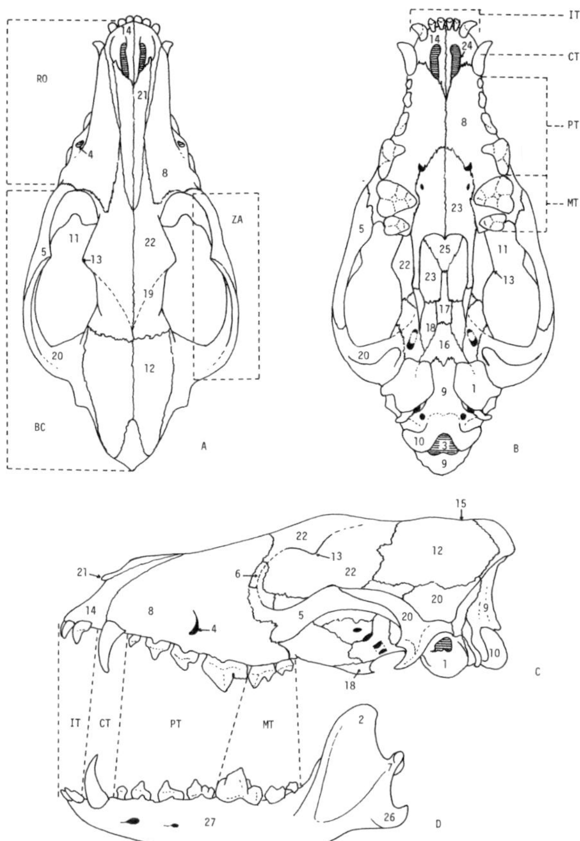

FIGURE 11. Dorsal (A), ventral (B), and lateral (C) view of a coyote skull plus its lower jaw (D) showing parts used in skull identification. Key to labeling of figures as follows:

BC—braincase	11—orbit
RO—rostrum	12—parietal
ZA—zygomatic arch	13—postorbital process
IT—incisor teeth	14—premaxillary
CT—canine teeth	15—sagittal crest
PT—premolar teeth	16—basisphenoid
MT—molar teeth	17—presphenoid
1—auditory bullae	18—pterygoid
2—coronoid process	19—temoral ridges
3—foramen magnum	20—squamosal
4—infraorbital foramen	21—nasal
5—jugal	22—frontal
6—lacrimal	23—palatine
7—mandibular condyle	24—incisive foramen
8—maxillary	25—vomer
9—occipital	26—angular process
10—occipital condyles	27—ramus

DIPLOID. Having a double set of chromosomes (2N); the normal chromosome number of cells (except for mature germ cells) in any individual derived from a fertilized egg.

DIMORPHISM. Occurrence of two distinct morphological types in a single population.

DISJUNCT POPULATION. A population of a species that is separated geographically from the main range of the species.

DIURNAL. Active during daylight hours. Opposite of nocturnal.

ECHOLOCATION. A sonar system used by most bats and cetaceans for locating objects by emitting sound pulses and receiving and identifying the echos of those sounds reflected by the objects.

ECOTONE. A zone of intergradation between ecological communities.

ECTOPARASITE. A parasite that lives on the exterior of its host.

EDWARDS PLATEAU. A region of west-central Texas known as the "Hill Country," bordered on the east and south by the Balcones Escarpment and on the west by the Pecos River.

ELECTROPHORESIS. A technique that separates the mixtures of protein and polypeptide molecules by their different rates of travel in solution in an electric field. The solution is generally held on a porous supporting medium such as a gel made of starch or polyacrylamide.

EMIGRATION. The movement of individuals away from a population. Opposite of immigration.

ENCEPHALOMYELITIS. Inflammation of the brain and spinal cord.

ENDEMIC. Pertaining to a mammal that is peculiar to a certain region.

ENDOPARASITE. A parasite that lives inside its host.

EPIPUBIC BONES. Paired bones that project anteriorly from the pelvic girdle into the abdominal wall of most marsupials.

ESTIVATE. The act of becoming dormant during the summer.

ESTRUS. The period in female mammals when ovulation occurs and the individual is receptive to mating.

ESTUARY. A river mouth where tidal action brings about a mixing of salt and fresh water.

ETHOLOGY. The study of animal behavior.

EXTIRPATE. To destroy, make extinct, or exterminate.

F_1 HYBRID. The offspring resulting from a cross between parents of different races or species.

F_2 HYBRID. The progeny produced by intercrossing F_1 individuals.

FERAL. Pertaining to formerly domesticated animals now living in a wild state.

FERRUGINOUS. Pertaining to or containing iron and resembling iron rust in color.

FETUS. The unborn offspring of viviparous mammals in the latter stages of development.

FORAMEN MAGNUM. The large opening at the back of the skull through which the spinal cord passes.

FORAMEN (pl. FORAMINA). Any opening, orifice, or perforation in a bone through which nerves or blood vessels pass.

FORBS. Herbaceous plants other than grasses or sedges.

FOSSORIAL. Pertaining to life under the surface of the ground.

FRONTAL BONES. The anteriormost pair of bones in the roof of the braincase, situated between the orbits posterior to the nasals and maxillae and anterior to the parietals.

FULVOUS. Tawny or dull yellow.

FUNDAMENTAL NUMBER (FN). The total number of chromosome arms, exclusive of the sex chromosomes, in a diploid cell. An acrocentric chromsome is counted as one; submetacentric and metacentric chromosomes are counted as two arms per chromosome.

GENE POOL. The total genetic information possessed by the reproductive members of a population.

GESTATION PERIOD. The length of time from fertilization until birth of a fetus.

GRAMINEAE. The grasses, a family of monocotyledenous plants.

GRANIVOROUS. Feeding on grains or seeds.

GRAZE. To feed on grass and other herbage by cropping and nibbling.

GREGARIOUS. Pertaining to social animals that live in groups or herds.

HALLUX. The first digit (big toe) of the hind limb.

HAMMOCK. A type of habitat consisting of low, sandy loam ridges scattered along the flood plains of the larger streams in eastern Texas. The vegetation is mixed and varied, consisting chiefly of white oak, water oak, magnolia, sweetgum, holly, yaupon, huckleberry, grapes, and mulberry.

HERBACEOUS. Resembling or pertaining to a herb, which is a seed plant that lacks a persistent, woody stem aboveground and dies at the end of the season.

HERBIVOROUS. Feeding primarily or principally on vegetation.

HIBERNACULA. Winter shelters where animals pass the winter in an inactive (torpid or dormant) state.

HIBERNATION. A seasonal period of dormancy in winter involving a lowering of all metabolic processes and a lessening of ability to regulate body temperature.

HISPID. Having a rough pelage characterized by bristles or stiff hairs.

HOME RANGE. The area that a mammal occupies during its life, not including migration, emigration, or unusual wanderings.

HOMING. The tendency of animals to return to their home area when experimentally displaced to another area.

HYDRIC. Characterized by or thriving in abundance of moisture.

IMMIGRATION. The movement of individuals into a population. Opposite of emigration.

IMPLANTATION. The embedding or attachment of the embryo to the lining of the uterus of the female mammal.

INCISORS. The anteriomost teeth in the jaws of most mammals. They are always rooted in the premaxillary bone of the upper jaw and on the front part of the lower jaw.

INFRAORBITAL FORAMEN. A foramen in the skull through the zygomatic process of the maxilla (in front of the orbit to the side of the rostrum).

INGUINAL. Pertaining to the region of the groin.

INSECTIVOROUS. Eating insects.

INTERFEMORAL MEMBRANE. The web of skin extending between the hind legs and frequently enclosing the tail of bats, also called uropatagium.

INTERORBITAL CONSTRICTION. The least distance across the top of the skull between the orbits.

JUGAL. The bone which forms the central section of the zygomatic arch and is located between the zygomatic process of the maxilla and the squamosal.

KARYOTYPE. The somatic chromosomal complement of an individual or species.

The term is usually applied to photomicrographs of the metaphase chromosomes arranged in a standard sequence (see page 46).

LABIAL SHELF. A thin, narrow, horizontally flattened projection of enamel extending along the side of a tooth closest to the lips.

LACRIMAL BONE. A small bone in the anterior wall of each orbit.

LACTATION. The secretion of milk by the mammary gland.

LEPIDOPTERA. A large order of scaly-winged insects, including the butterflies and moths.

LEPTOSPIROSIS. An infection with spirochetes of the genus *Leptospira*.

LITTER. The set of young born to a female following a pregnancy.

LOPH. A ridge on the grinding surface of a tooth formed by the elongation and fusion of cusps.

MAMMARY GLANDS or MAMMAE (sing. MAMMA). Milk-secreting glands unique to mammals.

MANDIBLE. The lower jaw, composed of a pair of bones (the dentaries) in mammals.

MANDIBULAR CONDYLE. The knob by which each mandible articulates with the skull.

MAST. Collectively nuts that serve as food for hogs and squirrels.

MAXILLA (pl. MAXILLAE) or MAXILLARY BONE. One of a pair of bones that forms part of the rostrum, palate, and zygomatic process and bears all upper teeth except the incisors.

MAXILLARY TOOTH ROW. A measurement of the alveolar distance from the anterior border of the anterior molar to the posterior border of the posterior molar.

MELANISTIC. Having an unusually dark pelage owing to increased amounts of black pigment.

MESAXONIC. Type of foot structure with the main axis of weight supported by a single digit, as in the Perissodactyla.

MESIC. Characterized by a moderate amount of moisture.

METACENTRIC. Designation for a chromosome with a centrally placed centromere.

MIDDEN. An accumulation of refuse about a dwelling place.

MIGRATION. A movement of animals involving a journey to a definite area and a return journey to the area from which the movement arose.

MILK TOOTH. Teeth of a young mammal which are shed and replaced by permanent teeth. Also known as deciduous teeth.

MIST NET. A net of fine mesh used to capture birds and bats.

MOLAR. Any of the posteriormost cheek teeth behind the premolars on each side of the jaws that have no deciduous precursors (milk teeth).

MONESTROUS. Pertaining to species that have only one period of estrus or heat per year.

MONOCOT PLANTS. A group of mostly herbaceous plants characterized by a single cotyledon, parallel-veined leaves, and stems and roots lacking a well-defined pith and cortex.

MONOGAMOUS. Consorting with only one mate. Opposite to polygamous.

MONOTYPIC. A taxonomic category containing but one immediately subordinate zoological unit, as a species containing but one (the nominate) subspecies.

MORPHOLOGY. A branch of biology that deals with structure and form of an organism at any stage of its life history.

NECTIVOROUS. Feeding on nectar.

NEMATODE. The round- or thread-worms of the Phylum Nematoda; includes both free-living as well as parasitic forms.

NICTITATING MEMBRANE. The "third eyelid," a thin membrane of the inner angle of the eye or below the eyelid in some species which can be extended over the surface of the eyeball.

NOCTURNAL. Active during the night. Opposite of diurnal.

OCCIPITAL BONES. The bone surrounding the foramen magnum that bears the occipital condyles.

OCCIPITAL CONDYLES. The two knobs on either side of the foramen magnum that articulate with the vertebral column.

OCHRACEOUS. Reddish yellow.

OMNIVOROUS. Having a diet that includes both animal and plant food.

ORBIT. The socket in the skull in which the eyeball is located.

ORBITAL RIM. A raised bony ridge around the margin of the orbit.

OVULATION. Discharge of an egg (ovum) from the ovary into the uterus.

OXBOW. A piece of land tranferred from one bank of a river to the other as a result of a shift in the river's channel. These channel shifts occur between bends in the river, and where the river straightens its course a horseshoe-shaped (or oxbow) lake is left behind. This phenomenon occurs commonly in the flood plain of larger rivers.

PALATE. The bony roof of the mouth.

PARAPATRIC. Pertaining to the ranges of species that are contiguous but not overlapping.

PARAXONIC. Type of foot structure with the main axis of weight distributed between a pair of similarly-sized digits, as in the Artiodactyla.

PARIETAL. Either of the pair of bones that forms the side and roof of the cranium posterior to the frontals and anterior to the occipital.

PARTURITION. Of or pertaining to birth.

PASSERINE BIRD. A very large order of small to medium-large perching birds containing about three-fifths of the known living species.

PATAGIUM. A membrane or fold of skin extending between the forelimbs and hindlimbs of flying squirrels.

PEDALFER SOIL. A soil rich in aluminum and iron, with few or no carbonates.

PEDICEL. An extension of the frontal bone from which the antler arises.

PEDOCAL SOIL. A soil rich in carbonates, especially those of lime.

PELAGE. Collectively, all the hairs on a mammal.

PELVIC. Pertaining to the hip girdle.

PINNA (pl. PINNAE). The external ear.

PLACENTA. A vascular organ that unites the fetus to the wall of the uterus.

PLANTIGRADE. Pertaining to walking with the whole sole of the foot touching the ground, as in bears and raccoons.

POLLEX. The first digit (thumb) of the hand.

POLYEMBRYONY. A reproductive mechanism in which several young are produced from a single egg fertilized by a single sperm.

POLYESTROUS. Pertaining to species that have three or more estrous cycles per year.

POLYGAMOUS. Having more than one mate at one time.

POSTNATAL. Development that occurs subsequent to birth.

POSTORBITAL CONSTRICTION. Least distance across the top of the skull posterior to the postorbital process.

POSTORBITAL PROCESS. A projection of the frontal bone which marks the posterior margin of the orbit.

POSTPARTUM HEAT. The condition in which a female comes into estrus again immediately after giving birth.

PRECOCIAL. Pertaining to young at birth that are capable of moving about and feeding with little parental assistance. Opposite to altricial.

PREMAXILLARY BONE. One of the paired bones at the anterior end of the upper jaw that bear the incisor teeth.

PREMOLAR. The cheek teeth located anterior to the molars and posterior to the canine. Present in both permanent and milk dentition.

PUBERTY. The period at which the generative organs become capable of exercising the function of reproduction.

RABIES. An acute, encephalitic viral infection transmitted to humans by the bite of a rabid animal.

REENTRANT ANGLE. The inward-pointing angles in the sides of certain types of high-crowned teeth; they make the teeth appear prism-shaped.

RIPARIAN. Associated with the bank of a natural watercourse, such as a river or stream.

ROOT. The portion of a tooth below the gum line that fits into the socket (alveolus).

ROSTRUM. The facial region of the skull anterior to the orbits.

RUSSET. Yellowish brown, light brown, or reddish brown.

SAGGITAL CREST. A median, longitudinal bony ridge on top of the braincase.

SALTATORIAL. Adapted for locomotion by leaping.

SAVANNA. A grassland containing scattered trees and drought-resistant undergrowth.

SAXICOLOUS. Pertaining to an animal that lives among rocks.

SCROTAL. The condition in males whereby the testes are enlarged and descended into the scrotum; indicative of reproductive activity.

SCUTES. Dermal plates which collectively make up the carapace of an armadillo.

SEBACEOUS GLAND. A gland, arising in association with a hair follicle, which produces and secretes a fatty substance.

SEDENTARY. Pertaining to animals that move about very little.

SEMIFOSSORIAL. Pertaining to mammals that are partially, but not fully, adapted for life underground (such as ground squirrels and badgers).

SEX CHROMOSOME. Either member of a pair of chromosomes responsible for sex determination; in mammals the X chromosome or Y chromosome.

SEXUAL DIMORPHISM. A pronounced difference, other than the organs of reproduction, in the morphology of the two sexes of a single species.

SPECIES. Groups of acutally (or potentially) interbreeding natural populations that are reproductively isolated from other such groups. Reproductive isolation implies that interbreeding between individuals of two species normally is prevented by intrinsic factors.

SPHENOPALATINE VACUITY. The space, visible on the venter of the skull posterior to the palate, between the junction of the basisphenoid-presphenoid bones and the pterygoid bone.

STEPPE. In reference to vast tracts of land that are generally level and without forests.

SUBMAXILLARY GLAND. A large salivary gland located below the mandible on each side of the jaw.

Submetacentric. Designation for a chromosome in which the centromere is nearer one end than the other.

Subspecies. A geographically defined aggregate of local populations which differs taxonomically from other such subdivisions of the species.

Supraorbital Process. A bony process on the top rim of each eye socket.

Sympatric. Pertaining to two or more populations which occupy overlapping geographical areas.

Tactile. Pertaining to the sense of touch.

Tamaulipan Biotic Province. One of seven biotic provinces in Texas (Blair, 1950), including the southern part of the state south of a line extending from Del Rio to San Antonio to Corpus Christi.

Taxonomy. The science of classifying organisms.

Temporal Ridges. A pair of ridges on top of the braincase which usually arise on the frontal bones near the postorbital processes and converge posteriorly to form the medium sagittal crest.

Terrestrial. Referring to mammals that live on land as opposed to living in the water.

Territory. An area defended by an individual or group. The behavior patterns associated with the defense of a territory is referred to as territoriality.

Texan Biotic Province. One of seven biotic provinces in Texas (Blair, 1950), representing a broad transitional region between the hardwood and pine forests of extreme eastern Texas and the grasslands of the western part of the state.

Torpor. A state of inactivity or dormancy accompanied by a reduction in the heart rate, body temperature and metabolism.

Tragus. The fleshy projection located in the lower portion of the ear of most bats.

Trematode. Parasitic flatworms (flukes) of the Class Trematoda, Phylum Platyhelminthes.

Trypanosomiasis. See Chagas' disease.

Tularemia. A bacterial infection of wild mammals (particularly rodents and lagomorphs) caused by *Pasteurella tularensis* and which may be transmitted to humans and some domesticated animals.

Tympanic Bulla. See auditory bullae.

Type Locality. The place where the type specimen (holotype) of a species or subspecies was collected.

Typhaceae. The cattails (genus *Typha*), a family of monocotyledenous plants.

Ungulate. A mammal having hooves, not claws.

Unicuspid. A tooth having a single cusp.

Uterus. A muscular expansion of the reproductive tract in female mammals where the embryo and fetus develop. The uterus opens externally by way of the vagina.

Vector. An agent, such as an insect, capable of mechanically or biologically transferring a pathogen from one organism to another.

Vibrissae. Long, stiff hairs that serve primarily as tactile receptors. Also known as whiskers.

Viviparous. Pertaining to those animals that give birth to live young.

Xeric. Characterized by a dry climate.

Zygomatic Arch. The bony arch, formed by the jugal bone and processes of the maxilla and squamosal, that encloses the orbit.

Zygomatic Process. The projection of the maxilla that forms the anterior portion of the zygomatic arch.

Literature Cited

Ables, E. D. 1969. Home-range studies of red foxes (*Vulpes vulpes*). *J. Mamm.* 50:108–120.

———. 1975. The ecology of the red fox in North America. In *The wild canids: their systematics, behavioral ecology and evolution*, ed. M. W. Fox, pp. 216–236. New York: Van Nostrand Reinhold Co. Behavioral Science Series. 508 pp.

Alexander, B. G. 1968. Movements of deer in northeast Texas. *J. Wildlife Mgmt.* 32:618–620.

Andelt, W. F., and P. S. Gipson. 1979. Home range, activity, and daily movements of coyotes. *J. Wildlife Mgmt.* 43:944–951.

———, D. P. Althoff, and P. S. Gipson. 1979. Movements of breeding coyotes with emphasis on den site relationships. *J. Mamm.* 60:568–575.

Anonymous. 1939. Plant 45 beaver in eastern Texas. *Texas Game, Fish, and Oyster Bull.* 2:1.

———. 1945. *Principal game birds and mammals of Texas, their distribution and management*. Austin, Texas: Press of Von Boeckmann-Jones Co. 149 pp.

———. 1952a. Game regions of Texas—the blackland prairie. *Texas Game and Fish* 10:6–8.

———. 1952b. Game regions of Texas—pine and postoak belt. *Texas Game and Fish* 10:16–17, 31.

———. 1976–77. *Texas Almanac and State Industrial Guide*. Dallas, Texas: A. H. Belo Corporation. 672 pp.

Baccus, J. T., and R. E. Greer. 1971. Additional records of *Baiomys taylori* (Rodentia: Cricetidae) for northern Texas. *Tex. J. Sci.* 23:148–149.

Bailey, E. P. 1974. Notes on the development, mating behavior, and vocalization of captive ringtails. *Southwestern Nat.* 19:117–119.

Bailey, V. 1905. *Biological survey of Texas*. N. Am. Fauna, vol. 25. Washington, D.C.: Dept. of Agriculture, Bureau of Biological Survey. 222 pp.

Baker, R. H. 1942. Notes on small mammals of eastern Texas. *J. Mamm.* 23:343.

———. 1943. May food habits of armadillos in eastern Texas. *Am. Midland Nat.* 29:379–380.

———. 1944a. An ecological study of tree squirrels in eastern Texas. *J. Mamm.* 25:8–24.

———. 1944b. The occurrence of *Mustela frenata arthuri* in Texas. *J. Mamm.* 25:319.

———. 1949. Mountain lion in southeastern Texas. *J. Mamm.* 30:199.

———. 1956. Remarks on the former distribution of animals in eastern Texas. *Tex. J. Sci.* 13:356–359.

———, and D. W. Lay. 1938. Notes on the mammals of Galveston and Mustang islands, Texas. *J. Mamm.* 19:505.

———, and C. C. Newman. 1942. Notes on a den site of a raccoon family. *J. Mamm.* 23:214–215.

———, ———, and F. Wilke. 1945. Food habits of the raccoon in eastern Texas. *J. Wildlife Mgmt.* 9:45–48.

Ballard, P. D., C. R. Ferguson, and E. D. Wilson. 1966. A study of the baculum growth and estrous cycle of the nutria. *Tex. J. Sci.* 18:120 (abstract).

Barbour, R. W., and W. H. Davis. 1969. *Bats of America*. Lexington: Univ. Press of Kentucky. 286 pp.

————, and ————. 1974. *Mammals of Kentucky*. Lexington: Univ. Press of Kentucky. 322 pp.

Barham, E. G., J. C. Sweeney, S. Leatherwood, R. K. Beggs, and C. L. Barham. 1979. Aerial census of the bottlenose dolphin, *Tursiops truncatus*, in a region of the Texas coast. *Fishery Bull.* 77:585–596.

Barnette, R. B. 1979. The mammals of the Big Thicket National Preserve. M.S. thesis, Texas A&M Univ., College Station. 118 pp.

Baumgardner, G. D., and D. J. Schmidly. 1981. Systematics of the southern races of two species of kangaroo rats (*Dipodomys compactus* and *D. ordii*). *Occas. Papers Mus. Texas Tech Univ.* 73:1–27.

Bekoff, M. 1977. *Canis latrans. Mammalian Species* 79:1–9. Am. Soc. Mamm.

Benke, A. 1973. Wild hogs—the ugliest Texans. *Texas Parks and Wildlife* 31:6–9.

Birkenholz, D. E. 1963. Movement and displacement in the rice rat. *Quart. J. Florida Acad. Sci.* 26:269–274.

Birney, E. C. 1973. Systematics of three species of woodrats (genus *Neotoma*) in central North America. *Misc. Publ. Mus. Nat. Hist. Univ. Kansas* 58:3–173.

Blair, W. F. 1941. Observations of the life history of *Baiomys taylori subater. J. Mamm.* 22:378–383.

————. 1949. Extensions of the known range of three species of Texas mammals. *J. Mamm.* 30:201–202.

————. 1950. The biotic provinces of Texas. *Tex. J. Sci.* 2:93–117.

————. 1952. Mammals of the Tamaulipan biotic province in Texas. *Tex. J. Sci.* 4:230–250.

Blankenship, T. L. 1979. Reproduction and population dynamics of the bobcat in Texas. M.S. thesis, Texas A&M Univ., College Station. 54 pp.

Bohlin, R. G., and E. G. Zimmerman. 1982. Genic differentiation of two chromosome races of the *Geomys bursarius* complex. *J. Mamm.* 63:218–228.

Boley, R. B., and T. E. Kennerly, Jr. 1969. Cellulolytic bacteria and reingestation in the plains pocket gopher, *Geomys bursarius. J. Mamm.* 50:348–349.

Bothma, J. duP., and J. G. Teer. 1977. Reproduction and productivity in South Texas cottontail rabbits. *Mammalia* 41:253–281.

Boydston, G., and F. Harwell. 1980. Big game harvest regulations (white-tailed deer harvest surveys). Big Game Investigations Job Performance Report (Job No. 4), Federal Aid Project No. W-109-R-3. Texas Parks and Wildlife Dept. Austin. 110 pp.

Bradshaw, W. N. 1965. Species discrimination in the *Peromyscus leucopus* group of mice. *Tex. J. Sci.* 17:278–293.

————. 1968. Progeny from experimental mating tests with mice of the *Peromyscus leucopus* group. *J. Mamm.* 49:475–480.

Bray, W. L. 1904. Forest resources of Texas. *U.S.D.A. For. Ser. Bull.* 47:1–71.

————. 1906. *Distribution and adaptation of the vegetation of Texas*. Bull. Univ. Texas, vol. 82. Austin. 108 pp.

Bridgewater, D. D. 1966. Laboratory breeding, early growth, development and behavior of *Citellus tridecemlineatus* (Rodentia). *Southwestern Nat.* 11:325–337.

————, and D. F. Penny. 1966. Predation by *Citellus tridecemlineatus* on other vertebrates. *J. Mamm.* 47:345–346.

Broadbrooks, H. E. 1952. Nest and behavior of short-tailed shrews, *Cryptotis parva. J. Mamm.* 33:241–243.

Brown, W. A. 1977. The influence of prescribed burning on small mammal populations of the Texas gulf coastal plains. M.S. thesis, Texas A&M Univ., College Station. 95 pp.

Brownlee, W. C. 1977. Status of the river otter (*Lutra canadensis*) in Texas. Spec. Report, Texas Parks and Wildlife Dept. Austin. 7 pp.

Buchanan, G. D. 1957. Variation in litter size of nine-banded armadillos. *J. Mamm.* 38:529.

————. 1958. The current range of the armadillo *Dasypus novemcinctus mexicanus* in the United States. *Tex. J. Sci.* 10:349–351.

————, and R. V. Talmadge. 1954. The geographic distribution of the armadillo in the United States. *Tex. J. Sci.* 6:142–150.

Buechner, H. K. 1942. Interrelationships between the pocket gopher and land use. *J. Mamm.* 23:346–348.

Burr, J. G. 1946. The rise and fall of the beaver. *Texas Game and Fish* 4:4–5, 17–19.

Caire, W., and E. G. Zimmerman. 1975. Chromosomal and morphological variation in the deer mouse, *Peromyscus maniculatus*, in Texas and Oklahoma. *Syst. Zool.* 24:89–95.

Caldwell, D. K., and M. C. Caldwell. 1972. *The world of the bottlenosed dolphin*. Philadelphia: J.B. Lippincott Co. 157 pp.

Calhoun, J. B. 1941. Distribution and food habits of mammals in the vicinity of Reelfoot Lake Biological Station, III. Discussion of the mammals recorded from the area. *J. Tennessee Acad. Sci.* 16:207–275.

Cameron, G. N. 1977. Experimental species removal: Demographic responses by *Sigmodon hispidus* and *Reithrodontomys fulvescens*. *J. Mamm.* 58:488–506.

————, and S. R. Spencer. 1981. *Sigmodon hispidus*. *Mammalian Species* 158:1–9. Am. Soc. Mamm.

————, W. B. Kincaid, and B. A. Carnes. 1979a. Experimental species removal: temporal activity patterns of *Sigmodon hispidus* and *Reithrodontomys fulvescens*. *J. Mamm.* 60:195–197.

————, W. B. Kincaid, C. A. Way, and J. O. Woodrow, Jr. 1979b. Daily movement patterns of *Sigmodon hispidus*. *Southwestern Nat.* 24:63–70.

Carley, C. 1979. *Status summary: the red wolf (Canis rufus)*. Endangered Species Report No. 7. U.S. Fish and Wildlife Service, Albuquerque, New Mexico. 36 pp.

Carter, D. C. 1962. The systematic status of the bat *Tadarida brasiliensis* (I. Geoffroy) and its related mainland forms. Ph.D. dissertation, Texas A&M Univ., College Station. 80 pp.

Chambers, W. T. 1934. Divisions of the pine forest belt of East Texas. *Economic Geog.* 33:19–21.

Chambless, L. F., and E. S. Nixon. 1975. Woody vegetation-soil relations in a bottomland forest of East Texas. *Tex. J. Sci.* 26:407–416.

Chapman, B. R., and R. L. Packard. 1974. An ecological study of Merriam's pocket mouse in southeastern Texas. *Southwestern Nat.* 19:281–291.

Chapman, J. A., J. G. Hockman, and M. M. Ojeda C. 1980. *Sylvilagus floridanus*. *Mammalian Species* 136:1–8. Am. Soc. Mamm.

Choate, J. R. 1972. Variation within and among populations of the short-tailed shrew in Connecticut. *J. Mamm.* 53:116–128.

Cleveland, A. G. 1970. The current geographic distribution of the armadillo in the United States. *Tex. J. Sci.* 22:90–92.

————. 1979. Natural history of the hispid cotton rat. In *Proc. First Welder Wild-*

life Foundation Symposium, ed. D. L. Drawe, pp. 229–241. Contr. B-7, Welder Wildlife Foundation, Sinton, Texas. 276 pp.

Cohen, W. E. 1982. A resource analysis of fur-bearing animals in Texas. Undergraduate fellow's thesis, Texas A&M Univ., College Station. 89 pp.

Collins, O. B., F. E. Smeins, and D. H. Riskind. 1975. Plant communities of the blackland prairie of Texas. In *Prairie: a multiple view*, ed., M. K. Wali, pp. 361–367. Grand Forks: Univ. N. Dakota Press. 433 pp.

Constantine, D. G. 1958. Ecological observations on lasiurine bats in Georgia. *J. Mamm.* 39:64–70.

————. 1966. Ecological observations on lasiurine bats in Iowa. *J. Mamm.* 47:34–41.

Coues, E. 1877. Fur bearing animals. A monograph of the North American Mustelidae. *U.S. Geol. and Geog. Surv. Territories* 8:1–348.

Crabb, W. D. 1941. Food habits of the prairie spotted skunk in southeastern Iowa. *J. Mamm.* 22:349–364.

————. 1944. Growth, development and seasonal weights of spotted skunks. *J. Mamm.* 25:213–221.

Cuyler, W. K. 1924. Observations on the habits of the striped skunk (*Mephitis mesomelas varians*). *J. Mamm.* 5:180–189.

Dalbey, F. C. 1980. Parapatric distribution of *Neotoma floridana* and *Neotoma micropus* in south central Texas: an ecological and morphological study. M.S. thesis, Southwest Texas State Univ., San Marcos. 82 pp.

Davis, D. E. 1947. Notes on commensal rats in Lavaca County, Texas. *J. Mamm.* 28:241–244.

Davis, R. B., C. F. Herreid II, and H. L. Short. 1962. Mexican free-tailed bats in Texas. *Ecol. Monographs* 32:311–364.

Davis, W. B. 1938. A heavy concentration of *Cryptotis*. *J. Mamm.* 19:499–500.

————. 1939. A new *Peromyscus* from Texas. *Occas. Papers Mus. Zool. Louisiana State Univ.* 13:1–2.

————. 1940a. Another heavy concentration of *Cryptotis* in Texas. *J. Mamm.* 21:213–214.

————. 1940b. *Distribution and variation of pocket gophers (genus Geomys) in the southwestern United States*. Bull. 590, Tex. Agric. Exp. Sta., College Station. 38 pp.

————. 1940c. Critical notes on Texas beavers. *J. Mamm.* 21:84–86.

————. 1942. The moles (genus *Scalopus*) of Texas. *Am. Midland Nat.* 27:380–386.

————. 1945. Texas skunks. *Texas Game and Fish* 3:8–11, 25–26.

————. 1946. Further notes on badgers. *J. Mamm.* 27:175.

————. 1951a. Eastern moles eaten by cottonmouth and gray fox. *J. Mamm.* 32:114–115.

————. 1951b. Texas skunks. *Texas Game and Fish* 9:18–21, 31.

————. 1956. Nutrias can mean trouble. *Texas Game and Fish* 14:15, 23.

————. 1958a. Distribution of nutria in Texas. *Texas Game and Fish* 16:22.

————. 1958b. Living fossil. *Texas Game and Fish* 16:8–10.

————. 1961. The female of *Mustela frenata texensis*. *J. Mamm.* 42:273.

————. 1974. *Mammals of Texas*. Texas Parks and Wildlife Dept., Bull. no. 41. Austin. 294 pp.

————, and L. Joeris. 1945. Notes on the life history of the little short-tailed shrew. *J. Mamm.* 26:136–138.

————, and G. H. Lowery, Jr. 1940. The systematic status of the Louisiana muskrat. *J. Mamm.* 21:212–213.

————, and J. L. Robertson, Jr. 1944. The mammals of Culbertson County, Texas. *J. Mamm.* 25:254–273.

————, R. R. Ramsey, and J. M. Arendale, Jr. 1938. Distribution of pocket gophers (*Geomys breviceps*) in relation to soils. *J. Mamm.* 19:412–418.

Debusk, J., and T. E. Kennerly, Jr. 1975. Homing in the cotton rat, *Sigmodon hispidus* Say and Ord. *Am. Midland Nat.* 93:149–157.

Desha, P. G. 1966. Observations on the burrow utilization of thirteen-lined ground squirrels. *Southwestern Nat.* 11:408–410.

DeViney, G. T. 1964. The unique mammary system of the nutria. *Tex. J. Sci.* 16:481–482 (abstract).

Dice, L. R. 1937. Fertility relations in the *Peromyscus leucopus* group of mice. *Contrib. Lab. Vert. Genet. Univ. Michigan* 4:1–3.

————. 1940. Relationships between the woodmouse and the cottonmouse in eastern Virginia. *J. Mamm.* 21:14–23.

Dolan, P. G., and D. C. Carter. 1977. *Glaucomys volans. Mammalian Species* 78:1–6. Am. Soc. Mamm.

Dresner, G. A. 1982. Lutra canadensis. Manuscript.

Dunaway, P. B. 1968. Life history and populational aspects of the eastern harvest mouse. *Am. Midland Nat.* 79:48–67.

Eisenberg, J. F. 1981. *The mammalian radiations: an analysis of trends in evolution, adaptation, and behavior.* Chicago: The Univ. of Chicago Press. 610 pp.

Ellis, L. S., V. E. Diersing, and D. F. Hoffmeister. 1978. Taxonomic status of short-tailed shrews (*Blarina*) in Illinois. *J. Mamm.* 59:305–311.

English, P. F. 1932. Some habits of the pocket gopher, *Geomys breviceps breviceps. J. Mamm.* 13:126–132.

Engstrom, M. D., D. J. Schmidly, and P. K. Fox. 1982. Nongeographic variation and discrimination of species within the *Peromyscus leucopus* species group in eastern Texas. *Tex. J. Sci.* 34:149–162.

Errington, P. L., and R. M. Berry. 1937. Tagging studies of red foxes. *J. Mamm.* 18:203–205.

Evans, E. F. 1952. Game regions of Texas—the coastal prairie. *Texas Game and Fish* 10:30–31.

Ewer, R. F. 1973. *The carnivores.* Ithaca, New York: Cornell Univ. Press. 494 pp.

Filice, G. A., R. N. Greenberg, and D. Fraser. 1977. Lack of observed association between armadillo contact and leprosy in humans. *Amer. J. Trop. Med. Hyg.* 26:137–139.

Fitch, H. S., P. Goodrum, and C. Newman. 1952. The armadillo in the southeastern United States. *J. Mamm.* 33:21–37.

Fritts, S. H., and J. A. Sealander. 1978a. Diets of bobcats in Arkansas with special reference to age and sex. *J. Wildlife Mgmt.* 42:533–539.

————, and ————. 1978b. Reproductive biology and population characteristics of bobcats in Arkansas. *J. Mamm.* 59:347–353.

Gardner, A. L. 1973. The systematics of the genus *Didelphis* (Marsupalia: Didelphidae) in North and Middle America. *Spec. Publ. Mus. Texas Tech Univ.* 4:3–81.

Genoways, H. H., and J. R. Choate. 1972. A multivariate analysis of systematic relationships among populations of the short-tailed shrew (genus *Blarina*) in Nebraska. *Syst. Zool.* 21:106–116.

————, J. C. Patton III, and J. R. Choate. 1977. Karyotypes of shrews of the genera *Cryptotis* and *Blarina* (Mammalia: Soricidae). *Experientia* 33:1294–1295.

George, S. B., J. R. Choate, and H. H. Genoways. 1981. Distribution and taxonomic status of *Blarina hylophaga* Elliot (Insectivora: Soricidae). *Ann. Carnegie Mus. Nat. Hist.* 50:493–513.

———, H. H. Genoways, J. R. Choate, and R. J. Baker. 1982. Karyotypic relationships within the short-tailed shrews, genus *Blarina*. *J. Mamm.* 63:639–643.

Gier, H. T. 1975. Ecology and behavior of the coyote (*Canis latrans*). In *The wild canids: their systematics, behavioral ecology and evolution*, ed. M. W. Fox., pp. 247–262. New York: Van Nostrand and Reinhold Co. Behavioral Science Series. 508 pp.

Gipson, P. S. 1974. Food habits of coyotes in Arkansas. *J. Wildlife Mgmt.* 38:848–853.

———, and J. A. Sealander. 1972. Home range and activity of the coyote (*Canis latrans frustror*) in Arkansas. *Proc. S.E. Assoc. Game & Fish Comm.* 26:82–83.

Glass, B. P. 1947. Geographic variation in *Perognathus hispidus*. *J. Mamm.* 28:174–179.

Goertz, J. W. 1963. Some biological notes on the Plains harvest mouse. *Proc. Okla. Acad. Sci.* 43:123–125.

Goodpasture, W. W., and D. F. Hoffmeister. 1952. Notes on the mammals of western Tennessee. *J. Mamm.* 33:159–184.

———, and ———. 1954. Life history of the golden mouse, *Peromyscus nuttalli*, in Kentucky. *J. Mamm.* 35:16–27.

Goodrum, P. 1937. Notes on the gray and fox squirrels of eastern Texas. *Proc. N. Am. Wildlife Conf.* 2:499–504.

———. 1938. Squirrel management in east Texas. *Proc. N. Am. Wildlife Conf.* 3:670–676.

———. 1940. *A population study of the gray squirrel in eastern Texas*. Bull. 591, Tex. Agric. Exp. Sta., College Station. 34 pp.

———. 1961. *The gray squirrel in Texas*. Texas Parks and Wildlife Dept., Bull. no. 42. Austin. 43 pp.

Gould, E. 1969. Communication in three genera of shrews (Soricidae): *Suncus, Blarina*, and *Cryptotis*. *Comm. Behav. Biol.*, Part A 3:11–31.

———, N. C. Negus, and A. Nowick. 1964. Evidence of echolocation in shrews. *J. Exp. Zool.* 156:19–38.

Gould, F. W. 1975. *Texas plants: a checklist and ecological summary*. Bull. MP-585, Tex. Agric. Exp. St., College Station. 121 pp. (revised).

———. 1978. *Common Texas grasses: an illustrated guide*. College Station: Texas A&M Univ. Press. 267 pp.

Gruber, J. A. 1981. Ecology of the Atlantic bottlenosed dolphin (*Tursiops truncatus*) in the Pass Cavallo area of Matagorda Bay, Texas. M.S. thesis, Texas A&M Univ., College Station. 182 pp.

Gunter, G. 1942. Contributions to the natural history of the bottlenose dolphin, *Tursiops truncatus* (Montague), on the Texas coast with particular reference to food habits. *J. Mamm.* 23:267–276.

———. 1954. Mammals of the Gulf of Mexico. In *The Gulf of Mexico, its origin, waters, and marine life*, ed. P. E. Galtsofff, pp. 543–551. U.S. Fish & Wildlife Serv. Fish. Bull. 89. 604 pp.

Haines, H. 1961. Seasonal changes in the reproductive organs of the cotton rat, *Sigmodon hispidus*. *Tex. J. Sci.* 13:219–230.

———. 1963. Geographical extent and duration of the cotton rat, *Sigmodon hispidus*, 1958–1960 fluctuation in Texas. *Ecology* 44:771–772.

———. 1971. Characteristics of a cotton rat (*Sigmodon hispidus*) population cycle. *Tex. J. Sci.* 23:3–27.

Hall, E. R. 1951. American weasels. *Univ. Kansas Publ. Mus. Nat. Hist.* 4:1–466.

———. 1981. *The mammals of North America.* 2 vols. New York: John Wiley & Sons, Inc. 1,181 pp.

———, and J. K. Jones, Jr. 1961. North American yellow bats, "Dasypterus," and a list of the named kinds of the genus *Lasiurus* Gray. *Univ. Kansas Publ. Mus. Nat. Hist.* 14:73–98.

———, and K. R. Kelson. 1959. *The mammals of North America.* New York: Ronald Press Company. 1,083 pp.

Halloran, A. F. 1941. A suggestion for mink management in Texas. *J. Mamm.* 22:449.

———. 1942. A surface nest and the young of *Sigmodon* in Texas. *J. Mamm.* 23:91.

Hamilton, W. J., Jr. 1938. Life history notes on the northern pine mouse. *J. Mamm.* 19:163–170.

Hanson, R. P., and L. Karstad. 1959. Feral swine in the southeastern United States. *J. Wildlife Mgmt.* 23:64–74.

Harwell, W. F., and H. G. Gore. 1982. White-tailed deer population trends. Big Game Investigations Job Performance Report (Report No. 1), Federal Aid Project No. W-109-R-S. Texas Parks and Wildlife Dept., Austin. 78 pp.

Henry, V. G. 1968. Length of estrous cycle and gestation in European wild hogs. *J. Wildlife Mgmt.* 32:406–408.

Hershkovitz, P. 1966. Catalog of living whales. *U.S. Nat. Mus. Bull.* 246:1–259.

Hoffmann, R. S., and J. K. Jones, Jr. 1970. Influence of Late-Glacial and Post-Glacial events on the distribution of Recent mammals on the northern Great Plains. In *Pleistocene and Recent environments of the central Great Plains*, ed. W. Dort, Jr., and J. K. Jones, Jr., pp 355–394. Lawrence: Univ. Kansas Press. 433 pp.

Hollister, N. 1911. *A systematic synopsis of the muskrats.* N. Am. Fauna, vol. 32. Washington, D.C.: Dept. of Agriculture, Bureau of Biological Survey. 47 pp.

———. 1925. The systematic name of the Texas armadillo. *J. Mamm.* 6:60.

Honeycutt, R. L., and D. J. Schmidly. 1979. Chromosomal and morphological variation in the plains pocket gopher, *Geomys bursarius*, in Texas and adjacent states. *Occas. Papers Mus. Texas Tech Univ.* 58:1–54.

Hooper, E. T. 1952. A systematic review of the harvest mice (genus *Reithrodontomys*) of Latin America. *Univ. Michigan Mus. Zool. Misc. Publ.* 77:1–255.

Howard, W. E. 1949. A means to distinguish skulls of coyotes and domestic dogs. *J. Mamm.* 30:169–171.

Hugghins, E. J. 1951. A survey of helminths and ectoparasites of roof and cotton rats in Brazos County, Texas. *Am. Midland Nat.* 46:230–244.

Humphrey, S. R. 1974. Zoogeography of the nine-banded armadillo (*Dasypus novemcinctus*) in the United States. *Bioscience* 24:457–462.

Hunsaker, D., II, G. G. Raun, and J. E. Swindells. 1959. Range expansion of *Baiomys taylori* in Texas. *J. Mamm.* 40:447–448.

Hunt, T. P. 1951. Breeding of *Cryptotis parva* in Texas. *J. Mamm.* 32:115–116.

———. 1959. Breeding habits of the swamp rabbit with notes on its life history. *J. Mamm.* 40:82–91.

Inglis, J. M. 1955. Population dynamics of the cotton rat (genus *Sigmodon*). M.S. thesis, Texas A&M Univ., College Station. 84 pp.

———, W. J. Clark, H. D. Irby, and D. M. Moehring. 1974. Preconstruction ecological and biological studies: Blue Hills Nuclear Power Plant environmental study. Typescript. College Station: Texas A&M Univ. 1,300 pp.

Jackson, A. 1964. Texotics. *Texas Game and Fish Comm.* 22:7–11.

Jenkins, S. H., and P. E. Busher. 1979. *Castor canadensis. Mammalian Species* 120:1–8. Am. Soc. Mamm.

Jennings, W. L. 1958. The ecological distribution of bats in Florida. Ph.D. dissertation, Univ. Florida, Gainesville. 126 pp.

Johnson, C. 1959. Selective adaptation for the color phases of the terrestrial snail *Helicina orbiculata. Tex. J. Sci.* 11:366–370.

Johnson, E. H. 1931. *The natural regions of Texas.* Univ. Texas Bull., vol. 3113. Austin. 148 pp.

Jones, C. 1977. *Plecotus rafinesquii. Mammalian Species* 69:1–4. Am. Soc. Mamm.

———, and R. D. Suttkus. 1975. Notes on the natural history of *Plecotus rafinesquii. Occas. Papers Mus. Zool. Louisiana State Univ.* 47:1–14.

Jones, J. K., Jr., D. C. Carter, and H. H. Genoways. 1979. Revised checklist of North American mammals north of Mexico, 1979. *Occas. Papers Mus. Texas Tech Univ.* 62:1–17.

Joule, J., and G. N. Cameron. 1974. Field estimation of demographic parameters: influence of *Sigmodon hispidus* population structure. *J. Mamm.* 55:309–318.

———, and ———. 1975. Species removal studies. I. Dispersal strategies of sympatric *Sigmodon hispidus* and *Reithrodontomys fulvescens* populations. *J. Mamm.* 56:378–396.

Kalmbach, E. R. 1943. *The armadillo: its relation to agriculture and game.* Texas Game, Fish, and Oyster Comm., Austin, Texas. 60 pp.

Kaye, S. V. 1961a. Movements of harvest mice with gold-198. *J. Mamm.* 42:323–337.

———. 1961b. Laboratory life history of the eastern harvest mouse. *Am. Midland Nat.* 66:439–451.

Kennerly, T. E., Jr. 1958. Comparisons of morphology and life history of two species of pocket gophers. *Tex. J. Sci.* 10:133–146.

———. 1963. Gene flow pattern and swimming ability of the pocket gopher. *Southwestern Nat.* 8:85–88.

———. 1964. Microenvironmental conditions of the pocket gopher burrow. *Tex. J. Sci.* 16:395–441.

Kincaid, W. B., and G. N. Cameron. 1982. Effects of species removal on resource utilization in a Texas rodent community. *J. Mamm.* 63:229–235.

Launchbaugh, J. R. 1955. Vegetational changes in the San Antonio Prairie. *Ecol. Monogr.* 25:39–57.

LaVal, R. K. 1970. Infraspecific relationships of bats of the species *Myotis austroriparius. J. Mamm.* 51:542–552.

———, and M. L. LaVal. 1979. Notes on reproduction, behavior, and abundance of the red bat *Lasiurus borealis. J. Mamm.* 60:209–212.

Lay, D. W. 1939. Fur resources of eastern Texas. *Texas Game, Fish and Oyster Bull.* 15:1–7.

———. 1942. Ecology of the opossum in eastern Texas. *J. Mamm.* 23:147–159.

———. 1943. Pines and bucks of East Texas. *Texas Game and Fish.* 1:4, 11.

———. 1945. Muskrat investigations in Texas. *J. Wildlife Mgmt.* 9:56–76.

———. 1954. More deer in east Texas. *Texas Game and Fish.* 12:8, 26.

———. 1965. Fruit utilization by deer in southern forests. *J. Wildlife Mgmt.* 29:370–375.

————. 1967. Deer range appraisal in eastern Texas. *J. Wildlife Mgmt.* 31:426–432.

————. 1969. Foods and feeding habits of white-tailed deer. In *White-tailed deer in the southern forest habitat,* ed. L. K. Halls, pp. 8–13. Nacogdoches, Texas: Southern Forest Experiment Station, Forest Service, USDA. 130 pp.

————, and R. H. Baker. 1938. Notes on the home range and ecology of the Attwater wood rat. *J. Mamm.* 19:418–423.

————, and T. O'Neil. 1942. Muskrats of the Texas coast. *J. Wildlife Mgmt.* 6:301–311.

Layne, J. N. 1959. Growth and development of the eastern harvest mouse, *Reithrodontomys humulis. Bull. Florida State Mus. Biol. Sci.* 4:61–82.

Leatherwood, J. S. 1975. Observations of feeding behavior of bottlenosed dolphins *Tursiops truncatus* in the northern Gulf of Mexico and *Tursiops* c.f. *T. gilli* off southern California, Baja California and Nayarit, Mexico. *Mar. Fish. Rev.* 37:10–16.

Lechleitner, R. R. 1959. Sex ratio, age classes and reproduction of the black-tailed jack rabbit. *J. Mamm.* 40:63–81.

Lee, M. R. 1969. A widely applicable technique for direct processing of bone marrow for chromosomes of vertebrates. *Stain Tech.* 44:155–158.

Liers, E. 1951. Notes on the river otter (*Lutra canadensis*). *J. Mamm.* 32:1–9.

Lilly, J. C. 1958. Some considerations regarding basic mechanisms of positive and negative types of motivations. *Am. Jour. Psychiatry* 115:498–504.

————. 1961. *Man and dolphin.* Garden City, N.Y.: Doubleday and Company, Inc. 312 pp.

Linzey, D. W., and R. L. Packard. 1977. *Ochrotomys nuttalli. Mammalian Species* 75:1–6. Am. Soc. Mamm.

Long, C. A. 1972. Taxonomic revision of the North American badger, *Taxidea taxus. J. Mamm.* 53:725–759.

————. 1973. *Taxidea taxus. Mamm. Species* 26:1–4. Am. Soc. Mamm.

Lotze, J., and S. Anderson. 1979. *Procyon lotor. Mammalian Species* 119:1–8. Am. Soc. Mamm.

Lowery, G. H., Jr. 1974. *The mammals of Louisiana and its adjacent waters.* Baton Rouge: Louisiana State Univ. Press. 565 pp.

————, and W. B. Davis. 1942. A revision of the fox squirrels of the lower Mississippi Valley and Texas. *Occas. Papers Mus. Zool. Louisiana State Univ.* 9:153–172.

Manaro, A. J. 1961. Observations on the behavior of the spotted skunk in Florida. *Quart. J. Florida Acad. Sci.* 24:59–63.

Marshall, A. D., and J. H. Jenkins. 1966. Movements and home ranges of bobcats as determined by radio-tracking in the upper coastal plain of west-central South Carolina. *Proc. S.E. Assoc. Game & Fish Comm.* 20:206–214.

McBee, K., and R. J. Baker. 1981. *Dasypus novemcinctus. Mammalian Species* 162:1–9. Am. Soc. Mamm.

McCarley, H. 1954a. Natural hybridization in the *Peromyscus leucopus* species group in eastern Texas. *Evolution* 8:314–323.

————. 1954b. The ecological distribution of the *Peromyscus leucopus* species group in eastern Texas. *Ecology* 35:375–379.

————. 1954c. Fluctuations and structure of *Peromyscus gossypinus* populations in eastern Texas. *J. Mamm.* 35:526–532.

————. 1958. Ecology, behavior, and population dynamics of *Peromyscus nuttalli* in eastern Texas. *Tex. J. Sci.* 10:147–171.

————. 1959a. A study of the dynamics of a population of *Peromyscus gossypinus* and *P. nuttalli* subjected to the effects of x-irradiation. *Am. Midland Nat.* 61:447–449.

————. 1959b. The effect of flooding on a marked population of *Peromyscus*. *J. Mamm.* 40:57–63.

————. 1959c. An unusually large nest of *Cryptotis parva*. *J. Mamm.* 40:243.

————. 1959d. The mammals of eastern Texas. *Tex. J. Sci.* 11:385–426.

————. 1962. The taxonomic status of wild *Canis* (Canidae) in the south central United States. *Southwestern Nat.* 7:227–235.

————. 1963. Distributional relationships of sympatric populations of *Peromyscus leucopus* and *P. gossypinus*. *Ecology* 44:787–788.

————. 1964. Ethological isolation in the cenospecies *Peromyscus leucopus*. *Evolution* 18:331–332.

————. 1966. Annual cycle, population dynamics, and adaptive behavior of *Citellus tridecemlineatus*. *J. Mamm.* 47:294–316.

————. 1978. Vocalizations of red wolves (*Canis rufus*). *J. Mamm.* 59:27–35.

————, and W. N. Bradshaw. 1953. New locality records for some mammals of eastern Texas. *J. Mamm.* 34:515–516.

————, and C. J. Carley. 1979. *Recent changes in distribution and status of wild red wolves (Canis rufus).* Endangered Species Report No. 4, U.S. Fish and Wildlife Service, Albuquerque, New Mexico. 38 pp.

McKnown, R., and E. D. Wilson. 1964. Population distribution and litter size of nutria captured at the Sheldon Reservoir, Houston, Texas. *Tex. J. Sci.* 16:488 (abstract).

McLeod, C. A. 1971. The Big Thicket forest of East Texas. *Tex. J. Sci.* 23:221–233.

McManus, J. J. 1974. *Didelphis virginiana. Mammalian Species* 40:1–6. Am. Soc. Mamm.

Mead, R. A. 1968. Reproduction in eastern forms of the spotted skunk (genus *Spilogale*). *J. Zool. London* 156:119–136.

Mengel, R. M. 1971. A study of dog-coyote hybrids and implications concerning hybridization in *Canis*. *J. Mamm.* 52:316–336.

Michael, E. D., and J. B. Birch. 1967. First Texas record of *Plecotus rafinesquii*. *J. Mamm.* 48:672.

————, R. L. Whisennand, and G. Anderson. 1970. A recent record of *Myotis austroriparius* from Texas. *J. Mamm.* 51:620.

Mitchell, J. L. 1961. Mink movements and populations on a Montana river. *J. Wildlife Mgmt.* 25:48–54.

Muul, I. 1968. Behavioral and physiological influences on the distribution of the flying squirrel, *Glaucomys volans*. *Misc. Publ. Mus. Zool. Univ. Michigan* 134:1–66.

Negus, N. C., E. Gould, and R. K. Chipman. 1961. Ecology of the rice rat, *Oryzomys palustris* (Harlan), on Breton Island, Gulf of Mexico, with a critique of the social stress theory. *Tulane Studies in Zool.* 8:95–123.

Nesbitt, W. H. 1975. Ecology of a feral dog pack on a wildlife refuge. In *The wild canids: their systematics, behavioral ecology and evolution*, ed. M. W. Fox, pp. 391–396. New York: Van Nostrand and Reinhold Co. Behavioral Science Series. 508 pp.

Newman, C. C., and R. H. Baker. 1942. Armadillo eats young rabbits. *J. Mamm.* 23:450.

Newman, H. H. 1913. The natural history of the nine-banded armadillo of Texas. *Am. Nat.* 47:513–539.

Nixon, E. S., L. F. Chambless, and J. L. Malloy. 1973. Woody vegetation of a palmetto (*Sabal minor*) area in Texas. *Tex. J. Sci.* 26:535–541.

Norton, W. G. 1981. The game and furbearing mammals of Big Thicket National Preserve. M.S. thesis, Texas A&M Univ., College Station. 122 pp.

O'Neil, T. 1949. *The muskrat in the Louisiana coastal marshes*. New Orleans: Louisana Dept. Wildlife and Fisheries. 152 pp.

Packard, R. L. 1960. Speciation and evolution of the pygmy mice, genus *Baiomys*. *Univ. Kansas Publ. Mus. Nat. Hist.* 9:579–670.

———. 1961. Additional records of mammals from eastern Texas. *Southwestern Nat.* 6:193–195.

———. 1963. Distribution of the blacktailed jackrabbit in eastern Texas. *Tex. J. Sci.* 15:107–110.

———. 1966. *Myotis austroriparius* in Texas. *J. Mamm.* 47:128.

———. 1968. An ecological study of the fulvous harvest mouse in eastern Texas. *Am. Midland Nat.* 79:68–88.

———. 1969. Taxonomic review of the golden mouse *Ochrotomys nuttalli*. *Univ. Kansas Misc. Publ. Mus. Nat. Hist.* 51:373–406.

———, and H. Garner. 1964. Arboreal nests of the golden mouse in eastern Texas. *J. Mamm.* 45:369–374.

Paradiso, J. L. 1965. Recent records of red wolves from the Gulf coast of Texas. *Southwestern Nat.* 10:318–319.

———. 1968. Canids recently collected in East Texas, with comments on the taxonomy of the red wolf. *Am. Midland Nat.* 80:529–534.

———, and R. M. Nowak. 1971. *A report on the taxonomic status and distribution of the red wolf*. Spec. Sci. Report 145:1–36, U.S. Dept. Int., Fish and Wildlife Serv.

———, and ———. 1972. *Canis rufus. Mammalian Species* 22:1–4. Am. Soc. Mamm.

Parmalee, P. W. 1953. Foods of the feral house cat in east-central Texas. *J. Wildlife Mgmt.* 17:375–376.

———. 1954. Food of the great horned owl and barn owl in east Texas. *Auk* 71:469–470.

Patton, R. F. 1974. Ecological and behavioral relationships of the skunks of Trans-Pecos Texas. Ph.D. dissertation, Texas A&M Univ., College Station. 199 pp.

Pearson, O. P. 1947. The rate of metabolism in some mammals. *Ecology* 28:127–145.

Penney, D. F., and E. G. Zimmerman. 1976. Genic divergence and local population differentiation by random drift in the pocket gopher *Geomys. Evolution* 30:473–483.

Perez, J. C., W. C. Haws, and C. H. Hatch. 1978. Resistance of woodrats (*Neotoma micropus*) to *Crotalus atrox* venom. *Toxicon* 16:198–200.

Pessin, L. J. 1933. Forest associations in the uplands of the lower Gulf coastal plain (longleaf pine belt). *Ecology* 14:1–13.

Peterson, R. L. 1946. Recent and Pleistocene mammalian fauna of Brazos County, Texas. *J. Mamm.* 27:162–169.

Petrides, G. A. 1950. The nutria comes to Texas. *Texas Game and Fish* 8:4–5, 27.

Pettus, D. 1957. Records of the deer mouse on the Gulf coastal plain. *J. Mamm.* 38:416–417.

Pimlott, D. H., and P. W. Joslin. 1968. The status and distribution of the red wolf. *Trans. N. Am. Wildlife and Nat. Res. Conf.* 33:373–389.

Pitts, R. M. 1978. Carnivorous behavior in pigmy mice (*Baiomys taylori*). *Bios* 49:107–108.

Pollack, E. M. 1951. Observations of New England bobcats. *J. Mamm.* 32:356–358.

Pournelle, G. H. 1952. Reproduction and early post-natal development of the cotton mouse, *Peromyscus gossypinus gossypinus. J. Mamm.* 33:1–20.

Rainey, D. G. 1956. Eastern woodrat, *Neotoma floridana*; life history and ecology. *Univ. Kansas Publ. Mus. Nat. Hist.* 8:535–646.

Ramsey, C. 1968. Texotic line-up. *Texas Parks and Wildlife* 25:3–7.

Raun, G. G. 1959. A new Texas locality for *Dipodomys ordi. J. Mamm.* 40:146–147.

————. 1966. A population of woodrats (*Neotoma micropus*) in southern Texas. *Tex. Mem. Mus. Bull.* 11:1–62.

————, and B. J. Wilks. 1961. Noteworthy records of the hog-nosed skunk (*Conepatus*) from Texas. *Tex. J. Sci.* 13:204–205.

————, and ————. 1964. Natural history of *Baiomys taylori* in southern Texas and competition with *Sigmodon hispidus* in a mixed population. *Tex. J. Sci.* 16:28–49.

Read, J. A. 1981. Geographic variation in the bobcat (*Felis rufus*) in the south central United States. M.S. thesis, Texas A&M Univ., College Station. 107 pp.

Rice, D. W. 1957. Life history and ecology of *Myotis austroriparius* in Florida. *J. Mamm.* 38:15–32.

Richardson, W. B. 1942. Ring-tailed cats (*Bassariscus astutus*): their growth and development. *J. Mamm.* 23:17–26.

Ride, W. D. L. 1964. A review of Australian fossil marsupials. *J. Royal Soc. Western Australia* 47:97–131.

Riley, G., and R. T. McBride. 1972. *A survey of the red wolf (Canis rufus).* Spec. Sci. Rep. 162:1–16. U.S. Dept. Int., Fish and Wildl. Serv.

————, and ————. 1975. A survey of the red wolf (*Canis rufus*). In *The wild canids: their systematics, behavioral ecology and evolution*, ed. M. W. Fox, pp. 263–277. New York: Van Nostrand and Reinhold Co. Behavioral Science Series. 508 pp.

Riskind, D. H., and O. B. Collins. 1975. The Blackland Prairie of Texas: conservation of representative climax remnants. In *Prairie: a multiple view*, ed. M. K. Wali, pp. 361–367. Grand Forks: Univ. N. Dakota Press. 433 pp.

Robbins, L. W., and R. J. Baker. 1978. Karyotypic data for African mammals, with a description of an *in vivo* bone marrow technique. Bull. Carnegie Mus. Nat. Hist. 6:188–210.

Rollings, C. T. 1945. Habits, foods and parasites of the bobcat in Minnesota. *J. Wildlife Mgmt.* 9:131–145.

Rue, L. L., III. 1968. *Game animals.* New York: Harper and Row. 655 pp.

Russell, D. N., and J. H. Shaw. 1971. Distribution and relative density of the red wolf in Texas. *Proc. S.E. Assoc. Game & Fish Comm.* 25:131–137.

————, and ————. 1972. Red wolf—situation critical. *Texas Parks and Wildlife*, 30:12–15.

St. Romain, P. A. 1975. Geographic variation in the white-footed mouse (*Peromyscus leucopus*) in Louisiana and eastern Texas. *Southwestern Nat.* 20:355–362.

————. 1976. Variation in the cotton mouse (*Peromyscus gossypinus*) in Louisiana. *Southwestern Nat.* 21:79–88.

Sargeant, A. B., and D. W. Warner. 1972. Movements and denning habits of a badger. *J. Mamm.* 53:207–210.

Schadler, M. H., and G. M. Butterstein. 1979. Reproduction in the pine vole, *Microtus pinetorum*. *J. Mamm.* 60:841–844.

Schmidly, D. J. 1974. *Peromyscus pectoralis*. *Mammalian Species* 49:1–3. Am. Soc. Mamm.

———. 1977. *The mammals of Trans-Pecos Texas*. College Station: Texas A&M Univ. Press. 225 pp.

———. 1981. *Marine mammals of the southeastern United States coast and the Gulf of Mexico*. FWS/OBS-80/41, U.S. Fish and Wildlife Service, Office of Biological Services, Washington, D.C. 163 pp.

———, and B. A. Melcher. 1974. Annotated checklist and key to the cetaceans of Texas waters. *Southwestern Nat.* 18:453–464.

———, and W. A. Brown. 1979. Systematics of short-tailed shrews (genus *Blarina*) in Texas. *Southwestern Nat.* 24:39–48.

———, B. R. Barnette, and J. A. Read. 1979. The mammals of Big Thicket National Preserve and East Texas. Report prepared for the Office of Natural Resources, Southwest Region, National Park Service, Santa Fe, New Mexico (Contract No. CX 700050442). 345 pp.

———, W. G. Norton, and G. A. Barber. 1980. The game and furbearing mammals of Big Thicket National Preserve with comments on the small mammal fauna of selected units. Report prepared for the Office of Natural Resources, Southwest Region, National Park Service, Santa Fe, New Mexico (Contract No. CX 70290019). 141 pp.

———, K. T. Wilkins, R. L. Honeycutt, and B. C. Weynand. 1977. The bats of East Texas. *Tex. J. Sci.* 28:127–143.

Schultz, J. G., C. D. Fisher, and S. Hightower. 1975. Recent records of the eastern big-eared bat (*Plecotus rafinesquii*) in eastern Texas. *Southwestern Nat.* 20:144–145.

Schwartz, A. 1955. The status of the species of the *brasiliensis* group of the genus *Tadarida*. *J. Mamm.* 36:106–109.

Schwartz, C. W., and E. R. Schwartz. 1981. *The wild mammals of Missouri*. revised edition. Columbia: Univ. of Missouri Press and Missouri Department of Conservation. 356 pp.

Schwarz, E., and H. K. Schwarz. 1943. The wild and commensal stocks of the house mouse, *Mus musculus* Linnaeus. *J. Mamm.* 24:59–72.

Sealander, J. A. 1979. *A guide to Arkansas mammals*. Conway, Arkansas: River Road Press. 313 pp.

Seton, E. T. 1926. *Lives of game animals*. Vol. 2. London, England: Constable and Co. 671 pp.

Shane, S. H. 1977. The population biology of the Atlantic bottlenose dolphin, *Tursiops truncatus*, in the Aransas Pass area of Texas. M.S. thesis, Texas A&M Univ., College Station. 239 pp.

———. 1980. Occurrence, movements, and distribution of bottlenose dolphins, *Tursiops truncatus*, in southern Texas. *Fishery Bull.* 78:593–601.

Sharp, H. F., Jr. 1967. Food ecology of the rice rat, *Oryzomys palustris* (Harlan), in a Georgia salt marsh. *J. Mamm.* 48:557–563.

Sheldon, W. G. 1950. Denning habits and home range of red foxes in New York state. *J. Wildlife Mgmt.* 14:33–42.

Sherman, H. B. 1930. Birth of the young of *Myotis austroriparius*. *J. Mamm.* 11:495–503.

Simpson, T. R. 1980. The influence of nutria on aquatic vegetation and waterfowl in East Texas. Ph.D. dissertation, Texas A&M Univ., College Station. 55 pp.

Smolen, M. J. 1981. *Microtus pinetorum. Mammalian Species* 147:1–7. Am. Soc. Mamm.

Sollberger, D. E. 1943. Notes on the breeding habits of the eastern flying squirrel (*Glaucomys volans volans*). *J. Mamm.* 24:163–173.

Spenrath, C. A., and R. K. LaVal. 1974. An ecological study of a resident population of *Tadarida brasiliensis* in eastern Texas. *Occas. Papers Mus. Texas Tech Univ.* 21:1–14.

Sperry, C. C. 1941. *Food habits of the coyote.* U.S. Fish and Wildlife Serv., Wildlife Res. Bull. 4:1–70.

Springer, M. D. 1975. Food habits of wild hogs on the Texas Gulf Coast. M.S. thesis, Texas A&M Univ., College Station. 71 pp.

Stephenson, G. K., P. D. Goodrum, and R. L. Packard. 1963. Small rodents as consumers of pine seed in East Texas uplands. *J. Forestry* 61:523–526.

Stickel, L. F., and W. H. Stickel. 1949. A *Sigmodon* and *Baiomys* population in ungrazed and unburned Texas prairie. *J. Mamm.* 30:141–150.

Storm, G. L. 1972. Daytime retreats and movements of skunks on farmlands in Illinois. *J. Wildlife Mgmt.* 36:31–45.

Stransky, J. J. 1969. Deer habitat quality of major forest types in the south. In *White-tailed deer in the southern forest habitat*, ed. L. K. Walls, pp 42–45. Nacogdoches, Texas: Southern Forest Experiment Station, Forest Service, USDA. 130 pp.

Strecker, J. K. 1924. The mammals of McLennan County, Texas. *Baylor Bull.* 27:3–20.

———. 1926a. The mammals of McLennan County, Texas (supplementary notes). *Contrib. Baylor Univ. Mus.* 9:1–15.

———. 1926b. Extension of range of the nine-banded armadillo. *J. Mamm.* 7:206–210.

———. 1927. The trade in deer skins in early Texas. *J. Mamm.* 8:106–110.

———. 1929. Notes on the Texas cotton and Attwater wood rats in Texas. *J. Mamm.* 10:216–220.

———, and W. J. Williams. 1929. Mammal notes from Sulphur River, Bowie County, Texas. *J. Mamm.* 10:259.

Streubel, D. P., and J. P. Fitzgerald. 1978. *Spermophilus tridecemlineatus. Mammalian Species* 103:1–5. Am. Soc. Mamm.

Sullivan, J. R., and E. S. Nixon. 1971. A vegetational analysis of an area in Nacogdoches County, Texas. *Tex. J. Sci.* 23:67–79.

Svihla, A. 1931a. Life history of the Texas rice rat (*Oryzomys palustris texensis*). *J. Mamm.* 12:238–242.

———. 1931b. Habits of the Louisiana mink (*Mustela vison vulgivagus*). *J. Mamm.* 12:366–368.

Svihla, R. D. 1929. Habits of *Sylvilagus aquaticus littoralis. J. Mamm.* 10:315–319.

Swank, W. G., and G. A. Petrides. 1954. Establishment and food habits of the nutria in Texas. *Ecology* 35:172–176.

Taber, F. W. 1945. Contribution on the life history and ecology of the nine-banded armadillo. *J. Mamm.* 26:211–226.

Talmage, R. V., and G. D. Buchanan. 1954. *The armadillo (Dasypus novemcinctus). A review of its natural history, ecology, anatomy, and reproductive physiology.* Monogr. in Biol., The Rice Institute, 41:1–135.

Tate, W. H., Jr. 1970. Movements of *Neotoma floridana attwateri* in Brazos County, Texas. M.S. thesis, Texas A&M Univ., College Station. 39 pp.

Taylor, R. J., and H. McCarley. 1963. Vertical distribution of *Peromyscus leucopus* and *P. gossypinus* under experimental conditions. *Southwestern Nat.* 8:107–108.

Taylor, W. P. 1943. The gray fox in captivity. *Texas Game and Fish* 1:12–13.

———. 1954. Food habits and notes on life history of the ring-tailed cat in Texas. *J. Mamm.* 35:55–63.

———, and W. B. Davis. 1947. *The mammals of Texas.* Texas Game, Fish, and Oyster Commission. Bull. no. 27. Austin. 79 pp.

———, and D. W. Lay. 1944. Ecological niches occupied by rabbits in eastern Texas. *Ecology* 25:120–121.

Terrel, T. L. 1972. The swamp rabbit (*Sylvilagus aquaticus*) in Indiana. *Am. Midland Nat.* 87:283–295.

Texas Parks and Wildlife Code. Special Pamphlet 1981–1982. St. Paul, Minnesota: West Publ. Co. 430 pp.

Tharp, B. C. 1926. *Structure of Texas vegetation east of the 98th meridian.* Univ. Texas Bull., no. 2606, Austin. 97 pp.

Throckmorton, M. 1946. The native mammals of Brazos County, Texas. M.S. thesis, Texas A&M Univ., College Station. 99 pp.

Toweill, D. E. 1976. Movements of ringtails in Texas' Edwards Plateau region. M.S. thesis, Texas A&M Univ., College Station. 76 pp.

Trapp, G. R. 1977. Some anatomical and behavioral adaptations of ringtails, *Bassariscus astutus.* *J. Mamm.* 53:549–557.

———, and D. L. Hallberg. 1975. Ecology of the gray fox (*Urocyon cinereoargenteus*): a review. In *The wild canids: their systematics, behavioral ecology and evolution,* ed. M. W. Fox, pp 164–178. New York: Van Nostrand and Reinhold Co. Behavioral Science Series. 508 pp.

Tucker, P. K., and D. J. Schmidly. 1981. Studies of a contact zone among three chromosomal races of *Geomys bursarius* in east Texas. *J. Mamm.* 62:258–272.

Van Gelder, R. G. 1959. A taxonomic revision of the spotted skunks (genus *Spilogale*). *Bull. Am. Mus. Nat. Hist.* 117:233–392.

Van Zyll de Jong, C. G. 1972. A systematic review of the Nearctic and Neotropical river otters (genus *Lutra,* Mustelidae, Carnivora). *Royal Ontario Mus. Life Sci. Contrib.* 80:1–104.

Verts, B. J. 1967. *The biology of the striped skunk.* Urbana: Univ. Illinois Press. 218 pp.

Waggoner, K. V. 1975. The effect of strip-mining and reclamation on small mammal communities. M.S. thesis, Texas A&M Univ., College Station. 74 pp.

———. 1978. The effects of lignite mining and reclamation on small populations in Texas. In *Surface mining and fish/wildlife needs in the eastern United States,* ed. D. E. Samuel, Jr., J. R. Stauffer, C. H. Hocutt, and W. T. Mason, Jr., pp 256–266. Proc. Symp. U.S. Fish and Wildl. Serv., Morgantown, W.V. FWS/OBS-78/81. 386 pp.

Walsh, G. P., E. E. Storrs, H. Burchfield, and E. H. Cottrell. 1975. Leprosy-like disease occurring naturally in armadillos. *J. Reticuloen. Soc.* 18:347–351.

Wang, L., and J. W. Hudson. 1966. Physiology of daily torpor in *Perognathus hispidus.* *Tex. J. Sci.* 18:120–121 (abstract).

Warner, S. R. 1926. Distribution of native plants and weeds on certain soil types in eastern Texas. *Bot. Gazette* 82:345–372.

Watkins, L. C. 1972. *Nycticeius humeralis.* *Mammalian Species* 23:1–4. Am. Soc. Mamm.

Weiser, R. S. 1975. Natural leprosy-like disease in armadillos: a boon to leprosy research? *J. Reticuloen. Soc.* 18:315–316.

Whitaker, J. O., Jr. 1974. *Cryptotis parva. Mammalian Species* 43:1–8. Am. Soc. Mamm.

Wilkins, K. T. 1977. The effects of highways on small mammals and other wildlife. M.S. thesis, Texas A&M Univ., College Station. 103 pp.

———, and D. J. Schmidly. 1977. *Composition of small mammal populations on highway rights-of-way in east Texas.* FHWA TX 197–1F, National Technical Information Service, Springfield, Virginia. 96 pp.

———, and ———. 1980. The effects of mowing of highway rights-of-way on small mammals. In *Environmental concerns in rights-of-way management: proceedings of second symposium, 1979,* ed. R. E. Tillman, pp 55-1–55-13. Electric Power Research Institute (EPRI) Report WS-78–141.

Wilks, B. J. 1963. Some aspects of the ecology and population dynamics of the pocket gopher (*Geomys bursarius*) in southern Texas. *Tex. J. Sci.* 15:241–283.

Williams, P. K. 1968. Social tendencies in *Perognathus hispidus. Tex. J. Sci.* 20:95–96.

Wilson, D. E. 1973. The systematic status of *Perognathus merriami* Allen. *Proc. Biol. Soc. Wash.* 86:175–192.

Wislocki, G. B. 1942. Studies on the growth of deer antlers. I. On the structure and histogenesis of the antler of the Virginia deer (*Odocoileus virginianus borealis*). *Amer. J. Anat.* 71:371–415.

———. 1943. Seasonal changes in the male reproductive tract of the Virginia deer (*Odocoileus virginianus borealis*) with a discussion of the factors controlling the antler-gonad periodicity. In *Essays in biology,* pp. 631–647. Berkeley: Univ. California Press.

Wolfe, J. L., and A. V. Linzey. 1977. *Peromyscus gossypinus. Mammalian Species* 70:1–5. Am. Soc. Mamm.

Wood, J. E. 1949. Reproductive patterns of the pocket gopher (*Geomys breviceps brazensis*). *J. Mamm.* 30:36–44.

———. 1952. The ecology of furbearers in the upland post oak region of eastern Texas. Ph.D. dissertation, Texas A&M Univ., College Station. 187 pp.

———. 1954. Food habits of furbearers in the upland post oak region of eastern Texas. *J. Mamm.,* 35:406–415.

———. 1955a. Notes on young pocket gophers. *J. Mamm.* 36:143–144.

———. 1955b. Notes on the reproduction and rate of increase of raccoons in the post oak region of Texas. *J. Wildlife Mgmt.* 19:409–410.

———. 1959. Relative estimates of fox population levels. *J. Wildlife Mgmt.* 23:53–63.

Yates, T. L., and D. J. Schmidly. 1977. Systematics of *Scalopus aquaticus* (Linnaeus) in Texas and adjacent states. *Occas. Papers Mus. Texas Tech Univ.* 45:1–36.

———, and ———. 1978. *Scalopus aquaticus. Mammalian Species* 105:1–4. Am. Soc. Mamm.

Yeager, L. E. 1938. Otters of the Delta hardwood region of Mississippi. *J. Mamm.* 19:195–201.

Zimmerman, E. G., and N. A. Gayden. 1981. Analysis of genic heterogeneity among local populations of the pocket gopher, *Geomys bursarius.* In *Mammalian population genetics,* ed. J. Joule and M. H. Smith, pp. 272–287. Athens: Univ. of Georgia Press. 380 pp.

Index

Pages containing full species accounts are given in boldface. Photographs and distribution maps of the species appear with the full account.